Close Relationships

Close Relationships

Pamela Regan, Ph.D.
California State University, Los Angeles

Routledge
Taylor & Francis Group

NEW YORK AND LONDON

Published in 2011
by Routledge
711 Third Avenue
New York, NY 10017
www.psypress.com
www.family-studies-arena.com

Published in Great Britain
by Routledge
27 Church Road
Hove, East Sussex BN3 2FA

Routledge is an imprint of the Taylor & Francis Group, an Informa business

Typeset in Times by RefineCatch Limited, Bungay, Suffolk, UK

Cover design by Aubergine Creative Design

Library of Congress Cataloging-in-Publication Data
Regan, Pamela C.
  Close relationships / Pamela Regan.
    p. cm.
  ISBN 978–0–415–87743–5 (hardback : alk. paper)—ISBN 978–0–415–87799–2 (pbk. : alk. paper)
  1. Interpersonal relations.   2. Interpersonal communication.   I. Title.
  HM1106.R428 2011
  302.2—dc22   2010026224

ISBN: 978–0–415–87743–5 (hbk)
ISBN: 978–0–415–87799–2 (pbk)

Brief Contents

Detailed Contents

Preface

Almost every single aspect of human behavior and development takes place in the context of relationships with other people, and relationships have an enormous impact on human health and well-being. Most people are aware of this, and eagerly seek information about love, sex, friendship, parenting, childcare, and other relationship topics and issues. Historically, they have turned to philosophers, theologians, and artists—novelists, poets, composers, and playwrights—for knowledge and advice. And today, of course, they can—and often do—turn to the ever-growing number of "pop" psychology books, self-help manuals, and relationship-themed talk shows and radio programs (usually offered by individuals with little to no actual training or scholarly qualifications). It is only in recent years that people have been able to turn to science for answers to their relationship questions and concerns. *Relationship science* is a relatively new, multidisciplinary field of inquiry specifically addressed to developing a systematic body of knowledge about interpersonal relationships.

CONTENTS

Because relationships influence our actions, thoughts, beliefs, and feelings, inform our growth and development, and affect virtually every outcome we experience in our lifetimes, anyone wishing to explore, understand, and predict these and other aspects of human behavior must have a solid foundation in relationship science. This textbook provides that foundation by serving as a brief but comprehensive introduction to the basic concepts and goals, methodologies, theories, and empirical findings of this exciting and relatively new field. The first section presents the fundamental principles of relationship science. We begin by discussing the basic facts and key concepts (including just what scientists mean by the term "relationship") and the research methods commonly used by scholars in this area. We then consider the uniquely social nature of human beings, including the many ways in which we come into the world "primed" to form relationships and the continuing impact that relationships have on our health and well-being across the life-span.

The next section of the text focuses on relationship development. First, we consider topics related to relationship "beginnings," including research on the preferences that guide people's partner choices and attraction in first encounters. Relationship initiation—including how people convey attraction, initiate a first encounter, and intensify commitment in both friendships and romantic relationships—is discussed next. Finally, we conduct an in-depth examination of theories of relationship development and maintenance, followed by an exploration of research on mate choice and marriage.

The third section of the text focuses on processes that occur between relational partners and that have important implications for their personal and interpersonal experiences. We begin by considering how cognitive (thinking) and affective (feeling) processes may influence men's and women's interpersonal opportunities, behaviors, and outcomes. We then explore communicative and supportive processes that arise between relationship partners and that have clear implications for their personal and interpersonal well-being. We end by discussing two processes that have received an enormous amount of attention from relationship scientists—loving and sexing. We examine the nature of love, discuss the two love types that have received the most scrutiny from scientists (namely, passionate and companionate love), and consider recent advancements in the neurochemistry of love. We also explore men's and women's sexual beliefs and attitudes, and we discuss sexuality—attraction, frequency, satisfaction, and communication—in beginning and established relationships.

The fourth and final section of the textbook focuses on relationship challenges, ranging from rejection and betrayal (including unrequited love, sexual disinterest, obsession and relational stalking, and infidelity), to aggression and violence (including physical, psychological, and sexual aggression in romantic relationships as well as peer victimization and bullying in school and the workplace), to conflict, dissolution, loss, and bereavement. We end by considering therapeutic interventions designed to help relationship partners overcome many of these challenges and alleviate distress.

DISTINCTIVE FEATURES

There are a number of features that make this book "special" and distinguish it from other textbooks currently on the market.

- **This text provides a strong foundation in *relationship science* for students in any discipline**
The material presented in this textbook is inherently relevant to students and other readers, as it captures what the majority are experiencing in their daily lives as they go about establishing, maintaining, and even dissolving close relationships. Importantly, this book not only provides students with a comprehensive survey of relationship phenomena but it also is strongly grounded in methodology and research design. Relationship science—any science—is based on sound knowledge and application of principles of research design and analysis. Yet the majority of available texts gloss over issues of methodology and analysis. Not only is this worrisome from a content perspective, but it prevents students from gaining a true understanding of how to interpret empirical findings and does not allow for active engagement in the research process. This book overcomes this limitation by devoting an entire chapter to research methodology, discussing analysis and measurement issues in most other chapters, and including multiple examples of measurement instruments and scales for self-use or for use in course-related research activities.

- **This text includes a number of pedagogical features designed to enhance the learning experience and keep the material accessible and interesting**
Every effort has been made to make this book as accessible and "reader friendly" as possible. For example, each chapter contains detailed illustrations, including figures, tables, and exhibits, that

serve to provide additional examples and explanations of the written material. Detailed outlines are also provided to help guide readers through the material, along with a list of key concepts (with page references) to assist readers in identifying and comprehending important terms, theories, and findings. Finally, each chapter concludes with a set of exploration exercises designed to provide students with the opportunity to actively explore the various concepts presented in the chapter in greater detail. In some instances, students are encouraged to apply the concepts to their own relationship experiences; in others, they are asked to function as scientists, collecting information about various interpersonal events and determining how well their results match those found by other researchers and presented in the textbook.

- **This text is multidisciplinary and inclusive**

Because relationships are complex and affected by a multitude of variables, relationship science utilizes theory and research from many different fields of inquiry. Consequently, the theory and research cited in this textbook are drawn from a wide variety of domains, including psychology and its subfields (e.g., clinical, community, developmental, health, personality, social), communication studies, family studies, developmental science (child development, gerontology, life-span development), marriage and family therapy, social work, sociology, anthropology, natural (biology, physiology, chemistry) and health (medicine, epidemiology) science, zoology, economics, and even philosophy, history, and theology. Most of the current texts focusing on relationship topics are written primarily from one perspective (e.g., psychology, sociology, communication studies). However, scientific understanding of relationship phenomena has been—and will continue to be—informed by research conducted within a wide array of disciplines. Thus, a multidisciplinary and inclusive focus is essential in textbooks purporting to examine interpersonal relationships.

- **This text includes information on many different relationship types**

People form multiple types of close relationships over their lifetimes (for example, with lovers or mates, family members, and friends), and these intimate associations play a particularly important role in promoting (or hindering) health, happiness, and other important outcomes. Yet most existing books on interpersonal relationships focus exclusively or primarily on one type of relationship—romantic relationships to the exclusion of friend and family relationships, family relationships to the exclusion of friend and romantic relationships, and so forth. This text presents information on theory and research relevant to a variety of relationship types, including friend, family or kin, and romantic or mating relationships, as well as the relationship experiences of a diversity of individuals (e.g., children, adolescents, young adults, mature adults, elderly adults; heterosexual and homosexual men and women; cross-cultural and multicultural samples of individuals).

INTENDED AUDIENCE

The field of relationship science is young, theory and research are burgeoning, and the study of relationship phenomena is not grounded in any one discipline. Consequently, instructors often find it difficult to organize and present to their students the many theories and empirical findings relevant to the topics they cover in their particular courses. This multidisciplinary textbook is designed to provide an organizational framework and basic foundation of relationship knowledge—guiding principles, key concepts, methodologies, theories, empirical research—that instructors in *any* field can use in their courses. For example, the material presented here is suitable for undergraduate- and graduate-level relationship courses offered in departments of psychology, communication studies, family studies, developmental science, marriage and family therapy, social work, sociology, anthropology, and any other social or behavioral science.

Ancillary Materials

Moreover, there is a companion website created just for instructors (located at http://www.psypress.com/textbook-resources) that contains a test item bank with both multiple-choice and essay questions, PowerPoint lecture outlines of each chapter, and reproductions of all figures, tables, and exhibits contained in the textbook.

ACKNOWLEDGMENTS

A number of people contributed to this endeavor. In particular, thanks are due to Debra Riegert (Senior Editor, Routledge/Psychology Press/Taylor & Francis) and Erin Flaherty (Editorial Assistant, Routledge/Psychology Press/Taylor & Francis), as well as to the following reviewers who generously contributed their expertise: Danu Anthony Stinson, University of Victoria, Canada; Susan Sprecher, Illinois State University, USA; Lawrence Ganong, University of Missouri-Columbia, USA; and other anonymous reviewers.

About the Author

Pamela Regan is Professor of Psychology at California State University, Los Angeles. She received her Ph.D. in Psychology from the University of Minnesota and her undergraduate degree in English from Williams College. Her research interest is in the area of interpersonal relationships, with an emphasis on passionate love, sexual desire, and mate preference. She has published more than 100 journal articles, book chapters, and reviews (and has given over 75 professional presentations) on the dynamics of sex, love, and human mating, and she is the author of *The Mating Game: A Primer on Love, Sex, and Marriage* (Sage, 2008) and the co-author (with Ellen Berscheid) of *The Psychology of Interpersonal Relationships* (Pearson, 2005) and *Lust: What We Know About Human Sexual Desire* (Sage, 1999). In 2007 she was honored with the Outstanding Professor Award by her university for excellence in instruction and professional achievement.

PART I
Principles of Relationship Science

This section of the text presents the guiding principles of relationship science. Chapter 1 presents the basic "facts" and key concepts of relationship science. Chapter 2 examines the research methods (designs, data collection methods, research settings, ethical principles) commonly employed by relationship scientists. Chapter 3 explores the fundamentally social nature of human beings, including the myriad ways in which the human infant enters the world innately predisposed to form relationships and the significant impact that interpersonal relationships have on human health and well-being.

Chapter 1
Basic Facts and Key Concepts

CHAPTER OUTLINE
_____

This chapter introduces some of the basic "facts" and key concepts of the field of relationship science. We begin by considering exactly what scientists mean when they refer to the concept of "relationship" and how they typically determine whether two people actually are involved in one. We also discuss the specific kinds of relationship that typically are investigated, and we examine the various factors that affect how partners interact with one another and the outcomes they experience. As you will see, relationship science represents one of the most challenging and uniquely rewarding fields of inquiry.

FACT #1: RELATIONSHIP SCIENTISTS STUDY RELATIONSHIPS

This may seem like a silly—perhaps even stupid—statement to make at the beginning of a textbook called *Close Relationships*. But the truth is that one of the biggest challenges faced by early scholars in the field was finding a common definition of the concept "relationship" that everyone could agree on. Without a common vocabulary—a shared understanding of basic concepts—it was virtually impossible for scientists interested in exploring relationship topics to effectively communicate with each other and to share their theoretical and empirical findings. This, in turn, made it difficult for the field to progress and develop a cumulative and coherent body of knowledge. By the late 1970s, in fact, things were so messy that scientist Robert Hinde described the study of interpersonal relationships as an endeavor "where the complexity of material makes it difficult to follow the same path twice, and where the conceptual jungle chokes the unwary" (1979, p. 6).

These sorts of messy conceptual issues are not solely the bane of scientists and academicians. Most of us, in fact, have probably faced a similar situation at some point in our lives, finding (to our surprise and even chagrin) that our understanding of what it means to have, or to be in, a relationship does not entirely match that of our partner. In fact, psychologist Ann Weber (1998) observed that one of the most difficult issues for scientists who study romantic breakups (her own area of research) is that some people deny that their relationships actually ended because, in their minds, "there was no relationship to break up" (p. 272). Similarly, people who engage in extrarelational sex or infidelity (a topic we will discuss in Chapter 12) often justify their behavior by claiming that they did not have an actual "relationship" with the other party. Public examples of this phenomenon abound. In 2001, for instance, one politician excused his extramarital affair by arguing, "In my opinion, we did not have a relationship. It would probably be her definition of a relationship versus mine" (Isikoff & Thomas, 2001). On hearing the politician's denial, the woman involved replied, "OK, what do you call a relationship? It's like I don't understand what he defines as a relationship" ("Flight attendant angered by Condit's definition of 'relationship,'" August 28, 2001). Definitions of what constitutes a "relationship" clearly differ among people in everyday use, and so it is no wonder that scientists have had an equally difficult time coming to terms with this concept.

Interaction: The Basic Ingredient of a Relationship

Fortunately, due to the pioneering efforts of several early social and behavioral scientists—including psychologist Harold Kelley and his colleagues, whose influential book *Close Relationships* (Kelley et al., 1983) provided much of the initial vocabulary of relationship science—there is now substantial agreement in the field about just what constitutes a "relationship." Specifically, most scholars believe that the basic ingredient of a relationship is interaction, which provides two people with an opportunity to establish mutual influence or *interdependence* (Berscheid & Reis, 1998). Thus, the concept of *relationship* refers to a state of interdependence that arises from ongoing interactions, and two people are "in a relationship" or "have a relationship" to the extent that they interact and mutually influence each other—how one partner behaves (i.e., acts, thinks, or feels) influences how the other partner behaves (i.e., acts, thinks, or feels), and vice versa. Essentially, when two people are in a relationship, there is a "ping-pong" of influence back and forth between them such that each partner's behaviors at a given point in time influence the other partner's behaviors at a later point in time (see Figure 1.1). Because this oscillating rhythm of mutual influence occurs over time, relationships are inherently dynamic and temporal in nature—they are composed of a series of events that occur between partners over time (Reis, Collins, & Berscheid, 2000). It can sometimes be difficult to distinguish between an "interaction" and a "relationship," but in general, an ***interaction episode*** involves an isolated exchange (or set of exchanges) that occurs within a limited span of

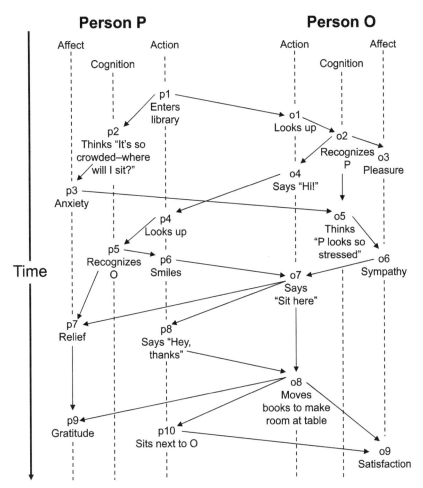

Fig. 1.1 An interaction between two individuals, P and O. As can be seen, not only are the affect (feeling), cognition (thinking), and action events within each person's chain of events causally connected, but the two chains are causally *interdependent* (shown by arrows connecting p and o events). In other words, the behaviors of one partner influence the behaviors of the other. This pattern of mutual influence constitutes evidence of their relationship.

Source: Kelley, H. H., Berscheid, E., Christensen, A., Harvey, J. H., Huston, T. L., Levinger, G., McClintock, E., Peplau, L. A., & Peterson, D. R. (2002). Analyzing close relationships. In H. H. Kelley, E. Berscheid, A. Christensen, J. H. Harvey, T. L. Huston, G. Levinger, E. McClintock, L. A. Peplau, & D. R. Peterson (Eds.), *Close relationships* (pp. 20–67). Clinton Corners, NY: Percheron Press. (Original work published 1983.) Copyright © 2002 by Percheron Press. Figure 2.1 adapted with permission of Eliot Werner Publications, Inc.

time, whereas a relationship involves repeated interactions over a longer duration of time (see Hinde, 1979, 1997; Homans, 1979).

Interaction is a necessary condition for a relationship to exist. This means that if two people seldom interact they do not have much of a relationship, and if there is no interaction whatsoever then there is no relationship—regardless of what they themselves might say or wish to believe. Consider the case of John Hinckley Jr., the man who attempted to assassinate President Ronald Reagan in 1981 in order to impress the actress Jodie Foster. Hinckley firmly believed that he and Foster were involved in a romantic relationship, asserting that "I am with Jodie spiritually every day and every night . . . We are a historical couple . . . I am Napoleon and she is Josephine. I am Romeo and she is Juliet" (Taylor, 1982). Although Hinckley had attempted to contact Foster on multiple occasions, she had never met him and insisted that there was no relationship. A similar scenario involving actress Halle Berry occurred more recently. In court documents filed in 2004, Berry revealed that Greg Broussard, a man who had repeatedly threatened her and against whom she later obtained a restraining order, had "imagined a relationship wherein he and I are engaged to be married" but that she did not know him and no such relationship existed (Hall, 2004). Relationship scientists would side with Foster and Berry. With no history of sustained interaction, with no established pattern of mutual influence or interdependence, neither Hinckley nor Broussard had a relationship with the objects of their misguided affection—the association existed only in the delusional fantasies of those two lone individuals. It is certainly not unusual for people to fantasize about having intimate connections with celebrities or fictional characters in television, movies, and literature (see Derrick, Gabriel, & Tippin, 2008). Most, however, do not mistake their one-sided fantasies for the reality of an actual relationship.

Two Additional Ingredients

All relationships involve interactions and, as we have discussed, interactions are a *necessary* condition for the existence of a relationship. However, interactions are not a *sufficient* condition—interaction alone does not constitute a relationship. Two other conditions must be met before scientists would be comfortable concluding that two people are in a "relationship."

The first condition is that the interactions must be unique in some way to the two people involved; that is, their interaction pattern must be different from the interaction patterns each has with other individuals *and* different from the interaction patterns of other sets of partners. In particular, their interactions cannot be role-based. In ***role-based interactions***, each person's behavior is influenced not by the partner's behavior but by social norms and prescriptions that govern the behavior of all people who assume that particular role (Hinde, 1979). Many of our interactions are role-based. For example, the interaction between a patient and a physician, a customer and a cashier, a citizen and a police officer, or a student and a teacher is largely dictated by their respective roles—and their behavior tends to be the same regardless of who the two individuals are, when and where the interaction occurs, or what their transaction involves (i.e., what ailments are being described and treated, what items are being purchased, what material is being taught and learned). Whether the patient is you, me, or someone else; the physician is Rebecca, Andrew, or Jane; and the reason for the visit is the flu, allergies, or a broken toe, the interaction follows much the same course because the behaviors of both individuals are primarily determined by their group membership and occupancy of particular social positions (in this instance, doctor and patient). Interactions between two people who are for the most part enacting their respective social roles—even over multiple occasions—do not constitute a relationship in the way scientists currently understand and use the term (though some scholars would label these ongoing associations ***formal*** or ***role-based relationships***; see Hinde, 1979).

The second condition is that the partners must have formed a ***mental representation*** of their relationship (often called a relationship schema); that is, they must have cognitively represented and organized their previous interactions and must hold them in memory. It is this mental representation of the relationship, developed over previous interactions, that allows the partners to respond to each other in their own unique, non-role-based way. You respond differently to your best friend than you do to other people, because the two of you have a history together that you hold in your memory—you can easily call up information about your friend's character, behavior, preferences, and values, as well as about your previous interactions, and this mental store of knowledge affects the current interactions you have with your friend and renders them different from those you have with other individuals.

In sum, in order for two people to be in a relationship, three conditions must be met:

- The two people must interact and influence each other's behaviors—that is, they must be interdependent.
- Their interaction must be unique and not based on the enactment of social roles—in other words, how the two interact with each other must be different from how they interact with other people, and must also be different from how other people interact.
- Their interaction history must be represented cognitively and held in memory—that is, as a result of their interaction(s), the partners must have formed a mental representation of their relationship, which influences their future interactions.

A relationship, then, does not reside within a single individual. Rather, a relationship "lives" in the interaction that takes place between two people (Berscheid & Regan, 2005).

Establishing Interdependence

Because relationship scientists are interested in studying relationships, and interdependence is the hallmark of a relationship, scholars in the field have developed several methods for determining whether two people are interdependent (i.e., whether their interactions are characterized by mutual influence). Currently, most researchers rely on self-report methods—they simply ask their study participants whether or not they have a relationship with a particular other person, or they have them respond to various questions about their "best friend," their "parent," or their "current romantic partner." Although people's reports about their relationships are not always accurate (an issue we will consider more fully in Chapter 2), this remains the most common method for establishing interdependence (and the presence of a relationship). Many different self-report measures will be presented throughout this textbook.

Alternately, researchers can collect information from *both* partners (called a ***dyad***) and look for evidence of mutual influence using special kinds of statistical analyses (see Kenny, Kashy, & Cook, 2006). The ***Actor–Partner Interdependence Model*** (APIM; Cook & Kenny, 2005; Kashy & Kenny, 2000) represents one increasingly popular strategy. The APIM recognizes that a person's experiences in a relationship are a function both of his or her own characteristics or properties (called the ***actor effect***) and the partner's characteristics or properties (called the ***partner effect***—this is a measure of influence). The APIM, illustrated in Figure 1.2, allows researchers to estimate both of these effects. Suppose we were interested in whether neuroticism (a concept we will consider in Chapter 8— essentially, it reflects a dispositional tendency to experience negative emotion) predicts friendship quality in children. At the beginning of the school year, we could assess two children's neuroticism levels using a standard personality inventory. At the end of the school year, we could assess the quality of the friendship between those two children (e.g., how much liking they report feeling for

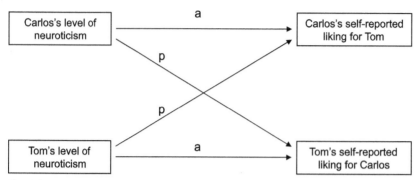

Fig. 1.2 The Actor–Partner Interdependence Model (APIM) proposed by David Kenny, Deborah Kashy, and William Cook (e.g., 2006) recognizes that a person's interpersonal outcomes are partly a reflection of his or her own characteristics (or prior behavior) and the characteristics or prior behavior of the relationship partner. Here, for example, the amount of liking that Carlos feels for his friend Tom is partly due to Carlos's own level of neuroticism (an actor effect, represented by the small "a" in the diagram) and partly due to Tom's level of neuroticism (a partner effect, represented by the small "p" in the diagram). Partner effects reflect interdependence or mutual influence—in this example, Tom is affected by Carlos, and Carlos is affected by Tom.

each other). The actor effect, depicted by the paths labeled *a* in the model, is a measure of how much each child's current feelings of friendship reflect his or her *own* level of neuroticism. In other words, the actor effect indicates how much of Carlos's liking for Tom is associated with Carlos's earlier level of neuroticism, and how much of Tom's liking for Carlos is associated with Tom's earlier level of neuroticism. The partner effect, depicted by the paths labeled *p* in the model, is a measure of how much each child's reports of liking reflect the *other* child's level of neuroticism. That is, the partner effect indicates how much of Carlos's liking for Tom reflects Tom's neuroticism, and how much of Tom's liking for Carlos reflects Carlos's neuroticism. These partner effects measure interdependence—the influence of each partner on the other.

Another method of establishing interdependence is to directly observe two people interacting over time and then examine their interaction pattern for signs of mutual influence. Relationship scientists have developed a number of special techniques—called ***time-series analyses***—that allow them to determine whether partners' responses exhibit interdependence (e.g., Bakeman & Gottman, 1997). Like the APIM, time-series analyses recognize that a person's behavior is often influenced by his or her own previous behavior (this corresponds to the actor effect in the APIM) as well as by the partner's previous behavior (this corresponds to the partner effect in the APIM and is a measure of influence). In time-series analyses, interdependence or mutual influence is established by determining that the behavior of each partner can be better predicted by the other partner's previous behavior than by his or her own previous behavior. Figure 1.3 illustrates this approach. Suppose we were interested in whether unhappily married couples have a tendency to reciprocate each other's negative behavior during arguments (we will consider this topic in greater detail in Chapter 15). We could find an unhappily married couple and then videotape the partners while they discussed an area of conflict in their relationship. We could then watch the videotapes and note the precise moment at which they exhibit various negative behaviors (e.g., anger, criticism, withdrawal, defensiveness). If we find, for example, that the husband's withdrawal behavior later in the interaction (say at Time 4) is better predicted by his wife's earlier (Time 3) criticism than by his own earlier (Time 3) defensiveness, then we have evidence that his behavior is dependent on hers. If the wife's behavior also can be better predicted from her husband's previous behavior than from her own previous behavior, the spouses are interdependent—they are influencing each other.

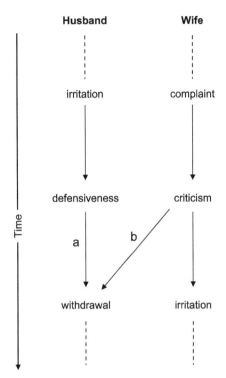

Fig. 1.3 Time-series analyses allow researchers to determine whether the behaviors of two partners (who are observed interacting over time) exhibit mutual influence. In this example, if the husband's withdrawal behavior later in the interaction is more strongly predicted by his wife's earlier criticism (represented by "b" in the diagram) than by his own earlier defensiveness (represented by "a" in the diagram), then she is influencing him. If the same pattern is found for the wife, the two partners are interdependent (their behaviors are causally connected and display mutual influence).

It is much easier to use self-reports from one person to establish the existence of a relationship (as opposed to gathering data from dyads, conducting behavioral observations over time, and so forth). However, the logic underlying the APIM, time-series analyses, and other dyadic techniques truly illustrates what it means to be interdependent—and these techniques have been successfully used to explore and uncover mutual influence in a variety of interpersonal domains.

FACT #2: RELATIONSHIP SCIENTISTS STUDY CERTAIN TYPES OF RELATIONSHIP

Just because relationship scientists study relationships does not mean that they are equally interested in all varieties. Each one of us forms associations with an enormous number of other individuals in the course of working, going to school, raising a family, taking care of a house, enjoying a hobby, traveling, and basically living our lives. But not all of these associations exert the same degree of impact on us—some are more influential than others, and it is these influential relationships that scientists are most interested in exploring.

Lovers, Family, and Friends

The relationships people form with lovers or mates, family members, and friends appear to play a particularly important role in promoting (or hindering) health, happiness, and other important life outcomes (see Chapter 3). Consequently, these three relationship varieties have received a great deal of attention from scientists.

Mating relationships (sometimes called romantic, dating, marital, or reproductive relationships) are differentiated from other relationships by the occurrence or potential occurrence of sexual involvement between the partners. Specifically, one of the distinguishing features of mating relationships is the fact that sexual exchanges and activities are viewed by the partners as a legitimate expectation for their relationship regardless of whether or not they are currently engaging in such activities (see Scanzoni, Polonko, Teachman, & Thompson, 1989). In other words, although sexual interaction is not a necessary feature of mating relationships, the occurrence of sexual activity within a mating relationship would not be unexpected or inappropriate—and this is what differentiates mating relationships from other relationship varieties (e.g., friendships, parent–child relationships). In addition, mating relationships—most notably marital or spousal relationships—are governed by an extensive array of social norms, expectations, and rules that regulate many aspects of the partners' union. For example, in the United States, marriage is considered a legal contract between the two partners, and each state specifies the requirements that must be met before a couple can legally wed (or legally divorce). Moreover, nearly all cultures endorse and enact social rituals and ceremonies to officially mark the beginning—and ending—of a marriage or other mating relationship (Ihinger-Tallman & Henderson, 2003). Similarly, the assumptions and roles associated with being a partner in a mating relationship (i.e., with being a husband or wife, boyfriend or girlfriend) tend to be more formalized than in many other relationship varieties. Chapters 7, 10, and 11, in particular, focus on this type of relationship.

Family relationships (sometimes called *kinship* or *kin relationships*) historically have been defined as partnerships or associations among people who are genetically or legally related—that is, who are connected by blood, adoption, or marriage (Comacchio, 2003; Ross, Mirowsky, & Goldsteen, 1990). Although definitions of family are changing, and increasing numbers of people now count their close friends and even their pets among their family members (e.g., Risley-Curtiss, Holley, & Wolf, 2006; also see Braithwaite et al., 2010), blood or genetic relatedness continues to be an essential feature of most people's understanding of what constitutes "family" (e.g., Widmer, 2006; for discussion, see Allan, 2008). Unlike other kinds of relationship, family relationships tend to be involuntary and thus are considered relatively permanent; we form these associations at birth or through adoption, marriage, or some other legal process, and therefore may have little choice in selecting our partners or dissolving our relationship with them (Dykstra, 2009; Munro & Munro, 2003). Similarly, there are a greater number of formal social and legal obligations and expectations for family relationships than there are for friendships and other types of more voluntary partnership. The dynamics of family relationships are discussed throughout the textbook.

A distinguishing feature of *friend relationships* is that they are voluntary; most people choose their friends but not everyone has the freedom to personally select his or her mate or family members. Moreover, there are far fewer social norms and obligations concerning friendships than there are for other, more socially structured and regulated partnerships (e.g., family and mating relationships). For example, as noted by Paul Wright (2003) in his review, there are no ceremonies surrounding the formation or dissolution of friend relationships, and the partners are generally free from social expectations that dictate how and when they should interact. Because friendships are less bounded by social, legal, and moral constraints than are family, mating, and other kinds of relationship, they are inherently more flexible (Allan, 2008)—how the partners define and understand their relationship, the activities and interactions in which they engage, and the expectations they have for their friendship largely are matters of personal choice and determination. Research generally reveals that the primary motivation for friendship involves fulfilling socio-emotional needs such as companionship, emotional support, affection, and intimacy (Blieszner & Adams, 1992; Hays, 1988; Oswald, Clark, & Kelly, 2004). Although these same needs may also be met in family and mating relationships, they tend not to be a distinguishing feature of those particular relationship varieties. (Indeed, as we will discuss in Chapter 7, individuals enter mating relationships for a variety of reasons, only some of which concern fulfillment of personal socio-emotional needs.) Although friendships historically have received less scholarly attention than mating and family relationships, this state of affairs is changing and there is now a growing body of research devoted to this important relationship variety.

Close Relationships

Of course, not all mating, family, and friend relationships are equally important. Friendly acquaintances, distant relatives, and casual dates or sex partners generally have less overall impact on our lives than, for example, best friends, parents or siblings, spouses, live-in boyfriends and girlfriends, and steady dates. Relationship scientists reserve the term *close relationship* for those more influential associations, and they typically differentiate between *subjectively close relationships* (often called *intimate relationships*) and *behaviorally close relationships* (see Ben-Ari & Lavee, 2007).

Subjectively Close (Intimate) Relationships. Some relationships are characterized by high levels of *subjective closeness*—that is, the partners feel close, connected, or bonded to one another. Subjective closeness is typically assessed via self-report. One of the most commonly used measures is the Inclusion of Other in the Self Scale (IOS) created by Arthur Aron, Elaine Aron, and Danny Smollan (1992). The IOS was derived from a theoretical view of closeness as an overlapping of selves and a sense of "oneness" with the other (e.g., Aron & Aron, 1996; Aron, Mashek, Aron, 2004), and it is intended to assess the degree to which an individual feels interconnected with his or her partner. As illustrated in Figure 1.4, the measure consists of seven pairs of circles (one representing the "self" and the other representing the "other" person) that overlap in varying degrees, and participants are asked to select the pair that best describes their relationship.

An alternate method for assessing subjective closeness is to simply ask participants to indicate the frequency and/or the intensity of intimacy, closeness, love, trust, caring, commitment, and other positive feelings, sentiments, and emotions that they currently experience for a specific relationship partner. The higher the score an individual reports on these scales, the greater the subjective closeness of his or her relationship.

Behaviorally Close (Highly Interdependent) Relationships. Unlike subjective closeness, which refers to feelings of closeness, behavioral closeness is tied to the partners' interaction pattern and refers to the extent to which they exhibit *high interdependence* or mutual influence. Four properties are necessary to establish a high level of interdependence (Kelley et al., 1983/2002):

- *Frequency of influence.* The partners must *frequently* influence each other's behavior (that is, they must affect each other on multiple occasions and not just once in a while at the occasional get-together). For example, two people who see each other once a year at a conference exert less influence on each other than two people who live together and interact on multiple occasions throughout the day, and their relationship would be considered less close.
- *Diversity of influence.* Each partner must influence a *diversity* (many different kinds) of the other partner's behaviors and outcomes. For example, a relationship between two people who only

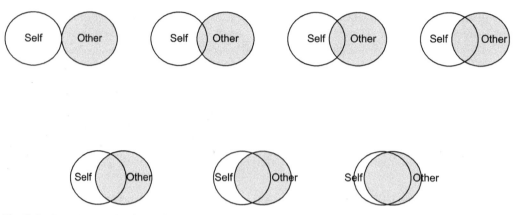

Fig. 1.4 The Inclusion of Other in the Self Scale.

Source: Copyright © 1992 by the American Psychological Association. Figure 1 reproduced with permission. Aron, A., Aron, E. N., & Smollan, D. (1992). Inclusion of Other in the Self Scale and the structure of interpersonal closeness. *Journal of Personality and Social Psychology, 63,* 596–612.

influence each other's work-related outcomes would be considered less close than a relationship in which each partner influences the books the other reads, the movies the other sees, the hobbies the other pursues, the academic choices the other makes, the attitudes and values the other holds, the neighborhood in which the other lives, the vacations the other takes, and so forth.

- *Strength of influence.* The partners' influence on each other must be *strong.* Strength of influence is indicated by the speed with which a person responds to the other, the magnitude (intensity) of the response to the other, and the number and importance of behaviors that are affected by the other. For example, Partner A exerts a fairly strong amount of influence on Partner B if a single behavior from Partner A produces an immediate and "big" reaction from Partner B, continues to affect Partner B over a long period of time, and influences Partner B's most important outcomes.
- *Duration of influence.* This frequency, diversity, and strength of influence must characterize the partners' interaction pattern for a relatively long *duration* of time. This means that two people assigned to the same cabin on a two-day camping trip might temporarily satisfy the frequency, diversity, and strength criteria—but because they do not satisfy the duration criterion, most researchers would not identify their relationship as a close one.

The most common measure of behavioral closeness is the Relationship Closeness Inventory (RCI; Berscheid, Snyder, & Omoto, 1989a, 1989b, 2004). The RCI is composed of three self-report subscales, equally weighted and summed to obtain a total closeness score. The Frequency subscale assesses the amount of time the partners spend together alone (without other people present). The Diversity subscale provides participants with a list of typical activities for their demographic group and assesses the number of activities the participants and their partners did together alone the previous week. For example, college students are asked how many times during the prior week they and their partners "attended class," "discussed things of a personal nature," and "went to a party" together. On the Strength subscale, participants are asked to indicate the degree of influence their partners have on their thoughts, feelings, actions, future plans, and goals (e.g., "how I spend my free time," "my overall happiness," "my school-related plans"). Relationship duration is measured but not included in the RCI total score.

In sum, there are two types of closeness we can experience in our interpersonal relationships—a type of closeness involving subjective feelings of connection and bondedness and/or positive affective experiences, and a type characterized by a high degree of behavioral interdependence. Some relationships possess both forms of closeness. Best friends may have a great deal of mutual influence on one another (behavioral closeness) as well as high levels of affection, liking, and felt intimacy (subjective closeness). Others possess one but not the other type of closeness. For example, the relationship between a person whose every obnoxious behavior negatively impacts the life of his or her long-suffering spouse would be considered behaviorally but not subjectively close (i.e., highly interdependent but not intimate), whereas the connection between a geographically distant but much-loved aunt and her nephew or niece would be viewed as subjectively but not behaviorally close (i.e., intimate but not highly interdependent).

Because relationship scientists typically focus on the interpersonal associations that have the most impact and influence on people's life outcomes—namely, the close relationships they form with mates, family members, and friends—the research and theory covered in this textbook are largely concerned with those relationship varieties. It is important to acknowledge, however, that other types of relationship can have a powerful impact on our lives, though many of them have yet to receive much systematic attention from scholars. For example, the relationships people form with companion animals often meet all of the criteria for closeness, and they appear to be strongly linked to beneficial health outcomes (Allen, 2009; Coren, 1998; Melson, 2001; Wilson & Turner, 1998; see photo below). People love, communicate with, care for, and support (and receive support

from) their pets, and they grieve their loss in much the same way that they mourn the loss of any other intimate partner. Indeed, in an increasingly mobile and urban world, where more and more of us are choosing to remain single and childless, where families move far apart, and where roughly half of all marriages end in divorce, some of the most enduring, stable, and committed relationships we have are the ones we establish with our pets. These associations are certainly deserving of much more scientific attention than they have yet received.

FACT #3: RELATIONSHIP SCIENCE IS NOT EASY

The fact that relationship scientists have successfully overcome most of the conceptual and methodological (see Chapter 2) challenges that have arisen does not mean that the road they travel is a smooth one. In reality it is not easy to be a relationship scientist, for a number of reasons.

Societal Taboos Against the Study of Relationships

The first reason is that relationship scientists have had to contend with widespread beliefs that often made it difficult to investigate relationship phenomena. In the United States, for instance, relationship topics were not considered appropriate subjects for scientific investigation, or were believed to be too complex and mysterious to yield to scientific analysis, even well into the twentieth century (for additional discussion, see Berscheid, 1986). Moreover, many people assumed that gaining scientific knowledge about relationship phenomena would somehow rob those phenomena of their intrinsic value, significance, and enjoyment. Interestingly, this assumption continues to rear its head today. For example, after *National Geographic* magazine published an article that reviewed scientific evidence about the nature of romantic love ("Love: The Chemical Reaction," February, 2006), one disillusioned reader wrote:

> Science has ruined everything for lovers and poets. Love is no longer a many-splendored thing, but a slosh of dopamine over a caudate nucleus. Your article enlightened me to what happened when I first saw my wife 46 years ago. It wasn't love; it was merely a squirt of dopamine.
> ("True love," March, 2006)

This man clearly blames relationship science for destroying one of the greatest and most mystical interpersonal experiences of his entire life!

Those groundbreaking scientists who bravely plunged ahead and studied relationship topics in the face of widespread social disapproval were punished. In 1975, for example, U.S. Senator William Proxmire gave the first of his infamous Golden Fleece Awards to the National Science Foundation for allocating grant money to two researchers who proposed to study interpersonal attraction and romantic love. In press releases announcing this dubious honor, Proxmire denounced the National Science Foundation for suggesting that "falling in love is a science" ("Ah, sweet mystery," March 24, 1975) and offered the following comments:

> Each month I have decided to offer a "golden fleece" award to the organization or person who has most utterly wasted your tax dollars. Last month's award went to the National Science Foundation for a study of why people fall in love. . . . Not only is this a question that cannot be answered, like what is infinity, [but] I'm not sure we want an answer. There should be some mysteries in life.
> (Proxmire, May, 1975)

Not surprisingly, the personal and professional fallout from this so-called "award" was devastating for the two investigators who received the National Science Foundation grants (see Berscheid, 2002; Hatfield, 2006). (Ironically, however, the media attention that the award generated actually increased the public's interest in scientific research on the topics of attraction and love.)

Studying interpersonal events and experiences in the face of these societal taboos has been (and to some extent continues to be) challenging for many relationship scientists.

Relationships are Complex

Another difficulty facing relationship scientists stems from the fact that relationships are incredibly complicated phenomena. Unlike other interpersonal phenomena which can be directly observed and which either occur or do not occur (e.g., compliance, helping), relationships are dynamic phenomena that unfold over time and that both encapsulate and are embedded in multiple other complicated phenomena (see Berscheid, 1986; Hinde, 1979, 1997; Reis et al., 2000). As a result, the study of relationships involves many levels of complexity, as illustrated in Figure 1.5.

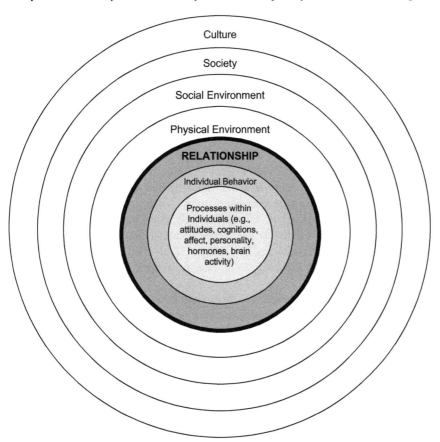

Fig. 1.5 Relationships are highly complex systems that exist in a hierarchy of other systems, including the physical environment (e.g., temperature, geography, crowding, economic conditions), the social environment (e.g., neighborhood, family, other people), and the larger society (e.g., United States) and culture (e.g., Western). Relationships also encompass a host of other systems, such as those residing in or associated with the individual partners. A change in any one of these systems tends to produce changes in the other systems.

Marital relationships, for example, are nested within an existing physical, social, and cultural environment that influences the nature of those marriages in many different ways. The presence or absence of children (a social environmental factor), the level of financial hardship the spouses face (a physical environmental factor), and the existing laws and customs regulating courtship, marriage, and divorce (a sociocultural factor) have implications for both the satisfaction and the stability of couples' unions. Marriages are also likely to be affected by the behaviors (e.g., negative, positive, communicative, supportive) and internal psychological and physical events (e.g., age, physical and mental health, mood, dispositional tendencies, personality traits) associated with each individual partner. In turn, marital relationships influence these other systems. As we will discuss in later chapters, marriage changes the partners' physical and mental properties (e.g., producing beneficial outcomes for some individuals and detrimental outcomes for others), influences their behavior (both alone and in interaction with one another), and alters their physical and social environments (e.g., by changing the spouses' degree of social integration, the quality and quantity of their social network, their living situation and economic state). Marriages also impact the larger sociocultural landscape. For instance, as increasing numbers of men and women delay marriage, have children out of wedlock, elect to cohabit (or remain single) rather than marry, and insist on choosing their partners on the basis of love, corresponding changes occur in social attitudes, customs, and even laws pertaining to mate selection, premarital sex, single parenthood, cohabiting and same-sex unions, and so forth.

In sum, no relationship exists in a vacuum—each one is involved in a dynamic exchange of influence with the other systems it encapsulates and in which it is embedded.

Relationship Phenomena are Multiply Determined

This brings us to the third reason why the job of the relationship scientist is particularly challenging—the inherent complexity of the aforementioned system guarantees that relationship phenomena are multiply determined. Consequently, in order to achieve any useful degree of understanding of interpersonal attraction, love, friendship development, marital satisfaction, conflict, bereavement, intimate partner violence, social support, divorce, or any other significant interpersonal experience, relationship scientists must explore a diversity of factors located at varying levels of analysis. In general, these factors fall into three broad classes or analytic levels (Hinde, 1979; Kelley et al., 1983; also see Dutton, 1985): personal factors, relational factors, and environmental factors (see Figure 1.6).

Personal factors are variables that are associated with the individual partners (often designated as P [Person] and O [Other]). These include personality traits or dispositional tendencies; belief systems, attitudes, preferences, and values; affective states; physical characteristics; mental health variables; hormonal or biological processes; and any other relatively enduring features or attributes that each partner brings to the relationship. For example, as we will see in later chapters, how satisfying a particular romantic relationship is partly reflects the age of the partners (satisfaction declines with age), their stable dispositions and traits (negative affectivity or neuroticism is associated with less satisfaction, and secure attachment style is associated with more satisfaction), their existing beliefs and expectations about love, romance, and relationships (those who idealize their relationship and each other tend to be happier), and a host of other person-level factors.

Relational (P × O) factors are located in neither partner but instead emerge from the partners' interactions or result from the combination of each partner's characteristics. Proximity, similarity, equity, mutual disclosure, and feelings of attraction between the partners, as well as their attributional patterns, communication styles, and conflict resolution strategies fall in this category. For

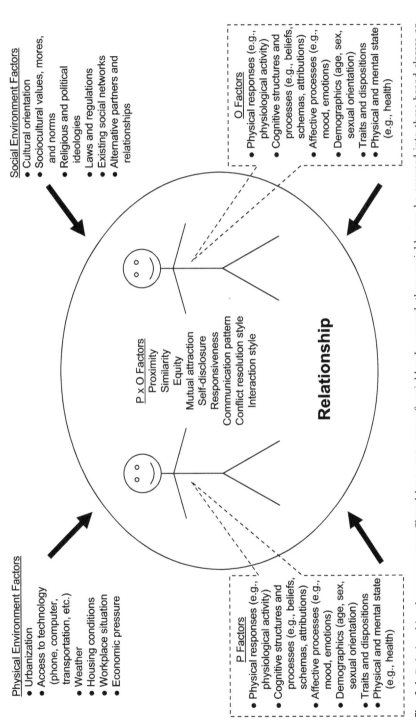

Fig. 1.6 Relationship phenomena are affected by a vast array of variables. In general, these variables can be grouped into three broad classes or analytic levels: (1) personal factors that are associated with the individual partners (Partner [P] and Other [O]), (2) relational (P × O) factors that reflect the combination of the two partners' characteristics (e.g., similarity) or that emerge from their interactions (e.g., responsiveness, conflict resolution style), and (3) environmental factors that are located in the physical and sociocultural environments surrounding the relationship.

The text within the figure reads:

Physical Environment Factors
• Urbanization
• Access to technology (phone, computer, transportation, etc.)
• Weather
• Housing conditions
• Workplace situation
• Economic pressure

Social Environment Factors
• Cultural orientation
• Sociocultural values, mores, and norms
• Religious and political ideologies
• Laws and regulations
• Existing social networks
• Alternative partners and relationships

O Factors
• Physical responses (e.g., physiological activity)
• Cognitive structures and processes (e.g., beliefs, schemas, attributions)
• Affective processes (e.g., mood, emotions)
• Demographics (age, sex, sexual orientation)
• Traits and dispositions
• Physical and mental state (e.g., health)

P Factors
• Physical responses (e.g., physiological activity)
• Cognitive structures and processes (e.g., beliefs, schemas, attributions)
• Affective processes (e.g., mood, emotions)
• Demographics (age, sex, sexual orientation)
• Traits and dispositions
• Physical and mental state (e.g., health)

P x O Factors
Proximity
Similarity
Equity
Mutual attraction
Self-disclosure
Responsiveness
Communication pattern
Conflict resolution style
Interaction style

Relationship

example, partners who consistently make unequal contributions to their relationship, and whose interactions are characterized by negative affect reciprocity and demand-withdrawal, are likely to experience dissatisfaction.

Environmental factors include variables located in the physical and social environments in which the relationship is embedded. These include the economic conditions of the partners (as well as the presence or absence of various material and physical resources), their occupational situation, other social objects (e.g., friends, family members, children, and alternative partners), social or religious customs, laws, cultural orientations, and the existing political climate. As we will discuss, social norms and cultural values dictate who we desire—and choose—for friendship and romance, laws determine who we can (and cannot) marry, economic hardship can make or break a marriage, and normative expectations about division of labor, sexuality, fidelity, violence, and other interpersonal events influence how happy our mating relationships, friendships, and family relationships ultimately end up being.

We will use this conceptual framework—a framework that classifies causal factors into personal, relational, and environmental variables—throughout the rest of the textbook. (But please keep in mind that relationship science, like any field, is an ongoing endeavor. As a result, not every single topic we will consider has been explored at each level of analysis and countless unanswered questions remain.)

Relationship Science is Multidisciplinary

Because relationships are complex and affected by a multitude of variables, relationship science draws on theory and research from many different fields of inquiry. Consequently, although most relationship scholars are trained (and earn their degrees) in one primary area, they must maintain currency in a number of other disciplines. The theory and research cited in this textbook thus are drawn from a wide variety of domains, including psychology and its subfields (e.g., clinical, community, developmental, health, personality, social), communication studies, family studies, developmental science (child development, gerontology, life-span development), marriage and family therapy, social work, sociology, anthropology, natural (biology, physiology, chemistry) and health (medicine, epidemiology) science, zoology, economics, and even philosophy, history, and theology. The fact that relationship science is multidisciplinary means that relationship scientists must be masters of many trades. This represents one of the greatest challenges for individual scholars but at the same time is one of the field's greatest strengths.

FACT #4: RELATIONSHIP SCIENCE IS IMPORTANT

> Relationships with others lie at the very core of human existence. Humans are conceived within relationships, born into relationships, and live their lives within relationships with others. Each individual's dependence on other people—for the realization of life itself, for survival during one of the longest gestation periods in the animal kingdom, for food and shelter and aid and comfort throughout the life cycle—is a fundamental fact of the human condition.
>
> (Berscheid & Peplau, 1983, p. 1)

Clearly, relationship scientists believe that relationships are important (or else they would not devote their careers to studying them). And most, if not all, people would agree. Ask any individual to specify the things that have brought the most joy (or the most pain) to his or her life, and interpersonal experiences will undoubtedly show up at the top of the list. We humans are fundamentally social creatures, designed to form and maintain close, intimate relationships with other people, and the ones we establish have immediate and lasting consequences on the quality of our lives (a fact we will examine more fully in Chapter 3 and revisit repeatedly throughout the remainder of the textbook). For this reason, relationship science is one of the most essential and deeply rewarding of endeavors.

SUMMARY

Relationship science possesses its own guiding principles and key concepts. For example, although numerous commonsense and idiosyncratic definitions of "relationship" exist, relationship scientists view interaction as the essential ingredient and consider two people to be in a relationship to the extent that they interact and mutually influence each other over time and in a unique way. Most researchers rely on self-report methods to establish interdependence, simply asking participants whether or not they have a relationship with a particular other person or having them respond to various questions about their "best friend" or their "current romantic partner." Other researchers collect dyadic data (that is, information from both partners in a given relationship) and look for evidence of mutual influence using several methods that are now available, such as the Actor–Partner Interdependence Model procedure and time-series analyses. Relationship scientists are most interested in exploring influential relationships; consequently, they have tended to devote most of their theoretical and empirical attention to close (intimate and/or highly interdependent) mating relationships, friendships, and family or kin relationships. The societal taboos that historically have hindered scientific examination of relationship phenomena, the complex nature of relationships (and the diversity of conditions that affect them), and the need to maintain currency in many different fields make relationship science one of the most challenging of endeavors—the fundamental importance of relationships to human life makes it one of the most rewarding.

KEY CONCEPTS

Interdependence (p. 4)
Relationship (p. 4)
Interaction episode (p. 5)
Role-based interactions (p. 6)
Formal (role-based) relationship (p. 6)
Mental representation (p. 7)
Dyad (p. 7)
Actor–Partner Interdependence Model (p. 7)
Actor effect (p. 7)
Partner effect (p. 7)
Time-series analyses (p. 8)
Mating relationships (p. 10)
Family (kinship) relationships (p. 10)

Friend relationships (p. 10)
Close relationship (p. 11)
Subjectively close (intimate) relationship (p. 11)
Subjective closeness (p. 11)
Behaviorally close relationship (p. 11)
High interdependence (p. 11)
Frequency of influence (p. 11)
Diversity of influence (p. 11)
Strength of influence (p. 12)
Duration of influence (p. 12)
Personal factors (p. 16)
Relational (P × O) factors (p. 16)
Environmental factors (p. 18)

EXPLORATION EXERCISES

These exercises are designed to allow you to explore in greater detail some of the concepts and issues discussed in this chapter. There are no right or wrong answers to these exercises—they are simply meant to provide an opportunity for discussion and debate.

1. One of the biggest challenges faced by early scholars interested in exploring relationship issues was coming up with a common conceptual vocabulary they all could agree on—including, for example, just what was meant by the concept of "relationship." Although today most scholars now agree about what constitutes a relationship, there is some evidence that people in general (that is, you and me) may sometimes disagree about what it means to have, or to be in, a relationship with someone. This exercise is designed to explore people's commonsense understandings of the concept of relationship. First, ask three or four people you know to answer the following question:

   What is a relationship? What does this term mean to you? Tell me in your own words how you would define this concept.

   Second, based on their responses, provide responses to the following questions: (1) How did they define the concept of relationship? What were the common themes or elements in their definitions? (2) Did their definition "match" the definition that most scientists now use? (3) Did you notice any differences of opinion among the responses? What were the most uncommon or distinct elements included in the definitions?
2. Many of the interactions we have with others as we go about our daily lives would be considered "role-based interactions." Describe two interactions you have had in the past week that were clearly role-based. What aspects about them helped you decide that they were indeed role-based?
3. The word "family" traditionally has been defined as a group of two or more people who are related by birth, marriage, or adoption (in fact, this is the definition employed by the U.S. Census Bureau). This definition leaves out many groupings some individuals would consider a family; in fact, there is evidence that people's understanding of what constitutes a "family" may be changing. This activity is designed to explore how people today understand the concept of family. To complete this exercise, you will first need to identify a group of 10 adults (strangers, friends, family members, or other students). Next, ask them to indicate which of the groupings of people listed on the next page they would consider a "family" (and you may make up other groupings, too). Record the total number of "yes" and "no" responses you received from your 10 participants in the place indicated.

Question: Is this a "family"?

Grouping	Yes	No
(a) a husband and wife and their biological children	_____	_____
(b) a husband and wife and their adopted children	_____	_____
(c) an unmarried man and woman and their biological children	_____	_____
(d) an unmarried man and woman living together as a couple	_____	_____
(e) two homosexual men living together as a couple	_____	_____
(f) two lesbian women living together and raising their child	_____	_____
(g) a mother, her child, and her grandmother	_____	_____
(h) a divorced man raising his child	_____	_____
(i) two best friends	_____	_____

What do your results tell you about how people understand the concept of family? Did everyone agree? Were there some groupings very few considered a "family"? Do you think that definitions will continue to evolve as society continues to change?

Chapter 2
Research Methods

Spend some time perusing the magazine aisle or self-help section at your local bookstore and you will be amazed at the sheer number of articles and books whose authors promise to provide solutions to important relationship problems and to share the knowledge needed to become a better parent, lover, friend, work colleague, and even pet owner. Relationship scientists are also interested in uncovering relationship truths and answering questions about relationships, but unlike most popular press writers—who tend to rely on anecdote, personal beliefs, or unfounded assumptions—they use specialized scientific methods for finding the answers. To a large extent, research methodology comprises the language of relationship science (or any science, for that matter). Principles of design and methodology allow scientists to develop and test their hypotheses and to communicate their results to other researchers and to the world at large. Therefore, knowledge of methodology is essential for anyone who wishes to be able to accurately interpret information about relationships. In this chapter, we consider the research methods commonly used by relationship scientists in their quest to understand—and make accurate predictions about—relationship phenomena.

FORMULATING A TESTABLE QUESTION

Before any investigation can begin, the researcher must first generate a *hypothesis*—a testable prediction about the relationship between two or more variables. If there is insufficient existing information about a relationship phenomenon to allow the researcher to generate a specific hypothesis, he or she may instead propose a more general *research question* that clearly specifies the variables of interest but does not make specific predictions about the associations among them. Some studies include both a general research question as well as a specific hypothesis about what the study will reveal. For example, communication scholars Paul Mongeau, Mary Claire Morr Serewicz, and Lona Ficara Therrien (2004) were interested in exploring the goals that young adults have for first dates. They had two general research questions: (1) what goals will college students report for their first dates? and (2) are there sex differences in first date goals? The researchers also generated a specific hypothesis; namely, that men would report more sexual first date goals than would women, and that women would report more romantic first date goals than would men. Table 2.1 provides additional examples of hypotheses and research questions from recent articles published in a variety of scientific journals.

Hypotheses and research questions may stem from a researcher's own personal experiences. For example, a scientist who is in a long-distance relationship may wonder whether couples who live far apart experience less (or more) relationship satisfaction than couples who live together. Another scholar whose best friend is in the process of obtaining a divorce may speculate about the impact of parental divorce on children's emotional adjustment. However, hypotheses and research questions are more commonly derived from existing research and theory. The fact that previous research had revealed that men are more likely than women to expect sex to occur on a first date, for example, contributed to Mongeau et al.'s (2004) hypothesis about sex differences in first date goals.

The essential feature of a hypothesis or research question is that it is *testable*. For example, consider the question "Is infidelity natural"? It is difficult to determine what data would constitute suitable evidence that infidelity is "natural," and virtually impossible to scientifically answer this question. However, consider the question "Are there sex differences in self-reported infidelity?" This question can be tested and answered in a variety of ways. We could, for example, do what Robert Michael and his colleagues (Michael, Gagnon, Laumann, & Kolata, 1994) did and obtain a sample of married adults living across the nation, ask them whether or not they have ever had sex with someone other than their spouse while they were married, and then compare the percentage of men and women who said "yes." Or we could gather a sample of college students involved in long-term dating relationships, ask them to report the number of times they had engaged in sexual

Table 2.1   Hypotheses and Research Questions

Below are some statements taken directly from a number of published articles. See if you can identify which statements reflect hypotheses (H) and which reflect research questions (RQ). Answers are at the bottom of the table.

Statement 1:   "The more similar spouses are to each other, the higher their levels of marital satisfaction and positive affect, and the lower their level of negative affect." (Gaunt, 2006, p. 1405)

Statement 2:   "Using an exclusively adolescent population, the present study sought to analyze dating violence victimization by region of the country in rural communities." (Marquart, Nannini, Edwards, Stanley, & Wayman, 2007, p. 648)

Statement 3:   "Men will overperceive women's sexual interest and women will underperceive men's sexual interest regardless of their degree of sexual interest in the target." (Koenig, Kirkpatrick, & Ketelaar, 2007, p. 415)

Statement 4:   "Children who form cross-racial/ethnic friendships would display greater levels of social competence such as relational inclusion and leadership compared with children who do not have cross-racial/ethnic friendships." (Kawabata & Crick, 2008, p. 1178)

Statement 5:   "The main aim of this study was to describe adolescents' perceptions and experiences of bullying: their thoughts about why children and adolescents are bullied, their ideas about why some bully others, and what they believe is important in order to stop bullying." (Frisén, Jonsson, & Persson, 2007, p. 749)

Statement 6:   "More satisfaction with division of labour by wives will be reported for couple- than family-initiated marriages." (Hortaçsu, 2007, p. 106)

Statement 7:   "Boys from divorced families will be more likely to be friendless and to be involved in a low-quality friendship than will boys from non-divorced families." (Lindsey, Colwell, Frabutt, & MacKinnon-Lewis, 2006, p. 48)

Statement 8:   "This study's first aim is to examine marital adjustment, spousal aggression, self-disclosure, and sexual satisfaction among former POWs [prisoners of war] and their wives." (Dekel, Enoch, & Solomon, 2008, p. 499)

Statement 9:   "Does the division of labor change across the transition to parenthood for lesbian couples, and, if so, what predicts this change?" (Goldberg & Perry-Jenkins, 2007, p. 302)

Statement 10: "More aggressive responses to betrayal would occur in the context of a romantic relationship when compared with a friendship." (Haden & Hojjat, 2006, p. 105)

Answers: 1 – H, 2 – RQ, 3 – H, 4 – H, 5 – RQ, 6 – H, 7 – H, 8 – RQ, 9 – RQ, 10 – H

activities with someone other than their partner during the relationship, and then compare the average (mean) number reported by men and the average number reported by women (e.g., Regan, 2000). The bottom line is that the researcher must be able to collect data that allow for the hypothesis or the research question to be tested.

DEFINING VARIABLES

In their hypotheses and research questions, researchers specify the variables—"infidelity," "sexual frequency," "social competence," "bullying," "marital satisfaction," "visual preference," and so forth—they are interested in exploring. Before any predictions about these variables can be tested, each variable must be precisely defined or *operationalized*. An **operational definition** is an exact, specific, and concrete definition of how the researcher chose to conceptualize and measure the variable. For example, the abstract variable "marital satisfaction" can be defined in a number of different ways. One researcher might measure marital satisfaction by asking participants to rate their overall happiness with their current spouse on a 7-point scale:

1	2	3	4	5	6	7
Not at all						*Extremely*
happy						*happy*

Another might operationalize marital satisfaction as scores on a multi-item questionnaire such as the Locke-Wallace Marital Adjustment Test (Locke & Wallace, 1959), the Dyadic Adjustment Scale (Spanier, 1976), or the Relationship Assessment Scale (Hendrick, 1988). And yet another might define marital satisfaction as the number of times couples engage in specific positive behaviors toward each other (e.g., holding hands, paying compliments) during a 10-day period. Each of these operational definitions has advantages and disadvantages. In fact, there is often no single, perfect method for operationally defining a variable. For this reason, scientists often ***multi-operationalize*** (i.e., employ multiple measures of) the variables included in their studies. Multi-operationalization increases the probability that a variable's meaning will be appropriately and completely "captured."

Operational definitions are extremely important, because they allow us to accurately interpret the results of a study. If, for example, we read a report that concludes that marital satisfaction changes over time, we need to know what the researchers meant by the term "marital satisfaction" and exactly how they measured it before we can evaluate the results.

SELECTING A RESEARCH STRATEGY

Once a hypothesis or research question has been formulated, and the variables of interest have been identified and defined, the researcher must decide how to go about implementing his or her investigation. In particular, he or she needs to select a research strategy. A ***research strategy*** concerns the way in which the researcher decides to investigate a question or hypothesis (in other words, how he or she frames the research question). Is the researcher interested in describing or illustrating a particular interpersonal event or phenomenon? Or establishing whether two variables are related or associated with one another? Or determining what causes a specific relational outcome? Depending on the researcher's primary scientific goal, he or she will adopt one of three different research strategies.

When the Goal is to Describe

Many investigations are designed to help the researcher illustrate or describe a phenomenon of interest. In ***descriptive research***, no variables are manipulated and the researcher often has not set out to specifically investigate a particular relationship among variables; rather, he or she is simply interested in describing people's behavior. For example, one recent descriptive investigation explored young adults' emotional responses to their very first romantic kiss (Regan, Shen, De La Peña, & Gosset, 2007). Participants in that study were asked to think back to their "very first romantic kiss ever" and to describe in a free response format (and in as much detail as possible) all of the feelings, emotions, and sentiments they recalled experiencing in the time period immediately before, during, and immediately after the kiss. Here are some examples of the data generated by this study:

> *From a male participant*: It was like fireworks were exploding in my mouth. It was a perfect moment. I felt euphoric and I will never forget that moment.

From a female participant: I felt comfortable and safe with this person because he was so gentle during the kiss. I also felt a little grossed out and disgusted because of the wet slimy lips. I think that was probably because it was new to me (now, I don't feel that way about kissing!).

It is common for free response data to be coded by the researcher and reduced to a quantitative (numeric) form. In this study, the researchers examined each free response for the presence or absence of particular kinds of positive and negative emotions. This allowed them to discover, for example, that the most common emotions experienced immediately prior to the first kiss were negative (e.g., anxiety, fear, uncertainty), and that more men than women reported experiencing positive emotions (e.g., joy, satisfaction, happiness) both during and after their very first kiss.

There are different types of descriptive research. ***Naturalistic or observational studies*** involve detailed observation of a participant sample in a natural or real-world setting. Psychologist Monica Moore's (1995) flirting research illustrates this type of descriptive investigation. In her study, Moore observed teenage girls in various public locations, including a shopping mall, an ice skating rink, and a swimming pool, as well as at school-related sporting events and parties. She recorded the type (e.g., smiling, hair flipping) and number of flirting behaviors that each girl demonstrated over a 30-minute period (see Table 2.2). In this way, she was able to identify the ways in which adolescent girls attempt to communicate romantic interest to potential partners. ***Survey research*** involves designing and administering a questionnaire to a sample of people in order to assess and describe their beliefs, attitudes, behaviors, and so forth. The national surveys conducted by sex researcher Alfred Kinsey and his colleagues (Kinsey, Pomeroy, & Martin, 1948; Kinsey, Pomeroy, Martin, & Gebhard, 1953) provide an example of this type of descriptive investigation. ***Archival research*** involves using data that were gathered by others. Public archives and statistical abstracts (e.g., census reports) provide data on marriage, divorce, births and deaths, and other important interpersonal events. Newspapers, journals, and diaries are another source of information about close relationships. For example, psychologist Paul Rosenblatt (1983) was able to explore relationship loss (and its associated grief and bereavement) in the lives of nineteenth-century men and women by examining diaries located in libraries throughout the United States.

Descriptive research is important for a number of reasons. Descriptive studies often serve as a springboard for future research because they provide basic information about the phenomenon of interest. A researcher who wishes to study courtship behavior must first understand the basic parameters of that phenomenon—how do people typically flirt, what kinds of behaviors do men and women "naturally" demonstrate in courtship settings? Descriptive research provides answers to those questions. In addition, naturalistic or observational studies often have high levels of something called ***external validity***, which means that the results are reflective of what actually occurs in the "real

Table 2.2 Top Five Most Common Nonverbal Flirting Behaviors Used by 100 Teenage Girls

Behavior	Frequency (%)
Hair flip	57
Type I glance (room or group encompassing glance)	49
Head toss	42
Type II glance (short, darting glance)	32
Smile	30

Source: Moore, M. M. (1995). Courtship signaling and adolescents: "Girls just wanna have fun"? *The Journal of Sex Research, 32,* 319–328. Copyright © 1995 by the Taylor and Francis Group, LLC.

world." At the same time, however, the researcher who conducts a naturalistic study has no control over the participant or the research situation, and therefore cannot make causal inferences (which, as we will discuss, is often of primary interest to a relationship scientist). Moreover, the researcher must decide which behaviors are of interest, select a suitable setting for observing these behaviors, and—most importantly—develop a coding system for recording and measuring the behaviors. These are often very time-consuming and challenging tasks.

Similarly, researchers who conduct surveys must decide how to obtain an appropriate sample of participants and how to maximize response rates so that no biases will be introduced into their results. Another major consideration in conducting survey research concerns the construction of the questionnaire. In particular, researchers must be very sensitive to the way in which questions are phrased and the type of response options allowed participants. For example, consider the following three questions, each designed to assess attitudes toward infidelity:

- "Is it morally appropriate for a married woman to violate the sanctity of her marriage vows and betray her husband by having sexual intercourse with another man?"
- "Is it acceptable for a woman to become romantically involved with someone other than her partner?"
- "Is it acceptable for married women to have affairs?"

The same participant is likely to provide different answers to these questions based entirely on how they are phrased. Survey researchers must work very hard to avoid bias when creating their questionnaires.

Archival research is also not without its difficulties. It can be extremely laborious, existing records may be difficult to locate and/or inaccurate, and the researcher is limited to the data at hand and therefore cannot ask additional questions or obtain further clarification of responses.

When the Goal is to Establish Association

Often, relationship researchers are interested in seeing whether two or more variables are related in some meaningful way. *Correlational research* involves measuring variables and looking for evidence of an association between them. This type of research does not allow scientists to determine whether one variable *causes* another, but simply to determine whether the variables *covary*. This is a very useful strategy when the researcher is dealing with variables that cannot be directly manipulated or controlled, including intra-individual variables (e.g., demographic or personality characteristics) and personal history variables (e.g., relationship status, length of relationship, previous relationship experiences).

Examples of correlational research abound in the relationship literature. Some questions that have been investigated include:

- Is neuroticism associated with marital satisfaction? (e.g., Donnellan, Conger, & Bryant, 2004).
- Is self-disclosure correlated with friendship quality? (e.g., Oswald & Clark, 2006).
- Is bullying associated with psychosocial adjustment among children? (e.g., Nishina, Juvonen, & Witkow, 2005).
- Is biological sex related to sexual attitudes? (e.g., Oliver & Hyde, 1993).
- Is relationship duration correlated with amount of passionate love? (Sprecher & Regan, 1998).
- Is social integration associated with mortality rates? (e.g., Engedal, 1996).

There are three types of correlations or associations that variables can demonstrate: positive, negative, and none (zero). A *positive correlation* between two variables means that they covary in a positive way; as scores on one variable (*X*) increase, so do scores on the other variable (*Y*). For example, as we will discuss in Chapter 11, researchers generally find a positive correlation between marital satisfaction and sexual satisfaction. That is, among a given sample of participants, those who score low on marital satisfaction also tend to score low on sexual satisfaction; those who score in the middle range on marital satisfaction tend to score in the middle range on sexual satisfaction; and those who score high on marital satisfaction tend to report correspondingly high levels of sexual satisfaction. A *negative correlation* between two variables means that they covary in a negative way; as scores on one variable (*X*) increase, scores on the other variable (*Y*) decrease. In Chapter 7 we will see that relationship researchers have consistently found a negative correlation between marital satisfaction and length of marriage. Specifically, the longer that married couples have been together, the lower their levels of marital satisfaction tend to be. A *zero correlation* means that the two variables are unrelated; there is no evidence of a significant association between them. For example, there is virtually no correlation between marital satisfaction and the height of the partners—in other words, very short, average, and very tall people do not differ in their levels of marital happiness.

Correlations not only have a direction but they also can range from weak to strong. The *correlation coefficient* (symbolized by *r*) is a statistic that provides a measure of the strength of the association between two variables. Correlation coefficients can range from −1.00 (a perfect negative correlation) to +1.00 (a perfect positive correlation), and the closer they are to those endpoints the stronger the association between the variables. Figure 2.1 illustrates the three types of correlation and their associated coefficients.

One of the most important things to remember about correlational studies is that they can establish covariation but not causation. All too often, researchers forget this essential methodological fact and find themselves drawing causal conclusions from correlational data (for additional discussion, see Baumrind, 1983). If we find, for example, that marital satisfaction and sexual satisfaction are positively correlated, it might be tempting to conclude that a happy marriage makes for a fulfilling sex life (in other words, marital satisfaction causes sexual satisfaction). But this would be a mistake. It is just as likely that a good sex life makes for a happy marriage (that is, sexual satisfaction causes marital satisfaction). Alternately, both marital and sexual satisfaction might be related to a third variable that is actually responsible for their observed correlation. For example, good communication skills might contribute to marital happiness and sexual fulfillment—thus, the reason that marital satisfaction and sexual satisfaction are associated is because they share this common underlying cause. For these reasons, we cannot draw causal conclusions from correlational research findings.

Now, having said this, there are specific correlational research strategies that do provide *clues* to causal relationships among variables. *Longitudinal (prospective) studies*, in which participants are measured at two or more points in time, are becoming more commonly utilized by relationship scientists. These studies are particularly valuable for two reasons. First, many relationship scholars are interested in how relationships change and develop over time, and longitudinal studies are specifically designed to provide developmental data. Second, longitudinal studies provide information about the temporal order in which events occur—and knowledge that one variable *X* precedes or happens before another variable *Y* suggests that *X* may, in fact, cause *Y*. For example, assume that a researcher uses the Strange Situation (a procedure we will discuss in the next chapter) to assess a group of children's attachment patterns, measures their social adjustment 4 years later, and finds that the two are associated (that is, that childhood attachment predicts social adjustment). Because

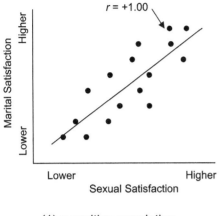

(1) a positive correlation

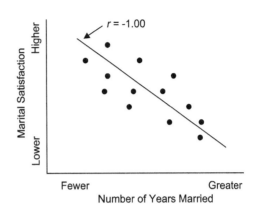

(2) a negative correlation

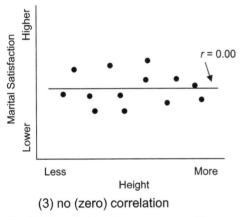

(3) no (zero) correlation

Fig. 2.1 Correlations. Scatter plots provide a graphic illustration of the relationship between two variables. The graphs here illustrate (1) a positive correlation, (2) a negative correlation, and (3) no correlation. Each point represents the position of a single participant's scores on the two measured variables. The solid straight lines depict what the correlations would look like if they were "perfect" (if X exactly predicted Y).

the design is longitudinal, and one variable clearly preceded the other, the researcher is justified in concluding that there may be a causal link between childhood attachment and subsequent social adjustment.

The bottom line, though, is that correlational studies simply demonstrate covariation—they may suggest, but they cannot absolutely determine, causal relationships.

When the Goal is to Determine Causation

Only a true experiment allows researchers to directly test and establish causal relationships among variables. In an ***experiment***, the researcher manipulates the causal variable X (called the ***independent variable***) to create groups of participants who differ in the level of that variable, and then measures and compares the groups in terms of their scores on some outcome Y (called the ***dependent variable***).

All other variables are kept constant (and thus their potential effects are controlled), either through direct experimental control or through random assignment of participants to the different levels of the independent variable. (***Random assignment*** means that each participant has an equal chance of being placed in the different groups created by the experimenter.) If the scores of the groups on the dependent variable are different, then the researcher can reasonably conclude that the manipulated variable X caused the measured variable Y, because the only difference between the groups was in their level of X.

For example, to test the hypothesis that similarity (the causal or independent variable) produces interpersonal attraction (the dependent variable), a researcher might bring a group of participants into the laboratory and randomly assign them to one of two conditions (each reflecting a different level of the independent variable): (1) an *experimental condition* in which they are told that they will take part in a "get acquainted" conversation with another person who shares several of their attitudes, interests, and hobbies, or (2) a *control condition* in which they are simply told that they will take part in a "get acquainted" conversation with another person. After exposing participants to one of these conditions, the researcher might ask them to answer a series of questions while they wait for the other person to arrive, including a question about how much they think they will like their conversation partner—their rating on this "liking" item is the measured or dependent variable. If liking ratings are higher in the experimental (similarity) condition than in the control condition, then support has been found for the hypothesis that similarity causes interpersonal attraction. Figure 2.2 illustrates this experimental study.

Now, this conclusion is only warranted if the experimenter has eliminated possible confounding. ***Confounding*** occurs when a variable other than the independent variable differs between the two groups and might influence scores on the dependent variable. For example, what if a female researcher conducted the sessions involving the participants assigned to the experimental group, whereas a male researcher conducted the sessions involving the control group? The sex of the

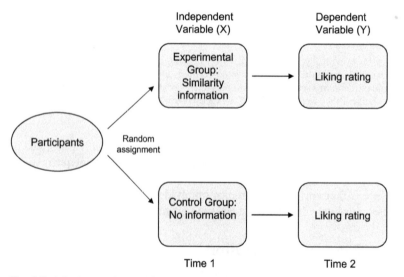

Fig. 2.2 A basic experimental design. To test the hypothesis that similarity produces liking, the researcher randomly assigns participants to an experimental (similarity information) or control (no information) group, and then measures subsequent behavior (liking ratings). If liking ratings are higher in the experimental group than in the control group, then support has been found for the hypothesis that similarity causes interpersonal attraction.

researcher represents a potential confound—it is possible that people's degree of liking for another individual, and the extent to which they feel comfortable expressing that preference, is affected by the sex of their "audience" (in this case, the researcher). Thus, any difference in interpersonal attraction ratings that is observed between the two groups may not reflect the influence of the independent variable, and the experimental results have been compromised. Similarly, what if a large number of participants in the similarity condition are securely attached, highly social extraverts who enjoy other people's company and expect to like every stranger they meet? What if most of the participants in the control condition stayed up late the night before and are too sleepy to pay much attention to the research situation? These individual difference variables may also influence scores on the dependent variable. The job of the experimenter is to eliminate possible confounding through **direct experimental control** (for example, by ensuring that participants are tested by the same researcher, during the same time of day, in the same room, and so on) and also through random assignment of participants to the different experimental conditions (which distributes any pre-existing individual differences—such as extraversion, sociability, and fatigue—evenly across the groups). By following these procedures, the experimenter can reasonably conclude that any difference in interpersonal attraction or liking ratings between the two groups is due solely to the influence of the independent variable (and the experiment would be said to have high *internal validity*).

Experimental designs provide the best opportunity for relationship researchers to determine causality. However, they do have a downside. For example, they are often costly and time-consuming to design and run. In addition, sometimes so much control is placed over the research situation that the experiment lacks external validity and it may be difficult to apply the results to the "real world." Finally, some variables simply cannot be manipulated. For example, we might wish to test the hypothesis that marriage influences personal happiness, but we cannot randomly assign participants to "married" and "single" groups, force them to live together for some period of time, and then measure their life satisfaction. Researchers can only experimentally investigate causal variables that they can control and manipulate.

CHOOSING A DATA COLLECTION METHOD

Once a relationship scientist has selected a research strategy, he or she must decide what kind of data to collect from the study participants. The **data collection method** refers to the source of the data. Regardless of the design, there are two broad categories of data collection method—self-report and observation.

Self-Report

Self-report methods involve asking people directly to report on their own experiences—behavior, affective reactions, attitudes, perceptions, thoughts, physical or mental state, and so forth. For example, if we were interested in measuring the amount of passionate love that a group of men and women felt for their partners, we might ask them to indicate how much they are currently in love with their partners, using the following response scale:

1	2	3	4	5	6	7
Not at all in love						*Extremely in love*

Alternately, we might administer a larger, multi-item scale such as the Passionate Love Scale (Hatfield & Sprecher, 1986a) to assess the amount of passionate love our participants currently experience. (The complete Passionate Love Scale is presented in Chapter 10.)

Many relationship researchers use self-report methods because they are relatively inexpensive and easy to administer. They also allow the researcher to obtain data directly from the source—and if we want to know how a person feels about his or her relationship, who better to ask than the person himself or herself? However, self-report methods rely on the researcher's ability to develop questions or select existing scales or measurement instruments that truly assess, reflect, or "capture" the behavior of interest. We have already discussed how questions that are poorly worded or easily misinterpreted by participants may yield meaningless data. For example, asking people to indicate the likelihood that they will "be unfaithful" to their current romantic partners presumes that all people define infidelity in the same manner. And yet there is evidence that they do not (e.g., Yarab, Allgeier, & Sensibaugh, 1999). Some people, for instance, consider sexual intercourse with another person to constitute infidelity, but they do not view flirting with another as an act of infidelity; others, however, view both flirting and sexual intercourse as acts of infidelity. It is the researcher's responsibility to make sure that participants have a clear understanding of the meaning of the item or set of items to which they are responding.

Self-report methods also rely on the participants' ability and willingness to report honestly and accurately about their own actions and feelings. People can only report what they are consciously aware of and what they are able to verbalize; they cannot report unconscious thoughts or feelings or those they cannot readily put into words (see Wilson, 1994). A study conducted by social psychologist Susan Sprecher (1989) provides a compelling illustration of the dangers of relying on self-report. In her study, men and women received information about an opposite-sex target who was presented as possessing high or low levels of physical attractiveness (and various other attributes). After rating the target's desirability as a dating partner, participants then were asked to indicate which attributes they believed had influenced their evaluations. Although men *reported* being more influenced than women by the target's physical appearance, the experimental data revealed that men and women were equally affected by the manipulation. That is, the physically attractive target was overwhelmingly preferred as a dating partner by both men and women. This suggests that people may be differentially aware of (or motivated to reveal) the factors that influence their perceptions and evaluations—an important consideration to keep in mind when evaluating self-report data.

Additionally, participants may have difficulty describing particular relationship events due to forgetfulness and other memory processes (Wiederman, 2004). For example, at the end of one longitudinal study of married couples (Vaillant & Vaillant, 1993), the researchers asked spouses to think back over their marriage and indicate how their satisfaction levels had changed over time. Because the researchers had measured marital satisfaction repeatedly during the study, they were able to compare spouses' recollections against their ongoing, prospective reports. The comparison indicated a clear memory bias. Specifically, spouses recalled a U-shaped or curvilinear pattern of satisfaction such that the high levels of happiness they experienced as newlyweds declined during the early years of their marriages but then returned to high levels in later years. However, an examination of their prospective reports indicated that marital satisfaction actually remained fairly stable over time (see Chapter 8 for additional discussion of memory biases for relationship events).

Participants also may distort aspects of their self-reports because of self-presentational concerns such as a desire to portray their experiences and their relationships as "normal," healthy, or adequate (see Orbuch & Harvey, 1991). A 1989 Gallup poll, for example, found that 84% of married respondents—when first asked—reported that they were "very satisfied" with their marriages;

however, further questioning revealed that 40% had actually considered leaving their partners and 20% said that their marriages were "bad" half of the time (see Olson, 1990). Assurances of anonymity, individual as opposed to group participation, and the use of self-administered questionnaires (as opposed to interviews) have been proposed as effective ways of reducing self-presentational concerns and enhancing the reliability of self-reports (Wiederman, 2006).

Structured Self-Reports of Daily Experiences. Another method for reducing the biases that can creep into self-reports is to ask participants to provide their observations almost immediately after a particular event of interest occurs, using structured questionnaires (Reis, 1994; Reis & Gable, 2000). One frequently used questionnaire is the Spouse Observation Checklist (SOC; see Weiss & Margolin, 1977). The SOC provides participants with a list of specific behaviors that reflect different categories of married life, including affection (e.g., "We held hands," "Spouse greeted me affectionately when I came home," "Spouse hugged or kissed me"), companionship (e.g., "We sat and read together," "We took a walk," "We played with our pets"), and so forth. At the end of each day, participants record the behaviors that occurred in their relationship during the preceding 24 hours. The Rochester Interaction Record (RIR), developed by psychologists Ladd Wheeler and Harry Reis (see Reis & Wheeler, 1991) is another structured self-report method. The RIR employs *event-contingent sampling*—that is, participants only provide reports when an event occurs that satisfies particular criteria (in this case, a social interaction lasting at least 10 minutes). Thus, every time a participant engages in a social interaction that lasts 10 minutes or longer, he or she records the event in a diary along with various evaluations (e.g., pleasantness of the interaction, degree of intimacy experienced during the interaction, emotional responses to the interaction).

In addition to minimizing response biases caused by faulty memory, structured daily experience questionnaires like the SOC and the RIR provide valuable information about people's thoughts, feelings, and activities in their everyday, ongoing lives and in their natural interaction settings.

Observation

The second data collection method used by relationship scientists is observation. ***Observational methods*** include all of the various procedures by which researchers directly observe or record the behavior of interest rather than rely on participants' self-reports. The flirting study described earlier in the chapter used an observational data collection method; specifically, Moore (1995) covertly observed her participants and discreetly recorded the number of times each girl displayed specific flirting behaviors. Some researchers use existing coding schemes to record their observations, rather than electing to go through the time-consuming and difficult process of developing their own. For example, scholars interested in relationship conflict frequently videotape couples having a discussion about an area of disagreement in their relationship and then code their behavior using one of a number of established behavioral coding systems, such as the Marital Interaction Coding System (MICS) developed by Robert L. Weiss and Kendra Summers (1983) or the Specific Affect Coding System developed by John Gottman and Lowell Krokoff (1989).

Researchers may also collect physiological data from their participants. Janice Kiecolt-Glaser, Cynthia Bane, Ronald Glaser, and William Malarkey (2003), for instance, were interested in whether various biological markers of stress could predict subsequent marital outcomes (including divorce). The researchers took blood samples from newlyweds while they discussed an area of conflict in their marriage and then analyzed the samples for levels of various stress hormones (e.g., epinephrine). When they re-contacted participants almost a decade later, they discovered that couples who had divorced had displayed higher levels of stress hormones during the earlier discussion than those who were still married.

Observational methods eliminate many of the biases that can occur with self-report methods. A married man or woman might not feel comfortable reporting strong negative emotions to a researcher (or to his or her spouse) during a conflict episode and thus may verbally misrepresent his or her true feelings. In this instance, observational methods—levels of stress hormones, physiological arousal, speech characteristics (interruptions, loudness), facial appearance, nonverbal behavior—would probably provide more accurate information about the participant's emotional state. However, observational methods possess their own set of difficulties. For example, people may alter their behavior if they discover that they are being observed, a situation known as *reactivity*; if this occurs, the data collected are unlikely to reflect participants' behavior as it naturally occurs.

Of course, in any one study a researcher may use an array of self-report and observational data collection methods. For example, a scientist interested in assessing passionate love might ask participants to indicate how in love they are with their partners on a 7-point scale (self-report), administer the Passionate Love Scale (self-report), record how often they touch their partners in a 10-minute period (observation), and measure their level of physiological arousal (e.g., heart rate, blood pressure, galvanic skin response) when sitting next to their partners (observation). It is often a very good idea to multi-operationalize a construct like passionate love because each measure provides a slightly different lens through which to view and assess the phenomenon.

SELECTING A RESEARCH SETTING

Once researchers have decided on a data collection method, they need to select a *research setting* in which to actually conduct their study and obtain data from participants. *Laboratory settings* include any setting or designated area established by the researcher to facilitate his or her ability to collect data (and, in the case of an experiment, to manipulate an independent variable and control any possible confounding variables). Laboratory settings range from the very simple and convenient (e.g., a researcher administers a social support scale to undergraduates seated at individual desks in an otherwise empty classroom) to the highly detailed and complex (e.g., a researcher seated behind a one-way mirror observes couples interacting in a laboratory room that has been carefully designed to resemble a "real" living room, complete with sofa, chairs, table, lamps, and bookcases). The benefit of laboratory settings is that they allow the researcher a degree of control often not possible in the outside world (and thus they usually provide higher levels of internal validity); the downside is that their artificial nature may cause participants to behave in an unnatural way (which compromises external validity).

Field settings are those that occur in the "real world" or the natural environment. Unlike most laboratory settings, field settings generally allow researchers to examine behavior as it naturally occurs. For example, in a recent study, psychologists Jamie Ostrov and Nicki Crick (2007) examined the association between different types of aggression and social adjustment among children. As part of their investigation, the researchers observed a group of 3- to 4-year-old children during recess on a preschool playground and recorded the extent to which each child engaged in physical (e.g., hitting, shoving) and relational (e.g., telling secrets, ending the friendship) aggression. Although the researchers had little control over the preschool setting and any outside events that spontaneously developed, it is likely that the behavior they observed reflected how children truly act during play episodes. Thus, what field settings lack in control of extraneous variables (and internal validity), they often make up for in external validity.

ANALYZING DATA AND INTERPRETING RESULTS

Once researchers have collected their data, they need to select an appropriate analytic strategy. Which one they choose will depend in part on their ***unit of analysis***. Some researchers opt to collect data and analyze responses from individuals as opposed to partners. For example, in a study of friendship quality, a random sample of individuals might be asked to think about their best friends (who are not participants in the study) and to rate their friendships on a number of dimensions (e.g., trust, disclosure, intimacy, warmth, closeness). There are several benefits to using an individual unit of analysis. For one thing, it is logistically easier to collect data from a group of individuals than it is to collect data from those individuals *and* their best friends, spouses, family members, or other relational partners (who may have conflicting schedules or other issues that make participation difficult). For another, most statistical procedures used by relationship scientists assume that the observations or pieces of data collected from study participants are ***independent***; this means that the responses given by one participant are not influenced by or related to those given by another participant. Violations of this important statistical assumption are likely to produce biased results (see Kenny & Judd, 1986). Because it is unlikely that a random sample of individuals will be related in any meaningful way to one another, use of an individual unit of analysis helps to ensure independent observations and reduce bias.

Other researchers choose to collect data and analyze the responses of dyads or couples. For example, a scientist interested in exploring marital communication might gather a sample of husband–wife pairs and solicit information from each spouse about the relationship. One of the primary benefits to adopting a dyadic unit of analysis is that it provides a much clearer view of the interpersonal processes that occur between relationship partners. When data about a relationship or about interpersonal, dyadic experiences are collected from only one individual (as they are when the researcher adopts an individual unit of analysis), the insights gained can be quite limited—after all, the researcher is getting one person's perspective about an event or experience that involves two people. For this reason, most relationship scientists would undoubtedly prefer to collect data from both partners. However, the primary difficulty with using a dyadic unit of analysis stems from the fact that researchers need to meet the assumption of independence in order to appropriately analyze their data and produce reliable results—but data that are collected from both relationship partners are rarely independent (see Gonzalez & Griffin, 1997). For example, it is highly likely that a husband's satisfaction with the overall level of communication in his marriage is related to his wife's satisfaction (and that her satisfaction with their level of communication has been influenced by or is associated with his).

Relationship scientists have proposed several solutions to this issue. One commonly used strategy has been to average the observations (scores) of both partners within the couple to create a set of "couple" observations. For example, the satisfaction ratings of both spouses could be averaged among the entire sample of married participants, and the researcher would be left with one set of "couple" scores for analysis. This strategy is not without its own set of problems. Fortunately, a number of conceptual and statistical developments (including the Actor–Partner Interdependence Model, discussed in Chapter 1) have made it easier for relationship scientists to analyze and interpret dyadic data (see Gonzalez & Griffin, 1997; Griffin & Gonzalez, 1995; Kenny, 1990; Kenny, Kashy, & Bolger, 1998; for a comprehensive review, see Kenny, Kashy, & Cook, 2006).

Statistical and Practical Significance

Regardless of which unit of analysis a researcher adopts, he or she will eventually subject the data to some sort of statistical analysis. Although there are a variety of methods available for analyzing data, each of them is designed to test whether the observed outcomes (e.g., the difference between the scores of the husbands and the scores of the wives; the difference between the scores of the experimental group and the scores of the control group; the correlations between variables) are "statistically significant" or whether they are simply due to chance (see, for example, Gravetter & Wallnau, 2007). Like other scientists, relationship researchers generally are willing to run no more than a 5% risk that their observed results are due to chance (as opposed to a real difference between groups or a real association between variables). Thus, a *statistically significant result* is one that is highly unlikely (specifically, less than 5% likely) to be the result of chance or coincidence.

Consider the study by Mongeau and his colleagues (2004) that we discussed earlier in this chapter. One of the hypotheses proposed in that investigation was that more men than women would report sexual first date goals. After collecting their data, the researchers found that 2% of the women and 13% of the men listed "sexual activity" as one of the reasons they had gone out on a first date. The results of the analysis revealed that this difference—2% versus 13%—was statistically significant, meaning that there was less than a one in twenty (5%) chance that it could have occurred by coincidence. Consequently, on the basis of their analysis and this statistically significant finding, the researchers concluded that their hypothesis was correct and that "men were more likely than women to report sexual activity goals" (p. 127). Of course, the slight possibility always remains that chance alone did create the observed difference—that in the general scheme of things, men and women do not possess different first date goals and that the difference found in this particular study was an anomaly (e.g., perhaps this specific sample of men and women was somehow different from other men and women, or the data collection method was flawed, or participants' reports were affected by a response bias). Statistical significance simply indicates that the results of a study are unlikely—but not totally impossible—to have been obtained by chance.

In general, a result that is published in a reputable scientific journal will be statistically significant. However, there is another type of significance that must be considered when interpreting research findings—*practical significance* or usefulness in real-world applications. Sometimes a statistical test might reveal that two groups differ, but the difference between them is of little practical value. For example, suppose that a relationship researcher administers a marital adjustment scale to two groups of distressed couples—an experimental (treatment) group who received 5 weeks of counseling and a control group who did not. The experimental group has an average adjustment score of 50, whereas the control group reports an average adjustment score of 40. The statistical analysis reveals that the difference in scores between the two groups is statistically significant. This result seems promising—until we realize that both groups still score in the "highly distressed" range. In this situation, the researcher might conclude that the treatment the couples received (that is, therapy or no therapy) affected their adjustment scores, but the effect was not large enough to be of any real clinical utility. A host of statistical techniques (called "estimation" or "effect size analyses") are now available to help relationship researchers and other scientists assess the practical significance of their results.

FOLLOWING ETHICAL PROCEDURES

In any discipline, scientists who wish to use human participants (and animal subjects, as well) in their studies are required to follow a number of ethical regulations and guidelines that have been developed for the protection of research participants. Although each discipline has its own official code of conduct and ethical procedures, they all share several fundamental principles (e.g., American Psychological Association, 2002; American Sociological Association, 1999; U.S.

Department of Health and Human Services, 2004). For example, a researcher cannot coerce, threaten, or otherwise force people to participate (or to continue participating) in a study. Researchers also cannot experiment on or collect data from people without their permission and without first providing them with the information they need to be able to make an informed decision about participation (such as requirements for participation, potential risks, and the procedures that are in place to reduce those risks). This is known as obtaining participants' *informed consent*. In addition, if the researcher employs *deception* (i.e., deliberately conceals the true nature of the study or the variables being examined from participants), he or she must conduct a post-study *debriefing* in which the deception is revealed, the rationale for using deception is explained, and any questions, concerns, or negative feelings participants have are resolved.

Because of the unique nature of their research, relationship scientists often face additional ethical challenges. For example, asking people to think systematically about their relationships may have unintended and even harmful effects (see, for example, Hughes & Surra, 2000; Surra, Curran, & Williams, 2009). This is particularly likely to occur when participation occurs over an extended period of time. The Boston Couples Study (e.g., Hill, Rubin, & Peplau, 1976), one of the first longitudinal investigations of courtship, provides a compelling illustration. In this study, a sample of dating couples completed extensive questionnaires (50 or more pages) that covered many aspects of their relationships, including patterns of self-disclosure, perceived problems in the relationship, sexual behavior and attitudes, feelings of romantic love and liking, and so forth. Questionnaires were administered to participants on four separate occasions over a 2-year period. At the end of the first year, participants also were asked whether they thought the study had had an impact on their relationship. Well over half of the couples said that it had. In discussing this finding, researchers Zick Rubin and Cynthia Mitchell (1976) noted that although most participants indicated that the impact was beneficial, some also reported that there were times during the course of the study where their participation proved difficult and painful, particularly when they learned things about their relationships, their own feelings, or their partners that they would rather not have known at the time. For example, one woman wrote, "At the time I cursed the study for destroying a lot of my fantasies about my boyfriend" (p. 22). From these and other findings, the researchers concluded that studying close relationships can have significant effects on those relationships:

> In the course of our research . . . it became increasingly clear that we "basic researchers" had been active agents in influencing the relationships of many of the couples we studied. By asking couples to scrutinize their relationships and by prompting them to discuss their relationships with one another, our study played a role in shaping these relationships. In some cases, our study served to strengthen a relationship; in other cases, to facilitate its dissolution.
>
> (Rubin & Mitchell, 1976, p. 17)

Another ethical dilemma that may arise during relationship research is that the investigator is sometimes unwittingly placed in the role of counselor by participants. People who take part in relationship studies often come to view the researcher not only as a scientist but also as a therapist. Because many researchers are not trained as relationship therapists, it would be highly unethical for them to act in that capacity and they must be prepared to provide referrals to appropriate counseling services.

In sum, like other scientists, relationship researchers must always obtain informed consent and follow all laws and ethical guidelines for conducting research with human participants. In addition, they must also consider, before beginning any investigation, whether they are justified in asking people to answer questions about their experiences in a particular relationship; they must address any ongoing concerns participants may develop during the course of their participation; they must refrain from providing counseling services unless specifically trained and licensed to do so; and they must refer participants to appropriate agencies or resources should the need arise. In short, relationship scientists must take whatever steps necessary to protect the welfare of their study participants and to ensure that those participants have an educational (and, hopefully, a rewarding) experience.

PUTTING IT ALL TOGETHER: AN EXAMPLE

In 1989, psychologists Russell Clark and Elaine Hatfield published the results of a study designed to explore sex differences in receptivity to sexual offers. As we present some of the pertinent details of their study, try to identify the key elements of research methodology we have discussed in this chapter; namely, the research strategy (is the study descriptive, correlational, or experimental?), data collection method (did the researchers collect self-report or observational data from their participants?), and research setting (did the research take place in the laboratory or out in the field?).

- *Background Information.* Existing theoretical and empirical literature reveals that "men are eager for sexual intercourse . . . [whereas] it is women who set limits on such activity" (p. 39).
- *Research Question.* "How receptive are [heterosexual] men versus women to sexual invitations? If a reasonably attractive man or woman approached members of the opposite sex and asked them for a date or a sexual encounter, how would men and women respond?" (pp. 47–48).
- *Method.* Male and female confederates (college students working for the researchers) volunteered to approach participants (48 men and 48 women) who were alone on campus and ask them one of three questions. Specifically:

   The confederates stood on one of five college quadrangles, and approached members of the opposite sex, who were total strangers. Only one requestor [confederate] made a request in each area at any one time. The requestors were instructed to approach only subjects who were attractive enough that they would be willing to actually sleep with them, if given the opportunity (assuming, of course, that they were appropriate on other grounds as well). . . . Once a subject was selected, the requestor approached him/her and said: "I have been noticing you around campus. I find you to be very attractive." The confederate then asked subjects one of three questions [randomly determined]: "Would you go out with me tonight?" "Would you come over to my apartment tonight?" or "Would you go to bed with me tonight?" (p. 49).

   The researchers also noted that all participants were "debriefed and thanked for their participation" (p. 50). The data consisted of the percentage of men and women participants who responded affirmatively (said "yes") to the specific invitation they received.

So, from this description, what do we know about the research strategy utilized in this study? Based on the information provided, this study is *experimental*. Clark and Hatfield (1989) were interested in whether the type of invitation men and women received from an opposite-sex stranger would influence their behavior (i.e., how receptive they would be to the offer). This research question was examined by creating three levels or conditions of the independent variable "type of invitation" (date, apartment, sex) and then randomly assigning participants to one of those three conditions.

The data collection method is a bit trickier to identify. At first glance, the method may appear to be self-report; after all, participants gave verbal responses to the invitation they received (that is, they either agreed to, or refused, the request). However, what was actually measured was participants' behavior—and it was observed and duly recorded by the confederates. Thus, the method of data collection is *observational*. Participants engaged in an observable behavior—they did not report what they would have done had they received a particular type of invitation; rather, they received an invitation and responded to it. The research setting is clearly outside of the laboratory in the *field*. Thus, this study represents a field experiment in which the researchers collected observational data. (And, in case you were wondering, the results revealed clear sex differences in receptiveness to sexual offers. About half of men and women accepted the date invitation; only 6% of the women accepted the invitation to go to the confederate's apartment (compared to 69% of the men); and not one woman— but a whopping 75% of the men—accepted the invitation to go to bed with the confederate.)

SUMMARY

This chapter considered the basic principles of research methodology used by relationship scientists. Researchers begin their investigations by formulating testable hypotheses or research questions and creating precise, operational definitions of the variables of interest. They then select a research strategy—is their goal to describe an interpersonal event, to establish covariation among variables, or to determine whether one variable causes another? Descriptive studies allow the researcher to explore and illustrate the parameters of a given event, behavior, or phenomenon. Correlational studies allow researchers to examine whether variables covary with one another; these designs often suggest, although they cannot determine, causal associations between variables. The most powerful weapon in the methodological arsenal of the relationship scientist is the true experiment, the only design that enables the researcher to test causation (i.e., whether one variable causes another). In addition to selecting a strategy, researchers must also choose between self-report and observational data collection methods; each has its pluses and minuses. Researchers then must decide whether to conduct their investigation in the controlled (but artificial) setting of the laboratory or in the natural (but decidedly uncontrollable) setting of the field. And, once they collect their data, they must select an appropriate statistical analysis for determining whether the results of their investigation are significant. Finally—and most importantly—researchers must treat their participants in an ethical manner to ensure that they have a rewarding and educational (or at least a benign) experience.

KEY CONCEPTS

Hypothesis (p. 23)
Research question (p. 23)
Operational definition (p. 24)
Multi-operationalize (p. 25)
Research strategy (p. 25)
Descriptive research (p. 25)
Naturalistic or observational studies (p. 26)
Survey research (p. 26)
Archival research (p. 26)
External validity (p. 26)

Correlational research (p. 27)
Positive correlation (p. 28)
Negative correlation (p. 28)
Zero correlation (p. 28)
Correlation coefficient (p. 28)
Longitudinal (prospective) studies (p. 28)
Experiment (p. 29)
Independent variable (p. 29)
Dependent variable (p. 29)
Random assignment (p. 30)

Confounding (p. 30)
Direct experimental control (p. 31)
Internal validity (p. 31)
Data collection method (p. 31)
Self-report methods (p. 31)
Observational methods (p. 33)
Reactivity (p. 34)
Research setting (p. 34)
Laboratory settings (p. 34)

Field settings (p. 34)
Unit of analysis (p. 35)
Independent observation (p. 35)
Statistically significant result (p. 36)
Practical significance (p. 36)
Informed consent (p. 37)
Deception (p. 37)
Debriefing (p. 37)

EXPLORATION EXERCISES

These exercises are designed to allow you to explore in greater detail some of the concepts and issues discussed in this chapter. There are no right or wrong answers to these exercises—they are simply meant to provide an opportunity for discussion and debate.

1. Find a recent article or news item that presents information about a relationship topic (magazines, newspapers, talk radio, or TV news shows are good sources). Then, identify the basic point or claim being made (in other words, what relationship issue is the focus of the article or news item?). Next, consider the evidence that the authors or journalists cite in support of their argument. Based on your knowledge of research methods, is the evidence solid? Do the results appear to be grounded in scientific methods, or based on anecdote or personal observation? Should the audience believe the information presented, or should they be skeptical?

2. Go to your library and select a recent journal article that explores a relationship topic (journals you might want to consider include *Personal Relationships* and the *Journal of Social and Personal Relationships*). Working on your own or with a classmate, describe: (a) the research question and/or hypothesis; (b) the research strategy the author(s) used to address this question (i.e., descriptive, correlational, experimental); and (c) any ethical considerations you feel are raised by the study.

3. Table 2.1 contains a list of statements taken directly from various published articles. Read each statement and then see if you can identify which ones reflect hypotheses and which ones reflect research questions. The answers are located at the bottom of the table.

Chapter 3
Our Social Nature

We humans are among the most social creatures in the entire animal kingdom. Reproductive technology notwithstanding, every single one of us owes our very existence to a relationship (however brief or fleeting) that once existed between two people. And we live our entire lives—beginning from the moment we enter the world at birth (and even earlier, if we consider the fact that we are, quite literally, connected to our mothers during pregnancy)—enmeshed in a complex web of interpersonal bonds and social associations. Most of us are aware of just how connected we are to other people, and just how significant relationships are to the quality of our lives. Surveys consistently reveal that the majority of us value our close relationships, consider them to be essential for our personal well-being, and are happiest and most satisfied when we maintain positive social ties to others (Diener & Oishi, 2005). We are so social, in fact, that relationship scientists now believe that this aspect of our nature was actually programed into the human design over evolutionary time:

> Evolutionary psychology places social interaction and social relationships squarely within the center of the action. In particular, social interactions and relationships surrounding mating, kinship, reciprocal alliances, coalitions, and hierarchies are especially critical, because all appear to have strong consequences for successful survival and reproduction. From an evolutionary perspective, the functions served by social relationships have been central to the design of the human mind.
>
> (Buss & Kenrick, 1998, p. 994)

In this chapter, we will consider the fundamental "social-ness" of human nature, beginning with an examination of our evolved need for interpersonal contact and connection. Next, we will discuss how human infants come into the world already "wired" to seek physical contact and to establish relational bonds with others. Finally, we will explore how the relationships we form have an enormous impact on our health and well-being during infancy and across the life-span.

RELATIONSHIPS: OUR EVOLUTIONARY HERITAGE

Although we often think of ourselves as occupying the top position in the animal kingdom, even a quick consideration of other species reveals that we are actually relatively unimpressive, at least in terms of physical abilities. We are not as fast, strong, or resilient as other mammals, and we lack many of the physical accoutrements that aid in survival (such as horns, claws, sharp teeth, and dense coats). Moreover, our offspring are born in an extremely fragile state, unable to run, climb, hide, or even feed themselves, and they remain fragile and immature for an extended length of time. Thus, as our early human ancestors were struggling to survive in a hostile environment (one lacking in such modern-day conveniences as houses, hospitals, and grocery stores), they could not have relied on sheer physical strength—because they did not possess great amounts of this, comparatively speaking. Instead, their survival would have depended more heavily on the ability to band together with other humans and work cooperatively to overcome the environmental hazards and obstacles that they faced.

Indeed, based on a consideration of our species' physical vulnerability, and of the many survival challenges faced by our ancestral forebears, some relationship scholars have proposed that the most important feature of our evolutionary heritage was—and still is—selection for small group living. For example, theorists Linnda Caporael and Marilynn Brewer (e.g., 1995) posit that coordinated group living has been the primary survival strategy of the human species from its earliest origins through the present day. They suggest that social organization provided a critical "buffer" between the individual organism and the (often harsh) demands of the physical environment, and they consequently conclude that:

> the species characteristics that we would expect to be biologically built in would be those associated with human sociality—propensities toward cooperativeness, group loyalty, adherence to socially learned norms, and fear of social exclusion.
>
> (Brewer & Caporael, 1990, pp. 240–241)

In other words, early humans who possessed features and attributes that facilitated successful social interaction and group living—who cooperated for food-gathering and defense, established enduring alliances, attracted mates and formed long-term pairbonds, and reared their young—survived, reproduced, and contributed to the genetic heritage of modern-day humans, whereas those who were unwilling or unable to form relationships with others did not (Brewer, 2004; Cosmides & Tooby, 1997). We are simply not adapted for survival as lone individuals, dyads, or even small family units. Rather, we are designed, both physically and mentally, for group living.

The Need to Belong

The *need to belong* represents one of the most interesting and basic aspects of our evolved mentality. Social psychologists Roy Baumeister and Mark Leary (e.g., 1995) propose that, over evolutionary time, our species developed a fundamental, powerful, and pervasive drive to form and maintain at least a minimum number of lasting, positive, and significant interpersonal attachments—a need to belong. These scholars cite a great deal of evidence in support of their hypothesis that humans are motivated to establish and maintain interpersonal bonds (also see Baumeister, Brewer, Tice, & Twenge, 2007; Leary & Cox, 2008). For example:

- People form social bonds quickly and easily. Even people in experimentally created groups (i.e., groups created randomly in the laboratory) quickly become cohesive, develop strong group loyalty and allegiance, and show decided preference for other group members.
- People are extremely reluctant to break or dissolve social bonds. Even when there is no objective reason for maintaining a particular relationship—as, for example, when a committee or training group fulfills its tasks and there is no further need for members to meet—people are often unwilling to let go of the relationships they have formed with each other.
- Social attachments exert substantial influence on how people think, and relationship issues are the focus of much of our cognitive activity. For example, people devote considerable cognitive processing to interpersonal interactions and relationships; they process information about relationship partners differently from how they process information about strangers or acquaintances; and they think more thoroughly (i.e., devote more cognitive effort to processing information) about relationship partners than they do about other individuals. (See Chapter 8 for additional discussion of this point.)
- Social bonds are strongly associated with people's emotional states—that is, with how they feel. Many of the strongest emotions that men and women experience are linked to belongingness issues. Being accepted, included, or welcomed usually produces positive emotions (e.g., happiness, satisfaction, elation), whereas being excluded, rejected, or ignored generally results in negative emotions (e.g., jealousy, depression, loneliness).

According to Baumeister and Leary, belongingness needs cannot be completely fulfilled by frequent interactions with a large number of casual (non-intimate) partners or by having an intimate attachment that lacks frequent interaction; rather, what we seem to need is frequent, positive interactions in the context of an ongoing and valued relationship. Table 3.1 illustrates this point.

In sum, relationship scholars believe that our social nature is "wired" into our biological makeup—indeed, that it is the very essence of what makes us human.

Table 3.1 The Need to Belong

Consider the following three relationship options. If you could only experience one of these relationship realities in your lifetime, which option would you choose?

Option A: You have frequent and positive interactions with many people, each one of whom is a stranger or casual acquaintance. Not one of them is a close friend or romantic partner.

Option B: You have a warm, truly intimate relationship with one other individual, but he/she lives far away and you hardly ever have the chance to interact in person.

Option C: You have several warm, intimate relationships with other people. You care about these people, feel they care about you, and interact with them frequently.

Which option did you choose? If you're like most people, you probably selected Option C—the option that allows you to experience positive interactions in the context of long-term, stable relationships. This illustrates the need to belong. Options A and B only partially satisfy our belongingness needs (Option A provides interaction in the absence of a close relationship bond, and Option B provides a close bond but little to no actual interaction).

THE HUMAN INFANT: BORN "READY TO RELATE"

Given that establishing social connections with others was critical to the survival of our species, it is not terribly surprising that we come into the world biologically "ready" to form relationships. Assuming normal gestation and prenatal development, all babies are born with a set of innate (unlearned) biological endowments that facilitate social interaction and relationship formation.

The Attachment System

The first of these important biological gifts is the *attachment system*. British clinician John Bowlby (e.g., 1953, 1969, 1973, 1988) originally proposed the evolutionary concept of *attachment*, defined as the innate and adaptive "propensity of human beings to make strong affectional bonds to particular others" (1977, p. 201). According to attachment theory, human infants enter the world predisposed to emotionally "bind" themselves to the mother, father, or other primary caregiver—in other words, to form relationships. This evolved predisposition manifests itself in a set of instinctive, goal-directed responses, called *attachment behaviors*, which serve to promote physical proximity to primary caregivers (called *attachment figures*) and thereby enhance the infants' chances of survival. Common attachment behaviors (most of which are present at birth or develop shortly thereafter) include crying, sucking, smiling, clinging, and following. Although these behaviors are seen most clearly in infants and very young children, people of all ages often exhibit the same or very similar responses, particularly when feeling distressed, ill, or frightened. According to Bowlby, such behaviors represent a normal and healthy response to stressful situations.

Three important lines of research contributed to Bowlby's belief that attachment is "an integral part of human nature" (1988, p. 27) whose biological function is protection:

- Clinical observations of the impact of disrupted parent–child relationships. During the 1930s and 1940s, Bowlby (e.g., 1944, 1951) and a number of other clinicians (e.g., Bender, 1948; Burlingham & Freud, 1942; Goldfarb, 1947; Levy, 1937; Spitz, 1946, 1949) noticed and began to document the harmful effects of prolonged hospitalization, institutional foster care, parental death, and other disruptions of the family relationship on children's personality development and socio-emotional functioning. These clinical observations highlighted the fundamental importance of the parent–child relationship and suggested that the quality of this relationship (e.g., present/absent, well-adjusted/maladjusted) produced a multitude of consequences that extended far beyond infancy.

- Ethological research on imprinting in birds. During the 1950s, Bowlby also became aware of Konrad Lorenz's (e.g., 1952) work on the instinctive "following" response in goslings and ducklings, which demonstrated the biological underpinnings of the relationships that develop between offspring and parents in many non-human species. This research suggested to Bowlby that humans may possess a similar set of instinctive responses related to the formation of enduring relationships.
- Psychological research on affectional responses in monkeys. At around the same time, Bowlby became aware of Harry Harlow's (e.g., 1958, 1959) seminal work on "contact comfort" in fostering the development of affectional responses in infant monkeys. Harlow's infant monkeys showed a marked preference for a soft, cloth-covered surrogate "mother" who provided no food over a hard, wire-covered surrogate who did provide food. This preference was particularly apparent when the infant monkeys were placed in strange or stressful situations, leading Harlow to conclude that one function of a parent is to "provide a haven of safety for the infant" (1958, p. 678). Applied to humans, this research suggested that physical closeness, contact, and felt security may be core components of the parent–child relationship.

Based largely on the evidence provided by these three areas of research, Bowlby posited that the survival and well-being of human infants—in both the ancestral environment of our species' earliest forebears and in the contemporary environment that surrounds us today—are to a large extent dependent on establishing a close, continuous relationship with one or a few individuals who can provide consistent physical and psychological protection and nurturance.

Differences in Attachment Pattern.   An infant's attachment behaviors are designed to "pull" supportive behavior from his or her primary attachment figures by activating an innate *caregiving system*, also presumed to constitute one of our species' biological inheritances. Indeed, Bowlby (e.g., 1977, 1988) noted that parents of crying babies generally experience a strong urge to behave in ways that reduce their infants' distress—for example, by cradling, feeding, stroking, or otherwise soothing the infant with some form of physical contact designed to convey safety, security, and comfort. Of course, not all parents respond to attachment displays in the same way; some are readily available, responsive, and supportive, whereas others provide inconsistent or unreliable care (or little care at all). Consequently, not all infants form the same kind of affective relationship or attachment with their primary caregiver.

   To assess qualitative differences in attachment, relationship scientists typically use the *Strange Situation procedure* developed by Bowlby's colleague and research associate Mary Ainsworth (e.g., Ainsworth, Blehar, Waters, & Wall, 1978). The Strange Situation activates the attachment system by exposing young children (typically between 12 and 18 months of age) to "strange" or unfamiliar people and settings in a laboratory situation. The procedure consists of eight episodes, all but the first of which last for approximately 3 minutes (these can be shortened if the child becomes too distressed). Specifically, following a brief, 30-second introduction to the laboratory room (Episode 1), the caregiver (typically the mother) and child are left alone for 3 minutes (Episode 2). A stranger then enters, remaining for 3 minutes in the room with both the mother and the child (Episode 3) and then signaling the mother to leave (Episode 4). After the child has been alone with the stranger for the requisite period of time, the mother returns and the stranger leaves (Episode 5). The mother exits once more, and the child is left alone in the room (Episode 6). Finally, the stranger re-enters the room (Episode 7) and is joined 3 minutes later by the mother (Episode 8).

The child's responses during this moderately stressful series of episodes are used to assess the quality of his or her attachment to the caregiver. Behaviors—particularly those enacted during the two reunion episodes—are scored for *proximity seeking* (i.e., efforts to gain or regain physical contact with the mother; e.g., directly approaching the mother upon reunion); *contact maintenance* (i.e., efforts to maintain self-initiated physical contact with the mother; e.g., after approaching the mother, continuing to gaze at her and cling to her skirt or pant leg); *avoidance* (i.e., any active avoidance of proximity to or interaction with the mother; e.g., turning the face away from the mother when she returns, refusing to make eye contact with her, pouting); *resistance* (i.e., negative behavior [often accompanied by anger] in response to the mother's contact attempts; e.g., refusing, slapping, or throwing a toy offered by the mother, clambering for contact and then pushing away from the mother when contact is offered); and *crying*.

Children typically display one of three kinds of behavior patterns during the Strange Situation, each of which is presumed to be the product of their history of interaction with the caregiver (Weinfield, Sroufe, Egeland, & Carlson, 1999): secure, insecure/resistant, or insecure/ avoidant. Children who display the **secure attachment** pattern display high levels of proximity-seeking and contact-maintaining behavior and little to no resistant or avoidant behavior. They tend to use the caregiver as a secure base for exploration in the unfamiliar room. When they become distressed, they actively seek contact with her and are readily comforted. When the caregiver is absent, secure children are not unduly upset but instead display a confident expectation of her return. This behavior pattern appears to be rooted in a history of reliable caregiving, sensitivity and responsiveness to the child's expressions of need, and cooperative interactions (Bakermans-Kranenburg, van IJzendoorn, & Juffer, 2003; Sroufe, 2005; van IJzendoorn & Sagi, 1999). About two-thirds of children observed in the U.S. demonstrate this pattern.

One-third of children show a pattern of insecure attachment, which has two forms. Children who display the **insecure/resistant attachment** (sometimes called the *anxious/resistant* or *anxious-ambivalent*) pattern appear unable to use the caregiver as a secure base for exploration. They engage in little exploration even in the caregiver's presence, preferring to maintain contact with her, and have low tolerance for threat. Interestingly, although these children become extremely distressed when the caregiver leaves the room during the two separation episodes, they angrily resist her efforts to provide comfort on returning. Such behavior may be grounded in a history of inconsistent, chaotic, "hit-or-miss" caregiving (Sroufe & Fleeson, 1988). **Insecure/avoidant** (also called *anxious/avoidant*) children treat the caregiver much as they do the stranger; they are not distressed when she leaves and they do not seek contact when she returns. In general, they show low levels of proximity-seeking or contact-maintaining behavior and high levels of active avoidance. This behavior pattern is believed to reflect a history of rejection and/or emotional unavailability from the caregiver, particularly during times of need (Sroufe, 2005; Sroufe & Fleeson, 1988).

Bowlby theorized that the quality of the child's early attachment relationship (i.e., secure, insecure) influences later relationships. Specifically, he suggested that from that first relationship the child comes to develop a set of internalized expectations and beliefs about what other people are like (e.g., trustworthy, responsive, available, supportive) as well as internalized views of himself or herself as valued and self-reliant or unworthy and incompetent. These **internal working models**, in turn, influence the child's interpersonal expectations and behaviors and, therefore, his or her subsequent relationship outcomes. We will consider this point in greater detail later in the chapter.

The attachment system is among the most significant of the human infant's biological inheritances, helping to ensure that he or she comes into the world ready to form relationships with others.

The Face Perceptual System

Not only do infants enter the world prepared to physically and emotionally attach themselves to their caregivers, but they come biologically endowed with the propensity and ability to actively attend and respond to the faces of other humans. Cognitive and developmental neuroscientists believe that infants are born with a rudimentary *face perceptual system* that is mediated by subcortical structures (e.g., the superior colliculus) and that causes newborns to orient toward any stimulus that is sufficiently "face-like" (Farah, 2000; Morton & Johnson, 1991; Quinn & Slater, 2003; Zuckerman & Rock, 1957). This specialized face-detecting module represents another of the infant's impressive biological gifts.

A growing body of evidence supports the contention that infants have some degree of innate perceptual knowledge about the human face. For example, newborn infants less than 40 minutes old will track a slowly moving, face-like stimulus with their head and eyes farther than they will track a stimulus with scrambled facial features or no features at all (Goren, Sarty, & Wu, 1975; Johnson, Dziurawiec, Ellis, & Morton, 1991; Simion, Valenza, & Umiltà, 1998; see Figure 3.1). Similarly, they will look longer at a schematic face with a natural T-shaped arrangement of internal features than at one with inverted features (Mondloch et al., 1999; Umiltà, Simion, & Valenza, 1996). Moreover, newborn infants who sustain brain damage prior to any extended visual experience with human faces—for instance, within one day of birth—demonstrate impaired face recognition, suggesting that at birth portions of the human brain are already uniquely committed for the processing of facial information (Farah, Rabinowitz, Quinn, & Liu, 2000).

By causing a newborn to selectively attend to face-like stimuli, the rudimentary face perceptual system ensures that the infant's developing cortex receives consistent exposure to the faces of other humans and thus is able to acquire and retain specific information about the visual characteristics of the human face (Johnson, 2001). In essence, the infant learns the "rules" of faces in general as well as of the specific faces seen most often in the environment, including their contour and the shape, movement, and spatial relations of their features (e.g., distance between their eyes; this latter

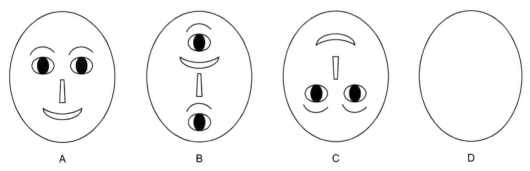

A   B   C   D

Fig. 3.1 Newborn infants will look longer at and orient more toward face-like objects (A) than less-face-like objects (B, C, and D). The fact that infants less than an hour old are able to detect the specific structural configuration of the face and to discriminate face-like patterns from non-face-like patterns suggests that they come into the world with a rudimentary face-detecting device that contains information about human facial structure and that supports attention to human faces.

class of information is called *second-order relational information*). Consequently, by 2 or 3 months of age, infants reared with a male primary caregiver tend to show a spontaneous preference for male rather than female faces, whereas those reared with female primary caregivers display recognition memory for individual female faces but not for individual male faces (Quinn, Yahr, Kuhn, Slater, & Pascalis, 2002; for discussion, see Ramsey-Rennels & Langlois, 2006). Similarly, as infants age, they become increasingly better at recognizing faces from the racial or ethnic group with which they are most familiar and increasingly worse at recognizing faces from other groups. Known as the *other-race effect*, this preferential recognition pattern begins at around 3 months and is firmly established by the time infants reach 9 months of age (Kelly et al., 2007; Sangrigoli & de Schonen, 2004). By 4 or 5 months of age, infants' attention is no longer automatically captured by the schematic "face-like" objects that captivate newborns; rather, they prefer to look at pictures of realistic faces whose internal features move rather than at unexpressive, still faces (Morton & Johnson, 1991). And by 7 months of age, infants are able to discriminate among faces on the basis of second-order relational information such as the distance between the eyes or the nose and mouth (Hayden, Bhatt, Reed, Corbly, & Joseph, 2007; Thompson, Madrid, Westbrook, & Johnston, 2001).

Clearly one of the most important tasks of the human perceptual system is recognition of the faces of other humans. Not only do a person's facial features provide the maximum number of cues that allow us to differentiate one individual from another, but the face communicates critical information about a person's feelings and intentions toward us (Darwin, 1872/1965; Ekman, 1993, 1997). It is extremely fitting, then, that human infants are born with some existing information about the structure of faces and a neural system that "expects" faces to be present in the environment and that supports attention to that particular type of stimulus. Faces are special objects in the infant's visual world—and they receive special attention.

Empathic Accuracy

Because the face provides the most significant clues to a person's thoughts, feelings, and behavioral intentions, face perception is vital to *empathic accuracy* or the ability to accurately decode the meaning or infer the content of another person's thoughts and feelings (Ickes, 1997, 2003). Empathic accuracy, in turn, is a key component of a larger skill set called *interpersonal sensitivity*, which refers to how well an individual "reads" other people and how appropriately he or she is able to respond to their cues (Hall & Andrzejewski, 2009). The ability to decode facial expressions is especially important for infants, who are not yet able to fully comprehend or produce language and thus are prevented from directly and verbally communicating with their caregivers and other humans.

Although empathic accuracy continues to develop well into adolescence and adulthood (see Eisenberg, Murphy, & Shepard, 1997; Thomas, De Bellis, Graham, & LaBar, 2007), research conducted with infants suggests that rudimentary forms of empathic accuracy arise within the first year of life. For example, even very young infants are able to process facial expression information and differentiate among different facial displays. Researchers generally find that by the time most infants reach 7 months of age, they can discriminate facial expressions of happiness from expressions of surprise, sadness, fear, and anger (e.g., Kotsoni, de Haan, & Johnson, 2001; Serrano, Iglesias, & Loeches, 1995; Young-Browne, Rosenfeld, & Horowitz, 1977; also see Kobiella, Grossmann, Reid, & Striano, 2008). Moreover, infants recognize that different *intensities* of the same expression (e.g., smiling) convey the same emotion (e.g., happiness), both within and across individuals (Bornstein & Arterberry, 2003). As observed by developmental researchers Marc Bornstein and Martha Arterberry (2003), "despite differences in amount of teeth showing, how crinkly the eyes are, or the extent of upturned lips, [to an infant] a smile is still a smile, and it projects happiness" (p. 586). Not surprisingly, recognition and discrimination of facial expressions by infants occurs most reliably when the presentation of the emotion is "natural"—that is, when it is dynamic (live-action) as opposed to static (photographic or pictorial) and includes vocal cues as well as facial displays (Montague & Walker-Andrews, 2001; Soken & Pick, 1999; Walker, 1982).

Infants are also exquisitely sensitive to eye contact, perhaps because the eyes serve as potent signals of people's emotional and mental states (Baron-Cohen, Wheelwright, & Jolliffe, 1997). In one study (Batki, Baron-Cohen, Wheelwright, Connellan, & Ahluwalia, 2000), a large sample of newborns less than 40 hours old were presented with two photographs of the same female face, one with the eyes open and the other with the eyes closed. The results indicated that the newborns spent a significantly greater amount of time gazing at the target when her eyes were open than when her eyes were closed. Indeed, by the second month of life, infants look at the eyes more than at any other internal feature of the human face (e.g., Maurer & Salapatek, 1976). Similarly, examination of infants' brain activity (e.g., event-related potentials or ERPs) during exposure to facial displays reveals enhanced cortical processing of faces when they are accompanied by direct eye contact as opposed to an averted gaze (Farroni, Johnson, & Csibra, 2004; Grossmann, Johnson, Farroni, & Csibra, 2007; also see Striano, Kopp, Grossmann, & Reid, 2006).

Not only can infants decode emotional information from other people's facial expressions, but there is abundant evidence that they rapidly learn to adjust their own behavior in response to that information. During face-to-face interactions, young infants smile more at adults who present a "happy" facial expression than they do at those who present a "sad" facial expression (D'Entremont & Muir, 1999). Infants also smile more at adults who make eye contact than adults who do not. In one experiment, researchers Sylvia Hains and Darwin Muir (1996) had an adult female confederate engage in a series of pleasant social interactions with a group of 5-month-old infants. During each interaction, the infant and the adult confederate sat in separate rooms but could see the other's head and shoulders via a large video monitor. Interactions were divided into four 1-minute phases. During the first and third phases of the interaction, the female confederate spoke, smiled, and maintained direct eye contact with the infant; during the second and fourth phases, she continued to speak and smile, but averted her gaze by looking away. As illustrated in Figure 3.2, infants altered their behavior as a function of the adult confederate's level of eye contact, smiling significantly more at her when she looked directly at them.

Similar results have been reported by researchers utilizing the ***still-face paradigm***, a methodological procedure which allows researchers to explore infants' sensitivity to changes in adults' facial expression as well as their capacity to regulate their own internal states (Tronick, 1989). The still-face paradigm consists of three age-appropriate, infant–adult interaction episodes, each lasting between 2 and 3 minutes: (1) a face-to-face episode during which the infant and adult (e.g., mother, caregiver, stranger) engage in normal social interaction; (2) a still-face episode during which the adult continues to look at the infant but assumes an affectively neutral, still face (a "poker" face) and remains unresponsive; and (3) a reunion episode during which the adult resumes normal, face-to-face interaction with the infant. Research reveals a robust ***still-face effect*** such that infants typically respond to the still-face episode with reductions in visual attention, smiling, and other positive affective displays, and with increases in crying and negative affect (Ellsworth, Muir, & Hains, 1993; Kisilevsky et al., 1998; Weinberg & Tronick, 1996).

Interestingly, infants not only attend and differentially respond to other people's facial expressions, but they also appear to be aware of the social significance of their *own* facial expressions. For example, in one early investigation (Eckerman & Rheingold, 1974), 10-month-old infants were placed with their mothers in an empty laboratory room that adjoined a second room containing an unfamiliar object (either a toy or another adult person). Infants were free to explore either room, to

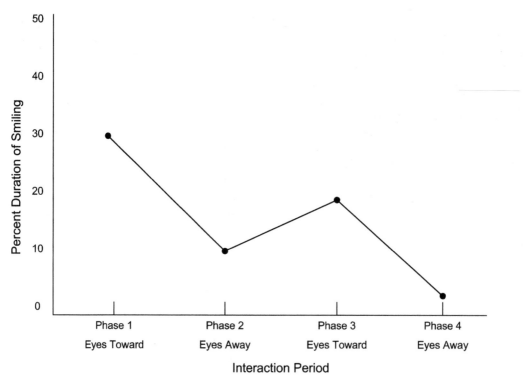

Fig. 3.2 Research reveals that infants are sensitive to, and adjust their behavior in accordance with, the emotional displays of other people. In an experiment conducted by Sylvia Hains and Darwin Muir (1996), an adult female confederate engaged in a series of pleasant social interactions with a group of 5-month-old infants. During the first and third phases of the interaction, she maintained direct eye contact with each infant; during the second and fourth phases, she averted her gaze by looking away. As can be seen, although smiling tended to generally decrease over time, infants smiled significantly more at the confederate when she maintained eye contact with them than when she did not.

Source: Hains, S. M. J., & Muir, D. W. (1996). Infant sensitivity to adult eye direction. *Child Development, 67,* 1940–1951. Copyright © 1996 by Wiley-Blackwell. Figure 1 adapted with permission.

approach the toy or adult stranger, or to remain near their mothers. Analysis of infants' behavioral responses to the unfamiliar object revealed that they both looked and smiled more frequently at the adult than at the toy. Similar findings were reported more recently by Susan Scanlon Jones and Tarja Raag (1989), who observed 18-month-old infants playing with a toy in the presence of their mothers and an adult stranger. Although infants smiled at all three objects—their mother, the stranger, and the toy—they directed the majority of their smiles (81%) at the two social objects (their mother [44%] and the stranger [37%]) rather than at the inanimate toy (19%). These results suggest that at some level infants are sensitive to the communicative content of their own facial displays of affect, insofar as they reserve those displays for other social objects.

The predisposition to be attentive to faces and to accurately interpret their expressions has important implications for social interaction and for bonding with caregivers and other humans. An infant, child, or adult who can accurately guess what another person is feeling and how he or she is likely to act can then adjust his or her own behavior accordingly; this is likely to facilitate attachment and to increase the probability of smooth, coordinated, and rewarding interactions.

Language

Although the capacity to communicate is not limited to the human species, the capacity to acquire and use language is uniquely human and in fact represents one of the most important of our species' biological inheritances. Numerous scholars have proposed that human infants are born with an innate language-acquisition device designed to facilitate species communication (see Bjorklund & Pellegrini, 2002; Crain & Pietroski, 2002). For example, the influential linguist Noam Chomsky (e.g., 1965, 1968, 2006) has long argued that all newborns enter the world biologically armed with some pre-existing knowledge of the structure of language. Called *Universal Grammar*, this set of basic grammatical principles is subsequently modified by experience into the specific natural language that is characteristic of the infant's environment. Similarly, in presenting his own conceptualization of language acquisition, neuroscientist Steven Pinker (1994, 1997; also see Pinker & Jackendoff, 2005) observed:

> The three-year-old . . . is a grammatical genius—master of most constructions, obeying rules far more often than flouting them, respecting language universals, erring in sensible, adultlike ways, and avoiding many kinds of errors altogether. How do they do it? Children of this age are notably incompetent at most other activities. We won't let them drive, vote, or go to school, and they can be flummoxed by no-brainer tasks like sorting beads in order of size . . . So they are not doing it by the sheer power of their overall acumen. Nor could they be imitating what they hear, or else they would never say *goed* or *Don't giggle me*. It is plausible that the basic organization of grammar is wired into the child's brain.
>
> (1994, pp. 276–277)

Scholars disagree over the precise nature of the evolved mental software that our species possesses for acquiring language. Some, like Chomsky and Pinker, contend that our innate endowment comes in the form of a specific language-learning mechanism; others maintain that we possess general learning mechanisms that can be used in the service of language acquisition and development but no special mechanism designed exclusively for that purpose (e.g., Christiansen & Chater, 2008; Palmer, 2000; for discussion, see Crain, Goro, & Thornton, 2006; Goldberg, 2008; Marcus & Rabagliati, 2009). This debate may never be fully resolved. However, although theorists continue to argue about the nature of the underlying mechanism, they do agree that the newborn brain is designed—somehow—to acquire language.

Evidence strongly supports this supposition. For example, infants are highly sensitive to several of the structural aspects of spoken language. Examination of the molar behavior (e.g., head turning, sucking rhythm) and brain activity (e.g., ERPs) of newborns reveals that they can: (1) detect changes in speech sounds (Brody, Zelazo, & Chaika, 1984; Cheour et al., 2002; Kujala et al., 2004); (2) distinguish between and retain memory for words heard up to 1 day earlier (Swain, Zelazo, & Clifton, 1993); and (3) perceive differences in words based on the number of syllables they contain, even when those words are in languages to which the infants have never been exposed (Bertoncini, Floccia, Nazzi, & Mehler, 1995; Bijeljac-Babic, Bertoncini, & Mehler, 1993; van Ooijen, Bertoncini, Sansavini, & Mehler, 1997). The ability to distinguish among speech sounds may even be present prior to birth. A study conducted by Anthony DeCasper and his colleagues (DeCasper, Lecanuet, Busnel, & Granier-Deferre, 1994) revealed that fetuses in the last month of gestation differentiated (as indicated by a reduction in heart rate) between rhymes their mothers had read aloud at an earlier time and new rhymes to which they had never been exposed.

In addition, infants show a bias for listening to human speech compared to other auditory signals. Psychologists Athena Vouloumanos and Janet Werker (2007) exposed a group of 2-day-old infants to two types of auditory stimuli: (1) speech stimuli consisting of one-syllable nonsense words (e.g., "lif"), and (2) non-speech stimuli consisting of non-vocal artificial sounds that retained the duration, pitch contour, amplitude, and intensity of the speech stimuli. To determine whether infants preferentially responded to the two sets of stimuli, the researchers employed a commonly used method called the ***high amplitude sucking (HAS) procedure*** (Jusczyk, 1985). In this procedure, infants are given a sterilized pacifier that is coupled to a pressure transducer. Following a silent baseline time period during which their normal range of sucking amplitude is established, they are presented with a stimulus (in this case, the speech or non-speech stimuli) every time they deliver suction in the upper 80% of their sucking amplitude range. Infants quickly learn that the presentation of the stimulus is contingent on their sucking behavior (i.e., "If I suck at this level, then I get to hear more of this type of stimulus"). Thus, their sucking amplitude can be used as a measure of preference. Using the HAS procedure, Vouloumanos and Werker (2007) found strong evidence that infants are biased to listen to speech; their neonate participants sucked significantly more on the pacifier to listen to the speech sounds than they did to listen to the non-speech sounds.

Other researchers also have found that infants demonstrate a preference for human speech. In one interesting investigation (Condon & Sander, 1974), a group of 14 newborns less than 2 days old were videotaped while an adult man or woman spoke a continuous sequence of words to them. The researchers then examined the videotapes and conducted a micro-analysis of the infants' overt body movements before, during, and after each utterance. This analysis revealed evidence of "interactional synchrony" such that as the sound elements in the adult's speech changed, the newborns moved their bodies by extending or retracting their elbows, altering their head position, rotating their hips or shoulders, adducting their toes, flexing their feet, and so forth. This correspondence was found regardless of whether the speaker was male or female and spoke words in English or Chinese. Tapping sounds and isolated vowel sounds, however, did not produce interactional synchrony, again providing evidence that infants are particularly responsive to the speech of other humans.

In sum, a wide array of research supports the proposition that human infants come into the world endowed with the mental software to acquire language.

THE IMPORTANCE OF SOCIAL INTERACTION

Given that we are designed to be social and that we actively seek and form connections with other humans from the moment we enter the world, it makes absolute sense that the relationships we establish during infancy (and beyond) have a significant and enduring impact on our subsequent health and development.

Early Interactions: Laying the Relational Foundation

None of these relationships is as significant and influential as the one the infant forms with his or her primary caregiver. This individual—usually the mother but sometimes the father, grandparent, older sibling, or other adult—not only serves as the infant's main source of sensory and motor stimulation in the time period immediately following birth, but also functions as the primary interaction partner and attachment figure throughout childhood (and thus is a major source of social, emotional, and communicative information). Consequently, how the caregiver responds to the infant affects virtually all aspects of that infant's physical, psychological, and social development (Richter, 2004). In general, sensitive and responsive caregiving appears to be the key ingredient in promoting optimal development. *Responsiveness* is generally defined as the caregiver's ability to monitor and recognize infant cues consistently and then to react to those cues promptly (i.e., within a fairly brief window of time following the child's behavior; e.g., 5 seconds), contingently (i.e., depending conceptually on the preceding child behavior; e.g., if the child picks up a cup, the caregiver refers to the cup), and appropriately (i.e., in a positive and meaningful way; e.g., "Yes, that's a cup") (Bornstein, Tamis-LeMonda, Hahn, & Haynes, 2008).

There is growing evidence that responsiveness is associated with a multitude of beneficial outcomes, including the development of (1) social competence (Kochanska, Forman, & Coy, 1999); (2) language skill and communicative competence (Gros-Louis, West, Goldstein, & King, 2006; Paavola, Kunnari, & Moilanen, 2005; Tamis-LeMonda, Bornstein, & Baumwell, 2001; Tamis-LeMonda, Bornstein, Baumwell, & Damast, 1996); and (3) cognitive and intellectual function (Bornstein & Tamis-LeMonda, 1997). For example, Leila Beckwith and Carol Rodning (1996) examined the association between maternal responsiveness and child language skill and social competence in a sample of 51 mother–child dyads. Specifically, when the children were 13 months old (and again when they were 20 months old), each mother–child pair was videotaped during a laboratory interaction based on the Strange Situation. These videotapes were examined and scored for evidence of *dyadic verbal reciprocity* during the first reunion episode (this served as a measure of the mother's responsiveness to the infant's vocalizations). Children's language skill was measured when they reached 36 months of age, and their social competence was evaluated at 60 months. Analysis of the data revealed that the measure of maternal responsiveness significantly predicted both developmental outcomes. That is, the more verbally responsive a mother was to her child's vocalizations during interaction, the higher her child subsequently scored on measures of social competence and expressive and receptive language skill.

Conversely, lack of responsiveness is associated with negative outcomes. For example, children raised in a *risky family environment*—a family situation characterized by overt conflict (manifested in recurrent episodes of anger and aggression) and deficient nurturing (reflected in cold and unsupportive interactions that are neglectful of the child's needs)—tend to have poor physical and mental health (see Repetti, Taylor, & Seeman, 2002). In addition, infants and young children raised in impoverished environments that do not allow for consistent, nurturing interactions with a primary caregiver—such as that found in many orphanages—often display impaired socio-emotional development along with deficits in physical growth, speech and language acquisition, and cognitive and intellectual functioning (see Kim, Shin, & White-Traut, 2003; Levin & Haines, 2007; MacLean, 2003). Indeed, after reviewing the existing orphanage studies, childhood trauma research, and animal deprivation and enrichment studies, child psychiatrist Bruce Perry (2002) concluded that young children (and young non-human mammals) need to have "both stable emotional attachments with and touch from primary adult caregivers, [as well as] spontaneous interactions with peers" (p. 79) in order to achieve optimal functioning. In other words, infants do not simply need appropriate physical and social stimulation; they also require sensitive, nurturant, and responsive care in the context of ongoing relationships with others. (This robust empirical finding certainly echoes and supports Baumeister and Leary's (1995) hypothesis that belongingness needs can only be fully satisfied through frequent positive interactions within a stable interpersonal bond.)

Attachment research provides additional evidence about the impact of early interactions on subsequent personal and interpersonal outcomes. Recall that infants whose attachment behaviors are consistently met with sensitive and responsive reactions from an emotionally and physically available caregiver are likely to develop a secure attachment bond (see Bowlby, 1988; Sroufe & Fleeson, 1988). This, in turn, has important developmental consequences. A review of longitudinal attachment studies conducted by psychologist Alan Sroufe (2005) revealed that, compared with children who were insecurely attached as infants, securely attached children develop: (1) greater *independence and self-reliance*; (2) a greater capacity for *emotional regulation* (e.g., higher self-confidence, self-esteem, and ego-resilience—defined as the ability to flexibly adjust expressions of feelings and impulses to suit situational requirements—as well as more effective coping strategies); and (3) greater *social competence* (e.g., they participate more actively in the peer group, are less often socially isolated, show greater empathy, develop more reciprocal and close friendships, and show stronger leadership qualities) by middle childhood and early adolescence. Sroufe (2005) concludes that "by instilling positive expectations concerning self and others, and by providing a platform for establishing successful close relationships and a viable social support network, early secure attachment promotes strength in the face of challenges and resilience following periods of trouble" (p. 360).

In sum, early social interactions play an important role in determining a child's developmental outcomes.

The Continuing Influence of Relationships

The relationships people form once they move beyond infancy and childhood also exert strong effects on health and well-being.

Social Integration.   There is compelling evidence that individuals who are socially integrated live longer and healthier lives. ***Social integration*** (sometimes called ***social cohesion***) refers to the extent of a person's social ties or connections, and its typical markers include marital status, degree of contact with friends and family, participation in formal and informal social and community organizations, and church membership (Kushner & Sterk, 2005). A number of large-scale epidemiological studies have documented an association between lack of social integration and ***mortality*** (for reviews, see Berkman, 1995; House, Landis, & Umberson, 1988). For example, in a longitudinal investigation conducted by Knut Engedal (1996), a random sample of 334 elderly residents (75 years of age or older) of Oslo, Norway who were living in their own homes completed various measures of mental and physical health as well as an index of social integration (number of social contacts each month). Three years later, the researcher examined official city registration records to determine which participants had died. The results revealed that degree of social integration significantly predicted survival status—the participants who were still living had received higher social contact scores 3 years earlier than those who had passed away. Similar results have been reported by other researchers (e.g., LaVeist, Sellers, Brown, & Nickerson, 1997). In addition to a reduced likelihood of death, socially connected people enjoy better health than their less connected counterparts. ***Morbidity*** (disease) rates are consistently higher among the more socially isolated (see Krantz & McCeney, 2002), and individuals with less extensive social integration tend to score lower on various markers of physical (e.g., fibrinogen concentration; Loucks, Berkman, Gruenewald, & Seeman, 2005; also see Loucks et al., 2006) and mental (e.g., Cott & Fox, 2001) health.

Not surprisingly, the size of an individual's ***social network***—composed of close associates, usually friends and family members, with whom one regularly interacts (Milardo, 1988; Milardo & Helms-Erikson, 2000)—is also associated with his or her likelihood of illness and death. People with larger social networks generally score higher on quality of life measures, are physically and mentally healthier, and live longer than those with smaller networks of close friends and family members (e.g., Barnes, de Leon, Wilson, Bienias, & Evans, 2004; García, Banegas, Pérez-Regadera, Cabrera,

& Rodríguez-Artalejo, 2005; Rutledge et al., 2008). For example, in one longitudinal investigation (Shye, Mullooly, Freeborn, & Pope, 1995), a sample of older (65 or more years of age) participants reported the number of people with whom they had "informal social contact" (this served as a measure of social network size). Fifteen years later, the researchers compared the survival rates of those who had earlier reported having small, medium, and large social networks. The greatest percentage of survivors (37%) was found for the group with the largest social network (the survival rates of those with medium and small social networks were 30% and 21%, respectively).

More recently, Traolach Brugha and colleagues (Brugha et al., 2005) explored the association between social network size and mental health among a sample of adults participating in the 2000 British National Household Survey. In this longitudinal study, men and women provided information about the size of their social networks (specifically, the total number of close relatives or friends they had) and were assessed for various psychiatric disorders; 18 months later, they were recontacted and the same information was collected. The results revealed that participants with a smaller social network (composed of three or fewer persons) at the initial assessment period demonstrated significantly worse mental health at the follow-up assessment, even after their initial level of mental health was taken into account. These findings—that the larger an individual's social network, the greater his or her chance of both good health and survival—are consistent with the results of studies examining the association between social integration and well-being.

Of course, social contact alone does not guarantee positive outcomes—rather, what appears to be most important is the nature or quality of that social contact. In accord with the research on social relationships and infant/child development we reviewed earlier, scientists have found that men and women whose social interactions are characterized by non-responsive, non-nurturant, critical, or demanding exchanges experience a multitude of harmful outcomes (see Seeman, 2000). Thus, just as was found for infants and children, integration into a warm and responsive community of others, and frequent contact with nurturing, sensitive partners, is what seems to be most beneficial for adults.

Loneliness. One of the most pernicious outcomes produced by an absence of satisfying social connections and close relationships is the psychologically aversive state of *loneliness*. In his seminal (1973) book, researcher Robert S. Weiss identified two types of loneliness: (1) the loneliness of *emotional isolation*, which is produced by the lack of a close emotional attachment and which can only be remedied by the formation of a new (or the renewal of a lost) attachment, and (2) the loneliness of *social isolation*, which is produced by the absence of an engaging social network and which can only be remedied by access to such a network. Both types of loneliness occur when people's desired pattern of social interactions or relationships does not match what they actually experience (Hawkley & Cacioppo, 2009; Peplau & Perlman, 1982). Loneliness is typically assessed via self-report, and the Revised UCLA Loneliness Scale (Russell, Peplau, & Cutrona, 1980) is one of the most commonly used measures. Sample items include "I lack companionship," "I am no longer close to anyone," "My social relationships are superficial," and "I feel isolated from others."

Loneliness is fairly pervasive; estimates in national surveys range from 11% to 26%, with the highest rates typically occurring among adolescents and young adults (Peplau, Russell, & Heim, 1979; Rubenstein & Shaver, 1982). Researchers generally find that higher levels of loneliness are associated with poorer mental health (e.g., greater depression and anxiety), physical health (e.g., increased risk for cardiovascular disease), physiological functioning (e.g., in response to stressors), and socio-emotional functioning (e.g., aggression, ineffective coping strategies) in children, adolescents, and adults (Buelga, Musitu, Murgui, Pons, & Howard, 2008; Cacioppo, Hughes, Waite,

Hawkley, & Thisted, 2006; Coplan, Closson, & Arbeau, 2007; Hawkley & Cacioppo, 2007; Liu & Guo, 2007).

The presence or absence of social ties clearly has significant consequences for the quality and even the quantity of human life.

Social Support. But precisely how does social integration (and its cousin, social network size) exert its influence on an individual's health and well-being? Relationship scientists now believe that *social support* is the mediating (causal) variable responsible for the social integration–health association (see Figure 3.3). Specifically, research suggests that people who possess a high degree of social integration (or a large social network) generally have access to high levels of social support; this social support, in turn, is what actually lowers mortality and morbidity risk. Social support is generally conceptualized as acts that reflect responsiveness to another's needs; more particularly, social support is defined as "acts that communicate caring; that validate the other's worth, feelings, or actions; or that facilitate adaptive coping with problems through the provision of information, assistance, or tangible resources" (Cutrona, 1996, p. 10).

Most studies find a positive association between social support and health outcomes (e.g., Pierce, Sarason, & Sarason, 1991; Sarason, Sarason, & Gurung, 2001; Uchino, Cacioppo, & Kiecolt-Glaser, 1996). However, some types of support may be more beneficial than others. In a recent study, Joann Reinhardt, Kathrin Boerner, and Amy Horowitz (2006) explored the association between different forms of social support—*emotional support* (support that involves expressions of concern, empathy, and intimacy) vs. *instrumental support* (support that involves the provision of material aid or physical assistance) and *perceived support* (the perception that social support is available if needed) vs. *received support* (the actual receipt of support from others)—and various measures of well-being (e.g., depressive symptomatology, adaptation to disability) among a sample of older adults who were experiencing age-related loss of vision. The results of their investigation revealed that both forms of emotional support—perceived and received—were strongly related to well-being. Specifically, the more emotional support (e.g., positive feedback, intimate interaction) that participants believed was potentially available from friends and family, the fewer depressive symptoms they exhibited and the better their adaptation to their vision loss. Similarly, the more emotional support that participants actually received from friends and family, the greater was their well-being (i.e., fewer depressive symptoms, higher adaptation to vision loss). The findings for instrumental support, however, were mixed. Higher amounts of perceived instrumental support (e.g., material aid, physical assistance) were associated with better adaptation to vision loss, but the amount of instrumental support that participants reported having actually received from others was associated with lower levels of well-being (i.e., the more material assistance participants received, the more symptoms of depression they reported). The researchers concluded that emotional support, as opposed to more tangible or instrumental forms of support, plays an important

Fig. 3.3 Relationship scientists believe that social support is responsible for the demonstrated association between social integration (and social network size) and health outcomes. That is, people who are highly socially integrated (and who possess a large social network) generally have access to higher levels of social support; this, in turn, lowers their risk of morbidity (disease) and mortality (death).

role in well-being, and that this is particularly the case among people wrestling with a serious health issue or a disability.

Other researchers also have identified occasions in which social support fails to be beneficial. For example, psychologists Niall Bolger, Adam Zuckerman, and Ronald Kessler (2000; also see Bolger & Amarel, 2007) observed that receiving social support may increase an individual's awareness that he or she is having difficulty coping and consequently lower his or her self-esteem. In addition, the receipt of social support may produce uncomfortable feelings of indebtedness and obligation to the support provider. These researchers have found evidence that *invisible social support*—support that occurs outside of the recipient's awareness or within his or her awareness but with sufficient subtlety that it is not interpreted as obviously "supportive"—is the most effective form of support and produces the clearest health benefits. We will consider the topic of social support in greater detail in Chapter 9.

SUMMARY

We humans are truly social animals. Not only are human infants born into an existing interpersonal reality, but they come bearing an extraordinary array of biological gifts that allow them to develop and sustain relationships with others in the social world. The innate need to belong impels each of us to form and maintain lasting interpersonal relationships; the attachment system predisposes us to quickly form strong bonds with important others and to engage in behaviors that promote close physical proximity; the face perceptual system enables us to attend and respond to the human face; empathic accuracy allows us to accurately decipher emotional and behavioral cues from other humans; and language allows us to communicate with our species and our relationship partners. These biological propensities promote social connectedness and enhance health and well-being in infancy, and they continue to play an important role in the development and maintenance of relationships as they unfold across the life-span. In addition, the relationships we form with others—in infancy and throughout our lives—have clear consequences for our mental and physical health and longevity. People who possess strong ties to the community and social institutions, and who have a supportive network of family, friends, and other close associates, tend to exhibit better health and to live longer than less-integrated individuals.

KEY CONCEPTS

Need to belong (p. 43)
Attachment system (p. 44)
Attachment (p. 44)
Attachment behavior (p. 44)
Attachment figure (p. 44)
Caregiving system (p. 45)
Strange Situation procedure (p. 45)
Secure attachment (p. 46)
Insecure/resistant attachment (p. 46)
Insecure/avoidant attachment (p. 46)
Internal working model (p. 46)
Face perceptual system (p. 47)

Second-order relational information (p. 48)
Other-race effect (p. 48)
Empathic accuracy (p. 48)
Interpersonal sensitivity (p. 48)
Still-face paradigm (p. 49)
Still-face effect (p. 49)
Universal Grammar (p. 51)
High amplitude sucking (HAS) procedure (p. 52)
Responsiveness (p. 53)
Dyadic verbal reciprocity (p. 53)
Risky family environment (p. 53)
Emotional regulation (p. 54)

EXPLORATION EXERCISES

These exercises are designed to allow you to explore in greater detail some of the concepts and issues discussed in this chapter. There are no right or wrong answers to these exercises—they are simply meant to provide an opportunity for discussion and debate.

1. Relationship scholars now believe that over evolutionary history, human beings developed a need to belong. Thus, it is no surprise that many of the strongest emotions that we experience are linked to issues of belongingness. Describe a situation from your own life in which your belongingness needs were met (i.e., you were accepted, included, welcomed). Now, describe a situation in which your belongingness needs were not met (i.e., you were rejected, excluded, ignored). How did the two situations make you feel? Compare and contrast your emotional response to the two situations.

2. This exercise is designed to illustrate the need to belong. Ask five people you know to consider the three relationship scenarios presented in Table 3.1. If they could only experience one of those relationship situations in their lifetimes, which one would they choose? For each person, indicate the selected option below. Then, sum up the total number of people who chose each of the various options.

	Option A	Option B	Option C
Person 1	____	____	____
Person 2	____	____	____
Person 3	____	____	____
Person 4	____	____	____
Person 5	____	____	____
Total:	____	____	____

Which option was the most commonly chosen? Which option was the least preferred? What does this say about the need to belong?

3. It is often said that "you can be lonely in a crowd." What does this saying mean? What type of loneliness is captured by this saying?

4. Think of a time in your own life when you needed help and when someone in your social network provided you with *effective* social support (that is, with support that actually was helpful to you). Now, think of a time when you needed help and when someone provided you with *unhelpful* social support (that is, with support that did not, in fact, help you). Compare those two situations. (a) What kind of social support was provided or offered in each situation? (b) Why do you think the support was helpful in the first situation and unhelpful in the second? How did the two situations differ? What could the person have done in the second situation to make his or her support efforts more helpful?

PART II
Relationship Development

This section of the textbook concerns the topic of relationship development. Chapter 4 focuses on relationship beginnings, with an emphasis on the factors that promote attention, attraction, and affiliation; Chapter 5 considers the ways in which individuals go about actually initiating relationships with others; Chapter 6 explores the major processes that propel relationship development; and Chapter 7 discusses marriage and mate selection.

It is important to keep in mind that most theory and research in this area focuses on *voluntary relationships* such as friendships and mating relationships in which the initiation (and subsequent development) of the relationship is primarily dependent on internal factors such as the degree to which the partners like each other. Such relationships typically are born within an *open interaction field* in which each potential partner is free to start (or refrain from initiating) the relationship (see Murstein, 1970). For example, a student attending an enormous lecture class, a woman surveying the other guests at a large holiday gathering, and a man reading profiles posted at an online dating service are all relatively free to select someone for an initial interaction (and potential relationship)—and, should a relationship then develop, they (or their partners) may elect to maintain or dissolve the association at any time. Because these relationships are heavily dependent on the partners' attraction to one another—a factor that can (and frequently does) change over time—they are of particular interest to scientists interested in developmental issues.

Of course, many relationships—including parent–child, student–teacher, coworker, and some mating relationships—are formed in *closed interaction fields* in which the partners are forced to interact by virtue of the environment. The initiation and subsequent development of these *involuntary relationships* are not dependent on the partners' level of attraction or liking for one another; rather, their association will continue as long as the external causal conditions that originally created it remain in place (or if the partners become sufficiently attracted to one another to maintain their relationship once the external constraints are lifted). For example, siblings growing up together in the same house are forced to interact regardless of their personal feelings (as are students and teachers, coworkers in the same office, or spouses in an arranged marriage). Involuntary relationships tend to be less subject to readily observable change than voluntary relationships; for that reason, questions of relationship development—initiation, progression, maintenance, and decline— have typically been investigated in voluntary relationships.

Chapter 4
Relationship Beginnings

What factors led to the formation of your closest friendship? How did you and your romantic partner first meet and become involved? What was it that initially attracted you to those individuals (and that initially attracted them to you)? In an open field situation, the partners must first *notice* each other before any relationship can develop; next, they must be sufficiently *attracted* to one another to wish to interact; and finally, they must *interact*. This chapter explores these three important aspects of relationship beginnings, focusing specifically on research designed to identify the factors that promote attention to, attraction to, and initial interaction between potential partners and thus contribute to the birth of a relationship.

WHO DO WE NOTICE? PRINCIPLES OF SELECTIVE ATTENTION

Several theorists have suggested that a relationship is born at the exact moment when one person first becomes aware of another person (e.g., Levinger & Snoek, 1972). However, as we discussed in Chapter 1, a true relationship requires mutual influence; thus, it is probably more accurate to locate a relationship's beginning in the moment in which two people first become consciously aware of each other. Because the human brain has limited conscious/attentional capacities, we cannot possibly be fully aware of all of the information our senses take in, and all the people we come in contact with, at any given moment (see Nørretranders, 1998). Consequently, some people are more likely than others to capture our attention. In closed field situations, attention is usually determined by situational pressures—for example, we notice the teacher standing in front of us in a classroom, or the person sitting next to us in a seminar, because he or she is in our immediate vicinity and the situation demands that we notice that teacher or that person. However, in an open field situation containing numerous potential interaction partners, two factors appear to be particularly important in focusing our attention on another person— novelty and importance.

In general, unexpected events and unfamiliar or *novel* people are more likely to capture our attention than are familiar or expected people and events. A student standing in line at the campus bookstore and surveying the crowd of other students is likely to notice someone wearing a bathing suit and striking a pose in the middle of the floor. The fact that we tend to notice novel others makes absolute sense from an evolutionary or adaptive perspective, because unfamiliar people have the potential to benefit or harm us. Is the bathing-suit-clad person a model on a photo shoot? Or is he/she in the midst of a psychotic breakdown? Our brains allow us to quickly identify—and make judgments about—the unfamiliar and unexpected, and the result of that determination (cute model vs. disturbed person) may influence whether we subsequently initiate an interaction or not.

Attention and awareness are also influenced by *importance*. We almost instantly judge some people to be more important to us than others. Specifically, given an array of potential partners competing for our precious and limited attentional resources, we are likely to award our attention to those individuals we believe have the power to influence our outcomes or to meet our own specific needs (e.g., Berscheid, Graziano, Monson, & Dermer, 1976; Erber & Fiske, 1984; also see Sunnafrank & Ramirez, 2004). For example, researchers have found that people with strong intimacy goals—who are focused on pursuing and achieving a high degree of emotional attachment, mutual dependence, and self-disclosure in their romantic relationships—tend to focus on intrinsic qualities (including warmth, expressiveness, openness, and humor) when evaluating a potential romantic partner (Sanderson, Keiter, Miles, & Yopyk, 2007). Similarly, men and women who are actively seeking a short-term sexual liaison and those seeking a committed dating relationship selectively attend to different attributes when considering someone for a potential relationship (e.g., Regan, Levin, Sprecher, Christopher, & Cate, 2000).

It is important to recognize that consciously attending to someone does not guarantee attraction. Nonetheless, awareness (in particular, mutual awareness) represents an important and necessary first step toward the establishment of a relationship—we cannot become attracted to, or initiate interaction with, someone we simply do not notice.

WHO DO WE LIKE? PRINCIPLES OF INTERPERSONAL ATTRACTION

Once we have noticed someone, a host of factors come into play to determine how positively we respond to that person. *Attraction*—liking or positive sentiment—is influenced by a number of variables. Some of these are associated with the other person (i.e., personal factors such as expressiveness, warmth, or physical attractiveness), some arise from the combination of the individual's and the other's characteristics (i.e., relational factors such as similarity), and others are located in the surrounding social or physical environment (i.e., environmental factors such as social norms).

Liking Those Who Possess Desirable Characteristics

Research reveals that we respond positively to people who possess particular kinds of attributes. The literature on mate preferences, for example, is enormous and encompasses a huge number of empirical studies, all of which indicate that men and women overwhelmingly prefer romantic partners who possess intelligence, emotional stability, warmth and expressiveness, an honest and trustworthy disposition, an exciting overall personality, and a physically attractive appearance. In two of the first documented examinations of mate preference, both conducted during the late 1930s and early 1940s, social scientists Harold Christensen (1947) and Reuben Hill (1945) asked college students at their respective universities to rank order a list of characteristics in terms of their importance in a romantic partner. The two most important attributes, according to both samples of participants, were "dependable character" and "emotional stability." Men and women also emphasized a "pleasing disposition" and "mutual attraction or love." Other researchers have since replicated these results using the same or very similar lists of features (e.g., Hudson & Henze, 1969; McGinnis, 1958; Regan, 1998c; Regan & Berscheid, 1997). Table 4.1 illustrates these findings.

Table 4.1   Top 10 Most Desired Characteristics in a Potential Marriage Partner

What Men Wanted	What Women Wanted
Good overall personality	Honesty and trustworthiness
Honesty and trustworthiness	Kindness and compassion
Attractive appearance	Good overall personality
Intelligence	Intelligence
Good health	Attentive to one's partner
Kindness and compassion	Good sense of humor
Good sense of humor	Self-confidence
Self-confidence	Good health
Attentive to one's partner	Attractive appearance
Easygoing nature	Easygoing nature

In this study, men and women were asked to rank order (from most to least desirable in a marriage partner) a list of attributes similar to the ones used by Christensen (1947), Hill (1945), and other early mate preference researchers. This table shows the top 10 most desired characteristics, arranged in order from most to least desirable. As can be seen from the results, men and women tend to desire similar attributes in a marriage partner, although there is some evidence that men rank external attributes such as appearance higher than do women.

Source: Regan, P. C., & Berscheid, E. (1997). Gender differences in characteristics desired in a potential sexual and marriage partner. *Journal of Psychology and Human Sexuality, 9(1)*, 25–37. Copyright © 1997 by the Haworth Press, Inc.

Similar results have been by reported by researchers examining friendship preferences. For example, Susan Sprecher and Pamela Regan (2002) asked a large sample of men and women to indicate their preferences for an array of characteristics in a potential same-sex friend as well as in a potential dating and marriage partner. Both sexes reported desiring a friend who possessed a great deal of the following attributes, in order of importance: sense of humor, expressiveness and openness, warmth and kindness, exciting personality, and intelligence. Moreover, both men and women indicated preferring a date or spouse with high levels of the exact same attributes (though in a slightly different order of importance). The researchers concluded that intrinsic attributes that reflect an ability and motivation to provide social and emotional support—like warmth, kindness, and expressiveness—may be fundamental to the establishment of all close interpersonal relationships.

In addition to exploring what people seek in potential partners, some researchers have examined the attributes that people seek to avoid. For example, social scientists Michael Cunningham, Anita Barbee, and Perri Druen (1996; also see Ault & Philhower, 2001; Cunningham, Druen, & Barbee, 1997; Cunningham, Shamblen, Barbee, & Ault, 2005) argue that the process of relationship formation requires individuals to evaluate potential partners not only in terms of the positive qualities they offer but also in terms of whether their negative qualities can be endured. Research on these undesirable partner attributes or *social allergens* reveals that men and women are repulsed by people who consistently violate social norms and rules of conduct, including drinking to excess, cheating at games, gossiping about others, arriving late all the time, and lying. In addition, they dislike potential partners who are oversexed—that is, who brag about sexual conquests or skills, constantly talk about or mention previous relationship partners, or gaze longingly at other men or women. People also seek to avoid individuals who have uncouth habits (e.g., demonstrate poor grooming, display poor table manners, stand too close or stare inappropriately, use a loud speaking voice). In sum, individuals are attracted to a potential partner who not only fulfills their desires, but who also manages to avoid doing the things that repulse them.

The Allure of Beauty.   Of all the attributes people can possess that can predispose us to like them, none is as powerful or alluring as physical attractiveness. The first unequivocal demonstration of the influence of physical appeal on interpersonal attraction was conducted in the late 1960s by social psychologists Elaine Hatfield (then Walster), Vera Aronson, Darcy Abrahams, and Leon Rottman (1966). In their study, incoming first-year students received information about a "Computer Dance" being offered as part of a series of university-sponsored activities for new students. Those who arrived to purchase advance tickets were asked to complete a questionnaire about their interests and characteristics, which they believed would be fed into a computer and used to pair them with another student—their date for the dance—who possessed similar attributes. (In actuality, students were randomly paired for the dance.) As each student went through the process of completing the questionnaire and purchasing a ticket, the four people supervising the activity (who were actually confederates working for the researchers) surreptitiously assessed his or her physical attractiveness. Later that week, the students arrived at the dance and met the partners who had been (randomly) assigned to them. Then, during intermission, they completed a questionnaire that asked, among other items, how much they liked their dates and whether or not they would like to go out with them again. The researchers had predicted a matching effect; that is, they expected that people would prefer partners at their own attractiveness level (for example, they hypothesized that moderately attractive people who happened to be assigned highly attractive dates would like their partners less than would moderately attractive people who happened to be assigned moderately attractive partners). However, this was not the case. For both men and women, and irrespective of their own level of attractiveness, the more physically appealing the date, the more he or she was liked and the more often participants wanted to go out with him or her again.

The impact of physical attractiveness on interpersonal attraction is extensive and not confined to the realm of dating and mating. Research reveals that attractive people are preferred in a wide variety of settings and receive preferential treatment in countless ways (for reviews, see Bull & Rumsey, 1988; Hatfield & Sprecher, 1986b; Langlois et al., 2000). Many scholars posit that this seemingly universal preference for beauty may stem from the *"beautiful is good" or physical attractiveness stereotype*—a strong and pervasive set of assumptions concerning the traits, attributes, and outcomes of attractive people (e.g., that they are more sensitive, kind, interesting, friendly, sociable, and outgoing, and that they will have "better" jobs, marriages, and lives, than less-attractive people). The stereotype was first identified and named in 1972 by social psychologists Karen Dion, Ellen Berscheid, and Elaine Walster (now Hatfield); since then, literally thousands of studies have confirmed that people do ascribe more favorable personality traits and more successful life outcomes to attractive people (for a review, see Eagly, Ashmore, Makhijani, & Longo, 1991). This may be one reason why physical attractiveness is such a potent predictor of interpersonal attraction.

Liking Those Who Are "Appropriate"

As we have seen, people like those who possess desirable characteristics. But what is the origin of these preferences? What makes a particular attribute appealing or a particular other person desirable as a friend or mate? Many relationship scholars posit that interpersonal attraction is strongly influenced by environmental factors that teach us the types of people who are "acceptable" for particular kinds of relationships, and the attributes that should be sought in a potential friend, mate, or other close relationship partner.

Some scientists adopt a sociocultural or social contextual theoretical perspective, focusing on *proximate environmental mechanisms*—causes located in the contemporary social, cultural, and historical environment—that appear to influence liking. These theorists posit that people learn the prevailing "rules" of attraction from exposure to *social and cultural scripts*, which are normative expectations that define and organize social experience and are used to guide and assess social behavior (e.g., Gagnon & Simon, 1973; Reiss, 1967, 1981, 1986; Simon & Gagnon, 1986), and through *social learning processes*, including the patterns of reinforcement and punishment that people receive for their interpersonal behavior (e.g., Hogben & Byrne, 1998; Mischel, 1966). Not only are a person's opportunities for interaction and relationship initiation influenced by family members, peers, other social network members, the media, the educational system, and political and religious ideologies, but those same social forces also shape his or her understanding of acceptable or appropriate interpersonal behavior (see Arriaga, Agnew, Capezza, & Lehmiller, 2008).

Attraction also may be shaped by a different kind of environmental pressure—one that existed a long time ago in the development of our species. Evolutionary theorists focus on forces that existed in the *environment of evolutionary adaptedness* or the ancestral environment in which our species developed its various adaptations (see Bowlby, 1969; Cosmides & Tooby, 1997; Symons, 1992). These theorists propose that the human mind was designed by the process of natural selection to solve *adaptive problems* or recurrent challenges in human evolutionary history that had consequences for survival and reproduction (Brewer & Caporael, 1990; Buss & Kenrick, 1998; Tooby & Cosmides, 1992). As we discussed in Chapter 3, many of these challenges were social or interpersonal in nature, including communicating and forming cooperative alliances with other humans, finding and retaining an appropriate mate, reproducing and rearing offspring, and so on. According to this perspective, modern-day humans prefer certain attributes in their potential friends and mates because those attributes were beneficial—that is, associated with higher rates of survival and/or reproductive success—in the ancestral environment. For example, early humans who were attracted to, and then formed friendships and mating relationships with, emotionally stable, intelligent, physically healthy partners survived longer and enjoyed greater reproductive success than those who selected less-suitable partners, and they passed the neural circuitry that governs those preferences along to us, their modern-day relatives.

Together, these two theoretical perspectives suggest that we are attracted to others whom the environment (both contemporary and ancestral) deems appropriate. Indeed, there is strong evidence that the media, parents, peers (particularly close friends), and other social forces are potent sources of information about attraction, love, romance, friendship, and other relational topics. For example, Leslie Baxter, Tim Dun, and Erin Sahlstein (2001) asked a sample of college students to keep a diary for 2 weeks in which they recorded any interactions they had with others in which rules for conducting relationships were communicated. An analysis of these diary records revealed that participants learned the "shoulds" and "should nots" of relating through (1) receiving unsolicited advice from their friends and other social network members; (2) observing the interpersonal behavior and outcomes of social network members; (3) gossiping with friends and network members; and (4) receiving direct sanctioning (reinforcement or punishment) for their own behavior from network members. In addition, a good portion of the rules that were communicated by friends and network members concerned "rules of eligibility" or the criteria that establish someone as a desirable romantic partner. For example, it was not considered appropriate to be attracted to or to date someone who was much older or much younger, who was already involved in a relationship with another person, who was on the "rebound" from a prior relationship, or who was closely connected to someone in the immediate social network (e.g., a friend's sibling, a friend's ex-partner).

There is also evidence that young adults' preferences are shaped not only by their peers but by the attitudes and expectations of their parents and the strength of their own cultural and familial orientation (see Daniels, 2002). In one study, psychologists Michaela Hynie, Richard Lalonde, and Nam Lee (2006) asked a sample of adult children of Chinese immigrants living in the U.S. or Canada to rate a series of "traditional" attributes in terms of their importance in a potential spouse. These attributes included the items *similar culture, similar religion, family reputation, parents' approval, chastity, strong cultural ties,* and *desires children.* Participants also completed two measures reflecting the influence of the social environment. The first was the Asian Values Scale, a 17-item measure of traditional Chinese values such as conformity, harmony, and emotional self-control (Kim, Atkinson, & Yang, 1999). Sample items include "The ability to control one's emotions is a sign of strength" and "Family's reputation is the primary social concern." The second was a scale assessing *family allocentrism,* defined as the degree to which a person feels connected to or interrelated with his or her family and the extent to which he or she is oriented to family norms (Lay et al., 1998). Sample items indicative of high allocentrism include "I am very similar to my parents" and "Knowing that I need to rely on my family makes me happy." The researchers then assessed one final source of social influence—namely, parental attitudes. They contacted participants' parents and had them rate the same seven traditional attribute items in terms of how important it was to them that their children find a mate with those characteristics. The results revealed a strong positive correlation between participants' mate preferences and all three sources of social influence. Specifically, the more importance participants placed on traditional attributes in a potential mate, the more strongly they endorsed the traditional values of their culture, the more connected they were with their family and the more oriented they were toward family norms, and the more importance their own parents placed on the same traditional attributes.

Moreover, cross-cultural research on mate preferences supports the idea that people tend to be attracted to others who are "appropriate." As predicted by evolutionary theories, the majority of men and women from around the world are attracted to romantic partners who possess the same core group of seemingly adaptive dispositional features (e.g., emotional stability, honesty and trustworthiness, expressiveness and warmth, a "dependable" character). In addition, in accord with social context theories, there is a strong tendency for individuals to prefer mates who possess attributes that reflect the prevailing social values of their respective cultures. For example, adults from collectivist cultures in the East and Middle East tend to find "practical" or "traditional" characteristics (e.g., family-oriented, chaste, neat) and demographic similarity (e.g., same religion, caste) more attractive than do adults from individualist cultures like the U.S. and other Western countries (Buss et al., 1990; Goodwin & Tang, 1991; Khallad, 2005; Sprecher & Chandak, 1992; Toro-Morn & Sprecher, 2003). The emphasis placed on these features is understandable when we consider that many collectivist cultures have a history of (and still practice) arranged marriage (see Chapter 7). Basing one's preferences on practical considerations, traditional social values, and demographic similarity increases the likelihood that the partners will be compatible and that the couple will receive approval and support from their families and other social groups.

Liking Those Who Are Familiar

Humans, along with most other species, tend to dislike the unfamiliar and like the familiar. This preference for the familiar probably represents an evolved or adaptive behavior; unfamiliar people, objects, and situations are potentially harmful, whereas those that are familiar have already been experienced and thus have known consequences.

Psychologist Robert Zajonc's (1968) seminal studies provided the first direct experimental evidence for the *mere exposure effect* (also called the *mere-repeated-exposure effect*); namely, the psychological phenomenon in which merely being exposed to a person (or an object) repeatedly is sufficient to produce a preference for that person (or object). In one experiment, for example, participants viewed a series of yearbook photographs of male college students as part of a study they believed concerned "visual memory." Each photograph was presented a different number of times (ranging from 1 to 25 exposures) for a period of 2 seconds throughout the course of the trial, and participants were then asked to indicate how much they liked the man in each photograph using a 7-point scale. The results revealed a significant positive association between frequency of exposure and liking ratings; the more often participants had seen a particular man's face, the more liking they reported feeling for him.

These findings have been replicated outside of the laboratory as well. Richard Moreland and Scott Beach (1992) conducted a field experiment in which four women confederates of similar appearance posed as college students in a large lecture class. To create differing levels of familiarity, one woman attended 5 sessions of class, another attended 10 sessions, another attended 15 sessions, and the fourth did not attend class at all. Additionally, to ensure that familiarity—and not other cues to likeability—was the only factor at work, the women did not interact in any way with the other students in the class. (They simply arrived at the lecture hall a few minutes before class, walked slowly down toward the front of the room, and sat where they could be seen by the other students.) At the end of the academic term, the researchers showed photographs of the four women to the students and asked them to estimate the probability that they would (1) like each woman and become friends with her and (2) enjoy spending time with her. In addition, students rated each woman on various trait dimensions (e.g., interesting/boring, attractive/unattractive, intelligent/unintelligent, honest/dishonest, sincere/insincere); these ratings were averaged to produce one general index of attraction. As expected, the results revealed a strong mere exposure effect—women who attended more class sessions received significantly higher scores on the attraction index, and the students reported that they would be significantly more likely to befriend them and to enjoy spending time with them.

The association between familiarity and interpersonal attraction has been extensively documented and is now one of the most robust findings in the literature (for reviews, see Bornstein, 1989;

Zajonc, 2001). However, there is an important caveat: if our initial reaction to someone is negative, repeated exposure to that person is unlikely to produce attraction. In general, familiarity appears to strengthen first responses, such that a person who is initially disliked comes to be disliked even more, and a person who is initially liked comes to be liked even more, with increased exposure (e.g., Perlman & Oskamp, 1971).

Liking Those Who Are Similar

Another important determinant of interpersonal attraction is the relational factor of *similarity*. Not only do people prefer potential partners who possess similar demographic characteristics, personality traits and dispositional tendencies, values and attitudes, and interests and hobbies (Markey & Markey, 2007; Regan et al., 2000; Sprecher & Regan, 2002), but similarity repeatedly has been shown to produce liking in laboratory experiments as well as in "real-life" contexts (e.g., Newcomb, 1961; for reviews, see Fehr, 2008; Montoya, Horton, & Kirchner, 2008).

Social psychologist Donn Byrne and his colleagues have conducted the most rigorous and extensive exploration of the similarity–attraction connection, concentrating on attitude similarity and generally employing a *bogus stranger experimental paradigm* (e.g., Byrne, 1971; Byrne, Baskett, & Hodges, 1971; Byrne & Griffitt, 1966; Smeaton, Byrne, & Murnen, 1989; for a review, see Byrne, 1997). Specifically, in the typical "bogus stranger" experiment, the researchers assess participants' attitudes on a variety of issues, perhaps as part of a class activity or assignment. Later in the academic term, participants are asked to evaluate an attitude survey ostensibly completed by another person (e.g., a student in a different class). In actuality there is no such other person; the responses on the attitude survey have been systematically varied by the researchers to represent different degrees of similarity to the participants' own (previously assessed) attitudes. After the participants have examined the attitudes of the supposed other person, they indicate their level of attraction to him or her. The results, across multiple studies with multiple participant samples (and age groups), are uniform and robust—attitude similarity generates attraction.

But why should similarity produce liking? Some relationship scholars have posited that the association between similarity and attraction may be the result of perceived familiarity. They reason that there is no one more familiar to each of us than ourselves; consequently, those who resemble us are inherently more familiar than those who do not resemble us, and this perception of familiarity is what produces attraction. Others have suggested that the similarity–attraction association is mediated by people's tendency to assume that similar others will like them (and dissimilar others will dislike them). In other words, it may not be similarity itself that enhances our attraction to another person, but rather the perception that a similar person will respond positively to us (e.g., Condon & Crano, 1988). Still others have proposed that similarity (especially of attitudes and beliefs) is reinforcing because it provides confirmation of our own particular way of perceiving the world; that is, we like similar others because those others provide *consensual validation* of our world view (e.g., Byrne & Clore, 1967; see Figure 4.1). Whatever the underlying mechanism, similarity has proven to be a powerful predictor of interpersonal attraction.

Liking Those Who Are Responsive

The responsiveness of two people to each other's behavior lies at the very heart of the concept of "relationship" (see Chapter 1). Thus, it is not terribly surprising that *responsiveness* is another variable that is strongly associated with interpersonal attraction. Research consistently reveals that men and women report greater liking for individuals who are responsive than for those who

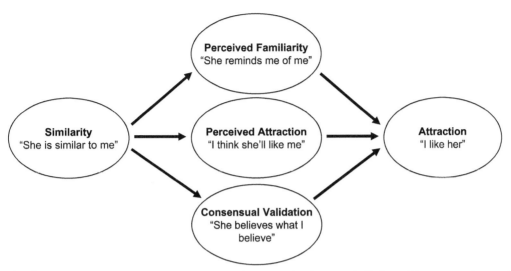

Fig. 4.1 Some relationship scientists believe that the association between similarity and interpersonal attraction may be the result of perceived familiarity, perceived attraction, and/or consensual validation. That is, people who are similar to us appear familiar, we tend to assume that they will respond positively to us, and they confirm our own world views (which is reinforcing to us). All three of these factors—perceived familiarity, perceived attraction, and consensual validation—generate feelings of liking.

are not (e.g., Davis & Holtgraves, 1984; Davis & Perkowitz, 1979; for a review, see Fehr, 2008). For example, communication scholars Doreen Baringer and James McCroskey (2000) found a strong, positive correlation between student responsiveness and attraction among a sample of teachers. Specifically, teachers expressed higher amounts of positive affect for students who engaged in interpersonal behaviors indicative of responsiveness (such as sitting closer, establishing eye contact, smiling, leaning forward, engaging in positive head nods) than they did for less-responsive students.

Similar results were reported more recently by psychologists Edward Lemay and Margaret Clark (2008). In their investigation, previously unacquainted college students completed an electronic survey in which they provided answers to a series of questions (e.g., "describe a unique accomplishment," "describe a humorous experience"). Students then reported in pairs for a laboratory session, where they were subsequently placed in separate rooms (ostensibly so that they could look over and change their survey responses in private). One of these students was then randomly assigned to either the *responsive condition* or the *neutral condition*. In the responsive condition, he or she was privately instructed by the researchers to behave in a positive manner toward the other participant, to act interested in and impressed by the other person, and to be friendly and encouraging. In the neutral condition, he or she was asked to behave in a neutral manner toward the other participant, to act not particularly interested in or impressed by the other, and to not be friendly or encouraging (but also to refrain from being mean or rude). The second student in each pair did not receive any instructions. Thus, each student pair consisted of one partner who was behaving in either a responsive or neutral manner (per experimental instructions), and another partner who was simply behaving naturally. Then, each pair of students was reunited for a 10-minute interaction during which they took turns sharing their answers to the survey questions. Finally, participants completed a number of rating scales, including a three-item measure designed to assess their level of attraction for one another (i.e., "I liked the other participant during the interaction," "I am interested in getting to know the other participant better," "I would like to start a friendship with the other participant"). The results revealed that responsiveness clearly generated attraction. Specifically, participants who interacted with a responsive partner (that is, a person who had been instructed to behave in a positive, friendly, and interested manner) reported more liking for that individual and expressed greater interest in pursuing a relationship with him or her than participants who interacted with a neutral partner.

One of the reasons we pay particular attention to another person's responsiveness may be because it imparts important information about the likelihood of a future relationship with him or her. People who are unresponsive—who avoid eye contact, refuse to respond (or respond inappropriately) when addressed by others, or remove themselves from social situations—are signaling a clear lack of interest in establishing a connection with us, and it makes sense that we would find them unappealing.

In sum, people tend to be attracted to individuals who possess desirable (and socially or culturally appropriate) characteristics, who resemble them along a number of dimensions, who are familiar, and who appear responsive. Before we leave the topic of interpersonal attraction and turn to a discussion of affiliation, it is important to acknowledge that much of the research in this area has focused on one factor (e.g., similarity, proximity) to the exclusion of others. However, in the "real world," these factors undoubtedly work together to influence attraction. They may even have additive effects. For example, we tend to like similar others and we also tend to perceive them as familiar (which, in turn, can generate additional liking). We may also perceive similar others as likely to be responsive to us (which can produce even more liking). Thus, there is no simple answer to the question of "who do we like"—attraction is a complex, multiply-determined phenomenon.

WHO DO WE APPROACH? PRINCIPLES OF AFFILIATION

In closed field settings, *affiliation* is not dependent on attraction developing between the partners—they will interact as long as the external situation demands it. In open field settings, however, feelings of attraction are the most usual motivation for voluntary attempts to initiate interaction with another person. But even in open field situations, attraction does not guarantee affiliation—people do not always approach others to whom they are attracted. Why? Relationship scholars have identified two additional factors which seem to play a significant role in determining affiliation—accessibility and receptivity.

Approaching Those Who Are Accessible

One of the realities people face as they go about selecting partners for friendship, romance, and other activities is that life rarely offers up an unlimited selection of interpersonal possibilities. Rather, as sociologist Alan Kerckhoff (1974) observed, people always make their selections from a *field of availables*—individuals who are available and accessible for interaction. Thus, who someone approaches for an initial encounter critically depends on the composition of his or her current field of availables. A person's field of availables, in turn, is affected by both the surrounding physical environment (i.e., physical proximity) and aspects of his or her social environment (i.e., social proximity and social influence).

Physical Proximity.   People who are available and readily accessible for interaction tend to be within close ***physical proximity***. The influence of physical proximity on relationship formation has been extensively documented, with numerous studies revealing that people who live close to one another are more likely to become friends than those who live even just a bit farther away (see Fehr, 2008). For example, in one frequently cited investigation, researchers Lucille Nahemow and M. Powell Lawton (1975) interviewed 270 residents of Dyckman Houses about various aspects of their friendship choices. (Dyckman Houses is an ethnically diverse public housing project located in New York City and consisting of several 14-story buildings, each with 12 apartments per story.) During the interview, each resident was asked to list his or her "best friends in the project" and to indicate where those individuals lived and how they had originally met. The results demonstrated that residential proximity played a critical role in the selection of friends. Of all the friends who were listed first by participants (i.e., their very best friend), 88% lived in the same building as they did, and nearly half lived on the participants' own floor. This pattern held across sexes and ethnic groups. Proximity also facilitated the beginning of those friendships; 52% of residents reported having met their current friends in the hallways, elevators, and entrance areas in their own buildings, and an additional 30% had met close by on the project grounds. In discussing their findings, the researchers concluded, "The proximity effect appears to be a powerful force in friendship formation and operates for people of all ages, races, and for both sexes" (p. 209).

Similar results were reported in another classic investigation conducted by sociologist Mady Wechsler Segal (1974), who focused on friendship choices among Maryland state police trainees. Trainees lived and attended classes in the police academy, and they were assigned to dorm rooms and classroom seats on the basis of the alphabetical order of their last names. Thus, the closer two trainees were to each other in alphabetical order, the physically closer they also were to each other (in other words, alphabetical order served as a measure of proximity). Trainees had known each other for approximately 6 weeks when they received a questionnaire from the researcher asking them to name their three "closest friends" on the force and to provide a variety of attitudinal, demographic, and related information. The results revealed that alphabetical ordering indeed was associated with friendship choices—the closer together in the alphabet any two trainees were, the more likely they were to name each other as their closest friend on the force (in fact, 45% of the "best friends" nominated by trainees were directly adjacent to them in alphabetical order). Moreover, proximity in the alphabet was a better predictor of friendship choice among the trainees than was similarity of age, marital status, religion, ethnicity, hobbies, and other characteristics often associated with interpersonal attraction and friendship choice.

Physical proximity provides the opportunity for interaction, which is a necessary condition for establishing a relationship. Proximity may also promote attraction between potential partners, through two primary mechanisms. The first mechanism is through *civility and courtesy norms* which govern social behavior among individuals in close physical proximity. These norms, coupled with the expectation of future interaction (and the knowledge that there will undoubtedly be consequences for our present behavior), may encourage us to treat our neighbors, classmates, and coworkers with consideration and respect. As noted by Beverley Fehr (2008) in her recent review of the friendship formation literature, many workplace and school settings also encourage cooperative and friendly exchanges between interactants. Consequently, initial exchanges among people in close proximity are likely to be pleasant and conducive to subsequent relationship development.

Proximity also may promote attraction through *similarity* (or the perception of similarity). As we have seen, similarity generally promotes positive sentiment, and people who live in the same neighborhood, attend the same school, and work in the same location are likely to resemble each other on important demographic, attitudinal, and trait dimensions. Indeed, Nahemow and Lawton (1975) found that 60% of the close friends nominated by participants in their study were in the same age category, 72% were of the same race or ethnicity, and 73% were of the same sex.

Although physical proximity is often described in textbooks as a fundamental "law" of affiliation (and attraction), it is important to recognize that proximity only provides the opportunity for interaction—it does not guarantee the *quality* of those interactions. The tendency to dislike those we are near is as strong as (and even stronger than) the tendency to like them. Ebbe Ebbesen, Glenn Kjos, and Vladimir Konecni (1976) asked a group of people living in a townhouse complex in southern California to indicate the residents they "liked most" (friends) and "disliked most" (enemies). Not surprisingly, the researchers found the classic proximity effect such that the probability of being chosen as a friend increased as the physical distance between people decreased. However, the association between physical proximity and enmity was even stronger; participants lived near a greater number of disliked than liked residents. The investigators attributed this finding to "environmental spoiling"—disliked others tended to violate civility and courtesy norms and behave in ways that spoiled the participants' living environment.

It is also important to recognize that people need not be physically close in order to initiate contact or interact with one another. Increasing numbers of people now use the Internet to search for friendship and romantic opportunities (McKenna, 2008), and many of them do so because of a lack of physical access to potential relationship partners (Madden & Lenhart, 2006). In the online world, proximity is a function of electronic or virtual space rather than physical location:

> In order for two people to meet online, they have to be in the same chat room at the same time (closest approximation to "real life" proximity), post messages on the same message board forum (one that archives past postings), be part of the same listserv (where users interact both on the list and off), or have the same software as other people (i.e., AOL's Instant Messenger or ICQ messaging software). Any one of these things [increases] the possibility of two people crossing paths and communicating.
>
> (Levine, 2000, p. 566)

This suggests that it is **interaction accessibility** and not actual physical proximity that is important in the beginning stages of relationship formation. Interestingly, although the Internet may have widened the pool of availables for many people, the same factors that generate attraction and a desire to affiliate in face-to-face situations also appear to produce attraction to potential online partners (e.g., similarity, familiarity or frequency of contact, physical attractiveness; see Levine, 2000; Sprecher, Schwartz, Harvey, & Hatfield, 2008). We will discuss this point further in the next chapter.

Social Proximity and Social Influence.   In addition to physical or virtual proximity, *social proximity*—how close potential partners are to each other in the social environment or the extent to which their social networks overlap—also influences affiliation. Relationship scholars Malcolm Parks and Leona Eggert (1991) propose that **communicative distance**, or the number of people in each individual's communication network that two persons must "go through" to reach each other for the first time, plays an important role in relationship beginnings. Specifically, they hypothesize that decreases in communicative distance (that is, increased social proximity) are associated with an increased probability of initial contact. To test this supposition, they asked high school and university students to provide the name of a same-sex friend and to list that friend's 12 closest network members. Participants then were asked to indicate how many of these network members they had met before meeting their friend. The results revealed that approximately two-thirds of the participants had met at least one member of their friend's social network prior to meeting their friend. It seems that we meet many of our future partners through our current ones.

The social environment affects interaction accessibility in other ways, as well. For instance, because social norms influence people's beliefs about who is an appropriate partner for various kinds of relationships, they also influence with whom people will actually attempt to interact. In addition, members of an individual's social network may actively facilitate initial encounters with desirable partners (and prevent encounters with those they deem undesirable). Research conducted by family studies scholars Eric Vernberg, Susan Beery, Keith Ewell, and David Abwender (1993) revealed that parents help their children meet new friends in several ways, such as by (1) becoming involved with the parents and families of other children, (2) enabling their children to spend time with potential friends (e.g., allowing them to invite a new acquaintance to the movies or over for dinner), (3) providing advice about how to initiate and behave in relationships, and (4) encouraging participation in activities with peers (e.g., team sports and school activities). Similarly, family members, "third parties" (a common friend or acquaintance), and even professional matchmakers (see Chapter 7) may arrange initial meetings between men and women in hopes that they will "hit it off" and enter a romantic relationship (Clark, Shaver, & Abrahams, 1999; Parks, 2007; also see Arriaga et al., 2008).

In sum, our opportunities for interacting with someone are strongly influenced not only by the nature of the physical environment, but also by the closeness of our social connection to that person and the extent to which others in our social network approve of and directly facilitate the initial encounter.

Approaching Those Who Are Receptive

A potential partner not only must be accessible for interaction but also must be receptive to our initiation attempts. A number of scholars interested in relationship beginnings have discussed the important role played by *receptivity* in determining whether one individual will attempt to affiliate with another (e.g., Davis, 1973). For example, Ted Huston and George Levinger (1978) proposed a two-factor model of affiliation:

> The person contemplating initiating an encounter must consider at least two factors: (a) the degree to which he [or she] finds the attributes of the potential partners attractive; and (b) the degree to which he [or she] anticipates they would find his [or her] attributes attractive and hence respond favorably to the initiative.
>
> (pp. 126–127)

Building upon Huston and Levinger's (1978) earlier model, Carrie Bredow, Rodney Cate, and Ted Huston (2008, pp. 12–13) have similarly proposed that the decision to make an overture to a potential partner is a function of both attraction and people's beliefs about whether the desired other is likely to reciprocate their interest and be open to their overture:

> The dual importance of attraction and concerns about reciprocation, as they combine to affect a person's propensity to make an overture, can be represented formally as follows . . .:

$$V = f (A \times P)$$

> where V is the strength of the valence of making an overture, A is the individual's attraction toward the other, and P is the would-be initiator's estimate of the probability that an overture will be accepted rather than rejected by the person. The probability of acceptance, in turn, is a

joint function of the potential initiators' perceptions of the other's openness to their motives for affiliation and their estimate of the likelihood the other will return their attraction.

Essentially, both of these models suggest that we are most likely to attempt to affiliate with another when we are highly attracted to that person and when we believe that he or she is attracted to us and open to the possibility of a relationship (and, thus, there is a good chance that he or she will be receptive to our overture).

Research supports these theoretical contentions. It appears that people are, in fact, most likely to initiate encounters (and potential relationships) with those they believe will respond favorably to their efforts. For example, in one investigation (Huston, 1973), male participants were presented with an array of photographs of women of varying levels of physical attractiveness (ranging from extremely attractive to above average in attractiveness). Half of the men were told that each woman pictured in the array would welcome the opportunity to date them, whereas the other half received no such assurance. Each participant was then given the opportunity to select a date from among the sample of women. The results revealed that the men who had been assured of acceptance chose the most physically attractive women in the array. Those who were unsure about whether the women would respond positively to them, however, chose one of the less physically attractive women (presumably because they felt that a less-attractive woman would be more likely than a highly attractive one to agree to go out with them). These findings demonstrate that people will generally not attempt to interact with someone they suspect might reject their overtures—it was only when receptivity was guaranteed that men felt free to select a partner based solely on the extent of their attraction to her.

Indeed, fear of rejection is one of the primary reasons people give for their failure to initiate a potential relationship. When Jacquie Vorauer and Rebecca Ratner (1996) asked a sample of men and women whether a fear of rejection had ever been a "significant obstacle" to them in pursuing a romantic relationship with another individual, the majority (76%) responded affirmatively. The researchers (pp. 491–492) then asked a second set of participants to imagine themselves in the following situation:

> You are at a party; currently, you are not seriously romantically involved with anyone. Early in the evening, you are introduced to a single person who could be a potential romantic partner. You learn from a brief conversation that you have a lot in common. In your opinion, the two of you are equally physically attractive. Toward the end of the evening, you find yourself alone in the kitchen with the person . . . Neither of you explicitly expresses a romantic interest in the other, or an interest in seeing the other again. You head back to join the group in the living room.

After reading the scenario, men and women indicated which of two possible alternatives explained their own and the other person's inaction: lack of romantic interest or fear of being rejected. Interestingly, the results provided strong evidence for ***pluralistic ignorance***, a phenomenon in which people observe others behaving similarly to themselves but attribute their own behavior and that of the others to very different underlying causes. In this case, participants attributed their own failure to make a romantic overture to fear of rejection (74%); however, they assumed that the other person's inactivity was caused by a lack of interest (71%). The anticipation of rejection appears at least partially responsible for the "disconnect" between people's attraction to another and their attempts to initiate interaction with that person.

In sum, in open field settings, people tend to approach those who are accessible for interaction and who they believe will be responsive to their initiation attempts.

SUMMARY

This chapter has explored the factors that promote attention to, attraction to, and initial interaction between potential partners and thus contribute to the birth of their relationship. Assuming an open field situation, we must first notice the other person before any relationship can begin. Two factors appear to influence whether or not we pay attention to a particular other person—novelty and importance. Assuming that we do, in fact, notice the other person we must then decide whether he or she is sufficiently attractive to warrant an interaction or potential relationship. Our determination will be based, in part, on the extent to which that person possesses desirable (and socially and/ or evolutionarily appropriate) characteristics and appears similar and familiar. If we find ourselves attracted to the individual, we may interact with him or her—or we may not. Attraction does not guarantee affiliation; whether or not we voluntarily interact with another in an open field setting is a function of the accessibility and perceived responsiveness of the potential partner as well as our own degree of attraction.

In reality, very few of our relationships develop in purely "open field" situations. Consequently, the processes of attention, attraction, and affiliation are interrelated and often do not occur in such a linear fashion. For example, attraction does not always precede interaction. We may notice and interact with someone because the social or physical environment demands it (e.g., we are in a closed field situation like a classroom, or a friend introduces us to a potential new friend or date, or we happen to end up standing next to someone on a crowded elevator and exchanging pleasantries). This interaction, in turn, may generate attraction as we discover that the person possesses a number of appealing characteristics (or repulsion as we uncover unpleasant traits). And these feelings of positive or negative sentiment are likely to influence whether or not we continue the interaction. Clearly, the birth of a relationship is a complex process.

KEY CONCEPTS

Voluntary relationships (p. 59)
Open interaction field (p. 59)
Closed interaction field (p. 59)
Involuntary relationships (p. 59)
Novelty (p. 62)
Importance (p. 62)
Attraction (p. 63)
Social allergens (p. 64)
Physical attractiveness ("beautiful is good")
 stereotype (p. 65)
Proximate environmental mechanisms (p. 65)
Social and cultural scripts (p. 65)
Social learning processes (p. 65)
Environment of evolutionary adaptedness (p. 65)
Adaptive problems (p. 65)
Family allocentrism (p. 66)

Familiarity effect (p. 67)
Mere exposure (mere-repeated-exposure)
 effect (p. 67)
Similarity effect (p. 68)
Bogus stranger experimental paradigm (p. 68)
Consensual validation (p. 68)
Responsiveness (p. 68)
Affiliation (p. 70)
Field of availables (p. 70)
Physical proximity (p. 70)
Civility and courtesy norms (p. 71)
Interaction accessibility (p. 72)
Social proximity (p. 72)
Communicative distance (p. 72)
Receptivity (p. 73)
Pluralistic ignorance (p. 74)

EXPLORATION EXERCISES

These exercises are designed to allow you to explore in greater detail some of the concepts and issues discussed in this chapter. There are no right or wrong answers to these exercises—they are simply meant to provide an opportunity for discussion and debate.

1. This exercise can be used to explore your own partner preferences—that is, the attributes that you find desirable or important in a partner (either a romantic partner or a friend—you choose). Below, you will find a list of characteristics that you might want a potential partner to possess. After you read over the entire list, rank order the attributes from most to least important (1 = most important characteristic to me, 2 = second most important characteristic to me, etc.).

Characteristic	Rank Order
Intelligent	_____
Kind and understanding	_____
High social status	_____
Emotionally stable	_____
Physically attractive	_____
Good sense of humor	_____
Honest and trustworthy	_____
Similar to you (interests, values, etc.)	_____
Cultured and refined	_____
Sexy looking	_____
Good earning potential	_____

   Which characteristics did you place at the top of your list? At the bottom? Do your preferences match what researchers have generally found?

2. Collect a sample of personal ads. What do people seek in a potential mate or romantic partner? What do they advertise? Make a list. Are there any similarities among your sample of writers? How do the preferences contained in the ads compare with research from self-report studies of mate preference?

3. Think back to when you first met your best friend (or, if you like, think back to when you met your current romantic partner). Consider the role that familiarity, similarity, responsiveness, and proximity (accessibility) played in helping your relationship get started.

Chapter 5
Relationship Initiation

CHAPTER OUTLINE

In the last chapter, we considered the factors that influence the likelihood of interaction between two people and, consequently, set the stage for the birth of a relationship. However, although interaction is a necessary ingredient for a relationship, it does not guarantee that one will actually develop. Once two people have noticed and become attracted to each other, and have had an initial encounter or series of encounters, their association is unlikely to develop beyond this very early stage unless they take steps to propel it forward—in other words, to move from "interaction" or "potential relationship" to "actual relationship." This chapter focuses on the ways in which people actively move beyond first encounters and initiate relationships with one another. Specifically, we will explore how men and women convey their interest in establishing a relationship to their potential partners, what happens during their initial encounters, how they go about intensifying their relationships and increasing their involvement, and the paths they follow to closeness and commitment. Because the majority of research on relationship initiation focuses on (heterosexual) romantic or mating relationships, it is important to recognize at the outset that most of the available information is limited to those types of relationship.

CONVEYING ATTRACTION

A person who wishes to establish a relationship with another individual must effectively convey his or her interest to the potential partner. A variety of nonverbal behaviors appear to communicate attraction across relationship contexts. For example, anthropologist David Givens (1978) observed male–female pairs of college students in initial encounters—some of which might have been "friendly" and others which might have been "romantic" in nature—ranging from having coffee together for the first time after class to conversing for the first time at a cafeteria table. Typical nonverbal behaviors displayed by both men and women included facing the partner, gazing directly at the partner as well as in a downward direction, and smiling. According to Givens, these nonverbal behaviors convey "an interest in the partner that is coupled with covert denials of aggressiveness and threat" (p. 355), and thus they serve as a powerful signal of liking.

Flirting

Similar results have been reported by researchers who have focused specifically on *flirting* or the communication of romantic and/or sexual interest. Psychologists Naomi McCormick and Andrew Jones (1989) conducted a descriptive field study in which they had trained confederates observe 70 pairs of unmarried men and women interacting in bars, taverns, and cocktail lounges. The confederates observed each couple for a period of 15 minutes while simultaneously coding their nonverbal behaviors. The results of these observations revealed that moving closer to the potential partner and gazing into his or her eyes was a particularly common flirting behavior. Other acts included smiling and laughing, as well as various "grooming activities" designed to call attention to oneself (such as self-touching, hair smoothing, abdomen tightening, back arching, and stretching). More recently, communication researchers Kori Egland, Brian Spitzberg, and Michelle Zormeier (1996) reported much the same results using a different methodology. In their investigation they asked 105 undergraduate students to report how frequently they used 60 specific "flirtation behaviors" with romantic partners. The top three most frequently utilized behaviors were smiling, engaging in extended eye contact, and being or looking attentive.

Although there are very few cross-cultural investigations of flirting behavior, existing studies suggest that men and women around the world advertise their interest in romance with the same basic repertoire of nonverbal behaviors. In a series of early investigations, for example, ethologist Irenäus Eibl-Eibesfeldt (e.g., 1975, 1989) surreptitiously filmed the social interactions of people from a variety of non-industrialized tribal cultures. He discovered that smiling was one of the most common ways in which both sexes conveyed romantic attraction to another person. In addition, women tended to engage in a particular sequence of nonverbal behaviors when flirting with men. Specifically, a woman would make brief eye contact with her partner, smile at him, and then display a behavior that Eibl-Eibesfeldt labeled the "eyebrow flash" (a quick arching of the eyebrows to widen the eyes followed by an immediate lowering of the brows). Immediately following the eyebrow flash, a woman would typically avert her gaze by tucking her chin down and to the side, put her hands on or near her mouth, and then smile or giggle. Although subsequent researchers generally have not found much evidence for the "eyebrow flash" as a flirting behavior among U.S. populations, smiling and eye contact do appear to be universal methods used by men and women to convey romantic interest.

Interpersonal touch can also serve to communicate romantic interest (e.g., Abrahams, 1994)—and some types of touch appear particularly potent. In one investigation, Josephine Lee and Laura Guerrero (2001) asked a large sample of undergraduate students to view videotapes depicting two work colleagues (one man and one woman) having a short conversation as they left the office at the end of the work week. The video segments were approximately 30 seconds long and ended with one of the actors touching the other as they said goodbye. The type of touch the actor displayed was systematically varied and included: (1) handshake, (2) clasping hands, (3) soft touch on the forearm, (4) arm around the shoulder, (5) arm around the waist, (6) soft touch on the cheek, (7) tapping the shoulder, and (8) pushing against the shoulder. In addition, half of the videotaped segments showed a woman touching her male colleague, and half showed a man touching his female colleague. Participants were randomly assigned to view one of the versions of the videotape (e.g., woman initiating handshake with man, man touching woman on the forearm; woman putting arm around man's shoulder, man touching woman on the cheek). After they viewed the videotape, participants then reported various impressions they had formed of the actor who engaged in the touching behavior, including his or her flirtatious intent (e.g., "The man was flirting with the woman") and romantic attraction (e.g., "The woman was attracted to the man," "The woman wanted a romantic relationship with the man"). The behavior that participants rated as reflecting the most flirtation and the most romantic attraction was the soft face touch, followed by the touch around the shoulder or waist, and then the soft touch on the forearm. The least flirtatious and romantic touches were the shoulder push, shoulder tap, and handshake. Thus, touching that is gentle and informal, and that occurs face-to-face or involves "hugging" behavior, appears to convey the most relational intent.

Does Flirting Work? But do these flirting behaviors actually "work"? Do glances, smiles, and gentle touches do what they are designed to do—that is, prompt romantic interest and overtures from potential mates? To answer this question, psychologist Monica Moore (1985) unobtrusively observed 40 women (ranging in estimated age from 18 to 35 years) in four different social settings: a local singles bar, a university snack bar, a university library, and a meeting at a university women's center. Women were selected for observation only if they were surrounded by at least 25 other people and if they were not accompanied by a man. During each hour-long observational period, both the type (e.g., smiling, sustained gazing, hair flipping, head tossing) and the number of flirting behaviors demonstrated by each woman were recorded.

There were several interesting results. First, Moore found that women's flirting behavior was context specific. That is, women in the singles bar (the most likely setting in which to meet a mate) flirted significantly more frequently than did women in the other three settings. In addition, women in the snack bar flirted more than did women in the library, who in turn flirted more than did women in the women's center (the least likely setting to meet a mate, assuming a heterosexual sample). Second, Moore found that women in the singles bar *increased* their rate of flirtatious display over the observational period; they flirted more as the hour passed. However, flirting behavior was constant (i.e., did not change over time) in the other three contexts. Third, and perhaps most important, the results revealed that women's flirting behaviors actually were quite effective at eliciting interest from potential mates. Specifically, regardless of the setting, the women who engaged in the most flirting behavior were also those who were approached most often by men.

Similar results were reported more recently by Lee Ann Renninger, Joel Wade, and Karl Grammer (2004), who were interested in exploring the effectiveness of men's flirting behavior. In this investigation, the researchers unobtrusively observed 38 men (ranging in age from 21 to 34 years) in bars located near college campuses. Men were selected for observation only if they were surrounded by at least 10 other people and were not seated in a booth or accompanied by a woman. During each 30-minute observation, the researchers recorded the men's nonverbal behavior and also determined whether or not the men successfully initiated romantic contact with a woman (defined as achieving at least 1 minute of continuous conversation). The results indicated that the men who successfully initiated romantic contact with women exhibited a greater number of particular kinds of nonverbal flirting behavior than men who did not establish romantic contact. Specifically, successful men directed more brief glances at their intended targets, engaged in a greater number of "space maximization" movements (positioning the body so that it takes up more space; e.g., extending one arm across an adjacent chair, stretching so that both arms extend straight up in the air), changed their location in the bar more frequently, and displayed greater amounts of non-reciprocated touching to surrounding men (e.g., playfully shoving, touching, or elbowing the ribs of other men). In discussing their findings, the researchers concluded that men who provide signals of their positive intentions (e.g., through glancing behaviors) and their status (e.g., through space maximization and non-reciprocated touch of male peers) receive preferential attention from women. Thus, for both sexes, flirting seems to be effective.

Cyber-Flirting: Conveying Attraction Online

Because flirting typically involves nonverbal behavior, most flirting occurs between people who are in close physical proximity and who therefore can engage in face-to-face interaction. Certainly it is easier for one person to convey romantic interest to another when the two individuals are in the same place, at the same time, with sufficient opportunity to see each other and to send and evaluate each other's courtship signals. But, as we discussed in Chapter 4, physical proximity and face-to-face interaction are not *required* to convey attraction. They are also not needed to initiate a romantic relationship with another person (or any kind of relationship, for that matter).

Computer-mediated communication or CMC is defined as communication that occurs online rather than in a face-to-face interaction setting. A number of forums for CMC exist, including chat rooms, newsgroups, bulletin boards, Multi-User Dungeons (MUDs), and Multi-User Dimensions, Object Oriented (MOOs). In some of these forums, social interaction occurs in "real time"—in chat rooms, MUDs, and MOOs, for example, the participants are online at the same time and their messages are typed, sent, and read in real time. In other forums, the communication does not occur in real time; participants who use email or subscribe to newsgroups may log on at their convenience and read and respond to messages when they choose. Irrespective of whether they occur in real time or not, all forms of online communication differ from traditional face-to-face interaction in several ways (e.g., Cooper & Sportolari, 1997; Haythornthwaite, Wellman, & Garton, 1998; Kiesler, Siegel, & McGuire, 1984). In particular, CMC lacks many of the auditory and visual cues that allow individuals to regulate their interactions and effectively communicate their intentions and feelings, including smiling, head nodding, eye contact, physical distance, touch, and tone and volume of voice. In addition, CMC provides limited information (if any) about the interactants' demographic characteristics (e.g., age, race or ethnicity, gender), personal features (e.g., physical attractiveness, height, weight, dress), or social attributes (e.g., socioeconomic status).

Because CMC users have a reduced array of traditional social cues on which to rely, they often use other methods for communicating their feelings of attraction to a potential date or mate (see

Levine, 2000; Whitty & Carr, 2003). In particular, language—both the content of messages and speed of responding to other people's communications—becomes highly important (Levine, 2000; Mantovani, 2001). Responding promptly (and appropriately) to another's messages and incorporating emoticons (☺), lexical surrogates ("hmm" or "ha ha ha"), and acronyms or narrative asides (such as <LOL> [laughing out loud] or <BRB> [be right back]) into one's own messages may serve to establish intimacy and convey feelings of interest and warmth. Online partners may also exchange picture and sound files to help further their connection.

Very little research has been conducted on how people actually flirt in online forums. However, one recent study conducted by psychologist Monica Whitty (2004) provides some information on the topic. In this investigation, more than 5000 men and women who used chat rooms were asked to report how frequently they engaged in six possible "online" flirting behaviors to indicate attraction to other people: (1) providing descriptions of their socioeconomic status (i.e., income, education, and/or occupation), (2) providing descriptions of their physical attractiveness, (3) providing descriptions of touching behavior, (4) initiating online conversation with the other person, (5) using emoticons to convey nonverbal cues (e.g., smiley faces [☺] or winks [;-)]), and (6) using acronyms (such as LOL for "laugh out loud" or "lots of laughs"). Of the six possible flirting behaviors, the two most frequently used were nonverbal in nature. Specifically, when considering their own *cyber-flirting* behavior, both men and women reported that they most often used nonverbal displays (in the form of emoticons) and represented laughter (in the form of acronyms) to convey their feelings of attraction to other individuals. Thus, regardless of whether their interactions occur face-to-face or online, most people seem to reply on nonverbal gestures to communicate romantic interest.

Although people can certainly flirt and initiate romances in an online environment, the majority of personal relationships that form online are not romantic in nature but rather tend to be friendship-based (see Parks & Floyd, 1996; Parks & Roberts, 1998). In fact, most young adults hold somewhat negative attitudes about using the Internet to find a date or mate (Anderson, 2005). This may be due in part to fears about the potential dangers or risks that can arise when using online forms of communication. Survey data indicate that both men and women worry about deception and personal safety when considering an online romance; in particular, they fear that putting their own personal information online (e.g., at a dating website) opens them up to potential risk, and they suspect that people they meet online may lie and misrepresent themselves (Donn & Sherman, 2002; Madden & Lenhart, 2006). There is evidence that these fears are justified: people do lie about their personal attributes (e.g., their age, appearance, and socioeconomic status) as well as their intentions, and some even sexually harass or "cyberstalk" other Internet users (Whitty & Carr, 2003, 2006).

Despite these potential dangers, online forums nonetheless represent a unique way to meet potential dates or mates in a setting that minimizes the social risks inherent in face-to-face interactions. This may prove especially beneficial for people who have few opportunities to meet potential partners, as well as for those who possess various stigmatizing characteristics that make it difficult for them to initially attract others (e.g., stuttering or vocal difficulties, lower levels of physical attractiveness), or who find the process of interpersonal communication challenging due to shyness or social anxiety (e.g., Lawson & Leck, 2006; Mantovani, 2001; Ward & Tracey, 2004). Indeed, in her recent review, Katelyn McKenna (2008) noted five ways in which online interactions facilitate relationship formation:

- *Relative absence of "gating" features.* Features that are readily perceived (e.g., attractiveness, age, and other physical attributes) tend to be highly important in face-to-face interactions; thus they serve as powerful gates to relationship initiation, letting some potential partners in and excluding others from consideration. When interactions take place in an online environment, however, these physical attributes or gating features are not usually apparent (online dating services are an exception), and they are less likely to become a barrier to relationship formation.

- *Increased feelings of anonymity.* In online environments, people often feel anonymous (even when they have posted personal information about themselves). Due to this sense of anonymity, they often disclose a great deal of revealing and intimate information about themselves (and far sooner than they would in face-to-face encounters). This, in turn, can serve to establish intimacy and form the basis for a relationship with an online partner. (Indeed, as we will discuss in the following chapter, self-disclosure and intimate communication are two of the most important determinants of relationship development.)

- *Increased control over interactions.* In an online setting, people can choose what personal information they share about themselves, plan what they will say, and edit their responses before sending them. In addition, they do not have to respond immediately to another's conversational gambits in the way they would have to during a face-to-face interaction.

- *Increased ability to discover similar others.* People can use the Internet to search for potential partners at their leisure. The fact that they are not bounded by geography or time increases the likelihood that they will discover potential partners who share their own particular interests.

- *Increased ability to know the partner prior to interaction.* By following another person's blog or message history in an online discussion forum or by reading someone's profile on a dating website prior to initiating contact, individuals can gain much more information about him or her than would normally be possible in traditional face-to-face settings.

The lack of gating features and increased anonymity, control, and knowledge that are afforded by online forums are likely to result in greater freedom of expression and intimacy between the potential cyber-partners during their initial interactions; this, in turn, may increase the likelihood that they will become involved and that their relationship will eventually move offline. There is much still to be learned about online relationship initiation, and this area promises to be an important source of future research.

INITIATING A RELATIONSHIP

Due to their voluntary and socially unstructured nature, most friend relationships do not have a formal "starting point." Most romantic relationships, however, do. After an initial face-to-face or online encounter or series of encounters, and assuming the successful communication of romantic interest, two people may decide to further their relationship by embarking on an "official" romantic interaction—the *first date*.

The First Date

Given the existence of the traditional (heterosexual) sexual script (see Chapter 11), it is not surprising that both men and women feel that it is more socially appropriate for a man to initiate a date than for a woman to do so (Green & Sandos, 1983; Ortiz-Torres, Williams, & Ehrhardt, 2003). Compared with women, men also report a greater willingness to initiate dates and a higher frequency of actual relationship initiations (Clark, Shaver, & Abrahams, 1999; Green & Sandos, 1983; McNamara & Grossman, 1991; Spreadbury, 1982).

There is some evidence, however, that many heterosexual men would like women to take a more active role in relationship initiation than the traditional script would seem to allow. Charlene Muehlenhard and Eric Miller (1988), for example, asked more than 200 undergraduate men to indicate their preferences with regard to three different approaches a woman might make to initiate a date: (1) *asking directly* for a date, (2) *hinting* for a date, and (3) simply *waiting* for the man to ask her out. Nearly all of the men preferred the more direct approaches. Specifically, 44% said that they preferred a woman to ask for a date, and 53% indicated that they preferred a woman to hint for a date. Only 3% of the men surveyed stated that they preferred a woman to adopt the passive approach of simply waiting to be asked out. In addition, provided that they liked the woman, nearly all of the men believed that the strategies of directly asking (99%) and hinting (93%) would result in a date. Few men (4%) believed that waiting would result in a date, even if they themselves liked the woman and wanted to go out with her. The initiation of a dating relationship clearly requires active efforts on the part of both individuals.

So what prevents individuals from pursuing dates with others to whom they are attracted? Recall from Chapter 4 that one of the primary reasons why people fail to take advantage of romantic opportunities concerns their fear of rejection and their tendency to fall prey to the attributional bias called pluralistic ignorance (e.g., Vorauer & Ratner, 1996). In addition, many individuals assume that they have adequately conveyed their attraction to a partner when in fact they have not. The **signal amplification bias** occurs when people believe that their overtures communicate more romantic interest to potential partners than is actually the case; consequently, they fail to realize that the partner may not be aware of their attraction (Vorauer, Cameron, Holmes, & Pearce, 2003). The following scenario illustrates how fear of rejection, coupled with both of the aforementioned attributional biases, can squelch the formation of a romantic relationship:

> Scott and Jen are two students who know each other casually and who run into each other one day on campus. Scott is attracted to Jen and would like to ask her out, so he decides to strike up a conversation. "Hey Jen," he says, "Good to see you. How's it going?" "Pretty good—things are kind of hectic this term, though," Jen responds, and the two chat about their classes and various other topics for the next 15 minutes. Finally, Jen looks at her watch and realizes that she's going to be late to her next class. "Listen, Scott," she says, "I've got to get going but I'll catch you later, okay?" As she races off to class, she thinks to herself, "He seems like such a nice guy. I wish he wanted to go out with me, but it's clear that he doesn't. If he were, he'd have asked me out by now. And there's no way I'm asking him out—he'd probably say no, I'd be totally humiliated, and then things would be all weird between us. I've got to move on and meet some other guys." Watching Jen leave, Scott thinks to himself, "I can't believe I made such a fool of myself. Could I have been any more obvious? I was practically falling all over her. She probably thinks I'm acting like some love-sick idiot. I have got to get myself under control and play it cool the next time we see each other."

In this fictitious scenario, both Scott and Jen are clearly afraid of being rejected. In addition, Jen has fallen prey to pluralistic ignorance. She has attributed her own failure to initiate a romance with Scott to her fear of rejection, and she has failed to realize that he might also be afraid of being rejected. Instead, she assumes that Scott's failure to ask her out stems from his lack of romantic interest in her. For his part, Scott has fallen prey to the signal amplification bias. He has grossly overestimated the amount of romantic attraction that his actions have conveyed to Jen (in fact, his "romantic" behavior has largely gone unnoticed by her!). Unfortunately, the fear of rejection and attributional biases exhibited by these two individuals may prevent them from initiating what could eventually develop into a satisfying and stable romantic relationship.

What Happens During a First Date?   Of course, many people overcome their hesitation or fears of rejection and successfully initiate a first date. So what happens during a "typical" first date? To find out, psychologists John Pryor and Thomas Merluzzi (1985) asked a sample of undergraduate students to list the "typical things that occur when a male and a female decide to go on a first date" (p. 365). Participants were instructed to generate *first date scripts*, events that happen in the "getting a date" stage as well as events that happen during the date itself. The following event sequence was viewed as typical during a first date initiation:

Step 1:   Notice each other (with the man noticing the woman first).
Step 2:   Get caught staring at each other.
Step 3:   Smile.
Step 4:   Find out about the other person from friends.
Step 5:   Create ways in which to "accidentally" run into each other.
Step 6:   Get introduced by a friend.
Step 7:   The woman says "hello" and the man begins the conversation.
Step 8:   Make an attempt during conversation to find common interests.
Step 9:   The man asks the woman for her phone number.
Step 10: The man phones the woman later to ask her out, beginning the conversation with "small talk" and then making arrangements for the date.

Both men and women generated this same type of sequence. Their scripts for the actual first date were similarly identical:

Step 1:   The man arrives to pick up the woman for the date.
Step 2:   The woman greets the man at the door.
Step 3:   They make conversation.
Step 4:   The woman introduces her date to parents/roommates and the two leave the house/apartment/dormitory.
Step 5:   They discuss where they will go on their date.
Step 6:   The two talk about common interests (i.e., make "small talk").
Step 7:   They go to a movie.
Step 8:   The man buys refreshments at the movie.
Step 9:   They then go get something to eat/drink and continue their conversation.
Step 10: The man takes the woman home.
Step 11: The man walks the woman to her door.
Step 12: They exchange complimentary views of the evening.
Step 13: If interested, the man asks to call again/the woman hopes the man asks to call again.
Step 14: They kiss.
Step 15: They say "goodnight" and thank each other for the evening.
Step 16: The man returns home.

More recent research (e.g., Laner & Ventrone, 2000) suggests that the essential features and format of first dates have remained largely unchanged over time, at least among U.S. samples.

Although men and women generally agree on the *sequencing* of events during the first date, they do hold slightly different expectations about the *type* of events that should occur. For example, although the "goodnight kiss" remains a fixed feature of the first date, heterosexual men often expect greater sexual involvement than do heterosexual women on a first date (Mongeau, Jacobsen, & Donnerstein, 2007; Mongeau & Johnson, 1995). Indeed, there is evidence that men and women may pursue different goals when initiating a romantic relationship. Catherine Clark, Phillip Shaver, and Matthew Abrahams (1999) asked a large sample of undergraduates to describe the goals they had pursued in their two most recent successful romantic relationships. The primary goal identified by the researchers concerned love; most men (84%) and women (81%) said that they had initiated the relationship in order to obtain a loving, caring, serious partnership. Other relatively common goals mentioned by equal numbers of both sexes included fun (cited by 18% of the men and 16% of the women) and learning (e.g., to experience dating, to get to know the other person [cited by 16% of the men and 18% of the women]). Only one sex difference was found. Far more men (30%) than women (8%) identified sexual intimacy—including kissing, intercourse, and just "following hormones"—as their motivation for initiating a dating relationship.

The different expectations that men and women may bring to their initial romantic interactions may result in misunderstanding and miscommunication. For example, a woman who wishes to convey her feelings of affection and liking for a new dating partner may smile at him and engage in other nonverbal displays. The woman's partner, whose goal may be one of sexual intimacy, may misinterpret her behavior as indicating sexual attraction. Indeed, research reveals that women are more likely than men to report having had their friendliness mistakenly perceived as a sign of sexual interest (Abbey, 1987). Men also are much more likely than women to perceive a number of interpersonal cues as signaling an interest in sex (e.g., Abbey, 1982; Abbey & Melby, 1986; Zellman & Goodchilds, 1983). For example, a study conducted by Robin Kowalski (1993) revealed that men imputed a higher desire for sexual intercourse than did women to a woman who was described as engaging in such common dating behaviors as accepting a man's invitation for a date, having dinner with him, maintaining eye contact with him, smiling at him, allowing him to pay for dinner, and complimenting him. Interestingly, women may also fall prey to perceptual biases with regard to sexual attraction; specifically, they tend to *underestimate* the extent of their partners' sexual interest (see Koenig, Kirkpatrick, & Ketelaar, 2007). Clearly, knowledge of the different ways in which men and women perceive interpersonal cues, along with direct and open communication of dating goals and desires, is essential between partners during the early stages of a romantic relationship.

INTENSIFYING A RELATIONSHIP

Only a very small portion of the first dates and other initial encounters that we have with potential partners actually will evolve into stable relationships. What strategies do men and women use when trying to move relationships beyond those beginning stages? To explore this question, communication scholar James Tolhuizen (1989) asked men and women to describe the things they said or did to intensify a romantic relationship and change it from "one of casual dating to one of serious and exclusive dating" (p. 418). Analysis of participants' free responses revealed that the most common strategy was to *increase contact*; more than 39% of the participants reported increasing the frequency and duration of their contact and interaction with the partner. Another commonly utilized method was *relationship negotiation* or direct discussion of the relationship, feelings between the partners, and the future of the relationship (29%). Participants also sought *social support and assistance* from individuals in their social networks, usually by asking for advice about how to proceed in intensifying the relationship (26%). Other strategies included *increasing the partner's rewards* (18% [e.g., paying compliments, doing favors]), *making a direct bid* for a more serious relationship (17% [e.g., directly requesting a more exclusive or serious relationship]), giving the partner *tokens of affection* (16% [e.g., giving gifts, cards, or other items that symbolize feelings of affection for the partner]), providing *verbal expressions of affection* (14% [e.g., declaring feelings of love, caring, or affection for the partner]), and *accepting a direct bid* for a more serious relationship (10% [e.g., agreeing to a direct request from the partner for a more exclusive relationship]). Not surprisingly, men and women differed slightly in the types of strategies they reported. Men were significantly more likely to report using verbal expressions of affection and making a direct relationship bid, whereas women were more likely to report using relationship negotiation and accepting a direct relationship bid.

Similar results were reported by Clark and colleagues (1999), who identified relationship intensification strategies from narratives provided by a large group of undergraduates. Participants reported engaging in a variety of behaviors to propel a relationship through its beginning stages. One of the most common categories of strategy involved *communication and emotional disclosure.* For example, the majority of participants said that they talked in person (94%), talked on the phone (54%), and spent time (85%) with the partner. *Direct and forward action* was also mentioned frequently; participants reported asking the other person directly to be their girlfriend or boyfriend (63%) and touching the other person (64% [e.g., kissing, hand holding]. As in Tolhuizen's study, participants also clearly used their social networks to promote the relationship. Approximately 86% reported that third parties helped to initiate and intensify the relationship by engaging in such activities as discovering whether a potential partner was available and/or interested, by introducing the two people, and by going out with them as the relationship began to develop.

More recently, Jon Hess, Amy Fannin, and Laura Pollom (2007) explored whether the strategies that people use to intensify their personal relationships are actually associated with their degree of commitment to those relationships. The researchers provided 200 young adults with a list of tactics for enhancing relationship closeness and asked them to indicate the frequency with which they used each one to promote the closeness of their relationship with a specific friend or romantic partner. These tactics were divided into three general categories: (1) tactics related to *openness*, which involved self-disclosure and efforts to create togetherness (e.g., "I tried to find or make opportunities to spend time with this person," "I was willing to discuss topics with this person that I wouldn't normally talk about with others;" "I joked around with this person to help build rapport"); (2) tactics related to *attention*, which reflected actively attending to the other and treating his or her disclosures with respect ("I tried not to forget things that this person told me," "I paid careful attention when this person was talking to me," "When this person spoke to me, I considered his or her message to be valuable and significant"); and (3) tactics related to *involvement*, which included intensifying interaction and fostering exclusivity with the other (e.g., "When doing something with this person, I tried to make the interaction last longer," "I tried to set up situations where just the two of us were together, instead of having other people around," "I asked this person lots of questions, so that the conversation would last longer"). Participants also completed measures of liking for their friends and romantic partners as well as a measure of commitment to the relationship. The results revealed a strong, positive association between relationship intensification tactics and both commitment and attraction. Specifically, the more frequently that participants reported using tactics designed to enhance closeness, the more deeply committed they were to their relationships and the more strongly they liked their partners.

In sum, individuals enact a number of behaviors as they attempt to intensify their association with another person and shape it into a more enduring relationship.

PATHWAYS TO COMMITMENT

Many relationships do not stand the test of time despite the best efforts of the partners to promote their development. Some relationships, however, will survive beyond the initial exchanges and continue along a path toward closeness and commitment.

Among Romantic Partners

Early evidence for how dating relationships progress over time was provided by Charles King and Andrew Christensen (1983), who surveyed a sample of undergraduate student couples about the occurrence of specific events in their relationships. The researchers found that developing romantic relationships are likely to progress through six consecutive stages. First, the partners express mutual attraction and affection and begin to spend an increasing amount of time together. Second, the partners themselves and the people in their social networks begin to view the two of them as "a couple." Third, the partners express feelings of love to one another and establish an exclusive relationship—for example, they end (or avoid entering) any other romantic associations and they make the decision to only date the current partner. Fourth, they begin to project their relationship into the future by considering moving in together and/or becoming engaged or getting married. Fifth, they begin to coordinate their time, money, and activities to pursue joint (as opposed to individual) interests. Finally, they make a more permanent commitment to one another through engagement, cohabitation, or marriage.

Although many couples follow the developmental sequence outlined by King and Christensen (1983), the amount of time they take to pass through the sequence may vary. A number of different courtship patterns or trajectories to commitment have been identified. For example, in one investigation, family scholar Catherine Surra (1985) asked a sample of young newlywed couples to retrospectively report on how the partners' commitment to each other had changed from the time they first met to the day of their wedding. Specifically, husbands and wives were instructed to estimate the chance of marriage (on a scale ranging from 0% to 100%) that they felt characterized their relationship from the date it began, during the subsequent months of courtship, and up until the wedding day (which naturally received a "chance-of-marriage" rating of 100%). These estimated chance-of-marriage values were placed on a graph that provided a pictorial view of each couple's pathway to commitment.

Surra (1985) then coded monthly chance-of-marriage values for each participant and derived a number of additional variables from the graphs, including length of courtship (number of months from the beginning of the relationship to the wedding day), degree of acceleration (number of months it took for the couple to move from a low [25%] to a high [75%] chance of marriage), number of turning points (upturns and downturns in the graph), and length of stage of involvement (number of months the couple spent in the casually dating, seriously dating, and engaged stages of involvement).

Analysis of the monthly chance-of-marriage values and the derived variables revealed four different courtship paths or trajectories to marital commitment. Couples on an *accelerated courtship* trajectory moved rapidly and smoothly to marriage, spent relatively little time dating prior to engagement, and experienced a higher index of upturns (turning points characterized by increased commitment) than did other couple types. *Accelerated-arrested courtship* couples also experienced a high number of upturns, which Surra (1985) hypothesized may provide momentum to the courtship process. The courtship of these couples was characterized by an even more rapid trajectory to marriage. Specifically, accelerated-arrested couples devoted very little time to dating, preferring to become engaged very quickly and then spending most (nearly 60%) of their courtship in this stage. Couples on a *prolonged courtship* trajectory to marital commitment demonstrated the reverse pattern; that is, they spent 65% of their courtship seriously dating and only 22% of it engaged. The *intermediate courtship* type fell somewhere in between the two accelerated types and the prolonged type in the smoothness and the rapidity of its progression toward commitment.

More recent research has revealed additional courtship paths as well as cultural differences in the length of courtship (e.g., Chang & Chan, 2007).

Among Friends

Although research on relationship progression has focused almost exclusively on romantic partnerships, there is some evidence that friendships also follow a variety of developmental trajectories to commitment. Communication scholar Amy Johnson and her colleagues (Johnson, Wittenberg, Villagran, Mazur, & Villagran, 2003) asked 30 university students to retrospectively report on how the closeness of their relationship with their current best friend had changed over time. As in the Surra (1985) study, participants used a graph to record the closeness levels (on a 100-point scale) that they felt characterized their relationship with their best friend from the day they first met (or the day of their "first remembered interaction") until the time of their participation in the study. Participants also provided information about the events associated with every turning point (i.e., downturn or upturn in closeness) they recorded in their graph.

Examination of these graphs revealed three primary trajectories to closeness among best friends (see Figure 5.1). The most common developmental trajectory was one of *steadily increasing closeness* over time with no downturns or noticeable decreases in closeness. In total, 40% of best friends displayed this pattern. The second most common developmental pattern consisted of a steady rise in closeness between friends followed by a downturn and then a subsequent rise (which sometimes but not always reached the previous level); this *rise-fall-recovery pattern* characterized 33% of friendships. Finally, 17% of best friendships demonstrated *multiple downturns in closeness within an overall pattern of increasing closeness.* [10% of best friendships did not fit into these three primary trajectories.] The most common reasons for increases or decreases in closeness, according to participants' reports, involved changes in shared activities, living situation (e.g., sharing a dorm room or apartment), self-disclosure and social support, and geographical distance. For example, upturns in closeness generally were associated with increased physical proximity to one another, spending increased time together in planned activities or just "hanging out," moving in together, doing favors for one another and providing emotional support in times of crisis, and sharing personal information.

Patricia Sias and Daniel Cahill (1998), who explored peer friendships in the workplace, also found that friendships follow various developmental trajectories. They asked 38 currently employed adults to nominate a coworker who they considered to be a "good or close friend" and to report the time it had taken their relationships to move from acquaintanceship to friendship, friendship to close friendship, and close friendship to very close friendship. The results revealed a great deal of variability in the length of time participants reported taking to reach each level of friendship. For example, although participants spent an average of 12 months transitioning from mere acquaintances to actual friends, some became friends in as little as 1 day whereas others took as long as 8 years. Similarly, participants became close friends anywhere from 1 month to 20 years after their first meeting (with an average time of 31 months), and they reported becoming very close friends from between 3 months to 9 years after their initial meeting (with an average time of 4 years).

In sum, there is no one path toward relationship permanence; partners may achieve commitment and closeness in a variety of ways.

SUMMARY

This chapter explored relationship initiation. Relationship researchers have discovered that during initial encounters, men and women engage in a number of behaviors designed to attract a potential friend or romantic partner. Eye contact, smiling, interpersonal touch, and other behaviors all serve to convey attraction and interest. Following these initial interactions, many individuals may further

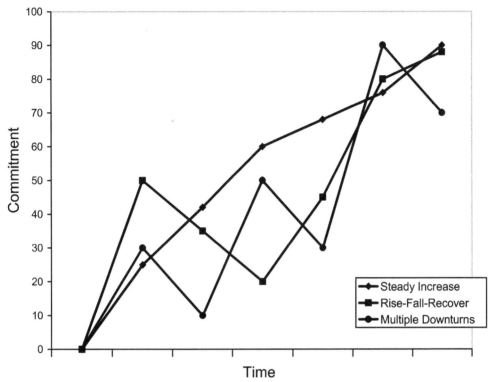

Fig. 5.1 Not all friendships follow the same path to commitment. Some friends experience a steady increase in commitment and closeness over time, whereas others experience a rapid rise followed by a subsequent period of decline and recovery. Still others find their relationships marked by multiple downturns within an overall pattern of increasing commitment.

Source: Johnson, A. J., Wittenberg, E., Villagran, M. M., Mazur, M., & Villagran, P. (2003). Relational progression as a dialectic: Examining turning points in communication among friends. *Communication Monographs, 70,* 230–249. Copyright © 2003 by The National Communication Association. Figures 1, 2, and 3 adapted by permission of Taylor and Francis Ltd (http://www.tandf.co.uk/journals) on behalf of The National Communication Association.

their relationship by embarking on a first date. Research indicates that a first date often involves a series of scripted behaviors and action sequences, in some instances including the communication of sexual attraction and the willingness to engage in some form of sexual contact (e.g., goodnight kiss). After a first date between romantic partners or a series of initial encounters between friends, one or both partners may attempt to intensify the relationship or propel it to a state of greater permanence using a variety of strategies. Assuming that the relationship does, in fact, endure beyond these beginning stages, friends and romantic partners may follow one of several different pathways to commitment and closeness. In the next chapter we consider theory and research about the actual processes that serve to move partners along their developmental trajectories.

KEY CONCEPTS

Flirting (p. 78)
Computer-mediated communication (p. 80)
Cyber-flirting (p. 81)

First date (p. 82)
Signal amplification bias (p. 83)
First date script (p. 84)

Accelerated courtship pattern (p. 87)   Prolonged courtship pattern (p. 87)
Accelerated-arrested courtship pattern (p. 87) Intermediate courtship pattern (p. 87)

EXPLORATION EXERCISES

These exercises are designed to allow you to explore in greater detail some of the concepts and issues discussed in this chapter. There are no right or wrong answers to these exercises—they are simply meant to provide an opportunity for discussion and debate.

1. This exercise is designed to explore how people convey romantic interest—that is, how they "flirt." Researchers have identified a number of nonverbal behaviors that appear to communicate attraction, including the following:

Facing the partner
Gazing directly at the partner
Moving close to the partner
Smiling/laughing
Making extended eye contact
Touching the partner
"Grooming" activities (self-touch, hair smoothing)
"Posturing" activities (abdomen tightening, back arching, stretching)

   For this exercise, you will need to select a setting in which you can observe men and women interacting in a natural setting (on campus, at a party, at a local hangout, etc.). Try to select a setting in which it is likely that the men and women you are observing are single and in search of a potential date. Select one pair and observe the partners for a period of 10 minutes. Which of the nonverbal behaviors listed above did they display? Do this for at least two other couples. What nonverbal behavior was the most common? Did the men and women you observed use different flirting behaviors?

2. Have you (or has someone you know) ever initiated a romantic relationship or a friendship in an online environment? If so, how did you communicate your interest in establishing a relationship? Discuss how you were able to convey intimacy, warmth, responsiveness, and interest in the absence of face-to-face interaction. What were the benefits, if any, to using computer-mediated communication as opposed to face-to-face communication? Were there any downsides or difficulties?

3. Either alone or working with your classmates, create a first date script in which you outline the sequence of events that occur during a "typical first date." Once you have generated your list, compare it to the typical first date script identified by researchers. How did your script differ from—or resemble—that one?

4. Relationship scholars have discovered a number of different friendship development patterns. For example, some friends become increasingly closer and more committed over time, progressing smoothly from acquaintanceship to friendship to best friend status. Other friends gradually become closer but then experience a downturn or decrease in closeness before becoming closer again. These different trajectories are illustrated in Figure 5.1. Think of your relationship with your best friend, starting from the time you first met to today, and focusing particularly on the turning points you can recall (the downturns or upturns in closeness the two of you experienced). What type of developmental trajectory has your relationship generally followed?

Chapter 6
Relationship Development

CHAPTER OUTLINE

In the previous chapter we discussed how initial encounters with potential partners can lead to the establishment of a more permanent, committed relationship. We also considered the strategies that men and women use to communicate their interest to a partner and to intensify the relationship. In this chapter we review the major theories that have been proposed to explain the processes that allow relationships to progress and develop over time.

THE SEQUENCE OF RELATIONSHIP DEVELOPMENT

Many of the earliest theories of relationship development proposed that partners move through a sequential series of stages that are associated with increasing amounts of commitment and involvement. Each stage was assumed to revolve around a particular developmental issue whose resolution propelled the partners into the next stage. Although most *stage models* focus on the development of romantic relationships, several are applicable to friendship development as well. Today, stage models have been replaced by process-oriented theories; nonetheless, they represent an important historical first step toward understanding relationship progression.

Filter Theory

Based on a longitudinal study of the courtship experiences of dating couples, Alan Kerckhoff and Keith Davis (1962) proposed that three sequential "filtering factors" operate during the process of relationship formation. According to *Filter Theory*, potential partners first are screened in terms of their similarity on *social attributes*, such as religion, education level, and socioeconomic class. People who are deemed to be too different with respect to these social attributes are filtered out from the field of potential long-term partners. Assuming that the potential partners pass through the first filter, they are then screened with respect to similarity on attitudes and values or *value consensus*. As before, those who are judged to be too dissimilar are filtered out. Finally, in the third filtering stage, partners are evaluated on *need complementarity* or whether they possess complementary or compatible traits, behavioral characteristics, or interpersonal styles.

The notion that different aspects of the "fit" between two partners would become important at different times in their relationship makes intuitive sense. For example, during the early stages of courtship or friendship formation, demographic similarity might be of utmost importance in promoting a dyad's relational growth. Later, as the partners begin to enter more committed or involved stages of romance or friendship, similarity on underlying values and belief systems, and compatibility with regard to interpersonal styles, might become more important in determining whether or not their relationship continues. However, although conceptually interesting, subsequent research generally has not supported this model of relationship development (e.g., Levinger, Senn, & Jorgensen, 1970; for a review, see Levinger, 1983).

The Wheel Theory of Love

Another early model of relationship development, this one devoted to romantic relationship progression, was proposed by sociologist Ira Reiss (e.g., 1960, 1980). According to his *Wheel Theory of Love*, the "mate-selecting process" involves four sequential but highly interrelated phases. During the initial stage, called *rapport*, potential partners assess the extent to which they feel at ease with, understand, and feel free to talk with each other. The process of establishing and feeling rapport is facilitated by similarity; Reiss suggests that we are most able to feel rapport for those who resemble us on key social and cultural variables (e.g., religious upbringing, educational background, socioeconomic status). Feelings of rapport, in turn, increase the likelihood that two people will begin a process of mutual *self-revelation* in which they reveal or disclose varying degrees of information about their values and belief systems to each other. These acts of self-revelation, in turn, contribute to *mutual dependency*, such that each partner becomes dependent on the other to fulfill his or her habits or obtain certain goals. For example, Reiss (1980) wrote, "One needs the other person as an audience for one's jokes, as a confidant(e) for the expression of one's fears and wishes, as a partner for one's sexual needs, and so forth" (p. 127). The fulfillment of goals or habits promotes satisfaction, and thus contributes to relationship maintenance. The fourth and final phase of development is called *intimacy need fulfillment*. Here, the partners evaluate whether their relationship and their interactions with each other satisfy basic intimacy needs, including love, sympathy, and support.

Stimulus-Value-Role Theory

Another popular early theory of relationship development, also addressed to romantic partnerships, was proposed by Bernard Murstein (e.g., 1970, 1976). *Stimulus-Value-Role Theory* suggests that couples progress through three stages. In the *stimulus stage*, the potential partners perceive each other's external attributes, physical appearance, and behavior, and each also evaluates his or her own attributes in terms of how attractive these might be to the other. Based on this comparison, each person estimates the likelihood that his or her attraction will be reciprocated and that future interaction with the other will be rewarding. If this estimate is favorable (i.e., if each believes that the other will like him or her and find his or her attributes desirable, and if each thinks that additional interaction will be rewarding), then the individuals are propelled into the next stage. During the *value stage*, the partners appraise their compatibility on various values and attitudes. This process of value appraisal allows them to continue to assess the potential benefits or rewards of the relationship. During the final *role stage*, the partners evaluate themselves and each other for suitability in various roles (e.g., spouse, parent). Although these stages are considered to be relatively distinct, Murstein (1987) also noted that individuals make stimulus, value, and role assessments of each other throughout the entire developmental journey; each factor simply becomes more prominent during a particular stage.

The Premarital Dyadic Formation Model

A similar developmental model was proposed by sociologist Robert Lewis (1972, 1973), who suggested that romantic relationships pass through six sequential phases on the road to commitment. According to the *Premarital Dyadic Formation Model*, the first phase involves the *perception of similarities* (e.g., in demographic background, values, interests, and personality) through observation and interaction. The perception of similarity, in turn, contributes to the achievement of *pair rapport*, which produces positive emotional and behavioral responses to the partner, promotes effective communication, and instills feelings of self-validation and satisfaction with the partner and the relationship. The rapport that partners develop propels them into the third phase of relationship progression—the *inducement of self-disclosure* of intimate personal events and experiences. Self-disclosure facilitates *role-taking* (the ability to understand the partner's perspective and empathize with his or her role in the interaction and the relationship), the fourth phase of development. The fifth phase concerns the achievement of *interpersonal role-fit*, in which the partners assess the extent of their similarity and complementarity in personality, needs, and roles. Finally, during the sixth phase of development, the partners achieve *dyadic crystallization*—they become increasingly involved with each other and committed to the relationship, and they form an identity as a committed couple.

Although historically interesting, stage models of relationship development have fallen out of scientific favor for a number of reasons. First, stage theorists do not agree on the number, the sequence, or even the characteristics of the various stages of relationship development (although most award similarity a central role in the early stages). Second, empirical research now reveals that not all relationships progress through the same stages or follow the same sequential order of development. Third, partners differ in the rate at which they pass through particular developmental stages; as we discussed in Chapter 5, some individuals become friends in as little as one day, whereas others take several years to achieve the same degree of closeness, and some dating couples move quickly to engagement and marriage whereas others follow a more leisurely path. And finally, a number of process models have been developed that appear to more accurately capture the how and why of relationship progression.

THE PROCESS OF RELATIONSHIP DEVELOPMENT

Most relationship scholars now agree that relationships develop gradually over time rather than by passing through a series of discrete stages. *Process models* suggest that relationship development is fueled by sometimes imperceptible changes in intimacy, self-disclosure, exchange of benefits and costs, and other interpersonal processes that occur between partners.

Self-Disclosure and Intimacy

Irwin Altman and Dalmas Taylor (1973) proposed one of the first process models of relationship progression. *Social Penetration Theory* targets *self-disclosure*—the reciprocal exchange of self-relevant information—as the fuel that propels partners along their developmental trajectory. Specifically, individuals are believed to become progressively closer and more committed to each other as they increase both the *depth* (the extent to which the disclosed information is intimate or personal, emotional, and detailed) and *breadth* (the variety of dimensions about which information is revealed) of their self-disclosure. At first, relationships are characterized by superficial, shallow exchanges in which the partners reveal relatively impersonal information (low depth) along a very few dimensions (low breadth). Meeting for the first time at a university-sponsored social event, for example, Wendy and Karen might exchange information about their majors, their musical preferences, and the quality of the band hired to play at the event. If these initial disclosures are rewarding and if each believes that future interactions will also be rewarding, then presumably they will progress to more intimate exchanges in which they reveal increasingly intimate, emotional, and detailed personal information about themselves along a greater number of dimensions. Following their enjoyable (and somewhat superficial) conversation at the party, Wendy and Karen might begin to meet a few times a week for coffee after class. During these interactions, Karen might disclose her ambivalent feelings about her choice of major and her fear that she will not be able to find a rewarding career. Wendy, in turn, might reveal the problems she is experiencing with her roommate and the secret crush she has on a classmate.

Other theorists have subsequently expanded this theory by proposing that it is not only the depth and the breadth of self-disclosure that propel a relationship along its developmental path but also how *responsive* each partner is to the other's disclosures. *Intimacy Theory*, developed by psychologist Harry Reis and his colleagues (Reis, Clark, & Holmes, 2004; Reis & Patrick, 1996; Reis & Shaver, 1988), posits that attentive, supportive responses that leave the partner feeling validated, understood, cared for, and accepted promote the growth of intimacy and the subsequent development of the relationship. These responses may be of a verbal or a nonverbal nature. In their review of the literature, Karen Prager and Linda Roberts (2004; also see Prager, 2000) observed that an individual who is engaged in an intimate interaction displays a host of behavioral cues that signal attentiveness and responsiveness to the partner as well as positive involvement in the interaction. These include increased eye contact, more forward lean and direct body orientation, more frequent head nods, increased physical proximity, greater facial expressiveness, longer speech duration, more frequent or more intense interruptions, and more intense paralinguistic cues (e.g., speaking rate, tone of voice, pauses, silences, laughter). Recent research reveals that people do, in fact, interpret these behavioral cues as communicating validation, understanding, and caring—in short, responsiveness (see Maisel, Gable, & Strachman, 2008).

Thus, in the above example, Wendy's timely acknowledgment of Karen's disclosures about her academic and job-related concerns, her appropriate expressions of sympathy, her verbal and nonverbal responsiveness and demonstrated willingness to continue the conversation, and her reciprocal disclosures all serve to communicate that she understands the situation and that she respects Karen's point of view. This, in turn, will increase Karen's sense of trust and security and will promote intimacy and the development of the relationship. To the extent that Wendy fails to reciprocate ("Hmmm. What did you say? I wasn't listening"), challenges ("I've never had those feelings about my future—I already know what I'm going to do with my life"), or dismisses ("Hey, I've got a lot on my mind right now and I really don't have time to listen to you complain about something so trivial") Karen's revelations, intimacy will decrease and the relationship may stall or be compromised. Thus, it is not simply the act of disclosing information or making personal revelations that contributes to relationship development. Rather, *reciprocal and responsive* disclosures that contribute to *feelings of intimacy*—in other words, verbal and nonverbal behaviors that reflect mutual perceptions of understanding, caring, and validation—are what encourage and sustain the growth of relationships.

Empirical Evidence. Many of these theoretical statements have received empirical support (for reviews, see Collins & Miller, 1994; Derlega, Winstead, & Greene, 2008). For example, self-disclosure—and the feelings of intimacy that it engenders—appears to play a pivotal role in the development and maintenance of friendships and family relationships (e.g., Bauminger, Finzi-Dottan, Chason, & Har-Even, 2008; Canary, Stafford, Hause, & Wallace, 1993; Duck & Miell, 1986; Fehr, 2004). Patricia Sias and Daniel Cahill (1998) asked a sample of men and women to identify a coworker they considered to be a "good or close friend" and to discuss the factors that they believed had propelled their relationships through three developmental phases: (1) *acquaintance to friend*, or the phase in which the coworker changed from being perceived merely as an acquaintance to being perceived as an actual friend, (2) *friend to close friend*, or the point at which the coworker changed from being considered a friend to being considered a close friend, (3) *close friend to very close friend*, or the point at which they began to view their coworker as a very close (or almost best) friend. The results revealed that all three transitions were marked by increases in self-disclosure and intimate communication. For example, many respondents believed that changes in the nature of their communication (including increased discussion of non-work topics such as hobbies, current events, and family, as well as an "easier," less formal style of relating), along with proximity and perceived similarity, helped them make the first transition from acquaintance to friend. The second transition (i.e., from friend to close friend) also was believed to be fueled by increased intimacy in communication style and content, by perceptions of even greater similarity, and by increased support and "outside" socializing. The third and final transition, according to participants, was driven primarily by increases in many of the factors that were important in the second transition (i.e., increases in intimate communication, outside socializing, and coping assistance for personal problems/issues). In addition, many respondents pointed to increased communication about work-related problems as helping them to transition from close friends to very close or almost best friends.

There is evidence that self-disclosure and expressions of intimacy serve a similar function in romantic relationships. Communication researchers Stephen Haas and Laura Stafford (1998) asked a convenience sample of men and women involved in committed (homosexual) romantic relationships to report on the behaviors that they used to maintain their relationships. Although participants generated a number of maintenance strategies, one of the most commonly cited was self-disclosure. Specifically, 57% of the sample specified open and honest communication about thoughts and feelings, including disclosures about the relationship, as an effective way to maintain the romantic relationship. Less "deep" communication, akin to "small talk," was mentioned by close to 25% as a means by which their relationships were maintained. Research conducted with heterosexual romantic partners corroborates these findings (for reviews, see Canary & Dainton, 2003; Dindia, 2000).

In addition, self-disclosure and intimacy appear to be integrally connected with both relationship satisfaction and stability. Research conducted with romantic partners and with friends generally reveals that people who self-disclose, who perceive their partners as self-disclosing, and who believe that their disclosures and confidences are understood by their partners experience greater satisfaction, closeness, commitment, need fulfillment, and love than people whose relationships contain lower levels of intimacy and disclosure (e.g., Laurenceau, Barrett, & Rovine, 2005; Meeks, Hendrick, & Hendrick, 1998; Morry, 2005; Prager & Buhrmester, 1998; Rosenfeld & Bowen, 1991; Sprecher & Hendrick, 2004). In one study, for example, Debra Oswald and Eddie Clark (2006) asked a sample of 148 same-sex friendship pairs to complete measures of openness (that is, disclosure; e.g., "How often do you share your private thoughts with your friend?"), satisfaction with the relationship (e.g., "To what extent are you currently satisfied with your friendship?"), and commitment to the relationship (e.g., "How committed are you to maintaining your friendship?"). Correlational analyses at the individual and dyadic level revealed strong positive associations between disclosure and relationship quality (i.e., satisfaction and commitment). Specifically, participants who self-disclosed tended also to be satisfied with and personally committed to the relationship (this is the individual-level correlation), and friendships characterized by high levels of open communication also exhibited high levels of satisfaction and commitment (this is the dyadic-level correlation).

In sum, the process of revealing oneself to another, particularly when accompanied by reciprocity and validation, appears to play an essential role in the progression of many relationships.

Social Exchange

Many theories of relationship development are grounded in principles of *social exchange* (e.g., Adams, 1965; Hatfield, Utne, & Traupmann, 1979; Homans, 1961; Walster, Walster, & Berscheid, 1978). These theories focus on the exchange of rewards and costs that occur between partners in ongoing relationships. Although a number of social exchange theories exist, each with its own particular terminology and "take" on the process of relationship development, all share a few basic assumptions.

Principle 1: Maximize Rewards, Minimize Costs. The first assumption is that individuals seek to maximize their rewards and minimize their costs in any given relationship. *Rewards* are anything that the individual considers valuable; they can range from the concrete and tangible to the abstract and intangible. For example, Bob's marriage with Vicki may provide him with a number of concrete benefits that he values, including financial security, sex, children, a partner to share in his hobbies and interests, and the social profit that comes from having an attractive and intelligent spouse. This relationship also may provide Bob with a variety of less tangible rewards, including love, emotional support, and the fulfillment of life goals involving marriage and father-hood. *Costs* are those things that the individual considers to be unrewarding or that involve time, effort, compromise, and lost opportunity. In order to maintain his relationship with Vicki, for instance, Bob contributes to the housework, shares parenting tasks, listens supportively to Vicki's complaints about her work colleagues, and spends vacations with his annoying in-laws.

Of course, what is rewarding or costly for one person may not be for another. The financial security afforded by a marital relationship may be rewarding to an unemployed artist but meaning-less to a highly successful business mogul; the affection and emotional support provided by a friend-ship may be valuable to a person with few other relationships but unimportant (or even costly) to another person with an extensive social network and less time to devote to relationship main-tenance. In addition, two individuals in a given relationship may not agree about the value of a particular reward or cost. For example, Bob may place greater worth than Vicki does on his contributions to the housework.

Principle 2: Relationships Are Dynamic. The second assumption shared by social exchange theories is that relationships are dynamic entities that fluctuate and change over time. Relational partners are assumed to engage in a continual process of evaluation in which they assess each other's gains and losses, profits and expenditures, and rewards and costs. This means that a relationship that is considered equitable and satisfying at one point in time may come to be viewed as less equitable and satisfying (and even as inequitable and dissatisfying) as the gains and losses of each partner change over time. This happens, in part, because of the shifting nature of rewards and costs. A particular event, behavior, or occurrence may become less rewarding and/or more costly as it occurs repeatedly or as the relationship progresses. Two people caught up in the thrill of a pas-sionate new romance might find sexual activity to be highly rewarding and not at all costly. Over time, as they become used to each other and the novelty of their passion decreases, they may come to view sexual activity as less rewarding. Similarly, two best friends in high school may find it easy and rewarding to devote hours every single day to talking and text messaging; when they leave school to enter the work force or college, however, daily communication may become more difficult to maintain and therefore less rewarding.

Principle 3: Evaluations Influence Relationship Development. Third, social exchange theories assume that the result of each partner's cost–benefit evaluation determines the course of the relationship. For example, two strangers might meet at a party. Following their initial contact, each person evaluates the immediate outcomes of that interaction and makes a prediction about the outcomes of future interactions. If these evaluations and predictions are positive ("I really enjoyed that interaction; we have so much in common, and he is so easy to talk to"), then the individuals are likely to continue down the path to interpersonal involvement. If the evaluations and predictions are negative ("That was the most boring conversation I've had in a long time; we have absolutely nothing in common, and she is completely uninteresting"), then the two are unlikely to maintain anything other than a superficial relationship; they may even cease to interact altogether.

Principle 4: Equity is the Key to Happiness. A fourth (and related) assumption made by social exchange theorists is that the partners' perceptions of the outcomes they obtain from their relationship are strongly associated with how satisfying and fulfilling they find that relationship to be. Exchange frameworks propose that people will be most satisfied with (and most likely to remain in) a relationship when they view it as equitable. *Equity* is achieved when both partners experience a roughly equal ratio of positive-to-negative outcomes; that is, when the ratio between the benefits derived from the relationship and the contributions (costs or investments) made to the relationship is similar for both partners:

$$\frac{\text{Vicki's rewards or benefits}}{\text{Vicki's costs or investments}} = \frac{\text{Bob's rewards or benefits}}{\text{Bob's costs or investments}}$$

It is the ratio of benefits to contributions that determines equity rather than the exact number that each partner receives or makes. Thus a relationship in which one partner receives more benefits than the other may still be equitable so long as he or she makes a correspondingly higher number of contributions.

According to this theoretical perspective, people who find themselves in an inequitable relationship—who are under-benefited or over-benefited relative to the partner—will experience distress and will seek to restore equity. Equity can be restored to a relationship in a number of ways. For example, a woman who believes that her best friend contributes much more to the relationship than she herself does may attempt to restore **actual equity**. She may increase her own contributions (e.g., by making an effort to return her friend's phone calls more promptly, by offering to help her friend move in to her new apartment) and/or decrease her own benefits (e.g., by asking her friend for advice and support less frequently). Alternately, she can try to restore **psychological equity** by changing her perceptions of the values of various rewards and costs so that the relationship appears more equitable. She may, for instance, convince herself that her own contributions to the relationship are higher ("Come to think of it, I do a lot of nice things for her, too, like that time I took care of her cat when she went on vacation") or that her friend's costs (and her own benefits) are lower ("It's not like I'm taking advantage of our friendship; she likes giving me advice and listening to my romantic problems"). Restoring psychological equity is often easier and less costly than is restoring actual equity, particularly when a person is over-benefited. And finally, if the distress caused by the inequity should prove too great, then she can simply *end the relationship*.

It is important to keep in mind that equity—just like rewards and costs—is to a large extent in the eye of the beholder. One partner may view the relationship as highly equitable (and consequently satisfying) while the other partner considers it to be highly inequitable (and therefore less satisfying). Such discrepancies are not all that uncommon, because people generally are much more aware of their own contributions to a relationship than they are of their partners' contributions. (We will consider this interesting cognitive phenomenon in greater detail in Chapter 8.)

Empirical Evidence.   Many of the principles set forth by social exchange theories have received empirical support. For example, there is evidence that the nature of rewards and costs shifts over time and within relationships. Sociologist Diane Felmlee (e.g., 1995, 1998, 2001a) has conducted research on what she labels "fatal attractions." Her work demonstrates that a partner's attributes that are seen as particularly attractive, rewarding, and valuable at the beginning of a relationship can later come to be viewed as unpleasant, costly, and detrimental to the relationship. For example, a man who values a new friend's "spontaneous and carefree" nature may later perceive that same attribute as an annoying "flightiness" or "unreliability." A woman who initially is attracted to her boyfriend's "firm convictions" and "strong character" may later come to view him as "domineering" and "bossy."

We also know that people differ in terms of what they consider costly and/or rewarding; in particular, there appear to be several sex differences. In one study, Constantine Sedikides, Mary Beth Oliver, and Keith Campbell (1994) asked a sample of heterosexual college students to list the five most important benefits they had enjoyed, and the five most serious costs they had incurred, as a result of all the romantic relationships they had personally experienced. Analysis of these lists revealed a variety of *benefits*, including the following:

- Companionship or affiliation (cited by 60% of the total sample).
- Sexual gratification (46%).
- Feeling loved or loving another (43%).
- Intimacy (42%).
- Relationship expertise or knowledge (40%).
- Self-growth and self-understanding (37%).
- Enhanced self-esteem (32%).
- Exclusivity (32%).
- Feeling secure (28%).
- Social support from the partner's friends or relatives (22%).

Although men and women reported experiencing similar kinds of benefits from their romantic relationships, significantly more men (65%) than women (26%) cited sexual gratification as a particularly important benefit. Conversely, significantly more women (49%) than men (14%) specified enhanced self-esteem (including higher self-respect and self-confidence) as a romantic relationship benefit.

Participants also generated a number of different *costs*, including the following:

- Loss of freedom to socialize (cited by 69% of the total sample).
- Loss of freedom to date (68%).
- Time and effort investment (27%).
- Nonsocial sacrifices, such as falling grades (24%).
- Loss of identity (22%).
- Feeling worse about oneself (22%).
- Stress and worry about the relationship (20%).
- Fights (16%).
- Increased dependence on the partner (13%).
- Monetary losses (12%).

As before, there were sex differences. More men than women cited loss of freedom to socialize (77% vs. 61%) and to date (83% vs. 56%), along with monetary losses (18% vs. 6%), as burdens associated with their romantic relationships. More women than men mentioned loss of identify (29% vs. 14%), feeling worse about themselves (29% vs. 14%), and increased dependence on the partner (23% vs. 3%) as important costs they had incurred in their relationships.

A second study conducted by the authors confirmed and extended the results of the first study. Specifically, women in the second study ranked the benefits of intimacy, self-growth and self-understanding, and enhanced self-esteem higher in importance than did men, whereas men ranked sexual gratification and learning about the other sex higher in importance than did women. Also in the second study, women regarded loss of identity, increased dependence on the partner, feeling worse about oneself, and loss of innocence about relationships and love as greater costs to romantic involvement than did men, who considered monetary losses and time and effort investment to be more serious costs than did women.

In addition to exploring perceptions of costs and benefits, researchers have examined the hypothesized association between equity and relationship satisfaction. People clearly *assume* that equity is an important determinant of relationship quality, *expect* to experience distress if confronted by inequity in close relationships, and *believe* that equity should be restored to inequitable relationships (e.g., Canary & Stafford, 1992; Dainton & Stafford, 1993; Haas & Stafford, 1998). College students in one study (Sprecher, 1992), for example, were asked to imagine that they were in a long-term romantic relationship that had recently become inequitable. First, they imagined that the inequity benefited their partner and thus that the relationship was one of *under-benefit* for them: "You feel that you are contributing more (in love, effort, time, emotions, tasks) than your partner is. In other words, you feel that you are currently getting a worse deal than your partner is" (p. 60). Next, they imagined the opposite situation—a relationship that was inequitable due to their own *over-benefit*. For each scenario, participants indicated how they would respond emotionally to the inequity. The results revealed that men and women expected to become distressed—to experience increased anger and depression and decreased happiness, contentment, satisfaction, and love—in response to under-benefiting inequity. In addition, although participants did not expect to experience a great deal of distress in response to over-benefiting inequity, they did expect their feelings of guilt to increase. Clearly, inequity is *believed* to be associated with distress and dissatisfaction.

However, there is mixed evidence about whether equity and satisfaction *actually* are associated in ongoing relationships. Some studies find that equity is associated with a higher degree of satisfaction than is inequity (e.g., DeMaris, 2007; Sprecher, Schmeeckle, & Felmlee, 2006; for a review, see Sprecher & Schwartz, 1994). However, other researchers find that inequity—specifically, over-benefit—is related to higher levels of satisfaction than is equity (as we might expect from Sprecher's 1992 belief study; e.g., Kamo, 1993).

Overall, then, research generally supports most of the tenets of the social exchange framework. These theories provide important insight into how the exchange of rewards and costs between partners can promote relationship development and continuity.

Interdependence

We have seen that the exchanges between partners—their disclosures and revelations, their contributions and benefits—can propel a relationship toward increasing closeness (or, alternately, toward dissatisfaction and dissolution). *Interdependence frameworks* also focus on partners' exchanges, their perceptions of rewards and costs, and the process by which they evaluate and regulate their relationship (see Holmes, 2000). In addition, these models add to our understanding of relationship development in two important ways. First, interdependence models distinguish between *relationship satisfaction* (how the partners feel about the relationship) and *relationship stability* (whether the relationship will be maintained over time). They recognize that a highly satisfying relationship may ultimately prove unstable, and that a deeply unsatisfying one can endure for a lifetime. Second, these frameworks propose that relationship outcomes are affected not only by what happens between the partners but also by external forces that can serve to cement or weaken the partners' bond. For example, sociocultural taboos against divorce may prevent an unhappily married couple from ending their union; legalization of same-sex marriage may enable another couple to publicly acknowledge their commitment to each other; and parental influence may strengthen (or destroy) the friendship between two children.

Interdependence Theory.   John Thibaut and Harold Kelley's (1959) *Interdependence Theory* proposes that two people involved in a relationship are interdependent with respect to the outcomes of their behavior; that is, the thoughts, feelings, and actions of one partner influence his or her own outcomes as well as those of the other partner. Because each partner generally cannot achieve his or her best possible *personal* outcome at the same time, some degree of compromise is necessary for both partners to obtain at least minimally satisfactory *joint* outcomes. Thus, as the relationship develops and the partners become familiar with each other's behavioral options and the joint outcomes associated with those options, they will discover the most mutually advantageous sets of behavioral combinations and they will then coordinate their behaviors accordingly in order to achieve mutually satisfying outcomes. This process of coordination is called **transformation** and is assumed to produce satisfaction and to enhance commitment to the relationship. For example, Alan may wish to spend most weekends volunteering at a local animal shelter (his optimal outcome), whereas Stacy prefers to stay home and relax (her optimal outcome). The two may compromise by selecting an option that provides both of them with a relatively good outcome, such as volunteering at the shelter on Saturdays and spending Sundays at home together (or volunteering one weekend and relaxing at home the next weekend).

The fact that partners coordinate their behaviors to achieve beneficial joint outcomes is not enough, however, to guarantee that their relationship will be satisfying or that it will endure. Interdependence Theory also proposes that relationship partners rely on two standards when evaluating the outcomes they are receiving from a relationship. The first, called **comparison level** (CL), is the standard against which a partner evaluates the attractiveness of a relationship or how satisfactory it is. The comparison level is determined by the individual's expectations about the level of outcomes (rewards and costs) that the relationship ought to provide, and it is influenced by personal experience as well as general knowledge of outcomes commonly experienced in that type of relationship. To the extent that the outcomes the person actually experiences in the current relationship meet or exceed what is expected (outcomes $\geq$ CL), he or she is likely to view the relationship as attractive and to be satisfied; to the extent that the outcomes fall short of expectations (outcomes < CL), dissatisfaction is likely to result. This means that it is possible for someone who benefits immensely from a relationship to nonetheless be unhappy—if he or she expects more. Conversely, it is possible for someone who appears to be in a highly unrewarding relationship to be relatively satisfied—if he or she believes things could be worse. Thus, like the social exchange theories, Interdependence Theory predicts that satisfaction is not determined solely by the sheer number or the total "goodness" of outcomes that a person receives from the relationship—rather, it is the positive or negative discrepancy of current outcomes from CL that determines satisfaction.

The second standard partners use when evaluating their interpersonal outcomes is called the **comparison level for alternatives** (CLalt). CLalt reflects the outcomes the partners feel that they could obtain from available alternatives to the present relationship (including having no relationship at all). The discrepancy between current outcomes and CLalt influences the likelihood that an individual will remain in the relationship. If a person's current outcomes meet or exceed his or her expected outcomes in the best available alternative relationship (outcomes $\geq$ CLalt), then the relationship is likely to endure. If current outcomes fall below perceived alternative outcomes (outcomes < CLalt), however, the relationship is vulnerable to dissolution. Thus, an unhappy relationship may persist, if there are no acceptable alternatives, and a blissful association may dissolve in the face of a particularly appealing alternative. Figure 6.1 illustrates different combinations of outcomes, CL, and CLalt.

Interdependence Theory thus proposes that both internal (e.g., satisfaction) and external (e.g., alternative partners) factors are implicated in whether a relationship survives or dissolves over time. According to this framework, the most stable relationships will be those in which partners do not expect a great deal (have a low CL) but actually get quite a lot (receive many positive outcomes) from the relationship (and consequently experience high levels of satisfaction) and have very few attractive alternatives to the relationship (have a low CLalt). These factors work together to produce a high level of **dependence** on the relationship; the partners need the relationship in order to obtain the outcomes they desire, and they have no other viable options for attaining those desired outcomes. Their dependence, in turn, promotes the stability and endurance of their union (see Figure 6.2).

(a) *A satisfying and stable relationship*—the individual's current outcomes exceed his or her expectations and also exceed the outcomes he or she believes are available from alternatives to the relationship.

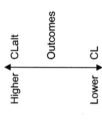

(b) *A satisfying but unstable relationship*—in this example, the individual's current outcomes exceed his or her expectations but do not exceed the outcomes he or she anticipates receiving from available alternatives to the relationship.

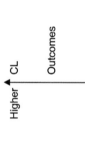

(c) *An unsatisfying and unstable relationship*—here, the individual's current outcomes are below his or her expectations and are also below the outcomes he or she believes are available from alternatives to the relationship.

(d) *An unsatisfying but stable relationship*—in this example, the individual's current outcomes are below what he or she expects to obtain from the relationship but they exceed the outcomes he or she anticipates receiving from available alternatives.

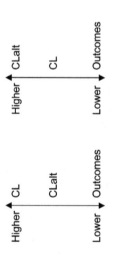

Fig. 6.1 Different combinations of outcomes, CL, and CLalt. Interdependence Theory predicts that relationship satisfaction and stability are a function of three factors: (1) the level of outcomes a person actually receives from the current relationship, (2) the outcomes a person expects to receive from the relationship (CL), and (3) the outcomes a person believes are available from alternatives to the current relationship. The positive or negative discrepancy between current outcomes and CL determines satisfaction, whereas the discrepancy between current outcomes and CLalt determines stability.

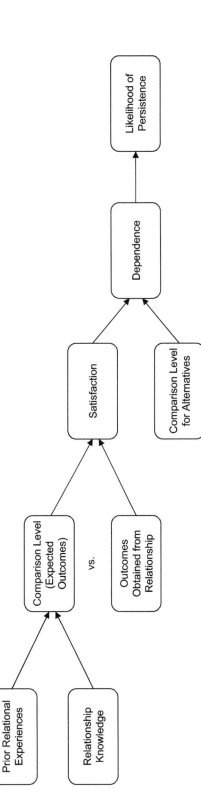

Fig. 6.2 Thibaut and Kelley's Interdependence Theory. Interdependence Theory predicts that relationships will endure to the extent that the partners are highly dependent on each other and the relationship for desirable outcomes. Dependence is a function of satisfaction with the relationship (which is highest when people's actual outcomes meet or exceed the outcomes they expect to obtain, i.e., their comparison level) and the comparison level for alternatives (or what is believed to be available from other relationships or partners). Thus, both internal (satisfaction) and external (quality and quantity of alternatives) forces determine whether a relationship will continue.

Interdependence Theory reminds us that the determinants of satisfaction and stability are not necessarily the same and that relationships develop as a function of changes in the partners' needs, motives, and expectations as well as shifts in the surrounding social environment.

Extensions of Interdependence Theory: Cohesiveness and Commitment.

Other theorists have elaborated on the basic principles of Interdependence Theory. For example, George Levinger's (e.g., 1965, 1976) *Marital Cohesiveness Model* posits that the strength and stability of the bond between partners is a function of two basic factors: the various inducements to remain in the relationship and the inducements to leave it (see Figure 6.3). *Inducements to remain* include all of the sources of *attractions* to the marriage and the spouse, which range from affectional rewards (e.g., love, companionship, sexual enjoyment), to socioeconomic rewards (e.g., income, material possessions, social prestige), to similarity between the spouses on important demographic dimensions. Other inducements to remain in a relationship include the restraints or *barriers* against its dissolution. Barriers derive from the social structure in which people live and from the social contracts into which they enter. For example, feelings of obligation to the partner, the marriage, and existing children; moral proscriptions stemming from religious values; and external pressures from kin, community, and social institutions all may serve as potent barriers to termination. *Inducements to leave* the relationship include the various attractions or rewards that can be obtained from *alternative relationships* (including no relationship at all). Essentially, this model proposes that "marital strength is a function of bars as well as bonds" (Levinger, 1965, p. 20). Thus, the bond between two people is likely to be ***cohesive*** (strong and stable) to the extent that they experience high attraction to the relationship, many barriers to terminating the relationship, and low attraction to alternative relationships. Although this model originally was addressed to marital relationships, it is certainly applicable to friendships and other relationship varieties.

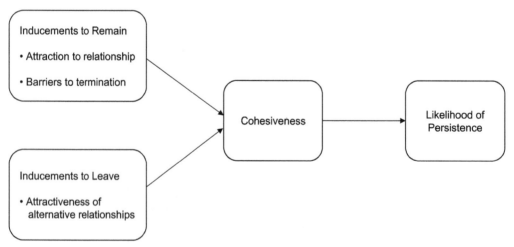

Fig. 6.3 Levinger's Marital Cohesiveness Model. Like Interdependence Theory, the Marital Cohesiveness Model proposes that both internal and external factors determine whether a relationship will endure over time. Highly cohesive relationships are the most likely to last. Cohesiveness (the strength of the relational bond between partners) is determined by the level of rewards and costs experienced in the relationship, which produces attraction; by the number of costs associated with terminating the relationship, or barriers; and by the presence or absence of acceptable alternatives to the relationship.

Another extension of Interdependence Theory—and one that has become the most influential contemporary model of relationship development—was proposed by Caryl Rusbult (1983; see also Rusbult & Buunk, 1993). Her *Investment Model* proposes that ***commitment***, defined as the individual's feelings of attachment to the partner and his or her intention and desire to remain in the relationship, is a function of three factors: (1) the person's level of ***satisfaction*** with the relationship, which is a function of rewards and costs (outcomes actually experienced) and comparison level (the level of outcomes people believe they deserve); (2) the perceived ***quality of alternatives*** to the relationship or the degree to which the individual believes that important needs could be met outside the relationship (e.g., by specific other people, by hobbies and other activities, by no relationship at all); and (3) the size of the person's ***investment*** in the relationship, which refers to the ways he or she is connected to the partner and bound to the relationship—these can be of a direct (e.g., time, emotional energy, personal sacrifice, reputation) or indirect (e.g., mutual friends, shared memories, shared possessions) nature (see Figure 6.4). Thus, this model proposes that people will feel committed to their relationship to the extent that they feel satisfied (i.e., their relationship provides abundant rewards, does not involve heavy costs, and closely matches their beliefs and assumptions about an ideal partnership), they believe that they have few and/or poor-quality alternatives to the relationship, and they have invested important resources in the relationship that serve as powerful inducements for its continuation. Commitment, in turn, influences whether or not the relationship will endure.

Empirical Evidence. There is strong support for many of the basic propositions just outlined (e.g., Attridge & Berscheid, 1994; Drigotas, Rusbult, & Verette, 1999; Goodfriend & Agnew, 2008; Kurdek, 2000, 2008; Rusbult, Johnson, & Morrow, 1986b; Rusbult, Martz, & Agnew, 1998). For example, researchers consistently find that relationship satisfaction is indeed higher when the partners' actual outcomes exceed their expectations (i.e., outcomes > CL). Marianne Dainton (2000)

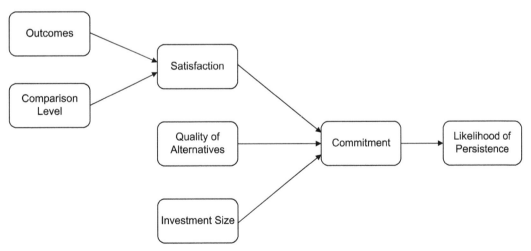

Fig. 6.4 Rusbult's Investment Model. Like Interdependence Theory and the Marital Cohesiveness Model, the Investment Model recognizes that the outcomes an individual obtains in his or her relationship, as well as the perceived quality of alternatives to that relationship, are important contributors to relationship stability. Specifically, this model proposes that people will feel committed to their relationships to the extent that they feel satisfied, believe that they have few good alternatives to the relationship, and have invested important resources in the relationship. This feeling of commitment, in turn, influences whether or not a relationship will last.

gave people currently involved in romantic relationships a list of everyday behavioral strategies that can be used to maintain or promote a relationship. These maintenance activities encompassed five general dimensions: *positivity* (e.g., behaving in a cheerful and optimistic manner), *openness* (e.g., engaging in self-disclosure or direct discussion of the relationship), *assurances* (e.g., providing messages stressing commitment to the partner and the relationship), *social networks* (e.g., relying on common friends and affiliations), and *sharing tasks* (e.g., being equally responsible for accomplishing tasks that the couple faces). For each activity, participants were asked to consider their partners' behavior and to indicate the extent to which their current relationships compared, either favorably or unfavorably, with their expectation levels. They also completed a measure of relationship satisfaction. The results revealed a strong positive correlation between expectation fulfillment and satisfaction; that is, the more an individual perceived his or her partner as using the various maintenance behaviors relative to his or her expectations, the more satisfied the individual was with the relationship.

A meta-analysis conducted by psychologists Benjamin Le and Christopher Agnew (2003) also provided support for several of the basic propositions of the Investment Model. (A **meta-analysis** is a quantitative technique that allows researchers to synthesize the results of many studies testing the same basic hypothesis. Because a meta-analysis uses data from multiple investigations, it usually provides a more reliable test of the hypothesis than would any one individual study.) Le and Agnew first searched the literature for published studies in which the researchers had collected measures of satisfaction, quality of alternatives, investment, and commitment. Overall, 31 studies utilizing participants in various types of romantic relationship (e.g., dating, engaged, cohabiting, married) were identified. Le and Agnew then gathered statistical information from each study and computed the average correlation across studies between commitment and its proposed bases (satisfaction, quality of alternatives, and investment). Their findings supported the Investment Model: across the more than 2400 romantic partners represented in the 31 studies, satisfaction level, quality of alternatives, and investment size consistently and strongly predicted commitment. Moreover, this result held across ethnic groups, for men and women, and for homosexual and heterosexual respondents alike. The more satisfied with and invested in their relationships participants were, and the lower the perceived quality of their alternatives, the stronger was their commitment to those relationships.

More recently, Susan Branje and her colleagues (Branje, Frijns, Finkenauer, Engels, & Meeus, 2007) conducted a study to test whether the Investment Model could also be applied to friendships. In their longitudinal investigation, the researchers asked 995 adolescents to report about aspects of their relationship with their best friend, including satisfaction (e.g., "I am satisfied with the relationship with my friend"), quality of alternatives to the friendship (e.g., "I have many opportunities to do things with others than my friend"), investment (e.g., "I lose a lot if the relationship with my friend gets worse"), and commitment (e.g., "I wish the relationship with my friend were to stay the way it is"). One year later, the researchers collected two measures of relationship stability. First, they determined whether participants still had the same best friend. Second, they had participants complete a scale designed to assess the desire to "switch" best friends (e.g., "I often think another best friend could make my life more interesting," "I am looking for a different best friend"). Interestingly, the results revealed that the associations among many of the variables were different for boys and girls. For example, all of the observed correlations were in the expected direction for female participants; the more satisfied with and invested in their friendships girls were, and the lower the perceived quality of their alternatives, the stronger was their reported commitment to those friendships. However, investment size was the only variable associated with commitment among boys. Also unexpected was the finding that commitment predicted only one of the two dimensions of relationship stability—desire to switch best friends. Participants who were less committed to their best friendships at Time 1 reported a greater desire to find a new best friend a year later at Time 2 (but they were not more likely to have actually chosen a new best friend during that time). In discussing their results, Branje and colleagues observed that girls and boys have different friendship experiences; in particular, girls' friendships tend to be more exclusive, emotionally involved, and intimate than boys' friendships. Consequently, they suggested that the Investment Model may be particularly useful for explaining the dynamics of exclusive dyadic relationships, such as those commonly observed between female friends (and, of course, romantic partners).

In sum, interdependence models provide a compelling view of relationship development. Both the internal characteristics of a relationship (satisfaction, perceptions of rewards and costs, investment level) and the external forces surrounding the partners (availability and quality of alternatives, presence or absence of societal barriers to divorce) influence whether the relationship continues.

SUMMARY

Recognizing that only a very few relationships survive beyond initial interactions, relationship scientists have devoted much time and effort to understanding the how and why of relationship development. In their quest, they have proposed a number of theoretical frameworks. Those who adopt a stage approach have charted the phases or stages of relational progression. Others have focused on the processes—self-disclosure and intimacy, exchange of rewards and costs, interdependence—that occur between partners and that fuel relationship development. Regardless of the framework utilized, researchers and theorists acknowledge that relationships are dynamic entities that fluctuate over time as a result not only of changes in the partners but also of alterations in the social environment and in the properties of the relationship itself.

KEY CONCEPTS

Stage models of relationship development (p. 92)
Filter Theory (p. 92)
Social attributes (p. 92)
Value consensus (p. 92)
Need complementarity (p. 92)
Wheel Theory of Love (p. 92)
Rapport (p. 92)
Self-revelation (p. 93)
Mutual dependency (p. 93)
Intimacy need fulfillment (p. 93)
Stimulus-Value-Role Theory (p. 93)
Stimulus stage (p. 93)
Value stage (p. 93)
Role stage (p. 93)
Premarital Dyadic Formation Model (p. 93)
Perception of similarities (p. 93)
Pair rapport (p. 93)
Inducement of self-disclosure (p. 93)
Role-taking (p. 93)

Interpersonal role-fit (p. 93)
Dyadic crystallization (p. 93)
Process models of relationship development (p. 94)
Social Penetration Theory (p. 94)
Self-disclosure (p. 94)
Depth of disclosure (p. 94)
Breadth of disclosure (p. 94)
Responsiveness (p. 94)
Intimacy Theory (p. 94)
Social exchange theories (p. 96)
Rewards (p. 96)
Costs (p. 97)
Equity (p. 97)
Actual equity (p. 98)
Psychological equity (p. 98)
Interdependence frameworks (p. 100)
Relationship satisfaction (p. 100)
Relationship stability (p. 100)

Interdependence Theory (p. 100)
Transformation (p. 101)
Comparison level (p. 101)
Comparison level for alternatives (p. 101)
Dependence (p. 101)
Marital Cohesiveness Model (p. 104)
Inducements to remain (p. 104)
Inducements to leave (p. 104)

Cohesiveness (p. 104)
Investment Model (p. 105)
Commitment (p. 105)
Satisfaction (p. 105)
Quality of alternatives (p. 105)
Investment (p. 105)
Meta-analysis (p. 106)

EXPLORATION EXERCISES

These exercises are designed to allow you to explore in greater detail some of the concepts and issues discussed in this chapter. There are no right or wrong answers to these exercises—they are simply meant to provide an opportunity for discussion and debate.

1. Make a list of your current close relationships. Select the one you feel is the closest relationship (for example, this may be your relationship with a best friend, or a relative, or a romantic partner). Using Social Penetration Theory and Intimacy Theory, explain how your relationship developed, using as many specific examples as you can recall.

2. According to equity theories of relationship development, inequity—situations in which one partner is giving or receiving more relative to the other partner—causes distress and can stall or negatively impact the partners' progression toward closeness. Have you ever been in an inequitable relationship, or experienced a time in which one of your relationships became inequitable (even temporarily)? How did you respond to the inequity? Does your response support theoretical assumptions or not?

3. On your own or with classmates, evaluate the following three statements from the perspective of Interdependence Theory:

Statement 1: "A good relationship will last forever."
Statement 2: "If he/she were really unhappy, then he/she would leave."
Statement 3: "If two people are truly happy together, nothing and no one can tear them apart."

Chapter 7
Mate Selection and Marriage

As we have seen in earlier chapters, some relationships pass beyond initial attraction and liking and continue to develop over time until they reach a state of relative permanence. Of all the types of established partnerships that exist, none has received as much scientific attention as the marital relationship. In this chapter we examine mate choice, marriage, and other forms of long-term romantic relationships. Because marriage historically has been viewed as a heterosexual relationship, much of the existing literature—and consequently much of the material presented in this chapter—is limited to the experiences and outcomes of heterosexual married couples.

THE NATURE OF MARRIAGE

Marriage is commonly defined as a long-term mating arrangement that is socially sanctioned and that involves economic, social, and reproductive cooperation between the partners. Although all known human societies practice and endorse this type of long-term pairing (Daly & Wilson, 1983; Goodwin, 1999), the customs and rituals surrounding the marriage ceremony vary widely from culture to culture (Ihinger-Tallman & Henderson, 2003). For example, the *gitanos* or *calé* of Spain and southern France prefer that men and women marry at a young age and place great value on female virginity. Gitano marriages often include an elaborate ceremony in which the bride is physically examined by a hired professional and/or by family members, and evidence of her virgin status then is publicly displayed to the wedding guests as a sign of her purity and moral decency (Gay y Blasco, 1997; Martin & Gamella, 2005). Other cultures follow different customs; the "honeymoon," for example, is a common feature of contemporary Western marriages but is virtually non-existent in other societies (Kalmijn, 1997).

Marriage rates have declined around the world, with the United States experiencing a particularly sharp decrease (Grad, 2006; Lester, 1996). For example, U.S. census data indicate that between the years 1935 and 1939, approximately 66% of men and 83% of women were married by the age of 25. Twenty years later, between 1955 and 1959, 51% of men and 65% of women were married by the time they reached 25 years of age. And two decades after this, between 1975 and 1979, only 37% of 25-year-old men and 50% of 25-year-old women were married (U.S. Census Bureau, 2007a). Currently, approximately one third of the adult U.S. population consists of single men and women who have never married; an additional 10% of adults are divorced and single (U.S. Census Bureau, 2007b, 2007c). Nonetheless, most unmarried men and women express a desire to marry, expect to marry at some point in their lives, and hold positive attitudes about the state of marriage and about married people in general (DePaulo & Morris, 2006; Frazier, Arikian, Benson, Losoff, & Maurer, 1996; Martin, Specter, Martin, & Martin, 2003).

The "Rules" of Marriage

Relationship scientists have identified four general "rules"—some of them codified into law, others reflecting unwritten social norms, standards, or guidelines—that men and women are expected to follow when choosing a marriage partner and entering and maintaining a marital union.

Monogamy.   One of the primary rules of marriage concerns the number of spouses an individual is permitted to wed. Around the world, both historically and in contemporary societies, *monogamy*—a marriage system in which two individuals (typically one man and one woman) pairbond—is the most commonly practiced form of marriage. However, other kinds of marriage system have been identified (see Fisher, 1989; Goodwin, 1999). *Polygamy*, a mating system in which multiple individuals pairbond, encompasses both polygyny and polyandry. In *polygyny* ("many females"), a man marries multiple women. In *polyandry* ("many males"), a woman marries multiple men. *Polygynandry* ("many females and males") or *cenogamy* is a mating system in which husbands and wives form a household and share the same spouses; in this type of group marriage, each man is considered married to all women, and each woman is considered married to all men.

One of the most comprehensive sources of cross-cultural information on mating systems is the *Ethnographic Atlas*. The *Atlas* contains data on various aspects of social and interpersonal life (e.g., family organization, mode of marriage, kinship terminology, community size) that characterize more than 1100 human societies located in Africa, the Mediterranean, Eurasia, the Pacific, North America, and South America. In 1967, ethnologist George Murdock presented information on a subset of 862 of those societies in a special edition of the journal *Ethnology*. Examination of this information, summarized in Table 7.1, reveals that polyandry is much less commonly endorsed than is either polygyny or monogamy. For example, fewer than 1% of societies explicitly permit a mating system based on a single woman marrying multiple husbands, but over 80% of the societies included in the *Atlas* permit at least some men to take multiple wives.

In all but a handful of human societies, then, women practice monogamy; that is, a woman marries one man at a time (although in polygynous societies, her spouse may have multiple wives). Similarly, although the ethnographic data at first glance suggest a high frequency of polygyny, a closer look reveals that men also tend to practice monogamy; they marry one woman at a time. Based on his own analysis of the *Atlas* data, Pierre van den Berghe (1979) reported that only about 10% of the men in polygynous societies actually have more than one wife. Thus, a more accurate interpretation is that most societies *permit* men to marry multiple wives but few men are able to attract more than one part-ner and sustain more than one mating relationship. This may be due in part to the fact that the number of marriageable men and women in most contemporary societies is roughly equal; consequently, there are very few "extra" women available with whom men can form polygynous unions. In addition, the

Table 7.1 Accepted Mating Systems in 862 Human Societies

Mating System	Practicing Societies	
	No.	%
Polygyny (multiple wives)	*713*	*82.7*
Generally practiced, within extended families	202	23.4
Generally practiced, within independent nuclear families	177	20.5
Occasionally practiced, within independent nuclear families	174	20.2
Occasionally practiced, within extended families	160	18.6
Monogamy (one husband–wife pair)	*137*	*15.9*
Within independent nuclear families	72	8.4
Within extended families	65	7.5
Polyandry (multiple husbands)	*4*	*0.5*
Within independent nuclear families	3	0.3
Within extended families	1	0.1
Unclassified	*8*	*0.9*

These frequencies represent percentages of societies endorsing polygyny, monogamy, and polyandry. It is important to remember that both polygynous and polyandrous societies also permit the formation of monogamous unions; thus, the most commonly accepted and practiced form of marriage is monogamy. These frequencies were tabulated by Regan (2008) from raw data presented in the *Ethnographic Atlas* (Murdock, 1967, pp. 170–231).

Source: Regan, P. (2008). *The mating game: A primer on love, sex, and marriage* (2nd ed.). Thousand Oaks, CA: Sage Publications. Copyright © 2008 by Sage Publications, Inc. Table 4.1 adapted with permission.

increased financial and social responsibilities engendered by having multiple wives (and offspring) make it difficult for most men to successfully sustain polygynous relationships. As noted by evolutionary scientists Martin Daly and Margo Wilson (1983, pp. 282–283):

> Polygynous unions remain rarer than monogamous ones . . . even within those societies that permit them. This is hardly surprising given male–male competition for wives and the pressures that are engendered when any substantial number of men are consigned to involuntary celibacy. Hence it is usually only a minority of wealthy, powerful men who have the means to acquire and maintain multiple wives.

After examining marriage, divorce, and remarriage rates across cultures, anthropologist Helen Fisher (1989) also concluded that monogamy is the primary marriage pattern for both men and women and that human societies generally exhibit a mate selection pattern of *serial pairbonding* or *serial monogamy* whereby men and women marry successive individual partners over their life-spans (as opposed to marrying one partner for the duration of their life-spans or many partners at a single time). In summarizing her findings, Fisher (1992, pp. 69, 72) observed:

> Because of the genetic advantages of polygyny for men and because so many societies permit polygyny, many anthropologists think that harem building is a badge of the human animal. I cannot agree . . . Both men and women have to be cajoled by riches to share a spouse. Whereas gorillas, horses, and animals of many other species *always* form harems, among human beings polygyny and polyandry seem to be optional opportunistic exceptions; monogamy is the rule. Human beings almost never have to be cajoled into pairing. Instead, we do this naturally. We flirt. We feel infatuation. We fall in love. We marry. And the vast majority of us marry only one person at a time. Pair-bonding is a trademark of the human animal.

Homogamy. A second (albeit unwritten) "rule" of marriage is the tendency for men and women to marry spouses who resemble them on a number of dimensions. Called *homogamy* or *assortment*, this tendency for similar individuals to pairbond has been extensively documented by relationship scientists (e.g., Blackwell & Lichter, 2004; Luo & Klohnen, 2005; Monden, 2007; van Leeuwen, van den Berg, & Boomsma, 2008; for reviews, see Berscheid & Reis, 1998; Buss, 1985; Murstein, 1980). For example, investigators have found positive correlations between spouses on demographic characteristics such as age, race or ethnicity, education level, socioeconomic status, and religion, as well as on a host of attitudes and values, personality traits, and cognitive abilities (e.g., IQ). Romantic partners even appear to resemble each other on physical attributes like attractiveness and health. The fact that we tend to prefer similar others may partly account for this general pairbonding tendency (see Chapter 4).

Exogamy. Another general norm of marriage is *exogamy* or the tendency for people to marry partners outside of their own familial or kinship group. All cultures have some form of *incest taboo* which prohibits sexual intercourse (and, consequently, marriage) between closely related individuals (Fisher, 1992; Frayser, 1989; Immerman & Mackey, 1997; Murdock, 1949), and many have laws designed to enforce this rule. In the United States, for example, marriage between parents and biological children, brothers and sisters, uncles and nieces, and aunts and nephews is illegal. In addition, over half of the states prohibit marriage between biological first cousins; the remaining states allow first cousin marriages or permit them only under particular circumstances (e.g., if the individuals are older than 65 years of age, are infertile, or have received genetic counseling, or if—as in Minnesota— the couple's aboriginal culture permits marriage between first cousins). Similar laws or customs exist in other countries, with most prohibiting sexual and/or marital relationships between immediate family members (e.g., between children and their parents, grandparents, and aunts and uncles). As in the U.S., however, greater latitude is extended with respect to first cousin marriages. For example, recent surveys conducted in Turkey, Jordan, Yemen, Afghanistan, and Pakistan revealed that approximately 20% to 50% of all marriages were between first cousins (e.g., Gunaid, Hummad, & Tamim, 2004; Kir, Gulec, Bakir, Hosgonul, & Tumerdem, 2005; Sueyoshi & Ohtsuka, 2003; Wahab & Ahmad, 2005; Wahab, Ahmad, & Shah, 2006). High rates of first cousin marriages have also been documented among Gypsy populations in Europe and Bedouin clans in the Middle East, perhaps due in part to the heavy emphasis placed by those groups on ethnic *endogamy* (e.g., selecting a mate from within one's own ethnic or clan affiliation; see Martin & Gamella, 2005; Raz & Atar, 2005).

Fidelity. A fourth rule of marriage also concerns sexual behavior. Not only is sexual intercourse considered a "normal" part of the marital relationship, but marital sex is assumed to be *exclusive* sex. That is, once an individual is married, the general presumption is that he or she will confine sexual activities to the marital relationship. Survey data indicate that most men and women possess strong expectations about marital *sexual exclusivity* or fidelity (e.g., Wiederman & Allgeier, 1996), disapprove of extramarital sex (e.g., Davis & Smith, 1991; Glenn & Weaver, 1979; Small, 1992), and express negative beliefs about "cheating spouses" (e.g., Sprecher, Regan, & McKinney, 1998). For example, sex researcher Robert Michael and his colleagues (Michael, Gagnon, Laumann, & Kolata, 1994) asked a U.S. sample of more than 3400 adults the following question: "What is your opinion about a married person having sexual relations with someone other than the marriage partner—is it always wrong, almost always wrong, sometimes wrong, or not wrong at all?" (p. 287). Their results revealed that 77% of the entire sample felt that extramarital sex was "always wrong"—a strong condemnation indeed.

Similar results were reported in a large cross-cultural investigation conducted by anthropologists Eric Widmer, Judith Treas, and Robert Newcomb (1998). These researchers contacted nationally representative samples of adults from 24 different countries and asked them to indicate whether it was acceptable for a married person to have "sexual relations with someone other than his or her husband or wife" (p. 252). Participants were given four response options: *always wrong*, *almost always wrong*, *wrong only sometimes*, and *not wrong at all*. Across all 24 countries, a majority (66%) of the participants agreed that extramarital sex was "always wrong." An additional 21% stated that extramarital sex was "almost always wrong." A mere 4% of the participants indicated believing that it was "not wrong at all" for married people to engage in sexual relations with another person. Similar results have been reported by other cross-cultural researchers (e.g., Haavio-Mannila & Kontula, 2003). Thus, there is a general consensus around the world that marital partners should be sexually exclusive. (As with many sexual attitudes (see Chapter 11), however, men are relatively more permissive than are women (e.g., Eisenman & Dantzker, 2006; Oliver & Hyde, 1993; Thompson, 1984).)

Understanding the "Rules": Social and Evolutionary Perspectives

Given the seemingly universal nature of these four "rules of marriage," relationship scientists have become interested in exploring their origins. Generally, scholars rely on the two general theoretical frameworks presented in Chapter 4. Recall that *social context theories* focus on proximal mechanisms— that is, forces located in the contemporary social, cultural, and historical milieu—that influence relationship choices and mating behavior. Social exchange or equity models, for example, conceptualize the process of mate selection as a marketplace in which people attempt to maximize their rewards and make social interaction as profitable as possible by exchanging their own assets—warmth and kindness, fidelity and trustworthiness, intelligence, humor, good looks, status, and so on—for desirable attributes in a partner (Murstein, 1970; Sprecher, 1998). Since people seek the best possible value in a potential marriage partner, but are constrained by what they themselves have to offer, this process generally will result in the pairing of individuals of roughly equal social "value" (i.e., homogamy). That is, those who possess a great many desirable characteristics, or who have high amounts of a few particularly valuable attributes, will be able to attract equally desirable others. Those who have fewer assets to offer potential mates may wish to establish mating relationships with highly desirable others, but will be unable to attract those highly attractive others and inevitably will form liaisons with less socially valuable partners. Thus, a consideration of the basic principles of social exchange suggests that people will seek a mate who possesses a host of socially desirable characteristics such as trustworthiness and fidelity, will moderate these preferences by taking into account their own attributes, and will ultimately pairbond with someone who is similar to them on important attribute dimensions.

Unlike social context theories, *evolutionary models* consider the ways in which contemporary mating behavior might be influenced by evolved psychological heuristics that were selected because they overcame obstacles to reproduction (and survival) located in the human ancestral past and therefore allowed our ancestors to make "appropriate" mating decisions. Recall that an appropriate mating decision, from an evolutionary perspective, is one that results in a high(er) probability of gene replication and the production of offspring who survive to reach reproductive maturity. According to this perspective, the human biological design favors the formation of enduring (long-term and committed) mating relationships. Specifically, because human offspring are characterized by a period of dependency that extends well beyond infancy, successful pairbonding and child rearing in the ancestral past depended for both sexes on the ability to select a fertile, healthy mate who could and would provide sustained social and emotional support, who would invest in the relationship and any offspring, and who would remain exclusively attached to the partner throughout the duration of the relationship. Those early humans who formed a committed, monogamous pairbond with an appropriate partner—one who was genetically and physically healthy, reproductively mature, emotionally stable, supportive, trustworthy, and sexually faithful—achieved greater reproductive success than those who did not; hence, the former's genes survived (see Chapters 3 and 4). This genetic legacy may explain why contemporary marriage is largely characterized by the "rules" of monogamy, homogamy, exogamy, and fidelity.

Types of Contemporary Marriage

Social and behavioral scientists have identified a number of dimensions along which marriages can vary. One dimension concerns the amount of personal choice an individual has in selecting a spouse. *Collectivist cultures* (including societies in Asia, the Middle East, and South America) typically limit the amount of freedom a man or woman has in choosing a marriage partner. These cultures are characterized by explicit and firm group boundaries, focus on group loyalty, solidarity, and shared activities, and generally require individual members to subordinate their personal goals to those of the group. Marriage is viewed primarily as a vehicle for maintaining social order and uniting families rather than as a means of fulfilling personal desires and uniting individuals (Goodwin, 1999; Hamon & Ingoldsby, 2003; Hatfield & Rapson, 1996). Given the emphasis placed on group cohesion and social unity, it is not surprising that many collectivist cultures practice (or historically have practiced) *arranged marriages* in which family members or matchmakers choose a mate for the individual. For example, in traditional east Asian and south Asian societies (e.g., Pakistan, India, Nepal), marriage is regarded as one of the most significant events in the human lifecycle and as an essential social and cultural duty, and many marriages are arranged or "semi-arranged" (Ghimire, Axinn, Yabiku, & Thornton, 2006; Medora, 2003). *Individualist cultures* (including the United States and northern and western Europe) typically allow an individual much greater freedom in the selection of a spouse. In these societies, people are fairly autonomous, group boundaries are flexible, and emphasis is placed on the fulfillment of personal goals in marriage and other life pursuits. Feelings of personal compatibility and mutual attraction between the partners, rather than meeting the needs of families or of society, serve as the primary motivation for marriage, and individuals generally select their own partners. *Free choice marriage* (also called *love-based marriage*) is the norm in those societies.

A second dimension along which marriages vary concerns the allocation of roles and responsibilities between the spouses in the marriage. ***Traditional marriages*** are those in which the spouses allocate roles and responsibilities on the basis of sex (e.g., Luepnitz, 1988; Rubin, 1976; Turner, 1970). The husband's role encompasses traditional "male" activities and traits. For example, he controls the economic aspects of family life and has the authority to make decisions for the entire family. The wife's role encompasses traditional "female" activities and traits. She is responsible for domestic tasks, including management of the house and children. Traditional relationships often involve little direct or overt expression of emotion between the spouses. Rather, each partner relies on relatives and same-sex friends for companionship and affection (Peplau, 1983). Television sitcoms that were popular in the U.S. during the 1950s through the 1970s showcase this type of marriage. *The Donna Reed Show, Father Knows Best, I Love Lucy, Leave it to Beaver, All in the Family, Happy Days,* and similar shows depicted marriages in which the husband worked outside the home and functioned as the sole "breadwinner," primary disciplinarian, and decision maker for the family, whereas the wife stayed at home, raised the children, and took care of domestic tasks such as cooking the family meals, shopping, and cleaning.

Another type of marriage exists, although it primarily occurs between spouses in individualist societies. Unlike traditional marriages in which tasks and roles are divided along gender lines, ***egalitarian, peer, or equal-status marriages*** are characterized by shared roles and responsibility in all aspects of married life (e.g., Gilbert, 1993; Scanzoni, Polonko, Teachman, & Thompson, 1989; Schwartz, 1994). Both the husband and wife are expected to contribute equally to the marital relationship—by providing social support and caregiving, affection and emotion, sexuality, financial resources, parenting skills, and domestic labor. U.S. television highlighted this kind of union in 1980s programs such as *The Cosby Show* (Clair and Heathcliff Huxtable) and *Roseanne* (Roseanne and Dan Conner), and, more recently, in shows like *Mad About You* (Paul and Jamie Buchman), *Medium* (Joe and Allison DuBois), *Friday Night Lights* (Eric and Tami Taylor), and *Desperate Housewives* (Lynette and Tom Scavo). Sociologists Pepper Schwartz and Virginia Rutter (1998) note that true peer marriages are relatively rare: "The potential for power sharing, obligation sharing, and resource sharing in marriage is real, though not commonly enacted. Pairs with the ambition of egalitarianism often fall short, into the "near peer" category" (p. 157). These "near peer" marriages usually involve a husband who helps with childcare and household labor, and a wife who provides financial resources and makes economic decisions, to a greater degree than would be expected in traditional marriages. Although truly egalitarian marriages may still be relatively uncommon, there is some evidence that partners who achieve them experience high levels of companionship and mutual respect as well as low levels of anger and conflict.

Division of Labor

Regardless of the type of marriage a couple has, it is likely that their division of household labor will reflect traditional sex-roles. Early studies—those conducted in the 1950s and 1960s—revealed a strict division of labor. Husbands specialized in "outside" tasks, including mowing the lawn, shoveling snow, and maintaining the car, whereas wives specialized in "inside" tasks, including cooking and cleaning (e.g., Blood & Wolfe, 1960). Research conducted four or five decades later demonstrates that the same task division continues to characterize modern marriages (Biernat & Wortman, 1991; Coltrane, 2000; Wilkie, Ferree, & Ratcliff, 1998).

In addition, although both sexes have a tendency to overestimate the amount of time they spend engaged in housework (Lee & Waite, 2005; Press & Townsley, 1998), there is overwhelming evidence that married women spend more time on domestic tasks than do married men (e.g., Baxter, 2005). For example, psychologists Sondra Solomon, Esther Rothblum, and Kimberly Balsam (2004) asked a large sample of married heterosexual couples (as well as homosexual couples in civil unions and homosexual couples not in civil unions) to report the number of hours each week they spent on housework. The results revealed that heterosexual married women spent significantly more time on housework than participants in any of the other groups—on average, married women engaged in housework approximately 11 to 20 hours a week, compared with the 6 to 10 hours reported by their spouses and partnered homosexual men and women. Even in *dual-earner marriages* (in which both the husband and wife work and make economic contributions to the family), women average approximately twice as many hours per week on housework as do men (Artis & Pavalko, 2003; Blair & Johnson, 1992; Solomon et al., 2004). After reviewing the existing literature, Scott Coltrane and Michele Adams (2003) concluded that "the average woman in the United States did about three times as much cooking, cleaning, laundry, and other routine housework in the 1990s as the average married man" (p. 472). Interestingly, although marriage places a seemingly unfair burden on women, research indicates that as long as both spouses believe that their expectations about the division of labor are being met and perceive the division as fair, they are likely to be satisfied with married life (e.g., Grote & Clark, 2001; Lennon & Rosenfield, 1994; Major, 1993; also see Milkie, Bianchi, Mattingly, & Robinson, 2002).

CHANGES IN THE NATURE OF MARRIAGE

The nature of marriage has changed over time. We have already discussed the fact that although most people hold positive attitudes about the state of marriage, marriage rates have declined around the world. A second change in the nature of marriage concerns the age at which people marry for the first time. Data collected by the U.S. Census Bureau (1998, 2005a, 2005b) reveal that age at first marriage is on the rise, with greater numbers of men and women delaying marriage until their mid to late 20s. For example, in 1958 the mean age at first marriage was approximately 23 years for men and 20 years for women. Two decades later, in 1978, the age at first marriage had increased to around 24 for men and 22 for women—a life-span delay of 1 to 2 full years. By 1998, men were marrying for the first time at around 27, and women were waiting to marry until they were 25. In 2005 men's average age at first marriage remained at 27, whereas women's had risen to 25.5. A similar trend has been observed in non-U.S. populations (e.g., Hortaçsu, Baştuğ, & Muhammetberdiev, 2001). For instance, over the past 30 years, the average age at first marriage has increased by 2 to 4 years among men and women in many Asian countries, including Thailand, Vietnam, Malaysia, Singapore, and Indonesia (see Williams & Philipguest, 2005).

A fairly recent change in the nature of marriage concerns the growing emphasis that most men and women place on their own happiness and personal fulfillment. Love and affection, rather than economic security, reproduction, or any other factor, have become the primary basis for marriage in the United States and other Western cultures. More than 40 years ago, social scientist William Kephart (1967) asked a sample of young men and women whether they would marry someone with whom they were not in love if that person possessed all of the other qualities they desired in a spouse. More than one third (35%) of the men and three fourths (76%) of the women responded affirmatively—they were willing to marry without love. However, by the mid-1980s there was evidence of a dramatic shift in attitude. When psychologists Jeffrey Simpson, Bruce Campbell, and Ellen Berscheid (1986) asked a group of young adults the very same question, only 14% of the men and 20% of the women indicated that they would marry someone they did not love if he or she was "perfect" in every other respect; that is, an overwhelming majority of participants considered love to be an essential prerequisite for marriage.

A similar attitude shift is occurring around the world. In the mid-1990s another group of researchers (Levine, Sato, Hashimoto, & Verma, 1995) asked a large sample of adults from 11 countries to answer the question first posed by Kephart (1967): "If a man/woman had all the qualities you desired, would you marry this person if you were not in love with him/her?" Although a greater number of participants from collectivist countries (e.g., India, Pakistan) than from individualist countries (e.g., United States, England) answered the question affirmatively, there was no country in which participants were completely willing to marry in the absence of love. In fact, sizeable numbers of men and women in every country reported that they would not enter a loveless marriage. For example, the percentage of participants who said "no" in response to the question was as follows: United States (86%), England (84%), Mexico (81%), Australia (80%), Philippines (64%), Japan (62%), Pakistan (39%), Thailand (34%), and India (24%).

The increased emphasis given to love as a basis for matrimony has produced other changes in the nature of marriage. In particular, attitude surveys and interviews indicate that growing numbers of young adults from cultures with a tradition of arranged marriage wish to select their own partners and to limit family involvement in the mate selection process (e.g., Schvaneveldt, Kerpelman, & Schvaneveldt, 2005; Zaidi & Shuraydi, 2002; for reviews, see Goodwin, 1999; Lieberman & Hatfield, 2006). Consequently, many of these cultures are experiencing a decrease in the number of arranged marriages (and a corresponding increase in the number of "love matches") that take place. For example, sociologist Fumie Kumagai (1995) reported that the ratio of arranged (*miai*) to love-based (*renai*) marriages in Japan shifted dramatically over the last half of the twentieth century. Specifically, during the time of World War II, approximately 70% of new marriages were arranged by parents whereas 30% were love-based or personal choice matches. By 1988, however, only 23% of new marriages were arranged; the rest either were completely love-based (75%) or reflected a combination of parental arrangement and personal choice (2%). Data collected more recently reveal an even greater decline in the proportion of arranged marriages: among Japanese couples marrying in 2005, only 6.4% reported an arranged marriage (National Institute of Population and Social Security Research, 2005, as cited in Farrer, Tsuchiya, & Bagrowicz, 2008). Similar changes have been documented in other countries (e.g., China, Nepal; Ghimire et al., 2006; Xu & Whyte, 1990). Clearly, men and women around the world not only want love in their marriages but also the freedom to choose their own spouses.

ALTERNATIVES TO MARRIAGE

Marriage is not the only option for men and women who seek to form a more or less permanent partnership with another person. Other types of long-term committed relationships exist.

Cohabitation

One of the most common (and increasingly popular) alternatives to marriage is *cohabitation*. Cohabitation resembles a marital relationship in that it is essentially a committed pairbond or monogamous union between two individuals who live together and who coordinate their economic, social, sexual (and sometimes reproductive) activities. Unlike marriage, however, cohabitation is not legally formalized (at least in the United States; in some countries, cohabiting couples can register their partnerships and obtain many of the same legal rights as married couples). Perhaps due in part to increasingly permissive social attitudes regarding premarital sex, rates of cohabitation in the United States, Canada, western Europe (e.g., Britain, Scotland), and other world regions are on the rise (see Bumpass & Lu, 2000; Goodwin, Christakopoulou, & Panagiotidou, 2006; Jamieson, Anderson, McCrone, Bechhofer, Stewart, & Li, 2002; Kiernan, 2004; Le Bourdais & Lapierre-Adamcyk, 2004). For example, a large national survey conducted in the U.S. revealed that only about 16% of men and 6% of women born between 1933 and 1942 had cohabited prior to marriage (Michael et al., 1994). This number increased to 33% for men and to 24% for women born in the decade between 1943 and 1952. More than half of the men (53%) and nearly half of the women (43%) born between 1953 and 1962 reported having cohabited prior to marriage, and two-thirds of men and women born between 1963 and 1974 had cohabited before marriage. Cohabitation has become so common, in fact, that the researchers concluded the following:

> . . . the path toward marriage, once so straight and narrow, has begun to meander and to have many side paths, one of which is being trodden into a well-traveled lane. That path is the pattern of living together before marriage. Like other recent studies, ours shows a marked shift toward living together rather than marriage as the first union of couples.
>
> (Michael et al., 1994, p. 96)

According to recent survey data compiled by the U.S. Census Bureau (2005c), there are currently more than 5 million cross-sex and more than 750,000 same-sex "unmarried partner households" in the United States. Cohabitation has joined marriage as an almost universal life experience.

Cohabitation may serve a variety of functions in developing relationships. For some couples, cohabitation may function as a replacement to marriage when marriage is not desirable or possible; for others, cohabitation may represent another phase or stage of relationship development; and for still others, cohabitation may serve as a "trial run" for marriage (Carmichael & Whittaker, 2007; Wu & Schimmele, 2003). The fact that most cohabiters expect to marry their partners (Brown, 2003; Brown & Booth, 1996; Bumpass, Sweet, & Cherlin, 1991)—and the majority eventually do (Smock & Gupta, 2002)—has led some scholars to propose that cohabitation allows couples to test their compatibility, iron out their differences, and thus strengthen their relationship before taking a formal (and legally binding) marriage vow.

Interestingly, however, existing research does not support this supposition. In actuality, premarital cohabitation appears to be associated with *negative* marital outcomes, including lower levels of satisfaction and commitment, poorer communication and supportive behavior, and greater amounts of conflict (e.g., Amato, Johnson, Booth, & Rogers, 2003; Cohan & Kleinbaum, 2002; Kline Rhoades, Stanley, & Markman, 2006; but see Brown, Sanchez, Nock, & Wright, 2006). For example, Galena Kline [now Kline Rhoades] and her colleagues (2004) compared three groups of married couples—those who had lived together before becoming engaged (before-engagement cohabiters), those who moved in together only after becoming engaged (after-engagement cohabiters), and those who did not live together until after getting married (non-premarital cohabiters)—on a number of measures of marital quality. Their results revealed that couples in the before-engagement group scored significantly lower than the other two groups of couples on a multi-item marital adjustment scale, suggesting that couples who begin cohabiting early in their relationship (i.e., before formalizing their commitment via engagement or marriage) are at greater risk for poor marital outcomes. This finding is so robust, in fact, that relationship scholars have labeled it the ***cohabitation effect***.

There is one dimension, however, on which cohabiters seem to experience more beneficial outcomes than their married counterparts—the division of household labor. In general, cohabitation is characterized by a more equal division of household labor than is marriage. Both homosexual and heterosexual cohabiters (as well as heterosexual married couples who cohabited prior to marriage) possess more egalitarian attitudes toward division of household labor and tend to demonstrate a more equitable allocation of household tasks than married couples who did not cohabit (Baxter, 2005; Clarkberg, Stolzenberg, & Waite, 1995; Davis, Greenstein, & Gerteisen Marks, 2007; Goldberg & Perry-Jenkins, 2007; for a review, see Kurdek, 2005b).

Despite these differences, existing research generally indicates that partners in all types of long-term committed relationship—whether heterosexual or homosexual, married or cohabiting—experience comparable outcomes in most dimensions of their relationships (for reviews, see Kurdek, 2005b; Peplau & Spalding, 2000). Moreover, the same factors that are associated with relational happiness among married heterosexual couples also are correlated with relational happiness among cohabiting heterosexual and homosexual couples (e.g., Kurdek, 2000, 2006b).

Same-Sex Partnerships

Like their heterosexual counterparts, most gay men and lesbian women strongly favor "couple-hood," seek committed, loving relationships, and affirm and celebrate their long-term partnerships with ceremonies, anniversaries, and other events that symbolically mark the importance of these unions in their lives (see Lannutti, 2005; Smart, 2007; Suter, Bergen, Daas, & Durham, 2006). For example, national surveys conducted by sociologist Janet Lever (1994, 1995) revealed that most homosexuals prefer long-term, monogamous relationships over other sexual or romantic arrangements. Her results also indicated that the majority of gay men (59%) and lesbians (70%) say that they would legally marry if allowed to do so. Same-sex marriage is currently legal in several countries outside the U.S., including Canada, the Netherlands, Norway, Spain, Belgium, and South Africa. Other countries around the world—such as Denmark, Finland, Sweden, Switzerland, Britain, France, Germany, Hungary, the Czech Republic, and New Zealand—do not permit same-sex marriages but do allow same-sex couples to legally register their unions (see Clarke & Finlay, 2004; Kauth, 2006; Ryan & DeMarco, 2003). These socially sanctioned partnerships provide coupled gay men and lesbians with access to many of the legal rights and responsibilities held by heterosexual married partners.

The issue of same-sex marriage is a hotly debated topic within the United States, with survey data revealing significant variability in people's attitudes toward marital unions between homosexual partners (e.g., Brumbaugh, Sanchez, Nock, & Wright, 2008). Although opinion polls conducted over the past decade suggest that the American public has become slightly more accepting of same-sex marriage (see Avery, Chase, Johansson, Litvak, Montero, & Wydra, 2007), the federal government currently does not sanction such unions. In 1996, Congress passed the ***Defense of Marriage Act*** (DOMA) which was then signed into law by President Bill Clinton. DOMA has two provisions, the first of which concerns the powers reserved to the states:

> No State, territory, or possession of the United States, or Indian tribe, shall be required to give effect to any public act, record, or judicial proceeding of any other State, territory, possession, or tribe respecting a relationship between persons of the same sex that is treated as a marriage under the laws of such other State, territory, possession, or tribe, or a right or claim arising from such relationship.
>
> (Pub. L. 104–199, sec 1, 100 Stat. 2419 [Sep. 21, 1996])

This provision means that no state (or other territory or political subdivision within the United States) is required to recognize same-sex marriages, even if those marriages were legally performed and licensed in another state. Thus, homosexual partners who obtain a marriage license in a state that recognizes same-sex marriage and who then move to a state that bans same-sex marriage will not be viewed as "married" under the laws of that state.

DOMA's second provision defines the concept of marriage (and spouse) for purposes of federal law:

> In determining the meaning of any Act of Congress, or of any ruling, regulation, or interpretation of the various administrative bureaus and agencies of the United States, the word "marriage" means only a legal union between one man and one woman as husband and wife, and the word "spouse" refers only to a person of the opposite sex who is a husband or a wife.
>
> (Pub. L. 104–199, sec 2, 100 Stat. 2419 [Sep. 21, 1996])

By explicitly defining marriage as a union between one man and one woman, DOMA prohibits the federal government from legally recognizing same-sex (or polygamous) marriages, even if those unions are legally recognized by individual states. This means that same-sex partners generally do not qualify for spousal benefits that are established by federal laws and regulations. For example, unlike heterosexual couples, homosexual couples cannot file joint federal income tax returns (and receive associated tax benefits) and they cannot receive Social Security benefits on one partner's death.

Since DOMA was signed into law, most states have adopted it as their own law or have passed amendments to their constitutions that have the same provisions as DOMA. Currently, five states (Connecticut, Iowa, Massachusetts, New Hampshire, and Vermont) and the District of Columbia are the only places in the U.S. that allow same-sex partners to legally marry. (In mid-2008, California also began to permit same-sex couples to marry, but the passage of Proposition 8—and subsequent 2009 ruling by the California Supreme Court—now prohibits same-sex couples from applying for marriage licenses. Although new licenses are currently unavailable, those granted prior to the 2009 ruling are legal.) However, other states (e.g., Hawaii, Maine, New Jersey) have enacted legislation permitting homosexual couples to enter *civil unions* (legally recognized unions that provide gay couples with the same basic rights, responsibilities, and benefits as heterosexual married couples) or to register their relationships as ***domestic partnerships*** (official unions that provide specific legal rights to partners in same-sex relationships). The future of same-sex marriage is not yet decided within the United States (or indeed, in many other countries).

MARITAL SATISFACTION

Marriage (and any long-term, committed relationship) usually is associated with personal happiness for both sexes. National surveys reveal that, at any given time, most Americans say that they are highly satisfied with their marriages (Amato et al., 2003; Campbell, Converse, & Rodgers, 1976; Veroff, Douvan, & Kulka, 1981), and married men and women appear equally satisfied (Faulkner, Davey, & Davey, 2005; Feeney, Peterson, & Noller, 1994; Litzinger & Gordon, 2005). For example, Rhonda Faulkner, Maureen Davey, and Adam Davey (2005) analyzed data from a sample of more than 1500 men and women in first-time marriages who rated their marital satisfaction, the amount of time they spent together talking or sharing an activity, and the likelihood that their marriages would end in divorce. The researchers summed participants' responses to these three items to create an overall measure of marital satisfaction on which scores could range from 1 to 21 (with 21 indicating the highest level of satisfaction). The results revealed that husbands and wives were extremely (and equally) happy with their marriages: the average score for husbands was 18.5 and the average score for wives was 18.4!

Whether married couples are able to *maintain* these happiness levels over time is another issue entirely. In exploring this question, relationship scientists have generally adopted one of two methodological approaches. *Cross-sectional studies* involve measuring (and comparing) the self-reported satisfaction or happiness of couples who have been married for different lengths of time at a single assessment point (e.g., Gilford, 1984; Gilford & Bengtson, 1979; Glass & Wright, 1977; Henry, Berg, Smith, & Florsheim, 2007; Rollins & Feldman, 1970; Sáez Sanz, 1984). Although initially popular among investigators and commonly utilized, these studies suffer from several serious problems that have reduced their use in recent years (see Glenn & Weaver, 1978). Among the most important is the fact that the spouses in each cohort or cross-sectional group are different from each other not only in terms of the age of their relationship but in a multitude of other ways as well (including their own physical age). Consequently, any difference in satisfaction between a group of couples in "younger" marriages and those in "older" marriages may be due to these other factors and not the duration of their marriages.

Only *longitudinal studies*, which follow the same couples through time, allow researchers to trace the temporal course of marital satisfaction. The use of longitudinal designs has increased dramatically in recent years, with most researchers assessing their married participants at two points fairly close together in time (e.g., Fisher & McNulty, 2008; Lu, 2006; Markides, Roberts-Jolly, Ray, Hoppe, & Rudkin, 1999; Paris & Luckey, 1966; Perren, von Wyl, Bürgin, Simoni, & von Klitzing, 2005). Although more informative than cross-sectional investigations, such *two-wave longitudinal studies* provide only limited information about the dynamics—the ebb and flow—of satisfaction over time. For example, in the course of their marriage, some couples may experience rises, declines, or plateaus in satisfaction, and others (perhaps most) may experience all three types of change; moreover, couples may experience these changes in different sequences, for different durations, and at different times. Because two-wave studies only explore the association between Time 1 and Time 2 satisfaction measurements, they permit only one of three conclusions: marital satisfaction stayed the same, decreased, or increased over that time period.

Satisfaction Trajectories

Multiple-wave longitudinal studies in which couples are assessed at more than two points over an extended period of time provide the most complete view of the dynamics of marital satisfaction. Multiple-wave investigations allow relationship scientists to use a set of statistical techniques called *growth curve analyses* to precisely chart the trajectory of change in marital happiness over time. In particular, these analyses provide two important pieces of information (*parameters*) about couples' satisfaction trajectories: the first parameter, called the *intercept*, reflects the partners' initial satisfaction level; the second parameter, the *slope*, reflects the rate of change (positive or negative) in the partners' subsequent satisfaction levels over time (see Karney, Bradbury, & Johnson, 1999; Kurdek, 2003; Raudenbush, Brennan, & Barnett, 1995). Depending on the number of assessments that take place, researchers can also determine whether the pattern of change in marital satisfaction is *linear* (i.e., the change is constant over time and there are no "bends" in the growth curve), *quadratic* (i.e., there is a phase of increased change that produces one bend in the growth curve), or *cubic* (i.e., there are two phases of increased change that produce two bends in the growth curve). Figure 7.1 illustrates these different satisfaction trajectories.

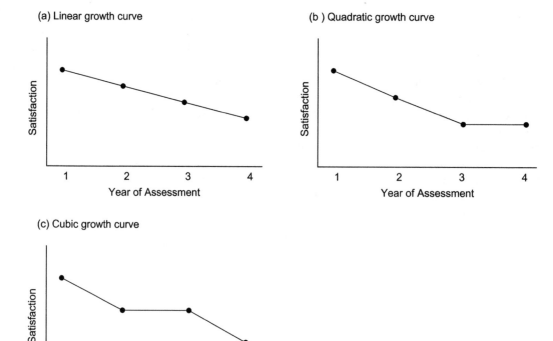

Fig. 7.1 Growth curve analyses of longitudinal data allow researchers to determine how marital satisfaction progresses or changes over time. If the satisfaction trajectory is linear, there are no "bends" in the growth curve and the rate of change is the same from assessment to assessment; that is, marital satisfaction changes steadily over time (a). If the pattern of change is quadratic, there is one bend in the growth curve; for example, marital satisfaction may decrease during the first several years of the relationship and then level off (b). If the pattern is cubic, there are two bends in the growth curve; for example, marital satisfaction may first decline, then level off, then decrease once again later (c).

This analytical technique was used by psychologists Benjamin Karney and Thomas Bradbury (1997), who asked a sample of 60 newlywed couples in their first marriages to complete four measures of marital satisfaction: (1) the Marital Adjustment Test (Locke & Wallace, 1959), which assesses spouses' global evaluation of their marriages, the amount of disagreement they experience across different areas of possible conflict, and various aspects of conflict resolution, cohesion, and communication; (2) the Quality Marriage Index (Norton, 1983), which asks spouses to rate the extent of their agreement with general statements about their marriage (e.g., "We have a good marriage," "I really feel like part of a team with my partner"); (3) the Kansas Marital Satisfaction scale (Schumm et al., 1986), a three-item measure that asks partners to rate their satisfaction with their marriage, their spouse, and their relationship with their spouse; and (4) a semantic differential scale in which spouses rated their feelings about their marriage on 15 adjective pairs (e.g., *bad–good*, *dissatisfied–satisfied*, *unpleasant–pleasant*). Participants completed all four measures at an initial assessment approximately 3 months after their marriages took place and then again at 6-month intervals over a 4-year period (this resulted in eight waves of data collection).

Growth curve analyses revealed a number of interesting findings. Examination of the intercepts (the starting point of each participant's satisfaction trajectory) revealed that husbands and wives reported relatively high marital satisfaction on all four measures as newlyweds. However, some spouses were clearly happier than others; the fact that the intercepts varied widely among participants indicated that there was substantial variability among husbands and wives in their initial levels of satisfaction. Examination of the slopes revealed that the marital satisfaction of both husbands and wives (as assessed by all four measures) declined linearly over time, with scores decreasing between 3% and 4% per year. As with initial satisfaction levels, individual differences were apparent—some participants experienced a more rapid decline in happiness than others, and a few participants (about 10%) experienced an increase in satisfaction over the first 4 years of marriage. Despite these individual differences, the satisfaction trajectories of wives and husbands within pairs did not differ; that is, a wife and her husband showed equivalent changes in satisfaction over time. Finally, Karney and Bradbury (1997) explored the relationship between the participants' satisfaction levels at the start of their marriages and their subsequent changes in satisfaction over time, something that growth curve analyses permit. Interestingly, they found that higher levels of initial satisfaction were associated with less steep declines in marital satisfaction. In explaining this finding, the researchers proposed that extremely high levels of happiness during the very beginning stages of marriage may serve a protective function, allowing spouses to maintain their positive feelings over time and thus experience a smaller decline in marital satisfaction.

Other long-term, multiple-wave studies have yielded similar results (e.g., Fisher & McNulty, 2008; Huston, McHale, & Crouter, 1986; Hirschberger, Srivastava, Marsh, Pape Cowan, & Cowan, 2009; Johnson & Bradbury, 1999; Kurdek, 1998, 1999, 2002, 2005a; Lawrence & Bradbury, 2007; Lawrence, Rothman, Cobb, Rothman, & Bradbury, 2008; Lindahl, Clements, & Markman, 1998; Umberson, Williams, Powers, Chen, & Campbell, 2005). For example, Lawrence Kurdek (e.g., 1999, 2002) followed 522 couples for a decade beginning from the time they were newlyweds (93 couples remained at the end of the 10-year period). At each annual assessment, participants completed a multi-item measure of marital quality. Growth curve analyses revealed that husbands and wives started their marriages with high levels of satisfaction and then exhibited a pattern of cubic change characterized by an initial accelerated decline, a stable plateau, and then a second accelerated decline. Specifically, couples' high newlywed levels of satisfaction declined fairly rapidly during the first 4 years of their marriages and then stabilized for awhile before declining again at about the eighth year of marriage (see Figure 7.2). Like the spouses in Karney and Bradbury's (1997) study, the husbands and wives in this investigation displayed similar satisfaction trajectories (though the wives had a steeper rate of linear—assessment to assessment—change).

In sum, longitudinal research consistently reveals that most newlywed couples (whether in their first or subsequent marriage) begin their married lives with a "honeymoon" period characterized by high amounts of satisfaction and well-being which then progressively decline during the next several years, stabilize for a period of time (often between the fourth and sixth years of marriage), and then continue to decline, assuming the couple stays together. In general, husbands and wives show the same changes in marital happiness. Finally, spouses with lower levels of satisfaction at the beginning of their marriages subsequently experience steeper declines in satisfaction than those who start their marriages at higher satisfaction levels. Of course, these results do not mean that, as time passes, marriage inevitably produces dissatisfaction for one or both spouses. In the majority of longitudinal investigations, spouses remained relatively content, with satisfaction scores that decreased over time but that were well above average at each assessment point. Thus, although happiness may decline during a marriage, it does not inevitably change into *un*happiness.

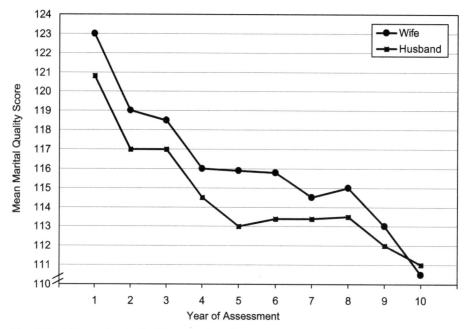

Fig. 7.2 A 10-year longitudinal investigation of marital satisfaction. Husbands and wives begin their marriages with extremely high initial levels of satisfaction, which then diminish significantly (though moderately) over time.

Source: Kurdek, L. A. (1999). The nature and predictors of the trajectory of change in marital quality for husbands and wives over the first 10 years of marriage, *Developmental Psychology*, 35, 1283–1296. Copyright © 1999 by the American Psychological Association. Figure 1 adapted with permission.

Factors Associated with Marital Happiness

Relationship scientists have identified a multitude of factors that are correlated with marital satisfaction. Many of these are personal factors—traits, dispositions, habits, beliefs, and other intra-individual attributes that an individual brings to his or her marriage (and other relationships) and that are associated with relationship success. Marital satisfaction is also associated with relational factors or characteristics that emerge from the joint properties of both partners and that reflect the combination of characteristics they bring to their interactions. For example, as we discussed in Chapter 6, there is overwhelming evidence that mutual, intimate, and responsive disclosure between partners not only contributes to the initial development of their relationship but also helps them to maintain their feelings of closeness and satisfaction over time. Parts III and IV of this textbook consider a variety of these (and other) personal and relational factors.

Environmental or contextual factors play a particularly significant role in marital satisfaction—despite the fact that most couples, as they go about their daily lives, probably are unaware of the powerful impact the physical and social environments have on their interpersonal outcomes. Two environmental factors in particular have been explored by relationship scientists: parenthood and economic hardship.

Parenthood. Of the many significant issues that spouses face during the course of their marriage, none has greater potential impact than the decision to become parents. A large literature about the impact of parenthood on marital quality exists, with the majority of studies finding that the transition to parenthood is marked by a reduction in marital satisfaction (e.g., Perren et al., 2005; for reviews, see Belsky, 1990, 2009; Sanders, Nicholson, & Floyd, 1997; Twenge, Campbell, & Foster, 2003).

For example, in one recent investigation, psychologist Erika Lawrence and her associates (Lawrence, Rothman, et al., 2008) assessed marital satisfaction levels among 104 couples at four points spanning approximately 39 months: during the beginning of their marriages (within the first 6 months), 1 month prior to the birth of their first child, 6 months after delivery, and then 6 months after that (i.e., 12 months postpartum). A sample of voluntarily childless, non-parent couples was assessed at similar points in time to provide a comparison group. As in previous marital satisfaction research, satisfaction levels were initially high and subsequently declined over time in all participant couples (husbands, wives, parents, non-parents). In addition, however, growth curve analyses revealed that parental status was significantly associated with husbands' and wives' satisfaction trajectories (specifically, with their rates of change in satisfaction). Even after controlling for initial levels of satisfaction, parents experienced steeper declines in marital satisfaction than did non-parents.

Interestingly, there is some evidence that spouses' marital satisfaction levels may increase once their children reach adulthood and leave home (see Gorchoff, John, & Helson, 2008).

Economic Hardship.   Some of the environmental pressures that couples face throughout their marriages result from decisions the partners deliberately and consciously make, such as the decision to become parents and raise a child together. Others are caused by forces over which they have little control (e.g., downsizing and subsequent job loss, changes in the local or national economy). A growing body of evidence, much of it collected by family scholar Rand Conger and his colleagues (for reviews, see Conger & Conger, 2002; Conger & Elder, 1994), demonstrates that stressful economic conditions can erode the quality of a marital relationship. During the late 1980s in rural Iowa, a severe downturn in the agricultural economy left many families on farms or in small towns facing foreclosures, unemployment, and increasingly harsh financial conditions. Conger and his colleagues (e.g., Conger et al., 1990; Conger, Rueter, & Elder, 1999) began a longitudinal study of 451 of those families, each consisting of a married couple with two school-aged children and an average annual income of around $30,000. At the first assessment, each husband and wife completed three measures of economic hardship which were combined to form a measure of *overall economic pressure*: (1) a measure of perceived ability to "make ends meet" each month (e.g., whether the couple had difficulty paying monthly bills, whether the spouses had any money left over at the end of the month); (2) a material needs index that assessed the couple's ability to purchase food, household items, clothing, medical care, and other basic items; and (3) a measure of the number of economic adjustments or cutbacks the couple had made during the past year in response to financial difficulties (e.g., giving up medical insurance). Each spouse also completed a five-item measure of *marital distress* that assessed the degree to which he or she had thought the marriage was "in trouble," considered obtaining a divorce or separation, discussed divorce or separation with a close friend, ever seriously suggested the idea of divorce to the partner, and talked about consulting a lawyer regarding divorce or separation. One year later, during the second assessment, participants completed an *emotional distress* inventory that measured the number of symptoms of depression, anxiety, and hostility they had experienced during the past week. Each couple also participated in an interaction task that enabled the researchers to observe their verbal and nonverbal behavior and assess their overall level of *marital conflict* (e.g., exchange of hostility, tense and uncomfortable silences, open conflict). Finally, during the third year of the study, spouses completed the same marital distress measure used in the first assessment.

The results were clear (see Figure 7.3). First, and not surprisingly, marital distress scores collected during the first and third assessment periods were positively correlated, indicating that couples who reported higher levels of marital distress at Time 1 were still distressed 2 years later at Time 3, whereas those who reported lower levels maintained those lower levels over time. Second, the economic pressure that spouses reported experiencing during the first assessment period not only was associated with their current levels of marital distress, but also predicted the amount of emotional distress (in the form of elevated symptoms of depression, anxiety, and hostility) each partner experienced the following year. Third, the emotional distress that husbands and wives experienced was significantly associated with their concurrent level of marital conflict (i.e., the negative nonverbal and verbal behavior they displayed during their interactions). And fourth, the amount of marital conflict that characterized the spouses' interaction patterns then contributed to their subsequent marital distress in year three of the study. In other words, these results provided evidence that adverse environmental conditions (in the form of financial hardship and economic pressure) produced personal distress and contributed to maladaptive interpersonal behaviors which, in turn, led to marital distress.

Conger and his colleagues also were interested in exploring ways to alter or effectively intervene in the economic stress process; in particular, they wondered whether social support might buffer the impact of economic pressure on the partners' levels of emotional distress (thereby disrupting the economic stress → emotional distress → marital conflict → marital distress pattern). It did. Couples who displayed higher levels of supportive behaviors toward each other during the Time 2 interaction task (e.g., who were cooperative, helpful, and sensitive, who listened attentively,

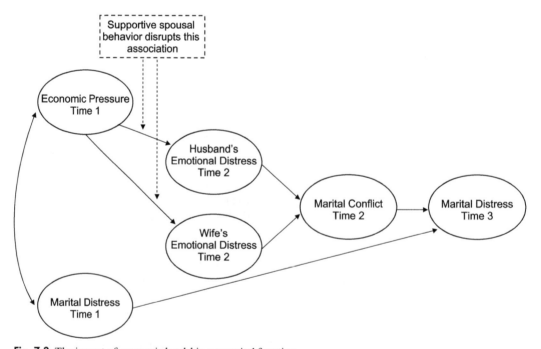

Fig. 7.3 The impact of economic hardship on marital function.

Source: Conger, R. D., Rueter, M. A., & Elder, G. H., Jr. (1999). Couple resilience to economic pressure. *Journal of Personality and Social Psychology, 76,* 54–71. Copyright © 1999 by the American Psychological Association. Figures 2 and 4 adapted with permission.

and who expressed approval of each other) did not experience increased levels of emotional distress in response to economic hardship. The researchers concluded that couples' resilience to economic hardship is associated with the provision of social support within the marriage:

> These results provide suggestive new information regarding specific properties of marriages that may be protective in the face of economic stress . . . Specifically, these findings suggest that, when faced with an immediate external stressor such as economic pressure, couples who engage in the nurturant and soothing behaviors included within the marital support construct are likely to be more resilient than those who do not.
>
> (Conger et al., 1999, p. 69)

Other researchers also have found associations between economic hardship and marital quality (e.g., Cutrona et al., 2003; Vinokur, Price, & Caplan, 1996).

In sum, the well-being of a relationship is strongly affected by pressures arising from the environmental context in which it is embedded—including those stemming from the oftentimes stressful transition from couplehood to parenthood or adverse financial and economic circumstances.

SUMMARY

Although a number of mating systems exist around the world, marriage—commonly defined socially and legally as a monogamous union between heterosexual partners—is a cross-cultural universal. Marriages can vary along a number of dimensions, and major alterations in the nature of marriage have occurred in both Western and non-Western societies. Among the most significant of these changes is an increased emphasis on love and mutual attraction as the basis for marriage and on personal (as opposed to family) choice in the selection of a marriage partner. Different types of long-term partnership exist, including cohabitation, civil unions, domestic partnerships, and marriage between same-sex partners, and research has revealed that they differ from heterosexual marriages in several ways (including a more equitable division of labor). Of all the empirical questions about marital relationships that have been asked, none has captured as much scientific attention as the course of marital satisfaction over time. A growing number of longitudinal studies reveal that satisfaction levels are relatively high in the early years of marriage, tend to decrease over time, are similar for husbands and wives, and are correlated with a variety of personal, relational, and environmental factors.

KEY CONCEPTS

Marriage (p. 110)

Monogamy (p. 110)

Polygamy (p. 110)

Polygyny (p. 110)

Polyandry (p. 111)

Polygynandry (p. 111)

Cenogamy (p. 111)

Ethnographic Atlas (p. 111)

Serial pairbonding or serial monogamy (p. 112)

Homogamy or assortment (p. 112)

Exogamy (p. 112)

Incest taboo (p. 112)

Endogamy (p. 113)

Sexual exclusivity (p. 113)

Collectivist cultures (p. 114)

Arranged marriage (p. 114)

Individualist cultures (p. 114)

Free choice or love-based marriage (p. 115)

Traditional marriage (p. 115)

Egalitarian, peer, or equal-status marriage (p. 115)

Dual-earner marriage (p. 116)

Cohabitation (p. 117)

Cohabitation effect (p. 118)

Defense of Marriage Act (p. 119)

Civil union (p. 120)

Domestic partnership (p. 120)

Cross-sectional studies (p. 121)

Longitudinal studies (p. 121)

Two-wave longitudinal studies (p. 121)

Multiple-wave longitudinal studies (p. 121)

Growth curve analyses (p. 121)

Parameters (p. 121)

Intercept (p. 121)

Slope (p. 121)

Linear satisfaction trajectory (p. 121)

Quadratic satisfaction trajectory (p. 121)

Cubic satisfaction trajectory (p. 121)

EXPLORATION EXERCISES

These exercises are designed to allow you to explore in greater detail some of the concepts and issues discussed in this chapter. There are no right or wrong answers to these exercises—they are simply meant to provide an opportunity for discussion and debate.

1. Discuss the various mating systems that occur throughout the world. Find examples of each system from modern or ancient civilizations (information should be available from the Internet or your campus or community library).

2. There is an old saying that goes something like this:

   Hogamous, higamous, man is polygamous
   Higamous, hogamous, woman is monogamous

   Evaluate this saying, using evidence from cross-cultural data on mating systems.

3. Researcher Robert Michael and his colleagues (Michael, Gagnon, Laumann, & Kolata, 1994) surveyed a large sample of adults living in the U.S. about their sexual attitudes and behaviors. One of their questions focused on infidelity, and they found that the majority of their participants held a very negative opinion about extramarital sex. This exercise is designed to explore attitudes toward infidelity among adults today. Find 10 adults—5 men and 5 women over 18 years old—and ask them to answer the following question (adapted from Michael et al.'s study):

   What is your opinion of a married person having sexual intercourse with someone other than the marriage partner—is it always wrong, sometimes wrong, or not wrong at all?

   Record the response of each of your participants using the grid on the next page. Then, sum up the total number of people who chose each of the various options.

	Always wrong	*Sometimes wrong*	*Not wrong at all*
Man 1	_____	_____	_____
Man 2	_____	_____	_____
Man 3	_____	_____	_____
Man 4	_____	_____	_____
Man 5	_____	_____	_____
Woman 1	_____	_____	_____
Woman 2	_____	_____	_____
Woman 3	_____	_____	_____
Woman 4	_____	_____	_____
Woman 5	_____	_____	_____
Men's Total:	_____	_____	_____
Women's Total:	_____	_____	_____
Overall Total:	_____	_____	_____

Based on these responses, provide answers to the following questions: (1) What was the most common attitude expressed by your participants? (2) Did their response pattern "match" the results found by earlier researchers? (3) Did men and women agree, or did they have different attitudes about infidelity?

4. Primetime television shows often include married couples among their cast of characters. Select three current television shows (either sitcoms or dramas) that include at least one married couple. Watch at least two episodes of each show. What type of marriage do these couples have? Next, find episodes of three television shows produced during an earlier decade (the 1990s, 1980s, 1970s, etc.) that include at least one married couple. Watch at least two episodes of each show. What type of marriage do these couples have? How have media depictions of married life changed over time? What impact do you think such depictions have on our own views of marriage?

PART III
Relationship Processes

This section of the textbook concerns relationship processes that shape people's interpersonal experiences and outcomes. Chapter 8 focuses on cognitive and affective processes, including relationship beliefs, positive illusions, attributions, and emotions, as well as stable dispositional tendencies related to thinking and feeling (such as adult attachment style, rejection sensitivity, and positive and negative affectivity). Chapter 9 considers communicative and supportive processes, including the ways in which caregiving and comfort are typically sought and provided as well as sex differences in intimacy, communication, and support. Chapter 10 examines the nature of love, with an emphasis on the two love types—passionate and companionate love—that have received the most attention from relationship scientists. Chapter 11 explores men's and women's sexual beliefs and attitudes, along with several aspects of sexuality—attraction, frequency, communication, and satisfaction—in beginning and established relationships.

Chapter 8
Thinking and Feeling

This chapter focuses on the related topics of *relationship cognition* and *relationship affect*—that is, on the perceptions, attributions, beliefs, and thoughts (cognition), and the feelings, sentiments, and emotions (affect), that people experience and express in their intimate relationships. These processes are deeply entwined (see Fitness & Strongman, 1991). What and how we think about our partners and our relationships influences how we feel about them. In turn, how we feel influences our beliefs and expectations, including the thoughts we generate and the conclusions we draw during interactions with our partners.

IMPLICIT RELATIONSHIP THEORIES

People develop a vast array of (not necessarily accurate) beliefs, expectations, values, attitudes, and assumptions about relationships from their own previous interpersonal experiences as well as from observing the relationships of their peers, family members, and others in society (see Chapter 4). This rich web of knowledge is organized and represented in memory in the form of cognitive structures called *relationship schemas* or *implicit relationship theories* that influence interpersonal behavior and are associated with relationship satisfaction and stability (Baldwin, 1992, 1995; Fletcher & Thomas, 1996; Knee, 1998).

Romantic Beliefs

One set of beliefs, related specifically to romantic relationships, encompasses five central notions about the nature of love and the characteristic features of romantic unions: the importance of love as a basis for marriage, the idea that love strikes without warning and often at first sight, the belief that there exists only one true love for each person, the idea that true love endures forever, and the notion that love can conquer all obstacles. The most thorough measure of these *romantic beliefs* was created by Susan Sprecher and Sandra Metts (1989), who drew on previous measurement instruments and theoretical statements about romantic ideology. The Romantic Beliefs Scale contains items that reflect the essential tenets of romanticism:

- *Love Finds a Way*: "If a relationship I have was meant to be, any obstacle can be overcome," "I believe if another person and I love each other we can overcome any differences or problems that may arise."
- *Love at First Sight*: "I am likely to fall in love almost immediately if I meet the right person," "When I find my 'true love' I will probably know it soon after we meet."
- *One and Only*: "There will be only one real love for me," "Once I experience 'true love,' I could never experience it again, to the same degree, with another person."
- *Idealization*: "The relationship I will have with my 'true love' will be nearly perfect," "The person I love will make a perfect romantic partner; for example, he/she will be completely accepting, loving, and understanding."

At least two personal factors—age and sex—are associated with romantic beliefs. For example, a descriptive study conducted by David Knox, Caroline Schacht, and Marty Zusman (1999) revealed that younger adults (19 years of age or younger) were more likely than their older counterparts (20 years of age or older) to believe in the phenomenon of "instant love" (54% vs. 36%) and to agree that "all problems can be solved if there is enough love" (61% vs. 43%). A similar age difference was reported more recently by another group of researchers (Medora, Larson, Hortaçsu, & Dave, 2002). There also appear to be fairly robust sex differences in romantic idealism, with men generally scoring higher than women on the Romantic Beliefs Scale (e.g., Sprecher & Metts, 1989, 1999; Weaver & Ganong, 2004).

Idealized romantic beliefs are associated with several aspects of relationship quality, including (not surprisingly) feelings of love for the partner. Men and women who strongly endorse the romantic ideal generally report higher levels of passionate love and liking for their partners than do their less-romantic counterparts, and they tend to fall in love with their partners at an earlier stage in their relationships (Sprecher & Metts, 1989). Moreover, highly romantic individuals think about the relationship more during a partner's absence (Cate, Koval, Lloyd, & Wilson, 1995) and express higher amounts of satisfaction with and commitment to the partner and the relationship (Sprecher & Metts, 1999; Weaver & Ganong, 2004; but see Metts, 2004). People who subscribe to a generalized romantic ideal may be more likely to feel passion, more eager to commit, and more inclined to view their partners and their relationships in a positive light than are their less overtly romantic counterparts.

Dysfunctional Relationship Beliefs

Although romanticized beliefs about love seem to be associated with positive affect and beneficial relationship experiences, other beliefs and assumptions can prove maladaptive. A set of six particularly harmful assumptions about intimate relationships have been identified by relationship scholars (Eidelson & Epstein, 1982; Epstein & Eidelson, 1981; Knee, Patrick, & Lonsbary, 2003). These *dysfunctional relationship beliefs* include the notions that:

- *Disagreement is Destructive*: Partners who truly love each other never fight, argue, or disagree; disagreements and conflicts are a sign of relationship distress, portend imminent dissolution, and reflect a lack of love and intimacy.
- *"Mindreading" is Expected and Essential*: Partners who truly understand and care about one another should be able to sense each other's needs, moods, and preferences without being told; partners who cannot easily "read" each other must not really love each other.
- *Partners (and Relationships) Cannot Change*: It is impossible for partners to change themselves or the quality of their relationship; if a relationship turns "sour," there is nothing anyone can do to make it better.
- *Relational Sex Should Be Perfect*: Sex between two loving partners should always be fulfilling and wonderful; partners should always desire each other sexually and find their sexual interactions to be completely satisfying.
- *Men and Women Are Fundamentally Different*: Men and women differ dramatically in their personalities and relationship needs; in heterosexual relationships, it is virtually impossible for the partners to ever figure each other out.
- *Partners Are Either Compatible (and Destined to be Together) or They Are Not*: Relationships are either destined to work or they are not; a successful relationship will seem "perfect" right from the start; if partners are meant for one another then the relationship will last, but if they are not then no amount of effort will make this happen.

Exhibit 8.1 contains items from the Relationship Belief Inventory (RBI), which is one of the most commonly used measures of dysfunctional relationship beliefs.

These global relationship beliefs may have a number of adverse interpersonal consequences. People who subscribe to the notion that a friend should be able to "read" their emotions easily and accurately, that family members should never argue or disagree, or that a romantic partner should be perpetually sexually desirable and desirous, might find themselves disappointed when their actual interpersonal experiences do not meet or exceed their expectations (in the words of Interdependence Theory, when outcomes fall below comparison level; see Chapter 6). Indeed, research reveals that scores on the RBI are negatively correlated with relationship satisfaction and adjustment among married and dating couples (Bradbury & Fincham, 1988; Emmelkamp, Krol, Sanderman, & Rüphan, 1987; Goodwin & Gaines, 2004; Haferkamp, 1994; Sullivan & Schwebel, 1995), as well as with young adults' expectations regarding future positive relationship outcomes (such as maintaining a long-lasting, happy, and mutually satisfying marriage; Dostal & Langhinrichsen-Rohling, 1997).

Exhibit 8.1 Sample Items from the Relationship Belief Inventory

The Relationship Belief Inventory, developed by Roy Eidelson and Norman Epstein (1982), is a 40-item inventory that assesses the extent to which people endorse five dysfunctional beliefs. Below are some sample items assessing each of these beliefs.

(1) Disagreement is Destructive

- *"When my partner and I disagree, I feel like our relationship is falling apart."*
- *"If your partner expresses disagreement with your ideas, he/she probably does not think highly of you."*

(2) "Mindreading" is Expected and Essential

- *"People who have a close relationship can sense each other's needs as if they could read each other's mind."*
- *"A partner should know what you are thinking or feeling without you having to tell."*

(3) Partners (and Relationships) Cannot Change

- *"I do not expect my partner to be able to change."*
- *"Damages done early in a relationship probably cannot be reversed."*

(4) Relational Sex Should Be Perfect

- *"A good sexual partner can get himself/herself aroused for sex whenever necessary."*
- *"I get upset if I think I have not completely satisfied my partner sexually."*

(5) Men and Women Are Fundamentally Different

- *"One of the major causes of marital problems is that men and women have different emotional needs."*
- *"You can't really understand someone of the opposite sex."*

SOURCE: Eidelson, R. J., & Epstein, N. (1982). Cognition and relationship maladjustment: Development of a measure of dysfunctional relationship beliefs. *Journal of Consulting and Clinical Psychology, 50,* 715–720. Copyright © 1982 by the American Psychological Association. Items reprinted with permission.

Dysfunctional cognitions also are associated with maladaptive responses to negative relationship events. One investigation (Knee, 1998) revealed that men and women who scored high on a measure of destiny beliefs (e.g., who believed that partners are meant to be together or they are not) reported greater use of ineffective coping strategies—including denial (e.g., pretending the upsetting event has not happened), mental disengagement (e.g., turning to work or other activities to take one's mind off the problem), and behavioral disengagement (e.g., reducing the amount of effort put into actively solving the problem)—when faced with an upsetting relationship event, than did participants who did not endorse such beliefs. Similarly, behavioral observations of married couples' conflict discussions demonstrates that spouses who hold maladaptive beliefs (as assessed on the RBI) are more likely to reciprocate, and less likely to respond positively to, each other's negative behavior (Bradbury & Fincham, 1993). In light of these findings, it is no wonder that many therapeutic interventions focus on replacing people's maladaptive beliefs with more functional expectations and assumptions about intimate relationships (see Chapter 15).

In sum, implicit relationship theories do appear to "influence one's relationship-relevant perceptions, emotions, and behavior in meaningful ways" (Knee et al., 2003, p. 45). In particular, people who rigidly adhere to dysfunctional beliefs seem less able (or willing) to cope with conflict and other interpersonal difficulties that arise in their relationships and more likely to experience dissatisfaction.

POSITIVE ILLUSIONS

In addition to generalized expectations and assumptions about close relationships, men and women also develop and possess beliefs about their own specific relationships, their own partners, and themselves. As we will discuss, many of these beliefs are illusory—they are more positive than can be logically sustained by objective reality or supported by the laws of probability. Such *positive illusions* have important implications—some good, some bad—for relationship experiences and outcomes.

About the Self

A vast body of social psychological research reveals that, as people go about their daily lives, they tend to interpret the situations they encounter and the events they experience in a decidedly self-centered, self-aggrandizing, and self-justifying way (Greenwald, 1980). For example, the majority of men and women possess *unrealistically positive self-views*—they judge positive traits as overwhelmingly more characteristic of themselves than negative traits; dismiss any unfavorable attributes they may have as inconsequential while at the same time emphasizing the uniqueness and importance of their favorable attributes; recall personal successes more readily than failures; take credit for positive outcomes while steadfastly denying responsibility for negative ones; and generally view themselves as "better" than the average person (and as better than they actually are viewed by others; for reviews, see Mezulis, Abramson, Hyde, & Hankin, 2004; Taylor & Brown, 1988). In addition, people often fall prey to an *illusion of control* consisting of exaggerated perceptions of their own ability to master and control events and situations that are solely or primarily determined by chance (e.g., Langer, 1975; for reviews, see Taylor & Brown, 1988; Thompson, 1999). Moreover, most individuals are *unrealistically optimistic* about the future, firmly believing that positive life events are more likely (and negative events are less likely) to happen to them than to others (Weinstein, 1980, 1984). Researchers have found that college students, for example, believe that they are significantly more likely than their peers to experience a wide array of positive outcomes, including liking their post-graduation jobs, earning a high starting salary, receiving a work-related award, owning their own homes, having their houses double in value within the first 5 years of ownership, achieving a long and happy marriage, and living past 80. Similarly, young adults believe that they are less likely than their peers to experience such negative life events as a getting mugged, being fired from a job, owning a "lemon," undergoing an early divorce, and falling prey to venereal disease, sterility, hepatitis, diabetes, lung cancer, high blood pressure, warts, sunstroke, vitamin deficiency, and the common cold (e.g., Dewberry, Ing, James, Nixon, & Richardson, 1990; Regan, Snyder, & Kassin, 1995; Weinstein, 1980, 1982, 1983, 1984).

These cognitive processes, collectively known as *self-serving biases* or *self-enhancement biases*, not only function to protect and enhance people's self-esteem (see Taylor & Brown, 1988, 1994) but also color perceptions of the events that occur in their closest and most intimate relationships. For example, two early investigations (Ross & Sicoly, 1979; Thompson & Kelley, 1981) demonstrated that married individuals routinely overestimate the extent of their own contributions, relative to their spouses, to a variety of joint marital activities (e.g., planning mutual leisure activities, carrying the conversation, resolving conflict, providing emotional support, initiating discussions about the relationship). Moreover, they more readily call to mind instances of the specific ways in which they (as opposed to their partners) contribute to each activity.

Research also demonstrates that people tend to adopt a self-serving orientation when interpreting and responding to negative relationship events. Judith Feeney and Andrew Hill (2006) asked a sample of dating or married couples to provide retrospective accounts of two hurtful relationship events—one perpetrated by the male partner and one perpetrated by the female partner—that had occurred during the previous year. Participants described the circumstances leading up to the event, what they or their partners said or did that was hurtful, and what happened after the event. The researchers then rated these accounts for the extent to which they (1) *highlighted* the severity of the event (e.g., by accentuating the victim's violated expectations, using strong language, or emphasizing intentionality; "He did it deliberately"); (2) *downplayed* the severity of the event (e.g., by noting extenuating circumstances, minimizing intentionality, or justifying the event; "I didn't mean to hurt her feelings"); and (3) contained evidence of *contrition* on the part of the perpetrator (e.g., discussion of the situation, apology for the event, acknowledgment of hurtful behavior, active attempts to make amends). The results provided clear evidence of self-serving bias. First, victims and perpetrators provided radically different accounts of the same hurtful event, with victims highlighting and perpetrators downplaying the event's severity and with victims perceiving less contrition on the part of perpetrators than perpetrators themselves reported expressing. Second, across events, the nature of participants' accounts shifted according to the role in which they found themselves. That is, after hurting a partner's feelings, men and women excused or justified their transgression by pointing to extenuating circumstances and emphasized the extent to which they had attempted to make amends for their hurtful behavior. However, after being hurt by a partner, those same men and women accentuated the extent of the harm they had suffered and were relatively unwilling to acknowledge the partner's positive efforts to atone for the transgression.

Although self-serving biases may benefit the individual partners by protecting their self-esteem, such cognitions may have additional, less-than-beneficial consequences for their relationship. For example, individuals who repeatedly overestimate their contributions to a friendship or romantic relationship may end up feeling under-benefited relative to their partners; over time, these feelings of inequity are likely to produce dissatisfaction and even contribute to the dissolution of the relationship (see Chapter 6). In addition, believing that "divorce won't happen to me," men and women who are overly optimistic about their chances of romantic happiness may not pay sufficient attention to identifying and avoiding common relational pitfalls (such as demand–withdraw and other dysfunctional interaction styles; see Chapter 15). Similarly, people who possess an exaggerated sense of their own control over their partners' behavior and the events in their close relationships may be ill-prepared to deal with conflict and other unexpected interpersonal situations that inevitably arise. Indeed, developmental researchers have found that mothers with high levels of illusory control—that is, who feel that they are able to control children's behavior more than is actually possible—demonstrate less behavioral sensitivity, responsiveness, and guidance, and exhibit more negative affect, when interacting with their own infants and toddlers (Donovan, Leavitt, & Walsh, 2000; Donovan, Taylor, & Leavitt, 2007).

About the Partner and the Relationship

People not only perceive their own attributes, behaviors, and future outcomes in an overly positive manner, but they also tend to idealize the characteristics of their intimate partners and relationships. Several *relationship-enhancement biases* have been identified. For example, research reveals a pervasive *memory bias* for relationship events, such that partners recall more positive experiences, fewer negative experiences, and greater improvement over time in relationship well-being than actually occurred (e.g., Halford, Keefer, & Osgarby, 2002; Karney & Coombs, 2000). A longitudinal study conducted by Susan Sprecher (1999) illustrates this phenomenon. In her 5-year investigation, a large sample of dating couples first completed a series of multi-item scales to assess their current levels of love, commitment, and satisfaction, as well as single-item measures of those same affective experiences (e.g., "In general, how satisfied are you with your relationship?"; these single-item scales were combined to form an overall index of positive feelings). Six months later, and then once during each of the following 3 years, participants completed the same measures of positive affect, thus allowing the researcher to assess *actual changes* in love, commitment, and satisfaction over time. In addition, at each follow-up participants also rated the extent to which their love and affection for the partner, commitment to the relationship, and satisfaction with the relationship had changed in the past year; these ratings allowed the researcher to measure *perceived changes* in positive affect over time. The results revealed a clear tendency to recast relationship history in a favorable manner. Specifically, at all four follow-up times participants reported that each specific experience—love and affection, satisfaction, and commitment—had significantly increased since they had last participated in the study. However, these perceptions were not substantiated by examination of participants' actual scores on measures of those same experiences taken over the course of the investigation. Scores on the multi-item measures of love, satisfaction, and commitment, and on the overall index of positive feelings, did not change between the first and second years, the second and third years, or any adjacent data collection waves, but instead remained uniformly high. In short, with each passing year participants maintained that their love (and satisfaction and commitment) had grown—even though it had not (see Figure 8.1).

Not only do people rewrite the history of their relationships, but they also tend to view those relationships (and their partners) in an overly positive manner (e.g., Barelds & Dijkstra, 2009; Buunk, 2001; Buunk & van der Eijnden, 1997; Murray & Holmes, 1999; Murray, Holmes, & Griffin, 1996a; Neff & Karney, 2002; Van Lange & Rusbult, 1995). A large body of research reveals that most of us:

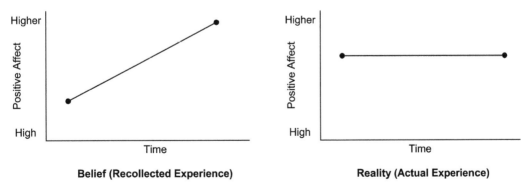

Fig. 8.1 Research reveals that partners tend to rewrite their relationship history so that it seems more positive than it actually was. Specifically, although partners in stable, satisfying relationships often do not experience significant increases over time in their (relatively high) scores on measures of positive affect (love, satisfaction, commitment), they typically remember such changes as having occurred. In other words, they believe that they love their partners more now than they did before (even though they do not).

- perceive our own relationships as superior to the relationships of other people;
- view our current partners more favorably than we view other possible partners;
- view our partners more positively than our partners view themselves;
- minimize any seeming faults that our partners possess by miscasting them as virtues ("Sure, she can seem kind of rude, but that's because she's so honest") or downplaying their significance ("He's not very communicative, but it's no big deal. He shows his love for me in many other ways");
- accentuate our partners' virtues by emphasizing their overall impact on the relationship ("Because she is so honest, I know I can trust her completely—she will never give me any reason to doubt her love").

In an early demonstration of *partner idealization*, scholars Sandra Murray, John Holmes, and Dale Griffin (1996a; also see Murray, Holmes, & Griffin, 1996b) asked both members of a sample of dating and married couples to rate themselves and each other on a variety of positive (e.g., kind and affectionate, tolerant and accepting, open and disclosing, responsive to my needs, intelligent and witty) and negative (e.g., critical and judgmental, controlling and dominant, thoughtless, lazy, moody) attributes. Participants also provided their perceptions of the ideal partner (i.e., how they would most prefer their current partner to score with respect to those attributes) and the typical or average partner (i.e., the extent to which they believed that each trait characterized the general population of partners). Ratings for negative attributes were reverse scored, and ratings across all of the traits then were summed and averaged to form a measure of overall impression favorability or positivity. Comparisons of these ratings (self, partner, perfect partner, average partner) provided evidence for the existence of positive illusions. First, participants' perceptions of the "perfect" partner were strongly linked to their perceptions of their current partner—the higher their expectations for the ideal partner, the more positive were their ratings of their own current dating partners or spouses (in other words, the more favorably they wanted their current partners to score on the attributes, the more favorably they perceived their partners as actually scoring). Second, participants' perceptions of their partners were significantly more positive than the partners' own self-perceptions; among both dating and married couples, individuals rated their partners more favorably (that is, higher on the positive traits and lower on the negative traits) than the partners rated themselves. And third, participants perceived their partners in a more favorable manner than they did the typical partner, rating their own partner's attributes more positively than the typical partner's attributes. Together, these findings suggest that most people "see their partners through the filters provided by their ideals, essentially seeing them . . . as they wish to see them" (Murray et al., 1996a, p. 86).

The idealization effect is not limited to perceptions of romantic partners. Research indicates that parents view their children as possessing more positive qualities than the average child (Cohen & Fowers, 2004; Wenger & Fowers, 2008). Similarly, adults rate their friends more favorably than those friends rate themselves (Toyama, 2002). Does the pervasive tendency the majority of us have to idealize our intimate partners mean that love—and friendship and parenthood—is blind? Not necessarily. For example, although the participants in Murray and colleagues' (1996a) study did indeed evaluate their partners more favorably than the partners rated themselves, the two sets of ratings were significantly correlated, indicating a fair degree of convergence between participants' impressions of a partner and that partner's own self-perceptions. Similarly, other researchers have found that most men and women, while maintaining an overwhelmingly positive view of a partner's *global* worth or character, nonetheless demonstrate a fairly accurate view of that person's *specific* strengths and weaknesses (Neff & Karney, 2002). In sum, people appear to see their partners as their partners see themselves—only better.

Interestingly, not everyone is equally likely to engage in relationship enhancement (or self-enhancement, for that matter). A key variable in the extent to which we view our partners and our relationships in an overly positive way is our current affective state. People who are unhappy—who are dissatisfied with their relationships or simply in the grips of a temporary bad mood—are less prone to idealization (Forgas, Levinger, & Moylan, 1994; Fowers, Lyons, Montel, & Shaked, 2001). In fact, dissatisfied individuals often demonstrate a ***negativity bias*** such that they anticipate unpleasant behavior from the partner, focus on the flawed or displeasing aspects of the partner's character, and remember and rewrite the history of the relationship in an unfavorable way (Halford et al., 2002; Vanzetti, Notarius, & NeeSmith, 1992; also see Tashiro & Frazier, 2007). The tendency for current feelings to influence cognitive appraisals of the partner and the relationship is called ***sentiment override*** (Weiss, 1980)—the individual's overarching positive or negative sentiment for the partner functions as a filter through which all aspects of the relationship are perceived, thus overriding the objective valence of specific partner actions or relationship events.

Like the illusions we hold about ourselves, the idealistic fantasies we weave around our partners and our relationships may have both beneficial and detrimental consequences. Some scholars have posited that reality—possessing an accurate, unbiased view of the partner and the relationship, warts and all—is the key to interpersonal happiness (e.g., De La Ronde & Swann, 1998; Swann, De La Ronde, & Hixon, 1994; Swann, Hixon, & De La Ronde, 1992). From this perspective, enhancement biases may contribute to relationship distress by blinding us to very real flaws in our partners' personalities and to potentially problematic interaction patterns. When these excessively positive visions are tested by the mundane and less-than-glamorous realities of daily interpersonal life, the disenchantment that follows may be so severe that it threatens the very survival of the relationship (we will discuss this possibility further in Chapter 14). Other scholars have adopted a different position, proposing that enhancement biases may contribute to interpersonal happiness by sustaining people's beliefs in their partners through difficult times and in the face of uncertain outcomes (e.g., Murray, 1999; Murray, Holmes, & Griffin, 2003). From this perspective, positive illusions serve a protective function by dispelling doubt about the partner and allowing individuals to feel secure and confident about the future of the relationship. Current evidence suggests that there is an element of truth in both perspectives. Partners are happiest and most satisfied when they are ***realistically idealistic***—that is, when they possess an accurate understanding of each other's most self-relevant attributes but maintain an exaggeratedly positive view of each other's overall character and their relationship.

ATTRIBUTIONS

Relationship scientists have identified another set of cognitive factors—specifically, the ***attributions*** or explanations that individuals make for a partner's behavior—that also appear to be associated with interpersonal function and well-being (Bradbury & Fincham, 1990; Fletcher & Fincham, 1991; Manusov, 1990). ***Causal attributions*** concern the perceived causes of behavior. When seeking to understand why his or her partner acted in a certain way, an individual makes a determination about ***locus*** (the extent to which the cause of the behavior rests in the partner as opposed to the external situation), ***stability*** (the extent to which the cause of the behavior is likely to change over time), and ***globality*** (the extent to which the cause of the behavior affects other areas of the relationship). ***Responsibility attributions*** concern the perceived responsibility or accountability for behavior. When considering the partner's action, the individual also comes to a conclusion about ***motivation*** (the extent to which the behavior reflects negative or positive, selfish or selfless, and harmful or harmless motives), *intention* (the extent to which the behavior is deliberate, voluntary, and freely chosen), and *blame* (the extent to which the behavior is justified by mitigating circumstances and therefore worthy of blame or praise).

In their exhaustive programs of research, Thomas Bradbury and Frank Fincham provide compelling evidence that these attributional dimensions are reliably associated with current relationship satisfaction and may even exert a causal influence on future relationship quality (e.g., Bradbury & Fincham, 1990; Bradbury, Fincham, & Beach, 2000; Fincham & Bradbury, 1992; Fincham, Harold, & Gano-Phillips, 2000; Fincham, Paleari, & Regalia, 2002; Karney & Bradbury, 2000). In particular, these researchers have found that people who are satisfied with their relationships generally explain the partner's positive behavior as being due to his or her internal disposition and believe that the cause of the behavior will be stable over time and globally influential in a variety of relational situations; moreover, they tend to perceive the positive behavior as freely chosen and intentional, and therefore worthy of praise (see Figure 8.2). At the same time, they generally attribute negative partner behavior to external circumstance or the partner's temporary state and believe that these circumstances or states will be unstable over time and specific to that one relational area. Moreover, they assume that the negative behavior was unintentional, and thus tend not to blame the partner for the behavior. By enhancing the impact of positive events and minimizing the impact of negative events, this particular set of attributions appears to promote relational well-being.

Dissatisfied partners make the opposite attributions. Specifically, they attribute each other's positive behaviors to situational (rather than dispositional) causes, assume that these causes are unstable and unlikely to be repeated, and believe that these causes are operative in one specific situation rather than in many or all relational situations (see Figure 8.3). Essentially, a partner who does something positive is perceived as "having acted unintentionally and with less positive and more negative intent, having little control over the cause of the event, being influenced by a temporary state rather than by a persisting trait, behaving involuntarily, being motivated by selfish concerns, being less deserving of praise, and having a less positive attitude toward the respondent" (Bradbury & Fincham, 1990, p. 5). Conversely, negative behaviors are attributed to the partner's enduring dispositional characteristics; these causes are believed to be stable over time and are perceived as globally influential across relational situations rather than as specific to one or a few situations. In addition, the partner is seen as having acted deliberately and with harmful intent, and consequently as deserving of blame. By discounting positive events and accentuating the impact of negative ones, these kinds of attributions promote relational distress.

Additional research reveals that attributional processes may play an important role in determining how well partners respond to stressful life events. For example, in one investigation, psychologists James Graham and Collie Conoley (2006) asked a sample of married couples to complete a variety of measures including a stress questionnaire that assessed the level of stress experienced by each partner within the past year (these numbers were combined to form a total accumulated stress score for the couple), a relationship attribution questionnaire that determined the extent to which the partners attributed negative spousal behaviors to internal, stable, and global causes, and a marital adjustment scale that provided an overall index of marital quality. The results revealed that relationship attributions *moderated* the association between marital quality and accumulated life stressors. This means that while the level of stress that the couples experienced was related to their marital quality, the relationship (between stress and marital quality) was partly dependent on the kind of attributions that the couples made for each other's behavior. Specifically, there was a strong and negative correlation between stress and marital quality among couples who made negative relationship attributions: couples who attributed their spouses' negative behavior to dispositional,

Relationship-Promoting Attributions

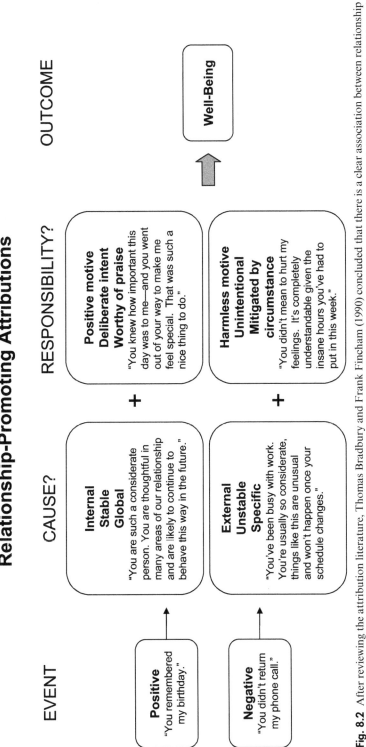

EVENT   CAUSE?   RESPONSIBILITY?   OUTCOME

Positive
"You remembered my birthday."

Internal
Stable
Global
"You are such a considerate person. You are thoughtful in many areas of our relationship and are likely to continue to behave this way in the future."

+

Positive motive
Deliberate intent
Worthy of praise
"You knew how important this day was to me—and you went out of your way to make me feel special. That was such a nice thing to do."

Well-Being

Negative
"You didn't return my phone call."

External
Unstable
Specific
"You've been busy with work. You're usually so considerate, things like this are unusual and won't happen once your schedule changes."

+

Harmless motive
Unintentional
Mitigated by circumstance
"You didn't mean to hurt my feelings. It's completely understandable given the insane hours you've had to put in this week."

Fig. 8.2 After reviewing the attribution literature, Thomas Bradbury and Frank Fincham (1990) concluded that there is a clear association between relationship satisfaction and attributional dimensions. People in satisfying or non-distressed relationships tend to attribute positive partner behaviors to internal, stable, and global causes, and to perceive the behaviors as freely chosen and worthy of praise. They tend to attribute negative partner behaviors to external, unstable, and specific causes, and to view them as unintentional and therefore not blameworthy. This set of attributions promotes relational well-being by enhancing the impact of positive events and minimizing the impact of negative events.

Relationship-Harming Attributions

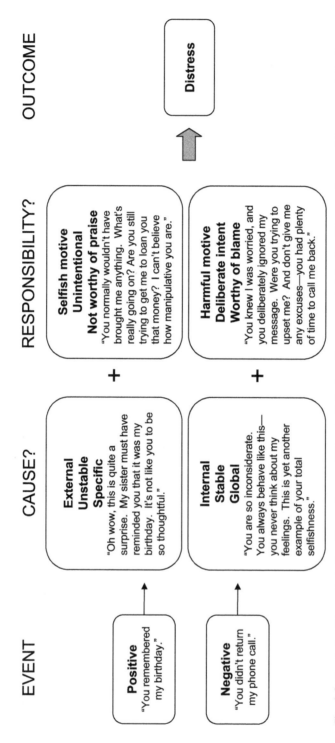

EVENT   CAUSE?   RESPONSIBILITY?   OUTCOME

Positive
"You remembered my birthday."

**External
Unstable
Specific**
"Oh wow, this is quite a surprise. My sister must have reminded you that it was my birthday. It's not like you to be so thoughtful."

\+

**Selfish motive
Unintentional
Not worthy of praise**
"You normally wouldn't have brought me anything. What's really going on? Are you still trying to get me to loan you that money? I can't believe how manipulative you are."

Negative
"You didn't return my phone call."

**Internal
Stable
Global**
"You are so inconsiderate. You always behave like this— you never think about my feelings. This is yet another example of your total selfishness."

\+

**Harmful motive
Deliberate intent
Worthy of blame**
"You knew I was worried, and you deliberately ignored my message. Were you trying to upset me? And don't give me any excuses—you had plenty of time to call me back."

Distress

Fig. 8.3 People in distressed relationships make very different attributions for a partner's behavior. They attribute positive partner behaviors to external, unstable, and specific causes, and view them as unintentional, motivated by selfish concerns, and not worthy of praise. Conversely, they attribute negative partner behaviors to internal, stable, and global causes, and perceive them as stemming from deliberate and harmful motives. This set of attributions diminishes or discounts the impact of positive events and accentuates the impact of negative events, thereby promoting relational distress.

stable, and global causes experienced lower levels of marital adjustment in the face of an accumulation of life stressors. However, stress and marital quality were unrelated among couples who made positive relationship attributions: couples who attributed their spouse's negative behavior to situational, unstable, and specific causes did not report lower levels of marital adjustment in the face of an accumulation of life stressors. The researchers concluded that "the presence of negative marital attributions appears to have the potential to make the relationship of couples more vulnerable to the impact of stressful events, while the presence of relationship-enhancing attributions appears to serve as a protective factor" (Graham & Conoley, 2006, pp. 237–238).

Clearly, the kinds of attributions that people make about their partners' behaviors are closely associated with both the overall quality of their relationships and how well those relationships can withstand negative life events. (Chapter 14 provides additional discussion of attributions, focusing on their role during conflict episodes.)

DISPOSITIONAL THINKING AND FEELING TENDENCIES

We have seen that people enter their relationships with pre-existing expectations and assumptions, develop specific beliefs about their partners, and make attributions for positive and negative events that arise during their unions—and that these expectations, beliefs, and attributions are associated with various interpersonal outcomes. In addition, relationship scientists have identified a number of relatively stable cognitive and affective dispositional tendencies—characteristic ways of perceiving, interpreting, and emotionally responding to interpersonal events—that have important relational implications. Four in particular have received a great deal of scrutiny: negative affectivity, positive affectivity, adult attachment style, and rejection sensitivity.

Negative Affectivity

Negative affectivity, also called *neuroticism* or *negative emotionality*, refers to a person's sensitivity to negative stimuli, propensity to experience negative emotions, and stability of behavior over time (Clark, Watson, & Mineka, 1994; Tellegen, 1985; Watson & Clark, 1984). Individuals high on negative affectivity hold unfavorable views of themselves and the world around them, tend to feel inadequate and dissatisfied, and are prone to frequent and intense negative emotions. They are generally moody, highly strung, sensitive, and touchy. People low on this disposition are emotionally stable and much less prone to negative emotional experiences. In general, they are calm, even-tempered, relaxed, and secure. The potential interpersonal correlates and consequences of negative affectivity have been examined most thoroughly in the realm of romantic relationships, with researchers consistently finding that this particular disposition predicts dissolution (e.g., Eysenck, 1980; Tucker, Kressin, Spiro, & Ruscio, 1998) and dissatisfaction or maladjustment (e.g., Barelds, 2005; Barelds & Barelds-Dijkstra, 2006; Bouchard, Lussier, & Sabourin, 1999; Donnellan, Assad, Robins, & Conger, 2007; Donnellan, Conger, & Bryant, 2004; Holland & Roisman, 2008; Karney & Bradbury, 1997).

In one classic longitudinal investigation, E. Lowell Kelly and James Conley (1987) followed a sample of 249 married couples from the time of their engagement during the 1930s to 1980. The first data collection took place during the period from 1935 to 1941. During these years, and prior to their marriage, the members of each couple were rated by five of their acquaintances on various personality traits, including neuroticism. In addition, after marriage, the spouses provided annual reports about their current levels of marital satisfaction (on a scale ranging from *extraordinarily happy* to *extremely unhappy*); these annual reports were averaged to provide a measure of marital satisfaction in early marriage. The second data collection occurred in 1954–55, and the third and final collection took place in 1980–81. During these two periods, husbands and wives were asked how satisfied they were with their marriage, whether they would still marry their spouse if they had their life to live over, whether they had ever regretted their marriage, and whether they had ever considered divorce or separation from their spouse. Responses to these four questions were then summed to create an overall index of marital satisfaction. At each of the various assessment times, the researchers also collected information on each couple's marital status (i.e., whether or not the spouses had gotten divorced). The results revealed that both marital outcomes—dissolution and satisfaction—were predicted by initial levels of neuroticism. For example, participants who divorced had higher pre-marriage levels of neuroticism than did their still-married counterparts. In addition, neuroticism was related to satisfaction among stably married couples (defined as couples who were still married at the time of any given assessment). Men and women who were higher in neuroticism at the beginning of the study reported more unhappiness and less satisfaction with their marriages early and later on in their lives than did men and women with lower levels of this trait.

In recent years, scientists have sought to discover why this particular disposition seems to negatively impact an individual's ability to find interpersonal happiness and stability. One possibility they have explored is that negative affectivity may contribute to dysfunctional exchanges between partners. For example, researcher Holly Hatton and her colleagues (Hatton, Donnellan, Maysn, Feldman, Larsen-Rife, & Conger, 2008; also see Donnellan, Larsen-Rife, & Conger, 2005) assessed the personality traits of a sample of young adults during their senior year in high school. A year after that initial assessment (and biannually for the next 6 years), participants engaged in an interaction with a close friend or romantic partner in which they discussed an area of disagreement in their relationship. These interactions were videotaped, and the researchers examined the participants' behavior for the presence of both positive (e.g., warmth, support, responsiveness) and negative (e.g., hostility, coercion, anger) features. The analyses revealed that negative emotionality significantly predicted both positive and negative interaction behavior. The higher a participant scored on negative affectivity, the more often he or she exhibited negative behavior and the less often he or she displayed positive behavior during the problem-solving discussion.

The evidence with respect to negative affectivity or neuroticism, then, is fairly straightforward. High levels of this personality trait are associated with relationship disruption and dissatisfaction. In addition, negative affectivity appears to manifest itself in maladaptive behaviors—including a failure to respond supportively and positively and a tendency to engage in coercive and negative acts—that are not at all conducive to relational well-being. Additional research exploring the relationship between this dispositional variable and social support is presented in Chapter 9.

Positive Affectivity

Positive affectivity (also called *extraversion* or *positive emotionality*) reflects the degree to which an individual responds positively to the social environment and experiences pleasant emotional states (Clark et al., 1994; Watson, 2002). People high on this personality dimension are actively and positively oriented toward the social environment. They seek out others, enjoy social interaction, behave in an outgoing and sociable manner, and tend to be cheerful, energetic, and self-confident. People low on positive affectivity or extraversion (sometimes referred to as *introverts*) are wary of social interaction, prefer solitary activities, and direct their attention inward to their own thoughts and feelings. Introverts are generally withdrawn, quiet, and reserved, and report lower levels of energy, self-confidence, and positive emotional experience.

Research reveals that positive affectivity or extraversion is positively correlated with the quality of children's peer relationships (e.g., Jensen-Campbell et al., 2002) and adults' friendships (e.g., Berry, Willingham, & Thayer, 2000; Neyer & Asendorpf, 2001). However, the results are inconclusive with respect to romantic relationships. For instance, although some researchers find that positive affectivity in one or both spouses is associated with *higher* levels of marital quality (e.g., Donnellan et al., 2004; Gordon & Baucom, 2009; Nemechek & Olson, 1996), others find that it is correlated with *lower* levels of adjustment and well-being (e.g., Bouchard et al., 1999; Lester, Haig, & Monello, 1989), and still others find no association at all between this dispositional tendency and marital satisfaction (e.g., Neyer & Voigt, 2004). The results are also mixed with respect to the association between positive affectivity and marital dissolution. Some researchers find that this personality trait is significantly associated with the likelihood of divorce. For example, psychologists Victor Jockin, Matt McGue, and David Lykken (1996) asked a sample of more than 3000 men and women who had been married at least once to complete a personality inventory that measured their levels of positive emotionality and various other traits. Participants also provided information about their marital histories, including whether or not they had ever divorced. The researchers then examined whether the participants' divorce status could be predicted reliably from their extraversion scores. The results indicated that it could be; that is, the higher men and women scored on positive emotionality, the greater the likelihood they had experienced marital dissolution. Other researchers, however, have not found any direct relationship between positive affectivity/extraversion and relationship termination (e.g., Kurdek, 1993).

Adult Attachment Style

Building on the theoretical foundation laid by John Bowlby (see Chapter 3), relationship scholars have proposed the concept of **adult attachment style** (Bartholomew & Horowitz, 1991; Collins, 1996; Hazan & Shaver, 1987), which refers to a person's characteristic beliefs, attitudes, and expectations about the self (worthy of love and support vs. not worthy of love and support), other people (available and supportive vs. unavailable and rejecting), and relationships (rewarding vs. punishing). Most attachment researchers and theorists now agree that four adult attachment styles exist, each reflecting the combination of two underlying dimensions (Feeney & Collins, 2003; see Figure 8.4). The **anxiety dimension** refers to the extent to which an individual worries or is concerned about being rejected or unloved by others; the **avoidance dimension** refers to the degree to which an individual actively avoids or approaches intimacy, connection, and closeness with others. Men and women who possess a **secure attachment style** have low levels of attachment-related anxiety and attachment-related avoidance. They believe that they are worthy of love and support and expect to receive these responses from others and they are comfortable with closeness and believe that relationships can be—and often are—highly rewarding. Men and women with a **preoccupied attachment style** (also called an **anxious/ambivalent** style) have a high level of attachment-related anxiety combined with a low level of attachment-related avoidance. These individuals are preoccupied with intimacy issues and have an exaggerated need for closeness with others yet at the same time are intensely anxious about being abandoned or rejected. People who possess a **dismissing-avoidant attachment style** demonstrate the opposite pattern; they have a low level of attachment-related anxiety and a high level of attachment-related avoidance. These self-reliant men and women value independence more than they do the formation of intimate relationships with others. Finally, individuals with a **fearful-avoidant attachment style** are high in both attachment-related anxiety and avoidance; these adults truly desire to form close, intimate bonds with others but at the same time are highly fearful of being rejected. As a result, they protect themselves from potential disappointment by maintaining distance from others and avoiding intimacy.

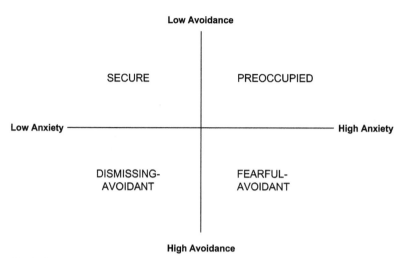

Fig. 8.4 Four adult attachment styles. Building on earlier work by Cindy Hazan and Phillip Shaver (1987), Kim Bartholomew (e.g., Bartholomew & Horowitz, 1991) proposed a typology of four adult attachment styles created by two underlying positive–negative dimensions (Model of Self and Model of Other). Subsequent theorists have maintained the four-category framework but have relabeled the underlying dimensions Anxiety and Avoidance (see Feeney & Collins, 2003).

As with positive and negative affectivity, most empirical work in the area of adult attachment style has been conducted with samples of dating or married couples. In general, this research reveals that the experiences that securely attached adults have within their romantic relationships are very different from those reported by insecure (i.e., preoccupied or avoidant) adults. Recent reviews (Collins & Feeney, 2004; Edelstein & Shaver, 2004; Feeney & Collins, 2003; Feeney, Noller, & Roberts, 2000) suggest the following conclusions:

- Compared with avoidant and preoccupied individuals, securely attached men and women report higher levels of satisfaction, trust, intimacy, love, and commitment in their dating and marital relationships.
- Securely attached adults experience lower levels of conflict, interpersonal difficulty, and negative affect than do insecurely attached adults (in fact, the experience of frequent negative emotion is quite common in the relationships of both preoccupied and avoidant men and women).
- Secure individuals exhibit more effective communication styles and display more adaptive and flexible patterns of self-disclosure than their insecure counterparts.
- Compared with avoidant and preoccupied men and women, securely attached adults are more likely to use positive and constructive problem-solving strategies (e.g., compromise, support, validation) for resolving conflict with their partners.

In addition to these qualitative differences in relationship experience, a study conducted by psychologist Nancy Collins (1996) provides evidence that people's attachment orientation biases the way they interpret and explain interpersonal events in their ongoing romantic relationships. Participants who were currently involved in a romantic relationship were asked to imagine that their partner had engaged in four potentially negative behaviors: not responding when the participant wanted to cuddle, not providing comfort when the participant was "feeling down," wanting to spend an evening by himself or herself, and leaving the participant standing alone at a party. After reading about each of these events, participants were asked to write a free-response explanation for the partner's behavior and to rate the extent to which the event would make them feel distressed (e.g., angry, hurt, disappointed, sad, unloved), nervous (e.g., nervous, confused, helpless), and unemotional or indifferent.

Analyses of the free response essays revealed that participants with different attachment styles provided very different cognitive interpretations of the event. Those who possessed a preoccupied attachment style explained the event in highly negative ways. Specifically, they were more likely than securely attached (and, in some cases, avoidant) participants to indicate that their partner was unresponsive, unloving, and untrustworthy and that the partner was purposely rejecting them. For example, when asked to explain why the partner would not want to cuddle, some gave responses such as the following: "He feels detached, doesn't want to be close to me," "She doesn't like me anymore," and "He's mad at me and this is his way of punishing me." Securely attached participants were more likely to give explanations and appraisals that minimized the negative impact of the event. An example was "She just had a bad day and wasn't in the mood to cuddle." Analysis of the emotional response data revealed that participants' attachment style also was associated with their affective reactions to the hypothetical relationship events. As expected, preoccupied participants reported exaggerated levels of negative emotion. They indicated that they would feel much more emotional distress, helplessness, and nervous confusion in the face of the various partner behaviors than did securely attached participants. Avoidant participants, on the other hand, reported that they would feel *less* distress than securely attached participants; in fact, the former's primary emotional response was indifference.

Taken altogether, these results suggest that when men and women with insecure (i.e., preoccupied or avoidant) attachment styles are faced with an interpersonal event that lends itself to a potentially negative interpretation, they are likely to respond cognitively and emotionally in ways that are unpleasant for their partner and harmful to the relationship. Craving closeness and validation from their partners—yet feeling unworthy of such responses—preoccupied individuals are only too ready to believe the worst. They assume that the event is caused by the partner's lack of love, concern, and trustworthiness, and they consequently experience overwhelming and excessive distress. Avoidant men and women also readily attribute negative motives to the partners, but their intense need for self-protection produces a very different emotional response—an uncommunicative display of stoic indifference. These cognitive and emotional responses are unlikely to produce beneficial outcomes for the partner or the relationship.

In sum, men and women with a secure attachment orientation enter their relationships expecting positive outcomes and then engage in behaviors that seem to promote intimacy and increase the likelihood that they actually will obtain those positive outcomes.

Rejection Sensitivity

Like adult attachment style, the concept of *rejection sensitivity* is also based heavily on Bowlby's attachment theory. Defined as the tendency to anxiously anticipate, readily perceive, and emotionally and behaviorally overreact to rejection from significant others, rejection sensitivity is presumed to develop as a self-protective response to early parental rejection (e.g., Downey, Bonica, & Rincon, 1999). Rejection sensitivity is assessed by asking individuals to imagine being in various situations that involve making requests or asking for assistance from acquaintances, romantic partners, or family members (e.g., asking a classmate to borrow his or her notes, asking a boyfriend/girlfriend to cohabit, asking parents for help in deciding what college programs to apply for). For each situation, participants are asked whether they would be concerned or anxious about the response to their request from the person or persons involved and whether they would expect the other(s) to honor or reject the request. People who are high in rejection sensitivity usually express anxiety and concern about the outcome of their request, coupled with an expectation of rejection; those who are low in rejection sensitivity report less anxiety and concern and express a calm expectation of assistance.

There is growing evidence that rejection-sensitive men and women essentially are primed to perceive rejection in the behavior of others—even when no rejection is intended. For example, in one study, Geraldine Downey and Scott Feldman (1996) asked a group of college students, each of whom had recently begun a new romantic relationship, to imagine that their partner had committed three insensitive but ambiguous actions that conceivably could have occurred for a number of reasons: had acted cool and distant, had begun to spend less time with them, and had been intolerant of something the participant did. Participants then indicated the extent to which they believed that each action reflected the partner's intentional desire to hurt them. The results revealed a positive correlation between rejection sensitivity (as assessed with the multi-item scale) and perceived hurtful intent; the more sensitive participants were to rejection, the greater the amount of hurtful intent they perceived in the partner's actions. Thus, it appears that men and women who anxiously anticipate rejection do actually "see" rejection in the actions of their intimate partners.

In addition, rejection sensitivity is associated with a number of negative interpersonal outcomes. For example, compared with people who are low in rejection sensitivity, rejection-sensitive people—and their partners—are less satisfied both with their romantic relationships (Downey & Feldman, 1996) and with their family relationships (Overall & Sibley, 2009). They are also more likely to be involved in unstable partnerships. In one longitudinal study (Downey, Freitas, Michaelis, & Khouri, 1998), dating couples completed a measure of rejection sensitivity and then were contacted 1 year later and asked to indicate their relationship status (i.e., whether the partners were still together). The results revealed that 44% of the couples who included a rejection-sensitive female partner had broken up, compared with 15% of the couples who included a non-rejection-sensitive female partner. Similarly, 42% of the couples who included a rejection-sensitive male partner had broken up over the 12-month period, compared with 15% of the couples who included a non-rejection-sensitive male partner. Dissolution is a common event in relationships involving at least one rejection-sensitive partner.

Rejection-sensitive men and women also tend to magnify the extent of their partner's dissatisfaction and lack of commitment; in other words, rejection-sensitive people believe that their dating partners are less satisfied and committed than is actually the case. In addition, they often exhibit behavior that can be potentially damaging to their romantic relationships and to their own psychological functioning. For example, research reveals a positive association between rejection sensitivity and the tendency to *self-silence* (Jack, 1991) or inhibit self-expression in intimate relationships (e.g., Purdie & Downey, 2000). A recent study conducted by psychologists Melinda Harper, Joseph Dickson, and Deborah Welsh (2006) demonstrated that men and women who were high in rejection sensitivity were more likely to report using a host of self-silencing behaviors in their interactions with their romantic partners including not voicing their feelings if doing so would cause disagreement, rarely expressing anger to their partners, and not expressing opinions or wishes that conflicted with those of their partners. These self-silencing behaviors, in turn, were associated with increased depressive symptoms. These results imply that individuals who are fearful of being rejected by their romantic partners suppress their personal voice and opinions in order to decrease the likelihood of conflict and maintain their relationships; unfortunately, this inhibition of self-expression may damage their own emotional health.

Other research has revealed that rejection-sensitive men and women tend to display hostile, jealous, emotionally unsupportive, and otherwise negative interpersonal behavior (according to their own and their partners' self-reports and laboratory observations of dyadic interaction). Interestingly, there appears to be a sex difference in how rejection-sensitive people manifest their insecurities within close romantic relationships. Specifically, men high in rejection sensitivity are more likely to display jealousy and suspicion and to seek to control their partners' contact with other people, whereas women high in rejection sensitivity are more likely to blame their partners unjustly and to display hostile and unsupportive behavior toward them (Downey & Feldman, 1996). There is also some evidence that rejection-sensitive men are more likely to engage in aggressive or coercive behaviors toward dating partners than are non-rejection-sensitive men (Downey, Feldman, & Ayduk, 2000).

In sum, rejection-sensitive people think about and respond to their partners in ways that appear to undermine the quality of their interactions and limit their chances of developing and maintaining satisfying and stable relationships.

SUMMARY

Over time and as a result of the interpersonal events we experience, each of us develops a host of relationship-relevant beliefs, attitudes, values, and expectations. We also hold beliefs and form attributions about ourselves and our own particular relationships and partners, and we possess a constellation of dispositional affective and cognitive tendencies that can influence our interpersonal behavior and the nature of the intimate associations we form with others. Some of these cognitive and affective processes and tendencies seem to promote positive interpersonal outcomes. For example, people who understand—and at the same time idealize the overall favorability of—their partners' self-relevant attributes tend to experience a great deal of relationship satisfaction and adjustment. Other cognitive and affective processes appear detrimental to relational well-being. Rigid adherence to dysfunctional relationship beliefs negatively impacts relational quality, as does consistent use of distress-maintaining attributions and high levels of negative affectivity, attachment insecurity, and rejection sensitivity. In sum, how we think and what we feel to some extent determines the quality of our relationships.

Of course, it is important to keep in mind that no single belief, attribution, or disposition inevitably determines what happens between partners or the fate of their relationship. Rather, it may be the particular constellation of beliefs, attributional patterns, and cognitive/affective tendencies that one person possesses, and how well those characteristics mesh with the enduring characteristics of his or her partner, that ultimately proves to have the greatest impact on any given relationship. Thus an extraverted, securely attached, interpersonally idealistic person may experience unhappiness, conflict, and instability, and an insecure, rejection-sensitive person who ascribes to dysfunctional relationship beliefs may find lasting love and satisfaction. In the realm of close relationships, anything is possible.

KEY CONCEPTS

Relationship cognition (p. 133)

Implicit relationship theories (p. 134)

Relationship affect (p. 133)

Romantic beliefs (p. 134)

Relationship schemas (p. 134)

Dysfunctional relationship beliefs (p. 135)

Positive illusions (p. 137)
Unrealistically positive self-views (p. 137)
Illusion of control (p. 137)
Unrealistic optimism (p. 137)
Self-serving biases (p. 137)
Self-enhancement biases (p. 137)
Relationship-enhancement biases (p. 139)
Memory bias (p. 139)
Partner idealization (p. 140)
Negativity bias (p. 141)
Sentiment override (p. 141)
Realistic idealism (p. 141)
Attributions (p. 141)
Causal attributions (p. 141)
Locus (p. 141)
Stability (p. 141)
Globality (p. 141)
Responsibility attributions (p. 141)
Motivation (p. 141)

Intention (p. 142)
Blame (p. 142)
Negative affectivity (neuroticism or negative emotionality) (p. 145)
Positive affectivity (extraversion or positive emotionality) (p. 146)
Introverts (p. 146)
Adult attachment style (p. 147)
Anxiety dimension (of attachment style) (p. 147)
Avoidance dimension (of attachment style) (p. 147)
Secure attachment style (p. 147)
Preoccupied (anxious/ambivalent) attachment style (p. 147)
Dismissing-avoidant attachment style (p. 147)
Fearful-avoidant attachment style (p. 147)
Rejection sensitivity (p. 149)
Self-silencing (p. 150)

EXPLORATION EXERCISES

These exercises are designed to allow you to explore in greater detail some of the concepts and issues discussed in this chapter. There are no right or wrong answers to these exercises—they are simply meant to provide an opportunity for discussion and debate.

1. How romantic are you? This exercise is a self-exploration activity designed to determine your level of romanticism—that is, the extent to which you endorse various idealized romantic beliefs. The following statements are included in the Romantic Beliefs Scale created by Susan Sprecher and Sandra Metts (these items were also presented earlier in this chapter). For each statement, indicate whether you find it to be generally true for you or generally false for you. Then add up your total number of "true" and "false" responses.

True   False
_____ _____ 1. If a relationship I have was meant to be, any obstacle can be overcome.
_____ _____ 2. I am likely to fall in love almost immediately if I meet the right person.
_____ _____ 3. There will be only one real love for me.
_____ _____ 4. The relationship I have with my "true love" will be nearly perfect.
_____ _____ 5. I believe that if another person and I love each other we can overcome any differences or problems that may arise.
_____ _____ 6. When I find my "true love" I will probably know it soon after we meet.
_____ _____ 7. Once I experience "true love," I could never experience it again, to the same degree, with another person.
_____ _____ 8. The person I love will make a perfect romantic partner; for example, he/she will be completely accepting, loving, and understanding.

How many "true" responses did you have? How many "false" responses? If you answered "true" to four or more of the statements, you are fairly romantic. If you answered "true" to fewer than four statements, you have a less idealistic (and perhaps more realistic?) vision of love.

2. Researchers have discovered that most of us adopt a self-serving orientation when we interpret and respond to negative events in our close personal relationships. For example, when our partner does something that hurts us, we often highlight or even exaggerate the severity of the incident and think that our partner is less sorry than he or she should be. And when we do something that hurts our partner, we tend to downplay or minimize the severity of the incident and emphasize or exaggerate the effort we made to atone for our behavior. Have you ever experienced this phenomenon yourself? Think back to a specific incident in which a close relationship partner (a good friend, a romantic partner, a relative, etc.) said or did something to you that was hurtful. Now, think of a specific incident in which you said or did something hurtful to that partner. How did you react in those two situations? Can you find any evidence, when you consider your reactions and those of your partner, that you (or your partner) adopted a self-serving orientation? What do you think the consequences of this interpersonal behavior pattern might be for your relationship over time (or for any relationship, really)?

3. We know that certain kinds of attributions are associated with relationship well-being, whereas others seem to promote relationship distress. Pick a positive interpersonal event that you have experienced recently (for example, perhaps one of your friends paid you a compliment, or a classmate agreed to lend you his or her lecture notes, or your boyfriend or girlfriend gave you an unexpected gift). Once you have selected a specific positive event, come up with examples of causal and responsibility attributions that you could make (or that you actually did make) that would promote your own satisfaction with the relationship. Now come up with examples of attributions you could make that would actually reduce your satisfaction with the relationship. Do the same for a negative interpersonal event you have experienced recently (that is, select a negative event and then come up with attributions you could make that would promote interpersonal well-being, and attributions you could make that would promote distress).

Chapter 9
Communicating and Supporting

CHAPTER OUTLINE

Effective communication is essential to the growth and maintenance of interpersonal relationships. In Chapter 1 we discussed how infants enter the world biologically prepared to attend (and respond) to the facial expressions and verbal behavior of other humans. This biological preparedness—the evolutionary inheritance of our species—promotes empathic accuracy and interpersonal sensitivity, which lie at the very heart of communicative competence. Communication, in fact, is one of the primary mechanisms through which relationships develop and are maintained over time (see Chapters 4–6). Recall that both men and women prefer and seek partners who possess high levels of interpersonal skill and responsiveness, employ a variety of verbal and nonverbal communicative strategies to convey interest to those potential mates and friends, and propel their budding relationships to deeper levels of intimacy and commitment through responsive self-disclosure and other forms of interpersonal exchange.

One particularly important aspect of communication that has captured the attention of relationship scientists concerns the provision and receipt of social support or caregiving. In this chapter we consider how people convey their needs for support to their intimate partners as well as the ways in which they go about providing comfort to distressed friends, lovers, and family members. We also discuss research on the consequences (both positive and negative) of social support, and explore various personal, relational, and environmental factors that are implicated in the caregiving process.

HOW DO PEOPLE ASK FOR (AND PROVIDE) SUPPORT?

People elicit support from their relationship partners in a variety of ways. As observed by relationship scholars Michael Cunningham and Anita Barbee (2000; also see Barbee, Rowatt, & Cunningham, 1998) in their review, these communicative strategies may be direct or indirect and verbal or nonverbal. Some ***direct support-seeking behaviors*** involve verbally asking for help. For example, an individual in distress may directly solicit help from the partner by talking about the problem in a factual manner, telling the partner about the problem, giving details about the situation, or disclosing the steps that have been taken to deal with the issue so far. Other direct behaviors are nonverbal; for instance, a person may show distress and convey a need for help through crying, furrowing his or her brow and making eye contact with the partner, or laying his or her head on the partner's shoulder. ***Indirect support-seeking behaviors*** also may be verbal or nonverbal. Indirect verbal tactics for activating caregiving include complaining about a situation or hinting that a problem exists without directly requesting assistance from the partner; indirect nonverbal strategies include subtly displaying negative affect or personal distress by sighing, sulking, or fidgeting. According to Cunningham and Barbee (2000), these indirect behaviors may protect the help-seeker's self-esteem because they do not explicitly acknowledge the need for assistance; at the same time, however, people who utilize indirect strategies run the risk of failing to effectively convey the nature or depth of the problem to the potential caregiver. Moreover, persistent use of indirect support-seeking behaviors such as complaining or sulking may annoy the partner and reduce the likelihood that he or she will provide the hoped-for assistance. (Indeed, research reveals that men and women whose partners display excessive needs for caregiving and support report higher levels of relationship dissatisfaction than those whose partners are less needy) (Cunningham, Shamblen, Barbee, & Ault, 2005).

People also differ in the ways in which they provide support to a partner in need (see Table 9.1). Most supportive or comforting behaviors fall into six general categories (Barbee & Cunningham, 1995; Burleson & Goldsmith, 1998; Cutrona, 1986; Dunkel-Schetter & Brooks, 2009). The first category includes ***emotional support*** behaviors. Specifically, when faced with a partner in distress, an individual may display verbal and nonverbal behaviors that communicate warmth, empathy, and concern, such as expressing caring and closeness and listening to the partner in a nonjudgmental and nurturing manner. ***Appraisal support*** (sometimes called ***esteem support***) is closely related to emotional support and is often subsumed into that category; this type of support involves communications that bolster, validate, and affirm the partner's sense of self-worth and competence. The third category includes behaviors that provide ***informational support***, such as giving advice, asking questions, or conveying information that helps the partner to better understand and cope with the stressful event or situation. The fourth category, ***instrumental support*** (sometimes called ***tangible***

Table 9.1 Types of Social Support

Type	Goal(s)	Example(s)
Emotional Support	Convey warmth, empathy, concern, and nurturance	"You're important to me" "I understand how you feel" "I care about you"
Appraisal Support	Bolster partner's self-worth and sense of competence	"I know you'll figure it out" "You deserve good things" "You're a survivor—you'll get through this"
Informational Support	Provide advice and information	"Here's what you should do . . ." "Have you tried doing this . . .?" "You really need to see a doctor"
Instrumental Support	Provide material aid or direct physical assistance	"Let me tie that bandage for you" "I can give you a loan" "Here's the way you do that . . ."
Companionship	Spend time with and be present for the partner	"I'm here if you need me" "I'm coming over right now" "You need a break—let's go for a jog"
Negative Support	Minimize, deny, or dismiss the situation	"It's no big deal—stop over-reacting" "I don't want to hear about this" "You have no one to blame but yourself for this situation"

support), involves the provision of material aid or other forms of direct physical assistance, and the fifth category, *companionship*, refers to providing comfort by spending time with, and being present for, the distressed partner. The sixth and final category, *negative support* behavior, includes verbal or nonverbal actions that deny, dismiss, or minimize the situation, assign blame to the partner, or discourage the partner from displaying negative emotion or seeking assistance.

WHICH TYPES OF SUPPORT ARE MOST HELPFUL?

Each of these different types of support has the potential to be helpful. For example, a student experiencing stress about the graduate school admission process may receive multiple forms of support from the people in his or her social network. Parents and other family members might pay the fees and proofread the written portion of the application (instrumental support), a close friend might suggest specific financial aid programs that are tailored to graduate students (informational support), and a dating partner might listen to the student's worries with empathy (emotional support), provide reassurance that "with your grades, you're sure to get in" (esteem support), and suggest a night at the movies when a study break is needed (companionship). Even negative support may be beneficial—when the student continues to display excessive worry about getting into graduate school, a friend's minimization and dismissal of the situation may be exactly what is needed to reduce stress (e.g., "I don't know what you're so worried about—you'll either get in or you won't. Until you find out, there's no point in even discussing it. You're just making yourself crazy for no reason. I'm through talking about this").

Nevertheless, a growing body of evidence—some of which we reviewed in Chapter 3—suggests that of all the various types of support that we may give our partners (or receive ourselves), emotional support is the most likely to alleviate distress, increase well-being, and produce other positive outcomes (e.g., Dunkel-Schetter, 1984; Kleiboer, Kuijer, Hox, Schreurs, & Bensing, 2006; Lehman, Ellard, & Wortman, 1986). For example, when researchers Gayle Dakof and Shelley Taylor (1990) asked a group of cancer patients to identify the most helpful things that their friends, family members, and spouses had "said or done to help you with your cancer" (p. 81), most of the helpful acts the patients specified reflected emotional support. Specifically, almost three-fourths of the helpful actions that participants indicated receiving from their spouses (74%), other family members (74%), and friends (72%) involved expressions of concern, empathy, affection, and validation.

Similar results were reported more recently by communication scholar Jessica Rack and her colleagues (Rack, Burleson, Bodie, Holmstrom, & Servaty-Seib, 2008). In this study bereaved college students who had experienced the death of a relationship partner (e.g., family member, close friend, romantic partner) were provided with a list of 16 specific types of social support and asked to rate how helpful they found each one to be in managing or alleviating their grief. According to the participants, the three most helpful types of supportive actions involved the provision of emotional support, including expressing care and concern for the bereaved individual ("I care about what happens to you," "I am concerned about how you feel," "I really care about how you are doing"), providing opportunities for the bereaved person to express his or her feelings ("I am a good listener if you need one," "If you want to talk, I will listen," "I really want to know how you are doing"), and offering supportive companionship (e.g., "I am here for you," "I am nearby if you need me," "I would be happy to stay with you if you'd like company"). Informational and negative support behaviors were perceived as particularly unhelpful. Participants rated giving advice ("You should keep busy," "When you feel bad you should exercise," "You should read self-help books") and minimizing the situation or dismissing their feelings ("It cannot be that bad," "It should not affect you," "You shouldn't let this get you down") as the least helpful forms of support. Thus, although different types of support may be beneficial in certain circumstances, emotional support is the one most consistently associated with positive outcomes.

Interestingly, emotional (and other types of) support may not even need to be experienced to prove helpful. As we discussed in Chapter 3, there is some evidence that *perceived support* (the perception that social support is available from the partner should it be needed) may have stronger links to well-being than *received support* (also called *enacted support*; this refers to the actual receipt of support from others). Sometimes simply knowing that another person is available to provide nurturance and warmth, advice and guidance, physical assistance and material aid, or mere companionship is enough to alleviate distress and enhance well-being.

When Helping Hurts: The Costs of Visible Support

Receiving support from a concerned and caring partner clearly has the power to provide multiple benefits to a person in need. However, support receipt also appears to carry some potential costs (see Vangelisti, 2009). Psychologist Niall Bolger and his colleagues (e.g., Bolger, Zuckerman, & Kessler, 2000; Gleason, Iida, Shrout, & Bolger, 2008; Shrout, Herman, & Bolger, 2006) have conducted a number of investigations of the daily support transactions that occur between partners during times of acute stress (e.g., while one member of the couple is preparing for the state bar examination). Using a daily diary methodology, these researchers had both members of each couple provide information about their own and the partner's provision of support, as well as their own mood states, at the end of every day for a specific period of time (e.g., a 1-month period). The results of the studies consistently revealed that men and women who received emotional support on any given day often experienced *increases* in mood states indicative of depression (e.g., feelings of sadness, discouragement, worthlessness, and hopelessness), anxiety (e.g., feelings of uneasiness, nervousness, anxiety, and edginess), and anger (e.g., feelings of resentment, annoyance, anger, and peevishness) on the following day. In other words, the act of being supported by an intimate partner was associated with subsequent *reductions* in participants' well-being. Interestingly, however, when participants were not aware that support had been provided—that is, when the partner indicated having given emotional support but the participant did not mention having received such support in his or her daily diary—depressed feelings were lower on the following day.

In explaining this somewhat surprising pattern of findings, Bolger and colleagues (e.g., 2000) point out that the conscious awareness that one has received support may (1) challenge a person's sense of competence and self-efficacy and consequently lower his or her self-esteem (after all, a successful, competent person could easily handle the situation and would not need so much help); (2) draw attention to and possibly even exacerbate the perceived magnitude of the problem or stressful situation (really, the problem must be almost insurmountable if it elicits this much help from the partner); and (3) produce unpleasant feelings of indebtedness to the partner or inequity in the relationship (how on earth will it be possible to "repay" the partner and "even things out" in the relationship?). Such beliefs and perceptions, in turn, are likely to increase negative affect, producing feelings of sadness, discouragement, anxiety, and even annoyance or irritation. Consequently, the researchers conclude that *invisible support*—support that is actually received by the recipient but that occurs without his or her awareness—produces the most positive benefits and is the most effective form of support transaction.

RELATIONAL AND ENVIRONMENTAL FACTORS ASSOCIATED WITH SUPPORT

Whether support is helpful or harmful is dependent not only on its visibility but also on a number of other contextual factors. Some of these are relational, and include the partners' history of supportive interactions, their level of interpersonal satisfaction, the degree of intimacy and equity that characterizes their relationship, and the "fit" or "match" between the type (and amount) of support sought by one partner and the type (and amount) actually provided by the other (Brock & Lawrence, 2009; Cutrona & Russell, 1990; Dunkel-Schetter & Skokan, 1990; Rini, Dunkel-Schetter, Hobel, Glynn, & Sandman, 2006; Sarason, Sarason, & Pierce, 1994). For example, research indicates that relationship satisfaction is significantly correlated with both perceived and enacted support. Men and women in satisfying romantic relationships tend to view their partners as more helpful and responsive, believe that support is more readily available, perceive existing levels of support as more adequate, and provide (and receive) greater and more effective support than their less-satisfied counterparts (e.g., Brunstein, Dangelmayer, & Schultheiss, 1996; Collins & Feeney, 2000; Iida, Seidman, Shrout, Fujita, & Bolger, 2008; Lawrence, Bunde, et al., 2008; Lawrence, Pederson, et al., 2008; Lemay, Clark, & Feeney, 2007).

Equity, reciprocity, and other relational variables also are implicated in the social support process. A daily diary study conducted by Masumi Iida, Niall Bolger, and colleagues (2008)—methodologically similar to the ones described in the preceding section—revealed that participants who received emotional support from their partners on a given day were significantly more likely to provide emotional support on that same day. In other words, people were more likely to give emotional support on days when they themselves received emotional support and less likely to give support on days when they did not receive support. A similar pattern emerged with respect to instrumental or practical support. This suggests that partners pay attention to issues of equity and reciprocity—to their interaction history, in fact—when deciding whether and how to provide support for one another.

Several environmental factors, including the amount of time partners spend together and the severity or ambiguity of the stressor, also have been targeted by relationship scholars interested in caregiving. For example, in their review of the cancer support literature, Camille Wortman and Christine Dunkel-Schetter (1979, 1987; also see Dunkel-Schetter, 1984) observed that men and women whose partners are in the throes of an acutely stressful victimizing event—such as the onset of cancer or some other life-threatening medical condition—often harbor negative feelings about the illness and the afflicted individual (including anger, anxiety, fear, sadness, feelings of personal vulnerability, and physical aversion). At the same time, however, they believe that these feelings should not be expressed to the partner and that doing so would be morally wrong and interpersonally irresponsible. Consequently, in an effort to be supportive, the would-be helpers tend to hide their true responses to the situation under a facade of forced cheerfulness, encouragement, and optimism. This places them in a state of conflict characterized by feelings of ambivalence, confusion, and discomfort, which unfortunately prevents them from providing effective support. For example, people typically avoid or reduce their level of contact with cancer patients (even those with whom they have loving, committed, and close relationships). Similarly, they tend to minimize the severity of the situation, discourage patients from openly communicating about the disease or their feelings, confine conversations to superficial topics, and otherwise behave in ways that are unintentionally damaging to the individuals in need. The nature of the stressor, then, plays an important role in determining the quality and quantity of support a person can expect to receive from his or her intimate associates. In general, most of us are better equipped to provide comfort to a partner dealing with daily hassles and other less acute stressors.

PERSONAL FACTORS ASSOCIATED WITH SUPPORT

Factors associated with the partners themselves also have the potential to influence the social support process. Relationship scholars have identified a number of cognitive, affective, dispositional, and other person-level variables that can render helping more (or less) likely to occur. For example, research on mood states and caregiving behavior among friends reveals that people who are put in a positive mood through experimental induction (e.g., by exposure to movie clips designed to evoke positive emotion) are much more likely to notice a partner's distress and provide effective support and problem-solving strategies than are people in an experimentally induced negative mood—in fact, saddened people are often so self-focused that they fail to even notice that their partners need support (and even when they do notice, they lack the energy to intervene; see Barbee et al., 1998; Cunningham & Barbee, 2000). Researchers interested in the correlates of chronic mood states such as depression have reported similar results; specifically, depressed men and women make fewer supportive statements to their romantic partners during problem-solving discussions (e.g., Gurung, Sarason, & Sarason, 1997).

Other personal factors, including adult attachment style and positive and negative affectivity, are also associated with support seeking and providing.

Adult Attachment Style: Secure People Tend to be Supportive People

It is hardly surprising that adult attachment style is correlated with caregiving behavior. The attachment system itself is designed to promote the formation of relational bonds and enhance safety and survival by ensuring a steady supply of social support. As we discussed in Chapter 3, attachment behaviors are innate, occur in response to stressful situations, are present throughout the life-span, and are specifically designed to elicit supportive, nurturing responses from our intimate partners. However, not all partners are equally responsive, and not all individuals are equally comfortable seeking support when they become distressed. These differences are closely associated with (and are believed to reflect) people's attachment histories. For example, research conducted with adults reveals that securely attached men and women respond more favorably to emotional support than do insecurely attached individuals (who tend to react more positively to instrumental caregiving behaviors; see Simpson, Winterheld, Rholes, & Oriña, 2007). Moreover, compared with people who possess an insecure attachment style, securely attached individuals provide more responsive and sensitive care to their partners, view social support as more readily available, perceive their partners as more effective caregivers, and are more likely to actively seek support for themselves when needed (e.g., Bachman & Bippus, 2005; Collins & Feeney, 2000; Kane et al., 2007; Kidd & Sheffield, 2005; Meyers & Landsberger, 2002; Millings & Walsh, 2009; for reviews, see Collins & Ford, 2010; Mikulincer & Shaver, 2009).

In one early investigation, Jeffrey Simpson, William Rholes, and Julia Nelligan (1992) examined the behavior of dating couples during a laboratory interaction. In this study, members of the couples first completed a self-report measure of attachment style. Next, the female member of each couple was informed that she soon would be exposed to a set of experimental procedures that "arouse considerable anxiety and distress in most people" (p. 437). She was not, however, told the specific nature of these procedures. Immediately following this anxiety-provoking manipulation, each woman was allowed to interact with her partner during a 5-minute "waiting" period. The couple's interactions were videotaped without their awareness and raters then viewed the videotapes and evaluated the behavior of both members of the couple during the 5-minute waiting period.

The results revealed that, for women, scores on the self-report attachment style measure were associated with support-seeking behavior. Specifically, among more secure women, increases in observer-rated anxiety were positively correlated with increased levels of observer-rated support seeking (i.e., women with higher levels of self-reported security sought more comfort and support from their partners as their anxiety increased, according to the behavioral observations of the raters). The reverse pattern was observed among more avoidant women; women with higher levels of self-reported avoidance demonstrated less support-seeking as their anxiety levels increased. Men's support-giving behavior also was predicted by their own attachment style. As their partners' levels of anxiety increased, more secure men offered more, and more avoidant men offered less, support. Similarly, as women discussed their feelings of anxiety more, secure men made more supportive remarks and avoidant men made fewer. These results demonstrate that differences in attachment style manifest themselves in behavioral differences during interaction between relational partners. In addition, these results highlight the fact that any interaction between two individuals (whether involving support seeking/giving or other types of exchange) will be influenced by the properties of both. As noted by the authors:

> More avoidant men, for example, cannot be characterized as cold, distant, or aloof *in general*. Although they do behave in this manner when their partner experiences higher levels of distress, their behavior is not the same when their partner's distress is lower.
>
> (Simpson et al., 1992, p. 442, emphasis in original)

Thus a person's attachment style, like other dispositional attributes, cannot be considered in isolation; rather, an individual's attachment style interacts with the situational context, and with the disposition of the other partner, to produce particular interaction behavior and interpersonal outcomes.

Positive Affectivity: Cheerful People Tend to be Supportive People

Relationship scholars also have found evidence linking another dispositional thinking and feeling tendency—positive affectivity—with how partners communicate and enact supportive exchanges with each another. In one study, researchers Carolyn Cutrona, Robert Hessling, and Julie Suhr (1997) assessed the extraversion (positive affectivity) levels of a sample of 100 married couples prior to observing each couple in a 10-minute interaction. These interactions took place in a laboratory furnished to resemble a comfortable living room. One partner was randomly chosen by the researchers to play the role of "support recipient." The support recipient was asked to describe a recent personally stressful situation to his or her spouse. The other member of the couple was assigned the role of "support provider." The support provider was instructed to simply listen to his or her partner and then react spontaneously and naturally. The two partners then switched roles and the process was repeated. These interactions were videotaped, and the researchers examined the support providers' verbal behavior for the presence of four types of supportive communication: *emotional support* (expressing love, concern, or empathy for the partner), *esteem support* (communicating respect for the partner and confidence in his or her abilities), *informational support* (providing information about the stressful situation or advice about how to deal with it), and *tangible aid* (providing or offering to provide goods, services, or other explicit forms of assistance needed to deal with the stressful situation). The frequencies with which these four types of support occurred during the interaction were summed to create an overall index of support behavior provided by each spouse.

The results revealed that this overall measure was positively correlated with levels of positive affectivity. Specifically, husbands and wives higher in extraversion made more positive supportive statements overall to their support-seeking spouses than did less-extraverted individuals—but they did not receive more support themselves from those spouses. In discussing this interesting pattern, Cutrona and her colleagues (1997) concluded:

> The results that emerged for extraversion [positive affectivity] highlight the importance of considering the personal characteristics of both the individual and his or her primary source of social support. Contrary to prediction, the extraversion of support *recipients* did not directly predict the amount of support they received from the spouse. Rather, the extraversion of support *providers* proved to be most important. Thus, a shy introvert who married a gregarious extravert might be amply supplied with a lifetime of social support, by virtue of his or her partner's interpersonally oriented nature.
>
> (p. 390, italics in original)

Further analyses also revealed that reciprocity of support was evident in the couples' behavior. That is, the more support a husband or wife *provided* during the first interaction, the more support he or she subsequently *received* during the second interaction—regardless of the level of extraversion of either spouse. This result suggests that people with high levels of positive affectivity may indirectly affect their own relational outcomes via the support they provide their partners; specifically, they tend to give their partners a great deal of social support, and their positive behaviors, in turn, seem to evoke corresponding supportive reactions from those partners.

Negative Affectivity: Unhappy People Tend to be Unsupportive People

Not surprisingly, negative affectivity appears to contribute to *unsupportive* exchanges between relationship partners. Using a procedure very similar to the one utilized by Cutrona and colleagues (1997), Lauri Pasch, Thomas Bradbury, and Joanne Davila (1997) examined the relationship between negative affectivity and supportive behavior in newlywed couples. Couples completed measures of marital satisfaction and negative affectivity and then were audio taped during two interactions. In the first interaction, one spouse was randomly selected to serve as the "helpee." The helpee was instructed to talk about an important personal characteristic, problem, or issue he or she would like to change about him- or herself (and that was not a source of tension in the marriage). The other spouse served as the "helper." The helper was simply asked to be involved in the discussion and to respond in whatever way he or she wished. The spouses then switched roles so that both had the opportunity to function as helper and helpee.

The verbal behaviors displayed by helpers and helpees were then examined for the presence of various positive and negative features. For example, *positive helpee behaviors* included offering a specific and clear analysis of the problem, expressing feelings related the problem, and asking for help or stating needs in a useful way. *Positive helper behaviors* included such instrumental acts as making specific suggestions and giving helpful advice as well as emotional acts ranging from providing reassurance, to giving encouragement, to conveying love and esteem to the helpee. *Negative helpee behaviors* ranged from making demands for help, to criticizing the helper, to whining or complaining about the situation. *Negative helper behaviors* consisted of criticizing or blaming the spouse and offering inconsiderate advice.

The analyses revealed that, for husbands, negative affectivity was negatively correlated with providing positive instrumental support to the helpee. That is, the higher a husband scored on this disposition, the less often he offered specific suggestions and gave helpful advice to his wife. A similar pattern was found among wives. The higher a wife scored on negative affectivity, the less often she displayed positive behavior—and the more often she displayed negative behavior—toward the helpee (her husband). Thus, men and women with high levels of negative affectivity seemed to provide support in a largely negative and unhelpful manner. The researchers then examined the audio taped conversations for evidence of "negative reciprocity" of social support behavior—that is, exchanges characterized by reciprocal displays of negative communications (for example, the helpee complains and the helper then criticizes; the helper blames and the helpee then demands help; see Chapter 15). Analysis of these data indicated that husbands who scored high on negative affectivity were more likely to reciprocate their wives' negative behavior when the husbands were in the role of helper; the husbands were also more likely to have their negative helper behavior reciprocated by their wives. The wives' level of negative affectivity, however, was not related to reciprocity of negative behavior. In discussing their entire set of results, Pasch and her colleagues (1997, p. 376) concluded:

> Although support provision is associated with negative affectivity for husbands and wives, it is the husband's negative affectivity that may have the most detrimental effect on actual interactions between husbands and wives. When husbands were in the role of providing support to their wives and when they were high in negative affectivity, social support interactions were characterized by extended sequences involving negative reciprocity. That is, husbands and wives were engaged in a cycle of negative support solicitation and provision to the extent that husbands were high in negative affectivity. These types of behavioral sequences have been

shown to be associated with poor marital outcome ... and it is plausible to assume that negative reciprocity occurring in the context of soliciting and providing social support may have negative consequences for the marriage and the individual.

In sum, the traits and dispositions of the partners in any given relationship—particularly their levels of positive and negative affectivity—may influence how they communicate during times of need as well as the quantity and quality of social support that they provide to each other.

SEX DIFFERENCES IN COMMUNICATING AND SUPPORTING

No person-level factor has received more attention from scholars interested in social support and communication than has biological sex. In general (as befits members of the same species), the interpersonal events, experiences, and outcomes of men and women are very similar. However, there is some evidence that men and women differ in the way they communicate and self-disclose, provide support to their partners, and create and maintain intimacy in their close relationships. For example, women engage in more "conversational maintenance" than do men; that is, in their conversations women are more likely than men to invite others to speak, to ask questions, encourage elaborations, respond to statements made by others, and display nonverbal behaviors that signal interest and involvement in the conversation (Wood, 2000). Women also are more likely than men to maintain conversational equality by including others in the conversation, expressing support (e.g., sympathy, agreement), and demonstrating responsiveness (e.g., eye contact, head nodding), whereas men are more likely than women to maintain conversational dominance by rerouting conversations to their own interests and agendas, interrupting others, and expressing themselves forcefully and authoritatively (Wood, 2009). In addition, men and women discuss different topics with their friends—women tend to talk about personal topics (feelings, relationships, problems) whereas men's conversations revolve around sports, vehicles, computers, work, and other non-personal topics (Fehr, 1996, 2000). Similarly, girls' and women's same-sex friendships are characterized by relatively greater levels of self-disclosure, intimacy, and support than are boys' and men's same-sex friendships (Bank & Hansford, 2000; Bauminger, Finzi-Dottan, Chason, & Har-Even, 2008; Fehr, 1996; Johnson, 2004). And finally, in heterosexual romantic relationships, women provide more comfort and helpful support to their partners—and are more responsive to their partners' changing needs for support—than men (Cutrona, 1996; Neff & Karney, 2005).

The Origin of Sex Differences in Supportive Communication: Different Cultures?

The origin of these sex differences has been the subject of some debate among the scientific community. Several explanations have been advanced. According to the ***different cultures thesis***, men and women approach relationships from a different cultural perspective and adopt a different set of standards, values, and beliefs with respect to their close relationships (e.g., Maccoby, 1990; Wood, 2007). Scholars who subscribe to this thesis observe that women traditionally are socialized to value interdependence, to establish intimacy through self-disclosure and affective communication, and to pursue communal goals within their close relationships. Conversely, men are socialized to value independence, to establish intimacy through shared activities, and to maintain power and autonomy in their close relationships. According to sociolinguist Deborah Tannen (e.g., 1990), for example, men and women inhabit separate worlds:

Intimacy is key in a world of connection where individuals negotiate complex networks of friendship, minimize differences, try to reach consensus, and avoid the appearance of superiority, which would highlight differences. In a world of status, *independence* is key, because a primary means of establishing status is to tell others what to do, and taking orders is a marker of low status. Though all humans need both intimacy and independence, women tend to focus on the first and men on the second. It is as if their lifeblood ran in different directions.

(p. 26, italics in original)

This fundamental difference between independence-oriented men and intimacy-oriented women is posited to have significant consequences in many relational domains, including communication and the expression of intimacy and social support. For example, Tannen (1990) suggested that in the world of women, "conversations are negotiations for closeness in which people try to seek and give confirmation and support, and to reach consensus" (p. 25). In the world of men, however, conversations serve a very different purpose; they are "negotiations in which people try to achieve and maintain the upper hand if they can, and protect themselves from others' attempts to put them down and push them around" (pp. 24–25). According to this framework, then, the different interpersonal experiences that men and women sometimes have stems from the vastly different worlds they inhabit, and the achievement of satisfying marital (and other cross-sex relational) outcomes is dependent on the ability of each sex to understand—and perhaps even learn how to effectively use—the other's culture-specific form of communication, intimacy expression, and support provision.

Although still prominent in popular literature and the media, the different cultures thesis has come under serious attack in recent years for a variety of reasons. First, much of the evidence cited by proponents of this framework is based on anecdote and subjective, first-person accounts that are not appropriate for scientifically testing hypotheses about common preferences or behavior patterns among groups of people. Second, a growing body of empirical research demonstrates that sex differences in communication, caregiving and support, and conceptions of intimacy are actually far fewer in number and much smaller in magnitude than would be predicted by the different cultures thesis. For example, after conducting a detailed review of the existing literature, communication scholar Brant Burleson (2003, pp. 13, 16) concluded:

Both men and women believe that the explicit elaboration and exploration of feelings is the best way to provide comfort to one another, and are themselves most comforted by such messages. . . . Although some small sex differences have been observed, these differences exist within much more substantial patterns of similarity, with both men and women assigning priority to the management of distressed feelings in support situations.

Indeed, a recent series of studies conducted by Erina MacGeorge and her colleagues provides evidence that men and women are more similar than they are different in their provision of, and responses to, supportive communication (MacGeorge, Graves, Feng, Gillihan, & Burleson, 2004). Adult participants in the first study read four scenarios describing a same-sex friend who was upset about a personal problem (i.e., being asked for a divorce by his or her spouse, receiving a poor performance evaluation at work, learning of the death of a high-school friend, and having to give a speech to a community group). After reading each scenario, participants were asked to respond to the situation as though their friends "were actually there in the room with you" (p. 153). These responses were tape-recorded and the researchers subsequently identified eight different types of communication made by the participants: *giving advice* ("If you're going to go ahead with the divorce, you should hire an attorney", "What you could do is practice your speech so when you go up there you'll feel more comfortable"), *expressing sympathy* ("I'm so sorry to hear about your friend," "Hey, if you need a shoulder to cry on, I'm here for you"), *asking questions* ("Have you considered seeing a marriage counselor?," "Have you talked with your boss yet?"), *offering help* ("I'd be happy to help if you need me", "You could always practice your speech on me"), *minimizing the situation* ("You seem to be making it worse than it really is," "I think you're blowing things a bit out of proportion"), *affirming or encouraging the other person* ("You're a fantastic public speaker, so I know you'll do great", "If your boss never told you what was expected, I don't see why you should have gotten such a poor evaluation"), *sharing a similar problem* ("I felt the same way when my friend died," "I know exactly how you feel—I got a really bad performance evaluation last year"), and *assigning blame* ("I hate to say this, but you really have no one to blame but yourself," "You should have gone to that public speaking workshop"). Contrary to the different cultures thesis, the results revealed very few sex differences. Although men gave advice proportionately more often than women and women were proportionately more likely than men to offer affirmation and help, the sexes did not differ in any of the other forms of support. Furthermore, both men and women largely gave support via advice and expressions of sympathy.

In a second study the researchers explored whether men and women differ in how they respond to supportive messages. College student participants in this study read two scenarios in which a "good friend" was portrayed as experiencing emotional distress over (1) the recently announced divorce of his or her parents and (2) the failure to receive an anticipated academic scholarship. After reading each scenario, participants received a list of comforting messages that varied in their degree of *person-centeredness* (i.e., the extent to which the message explicitly acknowledged, elaborated, and legitimized the feelings and perspective of the friend in distress). They then rated the messages for sensitivity and effectiveness, and these two measures were combined to provide an overall index of perceived message quality. The different cultures thesis would predict strong sex differences in perceptions of the quality of the messages—women, who come from a culture of intimacy, should respond more favorably to messages that focus on the verbalization of feelings and the provision of emotional support (i.e., highly person-centered messages), whereas men, who come from a culture of independence, should prefer messages that avoid the discussion of feelings and focus instead on instrumental solutions to the problem (i.e., less person-centered messages). Contrary to these predictions, the results revealed that both men and women evaluated messages that were highly person-centered much more positively than they did messages that were low in person-centeredness. In discussing these findings, MacGeorge and her colleagues (2004) observed that their results were consistent with those of other researchers who have also discovered more similarities than differences in men's and women's evaluations of supportive behaviors and communication skills, responses to supportive messages, and goals when providing support. They concluded, "At present, then, there appears to be virtually no relevant, credible evidence that supports the claim that men and women constitute different communication cultures or speech communities, especially with respect to supportive communication" (p. 172).

Or Different Abilities and/or Motivations?

In view of these and other empirical investigations, a number of theorists have suggested that it may be more accurate to view men and women as belonging to the same culture but as possessing differential communicative skill. The ***differential ability*** (or ***differential skill***) ***account*** posits that men and women hold similar views and expectations about communication, intimacy, and social support and approach their intimate relationships with similar goals and values, but that over the course of socialization women acquire more of the skills needed to produce behavior that fulfills those expectations and meets those goals (Kunkel & Burleson, 1999). There is strong evidence in support of this explanatory framework (for a review, see Burleson & Kunkel, 2006).

In addition to possessing different communicative abilities, men and women also may possess differential *motivation* to engage in emotionally supportive and intimate forms of communication. The **normative motivation account** recognizes that the provision of social support in contemporary American society is viewed as a feminine activity by both men and women (Kunkel & Burleson, 1999), and that most people are motivated to behave in accordance with the norms and expectations associated with their social roles (Eagly, 1987). To the extent that emotionally expressive, intimate, person-centered forms of communication and support provision are inconsistent with sociocultural notions of masculinity, men may be less motivated to engage in such behavior than are women—even if they are equally able.

A series of studies conducted by Brant Burleson, Amanda Holmstrom, and Cristina Gilstrap (2005) revealed a number of findings that support both of these more recent theoretical frameworks. First, men viewed highly person-centered messages as the most effective and supportive way of helping someone in emotional distress. Second, men viewed these communicative behaviors as a particularly feminine form of conduct. Third, men viewed other men who displayed these behaviors as relatively atypical (and they tended not to like them very much). In other words, in accord with the normative motivation account, the men in these studies possessed the knowledge that person-centered communication is the most useful and comprehensive way to provide emotional support but at the same time considered it to be a non-masculine way to behave. Fourth, Burleson and his colleagues found that men varied their own use of highly person-centered messages according to the sex of the person in distress; specifically, they indicated that they would be (and, in fact, they were) less likely to provide solace and other sensitive and sophisticated person-centered forms of support to another man than to a woman. This latter result also supports the normative motivation account—if men are simply less skilled at providing effective emotional support than are women, then they should generally prefer and provide less person-centered messages and they should prefer and provide these messages regardless of the sex of the person in distress. The fact that their choice of supportive message varied depending on the sex of the target demonstrated that the men in this study possessed the ability to alter their communicative displays to fit the context (i.e., displaying "feminine" support behavior with an emotionally distressed woman and electing to display "masculine" support behavior with an emotionally distressed man). However, the researchers also found evidence of differential skill—their studies revealed a consistent sex difference such that women were more likely than men to produce highly person-centered messages when comforting another person in distress (regardless of whether that individual was male or female).

Thus, a combination of differential ability as well as differential motivation—created and sustained by socialization forces and the prevailing sociocultural climate—probably contributes to the sex differences that relationship scientists have observed in the area of intimate and supportive communication behavior.

SUMMARY

The provision and receipt of social support involves a complex process of communication and exchange between relational partners. Consider, for example, an individual facing some problem or personal difficulty. In order for that individual to receive effective support from a friend, loved one, or other intimate partner, he or she must first recognize and acknowledge that distress is occurring, decide what type of support is needed, determine whether the partner is willing and/or able to provide the necessary assistance, and clearly communicate the need for help to that partner. At the same time, the partner must perceive the individual's distress, recognize that assistance is needed, identify the type of support that is likely to be most effective, evaluate whether he or she possesses the ability to provide that support, experience sufficient motivation to take action, and then actually enact the supportive behavior. The outcome of this complicated, multi-step communicative process is partly determined by the quality of the support itself (for example, whether it is enacted or perceived, emotional or informational, visible or invisible), as well as by a variety of personal (e.g., adult attachment style, positive and negative affectivity, biological sex), relational (e.g., satisfaction, equity, previous interactions and exchanges), and environmental (e.g., time, type of stressor) variables. In general, research reveals that social support transactions are most likely to produce beneficial outcomes when the type of assistance that is rendered matches the type that is sought, when support is given in such a way that the recipient feels valued, nurtured, and neither beholden nor incompetent, and when the transaction occurs in the context of a satisfying, equitable relationship.

KEY CONCEPTS

Direct support-seeking behaviors (p. 155)
Indirect support-seeking behaviors (p. 155)
Emotional support (p. 155)
Appraisal (esteem) support (p. 155)
Informational support (p. 155)
Instrumental (tangible) support (pp. 155–156)
Companionship (p. 156)
Negative support (p. 156)

Perceived support (p. 157)
Received (enacted) support (p. 157)
Invisible support (p. 158)
Different cultures thesis (p. 163)
Person-centeredness (p. 165)
Differential ability (skill) account (p. 165)
Normative motivation account (p. 166)

EXPLORATION EXERCISES

These exercises are designed to allow you to explore in greater detail some of the concepts and issues discussed in this chapter. There are no right or wrong answers to these exercises—they are simply meant to provide an opportunity for discussion and debate.

1. People employ a variety of behaviors—some indirect, some direct, some verbal, some nonverbal—when trying to obtain support from their partners. Think of five specific instances in which you attempted to elicit support from a close relationship partner. What did you do? How exactly did you communicate your need for support or assistance to your partner? Were your methods generally direct or indirect, verbal or nonverbal? Were they effective—did your efforts produce the support you wanted from your partner?

2. Table 9.1 lists different types of social support. Identify which of these types of support you have personally experienced, along with a specific instance. (Chances are, you've experienced all of them.) Which type of support was most beneficial to you? Were they all helpful, or were there some types of support that seemed to be particularly useful or positive? Did any of the types of support "backfire" and actually make you feel worse?

3. People often have a difficult time responding appropriately and supportively to a close partner who is experiencing an acute crisis or stressor (such as a life-threatening medical condition, the aftermath of an assault, or some other intensely victimizing event). Have you ever found yourself in this situation, either as the support provider or recipient? If you were the support provider, how did you respond? How did the situation make you feel? What did you do to provide support to the person in need? Do you think your efforts were successful? If you were the support recipient, how did the situation make you feel? What did the support provider do to help you? Were his or her efforts successful?

Chapter 10
Loving

CHAPTER OUTLINE

Like all great dramatic works, the story of each individual human life can often be whittled down to one fundamental *leitmotif*: the question of who loves us (and who does not), and when, where, and how love develops (or dissolves). Each of us owes the very fact of our existence to the attraction (whether it be affectionate or lustful, longstanding or fleeting) that once existed between two individuals, and our inherently social nature—our need to form positive, loving, supportive relationships with others—ensures that most of us will spend a good portion of our lives seeking an answer to that very question. Relationship scientists, too, have devoted considerable effort toward understanding love. This chapter presents their findings.

GENERAL THEORIES OF LOVE

Throughout history, scholars interested in exploring the nature of love have faced a pair of somewhat daunting tasks—first, identifying whether different types of love exist, and second, determining what features distinguish these types of love from one another. Existential psychologist Erich Fromm stated the issue clearly in his classic book *The Art of Loving* (1956, p. 18):

> This desire for interpersonal union is the most powerful striving in man. It is the most fundamental passion, it is the force which keeps the human race together, the clan, the family, society. The failure to achieve it means insanity or destruction—self-destruction or destruction of others. Without love, humanity could not exist for a day. Yet, if we call the achievement of interpersonal union "love," we find ourselves in a serious difficulty. Fusion can be achieved in different ways—and the differences are not less significant than what is common to the various forms of love. Should they all be called love? Or should we reserve the word "love" only for a specific kind of union . . .? As with all semantic difficulties, the answer can only be arbitrary. What matters is that we know what kind of union we are talking about when we speak of love.

The search to determine what is common across all love types and what is unique to each variety has consumed scholars from a variety of disciplines for many years.

Early Taxonomies

Early taxonomies of love were derived from personal observation and inductive reasoning, literature, and previous philosophical, theological, and scientific discourse. One of the earliest known treatises on the nature of love, a work entitled *The Art of Courtly Love*, appeared in France during the late twelfth century. Written by Andreas Capellanus (André le Chapelain), supposedly at royal behest, the three-part treatise considers the nature of love—its origins, manifestations, and effects; who can feel love; how love may be acquired, increased, decreased, and terminated; and what a lover ought to do if the beloved is unfaithful. Capellanus proposed two varieties of love. "Pure" love is less sexual, more cerebral, and more durable than "mixed" or "common" love:

> . . . one kind of love is pure, and one is called mixed. It is the pure love which binds together the hearts of two lovers with every feeling of delight. This kind consists in the contemplation of the mind and the affection of the heart; it goes as far as the kiss and the embrace and the modest contact with the nude lover, omitting the final solace, for that is not permitted to those who wish to love purely. This is the kind that anyone who is intent upon love ought to embrace with all his might, for this love goes on increasing without end, and we know that no one ever regretted

practicing it, and the more of it one has the more one wants. . . . But that is called mixed love which gets its effect from every delight of the flesh and culminates in the final act of Venus. What sort of love this is you may clearly see from what I have already said, for this kind quickly fails, and lasts but a short time, and one often regrets having practiced it . . . But I do not say this as though I meant to condemn mixed love, I merely wish to show which of the two is preferable. But mixed love, too, is real love, and it is praiseworthy, and we say that it is the source of all good things, although from it grave dangers threaten, too. Therefore I approve of both pure love and mixed love, but I prefer to practice pure love.

(1184/1960, pp. 122–123)

Once acquired, the effects of love (on the lover) are believed to be overwhelmingly positive and to include increased nobility of character, humility, a desire to perform services for others, gratitude, and fidelity. Although some contemporary literary critics have questioned Capellanus' motives in creating his treatise on love and whether he truly believed what he wrote, this work remains one of our earliest examples of discourse on the nature of love.

Other early scholars also proposed that multiple varieties of love exist, each containing specific distinguishing features. As illustrated in Figure 10.1, William James (1890/1950), the founder of American psychology, differentiated between maternal love and a form of (unnamed) love that was characterized by sexuality and exclusivity (i.e., directed toward one particular individual to the exclusion of all others). His contemporary, the German physician and pioneering sexologist Richard von Krafft-Ebing (1886/1945) identified four types of love: true love (a hardy mix of altruism, closeness, and sexuality), platonic love (based on compatibility), sensual love (a fleeting love based on sexual desire and romantic idealization), and sentimental love (about which he had little more to say other than that it was "nauseating" [p. 12]).

Several decades later, psychotherapist Albert Ellis (1954) proposed additional love varieties: "Love itself . . . includes many different types and degrees of affection, such as conjugal love, parental love, familial love, religious love, love of humanity, love of animals, love of things, self-love, sexual love, obsessive-compulsive love, etc." (p. 101). Existentialist Fromm agreed with Ellis that a diversity of loves existed and could be experienced by individuals over the life-span. According to his typology, love can be divided into two basic categories: real (or mature) love and pseudo-love. Varieties of real love include brotherly love, motherly love, fatherly love, erotic love, self-love, and love of God. Each of these love types contains four basic elements—care, responsibility, respect, and knowledge—along with particular unique features (e.g., motherly love is unconditional and altruistic, whereas erotic love is fragile and sexual). The pseudo-love types share some of the features of real love but are experienced by people with various personality disorders, who lack a strong sense of identity and who are incapable of engaging in "love between equals."

Unlike his contemporaries, theologian C. S. Lewis contented himself with just four types of love, each based on earlier distinctions made by Greek philosophers. In his engaging book *The Four Loves* (1960/1988), he proposed that Affection (called *storge* by the Greeks) is based on familiarity and repeated contact and resembles the strong attachment often seen between parents and children. This type of love is experienced for and by a wide variety of social objects, including family members, pets, acquaintances, and lovers. According to Lewis, affectionate love has a "comfortable, quiet nature" (p. 34) and consists of feelings of warmth, interpersonal comfort, and satisfaction in being together. The second variety of love depicted by Lewis is Friendship (or *philias*), a love type that is based on common interests, insights, or tastes, coupled with cooperation, mutual respect, and understanding. More than mere companionship, Lewis argued that Friendship develops when two people "discover that they are on the same secret road" (p. 67) and become kindred souls. Eros, or "that state which we call 'being in love'" (p. 91), is the

Theorist/Researcher	Proposed Nature of Love		
	No. of Types	Labels	Characteristic Features
Capellanus (1184)	2	Pure Common (mixed)	Durability, affection Fragility, sexuality
Krafft-Ebing (1886)	3 +	Sensual love True love Platonic love Sentimental love	Fragility, idealization, sexuality Durability, closeness, altruism, sexuality Compatibility Self-indulgent sentimentality
James (1890)	2	Love Maternal love	Exclusivity, sexual appetite, intensity "Passionate devotion," altruism

A. Ellis (1954)	11 +	Conjugal love, parental love
		  familial love, religious love,
		  sexual love, self-love, etc.
		Romantic love
			Unspecified
			
			Exclusivity, idealization,
			  emotional intensity, sexuality

Fromm (1956)	6 +	Real love(s):
		  Brotherly love
		  Motherly love
		  Fatherly love } care, respect,
		  Erotic love } responsibility,
		  Self-love } knowledge
		  Love of God
		Pseudo love(s):
		  Idolatrous love
		
		  Sentimental love
		  Etc.
			
			Universal
			Universal, unconditional, altruistic
			Universal, conditional
			Exclusive, fragile, sexual
			Self-focused
			Universal, oneness with God
			
			Idealization/worship, intensity,
			  sudden onset, fragility
			Idealization of (empty) relationship

Lewis (1960)	4	Affection
		
		Friendship
		
		Eros
		
		Charity
			Slow onset/growth, warmth,
			  comfortableness
			Similarity, durability, respect,
			  admiration
			Exclusivity, sexuality,
			  fragility, idealization,
			  cognitive preoccupation
			Tolerance, altruism

Fig. 10.1 A sample of early love taxonomies.

third variety of love. Containing a mixture of "sweetness" and "terror," Eros is characterized by sexuality, affection, idealization of and preoccupation with the beloved, and a very short life-span. The final love type is Charity, a selfless love based on tolerance, forbearance, and forgiveness; Charity involves no expectation of reward and desires only what is "simply best for the beloved" (p. 128).

All of these theorists agree that love is multifaceted—that is, that more than one variety of love exists—and all made progress toward specifying the characteristic manifestations of the various love types. However, they disagreed about the number of love varieties that exist, and, more importantly, none of their taxonomies was sufficiently developed to provide an adequate guide for empirical research (for example, by clearly and definitively specifying the causal antecedents and consequences of the individual love types). Recognizing the limitations of these earlier taxonomies, contemporary relationship scholars have increasingly relied on statistical techniques (usually factor analysis or cluster analysis) to help them identify the dimensions that underlie the reported experiences of individuals involved in love relationships. The assumption of researchers who adopt this *psychometric approach* is that identification of the common elements in the actual love experiences of people in ongoing relationships provides an effective way of distinguishing among different types of love.

Two of the most significant psychometrically derived classification schemes were developed by psychologist Robert Sternberg (e.g., 1986, 1988, 1998) and sociologist John Lee (e.g., 1973, 1988).

Sternberg's *Triangular Theory of Love*

On the basis of earlier social psychological theory and research on love as well as factor analysis of the self-reported experiences of men and women in dating relationships, Sternberg (e.g., 1986, 1998, 2006) proposed that love can be understood in terms of three basic components that form the vertices of a triangle: intimacy, passion, and decision/commitment (see Figure 10.2). The *intimacy component* is primarily emotional or affective in nature and involves feelings of warmth, closeness, connection, and bondedness in the love relationship. The *passion component* is motivational and consists of the drives that are involved in romantic and physical attraction, sexual consummation, and related phenomena. The *decision/commitment component* is largely cognitive and represents both the short-term decision that one individual loves another and the longer-term commitment to maintain that love over time.

Sternberg posited that these three love components differ with respect to a number of properties, including *stability*, *conscious controllability*, and *experiential salience*. For example, once present, the emotional intimacy component and the cognitive decision/commitment component both are usually quite stable in close relationships (that is, once they occur and become characteristic of a relationship, they tend to endure over time). However, the motivational passion component is presumed to be less stable and predictable. In addition, whereas people possess some degree of conscious control over the commitment that they make to a relationship, they generally have very little conscious control over the amount of passion that they experience for their partners (i.e., it is difficult to increase or decrease one's level of physical or sexual attraction to a partner). The three components also differ in terms of their experiential salience. Specifically, an individual is usually quite aware of the passion component, but awareness of the intimacy and decision/commitment components can be extremely variable. For example, a person may experience feelings of intimacy (e.g., closeness, connection, warmth) without explicitly being aware of those feelings or even being able to identify what he or she is feeling. Similarly, a person may not consciously realize the full extent of his or her commitment to the relationship and the partner.

Types of Love Relationship. The three basic components of love combine to produce eight different love types or experiences, summarized in Table 10.1. *Nonlove* encompasses casual interactions that are characterized by the absence (or very low levels) of all three love components. Most of our personal relationships (which are essentially casual associations) can be defined as nonlove. *Liking* relationships are essentially friendships that contain warmth, intimacy, closeness, and other positive emotional experiences but lack both passion and decision/commitment; we may care for the person and enjoy his or her company without feeling intense passion or a sustained commitment

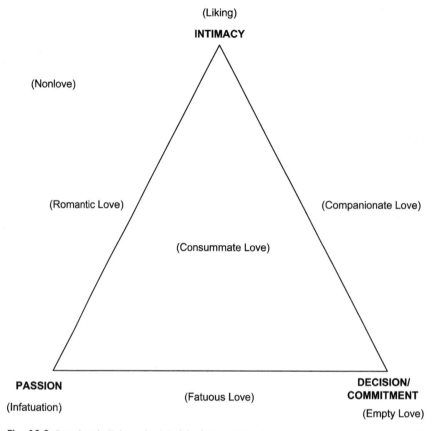

Fig. 10.2 Sternberg's Triangular Model of Love. The three components are indicated at the vertices of the triangle. The eight varieties of love produced by different combinations of the components are in parentheses.

Source: Sternberg, R. J. (1988). Triangulating love. In R. J. Sternberg & M. L. Barnes (Eds.), *The psychology of love* (pp. 119–138). New Haven, CT: Yale University Press. Copyright © 1988 by Yale University Press. Figure 6.2 adapted with permission.

to the relationship. *Infatuation* is described by Sternberg as an intense, "love at first sight" experience that is characterized by extreme attraction and arousal in the absence of any real emotional intimacy and decision/commitment. In *empty love* relationships, the partners are committed to each other and the relationship but lack an intimate emotional connection and passionate attraction. This type of love is often seen at the end of long-term relationships (or at the beginning of arranged marriages). *Romantic love* consists of feelings of closeness and connection (high intimacy) coupled with strong physical attraction. *Companionate love* is essentially a long-term, stable, and committed friendship that is characterized by high amounts of emotional intimacy, the decision to love the partner, and the commitment to remain in the relationship. This type of love is often seen in "best friendships" that are nonsexual or in long-term marriages in which sexual attraction has faded. Couples who experience *fatuous love* base their commitment to each other on passion rather than deep emotional intimacy. These "whirlwind" relationships are typically unstable and at risk for termination. Finally, *consummate love* results from the combination of all three components. According to Sternberg, this is the type of "complete" love many individuals strive to attain,

Table 10.1   Sternberg's Typology of Love Relationships

	Love Component		
Kind of Love Relationship	Intimacy	Passion	Decision/Commitment
Nonlove	Low	Low	Low
Liking	High	Low	Low
Infatuation	Low	High	Low
Empty Love	Low	Low	High
Romantic Love	High	High	Low
Companionate Love	High	Low	High
Fatuous Love	Low	High	High
Consummate Love	High	High	High

According to Sternberg (e.g., 1986), the three basic components of love—intimacy, passion, and decision/commitment—combine to produce eight different types of love relationship. For example, infatuation-based relationships are characterized by relatively high levels of passion but relatively low levels of intimacy and commitment, whereas companionate love relationships demonstrate the opposite pattern (i.e., high levels of intimacy and commitment coupled with low levels of passion).

particularly in their romantic relationships. Because the three basic components of love occur in varying degrees within a relationship, most love relationships will not fit cleanly into one particular category but will reflect some combination of categories.

Measurement.   Sternberg (1997, 1998) developed a 45-item scale to assess the three basic elements of love. The *Intimacy* subscale consists of 15 items designed to reflect feelings of warmth, support, self-disclosure, trust, and other aspects of intimate connection. Examples include "I feel close to _____," "I feel that I can really trust _____," "I feel that I really understand _____," "I have a warm relationship with _____," and "I share deeply personal information about myself with _____." The 15 items comprising the *Passion* subscale are designed to capture the more intense, physical, and exciting elements of romantic relationships, including "Just seeing _____ excites me," "I especially like physical contact with _____," "I find _____ to be very personally attractive," "I adore _____," and "I would rather be with _____ than with anyone else." The *Decision/Commitment* subscale contains 15 items that assess feelings of stability, commitment, and permanence. Examples include "I view my commitment to _____ as a solid one," "I have confidence in the stability of my relationship with _____," "I plan to continue in my relationship with _____," "I am certain of my love for _____," and "I will always feel a strong responsibility for _____."

Interestingly, although this scale was designed to measure three distinct aspects of love—intimacy, passion, and decision/commitment—empirical evidence suggests that it may actually measure one general love dimension. For example, psychologists Clyde and Susan Hendrick (1989) administered an early version of the Triangular Love Scale to a large sample of men and women. Their results indicated that the three subscales were highly intercorrelated, and also that the items formed a unifactorial scale. In other words, the scale appears to measure one global love dimension rather than three distinct elements or components of love. More recent attempts to validate the Triangular Love Scale have also produced equivocal results (see Sternberg, 1997). Perhaps for this reason, the scale has not received widespread use among relationship scientists interested in examining people's love experiences.

Lee's Colors of Love Typology

Another contemporary love classification scheme, and one that has produced a widely used measurement instrument, is the typology developed by Lee (e.g., 1973, 1977, 1988). In this novel approach each variety of love (or love style) is likened to a primary or secondary color. Like earlier theorists, Lee drew heavily on literature and philosophical discourse on the nature of love in developing his classification system and, like Sternberg, he also employed psychometric techniques (in this case, cluster analysis of love "symptoms" derived from literature and factor analysis of the results of a card-sorting task in which men and women sorted 1500 cards containing brief descriptions of love-related events, behaviors, ideas, or emotions to describe their own individual "love stories"). The results of Lee's analysis eventually produced a typology containing six styles or colors of love, each with characteristic features.

Primary and Secondary Love Styles. According to Lee, there are three primary colors or styles of loving. The first, *eros*, is an intensely emotional experience that is similar to passionate love. In fact, the most typical symptom of eros is an immediate and powerful attraction to the beloved individual. The erotic lover is "turned on" by a particular physical type, is prone to fall instantly and completely in love with a stranger (that is, experiences "love at first sight"), rapidly becomes preoccupied with pleasant thoughts about that individual, feels an intense need for daily contact with the beloved, and wishes the relationship to remain exclusive. Erotic love also has a strong sexual component; according to Lee, the typical erotic lover is "eager to get to know the beloved quickly, intensely—and undressed" (1988, p. 50). For example, not only does erotic love begin with a strong physical attraction, but the erotic lover usually seeks some form of sexual involvement fairly early in the relationship and enjoys expressing his or her affection through sexual contact.

The second primary color or style of love is *ludus* (or game-playing) love. The ludic lover views love as an entertaining game—one that is to be played with skill and often with several partners simultaneously. The typical ludic lover has no intention of including the current partner (or partners) in any future life plans or events, and dislikes any sign of growing involvement, need, or attachment from the partner. As the quintessential commitment-phobe, the ludic lover avoids seeing the partner too often, believes that lies and deception are justified, and expects the partner to remain in control of his or her emotions. In addition, ludic lovers tend to prefer a wide variety of physical types and view sexual activity as an opportunity for pleasure rather than for intense emotional bonding.

Storge is the third primary love style. Described by Lee (1973) as "love without fever or folly" (p. 77), storge resembles Lewis's concept of affection in that it is stable and based on a solid foundation of trust, respect, and friendship. Indeed, the typical storgic lover views and treats the partner as an "old friend," does not experience the intense emotions or physical attraction to the partner associated with erotic love, prefers to talk about and engage in shared interests with the partner rather than to express direct feelings, is shy about sex, and tends to demonstrate his or her affection in nonsexual ways.

Like the primary colors, these primary love styles can be combined to form secondary colors or styles of love. The three secondary styles identified by Lee contain features of the primaries but also possess their own unique characteristics. *Pragma*, a combination of storge and ludus, is "the love that goes shopping for a suitable mate" (Lee, 1973, p. 124). The pragmatic lover has a practical outlook to love and seeks a compatible partner. He or she creates a shopping list of desired features or attributes and selects a mate based on how well that individual fulfills the requirements (similarly, he or she will drop a partner who fails to "measure up" to expectations). Pragmatic love is essentially a faster-acting version of storge that has been quickened by the addition of ludus.

Mania, the combination of eros and ludus, is another secondary love style. Manic lovers lack the self-confidence associated with eros and the emotional self-control associated with ludus. This obsessive, jealous love style is characterized by self-defeating emotions, desperate attempts to force affection from the beloved, and the inability to believe in or trust any affection the loved one actually does display. The manic lover is eager, even desperate, to fall in love and to be loved. He or she begins immediately to imagine a future with the partner, wants to see the partner daily, tries to force the partner to show love and commitment, distrusts the partner's sincerity, and is extremely possessive. According to Lee (1973), people with a manic approach to love are "irrational, extremely jealous, obsessive, and often unhappy" (p. 15).

The last secondary color of love is *agape*, a combination of eros and storge. Agape is similar to Lewis's concept of charity, and represents an all-giving, selfless love style that implies an obligation to love and care for others without any expectation of reciprocity or reward. This love style is universal or inclusive in the sense that the typical agapic lover feels that everyone is worthy of love and that loving others is a duty of the mature person. With respect to their own personal love relationships, agapic lovers will unselfishly devote themselves to the partner, even stepping aside in favor of a rival who seems more likely to meet the partner's needs. Although Lee believed that many lovers respect and strive to attain the agapic ideal, he also believed that it was difficult to obtain in practice. That is, he felt that the give-and-take that characterizes most romantic relationships precludes the occurrence of purely altruistic love (although near-agapic experiences can and do occur).

Measurement. Lee's classification scheme inspired the development of several measurement instruments. The most well-known and commonly used is the 42-item Love Attitudes Scale (LAS) designed by the Hendricks and their colleagues (Hendrick & Hendrick, 1986; Hendrick, Hendrick, Foote, & Slapion-Foote, 1984). The LAS appears to reliably measure the six love styles and has subsequently been redesigned so that each of the items refers to a specific love relationship as opposed to more general attitudes about love (Hendrick & Hendrick, 1990). A shorter, 28-item version of the scale is also available (Hendrick, Hendrick, & Dicke, 1998). The complete scale, along with its shorter version, is reproduced in Exhibit 10.1.

The LAS is easy to administer and appears to reliably measure the six love styles proposed by Lee; consequently, it has been used in numerous empirical investigations. These studies reveal three general findings. First, in accord with other research demonstrating homogamy in mate selection (see Chapter 7), there is a tendency for individuals with similar love styles to pair; erotic lovers join with up with other erotic lovers, agapic people pair with other equally selfless lovers, and so on (e.g., Davis & Latty-Mann, 1987; Morrow, Clark, & Brock, 1995). Second, some love styles appear to be associated with relationship satisfaction. In particular, relationship satisfaction appears to be higher when partners possess an erotic, storgic, or agapic orientation to love, and lower when partners adopt a ludic love style (Fricker & Moore, 2002; Hendrick, Hendrick, & Adler, 1988; Meeks, Hendrick, & Hendrick, 1998). Third, there appear to be several individual and group differences in love style. For example, although sexual orientation does not appear to be associated with love styles (for a review, see Hendrick & Hendrick, 2006), there are fairly robust sex differences. Researchers commonly find that women score higher on the love styles of storge and pragma than do men, whereas men score higher on ludus (e.g., Dion & Dion, 1993; Hendrick & Hendrick, 1987, 1988, 1995; Hendrick et al., 1984, 1998; Le, 2005; Rotenberg & Korol, 1995; Sprecher & Toro-Morn, 2002). In addition, a number of recent investigations report higher scores among men than among women on the agapic love style (Hendrick & Hendrick, 2002; Lacey, Reifman, Scott, Harris, & Fitzpatrick, 2004; Lin & Huddleston-Casas, 2005; Neto & Pinto, 2003;

Exhibit 10.1 The Love Attitudes Scale

Instructions
Please answer the following items as honestly and accurately as possible. Whenever possible, answer the questions with your current dating partner in mind. If you are not currently dating anyone, answer the questions with your most recent partner in mind. Otherwise, answer in terms of what you think your responses would most likely be.

Response scale
1: strongly disagree; 2: moderately disagree; 3: neutral; 4: moderately agree; 5: strongly agree.

Items
Eros
  1. My partner and I were attracted to each other immediately after we first met.
 *2. My partner and I have the right physical "chemistry" between us.
  3. Our lovemaking is very intense and satisfying.
 *4. I feel that my partner and I were meant for each other.
  5. My partner and I became emotionally involved rather quickly.
 *6. My partner and I really understand each other.
 *7. My partner fits my ideal standards of physical beauty/handsomeness.

Ludus
  8. I try to keep my partner a little uncertain about my commitment to him/her.
 *9. I believe that what my partner doesn't know about me won't hurt him/her.
 *10. I have sometimes had to keep my partner from finding out about other lovers.
 11. I could get over my love affair with my partner pretty easily and quickly.
 *12. My partner would get upset if he/she knew of some of the things I've done with other people.
 13. When my partner gets too dependent on me, I want to back off a little.
 *14. I enjoy playing the "game of love" with my partner and a number of other partners.

Storge
 15. It is hard for me to say exactly when our friendship turned into love.
 16. To be genuine, our love first required *caring* for a while.
 17. I expect to always be friends with my partner.
 *18. Our love is the best kind because it grew out of a long friendship.
 *19. Our friendship merged gradually into love over time.
 *20. Our love is really a deep friendship, not a mysterious mystical emotion.
 *21. Our love relationship is the most satisfying because it developed from a good friendship.

Pragma
 22. I considered what my partner was going to become in life before I committed myself to him/her.
 23. I tried to plan my life carefully before choosing a partner.
 24. In choosing my partner, I believed it was best to love someone with a similar background.
 *25. A main consideration in choosing my partner was how he/she would reflect on my family.

*26. An important factor in choosing my partner was whether or not he/she would be a good parent.

*27. One consideration in choosing my partner was how he/she would reflect on my career.

*28. Before getting very involved with my partner, I tried to figure out how compatible his/her hereditary background would be with mine in case we ever had children.

Mania

29. When things aren't right with my partner and me, my stomach gets upset.

30. If my partner and I break up, I would get so depressed that I would even think of suicide.

31. Sometimes I get so excited about being in love with my partner that I can't sleep.

*32. When my partner doesn't pay attention to me, I feel sick all over.

*33. Since I've been in love with my partner, I've had trouble concentrating on anything else.

*34. I cannot relax if I suspect that my partner is with someone else.

*35. If my partner ignores me for a while, I sometimes do stupid things to try to get his/her attention back.

Agape

36. I try to always help my partner through difficult times.

*37. I would rather suffer myself than let my partner suffer.

*38. I cannot be happy unless I place my partner's happiness before my own.

*39. I am usually willing to sacrifice my own wishes to let my partner achieve his/hers.

40. Whatever I own is my partner's to use as he/she chooses.

41. When my partner gets angry with me, I still love him/her fully and unconditionally.

*42. I would endure all things for the sake of my partner.

Scoring

Starred items are included on the short form of the LAS. To find out your love style, add up your ratings for the items in each subscale. Divide this total by 7 (or by 4 if using the short form). Alternately, you may simply use your total scores for each subscale. You will have scores for the three primary love styles and for the three secondary love styles. Is your relationship characterized by one particular style of love? Or is it more complex than that?

NOTE: Response options have been reversed from original source. Starred items are included in the short form of the scale from Hendrick, Hendrick, and Dicke (1990).

SOURCE: Hendrick, C., & Hendrick, S. (1990). A relationship-specific version of the Love Attitudes Scale. *Journal of Social Behavior and Personality, 5,* 239–254. Copyright © 1990 by Select Press, Inc. Items adapted and reprinted with permission.

Sprecher & Toro-Morn, 2002). There also are multicultural and cross-cultural differences in love style. Within the United States, Asian American adults often score lower on eros and higher on pragma and storge than Caucasian, Latino, and African American adults (e.g., Dion & Dion, 1993; Hendrick & Hendrick, 1986). Latino groups, on the other hand, often score higher on ludus than Caucasian groups (e.g., Contreras, Hendrick, & Hendrick, 1996). And cross-cultural comparisons reveal that Chinese adults endorse a more pragmatic approach to love than do Americans (Sprecher & Toro-Morn, 2002).

These differences notwithstanding, it is important to keep in mind that not all individuals possess one approach to love, and the emotional tenor of any given relationship does not necessarily remain fixed over time. A man or woman may adopt numerous love styles, and a person's orientation to love may change over his or her lifetime or even during the course of a particular relationship. For example, the preoccupation and intense need associated with a manic love style may occur more often during the beginning stages of a romantic relationship, when the partners are uncertain as to their feelings and the future of their union. Later, these feelings may be replaced by more storgic or erotic feelings.

A final consideration to keep in mind when evaluating both Lee's and Sternberg's theories is that they were developed based on the self-reported experiences of adult men and women involved in romantic relationships. Thus these theories are more aptly considered taxonomies of adult romantic love; they (and their associated measurement instruments) may not adequately capture the kinds of love that people experience in other types of relationships (e.g., those with friends, family and kin, pets).

The Prototype Approach

Like the psychometric approach, the *prototype approach* to love is also empirically driven and involves collecting data directly from men and women about their love experiences. Unlike psychometric theorists, however, prototype researchers typically do not confine their investigations to romantic varieties of love, and they focus more specifically on people's knowledge and beliefs—their mental representations—of the concept of love. Researchers who utilize the prototype approach are interested in exploring what people think of when they are asked about love, how they differentiate love from related concepts (e.g., liking), how they form their conceptualizations of love, and how these conceptualizations or mental representations influence their behavior with relational partners.

The Hierarchy of Love.   Eleanor Rosch (e.g., 1973, 1975, 1978), an early pioneer in the use of prototype analysis, argued that natural language concepts (e.g., love, dog, apple) could be viewed as having both a vertical and a horizontal dimension. The *vertical dimension* reflects the hierarchical organization of concepts; that is, relations among different levels of concepts. Concepts at one level may be included within or subsumed by those at another, higher level. For example, the set of concepts "mammal," "dog," and "Collie" illustrate an abstract-to-concrete hierarchy with superordinate, basic, and subordinate levels.

Using the methods originally developed by Rosch, some researchers have investigated the hierarchical structure or vertical organization of the concept of love. Psychologist Phillip Shaver and his colleagues (Shaver, Schwartz, Kirson, & O'Connor, 1987), for instance, found evidence that "love" is a basic-level concept contained within the superordinate category of "emotion" and subsuming a variety of subordinate concepts that reflect types or varieties of love such as passion, infatuation, and liking (see Figure 10.3). In other words, most people consider passion, infatuation, and liking to be types of love, which, in turn, is viewed as a type of (positive) emotion.

The Prototype of Love.   Concepts also may be examined along a *horizontal dimension*. This dimension concerns the differentiation of concepts at the same level of inclusiveness (e.g., the dimension on which such subordinate level concepts as "Collie," "Golden Retriever," and "American Rat Terrier" vary). Rosch suggested that many natural language concepts have an internal structure whereby individual members of that category are ordered in terms of the

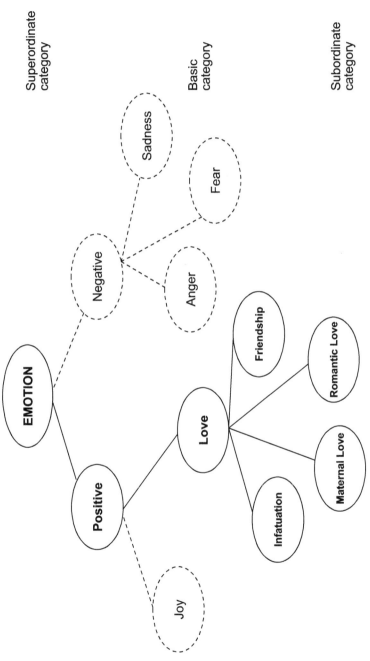

Fig. 10.3 The hierarchy of love and other emotions. Research conducted by Phillip Shaver, Beverley Fehr, and their colleagues (e.g., Fehr & Russell, 1991; Fischer, Shaver, & Carnochan, 1990; Shaver, Schwartz, Kirson, & O'Connor, 1987) suggests that *love* is a basic-level concept contained within the superordinate category of (positive) *emotion*. In addition, *love* appears to contain a variety of subordinate concepts that reflect types or varieties of love; of these, *maternal love* is viewed as the most prototypical.

Source: Shaver, P., Schwartz, J., Kirson, D., & O'Connor, C. (1987). Emotion knowledge: Further exploration of a prototype approach. *Journal of Personality and Social Psychology, 52,* 1061–1086. Copyright © 1987 by the American Psychological Association. Figure 1 adapted with permission.

degree to which they resemble the prototypic member of the category. A ***prototype*** is the best and clearest example of the concept (the "doggiest" dog—say, a Golden Retriever). People presumably decide whether a new item or experience belongs or "fits" within a particular concept by comparing the item with the concept's prototype. For example, in trying to decide whether or not he is in love with his partner, a man might compare the feelings ("I'm happy when she's with me," "I miss her when she's away," "I am very attracted to her"), thoughts ("I'm thinking about asking her to move in with me," "I wonder what our children would look like"), and actions ("I call her every day," "I plan my weekends so we can spend time together") he has experienced during their relationship with his prototype—his mental model—of "being in love." If what he is experiencing sufficiently matches his prototype, he is likely to conclude that he is, in fact, in love with his partner.

The prototype approach has been used extensively to explore the horizontal structure of a variety of interpersonal concepts, including love. Beverley Fehr and James Russell (1991; also see Fehr, 1994), for example, asked men and women to generate as many types of love as they could in a specified time and then asked another sample of individuals to rate these love varieties in terms of prototypicality or "goodness-of-example." Of the 93 subtypes generated, *maternal love* was rated as the best or most prototypical example of love, followed by *parental love, friendship, sisterly love, romantic love, brotherly love,* and *familial love. Infatuation,* along with *sexual love* and *puppy love,* was considered one of the least prototypical examples of love.

Researchers also have identified the prototypic features (as opposed to types) of love. In one early investigation, Fehr (1988) asked a group of participants to list the characteristics of the concept "love" and another group to rate how central each feature was to the concept. Features that her participants believed were central or prototypical to love included *trust, caring, honesty, friendship, respect, loyalty,* and *commitment.* Features that were considered peripheral or unimportant to the concept of love included *see only the other's good qualities, butterflies in stomach, uncertainty, dependency,* and *scary.*

Do people agree about the meaning of love? Within North America, the answer to this question is a resounding "yes." As noted by Fehr (2006) in her recent review of the prototype literature, there is a high degree of consistency across existing studies. Men and women in university and community samples from the west and east coasts of Canada and from the west coast of the United States possess a remarkably similar conceptualization of love—specifically, they agree that trust, caring, honesty, friendship, and respect are the most prototypical features of love. In addition, few individual differences in general conceptualizations of love have been identified. Fehr (2006) concluded that "the most striking finding in this literature is the extent of agreement on the prototype of love" (p. 233). However, it is important to note that until additional cross-cultural prototype analyses of love are conducted, we cannot draw any reliable conclusions about whether people around the world share a similar understanding of the meaning of love.

In sum, an examination of early scholarly discourse as well as more recent, empirically derived classification schemes reveals a few converging themes about the nature of love. First, all of the various theorists and researchers agree that the experience of love is intricately and importantly connected with the quality of individual human life, and that the study of love consequently has merit. Second, most theorists agree that multiple love types exist (although they disagree over precisely how many distinct varieties there are and what to call them), and this seems to dovetail nicely with people's commonsense or implicit theories of love and their reports of actual love experiences. In other words, love probably is best conceptualized as being composed of some number of subtypes or varieties of love rather than as one monolithic experience. Third, typologies of love and people's reports of their experiences in romantic relationships seem to suggest that love (or more specifically, adult romantic love) is composed at a minimum of two distinct varieties—a version that is intense, emotional, fleeting, and sexually charged, and a version that is durable, slow to develop, and infused with warmth and intimacy. These two types of love (variously called passionate, romantic, or erotic love and companionate, storgic, friendship-based, or affectionate love) have assumed special importance in contemporary relationship research, in part because their unique correlates or manifestations have been more clearly specified than have those of other varieties of love, and in part because of their presumed association with personal and species survival (as noted by Lewis, 1960/1988: "Without Eros none of us would have been begotten and without Affection none of us would have been reared" [p. 58]). We turn now to a consideration of these two special types of love.

PASSIONATE LOVE

Of all the many varieties of love that have been identified, ***passionate love*** has received the lion's share of attention from relationship scholars. The focus on this particular kind of love (and the corresponding lack of attention given to other types) is somewhat justified by the fact that passionate love appears to be a universal human experience. By young adulthood, most men and women report having been in love at least once (Regan, Durvasula, Howell, Ureño, & Rea, 2004), and researchers have found evidence that passionate love is experienced by people living in all cultures (Jankowiak, 1995; Jankowiak & Fischer, 1992; Sprecher, Aron, Hatfield, Cortese, Potapova, & Levitskaya, 1994). Moreover, as we discussed in Chapter 7, passionate love has become an essential part of the marriage contract in contemporary societies—most people say they will not marry without it and many people dissolve their relationships when it fades. In addition, and perhaps most importantly from a scientific perspective, passionate love appears to have several unique features that differentiate it from other varieties of love and that are amenable to empirical investigation.

Characteristic Features

Early theoretical statements about passionate love suggest that the experience of being in love with another is marked by a number of characteristic (and possibly even distinguishing) features, including a *swift and fairly sudden onset*, a *relatively brief life-span*, *idealization* of and *cognitive or mental preoccupation* with the beloved and/or the relationship, *intense and often fluctuating emotions*, *physiological arousal* and its associated bodily sensations, *sexual attraction*, and *exclusivity* or a focus on one specific individual (see Figure 10.4). For example, a substantial portion of English physician Havelock Ellis's many-volumed *Studies in the Psychology of Sex* is devoted to an examination of the relationship between love, sex, and marriage. Although his purpose was neither to develop a typology of love nor to discuss passionate love, Ellis nonetheless concluded that the love that frequently occurs between men and women is best viewed as a mixture of lust, or the physiological sexual impulse, and friendship, which includes other impulses of a more tender, affectionate nature (see, for example, 1933/1963, p. 234).

Sigmund Freud, one of Ellis's contemporaries and the founder of psychoanalytic theory, also associated passionate love or what he termed the "love-impulse" (1908/1963, p. 34) with sexual desire. According to psychoanalytic theory, passionate love is produced when the sexual instinct inherent within all individuals manifests itself as a psychical attachment to the current love-object. In other words, passionate love stems from a primitive, sexual urge and represents the suppression or sublimation of this sexual instinct. Freud later modified his view of this type of love to include an

Theorist	Label	Characteristic features
Andreas Capellanus (1184)	Common love	Emotional distress: "suffering" Cognitive preoccupation: "thinks about [beloved] continually" Sexual attraction: "desires of the flesh" Sexual intercourse: "the final act of Venus" Short duration: "quickly fails" Exclusivity: "they keep themselves for each other" Affection: "affection of the heart"
Richard von Krafft-Ebing (1886)	Sensual love	Idealization of beloved: "romantic idealizing [that] wraps the beloved object in the halo of perfection" Short duration: "never true and lasting" Sexual desire: "the fire of sensual feeling"
William James (1890)	Love	Sexual desire: "sexual appetite" Exclusivity: "the direction of the sexual instinct toward one individual tends to inhibit its application to other individuals"
Havelock Ellis (1897–1928, 1933)	Sexual love	Sexual desire: "lust" Affection: "friendship"
Sigmund Freud (1908, 1912)	Love-impulse	Sexual desire: "sensual passion" Affection: "tenderness"
Albert Ellis (1954)	Romantic love	Sexual desire (thwarted): "sexual teasing and blocking" Exclusivity: "one paramount love object" Idealization of beloved: "over-evaluates and fictionalizes" Emotional intensity: "goes from one violent passion to another" Short duration: "not sustained by the realities of either living or loving"
Theodor Reik (1944, 1945)	Love	Sexual desire: "sex-urge" Idealization of beloved: "the love-object appears as the personification of perfection" Emotional intensity: "like a virus in your blood" Short duration: "romance has to perish" Affection: "tenderness ... kindness"
Erich Fromm (1960)	Erotic love	Care: "active concern" Responsibility: "response to the needs of another" Respect: awareness of the other's "unique individuality" Knowledge: empathy, seeing the other "in his [her] own terms" Emotional intensity: "explosive" Short duration: "by its very nature short-lived" Exclusivity: "restricted to one person" Sexual desire: "desire for physical union"
C. S. Lewis (1960)	Erotic love (Eros)	Exclusivity: "Eros makes a man really want, not a woman, but one particular woman" Sexual desire: "sexual appetite," "the longing for a union which only the flesh can mediate" Cognitive preoccupation: "delighted pre-occupation with the Beloved" Idealization (of love and the love relationship): Eros "builds his own religion round the lovers [and] seems to sanction all sorts of actions they would not otherwise have dared" Short duration: "the most mortal of our loves" Affection

Fig. 10.4 Early theoretical statements about passionate love.

affiliative or affectionate component, ultimately concluding that "to ensure a fully normal attitude in love, two currents of feeling have to unite—we may describe them as the tender, affectionate feelings and the sensual feelings" (1912/1963, p. 59).

The view that sexual desire is an essential feature of passionate love is echoed by psychotherapist Albert Ellis in his classic work, *The American Sexual Tragedy* (1954). Following a thorough examination of the popular mass media of the time as well as a diverting excursion through the personal experiences of colleagues and friends and the free associations and dreams of his clients, he concluded, "Although *romantic* has become, in our day, virtually a synonym for *loving*, romantic love is actually a special type of love, and has several distinguishing features" (p. 101). According to Ellis, these distinguishing features include idealization of the beloved, intense and changeable emotions, fragility, exclusivity, and sexual desire. The latter was believed to be the most powerful antecedent of passionate love (1954, p. 113):

> Romantic love, again, is largely based on the sexual teasing and blocking of modern courtship. Its very intensity, to a large part, grows out of the generous promises combined with the niggardly actualities of sex fulfillment which exist during the courtship stages.

Ellis believed that the heady, emotionally volatile, idealized experience of passionate love was far more fleeting than the calm, steady, enduring, domestic love that characterized well-adjusted marital relationships. Indeed, the former was posited to survive only as long as sexual desire was permitted no outlet. Once the urgent pangs of desire were sated via intercourse, Ellis posited that passionate love would perish—"sexual and marital consummation indubitably, in the vast majority of instances, maims, bloodies, and finally kills romanticism until it is deader than—well, yesterday's romance" (p. 116).

Existentialist Fromm (1956) provides a similar conceptualization in his typology, stating that erotic love—"the craving for complete fusion, for union with one other person" (pp. 52–53)—shares four common features with all other forms of love (care, responsibility, respect, and knowledge) as well as several distinguishing characteristics. These include exclusivity ("completely individual attraction, unique between two specific persons," p. 57), emotional intensity, fragility, and sexual desire. Because sexual desire is so closely associated with erotic love, Fromm cautioned that many individuals are easily misled to conclude that they are in love with each other when in fact they simply desire one another sexually. We are only in love with the objects of our sexual desire when they are also the objects of our affection.

This theme is echoed by Lewis (1960/1988) in *The Four Loves*. Like other love types, erotic love or the "state which we call 'being in love'" (p. 91) was posited to contain affection. Lewis also concluded, as did Fromm, that passionate love is marked by exclusivity (even possessiveness), and that it contains a "carnal or animally sexual element" (p. 92) that essentially is an individualized sexual desire directed toward the beloved. And finally, he, too (p. 13), noted the short-lived or transitory nature of this variety of love:

> And all the time the grim joke is that this Eros whose voice seems to speak from the eternal realm is not himself necessarily even permanent. He is notoriously the most mortal of our loves. The world rings with complaints of his fickleness.

It is the transitory nature of passion, coupled with lovers' (unrealistic) beliefs in its permanence, that Lewis felt gave erotic love its unique blend of "strength, sweetness, terror and high port" (p. 115).

Contemporary relationship scholars have also emphasized the intense, emotional, idealistic, sexual, and fleeting nature of this type of love (see Hendrick & Hendrick, 1992, 2000; Regan, 1998b; Sternberg & Barnes, 1988; Sternberg & Weis, 2006). For example, Ellen Berscheid and Elaine Hatfield (then Walster; 1974; Walster & Berscheid, 1971)—among the first contemporary researchers to conduct a dialogue on the nature of passionate love—conceptualized this type of love as a fragile, temporary, intense phenomenon that blossoms when an individual is extremely aroused physiologically and when situational or contextual cues indicate that "passionate love" is the appropriate label for that arousal. These theorists suggested that a variety of physiologically arousing emotional experiences (including fear, rejection, frustration, hatred, excitement, and sexual gratification) can produce and enhance romantic attraction. In addition, they posited that sexuality is intricately linked with the experience of passionate love. More recent conceptualizations provided by these authors and their colleagues (e.g., Berscheid, 1988; Hatfield, 1988; Hatfield & Rapson, 1993; Regan & Berscheid, 1999) continue to emphasize the transitory nature of passionate love and more clearly target sexual desire (as opposed to other sexual phenomena) as one of its most important features.

Similarly, Dorothy Tennov (e.g., 1979, 1998) characterizes "limerence" or the state of being in love as a subjective experience marked by persistent, intrusive thought about the object of passionate desire (called the limerent object or "LO"), acute longing for reciprocation, mood fluctuations, intense awareness of the LO's actions, fear of rejection, shyness, physical reactions (such as "heartache"), emotional highs and lows depending on the LO's perceived reciprocity, and idealization of the LO's positive qualities. A particularly important hallmark of limerence is exclusivity. Like many other theorists, Tennov (1998) argues that there can be only one LO at a time, and that once an LO is selected, "limerence cements the reaction and locks the emotional gates against competitors" (1998, p. 86). In addition, she strongly believed that sexual feelings are a necessary part of the limerent experience, concluding:

> I am inclined toward the generalization that sexual attraction is an essential component of limerence. This sexual feeling may be combined with shyness, impotence or some form of sexual dysfunction or disinclination, or with some social unsuitability. But LO, in order to become LO, must stand in relation to the limerent as one for whom the limerent is a potential sex partner. Sexual attraction is not "enough," to be sure. Selection standards for limerence are, according to informants, not identical to those by which "mere" sexual partners are evaluated, and sex is seldom the main focus of limerence. Either the potential for sexual mating is felt to be there, however, or the state described is not limerence.
>
> (1979, pp. 24–25)

In sum, most love theorists view passionate love as a short-lived state that is characterized by idealization of the loved one, preoccupation or obsessive rumination about the relationship, and intense emotions. In addition, passionate love is considered an exclusive rather than an inclusive experience; that is, unlike other varieties of love, passionate love is generally felt for one particular individual (and people are presumed to be incapable of being in love with more than one individual at a time). And finally, most theoretical statements include the idea that passionate love is strongly rooted in sexual desire (which is often accompanied by other nonsexual, affectionate feelings).

Empirical Research

Most of these theoretical suppositions have received empirical support. For example, research conducted with dating couples reveals that idealization appears to play a role in the experience of passionate love—as we discussed in Chapter 8, men and women often perceive their romantic partners (and their romantic relationships) in an excessively positive light. In addition, there is evidence that passionate love is relatively fragile, or at least less durable than other varieties of love. Although feelings of passionate love initially may increase as a couple progresses from earlier to later courtship stages—

for example, from casual dating to steady dating or engagement (Hatfield & Sprecher, 1986a)—research conducted with dating and married couples generally finds that passionate love declines over longer periods of time (e.g., Hatfield, Traupmann, & Sprecher, 1984; Sprecher & Regan, 1998).

Passionate love also appears to be an intensely emotional experience. For example, men and women in one prototype study were asked to identify the basic characteristics of passionate love, further defined as the state of "being in love" with someone (Regan, Kocan, & Whitlock, 1998). Among the features they specified as particularly central to the concept of passionate love were such emotions as *happiness, joy or rapture, closeness, warmth, affection*, and *tenderness*. Participants also cited a number of physical sensations that are associated with the experience of intense emotion, including *giddiness* and a *racing heart*. Similarly, research with dating couples reveals that the greater the amount of passionate love that men and women feel for their dating partners, the more frequently they experience a host of positive emotions ranging from satisfaction and contentment to joy (Sprecher & Regan, 1998). Interestingly, although passionate love appears to be more strongly associated with positive emotional experience than with negative ones, there is one exception—jealousy. Both men and women associate jealousy with the state of being in love (Regan et al., 1998), and those who love passionately also tend to report feeling or having felt jealous (Sprecher & Regan, 1998).

The theoretical notion that sexual desire may be a distinguishing feature of passionate love has garnered the most empirical support. Certainly people *believe* that sexual attraction is an essential component of the state of being in love. When Robert Ridge and Ellen Berscheid (1989) asked a sample of undergraduates whether they thought that there was a difference between "being in love with" and "loving" another person, almost all (87%) emphatically claimed that there indeed was a difference between the two experiences—and that the difference had to do with sexual attraction (which they argued was part of the former and not the latter). Similar results were reported by Pamela Regan and her colleagues (1998), whose prototype analysis of the concept of passionate love revealed that out of the 119 features spontaneously generated by participants, *sexual desire* received the second highest frequency rating (65.8%; *trust* was first, cited by 80% of respondents). In other words, when thinking of passionate love, two-thirds of the participants automatically thought of sexual desire.

Person perception experiments provide additional support for these prototype results. Person perception experiments are commonly used in psychological research and essentially involve manipulating people's perceptions of a relationship and then measuring the impact of that manipulation on their subsequent evaluations and beliefs. In one such experiment, Regan (1998a, Experiment 2) provided a sample of undergraduate men and women with two self-report questionnaires ostensibly completed by "Rob" and "Nancy," a student couple enrolled at the same university. The members of this couple reported that they were currently passionately in love with each other, that they loved each other, or that they liked each other. Participants then estimated the likelihood that the partners experienced sexual desire for each other as well as the amount of desire that they felt for each other. The results revealed that both men and women believed that couples who were passionately in love were more *likely* to experience sexual desire, and experienced a greater *amount* of sexual desire, than couples who loved each other or who liked each other. Interestingly, sexual desire was believed to be no more likely in a "loving" relationship than in a "liking" relationship, and greater amounts of sexual desire were not believed to occur in loving relationships than in liking relationships. Again, it seems that sexual desire is viewed as an important feature of passionate love relationships—and not of relationships characterized by feelings of loving (i.e., companionate love) and/or liking (i.e., friendship).

Research conducted with individuals involved in ongoing romantic relationships, although relatively scarce, also supports the association between sexual desire and passionate love. For example, in one investigation (Regan, 2000), heterosexual dating couples indicated the amount of sexual desire, passionate love (further defined as the state of being "in love with" the partner), liking, and love they currently experienced in their relationships (assessed via single-item measures). The results revealed that sexual desire and passionate love were positively correlated; the more participants desired their dating partners sexually, the more they were in love with those partners. No associations were found between sexual desire and liking, or between sexual desire and loving.

Similar results were reported by Sarah Meyers and Ellen Berscheid (1996), who asked a large sample of men and women to list the initials of all the people they currently loved, the initials of all those with whom they were currently in love, and the initials of all those toward whom they currently felt sexual attraction or desire. The results indicated that 85% of the persons listed in the "in love" category also were listed in the "sexually desire" category, whereas only 2% of those listed in the "love" category (and not cross-listed in the "in love" category) were listed in the "sexually desire" category. In other words, the objects of participants' feelings of passionate love (but not their feelings of love) also tended to be the objects of their desire. The researchers also found evidence for the exclusive nature of passionate love; specifically, in accord with theoretical speculation, participants generally listed only one person in the "in love" category, though they listed many more in the other two categories.

Considered together, the results of these empirical investigations suggest that passionate love is a qualitatively different experience from other love varieties, and that exclusivity, fragility, idealization of the beloved, emotional intensity, and, in particular, sexual desire are among its distinguishing features.

Measurement

Researchers interested in measuring passionate love usually rely on self-report measures. Single-item measures typically ask respondents to report whether they are currently in love with their partner or to indicate the quantity or intensity of passionate love that they are currently experiencing for their partner (see Table 10.2). Such global, single-item measures are easy to use and appear to be relatively valid (Sprecher & Regan, 1998). However, many researchers choose to use larger multi-item scales that have been developed specifically to measure the various theoretically important dimensions of passionate love. Several multi-item passionate love scales have been constructed over the years (see, for example, Critelli, Myers, & Loos, 1986; Pam, Plutchik, & Conte, 1975; Swensen, 1961; Swensen & Gilner, 1963). The two most commonly used and theoretically grounded measures are the Erotic subscale of the Love Attitudes Scale (Hendrick & Hendrick, 1986) and the Passionate Love Scale developed by Elaine Hatfield and Susan Sprecher (1986a).

The Passionate Love Scale is arguably the most reliable and valid measure of passionate love currently available. Drawing on past theoretical conceptualizations, previously developed measures, and in-depth personal interviews, Hatfield and Sprecher crafted a series of items designed to assess the various components of the passionate love experience (see Exhibit 10.2). The items clearly reflect what theorists believe are the essential ingredients of passionate love: intense emotion and its associated physiological arousal ("I would feel deep despair if _____ left me," "Sometimes my body trembles with excitement at the sight of _____"), cognitive preoccupation ("_____ always seems to be on my mind"), idealization ("For me, _____ is the perfect romantic partner"), exclusivity ("I would rather be with _____ than with anyone else"), and sexual attraction ("I possess a powerful attraction for _____").

Table 10.2 Some Single-Item Measures of Passionate Love

1. Are you passionately in love with your partner right now?

    Yes   No

2. How much passionate love do you currently feel for _____?

1	2	3	4	5	6	7	8	9
None								A great deal

3. Rate the intensity of your feelings of passionate love for your current partner.

1	2	3	4	5	6	7	8	9
Not at all intense								Extremely intense

4. How deeply are you in love with _____?

1	2	3	4	5	6	7	8	9
Not at all deeply								Very deeply

5. How strong are your feelings of passionate love for your partner?

1	2	3	4	5	6	7	8	9
Very weak								Very strong

1	2	3	4	5	6	7	8	9
Not at all strong								Extremely strong

6. How often do you experience feelings of passionate love for your partner?

1	2	3	4	5	6	7	8	9
Never								Extremely often

Exhibit 10.2 The Passionate Love Scale

Instructions

We would like to know how you feel when you are *passionately in love* with someone. Please think of the person whom you love most passionately *right now*. If you are not in love right now, please think of the last person with whom you were in love. If you have never been in love, think of the person you came closest to caring for in that way. Try to tell us how you felt at the time when your feelings were the most intense.

Response scale

1	2	3	4	5	6	7	8	9
Not at all true				Moderately true				Definitely true

Items

1. Since I've been involved with _____, my emotions have been on a roller coaster.
2. I would feel deep despair if _____ left me.
3. Sometimes my body trembles with excitement at the sight of _____.

4. I take delight in studying the movements and angles of _____'s body.
5. Sometimes I can't control my thoughts; they are obsessively on _____.
6. I feel happy when I am doing something to make _____ happy.
7. I would rather be with _____ than with anyone else.
8. I'd get jealous if I thought _____ were falling in love with someone else.
9. No one else could love _____ like I do.
10. I yearn to know all about _____.
11. I want _____—physically, emotionally, mentally.
12. I will love _____ forever.
13. I melt when looking deeply into _____'s eyes.
14. I have an endless appetite for affection from _____.
15. For me, _____ is the perfect romantic partner.
16. _____ is the person who can make me feel the happiest.
17. I sense my body responding when _____ touches me.
18. I feel tender toward _____.
19. _____ always seems to be on my mind.
20. If I were separated from _____ for a long time, I would feel intensely lonely.
21. I sometimes find it difficult to concentrate on work because thoughts of _____ occupy my mind.
22. I want _____ to know me—my thoughts, my fears, and my hopes.
23. Knowing that _____ cares about me makes me feel complete.
24. I eagerly look for signs indicating _____'s desire for me.
25. If _____ were going through a difficult time, I would put away my own concerns to help him/her out.
26. _____ can make me feel effervescent and bubbly.
27. In the presence of _____, I yearn to touch and be touched.
28. An existence without _____ would be dark and dismal.
29. I possess a powerful attraction for _____.
30. I get extremely depressed when things don't go right in my relationship with _____.

Scoring

To find out your passionate love score, add up the ratings you gave to each item. Divide this total by 30.

SOURCE: Hatfield, E., & Sprecher, S. (1986a). Measuring passionate love in intimate relationships. *Journal of Adolescence, 9,* 383–410. Copyright © 1986 by Academic Press, Inc. Used with permission of Elsevier Ltd.

COMPANIONATE LOVE

Although scholars interested in love have devoted most of their attention to the passionate variety, they have also attempted to elucidate the nature of companionate love. Variously described as affectionate love, friendship-based love, and storge, *companionate love* reflects the "affection and tenderness we feel for those with whom our lives are deeply entwined" (Hatfield & Rapson, 1993,

p. 9). Berscheid (1985) observed that some love theorists conceptualize companionate love as a combination of altruistic love, attachment, and friendship. Indeed, Krafft-Ebing (1886/1945) called this type of love "true love" and stated that "it is rooted in the recognition of the moral and mental qualities of the beloved person, and is equally ready to share pleasures and sorrows and even to make sacrifices" (p. 12). This conceptualization resembles Lewis's (1960/1988) definition of Affection as well as the definitions proposed by several contemporary theorists (e.g., Brehm, 1985; Sternberg, 1988).

Characteristic Features

Companionate love is believed to be characterized by several basic features, including a *relatively slow onset*, *durability* or permanence, *interdependence*, and feelings of *affection*, *intimacy*, and *commitment*.

Research generally substantiates these theoretical predictions. For example, positive affect does appear to be a particularly strong feature of companionate love. Helmut Lamm and Ulrich Wiesmann (1997) asked university students to write down how they could tell that they "loved" (as opposed to "liked" or were "in love with") another person. The most common indicator of companionate love generated by the participants was *positive mood* (listed by 53%); distinctive indicators (i.e., elements that were listed significantly more frequently for "love" than for "like" or "in love") included such positive affective experiences as *trust* (41%), *tolerance* (21%), and *relaxedness or calmness* (12%). The participants in a study conducted by psychologist Donna Castañeda (1993) provided almost identical answers when asked to indicate the qualities and characteristics they believed to be important in a love relationship. Specifically, participants mentioned *trust*, *mutual respect*, *communication and sharing*, *honesty*, and *affection* along with a number of other positive emotions and experiences. Research with dating couples supports these survey results. Sprecher and Regan (1998) found that positive emotions (including joy, trust, liking, contentment, and satisfaction) were positively correlated with, and negative emotions (such as anger, hatred, anxiety, and loneliness) were negatively correlated with, the amount of companionate love reported by a sample of romantically involved couples. In addition, not only did companionate lovers feel high levels of *emotional* intimacy and warmth, but they also reported relatively more feelings of *sexual* intimacy (i.e., open communication with the partner about sexuality) than did passionate lovers. Thus, feelings of warmth, trust, and intimacy (emotional and, perhaps, sexual) are a hallmark of the companionate love experience.

In addition, there is some evidence that companionate love is durable and relatively impervious to the passage of time. The passionate love scores of the participants in Sprecher and Regan's (1998) study were negatively correlated with the age of their relationship (i.e., the longer they had been romantically involved with their partners, the less "in love" they claimed to be with those partners); however, their companionate love scores did not change as a function of the length of their relationship but remained uniformly high. Some relationship scientists speculate that companionate love may even grow stronger over time because it is grounded in intimacy processes (including caring, understanding, and attachment) that require time to develop fully (e.g., Hatfield & Rapson, 1993). Others propose that romantic relationships may progress in a linear fashion from passionate love to companionate love (e.g., Murstein, 1988; Reik, 1945). For example, Sternberg (1988) suggested, "Most romantic love relationships that do, in fact, survive eventually turn into companionate love relationships: the passion begins to melt, but the intimacy remains. Passion may be replaced over time by long-term and deeply felt commitment" (p. 127).

Measurement

Like passionate love, companionate love is typically assessed via self-report measures. These range from single-item measures (e.g., "How much caring, affectionate love do you feel for your partner?") to multi-item scales. For example, Sternberg (e.g., 1988) defined companionate love as the combination of intimacy and decision/commitment; thus, the 30 items included in the Intimacy and Decision/Commitment subscales of his larger love scale provide one measure of companionate love. The Storge subscale on the LAS also may assess this type of love. Perhaps the most commonly used measure of companionate love, however, is the 13-item Love Scale created by Zick Rubin (1970). Other researchers (e.g., Sprecher & Regan, 1998) have subsequently revised this scale by added items that assess interpersonal trust and removing items that reflected a more passionate love experience (see Exhibit 10.3).

Exhibit 10.3 The Companionate Love Scale

Instructions

Companionate love is a sturdy, durable type of love based on feelings of deep affection and caring. Some common terms for this type of love are *affectionate love, friendship love, true love,* and *attachment.*

We would like to know how you feel when you love someone this way. Please think of the person whom you love most companionately *right now.* If you do not love someone right now, please think of the last person you loved. If you have never loved someone, think of the person you came closest to caring for in that way.

Response scale

1	2	3	4	5	6	7	8	9
Not at all true				Moderately true				Definitely true

Items

1. I feel that I can confide in _____ about virtually everything.
2. I find it easy to ignore _____'s faults.
3. I would do almost anything for _____.
4. I would forgive _____ for practically anything.
5. I would greatly enjoy being confided in by _____.
6. I care about _____.
7. I feel that I can trust _____ completely.

Scoring

To find out your companionate love score, add up the ratings you gave to each item. Divide this total by 7.

SOURCE: Sprecher, S., & Regan, P. C. (1998). Passionate and companionate love in courting and young married couples. *Sociological Inquiry, 68,* 163–185. Copyright © 1998 by Blackwell Publishing, Inc. Items reprinted with permission of Wiley-Blackwell.

THE NEUROCHEMISTRY OF LOVE

In recent years, scientists have made concerted efforts to uncover the neurochemical underpinnings of love. Most have focused on the activity of specific *neurotransmitters* (electrochemical messages released by neurons or the cells of the nervous system). Researchers interested in passionate love have targeted the monoamines—in particular, serotonin, dopamine, and norepinephrine—due to their demonstrated relationship with mood and generalized arousal. For example, Helen Fisher (e.g., 1998, 2000, 2006) observed the following similarities between the experience of being in love and the psycho-physiological effects of the monoamines:

- People who are in love report focusing on specific events or objects associated with the beloved and remembering and musing over things that the beloved said or did. Increased levels of dopamine are associated with heightened attention, and increased levels of norepinephrine are associated with enhanced memory for new stimuli.
- People who are passionately in love often report feelings of euphoria and exhilaration coupled with heightened energy, loss of appetite, and sleeplessness. These same experiences are associated with increased concentrations of dopamine in the brain.
- People deep in the throes of passion report thinking about the loved one obsessively, and low levels of serotonin are implicated in the type of intrusive thinking that is associated with obsessive-compulsive disorder.

On the basis of these similarities, Fisher has suggested that passionate love is associated primarily with high levels of dopamine and norepinephrine and low levels of serotonin. There is some preliminary evidence in support of her hypothesis. One group of investigators (Marazziti, Akiskal, Rossi, & Cassano, 1999) found that a group of healthy people who were in the early phases of "falling in love" had approximately the same level of serotonin as did a group of people who had been diagnosed with obsessive-compulsive disorder; in addition, the serotonin levels of both of these groups of participants were significantly lower than those of a control group of healthy participants who were not currently in love (also see Kurup & Kurup, 2003). More recently, another study revealed that people who were intensely in love showed increased activity in dopamine-rich areas of the brain when they gazed at a photo of their beloved (Aron et al., 2005). Although additional research is needed, these findings suggest that the experience of passionate love may be associated with a particular neurochemical milieu.

Scientists also have begun to explore the neurochemical correlates of companionate love. Two neuropeptides, oxytocin and vasopressin, have come under scrutiny. Both vasopressin and oxytocin are associated with a variety of reproductive and caregiving behaviors in non-human mammals (see Hiller, 2004; Insel, 1997, 2000; Leckman & Herman, 2002). In addition, decreased levels of oxytocin and other alterations in the endocrine oxytocin and vasopressin systems have been observed in children diagnosed with autism, a developmental disorder characterized by severe social impairment and the inability to form interpersonal connections and lasting emotional attachments (Green et al., 2001). Based on these two lines of research, some scholars have hypothesized that oxytocin and vasopressin may be involved in the ability to form social attachments and to experience the deep feelings of affection and affiliation that are part and parcel of companionate love (Carter, 1998; Fisher, 2000; Leckman, Hrdy, Keverne, & Carter, 2006). As yet, however, this hypothesis has not been tested with healthy adult humans.

SUMMARY

Recognizing the important role that love plays in human life, many scholars have theorized about its nature. Early theorists derived their taxonomies from personal observation and inductive reasoning, literature, and previous philosophical, theological, and scientific discourse. Contemporary scholars have increasingly relied on statistical techniques to help them distinguish among different types of love; in general, their taxonomies are based on analyzing the self-reported experiences of people in ongoing love relationships as well as men's and women's common understandings and beliefs about love. This body of theoretical and empirical work reveals that many different ways of loving exist. Although relationship scientists continue to disagree about the exact number of love types that occur (and what to call them), all agree that at a minimum two distinct varieties exist—a version that is intense, emotional, fleeting, and sexually charged (passionate love), and a version that is durable, slow to develop, and infused with warmth and intimacy (companionate love).

KEY CONCEPTS

Psychometric approach (p. 173)
Triangular theory of love (p. 173)
Intimacy component (p. 173)
Passion component (p. 173)
Decision/commitment component (p. 173)
Stability property (p. 173)
Conscious controllability property (p. 173)
Experiential salience property (p. 173)
Nonlove (p. 173)
Liking (p. 173)
Infatuation (p. 174)
Empty love (p. 174)
Romantic love (p. 174)
Companionate love (p. 174)
Fatuous love (p. 174)

Consummate love (p. 174)
Erotic love style (eros) (p. 176)
Ludic love style (ludus) (p. 176)
Storgic love style (storge) (p. 176)
Pragmatic love style (pragma) (p. 176)
Manic love style (mania) (p. 177)
Agapic love style (agape) (p. 177)
Prototype approach (p. 180)
Vertical dimension (of a concept) (p. 180)
Horizontal dimension (of a concept) (p. 180)
Prototype (p. 182)
Passionate love (p. 183)
Companionate love (p. 190)
Neurotransmitters (p. 193)

EXPLORATION EXERCISES

These exercises are designed to allow you to explore in greater detail some of the concepts and issues discussed in this chapter. There are no right or wrong answers to these exercises—they are simply meant to provide an opportunity for discussion and debate.

1. Sternberg (e.g., 1986) proposes that three basic components—intimacy, passion, and decision/commitment—combine to form eight different types or varieties of love. Select two fictional relationships you have seen portrayed in media (e.g., books, plays, movies, television). Which type of love does each relationship illustrate? Describe each one in terms of the three components of love, citing specific examples to support your hypothesis.

2. What is your approach or orientation to love relationships? To answer this question, complete the Love Attitudes Scale (Exhibit 10.1 in this chapter). Follow the instructions and rate each item. Then sum the ratings you gave for each set of items (each subscale), as follows:

Items 1–7	Erotic love style	Total score = _____
Items 8–14	Ludic love style	Total score = _____
Items 15–21	Storgic love style	Total score = _____
Items 22–28	Pragmatic love style	Total score = _____
Items 29–35	Manic love style	Total score = _____
Items 36–42	Agapic love style	Total score = _____

Look at your total scores on each subscale. On which subscale(s) did you score highest? Lowest? Do your personal experiences match Lee's descriptions of the various love styles? Perhaps you had similar scores across all of the subscales. If this was the case, then your orientation to love cannot be easily captured by Lee's theory (or this scale); for example, you may be someone who approaches love differently depending on your partner or your current life situation.

3. What do people think of when they consider the concept of "love"? This exercise is designed to explore people's mental representations—their prototypes—of love. Find two volunteers. Ask each one to think of the concept of "love" and to list as many characteristics, attributes, or features of this concept as they can in two minutes (you'll need to time your volunteers). Then ask each volunteer to look over the list of features he or she generated and select the three features that are most important or central to the concept of love. Once you have collected these data from your volunteers, take a look at their responses. Do the features they selected match the results reported by Fehr (1988) in her prototype of love study? (Recall that her participants rated *trust*, *caring*, *honesty*, *friendship*, *respect*, *loyalty*, and *commitment* as central or prototypical features of love.)

4. Think of your current romantic partner (if you are not currently in a romantic relationship, think of your last romantic partner). Complete the Passionate Love Scale (Exhibit 10.2) and the Companionate Love Scale (Exhibit 10.3). Did you score above or below average (average = a score of 5 on both scales)? Do you think it is possible to feel both types of love—passionate and companionate—for another person?

5. Select one scene from a movie, television show, novel, or play that, in your opinion, best illustrates the concept of passionate love. Do the same for companionate love. Share your examples with the class and discuss the ways in which the scenes exemplify these two types of love.

Chapter 11
Sexing

Sexuality plays an important role in mating relationships. In the previous chapter, for instance, we saw how one particular sexual response—sexual desire—is associated with feelings of passionate love. This chapter focuses on *relational sex*, defined as sexual responses that occur within the context of ongoing romantic relationships. Relational sex is very different from other forms of sexuality such as individual sexual responses and casual sexual encounters between strangers or uncommitted partners. For example, although all three types of sexuality may stem from similar motives (including a need for physical release or the urge to satiate sexual desires), involve similar processes (such as physiological and genital arousal), and produce similar outcomes (including physical pleasure), relational sex has interpersonal meanings and consequences that other varieties of sexual experience do not. Unlike casual sex or solo sexual activities, sexual activities between relational partners may stem from feelings of love and intimacy; may serve to demonstrate or reaffirm the partners' commitment to each other; or may be used by the partners to restore equity or to shift the balance of power in their relationship (Cain et al., 2003; also see Sprecher & Regan, 2000). Sexual events that occur between partners in a romantic relationship thus have important nonsexual consequences for that relationship.

SEXUAL ATTITUDES

Well, I can't speak for anyone else, but for me, the only way I'd have sex with someone was if we were deeply in love. If two people are in love, then sex seems like a natural way to express those feelings.

– 19-year-old woman interviewed by the author

The decision to have sex is a personal choice that everyone should be free to make. Some people have sex just because they enjoy it, or because they have the chance to do it. That's fine; it's a personal decision. Other people, and I'm one of them, think that sex is best when it's done out of love, with someone you're involved with.

– 20-year-old man interviewed by the author

In the minds of many individuals, love and sex share an intimate connection. In fact, most men and women view intercourse and other sexual activities as most appropriate when they occur within the context of a committed, loving relationship. For example, in one of the first empirical investigations of sexual attitudes, sociologist Ira Reiss (1964) reported that men and women from a national probability sample of the U.S. population, as well as students from five high schools and colleges, were increasingly accepting of premarital sexual intercourse between two people as their relationship became characterized by correspondingly greater amounts of affection and commitment. Specifically, as the couple's relationship progressed from relatively little affection to strong affection, and then to love and engagement, participants believed that intercourse was more acceptable. Similar results were reported 20 years later by sociologists Susan Sprecher, Kathleen McKinney, Robert Walsh, and Carrie Anderson (1988), who found that increasing numbers of men and women viewed sexual intercourse between two people as acceptable as their relationship stage moved from the first date (28%), to casual dating (41%), to serious dating (72%), to pre-engagement (77%), and finally to engagement (82%).

Research reveals that U.S. society is becoming more ***sexually permissive*** (for a review, see Willetts, Sprecher, & Beck, 2004). In particular, although men and women continue to view sex as most appropriate when it occurs in the context of a committed and love-based relationship, there is a trend toward greater acceptance of sexual activity in casual dating relationships. Robert Sherwin and Sherry Corbett (1985), for example, examined college students' normative beliefs about sexual activity in various types of dating relationship. Three groups of students—the first surveyed in 1963, the second in 1971, and the third in 1978—were asked to indicate the extent to which various sexual activities generally were expected to play a part in the relationship between casually dating, steadily dating, and engaged couples. The results provided evidence for increasingly liberal campus sexual norms among both men and women over the 15-year period. For example, none of the men and women in the 1963 sample expected sexual intercourse to occur in a casual dating relationship; by 1978, however, 17% of the men and 9% of the women viewed intercourse as a normal part of casual dating.

A recent investigation by psychologists Brooke Wells and Jean Twenge (2005) confirmed these results. These researchers identified 45 individual research studies conducted in the U.S. between the years 1955 and 1989 that had examined attitudes toward premarital sex. For each study they then gathered information on the year of data collection and the proportion of participants who indicated approval of premarital intercourse. The results revealed that attitudes toward premarital sex became considerably more permissive over time; specifically, there was a positive correlation between year of publication and the percentage of participants endorsing premarital sex. For example, only 12% of young women surveyed during the mid-to-late 1950s (1955–1959) approved of premarital sex. By the mid-1980s, however, 73% of women approved of premarital sexual intercourse. Young men displayed a similar shift in attitude over time; 40% of men surveyed in the 1950s approved of premarital sex compared to 79% of men surveyed in the 1980s.

A similar trend toward sexual permissiveness is occurring in other societies around the world (e.g., Herlitz & Ramstedt, 2005; Widmer, Treas, & Newcomb, 1998). For example, one group of researchers (Le Gall, Mullet, & Shafighi, 2002) surveyed the sexual attitudes of a large sample of French men and women who represented four different age groups: *young adults* between the ages of 18 and 29, *adults* between the ages of 30 and 49, *middle-aged adults* between the ages of 50 and 64, and *older adults* between the ages of 65 and 89. All of the participants answered a series of questions designed to measure sexual permissiveness (e.g., "Casual sex is acceptable"). The researchers discovered that the two younger cohorts (young adults and adults) were significantly more permissive in their sexual attitudes than the two older cohorts (middle-aged and older adults)—and this difference was found for both men and women. Today, sexual intercourse clearly is considered a more acceptable part of the premarital interactions of men and women than it was in earlier generations.

Correlates of Sexual Attitudes

Relationship scientists have identified several correlates of attitudes toward premarital sex. One of the most potent is biological sex. Research generally reveals that men hold more permissive or positive attitudes toward uncommitted or casual sexual activity than do women (e.g., Oliver & Hyde, 1993). This sex difference is robust and has been documented in a number of different cultures (e.g., Mwaba & Naidoo, 2005; Odimegwu, 2005) and in various ethnic groups living in the United States (e.g., Eisenman & Dantzker, 2006; Hendrick, Hendrick, & Reich, 2006). For example, sociologists John Roche and Thomas Ramsbey (1993) asked a large sample of college students to indicate how appropriate they thought sexual intercourse would be between partners at five different stages of dating: dating with no particular affection (Stage 1), dating with affection but not love (Stage 2), dating and being in love (Stage 3), dating one person only and being in love (Stage 4), and engaged (Stage 5). Equally high numbers of men (76%) and women (67%) believed that sexual intercourse was appropriate between engaged partners (Stage 5), and equally low numbers (3% of the men, 0% of the women) felt that it was acceptable in the complete absence of commitment and affection (Stage 1). However, men and women clearly diverged in their attitudes about the role of sex in dating relationships in the other relationship stages. For example, 17% of the men, compared to only 1% of the women, believed that intercourse was appropriate when dating partners felt affection but not love (Stage 2). Similarly, many more men (44%) than women (15%) felt that sexual intercourse was acceptable when partners were dating and in love (Stage 3). Thus both sexes viewed intercourse as increasingly acceptable as a dating relationship became characterized by greater amounts of commitment and affection. However, men felt that sex was appropriate at earlier relationship stages than did women (in fact, more men than women simply believed that sex was appropriate—regardless of relationship stage).

Similar results were reported by Marita McCabe and John Collins (1984), who asked men and women to indicate how much sexual activity they desired at three stages of a romantic relationship: on the first date, after several dates had occurred, and when going steady. The researchers found—as we might expect—that men expressed a desire for a higher level of sexual activity at the earlier relationship stages (i.e., on the first date and after several dates) than did women. However, there was no difference in how much sexual activity men and women wanted at the *later* relationship stage of going steady. In other words, both sexes were willing for sexual activity to occur in a dating relationship, but men wanted this activity to begin earlier in the developmental trajectory of the relationship than did women, who felt that sex should wait until there was some evidence of commitment and emotional involvement.

Another important correlate of attitudes toward premarital sexual activity is culture. As noted by cross-cultural psychologist Robin Goodwin (1999), human societies vary considerably in the extent to which they permit premarital sex, and this is partly due to whether they are collectivist or individualist in orientation (see Chapter 7 for discussion of these cultural orientations). Goodwin's review indicates that young adults in collectivist cultures (e.g., Asia, the Middle East) strongly disapprove of premarital sex, whereas young adults from individualist cultures (e.g., Britain, Belgium, France, Scandinavian countries) tend to hold more permissive attitudes (also see Widmer et al., 1998; Yan, 2006). Indeed, Susan Sprecher and Elaine Hatfield (1995) asked more than 1500 college students from the United States, Russia, and Japan to indicate how acceptable they thought sexual intercourse was on a first date, when casually dating, when seriously dating, when pre-engaged, and when engaged to be married. Although participants from all three cultures disapproved of sex between uncommitted partners (those who were on a first date or those who were casually dating), American students generally were more tolerant of sexual activity between seriously dating, pre-engaged, and engaged partners than were Russian and Japanese students. In America, sex was deemed acceptable as soon as some evidence of the couple's commitment was present. In Russia and Japan, however, the fact that the couple was seriously involved or even engaged was insufficient justification for sexual activity—a marriage vow was required.

SEXUALITY AND THE ATTRACTION PROCESS

As we discussed in Chapter 4, there are a number of attributes or characteristics that people find particularly desirable in potential mates, including intelligence, honesty, a good sense of humor, emotional stability, and interpersonal warmth. Attributes that are related to sexuality, including a potential partner's "sex appeal," sexual history, and amount of prior sexual experience also appear to be important determinants of initial attraction.

Sex Appeal

Although many relationship scientists have explored the characteristics that people find attractive in potential mates, relatively few have investigated the factors that render someone particularly sexually appealing and that thus prompt initial attraction. In an effort to discover the specific features that create "*sex appeal*," social psychologists Pamela Regan and Ellen Berscheid (1995) asked a group of men and women to list all the characteristics that would make a man or woman sexually appealing to others. The results indicated that a woman's sex appeal was believed to be primarily a function of appearance (with 90% specifying this attribute), coupled with such dispositional dimensions as a good overall personality (cited by 23%), self-confidence (cited by 17%), and intelligence (mentioned by 15%). Examples of participants' responses included the following:

From a male participant: I think men want women to be willing, attractive, and interesting. It makes the desire stronger when he knows she wants the same thing, although not being able to get sex from her sometimes will do the same thing. Physically, I think a desirable woman would be soft, yet athletic, not fat, but not overly thin, with lots of curves and a nice face. A woman who is experienced and enjoys sex is more desirable than either an inexperienced, shy woman or else an overly experienced, "easy" woman.

From a male participant: Her appearance. Nothing else is needed. A man can be with any woman as long as he thinks she looks good. The easiest way to get a man interested in a woman is for his friends to say how good the girl looks. I truly feel that besides the body—no other characteristics are needed.

From a female participant: Definitely an attitude that portrays that she wants "it." Flirtation seems to help men become more interested. A confident characteristic that would suggest that she is good at "it." Overall attractiveness (skinny, tall, nice smile).

From a female participant: Could be very thin with long, thin legs, long hair, white teeth. Could be voluptuous—I guess what I'm getting down to is physical attraction.

Male sex appeal was presumed to be a function of a very similar constellation of features. Again, appearance was the most frequently mentioned characteristic (cited by 76%), followed by "sensitivity" or a compassionate, kind disposition (35%), a good overall personality (24%), and a sense of humor (18%):

From a male participant: I think a well-built, strong man would cause desire as opposed to a sloppy, overweight guy or a really skinny guy. I think women desire a guy who is open, honest, and is interested in pleasing them, instead of the opposite. I also think a woman desires men who appreciate her sexual appetites/preferences over ones who force their own wishes on her. Physical qualities would probably include muscles, and cleanliness or being well-groomed.

From a male participant: Women like men to be funny and caring. A major thing for women is that they want a man to be sensitive to their needs as women. Physical attractiveness is important to women, although they don't tend to show this as much as men do. I wish I knew more about this question myself—believe me!

From a female participant: A great fit body, and nice clothes. This doesn't mean that's all I'm looking for, but to be sexually attracted—yes.

From a female participant: Based on physical characteristics I would say the way a person looks such as his face, eyes, lips, and a well-toned body. A man must be caring, kind, and gentle. He must be able to show his feelings and let you know he cares about you.

In addition to overall physical appearance, specific physical features may be important elements of an individual's sexual attractiveness. For example, although the superficial facial features (including skin tone and pigment, eye color, and lip size) that are considered attractive vary widely across cultures, certain facial characteristics seem to be universally preferred. Men and women from a variety of cultures rate "average" faces with symmetrical features as especially desirable (e.g., Grammer & Thornhill, 1994; Jones & Hill, 1993; Langlois & Roggman, 1990). In addition, there are particular configurations of facial features that most adults find appealing. A series of studies conducted by Michael Cunningham and his colleagues (e.g., Cunningham, 1986; Cunningham, Barbee, & Pike, 1990) provides evidence that the most attractive male and female faces possess a combination of three types of attribute: neonate or babyish features (such as relatively large, wide-set eyes and a smallish nose), sexually mature features (including prominent cheekbones and thinner cheeks, and, in men, a strong chin), and expressive features (including a wide smile and high eyebrows).

Morphological (body) characteristics also may be important determinants of sex appeal. One of these characteristics is body fat distribution, which can be measured by computing a ratio of the circumference of the waist to the circumference of the hips. Before puberty, both sexes exhibit a similar *waist-to-hip ratio*; however, after puberty, women deposit more fat in the gluteofemoral region (buttocks and thighs) and men deposit more fat in the central and upper body regions (shoulders, abdomen, and nape of the neck). Typically, the waist-to-hip ratio ranges from .67 to .80 in healthy, pre-menopausal women (an hourglass shape), and from .80 to .90 in healthy men (a straighter shape). Research reveals that men and women of different ages, races, and cultural backgrounds assign higher attractiveness ratings to individuals who possess a waist-to-hip ratio that is typical or average for their sex—that is, an "hourglass" shape in women and a tapering "V" physique in men (e.g., Furnham, Tan, & McManus, 1997; Henss, 1995; Singh, 1993, 1994, 1995; Singh & Luis, 1995).

Thus, although many characteristics can make a person initially attractive and appealing to others, appearance seems to be the most important factor. And the significance people give to appearance is not surprising. The primary piece of information potential mates have about one another in first encounters is what they can see—each other's appearance.

Sexual Passion

Another sexual characteristic that has implications for attraction is sexual passion. Because most adults associate sexual desire with passionate love (see Chapter 10), we might expect men and women to prefer a partner who is capable of both experiencing and expressing feelings of sexual passion. Some evidence supports this hypothesis. For example, Susan Sprecher and Pamela Regan (2002) asked a large sample of men and women to indicate how much "sexual passion" they preferred in a potential dating or marriage partner. Participants were also asked to report how important it was that they obtain a partner with that particular level of sexual passion. No differences were found between men and women or between types of potential partner in the desired amount or importance of this particular sexual attribute. Participants preferred equally high levels (close to 8 on a 9-point scale) of sexual passion from both types of romantic partner, and they placed equal importance on obtaining these desired high levels.

Participants in another study (Regan, Levin, Sprecher, Christopher, & Cate, 2000) used percentiles to indicate where they would like their potential partners to rank on the characteristic "sexually passionate/high sex drive" relative to other same-sex individuals (e.g., a score of 50% indicated a preference for a partner who was "average" with respect to the characteristic). The results revealed that both men and women desired a romantic partner who ranked well above average. Specifically, men preferred that their potential mate possess more sexual passion and a higher sex drive than 80% of other women, and women preferred that their potential mate score higher on this attribute than 73% of other men. Family studies scholars Bron Ingoldsby, Paul Schvaneveldt, and Claudia Uribe (2003) obtained similar results when they asked a group of Ecuadoran men and women whether they would be willing to marry someone who "is not interested in sexual relations"—the majority (84.3%) indicated that they would not. These preferences make sense in light of the increasing sexual permissiveness that is developing around the world; that is, as sexual activity comes to be viewed as a more acceptable component of premarital relationships, it is no wonder that men and women prefer partners who possess sufficient sex drive to engage in that activity.

Sexual History

Sex appeal (and the features that comprise it) and sexual passion are not the only sexual characteristics that influence our attraction to another person. An individual's sexual history also influences how we evaluate him or her. In general, research reveals that men and women prefer their potential dates and mates to possess lower, rather than higher, levels of previous sexual experience. When Regan and Berscheid (1997) asked a group of men and women to rank order a list of characteristics in terms of their desirability in a potential romantic partner, "sexually available or 'easy'" was ranked as the *least* desirable attribute. Male participants in a study conducted by psychologists David Buss and David Schmitt (1993) also viewed such sexual attributes as "promiscuous" and "sexually experienced" as undesirable in a potential mate, and other studies continue to document this general finding (e.g., Bettor, Hendrick, & Hendrick, 1995; O'Sullivan, 1995; Sprecher, Regan, McKinney, Maxwell, & Wazienski, 1997).

When considering a potential spouse's sexual history, then, people clearly believe that "less is more." However, this does not necessarily mean that they desire partners who possess no sexual experience whatsoever. Indeed, data collected over the past several decades suggest that *chastity* (complete sexual inexperience) has become increasingly *un*important to both men and women. For example, in one of the earliest mate preference studies (Hill, 1945), men and women received a list of 18 attributes that they ranked in terms of importance in a romantic partner. Chastity, defined as "no previous sexual experience," was ranked 10th in importance—about halfway down the list. A replication study conducted some 20 years later (Hudson & Henze, 1969) revealed that chastity had fallen to 15th in importance. A decade later, another replication study (Hoyt & Hudson, 1981) indicated that chastity had continued its decline into irrelevance; women now ranked this attribute second to last (17th), and men ranked it dead last (18th) in importance. Thus, although a high level of sexual experience is not considered desirable, neither is complete and total sexual inexperience. Men and women apparently want someone with "just enough" sexual knowledge.

Some cultures, however, value chastity more than others. The results of one large cross-cultural mate preference study (Buss, 1989) indicate that people in several Asian countries (e.g., Taiwan, Japan, China, Indonesia, India) view chastity or "no previous sexual experience" as a relatively important attribute in a potential mate, whereas men and women in a variety of Western European countries (e.g., Belgium, France, Sweden, Italy, Greece, Norway) consider chastity to be irrelevant or even undesirable. Of course, what people say they want and what they themselves do are sometimes quite different. As noted by Goodwin (1999), premarital sex is quite common among both men and women in contemporary Eastern cultures; therefore, although chastity may be considered a desirable trait, it is not necessarily seen as an indispensable one.

THE FIRST SEXUAL ENCOUNTER

The first sexual encounter is usually a highly significant event in developing relationships. Interview data collected by Leslie Baxter and Connie Bullis (1986) demonstrate that the first sexual activities shared by a couple serve as an important marker signifying a change in the commitment level or developmental stage of their relationship. These researchers asked a sample of 40 dating couples to identify and discuss in detail all of the turning points in their relationship since the time of their first meeting. Thirteen general categories of relationship turning points subsequently were identified. One of these categories, labeled the "passion turning point" by the researchers, included four events—the couple's first kiss, their first episode of sexual intercourse, the first time they said "I love you," and what the researchers describe as the "whirlwind phenomenon" (essentially the experience of falling in love at first sight)—that couples indicated were important markers in influencing or signaling relationship commitment. Additional research by these and other investigators (e.g., Baxter & Pittman, 2001; also see Metts, 2004) further attests to the important role that first sexual events play in the early stages of romantic relationships.

The Decision to Have Sex for the First Time in a Relationship

What prompts a couple to become sexually active? Research suggests that partners weigh a number of factors when deciding whether to have sex for the first time with each other. The most important reason appears to be interpersonal in nature—specifically, emotional intimacy and closeness. For example, Scott Christopher and Rodney Cate (1984) asked a group of men and women to rate how important various considerations were in their decision to have sex for the first time in a premarital relationship. Their analysis revealed four general reasons underlying this decision. The first and most important reason involved *positive affection and communication*. For instance, people considered how much love they felt for the partner, the possibility that the relationship would result in marriage, and their level of commitment or involvement when deciding whether to have sex with the partner. *Arousal and receptivity*—including their own or the partner's level of sexual arousal immediately prior to intercourse and their receptivity to the partner's sexual advances—also played a role in the decision to have sex. A third factor concerned *obligation and pressure*. For example, feelings of obligation to have sex with the partner, as well as the partner's pressure or insistence on having sex, contributed to individuals' decisions about sexual involvement. Finally, people's sexual decisions were influenced by *circumstance*, ranging from the amount of drugs or alcohol they or their partner had consumed to the "specialness" of that particular date. These results suggest that although a number of factors clearly influence the decision to have sex, feelings of love and intimacy play an extremely important role.

Research on why people *refrain* from having sex with a particular partner also highlights the importance of the relationship's emotional tenor. In one study, Lucia O'Sullivan and Michelle Gaines (1998) surveyed a sample of college students who had the opportunity for sexual activity but had felt unsure or ambivalent about actually engaging in the activity. Participants were asked to describe the incident and to explain in detail their reasons for feeling ambivalent. Analysis of the free responses revealed that the most common reason given by men (35%) and women (49%) for feeling unsure about having sex with someone who clearly wanted them to do so concerned relationship and intimacy issues, including not feeling sufficient levels of commitment and being uncertain about their feelings for the partner.

Pathways to Sexual Involvement

At some point in their relationship, most couples do choose to become sexually intimate. This intimacy may take several forms, ranging from kissing and light petting to intercourse. In addition, some couples elect to engage in sexual activity relatively early in their relationship, while others wait until they have been together for a longer period of time and perhaps are engaged or even married.

Two teams of researchers, using different methodologies, have documented the different paths that couples follow as they move toward their first act of sexual intercourse. In the longitudinal Boston Couples Study (see Chapter 2), Anne Peplau and her colleagues (Peplau, Rubin, & Hill, 1977) surveyed a group of dating couples over a 2-year period about their sexual (and other) experiences. Christopher and Cate (1985) conducted a retrospective study in which they asked a sample of dating couples to think back over their relationship and report about various events and experiences. Despite their differing methods of data collection, the two research teams found strikingly similar results. For example, in both studies, some couples chose to abstain from sexual intercourse entirely and to limit their sexual interactions to non-intercourse activities (e.g., kissing, light petting). These couples, termed *sexually traditional* or *abstaining* by Peplau et al. (1977) and labeled *low involvement* by Christopher and Cate (1985), generally believed that love alone did not serve to justify sexual intercourse, that intercourse should be saved for marriage, and that abstinence from intercourse was a sign of love and respect between the partners. They also tended to hold conservative sexual attitudes and to have lower overall levels of sexual experience than did other couples.

Both research teams also found evidence of the other extreme—that is, couples who elected to engage in intercourse very early in their relationship (sometimes on the first date or after a few dates). *Sexually liberal* (Peplau et al., 1977) or *rapid involvement* (Christopher & Cate, 1985) couples viewed sex without love as acceptable and did not require commitment in order to have and enjoy intercourse. For these couples, the decision to have sexual intercourse stemmed primarily from physical pleasure and arousal motives rather than from any emotional concerns or relationship factors.

Other types of couple were identified as well. For example, Peplau et al. (1977) described a type of couple they termed *sexually moderate* or *later sex*. Partners in sexually moderate relationships were somewhere in between their traditional and liberal counterparts in terms of their attitudes and behavior. Although they generally chose to wait awhile before engaging in sexual intercourse, they also believed that sexual intercourse was acceptable if the two people loved each other—and they did not need a long-term commitment before becoming sexually involved. Love, rather than commitment per se, was sufficient justification for intercourse.

Christopher and Cate (1985) also described other couple types located between the rapid and low-involvement extremes. *Gradual involvement couples* engaged in sexual intercourse when they were considering becoming "couples," and demonstrated gradual increases in sexual intimacy as their relationships became progressively more committed. For example, as they moved from casual dating to steady dating, they engaged in correspondingly more intimate forms of sexual expression. *Delayed involvement couples*—the most common couple type identified by the researchers—also clearly associated sexual involvement with the level of commitment in their relationships. However, they held more conservative sexual attitudes than did the gradual involvement couples and demonstrated a very different pattern of sexual interaction. Specifically, delayed involvement couples engaged in extremely low levels of sexual activity until the partners made a commitment to each other and the relationship; once they were in a steady and monogamous union, they increased their level of sexual involvement. As noted by Christopher (2001), these couples "resolutely limit their sexual involvement until making a monogamous dating commitment. This level of commitment serves as a sexual watershed once reached, allowing them to explore their sexual involvement as fully as the other coitally experienced couples" (p. 87).

Clearly, commitment and emotional intimacy are intricately connected with sexuality in many dating relationships.

SEXUAL FREQUENCY

One topic that has received a great deal of attention from relationship scientists concerns the frequency with which partners engage in sexual intercourse (and other sexual activities). The majority of this research has utilized samples of married couples. Data collected over the past 60 years suggests that the average amount of sex that married couples have has not changed much over time. For example, during the late 1940s and early 1950s pioneering sex researcher Alfred Kinsey and his colleagues (Kinsey, Pomeroy, & Martin, 1948; Kinsey, Pomeroy, Martin, & Gebhard, 1953) surveyed more than 11,000 men and women living in the United States about a variety of sexual issues, including how often they engaged in sexual intercourse. They found that young married couples (between 16 and 25 years of age) tended to have sex between two and three times a week; slightly older couples (between 26 and 35 years of age) indicated engaging in intercourse about twice a week. Another survey conducted two decades later yielded similar sexual frequencies, with young couples (18–24 years of age) reporting sexual intercourse approximately three times a week (Hunt, 1974).

Couples surveyed during the 1990s resemble their counterparts from earlier decades in terms of their sexual activity rates. Like Kinsey and his colleagues, sex researchers Robert Michael, John Gagnon, Edward Laumann, and Gina Kolata (1994) conducted a national study of the sexual experiences of men and women living in the United States. One question asked participants to indicate how often they had engaged in sex during the previous 12 months. The possible response options were *not at all*, *once or twice*, *about once a month*, *two or three times a month*, *about once a week*, *two or three times a week*, and *four or more times a week*. Although participants were not asked to report the precise amount of sex in which they had engaged, the results were similar to those reported by previous researchers. Specifically, the response option endorsed by the highest percentages of married men (43%) and women (47%) was *two or three times a month*. The next most commonly endorsed option was *two or three times a week*, with 36% of married men and 32% of married women reporting having sex that frequently. Very small percentages of married men (1%) and women (3%) said they had absolutely no intercourse at all with their partners over the past year; similarly, few married men (7%) or women (7%) reported extremely high amounts of sexual activity (i.e., four or more times a week). Taken together, the results of these research endeavors suggest that most married couples (at least most younger married couples) tend to engage in sexual intercourse approximately one to three times a week. More recent research reveals similar frequency rates (e.g., Colson, Lemaire, Pinton, Hamidi, & Klein, 2006).

It is important to recognize, however, that tremendous variability exists both within and across individual couples. Not only does the rate of intercourse within any one couple often fluctuate over time, but researchers find that some married couples tend to engage in intercourse frequently (even on a daily basis), whereas others have sex very infrequently, if at all (Donnelly, 1993; Greenblat, 1983). For example, social scientist Cathy Greenblat (1983) asked 80 married participants to retrospectively report how often they engaged in intercourse each month during the first year of their marriage; recollected rates ranged from once a month (or an average of 12 times that year) to 45 times a month (or 540 times during that first year).

Sexual frequency also varies widely among homosexual couples. A group of Dutch researchers (Deenen, Gijs, & van Naerssen, 1994) asked more than 300 gay men who were currently involved in a committed relationship about their frequency of intercourse. Roughly one-third (30%) reported having sex less than once per week, 43% indicated having sex one to two times per week, 25% said they had sex three to five times per week, and a few (2%) reported having sex six or more times per week. Surveys conducted by Peplau and her colleagues (e.g., Peplau, Cochran, & Mays, 1997; Peplau, Cochran, Rook, & Padesky, 1978) reveal that lesbian couples also demonstrate a fair amount of variation in sexual frequency. In one investigation (Peplau et al., 1997), 11% of women in committed lesbian relationships reported having sex more than three times per week, 47% indicated having sex one to three times per week, and 41% said that they engaged in sexual activity less than once per week. Thus, irrespective of the sexual orientation of the partners, sexual frequency differs considerably among couples in established relationships.

In addition, certain *types* of couple engage in sexual activity more frequently than do others. In general, surveys reveal that cohabiting heterosexual couples and homosexual male couples tend to have sex (defined as genital contact) more frequently than do married couples, who in turn have sex more frequently than do homosexual female couples (e.g., Blumstein & Schwartz, 1983; Call, Sprecher, & Schwartz, 1995; Kurdek, 2006a; Rao & DeMaris, 1995; Solomon, Rothblum, & Balsam, 2005). And all of these couple types seem to engage in greater amounts of sexual activity than do single men and women. Recall that Michael et al. (1994) found that very few married men (1%) and women (3%) reported having no sex at all during the previous 12 months. Similarly, very few of the cohabiting men and women who participated in their study indicated having a sexless past year, but 23% of the single men and 32% of the single women reported engaging in no intercourse during the same time. In discussing their results, Michael et al. (1994, p. 118) concluded:

> We find that the critical factor that produces the most sexual activity is being part of a couple, whether it is a marriage or a cohabitation. Even though married life is not seen as very erotic, it is actually the social arrangement that produces the highest rate of partnered sexual activity among heterosexuals. What seems to produce the highest rates of partnered sex is an easily accessible partner.

Essentially, the state of singlehood is not as conducive to sexual activity as is marriage or cohabitation.

The Decline of Sexual Frequency over Time

The frequency with which couples engage in sex is associated both with their chronological ages and the age of their relationship. *Cross-sectional studies*, in which individuals from different age groups are surveyed about their sexual experiences, generally reveal that older couples engage in sexual intercourse less frequently than do younger couples (e.g., Brewis & Meyer, 2005; for reviews see Sprecher, Christopher, & Cate, 2006; Willetts et al., 2004). For example, sociologists Vaughn Call, Susan Sprecher, and Pepper Schwartz (1995) examined sexual frequency across the life-span using data gathered as part of the National Survey of Families and Households (a large-scale research endeavor consisting of personal interviews conducted with a national probability sample of 13,008 people). Their analyses were based on the 6785 respondents who were married and had a spouse living with them in the household, and the item of interest concerned how often the participants reported engaging in sexual intercourse with their spouse during the past month. The results revealed that the frequency of marital sex was negatively correlated with age. For example, married men and women from 19 to 24 years of age reported having intercourse approximately 12 times a month. Those in their early to mid-30s engaged in sexual activity close to 9 times a month. Respondents from 50 to 54 years of age indicated having intercourse an average of 5.5 times a month, those in their late 60s reported having sex a little over twice a month, and those who were 75 years of age or older engaged in intercourse less than once a month. Thus, increasing age was associated with decreasing levels of sexual activity. However, the authors also noted that although the older respondents definitely had less sex than their younger counterparts, they were far from asexual. About half of married adults between 65 and 74 of age were still having sex (just not perhaps every month).

Sexual frequency is also associated with the duration or age of a couple's relationship. Most studies demonstrate that the longer partners have been married or have cohabited, the less often they have sex (e.g., Rao & DeMaris, 1995; Samson, Levy, Dupras, & Tessier, 1991). This decline seems to be greatest during the first year of marriage, such that rates of sexual activity are typically very high during the newlywed phase and then undergo a dramatic decrease as the couple settles into married life. A longitudinal study conducted by researcher William James (1981) illustrates what has been termed the ***honeymoon effect***. James analyzed diaries and calendars kept by 21 newlywed couples, finding that couples had intercourse an average of 17 times during their very first month of marriage but only about 8 times a month by the end of the first year.

A similar decline in sexual frequency over time was observed by Laura Stafford, Susan Kline, and Caroline Rankin (2004), who analyzed data from the 1987–1988 and 1992–1994 National Survey of Families and Households. In this longitudinal investigation, three groups of heterosexual couples—couples who were married prior to the first wave of data collection and who were still married at the time of the second survey, couples who were cohabiting at both data collection times, and couples who were cohabiting at the time of the first survey but had married by the time of the second—were asked how often they and their partners had sex "during the past month" (p. 239) at two points in time (during 1987–1988 and then again 5 years later). The researchers found that there was a significant decrease in sexual frequency over time in all three groups (married couples, cohabiting couples, and cohabiting couples who transitioned to marriage). At the beginning of the study couples reported engaging in intercourse an average of 11 times per month. Five years later their frequency of sex had decreased to an average of 6 instances per month.

The lower level of sexual activity seen in older couples (and in older relationships) is undoubtedly due to a number of factors. For example, the various physical and psychological changes associated with the aging process (a personal factor), the loss of sexual novelty that develops from having intercourse with the same partner year after year (a relational factor), and stress, fatigue, and loss of privacy caused by the presence of children, child care activities, and heavy work schedules (environmental factors) all may limit a couple's desire and opportunity for sexual activity (Greenblat, 1983; Smith, 2006; Willetts et al., 2004).

SEXUAL SATISFACTION

Most partnered individuals—whether cohabiting or married, heterosexual or homosexual—report that they are satisfied with their sex lives (e.g., Blumstein & Schwartz, 1983; Kurdek, 1991; Lawrance & Byers, 1995; Michael et al., 1994). For example, psychologists Sandra Byers and Sheila MacNeil (2006) asked a sample of heterosexual men and women who were involved in long-term marital or cohabiting relationships to rate the sexual component of their relationships using five scales that included *good–bad, pleasant–unpleasant, positive–negative, satisfying–unsatisfying*, and *valuable–worthless*. These ratings were summed to create a global measure of *sexual satisfaction*. Participants made their evaluations at three different times over an 18-month period, and the researchers found that at all three times sexual satisfaction was uniformly high. Homosexual men and women appear equally satisfied sexually; more than 40% of the gay men (most of whom were partnered) in sociologist Janet Lever's (1994, 1995) large-scale surveys rated their current sex lives as "great" or "good," and more than 30% of the partnered lesbians indicated that their sex lives were "great."

One of the most important factors associated with sexual satisfaction is how often the partners engage in sexual activity. Heterosexual and homosexual couples who have more frequent sex generally report higher levels of sexual satisfaction than couples who have less frequent sex (e.g., Blumstein & Schwartz, 1983; Call et al., 1995; Lever, 1995; McNulty & Fisher, 2008; Young, Denny, Luquis, & Young, 1998; for reviews see Peplau, Fingerhut, & Beals, 2004; Sprecher & Cate, 2004). Sexual satisfaction is also associated with other sexual factors in a couple's relationship, including whether the partners experience orgasm (e.g., Haning et al., 2007; Perlman & Abramson, 1982; Pinney, Gerrard, & Denney, 1987; Tracy & Junginger, 2007; Young et al., 1998), when during the sexual interaction the partners reach orgasm (Darling, Davidson, & Cox, 1991), and the ratio of rewards (e.g., emotional intimacy, physical pleasure, feeling sexually desirable) to costs (e.g., time constraints, concerns about performance, discrepancies between sexual preferences and desired frequency) that partners receive from their sexual relationship (Byers, Demmons, & Lawrance, 1998; Byers & MacNeil, 2006; Kisler & Christopher, 2008). In general, couples tend to experience higher levels of sexual satisfaction when they engage in sex frequently, reach orgasm as a result of their activity and at about the same time, and obtain more sexual rewards than costs.

SEXUAL COMMUNICATION

Another factor that is closely connected to sexual satisfaction is sexual communication. The ability to effectively communicate with the partner about one's sexual needs, preferences, expectations, and attitudes is very important in established relationships. Not only is effective communication necessary for successfully negotiating the amount and type of a couple's sexual involvement, but it is also essential for maintaining the quality of their sexual relationship over time (Cupach & Comstock, 1990; Metts, Sprecher, & Regan, 1998).

One aspect of sexual communication that has received a great deal of attention from theorists and researchers is the *initiation* and *refusal* of sexual requests. In the *traditional* (heterosexual) *sexual script*, men are expected to initiate sexual activity, whereas women are expected to then accept or refuse these sexual requests (e.g., Gagnon & Simon, 1973; Reiss, 1981). Research indicates that men and women generally follow this script in their actual sexual interactions, with men functioning as the sexual initiators and women serving as the sexual regulators (Blumstein & Schwartz, 1983). For example, Shari Dworkin and Lucia O'Sullivan (2005) asked a sample of heterosexual men to describe the pattern of sexual initiation in their current romantic relationships. The most common pattern was *male-dominated*, with more than half (56%) of the men reporting that their sexual interactions followed the traditional script. Much smaller proportions of men reported an *egalitarian* pattern in which both partners initiated sex (25%) or a *female-dominated* pattern in which their partners initiated sex (19%). Interestingly, only one fourth of the men who reported following the traditional male-dominated initiation script wished to sustain this pattern; most (72%) desired to adopt a more egalitarian pattern with both partners equally responsible for initiating sexual activities. Over time, of course, women may become more comfortable initiating sexual activity with their partners.

Regardless of which partner does the initiating, most sexual initiation attempts that occur in long-term, committed relationships are successful; that is, most men and women respond positively to their partners' sexual invitations (Byers & Heinlein, 1989). These positive consent responses (as well as the initiation attempts) generally are communicated nonverbally and indirectly (e.g., Beres, Herold, & Maitland, 2004; Brown & Auerback, 1981; Byers & Heinlein, 1989; McCormick, 1979; Perper & Weis, 1987). It is unusual for individuals to explicitly and verbally request sex from their partners ("Hey, do you want to have sex?"); it is equally unusual for partners to consent to sexual invitations in a verbally explicit manner ("Why yes, I would love to have sex right now"). Rather, a person who desires sexual activity might play some romantic music, open a bottle of wine, and glance suggestively in the direction of the bedroom. The partner who receives this indirect invitation might smile, put down his or her book, and engage in other nonverbal behaviors that continue the sexual interaction without explicitly acknowledging acceptance (or even awareness) of the initial invitation.

Sexual *refusals*, however, do tend to be communicated verbally and directly. As noted by communication scholars William Cupach and Sandra Metts (1991), such directness "seems to fulfill simultaneously the goals of averting unwanted persistence of initiation by the partner and of maintaining the face of the rejected individual by offering an account" (p. 103). So how do couples ultimately resolve situations in which one partner wants sex and the other does not? Research suggests that couples employ several strategies for reaching amicable conclusions to these episodes—for example, they may mutually agree not to have sex, they may agree to postpone sex until a later time, or they may simply agree to disagree (and, of course, sometimes the reluctant partner may change his or her mind; Byers & Heinlein, 1989).

Whether initiations, refusals, and other aspects of sexual negotiation influence a couple's level of sexual satisfaction depends to a large extent on the communicative skill of the partners. It is not easy to be an effective sexual communicator. Successful communication about sexuality requires the ability both to *express* information about one's needs, desires, likes, and dislikes and to *solicit and receive* this information in a non-judgmental and non-defensive manner from the partner (D'Augelli & D'Augelli, 1985; Metts, 2003). This level of disclosure and intimacy requires a great deal of trust and acceptance, and may be difficult for couples to achieve. Many couples do, however, manage to express some aspects of their sexual feelings. In one study (Rubin, Hill, Peplau, & Dunkel-Schetter, 1980) researchers asked dating couples to report how much self-disclosure they experienced on a number of topics, including "my feelings about our sexual relationship." The majority (about three fourths) of men and women indicated having full disclosure on this topic with their partners. Thus, although open and honest communication about sexuality may seem like a difficult goal for couples to reach, it is certainly not impossible. Effective sexual communication is vital for maintaining the quality of the sexual relationship.

SEXUALITY AND RELATIONSHIP SATISFACTION

Not surprisingly, how people feel about their sex lives is related to how they feel about their relationships in general. All of the aspects of sexuality we have considered—sexual frequency, satisfaction, and communication—are associated with the *non*sexual dimensions of a relationship. For example, the frequency with which a couple has sexual intercourse is related to relationship satisfaction. Specifically, the more often a couple has sex, the more generally satisfied they are with the relationship (e.g., Call et al., 1995; Donnelly, 1993; Regan, 2000), the more they enjoy spending time together and sharing activities and hobbies (e.g., Blumstein & Schwartz, 1983; Sprecher, Metts, Burleson, Hatfield, & Thompson, 1995), and the more equitable and fair they perceive their relationship to be (Hatfield, Greenberger, Traupmann, & Lambert, 1982).

Similarly, a large (and increasingly multi- and cross-cultural) body of research indicates that there is a strong correlation between sexual satisfaction and relationship satisfaction (e.g., Butzer & Campbell, 2008; Byers, 2005; Byers & MacNeil, 2006; Henderson-King & Veroff, 1994; Litzinger & Gordon, 2005; MacNeil & Byers, 2005; for reviews, see Christopher & Sprecher, 2000; Kurdek, 1991; Peplau et al., 2004; Sprecher & Cate, 2004). Heterosexual and homosexual couples who are satisfied with their sexual relationship tend also to be satisfied with other areas of their partnership. In one study, for example, Kelli-An Lawrance and Sandra Byers (1995) asked close to 250 hetero-sexual men and women who were currently involved in long-term (mostly marital) relationships to rate their sexual relationships and their overall relationships on five 7-point bipolar scales: *good–bad, pleasant–unpleasant, positive–negative, satisfying–unsatisfying,* and *valuable–worthless*. They found a strong association between these two measures. Specifically, the more satisfied participants were with their sexual relationships (i.e., the more they rated them as good, pleasant, positive, etc.), the more satisfied they were with their relationships in general.

Of course, such correlational findings do not allow us to come to any firm conclusion about causality. That is, does good sex lead to a good relationship, or does a good relationship produce good sex? Several researchers have attempted to discover the nature of the causal connection between sexual and relationship satisfaction. To date, their efforts have met with limited success. For example, longitudinal investigations conducted by Sprecher (2002) and Byers (2005) demon-strated that sexual and relationship satisfaction covaried (that is, at any given point in time, people who were satisfied sexually also tended to be satisfied interpersonally) but were unable to conclu-sively support one particular causal direction. However, at least one recent study suggests that it is sexual satisfaction that contributes to relationship well-being (rather than the reverse). During five assessments spanning a 10-year period, Hsiu-Chen Yeh and colleagues (Yeh, Lorenz, Wickrama, Conger, & Elder, 2006) asked a sample of married couples to indicate how happy and satisfied they were with their marriages (these items were summed to create a measure of marital quality). Partici-pants also completed an eight-item scale that assessed sexual satisfaction (e.g., "My spouse and I have a wonderful sex life," "My spouse is happy with our sex life," "Sex isn't very important to me" [reverse scored]). The results revealed several interesting findings. First, sexual satisfaction was rela-tively stable over time; couples who were satisfied with their sex lives in 1990 tended to be satisfied a year later in 1991, and the year after that, and so on. (Marital quality proved equally stable.) Sec-ond, sexual satisfaction predicted later marital quality for both husbands and wives. Specifically, higher levels of sexual satisfaction at one assessment point (e.g., 1992) predicted an increase in mari-tal quality at the next assessment point (e.g., 1994). However, marital quality did not predict subse-quent levels of sexual satisfaction; in other words, participants' ratings of their marital happiness and satisfaction at one point in time were completely unrelated to how satisfied they were with their sex lives at a later point in time. In sum, although additional corroborating longitudinal research is needed, these results suggest that sexual satisfaction influences subsequent relational functioning (and not vice versa)—good sex leads to a good relationship.

SUMMARY

Sexuality plays an important role in mating relationships. Although there is a trend toward greater sexual permissiveness in many societies, most individuals continue to view sexual activity as most acceptable when it occurs between partners in committed (as opposed to casual or uncommitted) relationships. In general, men and women prefer as dates and mates others who possess moderate sexual experience (as opposed to none or extensive sexual experience), and they weigh a number of factors in deciding whether and when to become sexually active with their current partners. Couples follow different pathways to sexual involvement; some engage in sex relatively early in their relationships and others prefer to wait until they reach a later stage characterized by higher levels of commitment and intimacy. In marital and other established relationships, the amount of sex that couples have and how they communicate with each other about their sexual needs and wishes is intimately associated with their level of sexual satisfaction and with their happiness with the relationship.

KEY CONCEPTS

Relational sex (p. 196)
Sexual permissiveness (p. 197)
Sex appeal (p. 199)
Waist-to-hip ratio (p. 201)
Chastity (p. 202)
Sexually traditional or abstaining
  couples (p. 204)
Low involvement couples (p. 204)
Sexually liberal couples (p. 204)
Rapid involvement couples (p. 204)

Sexually moderate or later sex
  couples (p. 204)
Gradual involvement couples (p. 204)
Delayed involvement couples (p. 204)
Sexual frequency (p. 205)
Cross-sectional studies (p. 206)
Honeymoon effect (p. 207)
Sexual initiation (p. 208)
Sexual refusal (p. 208)
Traditional sexual script (p. 208)

EXPLORATION EXERCISES

These exercises are designed to allow you to explore in greater detail some of the concepts and issues discussed in this chapter. There are no right or wrong answers to these exercises—they are simply meant to provide an opportunity for discussion and debate.

1. Most societies have become more permissive over time in terms of sexual attitudes. For example, researchers have discovered that younger cohorts of adults tend to be more accepting of premarital sex than older cohorts of adults. This exercise is designed to explore attitudes toward premarital sex. Find 10 adults—five young adults between the ages of 18 and 29 and five older adults between the ages of 65 and 89—and ask them to answer the following question:

> *How acceptable is premarital sex—specifically, how acceptable is it for two people who are not married to engage in sexual intercourse with each other? Is it completely unacceptable, slightly unacceptable, slightly acceptable, or completely acceptable?*

Record the response of each of your participants using the grid overleaf. Then, sum up the total number of people who chose each of the various options.

	Completely unacceptable	Slightly unacceptable	Slightly acceptable	Completely acceptable
Young adult 1	_____	_____	_____	_____
Young adult 2	_____	_____	_____	_____
Young adult 3	_____	_____	_____	_____
Young adult 4	_____	_____	_____	_____
Young adult 5	_____	_____	_____	_____
Older adult 1	_____	_____	_____	_____
Older adult 2	_____	_____	_____	_____
Older adult 3	_____	_____	_____	_____
Older adult 4	_____	_____	_____	_____
Older adult 5	_____	_____	_____	_____
Young Total:	_____	_____	_____	_____
Older Total:	_____	_____	_____	_____

Based on these responses, provide answers to the following questions: (1) What was the most common attitude expressed by your two cohorts of participants? (2) Did your results "match" the results found by other researchers? (3) Did your two cohorts agree, or did they have different attitudes about premarital sex?

2. There is strong evidence that attitudes toward chastity (sexual inexperience) have changed fairly dramatically over time, at least in Western cultures. How might this change be related to other social changes (for example, the advent of birth control, media depictions of sexuality, and social norms about male and female sexuality)? Discuss this issue with your classmates.

3. Contrary to popular myths about the "swinging single," paired individuals often have more sex than their single counterparts. Why do you think that marriage and cohabitation might be more conducive to sexual expression than is singlehood?

PART IV
Relationship Challenges

People enter their relationships with a variety of expectations and standards. For example, most men and women expect friendships, romantic unions, and family relationships to be sources of support, positive emotion, and other beneficial personal and interpersonal outcomes, and they believe that the partners in those relationships should share life's experiences with one another, demonstrate sustained care, concern, respect, and loyalty, and provide advice and guidance when needed (e.g., Fehr, 2004; Hassebrauck & Fehr, 2002). As we have discussed in earlier chapters, when these relational standards are met, people are likely to experience interpersonal satisfaction; conversely, when expectations are not met, distress and dissatisfaction usually develop.

This section of the text focuses on *relational transgressions*—actions, behaviors, or events that (1) violate relationship norms, standards, and rules, (2) convey to the individual that the partner devalues the relationship, and (3) generally produce feelings of hurt and related negative emotions (e.g., anxiety, sadness, anger, shame; see Feeney, 2005; Leary, 2001; Metts, 1994; Vangelisti, 2001, 2006). Chapter 12 considers issues involving rejection and betrayal, Chapter 13 explores violence and aggression in intimate relationships, Chapter 14 examines the processes of conflict and dissolution, and Chapter 15 focuses on therapeutic interventions designed to assist partners in troubled relationships.

Chapter 12
Rejection and Betrayal

Throughout this text we have seen how the process of becoming intimately connected to another person provides an opportunity to experience love and satisfaction, to give and receive emotional and social support, and often—particularly if the relationship is a romantic one—to experience passion, joy, and excitement. All of these experiences, in turn, can enhance and promote an individual's psychological and physical well-being. But relationships can also be a potent source of emotional pain and psychological hurt, particularly when they involve rejection, deceit, or betrayal.

UNREQUITED LOVE: WHEN THE ONE WE LOVE DOES NOT LOVE US

Most of us have heard the sentiment, first expressed by Victorian poet Alfred Tennyson, that " 'tis better to have loved and lost than never to have loved at all." On the face of it, this seems like sound advice. As we discussed in Chapter 10, the experience of love—whether passionate or companionate—typically is associated with a wonderful and rewarding mix of positive outcomes, events, and feelings. However, love—particularly when it is *unrequited* or not reciprocated by the beloved—has the potential to be just as strongly associated with negative outcomes. In fact, of all the forms of interpersonal rejection that we can experience, perhaps none is as acutely painful as romantic rejection.

In one of the first empirical investigations exploring the dynamics of unrequited love, Roy Baumeister, Sara Wotman, and Arlene Stillwell (1993) asked a sample of college students to provide written accounts of situations in which they had experienced non-mutual romantic attraction. Each participant wrote two autobiographical stories—one from the perspective of the *would-be lover* who was romantically attracted to an uninterested other and one from the perspective of the *rejector* who did not reciprocate another's romantic attraction. Analysis of these written accounts revealed that unrequited lovers experienced a host of both positive and negative emotions. Many (44%) would-be suitors reported that their unreciprocated passion caused them pain, suffering, and disappointment; jealousy and anger (which were usually directed at the loved ones' chosen partners); and a sense of frustration. Similarly, 22% experienced worries and fears about rejection. In addition to these unpleasant experiences, however, the lovelorn suitors also reported many pleasant emotional outcomes; in fact, positive feelings far outweighed negative ones in the accounts they gave of their experience. For example, happiness, excitement, the blissful anticipation of seeing the beloved, sheer elation at the state of being in love, and other positive emotions were reported by the majority (98%) of would-be suitors. More than half (53%) also looked back on their unrequited love experiences with some degree of positive feeling. In explaining this finding, the researchers noted the following:

> Apparently, positive feelings can be remembered in a positive way even if the memory is linked to suffering and disappointment. People remember the warmth of their feelings for another person, and the memory is at least somewhat pleasant. Some of our participants expressed gladness at being able to preserve the friendship that could have been jeopardized if their romantic overtures had become too insistent. Others simply treasured the memory or retained a soft spot in their heart for the one they loved.
>
> (Baumeister & Wotman, 1992, p. 60)

When the researchers examined the experiences reported by the rejectors, however, they found little evidence of positive outcomes. Specifically, although roughly one-fourth (24%) of the rejectors reported feeling flattered by the attention of their admirers, the majority also viewed these unwanted advances as annoying (51%), felt uncomfortable about delivering rejection messages (61%), and experienced a host of negative emotions, including anger, frustration, and resentment (70%). In addition, their recollections of the entire experience were far less suffused with warmth, with only 33% indicating any positive affect in retrospect. The researchers concluded:

> Unlike the would-be lover, it was hard for the rejector to feel that his or her life had been enriched by this experience. For many, apparently, it was a useless and pointless set of aggrava-

tions. They were forced to respond to a situation they never wanted, and these responses were difficult for them, bringing uncertainty, guilt, aggravation, all of which went for naught. For some, a valued friendship was destroyed in the bargain. Thus they had plenty to resent and regret.

(Baumeister & Wotman, 1992, p. 62)

Other researchers have reported similar findings (e.g., Sinclair & Frieze, 2005). Unrequited love clearly is an emotionally difficult experience for both the rejector and the would-be suitor. Unfortunately, it also is a common event in the lives of adolescents and young adults (Hill, Blakemore, & Drumm, 1997), and—other than waiting patiently for the pain to pass with time—there appears to be no easy way to recover from the distress brought about by romantic rejection.

SEXUAL DISINTEREST: WHEN THE ONE WE DESIRE DOES NOT DESIRE US

Sexual disinterest represents another (often painful and distressing) form of interpersonal rejection. We have already reviewed research that suggests that sexual activity declines over time in most committed, long-term romantic relationships (see Chapter 11). One of the possible reasons for this decline is sexual disinterest—one or both partners experience reduced desire to engage in sexual activities with each another. Because many people routinely undergo fluctuations in their general level of sexual desire, and because sexual desire is associated with age, physical and mental health, drug use, hormonal variations, and a host of other personal factors, a reduction in one partner's level of sexual attraction to the other partner does not necessarily indicate that something is "wrong" with their relationship (Regan & Berscheid, 1999).

Sometimes, however, a reduction in sexual interest (particularly if it occurs suddenly and/or is sustained for a long period of time) may signal a relationship problem. Many clinicians and health professionals believe that sexual desire is strongly influenced by interpersonal or relational factors, including the emotions experienced within a relationship and/or directed toward a partner (e.g., Maurice, 2007; McCarthy, Ginsberg, & Fucito, 2006; Pietropinto, 1986). Indeed, a growing number of clinical case studies illustrate the corrosive impact of anger, hostility, anxiety, stress, and other emotions on sexual desire. For example, based on her pioneering case studies of men and women with sexual desire disorders, Helen Singer Kaplan (e.g., 1979, 1996) concluded that fears of rejection by the partner, poor communication, and power conflicts frequently produce anxiety and anger, which appear to rapidly and automatically activate an emotional "turn off" mechanism that suppresses sexual desire. Other scholars (e.g., Arnett, Prosen, & Toews, 1986; Trudel, 1991) similarly have observed that negative affect stemming from interpersonal conflict may elicit a stress response that causes diminished sexual desire.

Empirical research with clinical samples supports the prediction that diminished sexual desire often signals the existence of difficulties in a couple's relationship (e.g., Dennerstein, Koochaki, Barton, & Graziottin, 2006). In one early investigation, Freida Stuart, D. Corydon Hammond, and Marjorie Pett (1987) administered a marital adjustment scale to a sample of married women who were diagnosed with inhibited sexual desire (ISD), married women who reported normal sexual desire, and the spouses of women in both groups. The women in the ISD group had significantly lower marital adjustment scores than did women in the non-ISD group. Moreover, the spouses of women in the ISD group also reported significantly lower overall adjustment in their marriages than did the spouses of women in the non-ISD group.

Studies conducted with non-clinical samples confirm that relationship quality is associated with sexual interest in the partner. For example, Tore Hällström and Sverker Samuelsson (1990) conducted a longitudinal study in which they asked a large sample of married or cohabiting women to indicate (on two occasions 6 years apart) their present degree of sexual desire (i.e., whether they perceived it as strong, moderate, weak, or absent) and to report whether they received sufficient emotional support from their partner (yes/no) and had a "confiding" relationship with him (yes/no). The researchers found that a perceived lack of a confiding relationship with, and insufficient support from, the partner at the first assessment predicted a decrease in self-reported sexual desire over time. Similar results were reported more recently by Michael Brezsnyak and Mark Whisman (2004), who surveyed a sample of married couples and found that the amount of sexual desire that husbands and wives experienced for each other was strongly positively correlated with their level of relationship satisfaction (also see Davies, Katz, & Jackson, 1999; Regan, 2000).

In sum, clinical case studies and empirical research suggest that sexual desire may function as a "thermometer" to relationship quality. As with unrequited love, there is no easy cure for diminished sexual desire. However, recent clinical outcome studies suggest that the most effective therapeutic treatments are those that conceptualize sexual disinterest as a couple issue rather than as an individual problem, and that consequently incorporate techniques that involve both partners (such as communication skills training and sexual intimacy exercises; for a review, see Ullery, Millner, & Willingham, 2002). Although sexual disinterest is not necessarily a sign that a romantic relationship is in trouble, the interpersonal context clearly plays an important role in creating and sustaining sexual attraction between partners.

RELATIONAL STALKING: WHEN INTEREST BECOMES OBSESSION

A 32-year-old woman interviewed by the author of this textbook described the devastating effects of a romantic obsession:

> At first I thought it was sort of cute and romantic that he wanted to be with me all the time. He would ask me to give him a detailed account of my day, all the places I went, the people I talked with, the things I did. . . . I felt flattered that I had a boyfriend who loved me so much. But then it got out of hand. I mean, he wouldn't even let me drive to the store by myself! After we broke up, he began calling me at home, usually several times a night. He also started calling me at work, which made things difficult for me with my boss. So I stopped taking his calls at work and I changed to an unlisted number at home. I think what really made me realize that I needed to take some action and tell people what was going on was when he started spying on me. One morning, I was standing by the window looking outside and I noticed his car. He was just sitting there, watching me. I have no idea how long he had been there, but it really scared me. I felt trapped and violated.

Another interviewee, a 46-year-old man, provided a similar description of his experience:

> I met a woman I thought I liked. She was attractive, bright, seemed to have a good sense of humor and to be stable and well-grounded. We went out on a couple of dates and it turned out that we didn't have that much in common, so I didn't pursue the relationship. No big breakup or anything, we just weren't suited to each other. That should have been the end of it, but it

wasn't. She lived about 10 miles from me, and she would drive over to my neighborhood, park in front of my house, and then go jogging around the block for what seemed like hours. I would see her as she passed my house again and again, every single day. She began to eat in the local restaurants I frequented. She called my house and left messages about getting together to "work things out." She was everywhere I went and she did her best to invade every single moment of my day. My friends laughed about it and made jokes about what a lucky guy I was to have this woman chasing after me, but believe me it wasn't funny. Fortunately, I relocated due to my job and I haven't seen her since.

Most people at some time or another have experienced romantic or sexual rejection. And although these experiences are not pleasant, the majority of men and women manage to successfully negotiate them. In some cases, however, unreciprocated attraction is associated with obsessive thinking and inappropriate (and even violent) behavior (Meloy, 1989; Mintz, 1980; Sinclair & Frieze, 2002). ***Relational stalking*** is a harmful behavioral syndrome that involves one person (the pursuer or stalker) desiring and actively attempting to create or obtain an intimate relationship with another person (the target or victim) who either does not want this particular kind of relationship or who wants no relationship at all (see Emerson, Ferris, & Gardner, 1998; Spitzberg & Cupach, 2003). This phenomenon also has been called *obsessive relational intrusion* or ORI (Cupach & Spitzberg, 1998), *domestic stalking* (Dunn, 1999), *intimate partner stalking* (Tjaden & Thoennes, 2000), and *unwanted relationship pursuit* (Cupach & Spitzberg, 2008; Dutton & Winstead, 2006). Relational stalking behavior possesses three characteristic features: (1) intentional and persistent contact (or attempted contact) by the pursuer that is (2) unwanted and (3) psychologically aversive (unpleasant or offensive) to the recipient. In addition, although legal definitions vary across the U.S. (and other countries), relational stalking typically becomes a crime when it poses a credible threat that places the recipient in reasonable fear for his or her safety (see Cupach & Spitzberg, 2004; Meloy, 2007).

Surveys of college and community samples reveal that relational stalking is disturbingly common, with rates ranging from 12% to 40%, and with women at greater risk than men for this type of victimization (e.g., Coleman, 1997; Dressing, Kuehner, & Gass, 2005; Haugaard & Seri, 2003; Logan, Leukefeld, & Walker, 2000; Sheridan, Gillett, & Davies, 2002; Spitzberg & Cupach, 2003; Turmanis & Brown, 2006). In addition, sizeable numbers of men and women report having been the target of unwanted pursuit or "pre-stalking" behaviors including receiving undesired or unsolicited letters, notes, phone calls, visits, or gifts, or being followed or watched (Herold, Mantle, & Zemitis, 1979; Jason, Reichler, Easton, Neal, & Wilson, 1984; Roscoe, Strouse, & Goodwin, 1994). Most victims are acquainted with their stalkers; in fact, former romantic partners represent the largest category of relational stalkers (Spitzberg & Cupach, 2007).

Factors that Contribute to Relational Stalking

What factors contribute to relational stalking? There is some evidence that personality disorders, social skills deficits, and other individual or person-level factors increase the likelihood of engaging in unwanted pursuit (see Cupach & Spitzberg, 2008). Relational factors, however, appear to play the most important role. For example, relational stalking may emerge from the normal courtship process—in particular, from the indirect manner in which relationship initiation is typically enacted. As we discussed in Chapter 5, a person who wishes to convey romantic interest to another tends to rely on indirect cues to signal his or her attraction. These indirect behaviors—eye contact, smiling, casual conversational gambits—may pass unnoticed by the target (or may be noticed but not interpreted as a serious bid for a relationship); consequently, the target may fail to clearly communicate acceptance or rejection. In the absence of any direct and unequivocal response one way or the other, the pursuer may conclude that the target reciprocates his or her feelings and may persist in the pursuit behavior. Indeed, research conducted with college student samples reveals that men and women often engage in persistent pursuit or pre-stalking behaviors during the early stages of courtship (Sinclair & Frieze, 2002; Williams & Frieze, 2005) as well as after the unwanted termination of a romantic relationship (Dutton & Winstead, 2006). In addition, they often fail to accurately perceive the negative impact that their behavior has on the objects of their desire (Sinclair & Frieze, 2005; also see Davis, Ace, & Andra, 2000).

Similarly, pursuers often seek to promote their association with a target through the same interpersonal processes that characterize "normal" relationship development. For example, the development of most romantic relationships and friendships is marked by reciprocal and progressively deeper levels of self-disclosure, intimacy, social exchange, interdependence, and commitment (see Chapter 6). During interactions with the target, the pursuer may engage in behaviors that presumably convey and reflect these processes; from the pursuer's perspective, he or she is simply following the path of normal courtship and relationship progression. However, in relational stalking situations, the self-disclosure that occurs typically is one-sided, premature, and excessive. Additionally, hyperactive possessiveness takes the place of intimacy and closeness, and familiarity is created through violations of privacy rather than through the mutual exchanges that characterize normal relationship development. In sum:

> ORI [stalking] relationships are characterized by forms of intimacy that are distorted, exaggerated, accelerated, more intense, and more desperate, compared to the normal prototype for developing intimacy. Although the same dimensions of intimacy that characterize normal relations apply to ORI [stalking] relations, their manifestations are more forced, fabricated, prematurely escalated, and disinhibited.
>
> (Spitzberg & Cupach, 2002, p. 206)

The environmental or sociocultural context also promotes behaviors that are implicated in relational stalking. For example, a commonly held romantic assumption (and one that is frequently portrayed in movies, literature, and other media) is that "persistence pays." Hopeful suitors may continue in their efforts to gain affection from a seemingly uninterested partner because they believe that their persistence will ultimately be rewarded—in the face of their unwavering devotion, the beloved will eventually "come around" and return their affections.

By making it difficult for both pursuers and targets to recognize when pursuit behaviors have crossed out of the realm of "normal courtship," these contextual factors—the ambiguity that frequently surrounds relationship initiation, the occurrence of interpersonal processes that characterize "normal" relationship progression, and the cultural glorification of persistence in the face of romantic disinterest or rejection—create a situation that is conducive to relational stalking.

Pursuit Behaviors

Data gathered by Cupach and Spitzberg (1998, 2004, 2008; Spitzberg & Cupach, 1996, 2002) and others (e.g., Brewster, 2003; Turmanis & Brown, 2006) reveal that pursuers use a variety of tactics to promote relationships with their unwilling targets. Some of these strategies are *mildly intrusive*, including unexpectedly "showing up" at places frequented by the target, leaving repeated messages, giving gifts and other tokens of affection, using third parties to obtain information, and making exaggerated expressions of devotion or affection. Many of these milder forms of pursuit involve variations of flirting behavior and most targets consider them to be annoying but not terribly frightening or bothersome. *Moderately invasive* behaviors range from surveillance of the target (e.g., following, monitoring, or watching the target, driving by the target's home or place of work), trespassing, stealing information or property, intentionally sabotaging the target's reputation, and intruding on the target's friends and family. These forms of harassment are much more aggravating and distressing to the target. *Extremely intrusive or invasive* behaviors are those that are most likely to induce fear (in which case the behaviors would legally constitute stalking). These tactics include threatening to harm the target or his or her loved ones, physically restraining or assaulting the target, injuring or killing the target's pet(s), coercing or forcing the target to engage in sexual activities, damaging the target's property, and invading the target's home or work.

The milder forms of intrusive behavior are the most frequently experienced. For example, approximately 60% to 75% of the participants in Spitzberg and Cupach's studies, and 59% to 90% of the participants in an investigation conducted by criminologist Mary Brewster (2003), reported that their pursuer engaged in the following activities:

- Repeatedly called them on the phone.
- Sent letters or gifts.
- Asked them if they were seeing someone romantically.
- Called and hung up without speaking.
- Begged them for another chance.
- Watched or stared at them from a distance.
- Refused to take hints that he/she was not welcome.
- Made exaggerated claims about his or her affection.
- Gossiped or bragged about the supposed relationship with others.

About 10% to 40% of victims reported that their pursuer had engaged in the following less common but significantly more invasive and threatening behaviors:

- Threatening to cause physical harm to the target.
- Following the target from place to place.
- Damaging or stealing the target's property or possessions.
- Trespassing.
- Breaking into the target's home or apartment.
- Exposing himself or herself to the target.
- Forcing the target to engage in sexual behavior.
- Taking photos without the target's knowledge or consent.
- Recording conversations without the target's consent.

Responses to Victimization

Given the range of invasive and threatening actions in which pursuers commonly engage, it is hardly surprising that victims of relational stalking often experience a number of negative emotional reactions, including fear, anxiety, paranoia, depression, self-blame, and anger (e.g., Davis, Coker, & Sanderson, 2002; Mullen & Pathé, 1994; Pimlott-Kubiak & Cortina, 2003; Turmanis & Brown, 2006; Wallace & Silverman, 1996). In addition, they may change their lifestyle and patterns of social activity, develop a heightened distrust of others, and exhibit sleep disturbances, illness, and

other physical symptoms (Amar, 2006; Spitzberg & Cupach, 2001). Victims often face another difficult challenge—specifically, convincing others that they are, in fact, being stalked (see Leitz-Spitz,
2003). Because stalking emerges most commonly from pre-existing relationships, other people may
blame the victim for contributing to the situation (e.g., by "leading" the stalker on or not sufficiently communicating disinterest), may minimize the extent of the threat, and may disbelieve the
victim's claims of harassment (Sheridan, Gillett, Davies, Blaauw, & Patel, 2003).

One fundamental question for researchers in this area concerns coping responses to victimization. What responses, for example, are most effective at minimizing or eliminating stalking or intrusive behavior? What strategies can victims use to reduce their risk of negative outcomes in these
situations? Unfortunately, there is little systematic empirical work in this area. Some scholars have
attempted to identify the constellation of responses typically made by individuals who have been
harassed, stalked, or pursued (De Becker, 1998; Leitz-Spitz, 2003; Pathé, 2002; Spitzberg & Cupach,
1998, 2001). The results of their investigations suggest that one of the most common reactions is
avoidance—many targets simply ignore the situation or make no response at all. The prevalence of
this particular reaction may reflect the fact that most people lack a clear script for responding to
unwanted romantic attention. According to Baumeister and his colleagues (1993), this "*scriptlessness*"
often produces feelings of confusion and self-blame on the part of the target and contributes to
a passive avoidance of the would-be lover or the situation. Research reveals that targets also may
employ *direct confrontation*, which includes such actions as admonishing or attempting to reason with
the pursuer and requesting that he or she refrain from further contacts. *Retaliation* represents a third
strategy for dealing with unwanted attention. Retaliatory actions range from verbal threats and
attempts to belittle or shame the pursuer to physical violence. And finally, *formal protection* may be
sought from law enforcement officials, social workers and other professionals, or friends and family.

Each of these coping strategies carries a potential cost. For example, because avoidance is an
indirect and somewhat ambiguous strategy, the pursuer may fail to interpret it as rejection. Similarly, since the pursuer's goal is to connect with the target, direct confrontation by the target may
prove to the pursuer that persistence pays off—that is, that pursuit will eventually bring contact
with the object of obsession. Retaliation may demonstrate the target's lack of interest; however, it
may also anger the pursuer and push him or her to escalating levels of intrusion and threat. A similar outcome may be associated with formal protection efforts; for example, the seriousness of
obtaining a restraining order or having police intervene in the situation may trigger anger and
heightened aggression from the pursuer (as well as serve to demonstrate that he or she is finally
gaining the target's notice).

Although the effectiveness of the various types of coping responses is unknown to date, some
professionals believe that statements and actions that directly and unequivocally convey rejection
are most effective at managing unwanted attention (e.g., De Becker, 1998). For example, an individual should refuse gifts and other forms of attention offered by the pursuer, should directly state
his or her disinterest, and should cease all further contact and communication with that person. In
addition, targets should inform others of the situation, should document all stalking-related occurrences, should improve and/or increase security at their workplaces and homes, and should devise
a plan that allows for immediate escape if they feel threatened (see Leitz-Spitz, 2003).

INFIDELITY: WHEN THE ONE WE'VE CHOSEN CHEATS

As we discussed in Chapter 7, one of the most fundamental beliefs that people hold about marital
and other long-term, committed romantic relationships is that they should be *sexually exclusive*.

That is, once an individual is romantically committed to another, the general presumption is that he or she will engage in intercourse and other sexual activities only with the partner. And most people appear to not only believe this proscription but also to follow it. (An exception is gay men, who tend to hold relatively more permissive attitudes with respect to sexual infidelity and whose romantic relationships tend to be less sexually exclusive—see Peplau, Fingerhut, & Beals, 2004.) When Robert Michael and his colleagues (Michael, Gagnon, Laumann, & Kolata, 1994) asked participants to indicate how many sex partners they had had in the past year, the responses men and women gave clearly demonstrated "how likely people are to remain faithful to their sexual partners, whether or not they were married" (p. 101). Specifically, 95% of the married men and women, 75% of the never-married but cohabiting men and women, and 82% of the divorced and now cohabiting men and women had engaged in sexual activity with one and only one person (the partner) over the past 12 months. In fact, the people who reported multiple sex partners were, for the most part, single with no primary romantic partner. The researchers concluded, "Despite the popular myth that there is a great deal of adultery in marriage, our data and other reliable studies do not find it. Instead, a vast majority are faithful while the marriage is intact" (p. 89). The results of more recent surveys of married and dating couples continue to substantiate this basic relational fact (e.g., Knox, Vail-Smith, & Zusman, 2008; for reviews see Smith, 2006; Treas, 2003).

Factors that Contribute to Infidelity

However, although most people are sexually faithful to their partners, *infidelity* or *extrarelational sex* does occur. There are many reasons why an individual might engage in sexual activities with someone other than his or her primary partner. After reviewing the literature, scholars Julie Hall and Frank Fincham (2006) and Pepper Schwartz and Virginia Rutter (1998) identified a variety of person, relational, and environmental factors that are implicated in sexual infidelity. For example, extramarital sex is associated with biological sex; compared with women, men are more likely to report having engaged in an extramarital encounter (although this sex difference is most commonly found among older cohorts; see Wiederman, 1997). Environmental factors also are clearly linked with infidelity. Frequent travel, greater availability of alternative partners, and living in an urban setting are associated with a higher lifetime incidence of extramarital sex. Other powerful predictors of infidelity are relational, and include emotional or sexual incompatibility between the partners, interpersonal conflict or anger, problematic communication patterns, and lower levels of equity, commitment, and satisfaction.

A recent longitudinal study conducted by Elizabeth Allen and her colleagues (Allen et al., 2008) highlights the association between infidelity and relational factors. During an initial assessment, engaged couples participated in a brief problem-solving task in which they discussed and attempted to resolve two significant areas of conflict in their relationship. These interactions were videotaped and observers coded four aspects of each couple's interpersonal communication behavior: (1) positive communication (e.g., positive affect, support/validation), (2) negative communication (e.g., negative affect, denial), (3) emotional invalidation (e.g., insults, sarcasm), and (4) emotional validation (e.g., agreement, attribution of positive motives to the partner). Following this initial assessment, couples who subsequently married were re-contacted at yearly intervals for 8 years and asked to report whether or not they had ever been sexually unfaithful to their spouse. The results revealed that premarital communication behavior significantly predicted later marital infidelity. Compared to faithful couples, couples in which either the husband or wife eventually engaged in infidelity displayed lower levels of positive communication and higher levels of negative communication and emotional invalidation at the initial premarital assessment.

Other relational factors also appear to function as precursors to infidelity. Psychologists William Barta and Susan Kiene (2005) asked a group of men and women who had been unfaithful to their romantic partners to identify the reasons underlying their decision to be unfaithful. Participants were given four general categories of infidelity motivations: motives having to do with *relational dissatisfaction* (e.g., "I had 'fallen out of love with' my steady partner," "I wasn't sure if my steady partner was the right person for me"), motives involving *interpersonal neglect* (e.g., "I felt neglected by my steady partner," "My steady partner was emotionally distant"), motives concerning *sex* (e.g., "I wanted a greater variety of sexual partners," "I wanted more frequent sex"), and motives involving *anger* (e.g., "I wanted to 'get back at' my steady partner for something he or she did," "I wanted to prove to my steady partner that other people found me physically attractive"). Very few of the participants indicated that sex or anger motives played a role in their decision to be sexually unfaithful to their partners. Rather, their infidelity primarily stemmed from issues related to emotional compatibility with the partner and unhappiness with the romantic relationship: interpersonal dissatisfaction was the most highly rated reason for infidelity among both men and women, followed by neglect from the partner.

Responses to Infidelity

Just as infidelity may stem from a variety of motives and serve a number of different functions in people's lives, it is also associated with a great many outcomes. Some scholars have suggested that one-night stands, casual flings, and other forms of extrarelational sexual encounters may produce beneficial outcomes for the individual, including sheer physical pleasure, a feeling of personal growth, a sense of excitement and adventure, and the formation of an intense physical and/or emotional connection with the extrarelational partner (see Bringle & Buunk, 1991).

In general, however, most research indicates that the negative consequences of infidelity far outweigh any potential benefits. For example, the partner who engages in extrarelational sexual activity often experiences guilt and conflict about deceiving the other partner and violating moral or personal standards about exclusivity and fidelity, as well as anxiety and fear about sexually transmitted diseases, pregnancy, getting caught by the other partner, and so on (Bringle & Buunk, 1991; Spanier & Margolies, 1983). Indeed, a recent investigation conducted by Julie Hall and Frank Fincham (2009) revealed that men and women who had been unfaithful to their dating partners demonstrated higher levels of depression and lower levels of general psychological well-being, as well as greater guilt and shame about their behavior, than men and women who had not been unfaithful.

The cheated-on partner also experiences a number of negative emotional outcomes, including jealousy and anger, along with feelings of betrayal, self-doubt, and disappointment (Buunk, 1995; Charny & Parnass, 1995). Moreover, the relationship itself may not survive. Not only do people consider infidelity to be one of the most hurtful and destructive events that can occur in romantic relationships (Bachman & Guerrero, 2006; Feeney, 2004), but—as we will discuss in greater detail in Chapter 14—infidelity is one of the leading causes of relationship dissolution in the U.S. and around the world (e.g., Afifi, Falato, & Weiner, 2001; Amato & Rogers, 1997; Atkins, Baucom, & Jacobson, 2001; Betzig, 1989; Previti & Amato, 2004). This may explain why individuals who participate in extramarital relationships receive some form of punishment—from their spouses, family members or kin, or social authorities—in virtually all human societies (see Frayser, 1989). For example, a recent cross-cultural investigation conducted by anthropologists William Jankowiak and M. Diane Hardgrave (2007) revealed that equally high proportions of men and women sought to terminate a spouse's extramarital affair (in other words, both sexes were equally concerned about infidelity), and that the majority relied on physical violence to do so. Specifically, in 88% of the cultures sampled, men responded to infidelity with direct physical confrontation (e.g., beating the spouse or rival, or both); in 64% of cultures, women also responded to infidelity with physical violence. In sum, sexual infidelity is a potent and often quite destructive force in romantic relationships.

Sexual Jealousy

One of the most powerful consequences of infidelity or suspected infidelity is sexual jealousy. *Sexual jealousy* (also called *romantic jealousy*) is defined as an unpleasant psychological or emotional state that (1) arises when an important romantic relationship is threatened by a third party (a rival) and (2) motivates behavior designed to counter the threat (e.g., Daly & Wilson, 1983; Harris, 2009; White & Mullen, 1989). Anger and fear—including feelings of rage, hostility, anxiety, and worry—are commonly experienced by people who are in the throes of sexual jealousy (Guerrero, Trost, & Yoshimura, 2005).

Researchers who study sexual jealousy often ask participants to imagine their romantic partner engaging in *emotional infidelity* (e.g., forming a deep emotional attachment to or falling in love with someone else) or *sexual infidelity* (e.g., engaging in sexual activities or having intercourse with someone else) and then to indicate which type of infidelity would be the most upsetting. For example, participants in one study received the following instructions:

> Please think of a serious committed relationship that you have had in the past, that you currently have, or that you would like to have. Imagine that you discover that the person with whom you've become seriously involved became interested in someone else. What would distress or upset you more (please circle only one): (A) Imagining your partner forming a deep emotional attachment to that person. (B) Imagining your partner enjoying passionate sexual intercourse with that person.
>
> (Buss, Larsen, Westen, & Semmelroth, 1992, p. 252)

When faced with this kind of choice, both men and women usually (but not always) select the first option; that is, they say that their partners' emotional infidelity would be more upsetting than their sexual infidelity (e.g., Buss et al., 1999, Study 1; Harris, 2002; Wiederman & Kendall, 1999). However, two sex differences commonly are found. Specifically, although both sexes typically select emotional infidelity as most upsetting, more men than women select sexual infidelity, and more women than men choose emotional infidelity, as the most distressing event.

A study conducted by Christine Harris and Nicholas Christenfeld (1996) illustrates this pattern of results. These researchers asked college students to imagine their romantic partners engaging in sexual infidelity (i.e., "trying different sexual positions" with another person) and emotional infidelity (i.e., "falling in love" with another person). When asked which of the two types of infidelity would be most upsetting, the majority of women and men selected the emotional infidelity scenario. However, significantly more women (78%) than men (53%) chose the emotional infidelity scenario, and significantly more men (47%) than women (22%) selected the sexual infidelity scenario, as the most distressing situation.

The Origin of Sex Differences in Jealousy. The origin of these differences between men and women in jealousy responses has been the source of much debate in the scientific community. Evolutionary theorists argue that sex differences in jealousy are real and reflect the evolved mating psychologies of men and women, which are assumed to differ as a function of the different obstacles to reproductive success faced by ancestral men and women. As evolutionary scholars Martin Daly and Margo Wilson (1983, p.294) observe:

> The threat to a man's fitness resides in the risk of alien insemination of his adulterous wife, whereas the threat to a woman's fitness lies not so much in her adulterous husband's sexual contacts as in the risk that he will divert resources away from the wife and family. It follows that male jealousy should have evolved to be more specifically focused upon the sexual act, and female jealousy upon the loss of male attention and resources.

What does this mean? Recall the evolutionary hypothesis that reproductive success for both sexes is measured by the production of offspring who survive to reach reproductive maturity and who themselves then mate and perpetuate the individual's genetic makeup (see Chapters 3 and 7). From this perspective, modern men are more distressed by sexual infidelity than are women because in the evolutionary past that particular kind of infidelity jeopardized a man's ability to successfully reproduce and pass his own genetic material into the next generation. Essentially, a man whose partner was sexually unfaithful could have ended up providing resources to and raising another man's children—a genetic dead end. Modern women, on the other hand, are presumed to be more upset by emotional infidelity than are men because that type of infidelity jeopardized a woman's ability to obtain the steady supply of resources that she needed for her own and her children's survival (again, in the ancestral past). An emotionally unfaithful partner was likely to divert those important resources away from her and to the rival and any offspring the rival produced.

The evolutionary framework does not imply that infidelity in and of itself is less upsetting to one sex than to the other. On the contrary, as we have discussed throughout this textbook, humans are social creatures who possess a mind that is adapted for group living and for the formation of long-term, committed, and monogamous mating relationships. Consequently, *any* kind of behavior that threatens the primary romantic relationship is assumed to be distressing to both men and women. What the evolutionary framework suggests is that, to the extent that the sexes faced *different* obstacles to reproductive success over the expanse of human evolutionary history, they developed different psychological sensitivities to the two types of infidelity.

Other researchers believe that the commonly observed sex differences do not reflect the operation of specific evolved jealousy mechanisms in men and women but instead are primarily a function of **methodological artifact**; that is, they argue that the sex differences are not real but rather are created or magnified by the methods that researchers typically use to study jealousy (see DeSteno, Bartlett, Braverman, & Salovey, 2002; Harris, 2003; Sabini & Green, 2004). This criticism is valid. Researchers in this area typically employ hypothetical scenarios and a forced-choice methodology, and their study participants usually are very young adults and/or college students (many of whom may never have actually experienced a partner's infidelity). This is problematic for a number of reasons. First, sex differences usually occur only when participants are forced to choose one and only one type of infidelity as being the most distressing. Sex differences disappear when participants are allowed to evaluate each type of infidelity separately. When given rating scales rather than a forced-choice option, both men and women evaluate both types of infidelity as highly distressing (e.g., Cann & Baucom, 2004).

Second, it is very likely that what people *say* they would do or feel in response to a hypothetical and imaginary situation may be different from how they *actually* would respond if they were truly faced with the reality of a loved one's sexual or emotional betrayal. In an interesting study, Margit Berman and Patricia Frazier (2005) set out to test this idea. They selected two groups of participants—a group of men and women who had never to their knowledge been betrayed by their romantic partners and a group of men and women who actually had been betrayed by unfaithful romantic partners. Participants in the first group received the usual hypothetical scenario and forced-choice response option; they imagined that their current partners had been unfaithful and selected either sexual infidelity (i.e., the partner "enjoying sexual activities" with another person) or emotional infidelity (the partner's "emotional attachment" to another person) as most upsetting. Participants who had actually been betrayed were asked to think about their own partners' infidelity and to indicate whether the sexual behavior or the emotional attachment had distressed or upset them most. The response pattern for participants who had never been betrayed was similar to that typically reported by other researchers who use hypothetical scenarios; more men than women reported that knowledge of their partners' sexual activities would be more distressing than knowledge of an outside emotional attachment (and, conversely, more women than men said that emotional infidelity would be more distressing than sexual infidelity). However, participants who had actually experienced infidelity showed no such sex differences in their responses to the forced-choice question: equal percentages of men and women (53%) reported that the sexual aspect of their partners' infidelity was worse than the emotional aspect, and equal percentages (47%) indicated that the outside emotional attachment that their partners had formed was worse than their extrarelational sexual activities. The researchers concluded, "The findings reported above make clear the stark contrast between what college-aged men and women think they will feel if their romantic partners cheat on them and what they actually feel when such a betrayal occurs" (p. 1623). The hypothetical forced-choice paradigm obviously is seriously flawed, and more research clearly is needed on the nature of sexual jealousy as it occurs in actual ongoing romantic relationships.

Yet a third explanation for the observed sex differences has been proposed, this one focusing on the ways in which men and women cognitively interpret different types of infidelity. Several researchers (e.g., DeSteno & Salovey, 1996; Harris & Christenfeld, 1996) have noted that people possess different beliefs about the likelihood that the occurrence of one type of infidelity implies the occurrence of the other type for each sex. In Chapter 11 we reviewed evidence that men generally hold more positive attitudes about sex in the absence of love and commitment than do women; conversely, women, to a greater degree than men, prefer to engage in sexual intercourse only after the relationship is characterized by commitment and love. Because most people are aware of these existing sex differences in beliefs and preferences, it makes sense that (heterosexual) men would be relatively more upset by a partner's sexual infidelity than by her emotional infidelity, and that (heterosexual) women would demonstrate the reverse pattern. To men, a woman's sexual infidelity implies the presence of *both* sexual and emotional involvement (because they assume that women require emotional intimacy prior to entering a sexual relationship); consequently, this type of infidelity should be more disturbing than a woman's emotional infidelity (which implies emotional involvement alone). For women, the situation is reversed. Women may assume that a sexually unfaithful man is not necessarily emotionally involved with his partner but that an emotionally unfaithful man probably is sexually involved. Thus, a man's emotional infidelity (which implies both emotional and sexual involvement) is more upsetting to women than is his sexual infidelity (which implies only sexual involvement). Essentially, then, the argument is that each sex selects as most upsetting the type of infidelity that implies their partner's greatest degree of extrarelational involvement and that thus poses the greatest overall threat to the relationship.

The debate among researchers about sex differences in sexual jealousy may never be fully resolved. Nonetheless, we can draw some fairly firm conclusions about jealousy. First, sexual jealousy is a pervasive human response to real, imagined, or implied infidelity. *Both* men and women report experiencing considerable emotional distress when asked to imagine or to recall a romantic partner's infidelity. Second, jealousy is produced by *both* types of infidelity. Very few people remain unmoved when faced with their partners' real or imagined sexual infidelity, and very few people remain stoic and unaffected by their partners' emotional infidelity. Third, both sexes become upset by both types of infidelity. These issues are not in question.

SUMMARY

The close, intimate relationships we form with others throughout our lives can be a source of both highly rewarding and highly destructive outcomes. Sometimes we fall in love with someone who fails to return our affections. Sometimes a couple's sexual passion fades, or the partners become sexually or emotionally involved with someone else. Each of these transgressions is associated with a number of personal, relational, and environmental factors, and each produces a number of adverse consequences for the partners and their relationship.

KEY CONCEPTS

Relational transgressions (p. 213)
Unrequited love (p. 216)
Sexual disinterest (p. 217)
Relational stalking (p. 219)
Avoidance (p. 222)
Scriptlessness (p. 222)
Direct confrontation (p. 222)

Retaliation (p. 222)
Formal protection (p. 222)
Sexual exclusivity (p. 222)
Infidelity or extrarelational sex (p. 223)
Sexual (romantic) jealousy (p. 225)
Methodological artifact (p. 226)

EXPLORATION EXERCISES

These exercises are designed to allow you to explore in greater detail some of the concepts and issues discussed in this chapter. There are no right or wrong answers to these exercises—they are simply meant to provide an opportunity for discussion and debate.

1. Unrequited love appears to be a common human experience. Have you ever found yourself in this situation, either as the unrequited lover or as the unwilling object of affection? If so, take a few minutes and think back to your particular situation. How did you feel? What emotions do you recall experiencing? Make a list of as many of the sentiments, feelings, and emotions as you can remember. Were your feelings primarily positive, primarily negative, or a mixture of positive and negative? How well does your own experience match the experiences reported by participants in Baumeister et al.'s (1993) unrequited love study?

2. Some scholars have proposed that widely held romantic assumptions—including the notion that "persistence pays"—are implicated in relational stalking. Can you think of any media examples (drawn from literature, movies, or plays) in which persistence has, in fact, "paid" and the would-be suitor has eventually ended up winning the heart of his or her beloved? How might these portrayals potentially contribute to a relational stalking situation?

3. Relational stalking has been portrayed in a variety of movies, including *Fatal Attraction* (1987), *Fear* (1996), *Swimfan* (also called *Swimf@n*, 2002), *Enduring Love* (2004), *Obsessed* (2009), and a host of others. Select two movies that depict obsession and relational stalking and watch each one carefully. Using your knowledge of relational stalking, determine how well these cinematic portrayals match the features and characteristics of relational stalking identified by scientific research.

Chapter 13
Aggression and Violence

CHAPTER OUTLINE

In the previous chapter we reviewed research on rejection and betrayal, two highly unpleasant interpersonal experiences that shake the foundation of many close relationships. *Intimate partner violence*—violence occurring within romantic, marital, family, friend, and other intimate relationships—represents another deeply problematic (and disturbingly common) relational issue. Survey research reveals that minor acts of physical aggression (such as slapping, pushing, or shoving) occur in roughly one-third of dating relationships (Hines & Malley-Morrison, 2005). Severe acts of aggression also are quite prevalent. The U.S. Department of Justice (2008b) reports that about 12%

of victims of violent crime are assaulted by a relative (e.g., spouse, parent, child), with another 41% attacked by a personal acquaintance; in fact, only 38% of such crimes are committed by strangers. Although any intimate relationship carries the potential for violence, most researchers have focused on aggressive behavior that occurs between romantic partners; consequently, most of our discussion explores the dynamics of violence in dating and marital relationships. However, we also examine what is currently known about bullying and peer victimization, both among adults in the workplace and among children in school settings.

PHYSICAL AGGRESSION IN ROMANTIC RELATIONSHIPS

Different kinds of violence can occur in adult romantic relationships. One widely accepted typology was developed by Michael Johnson (e.g., Johnson, 1999, 2008; Kelly & Johnson, 2008). Based on thorough reviews of the literature and his own ongoing program of research, Johnson proposes that four basic varieties of intimate partner violence exist: situational couple violence, separation-instigated violence, coercive controlling violence, and violent resistance. Of these, situational couple violence and coercive controlling violence have received the most attention from relationship scientists.

Situational Couple Violence

One day my girlfriend was bugging me about something and she was going on and on. It was irritating so I turned away and tried to ignore her. She got so mad that she punched me in the arm with her fist.

      – 19-year-old man interviewed by the author

My best friend's boyfriend used to do mean things to her. He was always pinching her and grabbing her, kind of shoving her around physically. Sometimes she'd tell him to stop or she'd say "ow" really loud, and he'd always laugh it off like he was only teasing. It made me really uncomfortable.

      – 24-year-old woman interviewed by the author

My wife is a very, how shall I say this, "expressive" woman. I love her, but she has a tendency to kind of fly off the handle, especially when she's mad. Cursing, throwing stuff at me, and so on. Once she threw the remote control at me, and it got me right in the forehead. It hurt like a son of a gun. Fortunately, we don't argue all that often.

      – 32-year-old man interviewed by the author

It happened in college and it was an accident. I was teasing my boyfriend and calling him names. I don't know why. I knew he was getting really angry but I kept on doing it. I was only fooling around but all of a sudden he slapped me in the face. Basically, he just lost his cool and lashed out. I was more shocked than hurt—we both were.

      – 30-year-old woman interviewed by the author

These quotations describe the type of aggression that most typically occurs between romantic partners. ***Situational couple violence*** (sometimes called ***common couple violence*** or ***conflict-motivated violence***) refers to violent behavior that arises primarily in the context of interpersonal conflict (Ellis & Stuckless, 1996; Kelly & Johnson, 2008). This type of intimate partner violence is not accompanied by a chronic pattern of coercion, manipulation, and control but rather is associated with poor anger management, communication skill deficits, or ineffective conflict resolution strategies on the part of one or both partners. Situational couple violence typically erupts during a heated argument or disagreement during which one or both partners lose their tempers and impulsively resort to pushing, shoving, or other physical actions to resolve the conflict. Because these lapses of control are situational in nature (i.e., associated only with that particular argument), they tend to result in milder forms of physical aggression and do not commonly recur in the relationship.

Researchers interested in exploring situational couple violence typically use the 12-item Physical Assault Subscale of the revised Conflict Tactics Scale (CTS-2) developed by Murray Straus and his colleagues (Straus, Hamby, Boney-McCoy, & Sugarman, 1995). When responding to the items, participants indicate the frequency with which both they and their partners engaged in various physically violent actions during the past year, including:

- throwing something at the partner that could hurt;
- twisting the partner's arm or hair;
- pushing or shoving the partner;
- grabbing the partner;
- slapping the partner;
- using a knife or gun on the partner;
- punching or hitting the partner with something that could hurt;
- choking the partner;
- slamming the partner against a wall;
- beating up the partner;
- burning or scalding the partner on purpose;
- kicking the partner.

The first five items are considered to reflect relatively minor forms of physical aggression, whereas the last seven items are assumed to reflect more severe violence. The CTS-2 also includes an Injury Subscale which assesses the extent to which individuals are physically injured by their partners' violent behavior (e.g., "I went to a doctor because of a fight with my partner," "I had a sprain, bruise, or small cut because of a fight with my partner," "I had a broken bone from a fight with my partner").

Prevalence. Surveys of non-clinical samples (e.g., community or college student samples) reveal that fairly high (and roughly equal) proportions of men and women engage in situational couple violence (e.g., O'Leary & Williams, 2006; Straus & Ramirez, 2007; but see Archer, 2000). In one investigation, Straus (2004) asked more than 8000 students from 31 universities located around the world (e.g., Asia, the Middle East, Australia, New Zealand, Europe, South America, Canada, the United States) to complete the Physical Assault and Injury Subscales of the CTS-2. Although violence rates varied across samples (ranging from a low of 17% in the Braga, Portugal student sample to a high of 45% in the Louisiana, U.S. student sample), a substantial proportion of the participants (29%) reported having physically assaulted a dating partner in the previous 12 months. Most of these assaults were minor, such as slapping a partner or shoving a partner in anger; however, the rate of severe violence—ranging from punching, choking, and attacking the partner with weapons— was still disturbingly high (9%). Moreover, 7% of the students indicated that they had inflicted an injury on their dating partners (with men more likely than women to have inflicted severe injuries, e.g., broken bone, head trauma). Similar results were reported more recently by researchers James

McNulty and Julianne Hellmuth (2008), who administered items from the Physical Assault Subscale to a sample of newlywed couples; 36% of couples reporting having experienced at least one act of physical violence during the previous 12 months (see also Lawrence & Bradbury, 2007).

Although both men and women perpetrate situational couple violence, the sexes appear to differ in the type of violence they use. Psychologist John Archer (2002) conducted a meta-analysis using data from 58 previously published studies. Each study provided information on the occurrence of nine of the individual acts of physical violence measured by the original version of the CTS. These nine acts included throwing something; pushing, grabbing, or shoving; slapping; kicking, biting, or punching; hitting with an object; beating; choking or strangling; threatening with a gun or knife; and using a gun or knife. Archer's analysis of the numbers of men and women who inflicted each of these acts on their partners (according to those partners' self-reports) indicated that women were more likely than men to perpetrate acts of minor violence, whereas men were more likely than women to commit acts of severe violence. Specifically, a higher proportion of women than men engaged in four of the five acts of minor violence, including throwing something at the partner, hitting the partner with an object, slapping the partner, and kicking, biting, or punching the partner. Conversely, a higher proportion of men than women had perpetrated three of the four acts of severe violence, including beating, choking or strangling, and using a knife or a gun on their partners. Other researchers have found that men are more likely than women to repeatedly aggress against their partners, and that women are more likely than men to suffer physical injury as a result of their partners' aggressive behavior (Breiding, Black, & Ryan, 2008; Morse, 1995; Whitaker, Haileyesus, Swahn, & Saltzman, 2007). Thus, both sexes are aggressive—but women's aggression typically is less severe than is men's.

In sum, research on situational couple violence reveals that (minor) violence is a relatively common occurrence in romantic relationships and that both men and women can and do commit a variety of physically aggressive acts against their intimate partners.

Coercive Controlling Violence

Coercive controlling violence (also called *intimate terrorism* and commonly referred to as *domestic violence*, *spousal abuse*, or *battery*) is the type of intimate partner violence that is encountered most often by workers in agency settings such as hospitals and clinics, domestic violence shelters, public safety or law enforcement departments, and the legal system (Coker, Smith, McKeown, & King, 2000; Graham-Kevan & Archer, 2003; Johnson, 2006). Unlike situational couple violence, which typically arises in the context of interpersonal conflict and tends to involve minor forms of physical aggression, coercive controlling violence involves physical violence that is associated with a chronic pattern of emotionally abusive intimidation, coercion, and control (e.g., Kelly & Johnson, 2008). Coercively controlling and violent relationships typically involve one partner (the abuser) engaging in a persistent effort to frighten, manipulate, terrorize, hurt, humiliate, injure, and otherwise dominate and control the other partner (the victim). As illustrated in Table 13.1, abusers employ a variety of tactics in their quest for power and control, ranging from physical and emotional abuse, to economic or financial abuse, to isolation and denial (Hines, Brown, & Dunning, 2007; National Domestic Violence Hotline, 2008; Pence & Paymar, 1993; U.S. Department of Justice, 2008a). It is important to recognize that coercive controlling individuals do not necessarily use all of these tactics to dominate their partners; rather, they tend to use the combination they believe will be most effective at maintaining their control. For example, in many abusive relationships—particularly those with a history of prior physical violence—the abuser may no longer need to employ physical force to dominate the partner; as a result, coercive controlling violence does not always manifest itself in high levels of physical aggression (see Johnson, 2008).

Table 13.1   Coercive Controlling Violence: Tactics and Behavioral Examples

Tactic	Example(s)
Physical Abuse	Pushing, slapping, biting, hitting, choking, kicking, beating
Sexual Abuse	Forced sexual activities Insulting the partner in sexual ways Demanding sex after physical abuse Using weapons during sex
Emotional Abuse	Name-calling, insults, criticism Put-downs, public (or private) humiliation "Mind games" Making the partner think he/she is crazy Withdrawal of affection
Economic Abuse	Controlling finances Refusing to share money Preventing the partner from having or keeping a job
Social Isolation	Limiting the partner's outside activities Monitoring the partner's social contacts Trapping the partner in the home Preventing the partner from obtaining medical treatment Using jealousy to justify isolating the partner
Denial	Blaming the partner for the abuse Denying that the abuse happened Minimizing the extent of harm to the partner
Use of Children	Threatening or harming the children Using the children to relay messages Using the children to make the partner feel guilty
Use of Male Privilege (male abusers)	Treating the partner as a "servant" Making all the important decisions Defining men's and women's roles in the family
Use of the Domestic Violence System (female abusers)	Having the partner falsely arrested Falsely obtaining a restraining order Filing for sole custody of children
Coercion and Threats	Threatening to physically harm the partner Threatening to leave the partner Threatening to commit suicide Forcing the partner to drop abuse charges Forcing the partner to engage in illegal activities
Intimidation	Frightening or terrorizing the partner through looks, gestures, or actions Destroying the partner's property Abusing pets

Abusers employ a variety of tactics in their quest for power and control over their partners, ranging from emotional and financial abuse, to physical abuse, to intimidation, coercion, and threats (Hines, Brown, & Dunning, 2007; National Domestic Violence Hotline, 2008; Pence & Paymar, 1993; U.S. Department of Justice, 2008a).

Nature and Consequences.   There is strong evidence of sex asymmetry in coercive controlling violence; that is, among heterosexual couples, abusers are predominantly male and victims are predominantly female. In addition, although physical violence is not always present in high amounts throughout the relationship, it tends to occur with greater frequency than in relationships characterized by other types of intimate partner violence, is likely to escalate over time, and produces more serious consequences in terms of injury.

For example, Johnson (1999) derived a data set from interviews of married or formerly married women collected by Irene Frieze in the late 1970s (e.g., Frieze, 1983; Frieze & Browne, 1989; Frieze & McHugh, 1992). Frieze's sample included two groups of women: (1) an agency sample consisting of women who had sought assistance from a domestic violence shelter or who had filed Protection from Abuse Orders in court, and (2) a community sample of women who lived in the same neighborhoods as the agency sample. Each participant was extensively interviewed about the interpersonal dynamics of her marriage, including the extent to which her husband engaged in physical violence as well as various control tactics (e.g., threats, economic control, assertion of male privilege, isolation, emotional abuse). On the basis of the interview data, participants were subsequently divided into two relationship groups: (1) a group whose marriages contained physical violence coupled with coercive control (the domestic violence group) and (2) a group whose marriages contained conflict-motivated physical violence in the absence of coercion and control (the situational couple violence group). The results revealed that the two relationship groups differed in a number of ways. The first difference concerned the sex of the perpetrator. In the domestic violence group, almost all (97%) of the abuse was perpetrated by husbands (providing evidence of sex asymmetry in this type of intimate partner violence). However, in keeping with the results we reviewed earlier in the chapter, physical aggression was enacted by roughly equal proportions of husbands (55%) and wives (45%) in the situational couple violence group. The two groups also differed in the amount, severity, and developmental course of the physical violence they experienced in their marriages. On average, women in the domestic violence group reported experiencing 58 instances of physical violence at the hands of their husbands prior to the time of the interview session (compared to 14 instances reported by women in the situational couple violence group), and 76% had experienced severe or permanent injury (compared to 28% of women in the other group). In addition, 76% of the women in the domestic violence group indicated that their husbands' violence had escalated over the course of the relationship, whereas the majority of non-battered wives (54%) reported that their husbands' violent behavior had de-escalated over time.

Large-scale survey research conducted with samples drawn from the general population corroborates these findings. In one investigation, sociologist Joseph Michalski (2005) analyzed data on intimate partner violence collected as part of a national survey. Over 16,000 men and women involved in romantic relationships were asked whether their partners had ever engaged in acts of physical violence (e.g., "beaten you," "kicked, bit, or hit you with his/her fist," "choked you") and coercive control (e.g., "tried to limit your contact with family or friends," "put you down or called you names," "damaged or destroyed your possessions or property"). The results revealed that domestic violence was relatively infrequent; only 4% of the entire sample reported experiencing physical violence embedded in a pattern of coercive control (indeed, almost 90% of participants reported having never experienced physical aggression or coercive control from their partners). However, although the overall prevalence rate was low, the results confirmed the sex asymmetry observed earlier by Johnson (1999). Specifically, a significantly higher proportion of women (5.2%) than men (3.0%) reported having a violent and coercively controlling partner. Moreover, participants in coercive and controlling relationships experienced twice as many instances of physical violence as other participants, and the violence that occurred was more severe.

Many victims of domestic violence are forced to resort to aggression themselves in order to thwart the actions of their abusers (Henning, Renauer, & Holdford, 2006; Pagelow, 1981; Stuart et al., 2006). Called *violent resistance* (or *resistive/reactive violence*), this type of intimate partner violence is motivated by self-defense. Because most (heterosexual) abusers are male and most victims are female, it is not surprising that violent resistance is primarily enacted by women. For example, 96% of the abused women in Johnson's (1999) study (based on Frieze's data, e.g., 1983) had resorted to violence in an effort to protect themselves from injury from their abusive husbands. Unfortunately, self-protective violence may result in additional abuse; faced with physical resistance, an abusive partner may become enraged and perpetrate additional (and more severe) violence (Kelly & Johnson, 2008; Pagelow, 1981). Indeed, Ronet Bachman and Dianne Carmody's (1994) analysis of National Crime Victimization Survey data revealed that women who defended themselves against physical attacks from their intimate partners were twice as likely to sustain injuries as women who did not (also see Bachman, Saltzman, Thompson, & Carmody, 2002).

In addition to physical injury and trauma, victims of domestic violence experience a number of serious and adverse psychological outcomes. Women who are terrorized by their intimate partners often live in a state of chronic fear and anxiety; they also frequently report lowered self-esteem, depression, and symptoms of post-traumatic stress (e.g., Basile, Arias, Desai, & Thompson, 2004; Dobash & Dobash, 1979; Gelles & Harrop, 1989; Golding, 1999; Johnson & Leone, 2005; Tyson, Herting, & Randell, 2007). Although less is known about the consequences of domestic violence for male victims, there is evidence that men who are abused experience the same constellation of physical and psychological outcomes as their female counterparts (for reviews, see Dutton, 2007; Hines & Malley-Morrison, 2005). They may also experience an additional adverse consequence— re-victimization by a domestic violence system that is designed to assist female victims and that consequently often does not recognize that men, too, can be abused. When criminal justice scholars Denise Hines, Jan Brown, and Edward Dunning (2007) analyzed calls to a national domestic abuse hotline for men, they discovered that many male victims reported having sought help in the past but having been turned away, laughed at, not taken seriously, and treated as batterers (rather than victims) by agency workers. For many callers, this unfair treatment was as traumatic as the abuse itself.

Risk Factors. Many relationship scholars have sought to identify the risk factors or correlates of domestic abuse. In their comprehensive reviews of the existing literature, Denise Hines and Kathleen Malley-Morrison (2005) and Scott Christopher and Sally Lloyd (2000) discussed the following personal, relational, and environmental corrclates:

- Psychopathology: Male batterers are more likely than non-batterers to exhibit a variety of severe clinical disorders, ranging from major depression and anxiety to personality disorders (e.g., antisocial, borderline, narcissistic).
- Attitudes: Abusers (and, often, their victims) tend to endorse interpersonal violence and hold highly traditional attitudes toward marriage (e.g., they believe that husbands should be the dominant partner in marriage and that it is acceptable for a husband to hit a wife).
- Age: Intimate partner violence peaks among adults in their 20s and steadily declines in older cohorts.
- Alcohol use: Men who abuse alcohol are more likely to assault their romantic partners, and women who abuse alcohol are more likely to be assaulted by an intimate partner.
- Prior exposure to relational aggression: Women who were abused as children or who were exposed to inter-parental violence are more likely to experience domestic abuse later in

their own lives; men who witness inter-parental violence are more likely to be violent toward their female partners.

- Cohabitation: Compared with dating and married couples, couples who cohabit have higher rates of physical assault.
- Socioeconomic status: Low income, poverty, lower occupational status (e.g., blue collar or working class as opposed to white collar or middle class), and lower educational attainment are among the strongest predictors of domestic violence.
- Social isolation: Domestic abuse is more likely to occur when a couple is socially isolated and the partners have few sources of social support.

Domestic abuse is among the most pernicious forms of interpersonal violence that can arise in romantic relationships, and additional research on ways to prevent its occurrence and effectively combat its adverse effects is clearly needed.

SEXUAL AGGRESSION IN ROMANTIC RELATIONSHIPS

Sometimes the physical aggression that partners enact or experience within their romantic relationships is of a sexual nature or occurs concurrently with sexually aggressive acts. There are two broad categories of sexual aggression (see Christopher, 2001; Muehlenhard, Goggins, Jones, & Satterfield, 1991; Sprecher & McKinney, 1993). The first, *sexual coercion*, involves the use of verbal or psychological manipulation, pressure, or coercion to gain sexual compliance from another individual. Examples include pleading, verbally threatening to end the relationship, making the other person feel guilty for refusing sex, and continuing to persist in the face of the other's objections. Sexual coercion does not involve threats of physical harm or the use of physical force.

The second type of sexual aggression is *sexual assault* (also called sexual abuse or sexual violence). Sexual assault reflects "a direct power assertion" (Christopher, 2001, p. 134) on the part of one partner toward the other and includes both (1) sexual contact obtained with the threatened or actual use of physical force or bodily harm and (2) sexual acts committed with a partner who is unable to give consent (for example, due to intoxication or lack of consciousness). Scholars who have investigated the dynamics of sexually violent marital relationships have identified three distinct types of assault, each with its own characteristic features (see Finkelhor & Yllö, 1985; Groth, 1979; Monson & Langhinrichsen-Rohling, 1998; also see Marshall & Holtzworth-Munroe, 2002). The first, *battering rape* (also called *anger rape*), occurs in the context of a coercive and controlling relationship; that is, the victim experiences forced sex coupled with physical violence and coercive control. In some instances, the physical assault precedes the sexual violence, whereas in other instances the physical violence occurs during the sexual assault. In these relationships the perpetrator engages in multiple forms of aggression and often uses sex as a means to express anger and hurt the partner. The second type of sexual assault is *force-only rape* (or *power rape*). Force-only rape typically does not involve severe physical violence—the perpetrator generally is not physically abusive but will use force to obtain sex from an unwilling partner. In these relationships the perpetrator's intent is not to cause harm (although injury may result from the assault) but rather to exert dominance over the partner and control over the couple's sexual interactions. *Obsessive rape* (also called *sadistic rape*) is less common than the other two forms of sexual violence and is motivated by a sadistic desire to sexually torment and mistreat the partner. These perpetrators are obsessed with forcing their partners to engage in degrading, deviant, and painful sexual acts, take pleasure in their partners' humiliation, and are willing to use physical violence to achieve their sexual goals.

Prevalence

Research conducted over the past 40 years reveals that sexual aggression is a fairly common occurrence within dating relationships. An early study of undergraduate men, for example, revealed that 26% reported having made forceful attempts at intercourse while on dates that had, in turn, prompted a fighting, crying, or screaming response from their partners (Kanin, 1967). Two decades later, 25% of the men in a national survey of college students stated that they had used some form of sexual coercion or force on a dating partner (Koss, Gidycz, & Wisniewski, 1987). Today, these rates appear largely unchanged. Psychologists Christine Gidycz, Jennifer Warkentin, and Lindsay Orchowski (2007) asked 425 undergraduate men to answer a series of questions concerning their history of sexual aggression. Three types of sexually aggressive behaviors were assessed: (1) coercion (i.e., the use of authority, continual arguments, or pressure to coerce a woman into sexual intercourse), (2) sexually aggressive contact (i.e., the use of continual arguments, authority, or physical force to make a woman engage in non-intercourse sexual activities), and (3) rape or attempted rape (i.e., the use of alcohol, drugs, physical force, or threats of physical force to coerce a woman into sexual intercourse, including anal or oral sex). The results revealed that nearly 18% of the men reported perpetrating some form of sexual aggression. Specifically, 5.4% reported having used sexual coercion, 6.4% indicated having engaged in sexually aggressive contact, and fully 5.9% reported having committed rape or attempted rape. The majority of these sexual assaults involved dating partners (64.4%) or acquaintances (28.8%); only 6.8% of the victims were strangers.

Thus, contrary to popular opinion (which typically portrays sexual violence as an act perpetrated by strangers lurking in dark alleys), most victims of sexual assault are attacked by intimates. Indeed, the results of the 2003 National Crime Victim Survey (Calhoun, McCauley, & Crawford, 2006) indicated that 70% of perpetrators of rape, attempted rape, or sexual assault had an existing relationship with their victims at the time of the attack: 50% were acquaintances (e.g., dates, neighbors, classmates), 12% were spouses or committed romantic partners, and 8% were relatives. Similarly, almost all (95%) of the women surveyed by Robert Michael and his colleagues (Michael, Gagnon, Laumann, & Kolata, 1994) knew or were romantically involved with their attackers: only 4% of the respondents indicated that their male assailants were strangers who were unknown to them. In sum, most of the forced and unwanted sexual activities that women experience occur within the context of their existing relationships.

Although reliable estimates of marital rape are difficult to obtain, survey data from the U.S. and other world regions indicate that a sizeable proportion of marriages contain sexual violence (e.g., Garcia-Moreno, Jansen, Ellsberg, Heise, & Watts, 2006; Marshall & Holtzworth-Munroe, 2002). For example, a survey conducted in Great Britain by criminologists Kate Painter and David Farrington (1998) revealed that 13% of wives had experienced forced sexual intercourse with their husbands. Similar results were reported by William Parish and his colleagues (Parish, Luo, Laumann, Kew, & Yu, 2007), who examined the prevalence of unwanted sexual activities among a sample of more than 1100 married women in China. Almost one-third (32%) of the women reporting having experienced unwanted sexual intercourse with their husbands; of those women, 40% indicated that the activity had resulted in physical injury. For the majority of women, unwanted and harmful intercourse occurred repeatedly during their marriages (and over a period of 5 years, on average); a mere 9% reported only one episode of forced sex.

Origins and Consequences

The recognition that sexual violence occurs with some frequency within romantic relationships has created an interest in discovering the factors associated with this type of interpersonal aggression. One of the most potent correlates is biological sex. Most victims of sexual violence are female and most perpetrators are male. One national survey (Michael et al., 1994) revealed that many more women (22%) than men (2%) said they had experienced forced sexual activity at some time in their lives, and nearly all of the women (and one third of the men) who were forced reported being assaulted by men. Men and women also differ in their perceptions of sexual aggression. For example, when asked to evaluate date rape scenarios, men generally perceive a higher degree of sexual willingness on the part of the female target than do women. In addition, men typically believe the female target is more responsible for the assault—and the male target's behavior is more justified—than do women (e.g., Feltey, Ainslie, & Geib, 1991; Kowalski, 1992; Proite, Dannells, & Benton, 1993).

Personality characteristics also appear to be associated with rape perceptions and sexually aggressive behavior. For example, men who possess high levels of the trait *hypermasculinity* demonstrate an exaggerated adherence to a masculine gender role—they believe that violence is manly, view danger and risk taking as exciting, and endorse calloused sexual attitudes toward women (Mosher & Sirkin, 1984; see Exhibit 13.1). In addition, they have a more positive emotional response to rape depictions and are more likely to have engaged in sexually aggressive behavior than men who possess lower levels of this attribute (e.g., Beaver, Gold, & Prisco, 1992; Mosher & Anderson, 1986). Interestingly, there is some limited evidence that a similar personality construct may operate in women. Sarah Murnen and Donn Byrne (1991) found that women who scored high on the trait dimension of *hyperfemininity* (which reflects an exaggerated adherence to a stereotypic female gender role; see Exhibit 13.1) reported experiencing higher amounts of sexual coercion, and had a less-negative reaction to a coercive sex scenario, than women who scored low on hyperfemininity.

Exhibit 13.1 Hypermasculinity and Hyperfemininity

Some research has revealed a correlation between adherence to an exaggerated gender role and attitudes and personal experiences with sexual aggression. Sample questions from the scales developed to assess hypermasculinity and hyperfemininity are below. Each question contains a hypermasculine/feminine option (starred) and a non-hypermasculine/feminine option.

Hypermasculinity Scale

1. a. I hope to forget past unpleasant experiences with male aggression.
    b. I still enjoy remembering my first real fight.*
2. a. So-called prick teasers should be forgiven.
    b. Prick teasers should be raped.*
3. a. It's natural for men to get into fights.*
    b. Physical violence never solves an issue.
4. a. Some women are good for only one thing.*
    b. All women deserve the same respect as your own mother.
5. a. I'd rather gamble than play it safe.*
    b. I'd rather play it safe than gamble.

Hyperfemininity Scale

1. a. I like to play hard-to-get.*
   b. I don't like to play games in a relationship.
2. a. I seldom consider a relationship with a man as more important than my friendship with women.
   b. I have broken dates with female friends when a guy has asked me out.*
3. a. It's okay for a man to be a little forceful to get sex.*
   b. Any force used during sex is sexual coercion and should not be tolerated.
4. a. I never use my sexuality to manipulate men.
   b. I sometimes act sexy to get what I want from a man.*
5. a. I usually pay for my own expenses on a date.
   b. I expect the men I date to take care of my expenses.*

SOURCES: (1) Mosher, D. L., & Sirkin, M. (1984). Measuring a macho personality constellation. *Journal of Research in Personality, 18,* 150–163. Copyright © 1984 by Academic Press, Inc. Items reprinted with permission from Elsevier Ltd. (2) Murnen, S. K., & Byrne, D. (1991). Hyperfemininity: Measurement and initial validation of the construct. *The Journal of Sex Research, 28,* 479–489. Copyright © 1991 by Taylor & Francis Informa UK LTD—Journals. Items reprinted with permission of Taylor & Francis Informa UK LTD—Journals via Copyright Clearance Center.

A variety of social and cultural factors also may create an environment that is conducive to sexual aggression within romantic relationships (for reviews, see Christopher, 2001; Christopher & Kisler, 2004; Muehlenhard et al., 1991). For example, the ***sexual double standard***, which encompasses normative beliefs that men are sexual, that male sexuality is an uncontrollable and powerful force, and that women often offer token resistance to sex, may contribute to sexual aggression. Similarly, *legal and religious influences* are implicated in the occurrence of sexual coercion. Some ideologies promote the idea that husbands are entitled to have sex with their wives and that wives have no right to refuse their husbands' sexual requests. In fact, until 1976, husbands in some states in the U.S. could not be charged with raping their wives (and marital rape is still legal in many parts of the world). Other social influences that have been investigated and that are believed to foster sexual aggression include *sex role scripts* associated with heterosexual dating situations (e.g., men should control the progression of the relationship and any sexual interactions that occur); *socialization processes* that foster the acquisition of rape myths (e.g., Burt, 1980); and *peer group norms* that support and promote exploitative attitudes toward women and the use of coercive sexual strategies (e.g., Kanin, 1984, 1985; Martin & Hummer, 1989; also see Loh, Orchowski, Gidycz, & Elizaga, 2007).

Regardless of the origins of sexual aggression, the consequences for the victim are negative and diverse. In their respective reviews of the literature, Karen Calhoun, Jenna McCauley, and Megan Crawford (2006) and Zoë Peterson and Charlene Muehlenhard (2003) identified a host of acute (immediate) physical and psychological responses that victims of assault may experience including physical trauma and pain, fatigue, nausea, sleep disturbances, disorientation, and feelings of anxiety, fear, shame or embarrassment, guilt, humiliation, and anger. In addition to these immediate reactions, they noted that victims of assault often experience negative long-term outcomes. Some of these are physical in nature, and include chronic illness, disease, or unwanted pregnancy. Other consequences are interpersonal; victims often curtail their social activities, develop some sort of sexual dysfunction in their pre-existing romantic relationships, become significantly impaired in their ability to function at work or school, and experience disruption in their relationships with friends, family members, and romantic partners. The psychological consequences of sexual assault are equally adverse and range from depression, to fear and anxiety, to ***post-traumatic stress disorder*** or ***PTSD*** (a long-term reaction to traumatic events whose symptomatology includes re-experiencing the event mentally through distressing dreams or intrusive recollections; numbing or avoidance of thoughts, feelings, or memories related to the event; and increased arousal or hypervigilance).

Sexual aggression does occur between relational partners, and there is a strong and immediate need for additional research on the causes and consequences of this form of interpersonal violence.

PEER AGGRESSION AND VICTIMIZATION

As we have seen, physical, sexual, emotional, financial, and other forms of abuse can and do occur between romantic partners. However, it is not only within their intimate romantic or familial relationships that individuals run the risk of being exposed to violence—other interpersonal associations and partnerships can prove just as toxic. Abusive, aggressive, and harassing behavior may develop among coworkers, friends, and classmates. In fact, 7% of the college-age men and women in a study conducted by psychologist Jennifer Lento (2006) reported being physically victimized by their peers (for example, being shoved or pushed in anger), and 38% indicated having been psychologically victimized (through social exclusion, betrayal of secrets, manipulation, and so forth). Two particular types of peer victimization have received increasing scrutiny from relationship scholars—workplace bullying among adults and school bullying among children.

Bullying in the Workplace

Workplace or ***adult bullying*** (also called ***mobbing***; see Leymann, 1990) is a type of interpersonal aggression that occurs in the workplace and that consists of repeated and persistent negative actions from one person (or group of people) toward another person, typically but not always a subordinate (Adams & Crawford, 1992; Brodsky, 1976; Rayner & Hoel, 1997; Salin, 2003). Adult bullying has four characteristic features: (1) *intensity*, which refers to the number of different negative acts that targets experience (e.g., verbal abuse, ridicule, isolation, intimidation); (2) *repetition*, which refers to the frequency with which these negative acts occur; (3) *duration*, or the period of time over which the negative acts occur; and (4) *power disparity*, which refers to the power differential between the target and the perpetrator. Conflict that occurs once or that involves two individuals of relatively equal organizational status does not constitute bullying; rather, bullying is an escalating process that involves a more powerful perpetrator engaging in frequent (e.g., weekly) and prolonged (e.g., for 6 months) negative acts that are designed to humiliate, intimidate, frighten, or punish a less-powerful target (Einarsen, Hoel, Zapf, & Cooper, 2003; Leymann, 1990; Notelaers, Einarsen, De Witte, & Vermunt, 2006). Although scholars continue to debate the issue of intentionality—with some arguing that bullying requires conscious intent on the part of the bully and others arguing that the key element is the victim's reaction rather than the bully's intent—there is widespread agreement that the target must feel harassed and his or her work must be affected for a situation or series of events to constitute bullying (see Rayner & Hoel, 1997).

Based on their review of the literature, Charlotte Rayner and Helge Hoel (1997) suggest that bullying behaviors can be grouped into five basic categories: (1) *threats to professional status* (e.g., belittling of opinions, professional humiliation carried out in public, accusation regarding lack of effort); (2) *threats to personal standing* (e.g., name-calling, insults, intimidation, devaluation due to age); (3) *isolation* (e.g., preventing access to opportunities, physical or social isolation, withholding of information); (4) *overwork* (e.g., undue pressure, impossible deadlines, unnecessary disruptions); and (5) *destabilization* (e.g., failure to give credit when due, assignment to meaningless tasks, removal of responsibility, repeated reminders of blunders). These and other workplace bullying behaviors typically are assessed with the Negative Acts Questionnaire or NAQ (Einarsen & Hoel, 2001; Einarsen & Raknes, 1997). The NAQ is a self-report measure that asks respondents to indicate how often they have experienced three types of peer victimization in the workplace over the past 6 months. The first type of victimization includes negative actions that target the work and/or role of the employee, such as:

- persistent criticism of one's work and effort;
- repeated reminders of one's errors or mistakes;
- being ordered to do work below one's level of competence;
- being exposed to an unmanageable workload;
- excessive monitoring of one's work.

The NAQ also assesses negative actions that target the person directly. Examples include:

- insulting messages, telephone calls, or emails;
- having insulting or offensive remarks made about one's person (i.e., habits and background), attitudes, or personal life;
- being shouted at or being the target of spontaneous anger (or rage);
- being the subject of excessive teasing or sarcasm;
- threats of violence or personal abuse.

The final type of peer victimization assessed by the NAQ involves negative actions that are meant to isolate the employee, including:

- being ignored or facing a hostile reaction when one approaches;
- being ignored or excluded;
- having one's opinions and views ignored;
- being moved or transferred against one's will;
- someone withholding information which affects one's performance.

Recent research suggests that workplace harassment is fairly common. For example, large-scale surveys of workers conducted in the United States, Great Britain, and Finland reveal that approximately 10% of respondents report having been a target of workplace bullying (Hoel, Faragher, & Cooper, 2004; Lutgen-Sandvik, Tracy & Alberts, 2007; Salin, 2001). Rates climb when behavioral indices of bullying are used (as opposed to self-identification as a victim of bullying). For example, 28% of the workers in the U.S. survey and 24% of the workers in the Finland survey met the behavioral criteria for being bullied (as measured by the NAQ), though only about 9% of both samples self-identified as bullied.

There are a number of painful and lasting outcomes associated with workplace harassment. The targets of bullying often report sleep disturbances and cognitive impairments such as difficulty concentrating and remembering. In addition, they experience a variety of stress-related physical (e.g., sweating, shaking, feeling sick) and psychological (e.g., depression, anxiety, panic attacks, fear, anger, loss of self-confidence) outcomes (e.g., Hoel et al., 2004; Leymann & Gustafsson, 1996; Namie, 2007). For example, the results of one study revealed that 76% of bullying victims presented with PTSD symptoms, and almost one-third of those met all of the clinical criteria for PTSD (Mikkelsen & Einarsen, 2002).

Disruption of social and work-related activities is also common. In one recent investigation, psychologist Guy Notelaers and his colleagues (2006) surveyed more than 6000 workers from 18 organizations in Belgium about their workplace experiences. Participants completed both the NAQ and a questionnaire designed to measure four dimensions of work-related strain. The first dimension concerned the extent to which the respondents experienced *pleasure at work* (e.g., "I dread going to work" [reverse scored], "I'm pleased to start my day's work"); the second dimension reflected the *need for recovery from work* (e.g., "I find it difficult to relax at the end of a working day," "Because of my job, at the end of the working day I feel absolutely exhausted"); the third dimension concerned *work-related worrying* (e.g., "When I leave my work, I continue to worry about work problems," "I often lie awake at night pondering about things at work"); and the fourth dimension reflected *sleep quality* (e.g., "At night, more often than not, I am tossing and turning," "I often do not get a wink of sleep at night"). The results revealed significant associations between NAQ scores and all four measures of work-related strain. Specifically, compared with their non-victimized counterparts, the victims of workplace bullying reported experiencing less pleasure at work, a greater need for recovery from work, more worrying about work-related issues and events, and poorer sleep quality. Similar results have been observed with U.S. samples (e.g., Lutgen-Sandvik et al., 2007). Moreover, the harmful effects of bullying are not limited to the targets—their coworkers suffer, too. Employees who observe (but do not directly experience) bullying behavior report higher levels of job-related stress and lower levels of job satisfaction than employees who are not exposed to bullying (Lutgen-Sandvik et al., 2007; Vartia, 2001).

In sum, workplace bullying represents a severe and significant threat to adult health and well-being.

Bullying in School

Bullying (also called *peer abuse* or *peer harassment*) occurs when a child is exposed, repeatedly and over time, to negative actions from one or more similar-age peers (Finkelhor & Dziuba-Leatherman, 1994; Olweus, 1993). These actions may be physical (e.g., being hit, kicked, pushed, or shoved, or being threatened with physical harm), verbal (e.g., being called names), or relational (e.g., being the target of gossip or malicious rumors, being intentionally excluded from social events). An additional criterion of bullying is an imbalance of power between the target and the perpetrator(s)—"the student who is exposed to the negative actions has difficulty defending himself or herself" (Olweus, 1995, p. 197). Although both boys and girls engage in bullying, boys are more likely than girls to be bullies. In addition, boys tend to use physically aggressive behavior to intimidate their targets, whereas girls are more likely to use relational aggression (Pellegrini, 2002).

Bullying and victimization usually are assessed with self-report measures. The Olweus Bully/Victim Questionnaire (Olweus, 1993; Solberg & Olweus, 2003) presents children with a definition of bullying and then asks them to report the frequency with which they have received or enacted various forms of bullying behavior. Other measures avoid using such potentially reactive terms as "victim" or "bully" and instead simply ask students to report on their experiences with specific types of peer behavior (e.g., Arora, 1994; Crick & Grotpeter, 1996). For example, the Peer Victimization Scale (Neary & Joseph, 1994) contains two items that reflect general victimization ("picked on," "laughed at"), one item that assesses verbal victimization ("called bad names"), and one item that assesses physical victimization ("hit and pushed around"). Each item presents two types of hypothetical children (for example, the "picked on" item reads "Some kids are *not* picked on by other kids *BUT* other kids are *often* picked on by other kids"). Participants are asked to decide "which type of kid is most like you" and then to indicate whether the statement is "sort of true for me" or "really true for me." Scores on each item can range from 1 to 4, with higher scores indicating stronger feelings of peer victimization.

Survey data collected from a number of different countries, including the United States, reveal that bullying is a considerable problem in schools. One of the earliest investigations was conducted in the 1980s by psychologist Dan Olweus (1993), who surveyed more than 150,000 Norwegian and Swedish students about their experiences with peer aggression and victimization. The results of this pioneering study revealed that roughly 15% of students in the first through ninth grades were involved in bullying—approximately 9% as victims and 7% as aggressors. More recent investigations have yielded similar prevalence rates; specifically, about 6% to 15% of schoolchildren have experienced frequent (at least weekly) victimization at the hands of their peers (for a review, see Card & Hodges, 2008). Longitudinal studies of primary and secondary school students suggest that victimization rates decline over time. Overall rates of bullying and peer aggression appear to increase as students make the transition from fifth grade to middle school, decrease during the remainder of sixth grade, and continue to drop throughout seventh and eighth grade (Nylund, Bellmore, Nishina, & Graham, 2007; Pellegrini & Long, 2002; for a review, see Pellegrini, 2002). However, these studies have also revealed the existence of a small cohort of "stable victims"—that is, children who experience continued victimization across the primary and secondary school years (Nylund et al., 2007; Sweeting, Young, West, & Der, 2006).

Although existing research has focused almost exclusively on the experiences of school-aged children and adolescents, there is some evidence that peer victimization is also fairly prevalent among younger children (e.g., Troy & Sroufe, 1987). Child development scholars Nicki Crick, Juan Casas, and Hyon-Chin Ku (1999) asked preschool teachers to evaluate 129 of their pupils in terms of two types of victimization experience: (1) physical victimization ("This child gets pushed or shoved by peers," "This child gets hit, kicked, or pinched by peers") and (2) relational victimization ("This child gets ignored by playmates when they are mad at him/her," "This child gets left out of the group when someone is mad at him/her or wants to get back at him/her"). On the basis of these ratings, each child was classified as physically or relationally victimized or non-victimized. Most children were non-victimized; however, in accordance with rates observed in samples of older children, the researchers found that 16% of preschool children experienced physical victimization, and 12% experienced relational victimization, from their peers.

A number of factors appear to be associated with the likelihood of victimization. For example, in their thorough review of the literature, Noel Card and Ernest Hodges (2008) identified several personal factors that predict victimization, including physical weakness, social and communication skills deficits, and poor self-concept. Children who are victimized tend to be physically weaker than their peers. (However, other physical characteristics—including obesity, short stature, and wearing glasses—are not reliably related to victimization.) In addition, victimized children tend to display lower levels of assertiveness and less-effective conflict-management strategies, and they possess a poorer self-concept, than their non-victimized counterparts. Victimization is also associated with academic maladjustment. Children who are frequently targeted by aggressive peers often exhibit a lack of school enjoyment, tend to perceive school as an unsafe place, have high rates of school avoidance and absenteeism, and demonstrate low levels of academic ability and achievement. Relational and social environmental correlates include friendship quality and quantity and social acceptance or rejection. Friendship seems to serve a protective function; children with friends, particularly friends who possess physical strength and a high degree of social acceptance, are less likely to be victimized. Social acceptance (being liked) and rejection (being disliked) by peers is one of the most potent and robust correlates—children who are not well liked and who are rejected by their peers also tend to be victimized.

As noted by Card and Hodges (2008), many of these factors may serve as both a cause and a consequence of victimization. For example, a child who possesses a poor self-concept may be less likely to defend him- or herself against physical or verbal assault and thus may become an "easy target" for an aggressive peer; at the same time, frequent victimization is likely to contribute to a diminished self-concept. Similarly, poor academic achievement may put a child at risk for victimization (e.g., as a focal point for teasing) and victimization, in turn, may produce poor academic achievement (insofar as a child who is worried about being bullied at school is less able to focus on his or her academic work). Social status and victimization appear to operate in a similar mutually reinforcing cycle. Children who are rejected and not well liked by their peers become easy targets for bullies (who may even receive positive reinforcement from others for targeting those disliked children), and poor social status is a clear consequence of peer victimization.

Not surprisingly, the targets of bullying and peer aggression experience a number of adverse psychological outcomes, ranging from depression and suicide risk, to lowered self-esteem and life satisfaction, to social anxiety and symptoms of post-traumatic stress (Martin & Huebner, 2007; Olweus, 1993; Storch & Esposito, 2003; for a review, see Hawker & Boulton, 2000). Victimization is also associated with negative physical outcomes. For example, in one longitudinal study (Nishina, Juvonen, & Witkow, 2005), a large sample of sixth graders completed a measure of peer victimization (items included being called "bad names," being the target of rumors, and having one's property stolen or damaged, and so forth), along with several measures of psychosocial adjustment (depression, social anxiety, loneliness at school, and self-worth). Students also indicated the frequency with which they experienced a variety of physical symptoms, including headaches, upset stomach or nausea, and sore throat or coughs. Because data were collected during the fall semester and again during the spring semester, the researchers were able to assess the temporal relationships among the various measures. The results revealed that victimization during the fall semester predicted subsequent psychosocial adjustment and physical symptomatology in the spring semester. Specifically, students who perceived themselves as frequent targets of peer aggression at the beginning of the school year exhibited greater depression, social anxiety, and loneliness, lower self-worth, and more symptoms of physical illness at the end of the school year than students who did not view themselves as frequent targets.

Peer victimization is a widespread problem, and social scientists have proposed a number of intervention programs to combat bullying in the schools. Although research on the effectiveness of these programs is limited, the available evidence suggests that *comprehensive approaches* which view bullying as a systemic problem and which target all aspects of the system (i.e., school personnel, teachers, students, parents) are the most effective in deterring peer victimization (Card & Hodges, 2008; Olweus, 1993; Pellegrini, 2002; Smith, Schneider, Smith, & Ananiadou, 2004). The most widely used comprehensive approach is the anti-bullying program developed by Olweus (1993, 1995). This program requires intervention at the school, class, and individual level. For example, the school should regularly assess victimization rates, adopt a clear and strong anti-bullying policy, and have adults present in high-risk areas (e.g., bathrooms, hallways, playgrounds). Teachers and other school personnel should receive appropriate education (for example, on how to recognize the signs of victimization and on the impact and consequences of bullying), along with training regarding the school's policies with respect to bullying and strategies for effective intervention in bullying situations. The curriculum can also serve as a medium for change; for example, students might receive social skills training as part of their academic curriculum, and teachers might utilize collaborative activities and cooperative learning exercises in the classroom and tailor their educational materials to promote an anti-bullying attitude. The involvement of parents is equally important;

not only should parents receive education about the signs and impact of victimization but they should also be invited to work with school personnel to prevent and intervene in bullying situations. Students should also receive information about how to recognize victimization and about the impact of bullying; moreover, they should be encouraged to inform school personnel about victimization. Finally, in instances involving an individual aggressor and victim, there should be consistent enforcement of appropriate (non-aggressive) consequences for peer victimization, as well as individualized interventions (e.g., social skills training) and early involvement of parents of both the victim and the aggressor. These comprehensive intervention programs are difficult and costly to implement, and their effectiveness has yet to be conclusively demonstrated (see Merrell, Gueldner, Ross, & Isava, 2008). Nonetheless, such programs represent an important first step toward reducing peer victimization in schools.

SUMMARY

Aggression and violence are common themes running through many of our interpersonal relationships. Many romantic partners become angry and verbally or physically aggressive in the heat of an argument or conflict. Some men and women find themselves caught in a web of intimate terror—controlled, manipulated, and hurt by a coercive and violent partner. Even in relationships that are not characterized by situational couple violence or domestic abuse, aggressive incidents may occur. Sexual coercion and sexual assault, for example, are surprisingly common occurrences in dating and marital relationships. Peer relationships, too, can be quite violent. A growing body of research demonstrates that sizeable numbers of adults and children experience persistent victimization at the hands of aggressive peers. Each of these forms of relational aggression takes a considerable toll on the victims—they experience a host of detrimental psychological, physical, and social outcomes.

KEY CONCEPTS

Intimate partner violence (p. 229)
Situational couple violence (p. 230)
Common couple violence (p. 230)
Conflict-motivated violence (p. 230)
Coercive controlling violence (p. 232)
Intimate terrorism (domestic violence, spousal abuse, battery) (p. 232)
Violent resistance (p. 235)
Resistive/reactive violence (p. 235)
Sexual coercion (p. 236)
Sexual assault (p. 236)

Battering rape (anger rape) (p. 236)
Force-only rape (power rape) (p. 236)
Obsessive rape (sadistic rape) (p. 236)
Hypermasculinity (p. 238)
Hyperfemininity (p. 238)
Sexual double standard (p. 239)
Post-traumatic stress disorder (PTSD) (p. 240)
Workplace (adult) bullying (p. 240)
Mobbing (p. 240)
Bullying (peer abuse or harassment) (p. 242)

EXPLORATION EXERCISES

These exercises are designed to allow you to explore in greater detail some of the concepts and issues discussed in this chapter. There are no right or wrong answers to these exercises—they are simply meant to provide an opportunity for discussion and debate.

1. Describe situational couple violence. What factors do you think could contribute to this type of aggression in intimate relationships? At what point might situational couple violence become coercive controlling violence?
2. Researchers generally agree that sexual assault includes both sexual contact obtained by force (or the threat of force) and sexual contact with a partner who cannot give consent. Do you think this is an important distinction to make? Why or why not?
3. What are some of the characteristic features of workplace bullying? If someone came to you for advice on how to respond to workplace bullying, what would you say?

Chapter 14
Conflict and Loss

CHAPTER OUTLINE

Simply because all people are born into families and kin networks and actively seek (and eventually establish) long-term partnerships with friends, lovers, coworkers, and other individuals does not necessarily mean that those relationships will function smoothly or last forever. To the contrary, the process of relationship development is often "bumpy" and tension can easily arise between partners in even the most affectionate and committed of relationships. In this chapter we examine the topic of conflict, including the events that occur during conflict and how partners manage conflict. We also consider relationship loss—from the sequence of events involved in relationship dissolution to the ways in which people commonly respond to the demise of a friendship, marriage, or other intimate relationship.

CONFLICT

By their very nature, close relationships—that is, relationships in which there is a high degree of interaction and interdependence between the partners—provide a fertile breeding ground for interpersonal conflict. Partners who interact frequently and who exert a great deal of influence on each other have many opportunities to discover issues about which they disagree, attitudes, beliefs, and dispositions on which they differ, behaviors and habits they dislike, preferences and expectations they do not share, and a host of other incompatibilities.

The Nature and Frequency of Interpersonal Conflict

Given this array of potential sources of tension, it is no wonder that conflict is part and parcel of most people's relationship experiences. The majority of close friends argue with each other on a daily basis (Burk & Laursen, 2005; Laursen, 1993; also see Shulman & Laursen, 2002), and even preschool-aged children experience frequent disagreements with their playmates (e.g., Ljungberg, Horowitz, Jansson, Westlund, & Clarke, 2005). Similarly, surveys of community and college student populations reveal that nearly all married or dating couples report having differences of opinion, unpleasant disagreements, or arguments fairly often (Cramer, 2004; Hatch & Bulcroft, 2004; McGonagle, Kessler, & Schilling, 1992). Although it appears that almost any topic can become a source of disagreement between romantic partners, a study conducted by psychologist Lawrence Kurdek (1994) revealed that the specific issues over which homosexual and heterosexual couples fight tend to reflect six general conflict areas. These include: (1) *power* (e.g., lack of equality in the relationship, excessive demands or possessiveness, imbalance in allocation of household tasks); (2) *social issues* (e.g., political views and social issues, personal values); (3) *personal flaws* (e.g., personal grooming, driving style, drinking or smoking); (4) *distrust* (e.g., previous lovers, lack of trust, lying); (5) *intimacy* (e.g., sex, lack of affection); and (6) *personal distance* (e.g., frequent physical absence, job or school commitments).

Family interactions create a particularly rich environment for the development of conflict. On average, adolescents have two to three disagreements or differences of opinion with their parents over the course of a typical day (Adams & Laursen, 2007). The majority of these arguments involve relatively mundane, everyday issues, including household chores (e.g., helping around the house, taking care of possessions, keeping the house neat), room care (e.g., putting clothes away, cleaning one's room), homework and school performance (e.g., completing homework, grades), time management and curfews (e.g., getting up on time in the morning, coming home on time), and television viewing habits (Allison & Schultz, 2004; Smetana & Gaines, 1999). Parent–child conflict appears to reach its peak during the developmental period leading into adolescence (see Laursen, Coy, & Collins, 1998). For example, scholars Lilly Shanahan, Susan McHale, D. Wayne Osgood, and Ann Crouter (2007) conducted a longitudinal investigation designed to explore the trajectory of parent–child conflict from middle childhood to late adolescence. In this study a sample of first-born children in fourth or fifth grade and their second-born siblings (who were, on average, 3 years younger) reported how often, in the past year, they had experienced arguments, disagreements, or problems with their mothers and fathers across a variety of different domains (e.g., chores, appearance, homework/schoolwork, social life, bedtime/curfew, money). Data were collected over a 4-year period, with participating first-born

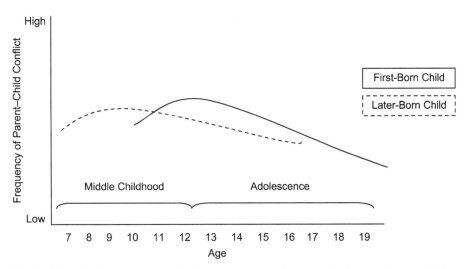

Fig. 14.1 Longitudinal research on the frequency of parent–child conflict generally reveals that conflict levels are closely tied to the transition to adolescence. First-born children typically experience their highest rates of conflict with parents when they leave middle childhood and enter adolescence. Second-born children, however, experience their highest rates of conflict when they themselves are still in middle childhood but their older siblings are transitioning to adolescence. Thus, in multiple-child families, it is the older child's entry into adolescence that seems to trigger elevated levels of parent–child conflict.

Source: Shanahan, L., McHale, S. M., Osgood, D. W., & Crouter, A. C. (2007). Conflict frequency with mothers and fathers from middle childhood to late adolescence: Within- and between-families comparisons. *Developmental Psychology, 43,* 539–550. Copyright © 2007 by the American Psychological Association. Figure 2 adapted with permission.

and second-born children providing their ratings once each year. The results revealed that the conflict trajectories of both sets of children were closely tied to the developmental status of the first-born child (see Figure 14.1). Specifically, among first-born children, conflict with mothers and fathers tended to peak at entry into adolescence (around age 13) and then declined thereafter. Second-born children's conflict trajectories mirrored those of their older siblings; that is, their own rates of conflict with parents also peaked when their older siblings entered adolescence and then diminished over time. These findings suggest that conflict develops differently between parents and children in multi-child families; in particular, the elevated level of parent–child conflict that occurs as first-borns enter adolescence appears to "spill over" into the relationship between parents and second-born children.

In addition to exploring what partners argue about and how often they disagree, relationship scholars have also charted the course of a typical conflict (see, for example, Christensen & Pasch, 1993). One of the earliest and most comprehensive models was proposed by Donald Peterson (1983/2002), who suggested that conflict is a contemporaneous process characterized by beginnings, middle phases, and endings. The model is presented in its entirety in Figure 14.2. (Figure 14.3 provides an illustration of the various stages using a specific conflict involving a hypothetical married couple.)

The Beginnings of Conflict: Predisposing Conditions and Initiating Events

According to Peterson (1983/2002), many conflicts are rooted in underlying or pre-existing conditions which set the stage for the occurrence of tension between partners. These *predisposing*

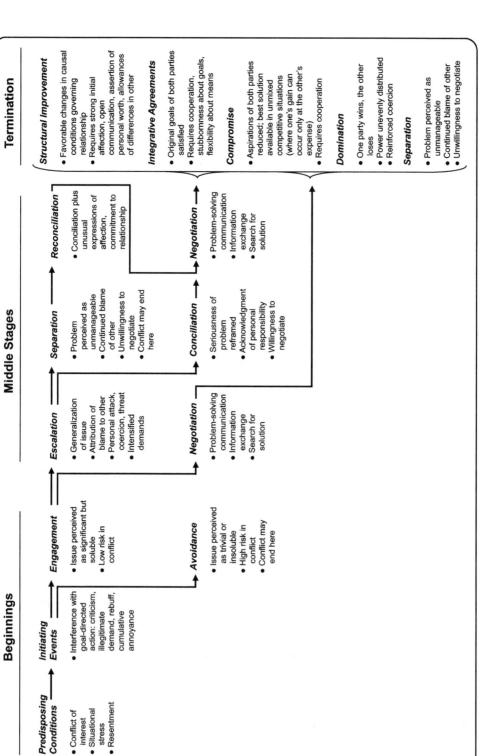

Fig. 14.2 The course of a conflict. According to Peterson (1983/2002), a conflict may take many possible courses from its beginnings, through its middle stages, to its termination. Arrows indicate the likely sequences, ending with avoidance or any of five possible terminations.

Source: Peterson, D. R. (2002). Conflict. In H. H. Kelley, E. Berscheid, A. Christensen, J. H. Harvey, T. L. Huston, G. Levinger, E. McClintock, L. A. Peplau, & D. R. Peterson, *Close relationships* (pp. 360–396). Clinton Corners, NY: Percheron Press. (Original work published 1983) Copyright © 2002 by Percheron Press. Figure 9.2 adapted with permission by Eliot Werner Publications, Inc.

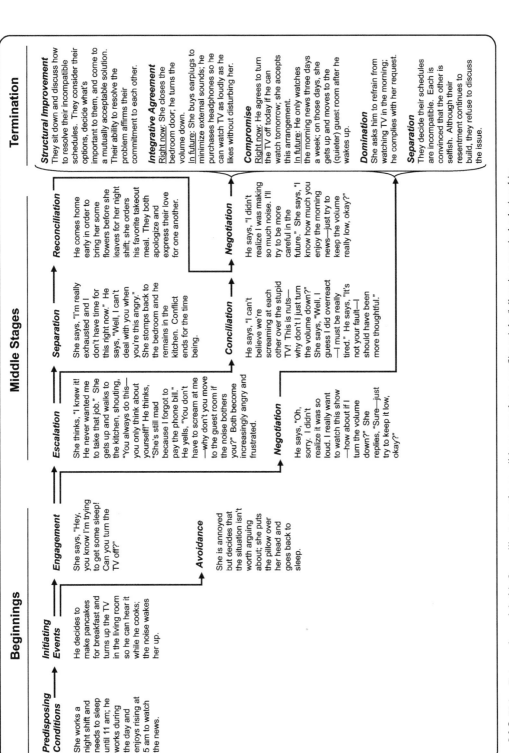

Fig. 14.3 Using Peterson's model, this figure illustrates the possible course that a conflict might follow in a marital relationship.

conditions include a variety of personal, relational, and environmental factors. For example, as we discussed in Chapter 8, individuals with high levels of negative affectivity, rejection sensitivity, or attachment anxiety often perceive and respond to interpersonal events in ways that increase the likelihood of open conflict. Opportunities for conflict also increase to the extent that the partners possess incompatible and highly valued goals (e.g., one partner wants to have children, the other does not); have dissimilar and strongly held attitudes, values, and preferences (e.g., one partner is firmly committed to reducing landfill waste, the other could not care less); or enact incompatible behavior patterns or habits (e.g., one partner stays up late, the other gets up early). Environmental stress—whether produced by the couple's physical situation (e.g., physical separation, crowded or unpleasant living arrangements, unceasing noise, scarce resources) or their social situation (e.g., presence or absence of social support, children and other family members, potential alternative partners)—constitutes yet another powerful precondition for conflict.

By themselves, these underlying predispositions to conflict do not inevitably lead to open disagreement or hostilities between partners. Two people with different long-term goals or habits, for example, frequently can and do co-exist quite peacefully. Similarly, a couple facing financial hardship, or caring for an elderly parent, or dealing with any of a number of other environmental stressors may enjoy a relatively conflict-free relationship. In order for general predispositions to be converted into open conflict, some *initiating event* must occur. Four classes of events tend to precipitate conflict:

- *Criticism* is defined as verbal or nonverbal acts by one partner that are perceived as demeaning or unfavorable by the other partner. For example, a father sitting down for breakfast might glance at his teenage son and remark, "Is that what you're wearing to school?" Whether the father intended to criticize his son is not important—what is important is that the son interprets the comment as critical. If he does, conflict is likely to erupt.
- *Illegitimate demands* refer to demands made by one partner that are perceived as unjust or unfair by the other partner. The father might demand that his son go upstairs and change into a suit and tie, and then threaten to ground him for a year if he refuses. Demands that fall outside of the common or normative expectations that both family members have of each other are likely to be perceived as unjust and consequently spark conflict.
- *Rebuffs* occur when one partner appeals to the other for a desired reaction and the other fails to respond as expected. For example, later that day the son might proudly bring his first "straight A" report card home to show his father—if his father merely grunts and then turns back to his newspaper, the son is likely to feel devalued, hurt, and upset.
- *Cumulative annoyance* develops when the actions of one partner exceed the other partner's tolerance threshold. Upstairs in his room, the son might begin to throw a ball against the wall. The first loud "thump" goes unnoticed, the second and third go ignored, but the fourth exceeds the father's threshold. "Stop that racket!" he yells. "Go outside if you want to play ball!"

The Choice to Avoid or Engage.   Once one of these initiating events has occurred, the partners have a choice—passive *conflict avoidance* or active *conflict engagement*. Whether partners respond passively or actively is partly a function of how significant and solvable they perceive their disagreement to be. Partners generally opt for avoidance when they perceive the risks of active dispute to be greater than the potential benefits. For example, if the issue over which they disagree is trivial or intractable, they may decide to simply withdraw from the situation and avoid discussing the issue. Conversely, partners often engage in conflict when they perceive an issue to be sufficiently important to require action and when they believe that interaction is likely to resolve the issue.

Regardless of whether partners choose to engage in conflict or avoid the situation entirely, they can do so in ways that are either beneficial or harmful to the health and well-being of their relationship—and this is related to their current feelings and level of commitment. Research conducted by Caryl Rusbult and her colleagues (e.g., Rusbult, 1987; Rusbult, Johnson, & Morrow, 1986a; Rusbult, Zembrodt, & Gunn, 1982; also see Oswald & Clark, 2006) reveals that people who are satisfied with and invested in their relationships typically respond to conflict-initiating events in a constructive manner. For example, when avoiding conflict, they demonstrate what Rusbult calls *loyalty*—they passively but optimistically wait for the situation to improve (e.g., hoping or praying for conditions to get better, "giving things some time"). When engaging in conflict, these individuals demonstrate *voice*, defined as actively and constructively attempting to improve the situation (e.g., urging the partner to change his or her behavior, seeking help, proposing solutions). People who are dissatisfied with their relationships, however, both avoid and engage in conflict in destructive ways, by either passively allowing conditions to deteriorate through *neglect* (e.g., ignoring the partner, leaving the room so as to avoid the argument, "letting things fall apart") or by actively harming the relationship through *exit* (e.g., threatening to end the relationship, screaming at the partner). Figure 14.4 illustrates these different responses. The willingness to respond to conflict-initiating events in a constructive manner (with loyalty or voice) rather than in destructive manner (with neglect or exit) is called *accommodation*. In essence, accommodation requires people to look beyond their immediate self-interest and the specific conflict facing them and consider long-term goals such as protecting their partners' well-being and maintaining the relationship (Rusbult, Verette, Whitney, Slovik, & Lipkus, 1991; Rusbult, Yovetich, & Verette, 1996; also see Rusbult, Bissonnette, Arriaga, & Cox, 1998).

The Middle Stages of Conflict: Negotiation vs. Escalation

If partners elect to actively engage in conflict, they pass into the middle stages of Peterson's model. Here, their interactions tend to follow one of two different paths. Some partners settle their disagreements smoothly through the use of *direct negotiation*; for example, each partner states his or her opinion or position and together they work toward a solution until some mutually acceptable outcome is obtained (this is similar to Rusbult's concept of voice). Other partners, however, are unable or unwilling to engage in this kind of straightforward problem-solving exchange; instead, their interaction *escalates* and the partners' behavior intensifies to the point of angry personal attacks, coercion, and even physical violence (this is similar to Rusbult's concept of exit). As we discussed in Chapter 13, partners sometimes lose their tempers during a heated argument and impulsively resort to pushing, shoving, and other physical actions to resolve their disagreement. Violent escalation is particularly likely to occur when the partners have multiple areas of conflict in their relationship and when they believe that the severity of the problems has worsened over time (Frye, 2006).

Once conflict has reached this level of intensity, it is difficult for most partners to move directly and cooperatively to resolution. Instead, an intermediate step must occur. This intermediate step usually takes the form of *conciliation*. Specifically, the partners engage in acts designed both to reduce the intensity of the negative emotions they experienced during the escalation phase and also to express their willingness to solve the problem (e.g., "This situation has gotten out of hand. I think I overreacted. Let's start over."). Alternately, *separation* may occur—partners may temporarily withdraw from open conflict if they believe the problem is insurmountable, if they continue to blame each other for the situation, or if they simply are unwilling to negotiate. Temporary

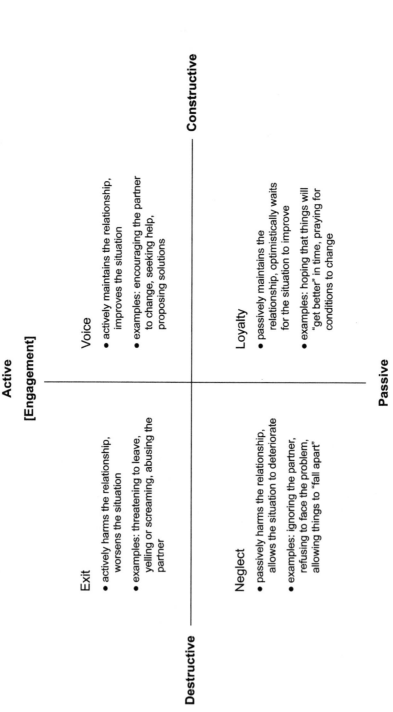

Fig. 14.4 Rusbult's typology of conflict responses. Research conducted by Caryl Rusbult (e.g., 1987) demonstrates that partners may avoid or engage in conflict in constructive or destructive ways. Partners who are unable to accommodate each other by inhibiting their destructive impulses and responding constructively to criticism, rebuffs, and other conflict-initiating events are likely to experience difficulty resolving their disagreements and less overall satisfaction with their relationship.

separation may lead to later *reconciliation*, which consists of conciliatory acts coupled with unusual or extreme expressions of affection and commitment.

The Importance of Attributions. Whether partners successfully negotiate and resolve their conflict or whether their initial disagreement escalates to increasingly angry and intense fighting is partly a function of the assumptions they make, and the conclusions they draw, about each other's behavior during their interaction. Recall from Chapter 8 that both ***causal attributions*** (explanations about the causes of a partner's behavior) and ***responsibility attributions*** (assumptions about the extent to which the partner is responsible for the behavior) are reliably associated with satisfaction, adjustment, and other important relationship outcomes (e.g., Bradbury & Fincham, 1990; Davey, Fincham, Beach, & Brody, 2001; Manusov, 1990). These particular attributions also play an important role in determining the course that a conflict interaction is likely to take. As illustrated in Figure 14.5, disagreements and arguments are likely to escalate and intensify to the extent that the partner's criticism, rebuff, or other negative behavior is attributed to internal, stable, and global causes and is perceived as intentionally hurtful, motivated by selfish concerns, and blameworthy. Indeed, a study conducted by psychologist Keith Sanford (2006) revealed that men and women who made negative causal and responsibility attributions for their spouses' behavior were more likely than those who did not to utilize contempt, criticism, and other negative forms of communication during discussions of important unresolved issues in their marriage (also see Davey et al., 2001). Similar results have been observed by researchers exploring the nature of parental attributions about children's behavior—parents who attribute their child's negative behavior to internal, stable, and global causes report a higher level of overt conflict in their recent interactions (Heatherington, Tolejko, McDonald, & Funk, 2007).

The reality is that partners in even the happiest and most stable of relationships often place different (and sometimes contradictory) interpretations on each other's behavior. This is especially likely to occur during times of interpersonal tension or strife. In their seminal article on conflict-related attributions in young couples, social scientists Bruce Orvis, Harold Kelley, and Deborah Butler (1976) identified and explained several basic attributional "facts" relevant to interpersonal conflict. First, during conflict, *attributional processes become activated* as each partner seeks to understand the cause of the conflict and of the other's behavior.

> Arriving home from work, Kate finds the front gate unlatched. "How many times do I have to remind Bobby not to leave the gate open? The dogs might get out. This is a busy street—doesn't he realize how dangerous it is?"
>
> "Why isn't she speaking to me?" Bobby wonders. "She's clearly angry about something. What have I done now?"

When the relationship is progressing smoothly, partners do not ask why; agreement does not need explaining. It is only when an unpleasant—or unexpected—event occurs that the flow of the relationship is interrupted and partners begin to actively search for an explanation.

Second, *the attribution process is selective and often biased*. During conflict, partners have a tendency to take a positive and benign view of their own behavior (as indeed they do on most occasions; see Chapter 8). Cognitively, they are able to quickly and easily access information that serves their own personal interests. Moreover, they genuinely believe that they possess an accurate understanding of the causes of each other's behavior and feel that their own behavior is justified.

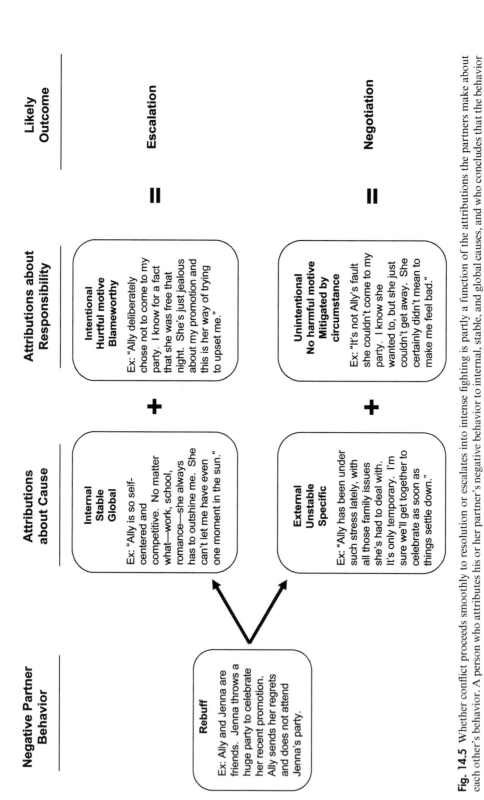

Fig. 14.5 Whether conflict proceeds smoothly to resolution or escalates into intense fighting is partly a function of the attributions the partners make about each other's behavior. A person who attributes his or her partner's negative behavior to internal, stable, and global causes, and who concludes that the behavior was intentional, selfishly motivated, and not mitigated by circumstance, is likely to become increasingly angry and upset. Conversely, a person who attributes his or her partner's negative behavior to external, unstable, and specific causes, and who does not assign high levels of responsibility or blame to the partner, is more likely to remain calm and to engage in direct negotiation with the partner.

"If he can't figure out why I'm not speaking to him, he's an idiot. It's not like I haven't asked him a thousand times to keep that gate closed. He knows how much I worry about the dogs getting out. This is so typical. He never listens to me, even though I always pay attention to what he wants. In fact, I can't remember a time when I got my way—it's always Bobby, Bobby, Bobby," Kate fumes.

"Is she still upset about last night? How many times does she expect me to apologize? It's not like I meant to be late. Besides, we got to the movie on time. This silent treatment stuff is completely childish. I wish she'd just grow up and tell me when she's angry. At least I have the decency to communicate openly about my feelings," Bobby sighs with exasperation.

Orvis and his colleagues (1976) noted that attributions can serve conflicting personal interests and still meet the criteria of plausibility because "ordinary events, including interpersonal behavior, readily lend themselves to different interpretations . . ., [and] the everyday attributor has great freedom to select from many different kinds of information and causes" (p. 380). In other words, faced with an unpleasant or unexpected relationship event, each partner has at his or her mental fingertips an array of seemingly plausible explanations, any one of which may further his or her own agenda.

Third, *the attributions that partners make during times of conflict can create "**attributional conflicts**"*—disagreements about the causes of behavior—that usually are not resolvable. Partners often disagree, not only about the ostensible conflict of interest, but also about the reasons for their behavior.

"I'm so angry with you," Kate yells. "I bet you left that gate open on purpose. You probably wanted the dogs to run away. You've never liked them—admit it!"

"What? How can you say that? I love those dogs. It was just a memory lapse. You know how forgetful I am—I never remember to lock anything. Besides, work is crazy right now. I've got a lot on my mind. I can't believe you think I would deliberately do something like that!" Bobby argues.

"It's true! You've always said you were a cat person. Even when we were dating, you never paid any attention to my dogs. And now that we're living together, you don't want them around. You'd be happy if they ran away," Kate cries.

"That is the most ridiculous thing I've ever heard. It's true I like cats, but I like dogs, too. And I've always treated those dogs well. In fact, I thought they were supposed to be *our* dogs—when did they become just yours?" Bobby yells.

Both partners in our example agree that Bobby forgot to latch the front gate. However, they disagree about the reasons for this event. Bobby honestly believes that he left the gate open because he was thinking about other things and simply forgot. Kate just as firmly believes that Bobby forgot because he secretly dislikes her dogs and wants them to run away. As noted by Orvis and his colleagues (1976), the multiple interpretations that can be given to any one behavior (there are many reasons why someone might leave a front gate unlocked), the relative inability of each partner to prove that a particular causal explanation is correct (how will Bobby ever conclusively demonstrate to Kate that his faulty memory—rather than some more nefarious motive—is to blame for the unlatched gate?), and the continuing conflict of interest itself (the unlatched gate) all "make it improbable that the actor and the partner can come to see eye-to-eye in the matter" (p. 381). During conflict, then, partners often find themselves with both a source of initial disagreement plus an additional source of conflict regarding attributions.

Fourth, "***meta-attributions***"—*explanations for explanations*—*may arise and create additional problems* for the partners. During conflict, each partner evaluates the credibility and validity of the attributions that the other makes for a particular behavior. When one partner gives a causal explanation that is not credible, that is illogical, or that seems particularly unconvincing, the other partner may wonder why it was given.

> "Wait a minute. His work isn't 'crazy' right now," Kate thinks. "In fact, this is their slow time. And he's not a forgetful sort of person. So why would he use that as his excuse for leaving the gate open? It doesn't make any sense. Something else must be going on, and I know what it is—he hates my dogs."

The issue of why a certain attribution was made may raise serious doubts about the giver of the attribution (e.g., his or her candor, trustworthiness, honesty, or perceptiveness) and about the future of the relationship, and may become yet another source of conflict between partners.

Investigations of the moment-by-moment thought processes that occur between partners during conflict episodes confirm that people's perceptions, attributions, and thoughts during conflict often are subjective, simplistic, and self-serving. In one study, for example, married couples visited a "family interaction lab" that was created by researchers Alan Sillars, Linda Roberts, Kenneth Leonard, and Tim Dun (2000). The lab resembled a combination living room and dining room, and each couple spent 15 minutes in this setting discussing one of their current unresolved disagreements. The spouses then went to separate rooms to view the videotape of their interaction. The videotape was designed to stop playing after each 20-second interval; when it did, participants reported what they remembered thinking and feeling at the time into a microphone. Analysis of these spontaneous thoughts revealed that individuals tended to treat their own inferences as objective observations ("She's attacking me," "He's lying"). They seemed unaware of the possibility that they might be mistaken in their assumptions and/or conclusions. Similarly, participants' thoughts showed little evidence of complex perspective taking. For example, only 3% of their thoughts had a mutual or relational focus (i.e., showed awareness of the interdependence between each partner's behavior), and only 5% of their thoughts focused on how the partner might be interpreting the situation. Furthermore, when participants did attempt to identify or acknowledge the partner's perspective, they tended to view that perspective in simplistic and undifferentiated terms ("He thinks he's right," "She knows I'm sick of talking about this"). Negative thoughts and feelings also occurred much more frequently than positive ones. And finally, both husbands and wives displayed a tendency to view their own communication during the conflict more favorably than that of their partner. Specifically, both spouses attributed positive acts (e.g., collaboration and cooperation, disclosure and openness, soliciting information, attending to the partner) more often to themselves than to the partner, and both attributed negative acts and intentions (e.g., confrontation, avoidance and withdrawal, topic shifting, stonewalling, lying, insincerity) more often to the partner than to themselves. The researchers concluded:

> A surprisingly high proportion of thoughts were negatively valenced and there was minimal evidence of attention to the inherent complexity and ambiguity that exists in the communicative process. Participants showed a tendency to construe their own and their partner's communicative acts as objectifiable behaviors with unequivocal meaning. Presumably, this is part of the problem that occurs when interaction does not go smoothly—people treat their inferences as objective observations.
>
> (Sillars et al., 2000, p. 496)

The attributions that people make about their own and their partners' behavior during conflict play an important role in determining whether or not they will progress smoothly toward a successful resolution of their disagreement.

The Endings of Conflict

All conflicts eventually end, and Peterson's (1983/2002) model presents five possible forms that those endings may take. Some are positive. For example, conflict may produce *structural improvement* in the relationship. Disagreements and arguments (particularly over personally relevant and significant issues) provide partners with an opportunity to learn new information about each other's goals, values, and needs as well as the expectations that each has about their relationship. Although these revelations may be disturbing, the couple may achieve a deeper level of intimacy. Indeed, dating couples interviewed by communication scholars John Siegert and Glen Stamp (1994) reported that their "first big fight" allowed them to clarify their feelings about each other and their relationship and left them with a newfound or increased sense of the extent of their commitment and interdependence. Another positive outcome is an *integrative agreement*, defined as a solution that simultaneously satisfies both partners' original goals. Peterson notes that purely integrative agreements are uncommon because it is difficult to reconcile truly divergent interests; rather, what usually happens is that the partners create an alternative that requires one or both to make some slight concessions but that still allows them both to satisfy their major goals. Other conflicts end with *compromise* as each partner reduces his or her wishes until a mutually acceptable alternative is found.

Of course, conflict does not always end well. Some disagreements or fights end in conquest or *domination*, with one partner continuing to pursue his or her own personal goals while the other capitulates. Over time, the repeated domination of one partner over another is likely to have a destructive impact on the relationship. In one investigation, Karen Kayser (1993; also see Kayser & Rao, 2006) asked a group of unhappily married individuals to identify the "critical turning points for the worse" in their relationships. The majority of participants cited instances in which their partners displayed overly controlling behavior, including unilateral decision making about both minor (e.g., how the participants should dress) and major (e.g., where the couple should live) issues without regard for the participants' opinion and feelings. Domination is related to power imbalances or asymmetries between the partners; the partner with the most resources and the least investment in or commitment to the relationship is the one who generally "wins."

The final possible ending involves *separation* or the withdrawal of one or both partners without immediate resolution of the conflict. This may be a useful step in attaining later resolution; time apart may allow tempers to cool and more creative solutions to occur to each partner. Often, however, withdrawal has a damaging effect—the partners become increasingly unhappy and their relationship may dissolve. The results of a study conducted by social scientist Duncan Cramer (2000) revealed a strong correlation between unresolved conflict and relationship satisfaction in dating couples; specifically, the more often that couples reported experiencing conflict that was not resolved, the less satisfied they were with their relationship.

Conflict Resolution Strategies. Whether conflict produces positive or negative outcomes depends, in part, on how the conflict is managed by the partners. For example, research generally reveals that the use of "*positive*" or constructive *conflict resolution strategies* promotes relationship well-being. Men and women whose partners employ *reason* (problem-solving and the use of rational argument, e.g., presenting alternatives, seeking solutions to the problem), *assertion* (direct expression of opinions or wants, e.g., clearly stating one's position, redirecting the conversation to the issue or topic, emphasizing points by gesture or eye contact), or *partner support* (acknowledgment of the partner's views, e.g., actively listening or questioning, expressing clear agreement with the partner, making compromises or concessions) are happier and more satisfied than individuals whose partners make less use of these strategies (e.g., Noller, Feeney, Bonnell, & Callan, 1994; for a review, see Cupach & Canary, 2003).

"Negative" conflict resolution strategies are associated with interpersonal distress and dissatisfaction (Noller et al., 1994). Negative strategies include *coercion*, defined as seeking control through the use of force (e.g., blame, threats, sarcasm, physical or verbal aggression); *manipulation*, defined as attempting to gain compliance by indirect or false means (e.g., providing misleading information, attempting to make the partner feel guilty or defensive, feigning sincerity or various mood states); and *avoidance*, characterized by a physical and/or emotional retreat from the situation (e.g., changing or avoiding the topic, avoiding eye contact, minimizing the situation by joking).

Obviously there is no "hidden secret" to resolving conflict, and no one strategy will work well for all couples. However, the available literature provides some helpful hints. First, successful conflict management requires open and honest communication in which both partners clearly express their opinions, positions, and wants. Second, the partners should remain focused on the issue or situation at hand. Third, each partner must attempt to understand the other's perspective and try to recognize his or her own contribution to the interaction and the partner's responses. Fourth, the partners should try to express positive affect whenever possible and to suppress (or at least not reciprocate) negative feelings and expressions. Finally, the partners' goal should be to reach an equitable solution rather than a win–lose one, and both must be willing to compromise and negotiate in service of that goal.

LOSS

Conflict, distress-maintaining attributions, and negative conflict resolution strategies certainly can create intense unhappiness and contribute to the demise of a relationship. However, even stable and satisfying relationships end. Although there is little information on the rates of friendship dissolution, an early survey conducted by Suzanna Rose (1984) revealed that the majority (57%) of college-age men and women reported having ended a "close friendship" within the past 5 years. Similarly, research indicates that over 50% of all first marriages and approximately 60% of all remarriages in the U.S. end in divorce or permanent separation (Castro-Martin & Bumpass, 1989; Henley & Pasley, 2003; Michael, Gagnon, Laumann, & Kolata, 1994). Between 1950 and the mid-1980s, the divorce rate rose steadily; since that time, it has remained fairly steady and currently falls at 3.6 divorces per 1000 people in the population (U.S. Census Bureau, 2007d). Although the United States has one of the highest divorce rates in the world, rising divorce rates now characterize many other nations as well, including Canada, Japan, France, Germany, Italy, the Netherlands, Spain, and the United Kingdom (U.S. Census Bureau, 2007e).

Interestingly, some kinds of committed romantic relationship appear more prone to dissolution than others. National surveys indicate that heterosexual married couples are less likely to end their relationships than are heterosexual and homosexual cohabiting couples (see Blumstein & Schwartz, 1983). For example, in one recent study, psychologist Lawrence Kurdek (2004) compared the rate of relationship dissolution among three groups of participants: cohabiting gay male couples, cohabiting lesbian couples, and heterosexual married couples. His results revealed that significantly more of the cohabiting homosexual couples (19% of the gay male couples and 24% of the lesbian couples) than of the heterosexual married couples (15%) had ended their relationships.

Close relationship loss is a common life experience for most people.

Why Do Relationships End?

Researchers have identified a wide array of factors that are associated with the likelihood of relationship dissolution. Recall from Chapter 8 that various dispositional variables (e.g., negative affectivity, rejection sensitivity) are implicated in relationship disruption. Other personal factors are demographic. For example, recent reviews of the divorce literature indicate that age at marriage is one of the most consistent predictors of dissolution: men and women who marry at younger ages have an increased risk of divorce (e.g., Rodrigues, Hall, & Fincham, 2006; Teachman, Tedrow, & Hall, 2006).

Relational factors are also implicated in the demise of many relationships. A number of scholars have suggested that ***disengagement*** is one of the key mechanisms through which initially satisfying relationships become unstable and at risk for termination (Barry, Lawrence, & Langer, 2008). Signs of disengagement include: (1) *emotional indifference*, or a lack of strong positive (e.g., love) or negative (e.g., anger) emotions directed toward the partner; (2) *cognitive disconnection*, including viewing the partner as unresponsive, detached, or different from oneself, psychologically distancing oneself from the partner, and paying less attention to the partner; and (3) *behavioral distancing*, such as reducing levels of communication and involvement in the partner's life and interacting in less intimate ways (Barry et al., 2008; Gottman, 1999; Hess, 2002; Kayser & Rao, 2006). (Table 14.1

Table 14.1   Relationship Disengagement

The following items and response scale are adapted from Karen Kayser's (1990, 1996) 21-item Marital Disaffection Scale. Higher scores indicate greater levels of emotional estrangement, apathy, and indifference toward the partner.

Response Scale

1	2	3	4	5
Not at all true				Very true

Items
1. I often feel lonely even though I am with my partner.
2. I miss my partner when we're not together for a couple of days. [reverse-scored]
3. I find myself withdrawing more and more from my partner.
4. Apathy and indifference best describe my feelings toward my partner.
5. I would prefer to spend less time with my partner.
6. I am not as concerned about fulfilling my obligations and responsibilities in my relationship as I was in the past.
7. There are times when I do not feel a great deal of love and affection for my partner.
8. Most of the time I feel very close to my partner. [reverse-scored]
9. I find it difficult to confide in my partner about a number of things.
10. I seem to enjoy just being with my partner. [reverse-scored]

Scoring
Answer each item using the scale provided. Reverse your scores for items 2, 8, and 10 (e.g., an original score of 5 becomes a new score of 1; an original score of 4 becomes a new score of 2; and so forth). Add up the scores.

Source: Kersten, K. K. (1990). The process of marital disaffection: Interventions at various stages. *Family Relations, 39,* 257–265. Copyright © 1990 by the National Council on Family Relations. Permission granted by Wiley-Blackwell. Table 1 items reprinted with permission.

presents sample items from one of the available measures of disengagement.) Research reveals a strong association between these experiences and relationship instability. For example, after conducting in-depth interviews of unhappily married men and women, Kayser (1996) concluded that a "gradual loss of emotional attachment, a decline in caring, [and] an increasing sense of apathy and indifference toward one's partner" (pp. 83–84) played a pivotal role in her participants' decision to leave their marriages. Similar results were reported more recently by Ted Huston and his colleagues (Huston, 2009; Huston, Caughlin, Houts, Smith, & George, 2001), who observed that the daily realities of married life often test (and sometimes destroy) spouses' romanticized illusions about each other and their relationship. These scientists found evidence that disillusionment—as reflected in declining feelings of love, lowered rates of affectionate behavior, increasing ambivalence about the relationship, and the growing conviction that one's partner is not responsive—distinguishes couples who divorce from those who remain together.

Across cultures, a particularly common interpersonal cause for the dissolution of romantic partnerships involves the violation of one of the most fundamental expectations people hold for that type of relationship—fidelity. When Laura Betzig (1989) examined reasons for divorce in a sample of 160 societies around the world, she discovered that infidelity or adultery was the single most common cause of conjugal dissolution, mentioned in 88 societies (or 55% of the sample). Interestingly, polygyny—a husband electing to add another wife to the household—and subsequent co-spouse conflict was the eighth most commonly reported cause of marital dissolution, cited by 16% of societies. Betzig (1989, p. 661) noted:

> Polygyny in effect legitimizes what would be extramarital sex on the part of a husband. The result is that, to a wife, the most important "other women" are cowives rather than lovers. When a husband has added too many of them or neglected her to favor them, a woman may divorce him.

Other researchers have also found lower rates of marital satisfaction and increased rates of psychological distress among wives in polygynous marriages than among wives in monogamous marriages (Al-Krenawi & Graham, 2006); this provides additional evidence that polygyny may not be conducive to optimal marital functioning and thus may contribute to relationship dissolution.

As would be predicted from Interdependence Theory and its offshoots (see Chapter 6), there is evidence that factors in the social environment surrounding a relationship—including the number and quality of available alternatives and the relative approval or disapproval for the relationship from the partners' social networks—also affect its stability (see Sprecher, Felmlee, Orbuch, & Willetts, 2001; Sprecher, Felmlee, Schmeeckle, & Shu, 2006). Diane Felmlee (2001b), for example, asked a large sample of university students to consider various alternatives to their present dating relationship (such as beginning a relationship with a new person, dating several other people, and spending time with friends) and then to indicate how those alternatives compared with the current relationship. Participants also rated the extent to which members of their social network (including their own family and friends and the partner's family and friends) approved of the relationship. Four months after providing these ratings, participants were re-contacted and their relationship status was assessed. The results revealed that initial perceptions both of available alternatives and social network approval significantly predicted subsequent breakup. Specifically, the more favorable the alternatives to the dating relationship that participants believed they had at Time 1, and the less approval for the relationship they perceived from their own friends and from their partners' family members, the more likely they were to have ended the relationship four months later at Time

2. Other researchers have found similar results (e.g., Etcheverry, Le, & Charania, 2008; Rusbult et al., 1982).

In addition, the larger sociocultural context can influence the stability of the relationships embedded within it. Several scholars have posited that the increased economic independence of women, the reduction of legal barriers to divorce (e.g., "no fault" divorce laws), the reduced social stigma associated with divorce, and other social changes that occurred in the U.S. during the twentieth century have made it easier for individuals involved in unhappy marriages to dissolve their unions (see Amato & Irving, 2006; Berscheid & Campbell, 1981).

These are only a few of the many factors that can contribute to the demise of the association between two people.

The Process of Relationship Dissolution

A number of models of relationship termination have been proposed, with most of them focusing on the dissolution of romantic unions. For example, clinical researcher John Gottman (e.g., 1994a; Carrère & Gottman, 1999; Gottman & Levenson, 1992) proposed that spouses experience a cascade of events that propel them along the path toward divorce (see Figure 14.6). According to his *cascade model of marital dissolution*, the dissolution process begins when the partners experience a flooding of negativity—they become overwhelmed by the ferocity of their own and the other's negative emotion. Flooding is followed by the perception that the marital problems are so severe that they cannot be easily resolved; this, in turn, leads to a desire to deal with the problems individually, rather than collaboratively with the spouse. As the partners turn away from the marriage and each other, they establish separate or parallel lives in which they become increasingly less likely to

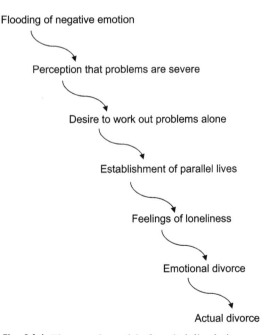

Flooding of negative emotion

Perception that problems are severe

Desire to work out problems alone

Establishment of parallel lives

Feelings of loneliness

Emotional divorce

Actual divorce

Fig. 14.6 The cascade model of marital dissolution proposed by Gottman (e.g., 1994a) suggests that unhappily married partners gradually turn away from each other over time, eventually experiencing emotional (and often physical) separation.

interact, communicate, and spend time together. Feelings of loneliness ensue. Together, this cascading series of events leads to what Gottman calls an "emotional divorce" (similar in character to the concept of disengagement we reviewed earlier) that ultimately results in dissolution.

Another model of relationship termination was proposed by scholar Steve Duck (1982; Rollie & Duck, 2006), who suggested that romantic relationships undergo five interrelated phases of disengagement and dissolution, each characterized by different processes and patterns of communication and interaction (see Figure 14.7). The ***intrapsychic phase*** begins when the individual crosses a threshold of "unbearable dissatisfaction" and begins to privately assess the partner's behavior, the quality of the relationship, the costs of termination, and possible alternatives to the relationship. If the decision is made to disclose these private thoughts to the partner, the next set of processes are engaged. During the ***dyadic phase***, the partners express their feelings, provide explanations for events, discuss their differences, and choose between repairing or dissolving their union. If the decision is to end the relationship, they enter the ***social phase***. Here, the partners reveal the actual (or impending) breakup to others in their social networks and deal with the social repercussions (e.g., judgment, possible disapproval, their own "newly single" status). During the ***grave-dressing phase***, each individual retrospectively examines the relationship's progression and demise, and creates an acceptable personal story that "tidies up" the associated memories. The final phase, called ***resurrection***, centers around adaptation and adjustment to the relationship's demise; here, the individuals confront the loss of what once was a valued connection with another person, experience self-growth, and ready themselves for future romance.

Empirical research supports several aspects of these models. Dina Battaglia, Francis Richard, Darcee Datteri, and Charles Lord (1998) asked a sample of undergraduate men and women (most of whom had experienced a breakup) to generate a script about the sequence of events that typically occur during the process of dissolving a romantic relationship. In accord with both Gottman's (e.g., 1994a) and Duck's (e.g., 1982) models, participants specified negative emotions (e.g., frustration, annoyance) and loss of interest, followed by a private assessment of the situation and a consideration of other possible partners, as occurring early in the dissolution process. Moreover, they cited emotional detachment, "officially" breaking up, and recovering or gaining a sense of closure as the final events. In addition, however, participants' scripts reflected the cyclical nature of relationship termination—a pattern that is not readily captured by the existing, and largely sequential, models. Specifically, they described partners as repeatedly vacillating between approach behaviors (such as communication, trying to work things out, and getting back together) and avoidance behaviors (including acting distant, physically avoiding each other, and deciding to date other people) before finally breaking up.

Disengagement Strategies.   Other relationship scholars, rather than exploring the phases or processes of relationship dissolution, have investigated the tactics—called ***disengagement strategies***—that people utilize when actually attempting to end a relationship. A series of studies conducted by Leslie Baxter (1985) suggested that disengagement strategies vary along two basic dimensions. The first, called ***indirectness vs. directness***, refers to the extent to which the person's desire to exit the relationship is made clear to the other partner. Direct strategies explicitly make clear the desire to end the relationship, whereas indirect strategies do not. The second dimension is called ***other-orientation vs. self-orientation*** and indicates the degree to which the disengager (the person attempting to end the relationship) tries to avoid hurting the partner. Other-oriented strategies demonstrate a desire to avoid embarrassing or manipulating the partner; self-oriented strategies display concern for the self at the expense of the partner. These two dimensions combine to form four categories of disengagement strategy, illustrated in Figure 14.8.

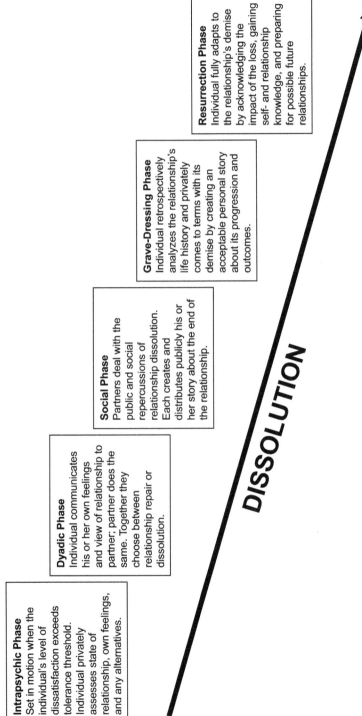

Intrapsychic Phase
Set in motion when the individual's level of dissatisfaction exceeds tolerance threshold. Individual privately assesses state of relationship, own feelings, and any alternatives.

Dyadic Phase
Individual communicates his or her own feelings and view of relationship to partner; partner does the same. Together they choose between relationship repair or dissolution.

Social Phase
Partners deal with the public and social repercussions of relationship dissolution. Each creates and distributes publicly his or her story about the end of the relationship.

Grave-Dressing Phase
Individual retrospectively analyzes the relationship's life history and privately comes to terms with its demise by creating an acceptable personal story about its progression and outcomes.

Resurrection Phase
Individual fully adapts to the relationship's demise by acknowledging the impact of the loss, gaining self- and relationship knowledge, and preparing for possible future relationships.

DISSOLUTION

Fig. 14.7 Duck (e.g., 1982; Rollie & Duck, 2006) proposes that relationships undergo five interrelated phases in the process of dissolving. Each phase is characterized by different patterns of communication and interaction between the partners. It is important to recognize that relationships may not follow this set sequence; rather, the processes characterizing each phase may overlap considerably and even occur simultaneously.

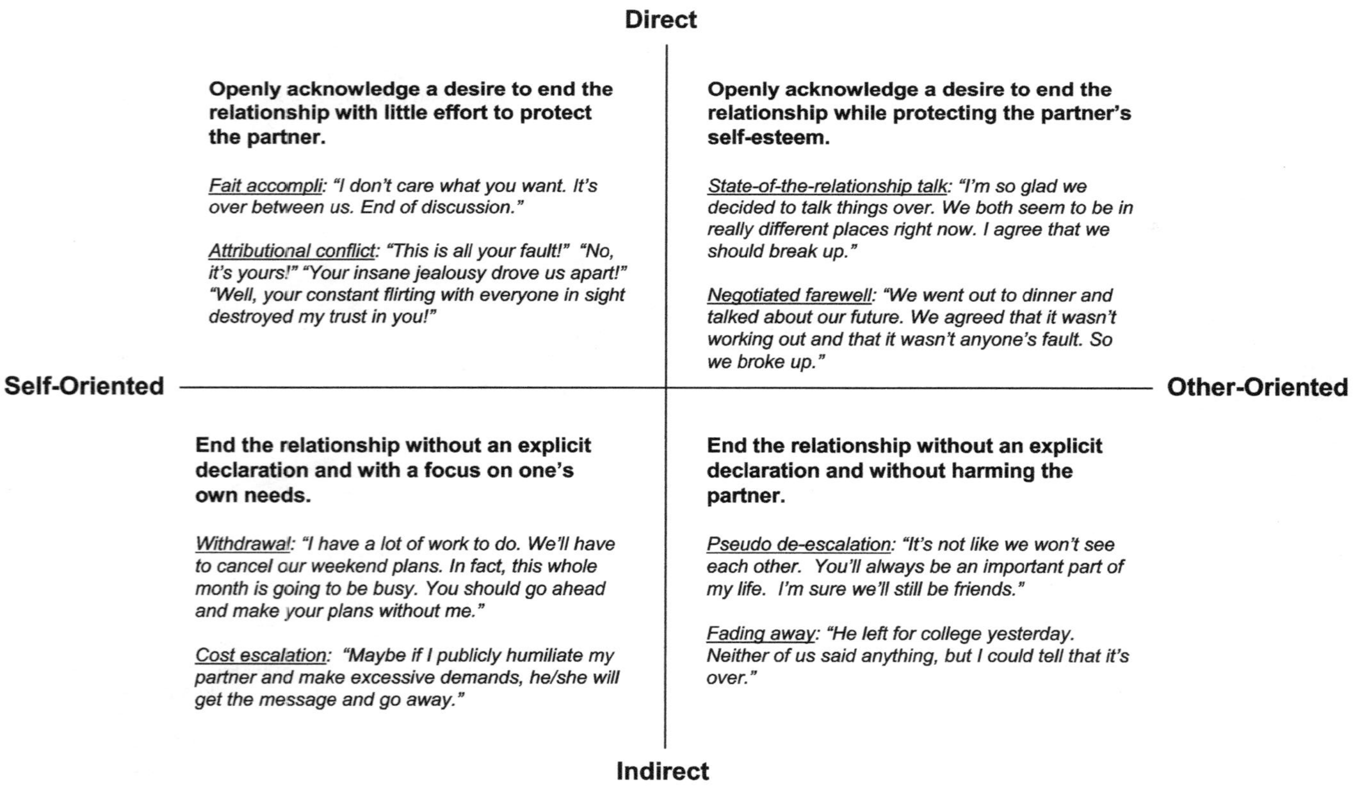

Direct

Self-Oriented

Openly acknowledge a desire to end the relationship with little effort to protect the partner.

Fait accompli: "I don't care what you want. It's over between us. End of discussion."

Attributional conflict: "This is all your fault!" "No, it's yours!" "Your insane jealousy drove us apart!" "Well, your constant flirting with everyone in sight destroyed my trust in you!"

Openly acknowledge a desire to end the relationship while protecting the partner's self-esteem.

State-of-the-relationship talk: "I'm so glad we decided to talk things over. We both seem to be in really different places right now. I agree that we should break up."

Negotiated farewell: "We went out to dinner and talked about our future. We agreed that it wasn't working out and that it wasn't anyone's fault. So we broke up."

Other-Oriented

End the relationship without an explicit declaration and with a focus on one's own needs.

Withdrawal: "I have a lot of work to do. We'll have to cancel our weekend plans. In fact, this whole month is going to be busy. You should go ahead and make your plans without me."

Cost escalation: "Maybe if I publicly humiliate my partner and make excessive demands, he/she will get the message and go away."

End the relationship without an explicit declaration and without harming the partner.

Pseudo de-escalation: "It's not like we won't see each other. You'll always be an important part of my life. I'm sure we'll still be friends."

Fading away: "He left for college yesterday. Neither of us said anything, but I could tell that it's over."

Indirect

Fig. 14.8 Baxter's model of disengagement strategies. Research conducted by Leslie Baxter (1985) suggests that the ways in which people disengage from a relationship vary along two primary dimensions. The *direct/indirect* dimension concerns whether the individual makes his or her desire to end the relationship clear to the partner. The *self-/other-oriented* dimension concerns the degree to which the individual focuses on protecting the self or the partner. These two dimensions combine to form four categories of disengagement strategy.

The first category encompasses strategies that are *direct and other-oriented*. In using the "state of the relationship talk," one or both partners explicitly acknowledge their dissatisfaction and desire to end the relationship—and they do so in a face-saving context of mutual discussion and agreement to exit. The "negotiated farewell" is a similar strategy that involves an explicit communication that formally ends the relationship and that allows each partner to share responsibility for the breakup. These strategies directly and openly express the goal of termination in a manner that saves face for both partners.

The second category contains strategies that are *direct and self-oriented*. Here, the disengager explicitly states his or her desire to end the relationship and makes little to no effort to avoid hurting, embarrassing, or manipulating the partner. "Fait accompli" occurs when the disengager declares that the relationship is over with no opportunity for discussion or compromise. "Attributional conflict" is a strategy in which both partners wish to end the relationship but cannot agree about why the breakup is necessary and thus blame each other (often bitterly) for its occurrence. People who use these strategies openly call for the termination of the relationship but often accomplish that goal at their partner's expense.

The third category contains strategies that are considered *indirect and self-oriented*. Here, an individual attempts to end the relationship without explicitly stating that goal and with an overwhelming concern for his or her own feelings and needs (as opposed to those of the partner). "Withdrawal" involves reducing the frequency and/or the intimacy of contact with the partner without telling the partner the real reason for the disengagement (i.e., the desire to end the relationship). A second indirect/self-oriented strategy is that of "cost escalation," which occurs when the person wishing to exit the relationship attempts to increase the relationship costs of the partner, thereby driving him or her away. People who use these strategies are avoiding any explicit discussion of relationship termination while at the same time focusing on their own needs and feelings.

The fourth category contains *indirect and other-oriented* strategies that attempt to accomplish a breakup without an explicit declaration and without excessive harm to either partner. One example is "pseudo de-escalation," when one or both partners (falsely) declare that they desire a transformed but less close relationship rather than a final and complete separation. Another is "fading away," when both partners implicitly understand that the relationship is over (but never directly acknowledge this state of affairs).

Baxter (1985) pointed out that the process of relationship disengagement is multifaceted and complex and that it is possible for one person to use numerous strategies when attempting to end a specific relationship. Indeed, research conducted by sociologist Diane Vaughn (1986) revealed that breakup "initiators" tend to employ a variety of indirect dissolution tactics, including waiting for the partner to behave badly and then seizing upon this "fatal mistake" as evidence that the relationship is flawed and should be terminated; decreasing the amount of interaction with the partner while simultaneously increasing the amount of interaction with others; and violating important and previously agreed-upon relationship rules such as fidelity.

Accounts: Telling the Story of the Relationship's Demise.

One important element in the process of relationship dissolution (and subsequent recovery from loss) is the making of **accounts**. Accounts are explanatory scripts that present the plot, introduce the characters and their patterns of interaction, and tell the "why" of the breakup. Like a novel, play, or some other type of dramatic presentation, accounts tell a story—in this case, that of the relationship and its demise.

According to account scholars John Harvey, Ann Weber, and their colleagues (e.g., Harvey & Fine, 2006; Harvey, Weber, Galvin, Huszti, & Garnick, 1986; Weber, 1998), people create accounts for a variety of reasons. First, account making allows individuals to reduce or eliminate the uncertainty and ambiguity that frequently accompany breakups. He says, "I know why we broke up. She was too jealous. There's no doubt in my mind that this is what killed our relationship." She says, "It's not like any one thing destroyed our relationship. It was more like a lot of little things that built up over time. We just weren't right for each other."

Accounts are not always accurate, and the individuals involved may create vastly different accounts of the same situation. Nonetheless, accounts allow their creators to clarify their understanding of the breakup, to establish blame or exoneration about an event, and to satisfy their need for control and information.

Second, accounts fulfill what Harvey, Weber, and their colleagues termed a "social-presentational" function that may protect and enhance the individual's self-esteem. During and after a breakup, people often are motivated to present the stories of their relationship to the members of their social network. By influencing the interpretations that others have of the individual and the events of the breakup, accounts may result in social support, sympathy, and other positive outcomes. The husband who tells his best friend that he has forgiven his wife's infidelity and that he accepts responsibility for driving her into the arms of another man projects an image of charity and martyrdom that may produce expressions of admiration and respect from his friend. The unfaithful wife who confesses her "weakness" and tells her best friend what a "horrible person" she is projects an image of need that may result in the provision of support: "So you made a mistake," the friend reassures her. "You're only human."

And third, accounts serve as a potent vehicle for emotional release. In telling the story of the relationship's demise, individuals may experience a cathartic purging of feelings of guilt, anger, depression, loneliness, insecurity, and confusion: "Here's what happened to me, and here's how I feel about it," the wounded party cries, giving voice to thoughts and pent-up emotions that he or she may not have had the opportunity to express during the breakup itself.

There is some limited empirical evidence suggesting that accounts may play an important role in helping people adjust to the end of a relationship. In one investigation, researchers Jody Koenig Kellas and Valerie Manusov (2003) asked a sample of 90 undergraduate students who had experienced the termination of an important romantic relationship to "tell the story" of the breakup in a written narrative. These written narratives were then rated for various aspects of completeness, including the extent to which they were coherent, presented the events in a sequential and episodic manner, attributed responsibility to the characters in the story, evoked and made sense of affect or emotions, and developed characters relevant to the story. Participants also completed a scale that assessed their overall adjustment to the loss of their important love relationship. The researchers found that both the coherence of a participant's narrative and the extent to which he or she segmented the events in a sequential and episodic manner were positively related to overall adjustment. That is, participants whose accounts of relationship dissolution made sense, hung together, were structured in an organized manner, and were supplemented with examples displayed higher levels of adjustment to the loss of their romantic relationships. These findings suggest that the ability to conceptually organize and understand a breakup may relate to the process of adjusting to relationship loss.

Reactions to Relationship Loss

People respond to the demise of a romantic relationship in a number of different ways. For example, men and women undergoing a divorce often experience depression, anxiety, lowered self-esteem, and other symptoms of psychological distress, as well as feelings of social isolation (Henley & Pasley, 2003). However, positive responses to divorce are also relatively common. Substantial proportions of divorced adults report beneficial changes in their relationships (including more frequent and more intimate interaction with friends, family members, and other social network members) and themselves (such as personal growth and greater autonomy, self-reliance, and self-esteem) following the dissolution of their marriages (see Tashiro, Frazier, & Berman, 2006). Similarly, although most children whose parents have divorced experience various emotional, behavioral, and academic difficulties, these problems tend to peak in the time period leading up to their parents' actual physical separation and are usually short-lived (Demo & Supple, 2003). Moreover, many children also report positive outcomes ranging from improvements in their relationship with both the custodial and the non-custodial parent, to closer relationships with siblings, to enhanced maturity, independence, and self-reliance; they also demonstrate increases in social competence and general relationship skills (Tashiro et al., 2006).

Similar positive responses have been identified by researchers investigating non-marital relationship dissolution. Psychologists Ty Tashiro and Patricia Frazier (2003) surveyed 92 men and women who recently had experienced the breakup of a dating relationship. Each participant was asked to describe the positive changes (if any) that had occurred as a result of the breakup. On average, participants reported experiencing five positive changes in themselves (e.g., increased self-confidence, self-reliance, independence, and willingness to experience and express emotion), their interpersonal dynamics (e.g., greater relationship knowledge, improved communication skills), and their surrounding social environment (e.g., improved friendships and family relationships).

Interestingly, there appear to be sex differences in emotional responses to romantic relationship dissolution. In particular, researchers generally find that women demonstrate greater emotional recovery and adjustment following divorce than do men. This robust finding is commonly attributed to three factors (see Braver, Shapiro, & Goodman, 2006). First, women tend to be more successful than men at accessing and using social support networks that buffer the stresses accompanying divorce. Second, women are less likely than men to rely on harmful or ineffective methods of coping with divorce-related stress (e.g., alcohol, drugs). Third, women are more likely than men to initiate divorce, and the initiating spouse typically experiences high levels of stress in the period leading up to the decision to divorce and then corresponding levels of relief following this decision (whereas the non-initiating spouse— typically the husband—experiences the greatest stress following the decision to divorce).

In addition to exploring reactions to the dissolution of marital and other romantic relationships, scientists have investigated responses and adjustment to the loss of an intimate partner due to death. Shock, helplessness, depression, and other symptoms of emotional distress are among most common initial responses among individuals who have lost a spouse (Farnsworth, Lund, & Pett, 1989; Stroebe & Stroebe, 1987). Researchers have also found, however, that there is a great deal of variability in the intensity and duration of distress experienced by widowed men and women. In one longitudinal study George Bonanno and his colleagues (Bonanno et al., 2002; Bonanno, Wortman, & Nesse, 2004) examined changes in depression and adjustment among a sample of adults before and after the death of their spouses. Their results revealed five core bereavement trajectories: (1) the *resilient* trajectory, demonstrated by 46% of the sample, was characterized by low levels of depression and other grief symptoms; (2) the *chronic grief* trajectory (16%) was characterized by elevated (and enduring) levels of depression following the loss; (3) the *common grief* trajectory (11%) involved increased depression immediately following the partner's death which then gradually diminished over time; (4) the *depressed-improved* trajectory (10%) was a pattern in which the death of the spouse resulted in a reduction of pre-loss depression levels (a finding the researchers attributed to the fact that these individuals typically reported negative and ambivalent feelings about their marriages and thus the partner's death may have brought an end to their stressful situation); and (5) the *chronic depression* trajectory (8%) was characterized by relatively high levels of depression both before and after the death of the spouse. In sum, there appears to be no "normal" or "universal" way of responding to a major interpersonal loss—rather, people react to the death of a partner or a relationship in many different ways.

One type of loss, however, that does appear to be universally traumatizing is *ambiguous loss*, which occurs when people are uncertain or lack definite knowledge about the whereabouts or status of a loved one (Boss, 2006, 2007). Two primary types of ambiguous loss have been identified. In the first the partner is perceived as physically absent but psychologically or emotionally present; this interpersonal situation is experienced by adults and children whose loved ones have gone missing as a result of military action, civil war, terrorist acts, abduction, adoption, or social welfare intervention (e.g., DeYoung & Buzzi, 2003; Huebner, Mancini, Wilcox, Grass, & Grass, 2007; Lee & Whiting, 2007). In the second type of ambiguous loss the partner is physically present but perceived as psychologically absent due to debilitating physical disease, mental disorder, or substance addiction (e.g., Boss & Couden, 2002; O'Brien, 2007). The ambiguity and uncertainty surrounding both of these situations prevents most people from resolving their feelings about the loss (which may or may not be "real"), redefining their relationship with the partner (who may or may not be gone), and enacting many of the socially normative and supportive mourning rituals that accompany permanent, decisive loss. In essence, the bereaved individual is left "frozen in grief" and unable to access coping and decision-making processes that would enable him or her to achieve closure (Boss, 1999).

People who experience relationship losses that are not socially acknowledged or validated also may have difficulty coping with their bereavement. *Disenfranchised grief* occurs when one's right, need, or capacity to grieve is not commonly recognized by society (Doka, 1989, 2008). When a loss is socially devalued (such as the death of a beloved companion animal, an ex-partner, a homosexual partner, an abusive or violent parent or spouse, or an unborn child) or socially stigmatized (for example, death resulting from suicide, murder, drug use, AIDS, or capital punishment), or when the bereaved individual is perceived as lacking the capacity or need to grieve (for example, young children, mentally disabled persons, the elderly, military or police personnel), little sympathy and social support are typically provided following the loss (Murray, 2003). This makes it difficult for many individuals to publicly mourn, resolve their feelings about the lost partner, and lay the relationship to rest.

SUMMARY

Conflict and disagreements are part and parcel of close relationships. Whether a relationship survives conflict is to a large extent determined by how that conflict is managed. People who communicate their own needs and feelings clearly and who acknowledge and support those of their partners are more likely to resolve conflict (and accomplish termination, if they elect to dissolve their relationship) in a manner that benefits both themselves and their partners. Research reveals that there is no single, universal reaction to the loss of a valued intimate relationship; rather, a variety of both positive and negative responses and outcomes are possible.

KEY CONCEPTS

Predisposing conditions (pp. 249–252)	Cumulative annoyance (p. 252)
Initiating events (p. 252)	Conflict avoidance (p. 252)
Criticism (p. 252)	Conflict engagement (p. 252)
Illegitimate demands (p. 252)	Loyalty (p. 253)
Rebuffs (p. 252)	Voice (p. 253)

EXPLORATION EXERCISES

These exercises are designed to allow you to explore in greater detail some of the concepts and issues discussed in this chapter. There are no right or wrong answers to these exercises—they are simply meant to provide an opportunity for discussion and debate.

1. Think of a recent conflict, argument, or disagreement you had with a close relationship partner (a good friend, romantic partner, or relative). Using Peterson's (1983/2002) model (outlined in Figures 14.2 and 14.3), chart the course of your conflict. Be as specific as possible, so that you are able to create a conflict progression chart similar to Figure 14.3.

2. Relationship scholars propose that conflicts may end in five different ways (structural improvement, integrative agreement, compromise, domination, separation). Using specific examples from your own life, illustrate and discuss each possible ending. Which ending did you find to be the most satisfying or beneficial (to you, to your partner, to your relationship)? Which one had the most harmful consequences?

3. Many of us hold fairly negative attitudes toward prenuptial agreements—yet partners make these agreements prior to marriage in an effort to establish a set of mutually agreed-upon rules of conduct and thus to avoid future conflict and disagreement. Working together with a classmate, construct a prenuptial agreement. You may pretend to be an engaged couple or two attorneys representing the partners' interests. As you draft the agreement, consider as many aspects of married life as you can (for example, finances; children—number, care and discipline, education, religion, etc.; family vacations; pets; living arrangements; division of labor/household chores; and so forth).

4. People may dissolve their close relationships in a number of different ways, several of which are outlined by Baxter's (1985) model. For this exercise, you will need to think of two relationships—one with a romantic partner and one with a friend—that you once were involved in but

that have now ended. How did those relationships dissolve? For each, and regardless of your own role (i.e., whether you were the leaver or the one who was left) consider whether the ending was primarily other-oriented or self-oriented, and primarily direct or indirect. What specific strategy do you think best exemplifies each of your two dissolution situations (e.g., fait accompli, negotiated farewell, withdrawal, fading away)? Compare the two situations in terms of the type of strategy used, your own response, your partner's reactions, and so forth. In general, do you think that there is a difference between how people typically end friendships and how they end romantic relationships?

Chapter 15
Intervention

There is no doubt that most people value their romantic partnerships, friendships, and family relationships and invest a good deal of time and energy into making them "work." Nonetheless, as we saw in the previous chapter, most spouses, friends, and family members argue, disagree, and experience episodes of heightened conflict and tension during the course of their relationships. When people become highly dissatisfied or suspect that their relationship is in real trouble—particularly in the case of romantic partnerships—some of them will seek assistance from a professional in hopes of determining whether or not their relationship is "workable" and preventing dissolution or separation from occurring (see Doss, Simpson, & Christensen, 2004).

In this chapter we explore the topic of relationship intervention, including the ways therapists identify and treat troubled relationships and whether therapy truly can provide help for couples in distress. Because the majority of research in this area has focused on therapeutic interventions for troubled marital (and other long-term, committed romantic) relationships, our discussion also focuses on that particular relationship variety.

IDENTIFYING DISTRESSED RELATIONSHIPS

Before a therapist can effectively intervene in a troubled relationship, he or she must first identify the dysfunctional thoughts, feelings, and behaviors that are contributing to the partners' distress. Some of these have been discussed in earlier chapters. For example, in Chapters 8 and 14, we saw how the way in which partners interpret each other's behavior is associated with the overall health of their relationship. For example, couples who routinely make attributions that discount positive partner behaviors and accentuate negative partner behaviors (both in general and in conflict situations) are more likely to experience distress than are couples who do not fall prey to these dysfunctional processes.

Dysfunctional Interaction Styles

Relationship scholars have identified several specific interaction styles that prevent men and women from successfully resolving interpersonal conflict and achieving satisfactory outcomes in their relationships. Many of these involve the affective behavior (i.e., feelings, emotions, and sentiments) that the partners display during times of active disagreement. Based on extensive observation and analysis of the interaction behavior of happily and unhappily married couples, clinical researcher John Gottman (e.g., 1994b, 1999; Coan & Gottman, 2007) identified four ways of interacting that are particularly corrosive to interpersonal happiness—criticism, contempt, defensiveness, and withdrawal. (These behaviors are so lethal to relationship well-being that Gottman called them "The Four Horsemen of the Apocalypse" in reference to the four horsemen that personify Pestilence, War, Famine, and Death in the New Testament's *Book of Revelation*.)

Criticism refers to "super-charged" complaints that suggest some deep-seated personality defect or character flaw in the partner: "Why did you say you'd baby sit when you knew we had plans to go away this weekend? You are so selfish. You always think about yourself and what you want to do. You never think about me." Forms of criticism include *blaming*, in which the individual assigns fault along with a personal attack or global accusation ("Now the weekend is ruined. This is all your fault—you never think to check with me before making plans"); *character attacks*, in which the individual criticizes the partner's personality or abilities in very general ways ("You are completely self-centered. You are absolutely incapable of seeing things from another person's perspective"); and *kitchen sinking*, which involves the making of a long list of complaints to illustrate the incompetencies or personality defects of the partner ("You never ask me what I want to do, and you never seek my opinion, and you never check with me before making plans, and you always do what you want . . ."). According to Gottman, few couples can completely avoid complaining about things they wish were otherwise or expressing their dissatisfaction with a particular situation. Consequently, the airing of complaints about specific events or actions is "normal" and actually can be a healthy activity to the extent that it facilitates open communication and produces positive change in the relationship. However, complaints that place blame on the partner and attack his or her personality or character are likely to sabotage the overall well-being of the couple's union.

If unresolved, criticism is usually followed by ***contempt***—statements or actions that are directly intended to insult the partner and inflict psychological damage. Some of the most common signs of contempt include insults and name-calling, hostile humor, mockery, and body language that communicates a lack of respect for the partner (e.g., sneering, rolling one's eyes, curling the upper lip, raising the eyebrows). Contempt is particularly damaging because once it enters the relationship the partners experience what Gottman called the "immediate decay of admiration" (p. 1994b, 80)— they find it nearly impossible to remember even one of each other's positive qualities or behaviors. Contempt is so corrosive to a relationship's health that Gottman stated that it ought to be banned from all marital interactions.

When faced with a partner's criticism and contempt, it is difficult for the other partner not to become defensive. ***Defensiveness*** refers to feeling victimized, unfairly treated, or attacked by the partner, particularly during times of conflict or disagreement. Forms of defensiveness include *denying responsibility* ("It's not my fault we ran out of milk. I can't be responsible for every little thing in this house"), *making excuses* ("I couldn't go to the store because my boss kept me late at work tonight and there wasn't time"), *cross-complaining* ("Well, if you'd remember to make a grocery list, we wouldn't run out of the things we need"), *minimization* ("Hey, it's not the end of the world. We can always have eggs for breakfast instead of cereal"), and *aggressive defenses* (vehement denials that come across as childish, as in "I never said I'd go to the store!" "Yes, you did!" "No, I didn't!"). In addition, partners who are feeling defensive have a tendency to endlessly reiterate their own positions without truly listening to what the other is saying ("As I said before . . .") and to make what Gottman called "yes-but statements" in which they admit to their behavior but then claim that it was morally justified ("Yes, it's true I didn't go to the store but that's because I was waiting for you to give me the grocery list"). There are also nonverbal actions that are frequently associated with defensiveness, such as using a whiny or high-pitched tone of voice, shifting the body from side-to-side, folding the arms across the chest, and giving a false smile in which the corners of the mouth rise but the eyes do not change.

The final "horseman" identified by Gottman is ***withdrawal*** or ***stonewalling***, which essentially involves removing oneself from the interaction in a way that conveys cold disapproval, icy distance, and smugness. When stonewalling, a person's face typically appears "frozen" or stiff; the jaw may be clenched and the neck muscles strained, or the face may be deliberately calm and composed so as to seem emotionally neutral. Withdrawal may occur in a variety of forms. For example, when faced with a partner's criticism or contempt, some individuals fail to respond or react at all (e.g., they may shrug their shoulders, turn away, and pick up a book or magazine). Others may offer monosyllabic responses ("Hmm"), verbally refuse to engage in the interaction ("Whatever," "I guess you're always right"), or display what Gottman calls "active away behaviors" that communicate an unwillingness to pay attention to the partner (e.g., examining or playing with one's hair, cleaning one's fingernails). Still others may physically remove themselves from the situation by walking away or leaving the room. Because it involves a refusal to communicate, habitual withdrawal is often a sign of a severely dysfunctional relationship.

Clinical research reveals that all four of these interaction styles are associated with marital dissatisfaction. For example, in one early investigation (Gottman & Krokoff, 1989), a sample of married couples completed measures of marital satisfaction and subsequently were videotaped for 15 minutes while they discussed an ongoing area of disagreement in their marriage. Observers then examined these videotaped interactions for the presence and amount of each of the aforementioned negative behaviors: (1) *criticism* (e.g., hostile statements expressing unambiguous dislike or disapproval of the partner's behavior and made in an irritated or hostile tone of voice), (2) *contempt* (mockery, sarcasm, insults, ridicule, derision, and other verbal content, tone of voice, facial expressions, gestures, and body movements indicative of contempt), (3) *defensiveness* (e.g., excuse making, denying responsibility), and (4) *withdrawal* (e.g., non-responsiveness to the partner, not tracking the partner's comments or conversation, turning off or away from the partner, incoherent talk). The results revealed that the frequency with which husbands and wives expressed criticism and contempt during the interaction was negatively correlated both with their own and with their spouses' marital happiness; in other words, the more often that a man criticized or displayed contempt for his wife, or a woman criticized or displayed contempt for her husband, the less satisfied both were with the quality of their marriage. In addition, the more often a wife withdrew from her husband during the interaction, and the more often a husband demonstrated defensiveness toward his wife, the less satisfied both partners were with their marriage. These four interaction styles clearly are associated with marital unhappiness.

Negative Affect Reciprocity

Unhappy couples also frequently display *negative affect reciprocity*, defined as a behavior sequence in which one partner's expression of negative affect is subsequently reciprocated by the other partner (Carstensen, Gottman, & Levenson, 1995; for a review, see Gottman, 1998). Unfortunately, partners who return each other's negative behavior can find themselves trapped in an extended (and quite destructive) cycle of negativity:

"Did you remember to pay the phone bill? I'd hate for us to get hit with another late fee."

"You're never going to let me forget that I forgot to pay the bills last month, are you?! For Pete's sake, it only happened once. Stop bringing it up all the time."

"Well, someone needs to be responsible about money in this relationship. And besides, you're the one who's always harping about the importance of being on time for things."

"That's rich, coming from someone who's never on time for anything. And thanks, by the way, for letting me know that you were running late tonight—so glad I got that call and was able to save dinner. Oh wait, that's right, you didn't call, and our dinner was ruined."

"You don't need to be sarcastic—believe me, I got the message loud and clear when you threw everything in the trash as soon as I walked in the kitchen."

"Well, if you'd taken the time to call and let me know you'd be late, maybe there would have been something edible left to eat. Guess they don't have phones at your office."

Happy couples also sometimes display negative affect reciprocity in their interactions. Unlike unhappy couples, however, who become absorbed by negativity and find it difficult to exit this state, happy couples are able to step out of the destructive cycle. One partner simply does not return the other partner's negative affect but instead responds positively or neutrally:

"Did you remember to pay the phone bill? I'd hate for us to get hit with another late fee."

"You're never going to let me forget that I forgot to pay the bills last month, are you?! For Pete's sake, it only happened once. Stop bringing it up all the time."

"I guess I have mentioned it a lot lately. Sorry about that. I think I've become kind of obsessed over our finances lately—I'm just so excited about the possibility of us actually being able to buy a house this year."

"I'm sorry, too. I shouldn't have snapped at you. We do need to be careful with our money—the more we save, the closer we are to owning our own home. I can't wait!"

Both distressed and non-distressed couples attempt to disrupt negative interactions through the use of *repair attempts*—humor, distraction, information exchange, appeals to basic values and marital expectations, finding areas of common ground, and other interpersonal processes that are designed to repair the interaction by reducing its level of overt negativity and channeling it in a more positive direction (Gottman, 1998, 1999). In both of the examples above, the second partner has attempted to divert the negative flow of the interaction by saying, probably with some irritation, "Stop bringing [my failure to pay the bill last month] up all the time." Repair attempts such as this one usually have two components—a positive (and expressed) communicative component specifically designed to repair the interaction ("Stop bringing it up all the time") and an associated negative nonverbal component (irritation). Interestingly, what appears to distinguish couples in distressed and non-distressed relationships is which aspect of the repair attempt they focus on—happy couples attend primarily to the positive communicative component (the content of what has been said) and thus are able to respond neutrally or positively to the partner ("Sorry . . ."), whereas unhappy couples focus on the accompanying negative nonverbal component (gestures, body language, tone of voice, etc.) and consequently respond in a like manner ("You're the one who's always harping . . ."). In discussing this pattern, Gottman observed that "reciprocated negative affective interaction is an absorbing state for dissatisfied couples . . . it is a state that is difficult to exit once entered" (1998, p. 179).

Demand–Withdraw Pattern

One interaction style that is particularly characteristic of distressed marriages is the ***demand–withdraw pattern*** of communication (e.g., Heavey, Christensen, & Malamuth, 1995; Uebelacker, Courtnage, & Whisman, 2003; Wegner, 2005). In this pattern one partner desires change and approaches the other about it, while the other partner avoids confrontation and withdraws from the issue or conflict. Across methodologies, samples, and cultures, researchers consistently find that the demand–withdraw pattern is strongly and negatively correlated with concurrent measures of relationship satisfaction; that is, the more frequently partners indicate engaging in this interaction pattern (on self-report measures) or overtly display the pattern (in laboratory observations), the lower they score on measures of marital satisfaction, adjustment, and well-being (Christensen, Eldridge, Bokel Catta-Preta, Lim, & Santagata, 2006; Guay, Boisvert, & Freeston, 2003; for a review, see Eldridge & Christensen, 2002).

One of the most frequently investigated questions about the demand–withdraw pattern concerns the extent to which demanding and withdrawing behaviors are sex-linked (i.e., associated with an individual's biological sex). Although both men and women can and do take on the roles of demander and withdrawer during interaction, research with dating, cohabiting, and married couples demonstrates that women typically demand and men typically withdraw (Christensen & Heavey, 1990; Gottman & Levenson, 1988; see Eldridge & Christensen, 2002). However, recent investigations suggest that this sex difference is moderated by several other factors, including the couple's level of distress (a relationship factor), whose issue is being discussed (a situational or contextual factor), and even the cultural environment in which the couple resides (a broader social environmental factor).

A recent study conducted by Kathleen Eldridge and her colleagues (Eldridge, Sevier, Jones, Atkins, & Christensen, 2007) illustrates these findings. The participant sample included married couples who were either severely distressed (i.e., were seeking marital therapy and who scored in the severely distressed range on three different measures of marital satisfaction) or non-distressed (i.e., scored in the normal range on the marital satisfaction measures). Prior to participating in the laboratory portion of the study, each spouse received a list of common areas of couple conflict and selected the one area he or she found most dissatisfying in the marriage. Together, the spouses then engaged in a videotaped laboratory interaction in which they discussed each of these problematic marital issues—the one chosen by the husband and the one selected by the wife. The researchers assessed the extent of the demand–withdraw behavior that occurred during the interaction with a self-report measure administered to the participants immediately following their discussions and also via behavioral observation and coding of the videotapes. Analysis of the self-report and observational data revealed several significant results. First, not surprisingly, couples in the distressed group scored significantly higher than those in the non-distressed group on both measures of demand–withdraw. This finding replicates earlier research demonstrating an association between marital dissatisfaction and the occurrence of the demand–withdraw pattern during conflict. Second, although sex differences were clearly evident—in general (across the two discussions), wives demanded more than husbands, husbands withdrew more than wives, and the wife-demand/ husband-withdraw pattern occurred more frequently than did the husband-demand/wife-withdraw pattern—these sex differences were moderated both by the level of distress that characterized the couple and by the structure of the conflict (whose topic was under discussion). Specifically, as can be seen in Figure 15.1, the wife-demand/husband-withdraw pattern was more common than the husband-demand/wife-withdraw pattern only among couples in distressed marriages; the two patterns were equally likely to occur among non-distressed (happily married) couples. In addition,

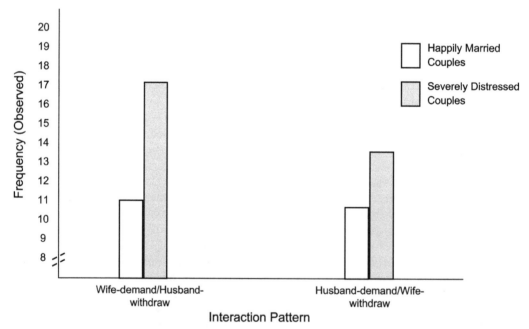

Fig. 15.1 Research reveals that the "typical" sex-linked demand–withdraw pattern tends to occur only among highly distressed couples. Specifically, laboratory investigations of conflict interactions demonstrate that the wife-demand/husband-withdraw pattern is more likely than the husband-demand/wife-withdraw pattern among unhappily married couples; both patterns occur with equal (and lower) frequency among happily married couples.

Source: Eldridge, K. A., Sevier, M., Jones, J., Atkins, D. C., & Christensen, A. (2007). Demand–withdraw communication in severely distressed, moderately distressed, and nondistressed couples: Rigidity and polarity during relationship and personal problem discussions. *Journal of Family Psychology, 21,* 218–226. Copyright © 2007 by the American Psychological Association. Data from Table 2, p. 222, used with permission.

the wife-demand/husband-withdraw pattern occurred more frequently than the husband-demand/wife-withdraw pattern among discussions of wife-chosen problem areas, whereas the two patterns were equally likely to occur among discussions of husband-chosen topics. In other words, as illustrated in Figure 15.2, wives demand (and husbands withdraw) more when the topic is one that is particularly important to the wife, and wives and husbands demand equally when the topic is one that is particularly important to the husband. Other relationship scientists have reported similar results (e.g., Christensen & Heavey, 1990; Heavey, Layne, & Christensen, 1993; Sagrestano, Christensen, & Heavey, 1998; Vogel & Karney, 2002).

Additional research suggests that the occurrence of demand and withdraw responses is also associated with the cultural context in which marriages are embedded. For example, Uzma Rehman and Amy Holtzworth-Munroe (2006) found that couples from Pakistan—a traditional, patriarchal culture characterized by rigid sex roles and inequitable distribution of power (e.g., financial, educational, political, legal) between the sexes—were less likely to engage in wife-demand/husband-withdraw behavior and more likely to display husband-demand/wife-withdraw behavior during a laboratory conflict interaction than were couples from the United States. Moreover, an analysis of each spouse's demanding behaviors revealed that the style in which demands were made changed as a function of cultural context. Both American wives and Pakistani husbands were more likely than their spouses to make aggressive demands (e.g., demands for change made in an angry, hostile, domineering, or contemptuous tone of voice). Pakistani wives, on the other hand, were more likely

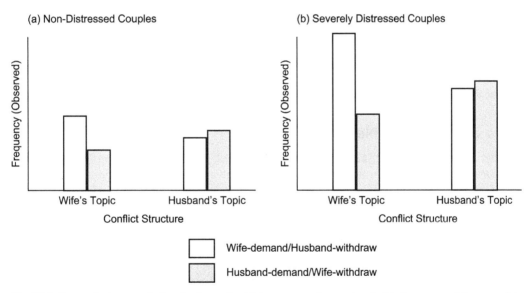

Fig. 15.2 Research also reveals that the demand–withdraw pattern is associated with the structural features of the conflict, including whose issue is being discussed. When the issue is one that is important to the wife, the wife-demand/husband-withdraw pattern occurs more frequently than the husband-demand/wife-withdraw pattern. However, when the issue is one that is important to the husband, both patterns are equally likely to occur (that is, husbands demand as often as wives). These results occur regardless of the couple's level of distress.

Source: Eldridge, K. A., Sevier, M., Jones, J., Atkins, D. C., & Christensen, A. (2007). Demand–withdraw communication in severely distressed, moderately distressed, and nondistressed couples: Rigidity and polarity during relationship and personal problem discussions. *Journal of Family Psychology, 21,* 218–226. Copyright © 2007 by the American Psychological Association. Figure 1 adapted with permission.

than their husbands and than American wives to make non-assertive demands (e.g., requests for change made in a flirtatious, seductive, or pleading manner). In discussing the results, the researchers concluded that demanding and withdrawing behaviors cannot be understood outside of the sociocultural context in which they occur:

> Our results suggest that some well-established findings in the marital literature (i.e., increasing levels of demand-withdraw are related to decreasing marital satisfaction) will apply even to relationships in very different cultures . . . On the other hand, our results suggest that other well-established findings in the marital literature (i.e., wives are more likely to be in the demanding role and husbands in the withdrawing role) may be culture-specific. Thus, it is vital that couples therapists recognize that the generalizability of much of what we know to be true regarding how couples communicate is unknown when one goes beyond the context of the Western world.
>
> (Rehman & Holtzworth-Munroe, 2006, p. 764)

The majority of research investigating the demand–withdraw pattern has been conducted with married (or otherwise romantically involved) couples. However, there is a small body of work focusing on family relationships. Some scholars have explored the demand–withdraw interaction pattern within the family system as a whole, finding that young (college-aged) adults who witness high levels of demand–withdraw behavior between their parents experience more symptoms indicative of mental distress (e.g., nervousness, worry, tension, irritability, depression, fatigue) and lower levels of satisfaction with their family relationships (Schrodt & Afifi, 2007). Similarly, parents and adolescents who report high levels of either parent-demand/child-withdraw or child-demand/parent-withdraw interaction behavior are less satisfied with the quality of their relationships than are parents and adolescents who report lower levels of demand–withdraw behavior (Caughlin & Malis, 2004).

Taken as a whole, these results demonstrate that demand–withdraw is one of the most destructive patterns of interaction in marriages and in families.

Ratio of Positive to Negative Behavior

Another factor that distinguishes unhappy from happy couples is the *ratio of positive to negative behavior* that they display during conflict or problem-solving discussions. A series of laboratory investigations conducted by Gottman and his colleagues (e.g., Gottman & Levenson, 1992) has consistently revealed that couples in stable, satisfying relationships typically engage in about five positive behaviors for every negative behavior—in other words, they show a 5:1 ratio of positive to negative affect and behavior in their interactions. Couples who are unhappy and prone to divorce, however, show a positive to negative ratio of 0.8:1 (i.e., slightly more negative than positive behavior).

Gottman's research suggests that couples may achieve the 5:1 ratio of positive to negative behavior in several different ways (Gottman, 1993; also see Bodenmann, Gottman, & Backman, 1997). For example, during disagreements, *volatile couples* tend to confront the conflict openly, argue heatedly, and spend most of their time enthusiastically trying to persuade one another about the validity of their own opinion or viewpoint. These couples are passionate and extremely emotionally expressive, and are more likely than other couples to display and to reciprocate both positive (e.g., affection, humor, interest) and negative (e.g., tension, anger) affect. They achieve the 5:1 ratio by engaging in high levels of intensely negative affective behavior and even higher levels of intensely positive affective behavior. The other couple types demonstrate less-frequent positive and negative affect and have more neutral interactions. Like volatile couples, ***validating couples*** also confront conflict and display emotion openly, but their discussions are characterized by less affective intensity and greater ease and calm. Recognition and support—though not necessarily endorsement—of the partner's feelings, statements, or description of a problem or issue is a fundamental theme in the interactions of these couples; indeed, in their conversations "there is often the sense that, although there is disagreement between them, they are both working together on a problem" (Gottman, 1993, p. 10). Validators achieve the 5:1 ratio by mixing a moderate amount of positive affect with a moderate but lower amount of negative affect. ***Avoider couples*** demonstrate the lowest levels of expressed emotion and the highest levels of neutral affect, essentially achieving the 5:1 ratio by avoiding negativity. These couples tend to minimize the importance of disagreement, feel that any differences they have are relatively easy to accept or ignore in light of their fundamental similarities, do not have specific conflict resolution strategies (e.g., they prefer to "let things work themselves out"), and make little effort to actively persuade each other or problem solve. Avoiders experience a great deal of calm interaction, but the result is a marriage characterized by some degree of emotional distance between the partners.

Regardless of how a couple achieves the "happy ratio," many clinical researchers and practitioners now believe that it is optimal for relationship well-being.

Failed Bids for Emotional Connection

How couples respond to each other during times of conflict obviously plays an important role in the overall health of their relationship. Interestingly, the seemingly trivial, mundane events that occur during their everyday interactions may be equally important. A growing number of relationship scholars have noted that partners often make an effort to establish intimacy and to connect with each other emotionally as they go about their daily lives and engage in their ordinary interactions (see Wile, 1993). For example, after examining hours of videotaped interactions between married couples, John Gottman and Janice Driver (2005) identified a variety of verbal and nonverbal ways in which partners demand emotional involvement from each other. These ***bids for emotional connection*** included:

- Bids for attention: "That's a strange-looking little dog over there."
- Bids for interest: "Doesn't your parents' dog look a little bit like that?"
- Bids for enthusiastic engagement: "Hey, maybe we should think about getting a dog."
- Bids for extended conversation: "Have you heard from your parents lately? The last time we saw them they were about to re-paint the house."
- Bids for play: [reaching out and tickling the partner] "I've been thinking about doing that all day!"
- Bids for humor: "That dog reminds me of a joke I heard. A poodle walks into a bar . . ."
- Bids for affection: [reaching for the partner's hand, etc.] "How about a kiss?"
- Bids for emotional support; "I'm kind of worried about my job. I don't think my new boss likes me."
- Bids for self-disclosure: "What is your favorite kind of dog—big or little?"

Partners can respond to each other's bids for emotional connection in three basic ways. First, they may display what Gottman and Driver (2005) called "turning toward" responses in which they react in an appropriate manner to the bid for connection; such responses can range from lower levels of acknowledgment (e.g., a grunt to indicate that they have heard the partner's statement or question) to wholehearted and enthusiastic replies. Second, partners may respond by "turning away" from the bid for connection. For example, they may simply ignore the other's statements or actions. And finally, partners may engage in "turning against" responses in which they display an irritable, hostile, or negative reaction to the bid for emotional connection (e.g., "Would you stop bothering me? I'm trying to read").

These everyday exchanges between partners may have important consequences for the health and well-being of their relationship. For example, partners who consistently acknowledge and respond positively to each other's bids for emotional connection may build up a reservoir of positive affect that can help them successfully weather stormy periods in their relationship. Partners with a history of failed bids for connection, however, may not have sufficient positive emotional reserves to fall back on when experiencing a major disagreement and thus may be more likely to use ineffective conflict resolution strategies. Indeed, in a series of studies Gottman and Driver (2005; Driver & Gottman, 2004) found that the more positive everyday moments that partners shared—for instance, the greater their frequency of playful bids for affection and enthusiastic responses to those bids—the more likely they were to display positive affect and humor during an argument. Conversely, the more often that partners turned away from each other's bids for emotional connection during everyday interactions, the more likely they were to display negative affective and behavioral responses during conflict (including criticism, contempt, defensiveness, and withdrawal). In discussing the results of their studies, the researchers concluded that it is important for relationship therapists to address not just how couples manage conflict but also how they respond to each other in their everyday interactions:

> Clinically, we are suggesting that the therapist specifically look with the couple at *failed bids for emotional connection* that happened during the week as well as conflicts that are upsetting to the couple. This suggests a therapeutic focus beyond the conflict context. . . . The bids and turning unit can help people become more attentive and mindful to this mundane part of their everyday relationship, to the everyday times when they are just "hanging out," when nothing important seems to be happening but when actually very important things are happening. It is our clinical experience that failed bids for connection and subsequent loneliness are a major source of marital conflict. Just helping a couple become mindful of these moments and investigating the "anatomies" of bidding and turning can provide insight that is capable of changing the nature of marital intimacy and the nature of conflict interactions as well.
>
> (Gottman & Driver, 2005, p. 76)

TREATING DISTRESSED RELATIONSHIPS

Not every couple who enters a therapist's office seeking help will actually receive it. Reputable clinicians and counselors will first take steps to determine whether the treatment approach they offer is likely to provide relief to the couple. In some cases, the answer will be "no" and the couple will be referred to another professional or encouraged to try a different form of treatment. For example, partners who are dealing with a sexual issue are often referred to a sex therapist. Couples whose relationships are characterized by alcohol, drug addiction, or physical violence also need immediate treatment from a professional who is trained to deal with those particular issues—physical abuse, in particular, is often a clear contra-indication for most of the therapies discussed below, including both integrative behavioral and emotionally focused therapies (see Dimidjian, Martell, & Christensen, 2008; Johnson, 2008). And some couples may not wish to repair their relationship but instead enter therapy in hopes of finding a way in which to end their partnership amicably; in those cases, referral to a legal, family, or mental health professional who specializes in relationship dissolution or divorce mediation is in order. However, assuming that the couple wishes to maintain the relationship and is not dealing with any of the specific problems previously mentioned, there are several different types of therapy available.

Behavioral Couple Therapy

Behavioral couple therapy (BCT) is based on the idea that the rewards and costs that partners experience in their interactions with each other determine how satisfied they are with their relationship (Simpson, Gattis, & Christensen, 2003). The goal of BCT is to modify partners' behavior using principles derived from social learning theory and social exchange theory. There are three major components of the typical BCT therapeutic program—*behavior exchange*, *communication training*, and *problem-solving training*. In behavior exchange, clients are taught to identify the partner behaviors they find desirable or offensive, to monitor their own and their partners' behaviors, to increase their awareness of the consequences of their own behavior, and to show appropriate acknowledgment of their partners' positive behavior. For example, the therapist might have each partner create a list of behaviors that he or she believes that the other would like, such as being complimented, receiving a gift, or getting a shoulder massage. The other partner rates those behaviors in terms of their desirability, and a set of highly rewarding or positive behaviors is generated for each spouse. The therapist then encourages the partners to engage in those positive actions—either by doing one or more each day or by setting aside a "caring day" to enact multiple behaviors—and provides appropriate assistance and support as needed.

BCT also involves teaching couples effective communication skills, including how to develop and make use of active listening skills and how to express themselves without blame and accusation. For example, members of a distressed couple might be instructed in how to replace statements that express blame and generalizations about the partner's behavior ("You never listen to me") with "I statements" that convey how the partner's behavior makes them feel ("When you don't answer me, it makes me feel as if I'm unimportant to you") and that contain specific requests ("It would make me happy if you would ask me about my day during dinner"). In addition to learning specific communication skills, couples receive training in effective problem solving, including how to clearly and concretely define problems and issues, how to collaboratively brainstorm and generate possible solutions to those issues, how to negotiate and compromise on possible solutions, how to actually implement the proposed solution, and how to evaluate the effectiveness of the solution.

Cognitive-Behavioral Couple Therapy

Cognitive-behavioral couple therapy (CBCT) grew out of the recognition that it is not just negative behavior that can create discord between relationship partners but also how they interpret that behavior and the meaning they place on it (e.g., Baucom & Epstein, 1990; Baucom, Epstein, & Rankin, 1995). In addition to traditional BCT techniques, CBCT uses *cognitive restructuring* to facilitate the partners' ability to recognize, systematically evaluate, and change their maladaptive cognitions, assumptions, and expectations about each other, their relationship, and relationships in general. For example, when clients make sweeping negative generalizations about their partners' behavior ("She never listens to me"), the therapist might ask them to search for exceptions ("Is it true that she really *never* listens to you? Can you think of one instance when she did?"). When clients make negative attributions about their partners' behavior ("I had a bad headache—I just needed some peace and quiet and he had the music turned up even though I was clearly feeling ill"), the therapist might challenge them to seek an alternative explanation for the same behavior ("Is it possible that he didn't know you had a headache? Did you directly communicate this information to him?"). And the therapist might help clients identify the unrealistic standards and beliefs they hold about relationships (see Chapter 8)—such as the assumption that "People who love each other never argue"—and then assist them in replacing these standards with more realistic expectations ("Conflict occurs in even the most loving and stable of relationships").

Integrative Behavioral Couple Therapy

The most recent adaptation of BCT is called *integrative behavioral couple therapy* (IBCT). This therapeutic approach was developed by Neil Jacobson and Andrew Christensen (1996; Christensen & Jacobson, 2000; Jacobson, Christensen, Prince, Cordova, & Eldridge, 2000) after they observed that many couples experience issues, problems, or incompatibilities that are not amenable to change and thus cannot readily be resolved (and indeed are often exacerbated) by traditional BCT and CBCT approaches, which focus on change as the primary mechanism for the alleviation of distress. IBCT often is referred to as "acceptance therapy" because it integrates the basic premises and behavioral and cognitive techniques of BCT and CBCT with strategies that are designed to promote the partners' acceptance of each other's entire personality as well as tolerance of each other's behavior:

> Acceptance is not a grudging resignation about the state of one's relationship. It is not a woeful surrender to a miserable status quo. In contrast, acceptance provides a hopeful alternative to couples faced with problems that are not amenable to typical change strategies. Moreover, acceptance can also provide a method by which couples use problems—once experienced as divisive and damaging—as vehicles for greater intimacy and closeness.
>
> (Dimidjian et al., 2008, p. 74)

The goal of acceptance therapy is for partners to learn how to change their expectations about the relationship and the partner, modify their behavior to better meet each other's needs, improve their communication and problem-solving skills, and learn how to better accept each other's total personalities and better tolerate any differences that cannot easily be overcome. Consequently, IBCT therapists use traditional behaviorally oriented techniques (e.g., behavior exchange, communication skills and problem-solving training) coupled with techniques specifically designed to increase acceptance and tolerance. For example, one *acceptance technique* therapists commonly use is to encourage couples to replace *hard disclosures* that convey anger and resentment and place the speaker in the dominant role (e.g., "You never take the time to ask me about how my day went. You think only of yourself. You are so incredibly selfish. I am so sick and tired of this") with *soft disclosures* that express the vulnerability and hurt hiding behind the anger (e.g., "I feel like my needs don't matter in this relationship. Like what I do and how I spend my time isn't important. Sometimes I feel unappreciated and really alone"). By allowing both partners to feel as if they are being heard by one another in an atmosphere of neutrality and empathy rather than one of dominance, blame, and anger, this technique encourages mutual acceptance. Additionally, therapists utilize *tolerance strategies*—including pointing out the positive features of negative partner behavior and having couples practice negative behavior during therapy sessions—to desensitize the partners to each other's negative behavior and to sensitize them to the impact of their own negative behavior.

Emotionally Focused Couple Therapy

In contrast to the behavioral therapies previously discussed, *emotionally focused couple therapy* (ECT) is rooted in principles of attachment theory, including the basic premise that all people possess an innate need to form strong, intimate, warm bonds to particular individuals and that failure to meet this need and/or disruption of these bonds will produce distress (see Chapter 3). Developed by Leslie Greenberg and Susan Johnson (1988; Johnson, 2004, 2008; Johnson & Greenberg, 1995), ECT recognizes that the partner functions as a primary and important attachment figure, and that negative relationship events and the emotions that accompany these events thus often reflect the operation of underlying attachment-related issues. For example, one of the reasons that people respond to a partner's expressions of contempt with anguish and diminished feelings of relational well-being is in part because such expressions directly convey that the partner considers them unworthy of love, affection, and care. Similarly, interaction patterns that reflect absence and/or a failure or unwillingness to respond to a partner's needs—such as withdrawal or stonewalling—increase separation distress and threaten attachment security. Other rigid interaction patterns, like the demand–withdraw pattern, also maintain feelings of insecurity and make it difficult for the partners to experience emotional bonding.

The goal of ECT is to enable the partners to achieve a secure attachment bond characterized by mutual emotional accessibility and responsiveness. In therapy, partners are encouraged to identify and express their underlying needs, expectations, and emotional experiences (such as their expectations about partner caregiving and fears about partner abandonment). As the therapeutic process progresses, the partners gain valuable information about themselves and each other, and are then able, with the help of the therapist, to develop interaction patterns that are more likely to satisfy their underlying attachment needs. They may even create "attachment rituals" designed to soothe each other or connect after time apart (Johnson, 2009). For example, the therapist might help Deborah, who is angry and hurt because her husband Jim has chosen to return to work after years of retirement, recognize and access her underlying fear of abandonment and then express this fear directly to Jim, rather than her surface anger and hurt ("I feel that you don't want to be with me—that your decision to go back to work means that you aren't happy at home. I need reassurance that I matter to you, that you need me, and that you aren't turning away from me. I feel alone in this marriage and that scares me.") Once he recognizes that fear is at the root of Deborah's anger and upset, Jim might be able to respond with greater support and caring and less defensiveness and withdrawal ("I do have a tendency to shut you out. I didn't realize that you were lonely and that my returning to work made you feel unloved and abandoned. I just saw you as critical and angry all the time—I didn't see your hurt and sadness. I want to be close to you, but I enjoy working and I need you to understand that it doesn't mean I don't want to be with you."). Together, the two of them may establish a more functional interaction pattern that better meets their basic attachment needs.

DOES THERAPY WORK?

Clinical researchers have attempted to address the question of whether couple therapy "works" in a number of ways. The most common method involves comparing distressed couples who receive therapy with distressed couples who do not receive therapy on various measures of well-being and adjustment. If the couples who received therapy (the treatment group) score significantly higher on measures of satisfaction or significantly lower on measures of distress than the couples who did not receive therapy (the no-treatment control group), then the researchers can conclude that therapy is effective. The results of studies that have employed this type of comparison consistently reveal that therapy is better than no therapy at all; that is, treatment couples generally show less distress and better overall adjustment than control group couples (e.g., Baucom, Hahlweg, & Kuschel, 2003; Dunn & Schwebel, 1995; Shadish & Baldwin, 2005).

However, in their exhaustive review of the marital therapy literature, Andrew Christensen and Christopher Heavey (1999) observed that simply demonstrating that there is a statistically significant difference between treatment couples and control group couples does not provide conclusive evidence that therapy is effective. For example, it is possible for the couples who received treatment to be less distressed than the couples who did not and yet still show significant levels of dysfunction; in other words, although the therapy has improved their situation relative to the control group, it has not fully alleviated their distress. Consequently, it is important to assess therapeutic effectiveness by evaluating treatment couples against an absolute standard—such as whether they obtain satisfaction, adjustment, or well-being scores in the "normal" range following treatment—rather than by simply comparing their scores to those of a control group. (See Chapter 2 for additional discussion of the distinction between statistical and practical significance.)

It is equally important to assess how long any therapy-induced improvements can be expected to last. Behavioral couple therapy has received the most attention and its positive effects have been the most thoroughly documented (e.g., Hahlweg & Markman, 1988; Shadish & Baldwin, 2005). For example, a meta-analysis of treatment outcome studies conducted by Michael Byrne, Alan Carr, and Marie Clark (2004) revealed that BCT significantly improved relationship satisfaction in 66% of couples, with 62% falling in the non-distressed range and about half (54%) maintaining these gains over follow-up periods lasting from 6 months to 4 years after treatment. Similar results were found for emotionally focused couple therapy. Specifically, 73% of couples who received ECT demonstrated significant increases in relationship satisfaction following treatment, with 51% falling in the non-distressed range and 53% continuing to exhibit recovery (i.e., non-distress) 2 months to 2 years later. In interpreting these findings it is important to recognize that most of the existing research has focused on middle-class, heterosexual couples involved in their first marriages. Thus little is known about the overall effectiveness of couple therapy in other types of relationships.

In addition to examining the average rates of improvement and/or recovery among couples who have completed therapy, several relationship scholars have sought to map the typical trajectory or pattern of recovery that couples experience while undergoing therapy. Does improvement occur gradually, for example, over the course of a therapeutic program or do couples experience surges early or late in treatment? To explore this question, Christensen and his colleagues (e.g., Christensen et al., 2004; Christensen, Atkins, Yi, Baucom, & George, 2006) conducted a longitudinal investigation in which 134 severely and chronically distressed married couples were randomly assigned to receive either traditional behavioral couple therapy or integrative behavioral couple therapy for a maximum of 26 sessions (on average, couples participated in 23 sessions spread across a period of 9 months). Assessments of relationship adjustment were taken throughout the intervention process, beginning with the couple's initial intake session, then again at 13 weeks and 26 weeks, and finally during the last therapy session. After the termination of therapy, four additional follow-up assessments were made at approximately 6, 12, 18, and 24 months.

The results revealed that the two groups of couples did not differ in overall adjustment following completion of their respective courses of therapy—both traditional and integrative behavioral therapies produced significant and equal improvements in couples' level of marital satisfaction. However, as illustrated in Figure 15.3, the trajectory of the two groups' change in satisfaction—that

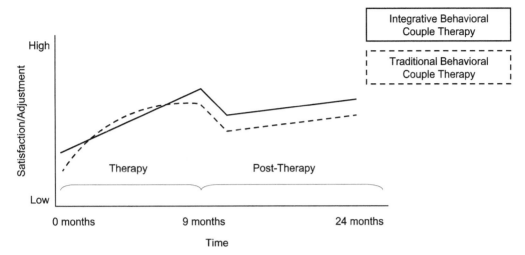

Fig. 15.3 Longitudinal research reveals different satisfaction trajectories among couples who receive traditional behavioral therapy and those who receive integrative behavioral therapy. Specifically, traditional behavioral couple therapy tends to produce rapid initial gains in satisfaction which then plateau later on in treatment, whereas integrative behavioral couple therapy produces slow but steady improvement over the entire course of treatment. Regardless of which therapy they have received, most couples experience a fairly sharp reduction in adjustment immediately following the termination of treatment, and then slow improvements in functioning over time.

Sources: (1) Christensen, A., Atkins, D. C., Berns, S., Wheeler, J., Baucom, D. H., & Simpson, L. E. (2004). Traditional versus integrative behavioral couple therapy for significantly and chronically distressed married couples. *Journal of Consulting and Clinical Psychology, 72,* 176–191. Copyright © 2004 by the American Psychological Association. Figure 1 adapted with permission. (2) Christensen, A., Atkins, D. C., Yi, J., Baucom, D. H., & George, W. H. (2006). Couple and individual adjustment for 2 years following a randomized clinical trial comparing traditional versus integrative behavioral couple therapy. *Journal of Consulting and Clinical Psychology, 74,* 1180–1191. Copyright © 2006 by the American Psychological Association. Figure 2 adapted with permission.

is, *how* the couples changed over time—was significantly different. Couples who received traditional behavioral couple therapy tended to improve rapidly early on in treatment but then experienced a plateau or leveling off in their level of satisfaction, whereas those who received integrative behavioral couple therapy demonstrated slow but steady improvement over the course of therapy. Analysis of the post-treatment, follow-up data revealed what the researchers labeled a "hockey stick shape" trajectory of change for both sets of couples such that satisfaction sharply decreased immediately after the conclusion of therapy and then gradually increased over the following 2 years. As noted by these researchers and others (e.g., Halford, 2001), the initial rapid increase in adjustment experienced by couples who received traditional behavioral therapy is likely the result of the emphasis on behavior exchange that characterizes the early stages of this type of therapy; behavior exchange techniques immediately increase the number of positive actions partners display toward each other and thus may produce an initial "boost" of satisfaction. Later on in therapy, as couples focus on their more enduring and intractable problems, the initial increase in satisfaction may level off. In contrast, integrative couple therapy tends to focus immediately on enduring and intractable problems; such therapy is unlikely to produce a quick boost of well-being but instead leads to slow and steady improvement over time.

SUMMARY

The decision to form a long-term partnership with another individual is one of the most significant decisions that any person will make in the course of his or her life. For this reason, it is essential for couples (and family members) to be able to find effective treatment when they experience distress. Therapists and clinical researchers have successfully identified a number of dysfunctional behaviors that can adversely impact relationship well-being. In addition they have developed several different types of therapeutic interventions that may help couples modify their behavior and increase their satisfaction. Although not all couples or families will benefit from therapy, research generally reveals that most interventions are moderately successful, at least in the short term.

KEY CONCEPTS

Criticism (p. 274)
Contempt (p. 275)
Defensiveness (p. 275)
Withdrawal or stonewalling (p. 275)
Negative affect reciprocity (p. 276)
Repair attempts (p. 276)
Demand–withdraw pattern (p. 277)
Ratio of positive to negative behavior (p. 280)
Volatile couples (p. 280)
Validating couples (p. 281)
Avoider couples (p. 281)
Bids for emotional connection (p. 281)

Behavioral couple therapy (p. 283)
Behavior exchange (p. 283)
Communication training (p. 283)
Problem-solving training (p. 283)
Cognitive-behavioral couple therapy (p. 283)
Cognitive restructuring (p. 283)
Integrative behavioral couple therapy (p. 284)
Acceptance techniques (p. 284)
Hard disclosures (p. 284)
Soft disclosures (p. 284)
Tolerance strategies (p. 284)
Emotionally focused couple therapy (p. 285)

EXPLORATION EXERCISES

These exercises are designed to allow you to explore in greater detail some of the concepts and issues discussed in this chapter. There are no right or wrong answers to these exercises—they are simply meant to provide an opportunity for discussion and debate.

1. Partners in even the most satisfying, well-adjusted, healthy relationship sometimes engage in destructive interaction behaviors (particularly during times of conflict). Using one of your own relationships, give a specific example (if you can) of a time in which you or your partner displayed each of the four dysfunctional interaction behaviors described in the textbook.
2. Working with a classmate or two, come up with specific examples of the various bids for emotional connection outlined in this chapter. What purpose do these bids serve in our close relationships? Think of a time when you made a bid for emotional connection and your partner did not respond in an appropriate or positive manner. How did this make you feel? Think of another time in which your partner did respond positively and appropriately to your bid for emotional connection. How did this make you feel? Compare and contrast those two different experiences.
3. If you were involved in a distressed relationship, and you had to choose one and only one type of therapy to enter with your partner, which one would you choose? Why? Discuss your choice with your classmates.

References

Abbey, A. (1982). Sex differences in attributions for friendly behavior: Do males misperceive females' friendliness? *Journal of Personality and Social Psychology, 42*, 830–838.

Abbey, A. (1987). Misperceptions of friendly behavior as sexual interest: A survey of naturally occurring incidents. *Psychology of Women Quarterly, 11*, 173–194.

Abbey, A., & Melby, C. (1986). The effects of nonverbal cues on gender differences in perceptions of sexual intent. *Sex Roles, 15*, 283–298.

Abrahams, M. F. (1994). Perceiving flirtatious communication: An exploration of the perceptual dimensions underlying judgments of flirtatiousness. *Journal of Sex Research, 31*, 283–292.

Adams, A., & Crawford, N. (1992). *Bullying at work: How to confront and overcome it*. London: Virago Press.

Adams, J. S. (1965). Inequity in social exchange. In L. Berkowitz (Ed.), *Advances in experimental social psychology* (Vol. 2, pp. 267–299). New York: Academic Press.

Adams, R. E., & Laursen, B. (2007). The correlates of conflict: Disagreement is not necessarily detrimental. *Journal of Family Psychology, 21*, 445–458.

Afifi, W. A., Falato, W. L., & Weiner, J. L. (2001). Identity concerns following a severe relational transgression: The role of discovery method for the relational outcomes of infidelity. *Journal of Social and Personal Relationships, 18*, 291–308.

Ah, sweet mystery. (1975, March 24). *Time*. Retrieved July 3, 2008 from http://www.time.com/time/magazine

Ainsworth, M. D. S., Blehar, M. C., Waters, E., & Wall, S. (1978). *Patterns of attachment: A psychological study of the strange situation*. Hillsdale, NJ: Lawrence Erlbaum Associates Inc.

Al-Krenawi, A., & Graham, J. R. (2006). A comparison of family functioning, life and marital satisfaction, and mental health of women in polygamous and monogamous marriages. *International Journal of Social Psychiatry, 52*, 5–17.

Allan, G. (2008). Flexibility, friendship, and family. *Personal Relationships, 15*, 1–16.

Allen, E. S., Kline Rhoades, G., Stanley, S. M., Markman, H. J., Williams, T., Melton, J., & Clements, M. L. (2008). Premarital precursors of marital infidelity. *Family Process, 47*, 243–259.

Allen, K. (2009). Pet–human relationships. In H. T. Reis & S. K. Sprecher (Eds.), *Encyclopedia of human relationships* (Vol. 3, pp. 1234–1237). Thousand Oaks, CA: Sage Publications.

Allison, B. N., & Schultz, J. B. (2004). Parent-adolescent conflict in early adolescence. *Adolescence, 39,* 101–119.

Altman, I., & Taylor, D. A. (1973). *Social penetration: The development of interpersonal relationships.* New York: Holt, Rinehart & Winston.

Amar, A. F. (2006). College women's experiences of stalking: Mental health symptoms and changes in routine. *Archives of Psychiatric Nursing, 20,* 108–116.

Amato, P. R., & Irving, S. (2006). Historical trends in divorce in the United States. In M. A. Fine & J. H. Harvey (Eds.), *Handbook of divorce and dissolution* (pp. 41–57). Mahwah, NJ: Lawrence Erlbaum Associates Inc.

Amato, P. R., Johnson, D. R., Booth, A., & Rogers, S. J. (2003). Continuity and change in marital quality between 1980 and 2000. *Journal of Marriage and Family, 65,* 1–22.

Amato, P. R., & Rogers, S. J. (1997). A longitudinal study of marital problems and subsequent divorce. *Journal of Marriage and the Family, 59,* 612–624.

American Psychological Association. (2002). *Ethical principles of psychologists and code of conduct.* Retrieved July 13, 2008, from http://www.apa.org/ethics/code2002.html

American Sociological Association (1999). *Code of ethics and policies and procedures of the ASA Committee on Professional Ethics.* Washington, DC: American Sociological Association.

Anderson, T. L. (2005). Relationships among Internet attitudes, Internet use, romantic beliefs, and perceptions of online romantic relationships. *CyberPsychology & Behavior, 8,* 521–531.

Archer, J. (2000). Sex differences in aggression between heterosexual partners: A meta-analysis. *Psychological Bulletin, 126,* 651–680.

Archer, J. (2002). Sex differences in physically aggressive acts between heterosexual partners: A meta-analytic review. *Aggression and Violent Behavior, 7,* 313–351.

Arnett, J. L., Prosen, H., & Toews, J. A. (1986). Loss of libido due to stress. *Medical Aspects of Human Sexuality, 20,* 140–148.

Aron, A., & Aron, E. N. (1996). Self and self-expansion in relationships. In G. J. O. Fletcher & J. Fitness (Eds.), *Knowledge structures in close relationships: A social psychological approach* (pp. 325–344). Mahwah, NJ: Lawrence Erlbaum Associates Inc.

Aron, A., Aron, E. N., & Smollan, D. (1992). Inclusion of Other in the Self Scale and the structure of interpersonal closeness. *Journal of Personality and Social Psychology, 63,* 596–612.

Aron, A., Fisher, H., Mashek, D. J., Strong, G., Li, H., & Brown, L. L. (2005). Reward, motivation, and emotion systems associated with early-stage intense romantic love. *Journal of Neurophysiology, 94,* 327–337.

Aron, A. P., Mashek, D. J., & Aron, E. N. (2004). Closeness as including other in the self. In D. Mashek & A. Aron (Eds.), *Handbook of closeness and intimacy* (pp. 27–41). Mahwah, NJ: Lawrence Erlbaum Associates Inc.

Arora, T. (1994). Measuring bullying with the "life in school" checklist. *Pastoral Care, 12,* 11–16.

Arriaga, X. B., Agnew, C. R., Capezza, N. M., & Lehmiller, J. J. (2008). The social and physical environment of relationship initiation: An interdependence analysis. In S. Sprecher, A. Wenzel, & J. Harvey (Eds.), *Handbook of relationship initiation* (pp. 197–215). New York: Psychology Press.

Artis, J. E., & Pavalko, E. K. (2003). Explaining the decline in women's household labor: Individual change and cohort effects. *Journal of Marriage and Family, 65,* 746–761.

Atkins, D. C., Baucom, D. H., & Jacobson, N. S. (2001). Understanding infidelity: Correlates in a national random sample. *Journal of Family Psychology, 15,* 735–749.

Attridge, M., & Berscheid, E. (1994). Entitlement in romantic relationships in the United States: A social exchange perspective. In M. J. Lerner & G. Mikula (Eds.), *Entitlement and the affectional bond: Justice in close relationships* (pp. 117–148). New York: Plenum.

Ault, L. K., & Philhower, C. (2001, July). *Allergen avoidance: Qualities in romantic partners that are shunned by lovers and their parents.* Paper presented at the joint conference of the International Network on Personal Relationships and the International Society for the Study of Personal Relationships, Prescott, AZ.

Avery, A., Chase, J., Johansson, L., Litvak, S., Montero, D., & Wydra, M. (2007). America's changing attitudes toward homosexuality, civil unions, and same-gender marriage: 1977–2004. *Social Work, 52*, 71–79.

Bachman, G. F., & Bippus, A. M. (2005). Evaluations of supportive messages provided by friends and romantic partners: An attachment theory approach. *Communication Reports, 18*, 85–94.

Bachman, G. F., & Guerrero, L. K. (2006). Relational quality and communicative responses following hurtful events in dating relationships: An expectancy violations analysis. *Journal of Social and Personal Relationships, 23*, 943–963.

Bachman, R., & Carmody, D. C. (1994). Fighting fire with fire: The effects of victim resistance in intimate versus stranger perpetrated assaults against females. *Journal of Family Violence, 9*, 317–331.

Bachman, R., Saltzman, L. E., Thompson, M. P., & Carmody, D. C. (2002). Disentangling the effects of self-protective behaviors on the risk of injury in assaults against women. *Journal of Quantitative Criminology, 18*, 135–157.

Bakeman, R., & Gottman, J. M. (1997). *Observing interaction: An introduction to sequential analysis* (2nd ed.). New York: Cambridge University Press.

Bakermans-Kranenburg, M. J., van IJzendoorn, M. H., & Juffer, F. (2003). Less is more: Meta-analyses of sensitivity and attachment interventions in early childhood. *Psychological Bulletin, 129*, 195–215.

Baldwin, M. W. (1992). Relational schemas and the processing of social information. *Psychological Bulletin, 112*, 461–484.

Baldwin, M. W. (1995). Relational schemas and cognition in close relationships. *Journal of Social and Personal Relationships, 12*, 547–552.

Bank, B. J., & Hansford, S. L. (2000). Gender and friendship: Why are men's best same-sex friendships less intimate and supportive? *Personal Relationships, 7*, 63–78.

Barbee, A. P., & Cunningham, M. R. (1995). An experimental approach to social support communication: Interactive coping in close relationships. *Communication Yearbook, 18*, 381–413.

Barbee, A. P., Rowatt, T. L., & Cunningham, M. R. (1998). When a friend is in need: Feelings about seeking, giving, and receiving social support. In P. A. Andersen & L. K. Guerrero (Eds.), *Handbook of communication and emotion: Research, theory, applications, and contexts* (pp. 281–301). Orlando, FL: Academic Press.

Barelds, D. P. H. (2005). Self and partner personality in intimate relationships. *European Journal of Personality, 19*, 501–518.

Barelds, D. P. H., & Barelds-Dijkstra, P. (2006). Partner personality in distressed relationships. *Clinical Psychology and Psychotherapy, 13*, 392–396.

Barelds, D. P. H., & Dijkstra, P. (2009). Positive illusions about a partner's physical attractiveness and relationship quality. *Personal Relationships, 16*, 263–283.

Baringer, D. K., & McCroskey, J. C. (2000). Immediacy in the classroom: Student immediacy. *Communication Education, 49*, 178–186.

Barnes, L. L., de Leon, C. F. M., Wilson, R. S., Bienias, J. L., & Evans, D. A. (2004). Social resources and cognitive decline in a population of older African Americans and whites. *Neurology, 63*, 2322–2326.

Baron-Cohen, S., Wheelwright, S., & Jolliffe, T. (1997). Is there a "language of the eyes"? Evidence from normal adults, and adults with autism or Asperger syndrome. *Visual Cognition, 4*, 311–331.

Barry, R. A., Lawrence, E., & Langer, A. (2008). Conceptualization and assessment of disengagement in romantic relationships. *Personal Relationships, 15*, 297–315.

Barta, W. D., & Kiene, S. M. (2005). Motivations for infidelity in heterosexual dating couples: The roles of gender, personality differences, and sociosexual orientation. *Journal of Social and Personal Relationships, 22*, 339–360.

Bartholomew, K., & Horowitz, L. M. (1991). Attachment styles among young adults: A test of a four-category model. *Journal of Personality and Social Psychology, 61*, 226–244.

Basile, K. C., Arias, I., Desai, S., & Thompson, M. P. (2004). The differential association of intimate partner physical, sexual, psychological, and stalking violence and posttraumatic stress symptoms in a nationally representative sample of women. *Journal of Traumatic Stress, 17*, 413–421.

Batki, A., Baron-Cohen, S., Wheelwright, S., Connellan, J., & Ahluwalia, J. (2000). Is there an innate gaze module? Evidence from human neonates. *Infant Behavior & Development, 23*, 223–229.

Battaglia, D. M., Richard, F. D., Datteri, D. L., & Lord, C. G. (1998). Breaking up is (relatively) easy to do: A script for the dissolution of close relationships. *Journal of Social and Personal Relationships, 15*, 829–845.

Baucom, D. H., & Epstein, N. (1990). *Cognitive-behavioral marital therapy*. New York: Brunner/Mazel.

Baucom, D. H., Epstein, N., & Rankin, L. A. (1995). Cognitive aspects of cognitive-behavioral marital therapy. In N. S. Jacobson & A. S. Gurman (Eds.), *Clinical handbook of couple therapy* (pp. 65–90). New York: Guilford Press.

Baucom, D. H., Hahlweg, K., & Kuschel, A. (2003). Are waiting-list control groups needed in future marital therapy outcome research? *Behavior Therapy, 34*, 179–188.

Baumeister, R. F., Brewer, L. E., Tice, D. M., & Twenge, J. M. (2007). Thwarting the need to belong: Understanding the interpersonal and inner effects of social exclusion. *Social and Personality Psychology Compass, 1*, 506–520.

Baumeister, R. F., & Leary, M. R. (1995). The need to belong: Desire for interpersonal attachments as a fundamental human motivation. *Psychological Bulletin, 117*, 497–529.

Baumeister, R. F., & Wotman, S. R. (1992). *Breaking hearts: The two sides of unrequited love*. New York: Guilford Press.

Baumeister, R. F., Wotman, S. R., & Stillwell, A. M. (1993). Unrequited love: On heartbreak, anger, guilt, scriptlessness, and humiliation. *Journal of Personality and Social Psychology, 64*, 377–394.

Bauminger, N., Finzi-Dottan, R., Chason, S., & Har-Even, D. (2008). Intimacy in adolescent friendship: The roles of attachment, coherence, and self-disclosure. *Journal of Social and Personal Relationships, 25*, 409–428.

Baumrind, D. (1983). Specious causal attributions in the social sciences: The reformulated stepping-stone theory of heroin use as an exemplar. *Journal of Personality and Social Psychology, 45*, 1289–1298.

Baxter, J. (2005). To marry or not to marry: Marital status and the household division of labor. *Journal of Family Issues, 26*, 300–321.

Baxter, L. A. (1985). Accomplishing relationship disengagement. In S. Duck & D. Perlman (Eds.), *Understanding personal relationships: An interdisciplinary approach* (pp. 243–265). London: Sage Publications.

Baxter, L. A., & Bullis, C. (1986). Turning points in developing romantic relationships. *Human Communication Research, 12*, 469–493.

Baxter, L. A., Dun, T., & Sahlstein, E. (2001). Rules for relating communicated among social network members. *Journal of Social and Personal Relationships, 18*, 173–199.

Baxter, L. A., & Pittman, G. (2001). Communicatively remembering turning points of relational development in heterosexual romantic relationships. *Communication Reports, 14*, 1–17.

Beaver, E. D., Gold, S. R., & Prisco, A. G. (1992). Priming macho attitudes and emotions. *Journal of Interpersonal Violence, 7*, 321–333.

Beckwith, L., & Rodning, C. (1996). Dyadic processes between mothers and preterm infants: Development at ages 2 to 5 years. *Infant Mental Health Journal, 17*, 322–333.

Belsky, J. (1990). Children and marriage. In F. D. Fincham & T. N. Bradbury (Eds.), *The psychology of marriage: Basic issues and applications* (pp.172–200). New York: Guilford Press.

Belsky, J. (2009). Parenthood, transition to. In H. T. Reis & S. K. Sprecher (Eds.), *Encyclopedia of human relationships* (Vol. 3, pp. 1204–1207). Thousand Oaks, CA: Sage Publications.

Ben-Ari, A., & Lavee, Y. (2007). Dyadic closeness in marriage: From the inside story to a conceptual model. *Journal of Social and Personal Relationships, 24*, 627–644.

Bender, L. (1948). Genesis of hostility in children. *American Journal of Psychiatry, 105*, 241–245.

Beres, M. A., Herold, E., & Maitland, S. B. (2004). Sexual consent behaviors in same-sex relationships. *Archives of Sexual Behavior, 33*, 475–486.

Berkman, L. F. (1995). The role of social relations in health promotion. *Psychosomatic Medicine, 57*, 245–254.

Berman, M. I., & Frazier, P. A. (2005). Relationship power and betrayal experience as predictors of reactions to infidelity. *Personality and Social Psychology Bulletin, 31*, 1617–1627.

Berry, D. S., Willingham, J. K., & Thayer, C. A. (2000). Affect and personality as predictors of conflict and closeness in young adults' friendships. *Journal of Research in Personality, 34*, 84–107.

Berscheid, E. (1985). Interpersonal attraction. In G. Lindzey & E. Aronson (Eds.), *The handbook of social psychology* (3rd ed., Vol. 2, pp. 413–484). New York: Random House.

Berscheid, E. (1986). Mea culpas and lamentations: Sir Francis, Sir Isaac, and "the slow progress of soft psychology." In R. Gilmour & S. Duck (Eds.), *The emerging field of personal relationships* (pp. 267–286). Hillsdale, NJ: Lawrence Erlbaum Associates Inc.

Berscheid, E. (1988). Some comments on love's anatomy: Or, whatever happened to old-fashioned lust? In R. J. Sternberg & M. L. Barnes (Eds.), *The psychology of love* (pp. 359–374). New Haven, CT: Yale University Press.

Berscheid, E. (2002). On stepping on land mines. In R. J. Sternberg (Ed.), *Psychologists defying the crowd: Stories of those who battled the establishment and won* (pp. 32–45). Washington, DC: American Psychological Association.

Berscheid, E., & Campbell, B. (1981). The changing longevity of heterosexual close relationships. In M. J. Lerner & S. C. Lerner (Eds.), *The justice motive in social behavior* (pp. 209–234). New York: Plenum Press.

Berscheid, E., Graziano, W., Monson, T., & Dermer, M. (1976). Outcome dependency: Attention, attribution and attraction. *Journal of Personality and Social Psychology, 34*, 978–989.

Berscheid, E., & Peplau, L. A. (1983). The emerging science of relationships. In H. H. Kelley, E. Berscheid, A. Christensen, J. H. Harvey, T. L. Huston, G. Levinger, E. McClintock, L. A. Peplau, & D. R. Peterson (Eds.), *Close relationships* (pp. 1–19). New York: W. H. Freeman & Company.

Berscheid, E., & Regan, P. (2005). *The psychology of interpersonal relationships*. Mahwah, NJ: Prentice-Hall.

Berscheid, E., & Reis, H. T. (1998). Attraction and close relationships. In D. T. Gilbert, S. T. Fiske, & G. Lindzey (Eds.), *The handbook of social psychology* (4th ed., Vol. 2, pp. 193–281). Boston, MA: McGraw-Hill.

Berscheid, E., Snyder, M., & Omoto, A. M. (1989a). Issues in studying relationships: Conceptualizing and measuring closeness. In C. Hendrick (Ed.), *Close relationships: Vol. 10. Review of personality and social psychology* (pp. 63–91). Newbury Park, CA: Sage Publications.

Berscheid, E., Snyder, M., & Omoto, A. M. (1989b). The Relationship Closeness Inventory: Assessing the closeness of interpersonal relationships. *Journal of Personality and Social Psychology, 57*, 792–807.

Berscheid, E., Snyder, M., & Omoto, A. M. (2004). Measuring closeness: The Relationship Closeness Inventory (RCI) revisited. In D. Mashek & A. Aron (Eds.), *Handbook of closeness and intimacy* (pp. 81–101). Mahwah, NJ: Lawrence Erlbaum Associates Inc.

Berscheid, E., & Walster, E. (1974). A little bit about love. In T. L. Huston (Ed.), *Foundations of interpersonal attraction* (pp. 355–381). New York: Academic Press.

Bertoncini, J., Floccia, C., Nazzi, T., & Mehler, J. (1995). Morae and syllables: Rhythmical basis of speech representations in neonates. *Language and Speech, 38*, 311–329.

Bettor, L., Hendrick, S. S., & Hendrick, C. (1995). Gender and sexual standards in dating relationships. *Personal Relationships, 2*, 359–369.

Betzig, L. (1989). Causes of conjugal dissolution: A cross-cultural study. *Current Anthropology, 30*, 654–676.

Biernat, M., & Wortman, C. B. (1991). Sharing of home responsibilities between professionally employed women and their husbands. *Journal of Personality and Social Psychology, 60*, 844–860.

Bijeljac-Babic, R., Bertoncini, J., & Mehler, J. (1993). How do 4-day-old infants categorize multisyllabic utterances? *Developmental Psychology, 29*, 711–721.

Bjorklund, D. F., & Pellegrini, A. D. (2002). Prepared to learn. In D. F. Bjorklund & A. D. Pellegrini (Eds.), *The origins of human nature: Evolutionary developmental psychology* (pp. 147–191). Washington, DC: American Psychological Association.

Blackwell, D. L., & Lichter, D. T. (2004). Homogamy among dating, cohabiting, and married couples. *Sociological Quarterly, 45*, 719–737.

Blair, S. L., & Johnson, M. P. (1992). Wives' perceptions of the fairness of the division of household labor: The intersection of housework and ideology. *Journal of Marriage & the Family, 54*, 570–581.

Blieszner, R., & Adams, R. G. (1992). *Adult friendship*. Newbury Park, CA: Sage Publications.

Blood, R. O. Jr., & Wolfe, D. M. (1960). *Husbands and wives: The dynamics of married living*. Glencoe, IL: Free Press.

Blumstein, P., & Schwartz, P. (1983). *American couples*. New York: William Morrow.

Bodenmann, G., Gottman, J. M., & Backman, H. (1997). A Swiss replication of Gottman's couple typology. *Swiss Journal of Psychology, 56*, 205–216.

Bolger, N., & Amarel, D. (2007). Effects of social support visibility on adjustment to stress: Experimental evidence. *Journal of Personality and Social Psychology, 92*, 458–475.

Bolger, N., Zuckerman, A., & Kessler, R. C. (2000). Invisible support and adjustment to stress. *Journal of Personality and Social Psychology, 79*, 953–961.

Bonanno, G. A., Wortman, C. B., Lehman, D. R., Tweed, R. G., Haring, M., Sonnega, J., Carr, D., & Nesse, R. M. (2002). Resilience to loss and chronic grief: A prospective study from preloss to 18-months postloss. *Journal of Personality and Social Psychology, 83*, 1150–1164.

Bonanno, G. A., Wortman, C. B., & Nesse, R. M. (2004). Prospective patterns of resilience and maladjustment during widowhood. *Psychology and Aging, 19*, 260–271.

Bornstein, M. H., & Arterberry, M. E. (2003). Recognition, discrimination and categorization of smiling by 5-month-old infants. *Developmental Science, 6*, 585–599.

Bornstein, M. H., & Tamis-LeMonda, C. S. (1997). Maternal responsiveness and infant mental abilities: Specific predictive relations. *Infant Behavior & Development, 20*, 283–296.

Bornstein, M. H., Tamis-LeMonda, C. S., Hahn, C-S., & Haynes, O. M. (2008). Maternal responsiveness to young children at three ages: Longitudinal analysis of a multidimensional, modular, and specific parenting construct. *Developmental Psychology, 44*, 867–874.

Bornstein, R. F. (1989). Exposure and affect: Overview and meta-analysis of research, 1968–1987. *Psychological Bulletin, 106*, 265–289.

Boss, P. (1999). *Ambiguous loss: Learning to live with unresolved grief*. Cambridge, MA: Harvard University Press.

Boss, P. (2006). *Loss, trauma, and resilience: Therapeutic work with ambiguous loss*. New York: W. W. Norton & Co.

Boss, P. (2007). Ambiguous loss theory: Challenges for scholars and practitioners. *Family Relations, 56*, 105–111.

Boss, P., & Couden, B. (2002). Ambiguous loss from chronic physical illness: Clinical interventions with individuals, couples and families. *Journal of Clinical Psychology, 58*, 1351–1360.

Bouchard, G., Lussier, Y., & Sabourin, S. (1999). Personality and marital adjustment: Utility of the five-factor model of personality. *Journal of Marriage and the Family, 61*, 651–660.

Bowlby, J. (1944). Forty-four juvenile thieves: Their characteristics and home-life (II). *International Journal of Psycho-Analysis, 25*, 107–128.

Bowlby, J. (1951). Maternal care and mental health. *Bulletin of the World Health Organization, 3*, 355–533.

Bowlby, J. (1953). Some pathological processes set in train by early mother–child separation. *Journal of Mental Science, 99*, 265–272.

Bowlby, J. (1969). *Attachment and loss: Vol. 1. Attachment.* New York: Basic Books.

Bowlby, J. (1973). Affectional bonds: Their nature and origin. In R. S. Weiss (Ed.), *Loneliness: The experience of emotional and social isolation* (pp. 38–52). Cambridge, MA: MIT Press.

Bowlby, J. (1977). The making and breaking of affectional bonds: I. Aetiology and psychopathology in the light of attachment theory. *British Journal of Psychiatry, 130*, 201–210.

Bowlby, J. (1988). *A secure base: Clinical applications of attachment theory.* London: Routledge.

Bradbury, T. N., & Fincham, F. D. (1988). Individual difference variables in close relationships: A contextual model of marriage as an integrative framework. *Journal of Personality and Social Psychology, 4*, 713–721.

Bradbury, T. N., & Fincham, F. D. (1990). Attributions in marriage: Review and critique. *Psychological Bulletin, 107*, 3–33.

Bradbury, T. N., & Fincham, F. D. (1993). Assessing dysfunctional cognition in marriage: A reconsideration of the Relationship Belief Inventory. *Psychological Assessment, 5*, 92–101.

Bradbury, T. N., Fincham, F. D., & Beach, S. R. H. (2000). Research on the nature and determinants of marital satisfaction: A decade in review. *Journal of Marriage and the Family, 62*, 964–980.

Braithwaite, D. O., Bach, B. W., Baxter, L. A., DiVerniero, R., Hammonds, J. R., Hosek, A. M., Willer, E. K., & Wolf, B. M. (2010). Constructing family: A typology of voluntary kin. *Journal of Social and Personal Relationships, 27*, 388–407.

Branje, S. J. T., Frijns, T., Finkenauer, C., Engels, R., & Meeus, W. (2007). You are my best friend: Commitment and stability in adolescents' same-sex friendships. *Personal Relationships, 14*, 587–603.

Braver, S. L., Shapiro, J. R., & Goodman, M. R. (2006). Consequences of divorce for parents. In M. A. Fine & J. H. Harvey (Eds.), *Handbook of divorce and dissolution* (pp. 313–337). Mahwah, NJ: Lawrence Erlbaum Associates Inc.

Bredow, C. A., Cate, R. M., & Huston, T. L. (2008). Have we met before? A conceptual model of first romantic encounters. In S. Sprecher, A. Wenzel, & J. Harvey (Eds.), *Handbook of relationship initiation* (pp. 3–28). New York: Psychology Press.

Brehm, S. S. (1985). *Intimate relationships.* New York: Random House.

Breiding, M. J., Black, M. C., & Ryan, G. W. (2008). Prevalence and risk factors of intimate partner violence in eighteen U.S. states/territories, 2005. *American Journal of Preventive Medicine, 34*, 112–118.

Brewer, M. B. (2004). Taking the social origins of human nature seriously: Toward a more imperialist social psychology. *Personality and Social Psychology Review, 8*, 107–113.

Brewer, M. B., & Caporael, L. R. (1990). Selfish genes vs. selfish people: Sociobiology as origin myth. *Motivation and Emotion, 14*, 237–243.

Brewis, A., & Meyer, M. (2005). Marital coitus across the life course. *Journal of Biosocial Science, 37*, 499–518.

Brewster, M. P. (2003). Power and control dynamics in prestalking and stalking situations. *Journal of Family Violence, 18*, 207–217.

Brezsnyak, M., & Whisman, M. A. (2004). Sexual desire and relationship functioning: The effects of marital satisfaction and power. *Journal of Sex & Marital Therapy, 30*, 199–217.

Bringle, R. G., & Buunk, B. P. (1991). Extradyadic relationships and sexual jealousy. In K. McKinney & S. Sprecher (Eds.), *Sexuality in close relationships* (pp. 135–153). Hillsdale, NJ: Lawrence Erlbaum Associates Inc.

Brock, R. L., & Lawrence, E. (2009). Too much of a good thing: Underprovision versus overprovision of partner support. *Journal of Family Psychology, 23*, 181–192.

Brodsky, C. M. (1976). *The harassed worker.* Lexington, MA: D. C. Heath.

Brody, L. R., Zelazo, P. R., & Chaika, H. (1984). Habituation–dishabituation to speech in the neonate. *Developmental Psychology, 20*, 114–119.

Brown, M., & Auerback, A. (1981). Communication patterns in initiation of marital sex. *Medical Aspects of Human Sexuality, 15*, 105–117.

Brown, S. L. (2003). Relationship quality dynamics of cohabiting unions. *Journal of Family Issues, 24*, 583–601.

Brown, S. L., & Booth, A. (1996). Cohabitation versus marriage: A comparison of relationship quality. *Journal of Marriage & the Family, 58*, 668–678.

Brown, S. L., Sanchez, L. A., Nock, S. L., & Wright, J. D. (2006). Links between premarital cohabitation and subsequent marital quality, stability, and divorce. *Social Science Research, 35*, 454–470.

Brugha, T. S., Weich, S., Singleton, N., Lewis, G., Bebbington, P. E., Jenkins, R., & Meltzer, H. (2005). Primary group size, social support, gender and future mental health status in a prospective study of people living in private households throughout Great Britain. *Psychological Medicine, 35*, 705–714.

Brumbaugh, S. M., Sanchez, L. A., Nock, S. L., & Wright, J. D. (2008). Attitudes toward gay marriage in states undergoing marriage law transformation. *Journal of Marriage and Family, 70*, 345–359.

Brunstein, J. C., Dangelmayer, G., & Schultheiss, O. C. (1996). Personal goals and social support in close relationships: Effects on relationship mood and marital satisfaction. *Journal of Personality and Social Psychology, 71*, 1006–1019.

Buelga, S., Musitu, G., Murgui, S., Pons, J., & Howard, V. (2008). Reputation, loneliness, satisfaction with life and aggressive behavior in adolescence. *The Spanish Journal of Psychology, 11*, 192–200.

Bull, R., & Rumsey, N. (1988). *The social psychology of facial appearance.* New York: Springer-Verlag.

Bumpass, L. L., & Lu, H. (2000). Trends in cohabitation and implications for children's family contexts in the United States. *Population Studies, 54*, 29–41.

Bumpass, L. L., Sweet, J. A., & Cherlin, A. (1991). The role of cohabitation in declining rates of marriage. *Journal of Marriage & the Family, 53*, 913–927.

Burk, W. J., & Laursen, B. (2005). Adolescent perceptions of friendship and their associations with individual adjustment. *International Journal of Behavioral Development, 29*, 156–164.

Burleson, B. R. (2003). The experience and effects of emotional support: What the study of cultural and gender differences can tell us about close relationships, emotion, and interpersonal communication. *Personal Relationships, 10*, 1–23.

Burleson, B. R., & Goldsmith, D. J. (1998). How the comforting process works: Alleviating emotional distress through conversationally induced reappraisals. In P. A. Andersen & L. K. Guerrero (Eds.), *Handbook of communication and emotion: Research, theory, applications, and contexts* (pp. 245–280). Orlando, FL: Academic Press.

Burleson, B. R., Holmstrom, A. J., & Gilstrap, C. M. (2005). "Guys can't say *that* to guys": Four experiments assessing the normative motivation account for deficiencies in the emotional support provided by men. *Communication Monographs, 72*, 468–501.

Burleson, B. R., & Kunkel, A. W. (2006). Revisiting the different cultures thesis: An assessment of sex differences and similarities in supportive communication. In K. Dindia & D. J. Canary (Eds.), *Sex differences and similarities in communication* (2nd ed., pp. 137–159). Mahwah, NJ: Lawrence Erlbaum Associates Inc.

Burlingham, D., & Freud, A. (1942). *Young children in war-time: A year's work in a residential war nursery.* London: G. Allen & Unwin Ltd.

Burt, M. R. (1980). Cultural myths and supports for rape. *Journal of Personality and Social Psychology, 38*, 217–230.

Buss, D. M. (1985). Human mate selection. *American Scientist, 73*, 47–51.

Buss, D. M. (1989). Sex differences in human mate preferences: Evolutionary hypotheses tested in 37 cultures. *Behavioral and Brain Sciences, 12*, 1–49.

Buss, D. M., et al. (1990). International preferences in selecting mates: A study of 37 cultures. *Journal of Cross-Cultural Psychology, 21*, 5–47.

Buss, D. M., & Kenrick, D. T. (1998). Evolutionary social psychology. In D. T. Gilbert, S. T. Fiske, & G. Lindzey (Eds.), *The handbook of social psychology* (4th ed., Vol. 2, pp. 982–1026). Boston: McGraw-Hill.

Buss, D. M., Larsen, R. J., Westen, D., & Semmelroth, J. (1992). Sex differences in jealousy: Evolution, physiology, and psychology. *Psychological Science, 3*, 251–255.

Buss, D. M., & Schmitt, D. P. (1993). Sexual strategies theory: An evolutionary perspective on human mating. *Psychological Review, 100*, 204–232.

Buss, D. M., Shackelford, T. K., Kirkpatrick, L. A., Choe, J. C., Lim, H. K., Hasegawa, M., Hasegawa, T., & Bennett, K. (1999). Jealousy and the nature of beliefs about infidelity: Tests of competing hypotheses about sex differences in the United States, Korea, and Japan. *Personal Relationships, 6*, 125–150.

Butzer, B., & Campbell, L. (2008). Adult attachment, sexual satisfaction, and relationship satisfaction: A study of married couples. *Personal Relationships, 15*, 141–154.

Buunk, B. P. (1995). Sex, self-esteem, dependency and extradyadic sexual experience as related to jealousy responses. *Journal of Social and Personal Relationships, 12*, 147–153.

Buunk, B. P. (2001). Perceived superiority of one's own relationship and perceived prevalence of happy and unhappy relationships. *British Journal of Social Psychology, 40*, 565–574.

Buunk, B. P., & van der Eijnden, R. J. J. M. (1997). Perceived prevalence, perceived superiority, and relationship satisfaction: Most relationships are good, but ours is the best. *Personality and Social Psychology Bulletin, 23*, 219–228.

Byers, E. S. (2005). Relationship satisfaction and sexual satisfaction: A longitudinal study of individuals in long-term relationships. *The Journal of Sex Research, 42*, 113–118.

Byers, E. S., Demmons, S., & Lawrance, K. (1998). Sexual satisfaction within dating relationships: A test of the interpersonal exchange model of sexual satisfaction. *Journal of Social and Personal Relationships, 15*, 257–267.

Byers, E. S., & Heinlein, L. (1989). Predicting initiations and refusals of sexual activities in married and cohabiting heterosexual couples. *Journal of Sex Research, 26*, 210–231.

Byers, E. S., & MacNeil, S. (2006). Further validation of the interpersonal exchange model of sexual satisfaction. *Journal of Sex & Marital Therapy, 32*, 53–69.

Byrne, D. (1971). *The attraction paradigm.* New York: Academic Press.

Byrne, D. (1997). An overview (and underview) of research and theory within the attraction paradigm. *Journal of Social and Personal Relationships, 14*, 417–431.

Byrne, D., Baskett, G. D., & Hodges, L. (1971). Behavioral indicators of interpersonal attraction. *Journal of Applied Social Psychology, 1*, 137–149.

Byrne, D., & Clore, G. L., Jr. (1967). Effectance arousal and attraction. *Journal of Personality and Social Psychology, 6*, 1–18.

Byrne, D., & Griffitt, W. (1966). A developmental investigation of the law of attraction. *Journal of Personality and Social Psychology, 4,* 699–702.

Byrne, M., Carr, A., & Clark, M. (2004). The efficacy of behavioral couples therapy and emotionally focused therapy for couple distress. *Contemporary Family Therapy, 26,* 361–387.

Cacioppo, J. T., Hughes, M. E., Waite, L. J., Hawkley, L. C., & Thisted, R. A. (2006). Loneliness as a specific risk factor for depressive symptoms: Cross-sectional and longitudinal analyses. *Psychology and Aging, 21,* 140–151.

Cain, V. S., Johannes, C. B., Avis, N. E., Mohr, B., Schocken, M., Skurnick, J., & Ory, M. (2003). Sexual functioning and practices in a multi-ethnic study of midlife women: Baseline results from SWAN. *The Journal of Sex Research, 40,* 266–276.

Calhoun, K. S., McCauley, J., & Crawford, M. E. (2006). Sexual assault. In R. D. McAnulty & M. M. Burnette (Eds.), *Sex and sexuality. Vol. 3. Sexual deviation and sexual offenses* (pp. 97–130). Westport, CT: Praeger.

Call, V., Sprecher, S., & Schwartz, P. (1995). The incidence and frequency of marital sex in a national sample. *Journal of Marriage and the Family, 57,* 639–650.

Campbell, A., Converse, D. E., & Rodgers, W. L. (1976). *The quality of American life.* New York: Russell Sage Foundation.

Canary, D. J., & Dainton, M. (Eds.). (2003). *Maintaining relationships through communication: Relational, contextual, and cultural variations.* Mahwah, NJ: Lawrence Erlbaum Associates Inc.

Canary, D. J., & Stafford, L. (1992). Relational maintenance strategies and equity in marriage. *Communication Monographs, 59,* 243–267.

Canary, D. J., Stafford, L., Hause, K. S., & Wallace, L. A. (1993). An inductive analysis of relational maintenance strategies: Comparisons among lovers, relatives, friends, and others. *Communication Research Reports, 10,* 5–14.

Cann, A., & Baucom, T. R. (2004). Former partners and new rivals as threats to a relationship: Infidelity type, gender, and commitment as factors related to distress and forgiveness. *Personal Relationships, 11,* 305–318.

Capellanus, A. (1960). *The art of courtly love* (J. J. Parry, Trans.). New York: Columbia University Press. (Original work created approximately 1184.)

Caporael, L. R., & Brewer, M. B. (1995). Hierarchical evolutionary theory: There *is* an alternative, and it's not creationism. *Psychological Inquiry, 6,* 31–34.

Card, N. A., & Hodges, E. V. E. (2008). Peer victimization among schoolchildren: Correlations, causes, consequences, and considerations in assessment and intervention. *School Psychology Quarterly, 23,* 451–461.

Carmichael, G. A., & Whittaker, A. (2007). Living together in Australia: Qualitative insights into a complex phenomenon. *Journal of Family Studies, 13,* 202–223.

Carrère, S., & Gottman, J. M. (1999). Predicting the future of marriages. In E. M. Hetherington (Ed.), *Coping with divorce, single parenting, and remarriage: A risk and resiliency perspective* (pp. 3–22). Hillsdale, NJ: Lawrence Erlbaum Associates Inc.

Carstensen, L. L., Gottman, J. M., & Levenson, R. W. (1995). Emotional behavior in long-term marriage. *Psychology and Aging, 10,* 140–149.

Carter, C. S. (1998). Neuroendocrine perspectives on social attachment and love. *Psychoneuroendocrinology, 23,* 779–818.

Castañeda, D. M. (1993). The meaning of romantic love among Mexican-Americans. *Journal of Social Behavior and Personality, 8,* 257–272.

Castro-Martin, T., & Bumpass, L. (1989). Recent trends in marital disruption. *Demography, 26,* 37–51.

Cate, R. M., Koval, J., Lloyd, S. A., & Wilson, G. (1995). Assessment of relationship thinking in dating relationships. *Personal Relationships, 2,* 77–95.

Caughlin, J. P., & Malis, R. S. (2004). Demand/withdraw communication between parents and adolescents as a correlate of relational satisfaction. *Communication Reports, 17*, 59–71.

Chang, S., & Chan, C. (2007). Perceptions of commitment change during mate selection: The case of Taiwanese newlyweds. *Journal of Social and Personal Relationships, 24*, 55–68.

Charny, I. W., & Parnass, S. (1995). The impact of extramarital relationships on the continuation of marriages. *Journal of Sex & Marital Therapy, 21*, 100–115.

Cheour, M., Martynova, O., Näätänen, R., Erkkola, R., Sillanpää, M., Kero, P., Raz, A., Kaipio, M. L., Hiltunen, J., Aaltonen, O., Savela, J., & Hämäläinen, H. (2002). Speech sounds learned by sleeping newborns. *Nature, 415*, 599–600.

Chomsky, N. (1965). *Aspects of the theory of syntax*. Cambridge, MA: MIT Press.

Chomsky, N. (1968). Language and the mind. *Psychology Today, 1*, 48–51, 66–68.

Chomsky, N. (2006). *Language and mind* (3rd ed.). New York: Cambridge University Press.

Christensen, A., Atkins, D. C., Berns, S., Wheeler, J., Baucom, D. H., & Simpson, L. E. (2004). Traditional versus integrative behavioral couple therapy for significantly and chronically distressed married couples. *Journal of Consulting and Clinical Psychology, 72*, 176–191.

Christensen, A., Atkins, D. C., Yi, J., Baucom, D. H., & George, W. H. (2006). Couple and individual adjustment for 2 years following a randomized clinical trial comparing traditional versus integrative behavioral couple therapy. *Journal of Consulting and Clinical Psychology, 74*, 1180–1191.

Christensen, A., Eldridge, K., Bokel Catta-Preta, A., Lim, V. R., & Santagata, R. (2006). Cross-cultural consistency of the demand/withdraw interaction pattern in couples. *Journal of Marriage and Family, 68*, 1029–1044.

Christensen, A., & Heavey, C. L. (1990). Gender and social structure in the demand/withdraw pattern of marital conflict. *Journal of Personality and Social Psychology, 59*, 73–81.

Christensen, A., & Heavey, C. L. (1999). Interventions for couples. *Annual Review of Psychology, 50*, 165–190.

Christensen, A., & Jacobson, N. S. (2000). *Reconcilable differences*. New York: Guilford Press.

Christensen, A., & Pasch, L. (1993). The sequence of marital conflict: An analysis of seven phases of marital conflict in distressed and nondistressed couples. *Clinical Psychology Review, 13*, 3–14.

Christensen, H. T. (1947). Student views on mate selection. *Marriage and Family Living, 9*, 85–88.

Christiansen, M. H., & Chater, N. (2008). Language as shaped by the brain. *Behavioral and Brain Sciences, 31*, 489–558.

Christopher, F. S. (2001). *To dance the dance: A symbolic interactional exploration of premarital sexuality*. Mahwah, NJ: Lawrence Erlbaum Associates Inc.

Christopher, F. S., & Cate, R. M. (1984). Factors involved in premarital sexual decision-making. *Journal of Sex Research, 20*, 363–376.

Christopher, F. S., & Cate, R. M. (1985). Premarital sexual pathways and relationship development. *Journal of Social and Personal Relationships, 2*, 271–288.

Christopher, F. S., & Kisler, T. S. (2004). Sexual aggression in romantic relationships. In J. H. Harvey, A. Wenzel, & S. Sprecher (Eds.), *The handbook of sexuality in close relationships* (pp. 287–309). Mahwah, NJ: Lawrence Erlbaum Associates Inc.

Christopher, F. S., & Lloyd, S. A. (2000). Physical and sexual aggression in relationships. In C. Hendrick & S. S. Hendrick (Eds.), *Close relationships: A sourcebook* (pp. 331–343). Thousand Oaks, CA: Sage Publications.

Christopher, F. S., & Sprecher, S. (2000). Sexuality in marriage, family, and other relationships: A decade review. *Journal of Marriage and the Family, 62*, 999–1017.

Clark, C. L., Shaver, P. R., & Abrahams, M. F. (1999). Strategic behaviors in romantic relationship initiation. *Personality and Social Psychology Bulletin, 25*, 707–720.

Clark, L. A., Watson, D., & Mineka, S. (1994). Temperament, personality, and the mood and anxiety disorders. *Journal of Abnormal Psychology, 103*, 103–116.

Clark, R. D., & Hatfield, E. (1989). Gender differences in receptivity to sexual offers. *Journal of Psychology & Human Sexuality, 2*, 39–55.

Clarkberg, M., Stolzenberg, R. M., & Waite, L. J. (1995). Attitudes, values, and entrance into cohabitational versus marital unions. *Social Forces, 74*, 609–632.

Clarke, V., & Finlay, S-J. (2004). For better or worse? Lesbian and gay marriage. *Feminism & Psychology, 14*, 17–23.

Coan, J. A., & Gottman, J. M. (2007). The Specific Affect Coding System (SPAFF). In J. A. Coan & J. J. B. Allen (Eds.), *Handbook of emotion elicitation and assessment* (pp. 267–285). New York: Oxford University Press.

Cohan, C. L., & Kleinbaum, S. (2002). Toward a greater understanding of the cohabitation effect: Premarital cohabitation and marital communication. *Journal of Marriage and Family, 64*, 180–192.

Cohen, J. D., & Fowers, B. J. (2004). Blood, sweat, and tears: Biological ties and self-investment as sources of positive illusions about children and stepchildren. *Journal of Divorce & Remarriage, 42*, 39–59.

Coker, A. L., Smith, P. H., McKeown, R. E., & King, M. J. (2000). Frequency and correlates of intimate partner violence by type: Physical, sexual, and psychological battering. *American Journal of Public Health, 90*, 553–559.

Coleman, F. L. (1997). Stalking behavior and the cycle of domestic violence. *Journal of Interpersonal Violence, 12*, 420–432.

Collins, N. L. (1996). Working models of attachment: Implications for explanation, emotion, and behavior. *Journal of Personality and Social Psychology, 71*, 810–832.

Collins, N. L., & Feeney, B. C. (2000). A safe haven: An attachment theory perspective on support seeking and caregiving in intimate relationships. *Journal of Personality and Social Psychology, 78*, 1053–1073.

Collins, N. L., & Feeney, B. C. (2004). An attachment theory perspective on closeness and intimacy. In D. J. Mashek & A. Aron (Eds.), *Handbook of closeness and intimacy* (pp. 163–187). Mahwah, NJ: Lawrence Erlbaum Associates Inc.

Collins, N. L., & Ford, M. B. (2010). Responding to the needs of others: The caregiving behavioral system in intimate relationships. *Journal of Social and Personal Relationships, 27*, 235–244.

Collins, N. L., & Miller, L. C. (1994). Self-disclosure and liking: A meta-analytical review. *Psychological Bulletin, 116*, 457–475.

Colson, M-H., Lemaire, A., Pinton, P., Hamidi, K., & Klein, P. (2006). Sexual behaviors and mental perception, satisfaction and expectations of sex life in men and women in France. *Journal of Sexual Medicine, 3*, 121–131.

Coltrane, S. (2000). Research on household labor: Modeling and measuring the social embeddedness of routine family work. *Journal of Marriage & the Family, 62*, 1208–1233.

Coltrane, S., & Adams, M. (2003). Division of labor. In J. J. Ponzetti Jr. (Ed.), *International encyclopedia of marriage and family* (2nd ed., Vol. 1, pp. 470–475). New York: Macmillan Reference USA.

Comacchio, C. (2003). Family, history of. In J. J. Ponzetti Jr. (Ed.), *International encyclopedia of marriage and family* (2nd ed., Vol. 2, pp. 555–559). New York: Macmillan Reference USA.

Condon, J. W., & Crano, W. D. (1988). Inferred evaluation and the relation between attitude similarity and interpersonal attraction. *Journal of Personality and Social Psychology, 54*, 789–797.

Condon, W. S., & Sander, L. W. (1974). Synchrony demonstrated between movements of the neonate and adult speech. *Child Development, 45*, 456–462.

Conger, R. D., & Conger, K. J. (2002). Resilience in Midwestern families: Selected findings from the first decade of a prospective, longitudinal study. *Journal of Marriage and Family, 64*, 361–373.

Conger, R. D., & Elder, G. H. Jr. (Eds.). (1994). *Families in troubled times: Adapting to change in rural America*. New York: Aldine de Gruyter.

Conger, R. D., Elder, G. H. Jr., Lorenz, F. O., Conger, K. J., Simons, R. L., Whitbeck, L. B., Huck, S., & Melby, J. N. (1990). Linking economic hardship to marital quality and instability. *Journal of Marriage and Family, 52*, 643–656.

Conger, R. D., Rueter, M. A., & Elder, G. H., Jr. (1999). Couple resilience to economic pressure. *Journal of Personality and Social Psychology, 76*, 54–71.

Contreras, R., Hendrick, S. S., & Hendrick, C. (1996). Perspectives on marital love and satisfaction in Mexican American and Anglo couples. *Journal of Counseling and Development, 74*, 408–415.

Cook, W. L., & Kenny, D. A. (2005). The Actor–Partner Interdependence Model: A model of bidirectional effects in developmental studies. *International Journal of Behavioral Development, 29*, 101–109.

Cooper, A., & Sportolari, L. (1997). Romance in cyberspace: Understanding on-line attraction. *Journal of Sex Education and Therapy, 22*, 7–14.

Coplan, R. J., Closson, L. M., & Arbeau, K. A. (2007). Gender differences in the behavioral associates of loneliness and social dissatisfaction in kindergarten. *Journal of Child Psychology and Psychiatry, 48*, 988–995.

Coren, S. (1998). *Why we love the dogs we do*. New York: Free Press.

Cosmides, L., & Tooby, J. (1997). *Evolutionary psychology: A primer* [online]. Retrieved from http://www.psych.ucsb.edu/research/cep/primer.html

Cott, C. A., & Fox, M. T. (2001). Health and happiness for elderly institutionalized Canadians. *Canadian Journal on Aging, 20*, 517–535.

Crain, S., Goro, T., & Thornton, R. (2006). Language acquisition is language change. *Journal of Psycholinguistic Research, 35*, 31–49.

Crain, S., & Pietroski, P. (2002). Why language acquisition is a snap. *The Linguistic Review, 19*, 163–183.

Cramer, D. (2000). Relationship satisfaction and conflict style in romantic relationships. *The Journal of Psychology, 134*, 337–341.

Cramer, D. (2004). Emotional support, conflict, depression, and relationship satisfaction in a romantic partner. *The Journal of Psychology, 138*, 532–542.

Crick, N. R., Casas, J. F., & Ku, H-C. (1999). Relational and physical forms of peer victimization in preschool. *Developmental Psychology, 35*, 376–385.

Crick, N. R., & Grotpeter, J. K. (1996). Children's treatment by peers: Victims of relational and overt aggression. *Development and Psychopathology, 8*, 367–380.

Critelli, J. W., Myers, E. J., & Loos, V. E. (1986). The components of love: Romantic attraction and sex role orientation. *Journal of Personality, 54*, 354–370.

Cunningham, M. R. (1986). Measuring the physical in physical attractiveness: Quasi-experiments on the sociobiology of female facial beauty. *Journal of Personality and Social Psychology, 50*, 925–935.

Cunningham, M. R., & Barbee, A. P. (2000). Social support. In C. Hendrick & S. S. Hendrick (Eds.), *Close relationships: A sourcebook* (pp. 273–285). Thousand Oaks, CA: Sage Publications.

Cunningham, M. R., Barbee, A. P., & Druen, P. B. (1996). Social allergens and the reactions that they produce: Escalation of annoyance and disgust in love and work. In R. M. Kowalski (Ed.), *Aversive interpersonal behaviors* (pp. 189–214). New York: Plenum.

Cunningham, M. R., Barbee, A. P., & Pike, C. L. (1990). What do women want? Facialmetric assessment of multiple motives in the perception of male facial physical attractiveness. *Journal of Personality and Social Psychology, 59*, 61–72.

Cunningham, M. R., Druen, P. B., & Barbee, A. P. (1997). Angels, mentors, and friends: Trade-offs among evolutionary, social, and individual variables in physical appearance. In J. A. Simpson & D. T. Kenrick (Eds.), *Evolutionary social psychology* (pp. 109–140). Mahwah, NJ: Lawrence Erlbaum Associates Inc.

Cunningham, M. R., Shamblen, S. R., Barbee, A. P., & Ault, L. K. (2005). Social allergies in romantic relationships: Behavioral repetition, emotional sensitization, and dissatisfaction in dating couples. *Personal Relationships, 12*, 273–295.

Cupach, W. R., & Canary, D. J. (2003). Conflict: Couple relationships. In J. J. Ponzetti Jr. (Ed.), *International encyclopedia of marriage and family* (2nd ed., Vol. 1, pp. 355–360). New York: Macmillan Reference USA.

Cupach, W. R., & Comstock, J. (1990). Satisfaction with sexual communication in marriage: Links to sexual satisfaction and dyadic adjustment. *Journal of Social and Personal Relationships, 7*, 179–186.

Cupach, W. R., & Metts, S. (1991). Sexuality and communication in close relationships. In K. McKinney & S. Sprecher (Eds.), *Sexuality in close relationships* (pp. 93–110). Hillsdale, NJ: Lawrence Erlbaum Associates Inc.

Cupach, W. R., & Spitzberg, B. H. (1998). Obsessive relational intrusion and stalking. In B. H. Spitzberg & W. R. Cupach (Eds.), *The dark side of close relationships* (pp. 233–263). Mahwah, NJ: Lawrence Erlbaum Associates Inc.

Cupach, W. R., & Spitzberg, B. H. (2004). *The dark side of relational pursuit: From attraction to obsession and stalking*. Mahwah, NJ: Lawrence Erlbaum Associates Inc.

Cupach, W. R., & Spitzberg, B. H. (2008). "Thanks, but no thanks . . ." The occurrence and management of unwanted relationship pursuit. In S. Sprecher, A. Wenzel, & J. Harvey (Eds.), *Handbook of relationship initiation* (pp. 409–424). New York: Psychology Press.

Cutrona, C. E. (1986). Behavioral manifestations of social support: A microanalytic investigation. *Journal of Personality and Social Psychology, 51*, 201–208.

Cutrona, C. E. (1996). *Social support in couples: Marriage as a resource in times of stress*. Thousand Oaks, CA: Sage Publications.

Cutrona, C. E., Hessling, R. M., & Suhr, J. A. (1997). The influence of husband and wife personality on marital social support interactions. *Personal Relationships, 4*, 379–393.

Cutrona, C. E., & Russell, D. W. (1990). Type of social support and specific stress: Toward a theory of optimal matching. In B. R. Sarason, I. G. Sarason, & G. R. Pierce (Eds.), *Social support: An interactional view* (pp. 319–366). New York: Wiley.

Cutrona, C. E., Russell, D. W., Abraham, W. T., Gardner, K. A., Melby, J. N., Bryant, C., & Conger, R. D. (2003). Neighborhood context and financial strain as predictors of marital interaction and marital quality in African American couples. *Personal Relationships, 10*, 389–409.

Dainton, M. (2000). Maintenance behaviors, expectations for maintenance, and satisfaction: Linking comparison levels to relational maintenance strategies. *Journal of Social and Personal Relationships, 17*, 827–842.

Dainton, M., & Stafford, L. (1993). Routine maintenance behaviors: A comparison of relationship type, partner similarity, and sex differences. *Journal of Social and Personal Relationships, 10*, 255–272.

Dakof, G. A., & Taylor, S. E. (1990). Victims' perceptions of social support: What is helpful from whom? *Journal of Personality and Social Psychology, 58*, 80–89.

Daly, M., & Wilson, M. (1983). *Sex, evolution, and behavior* (2nd ed.). Belmont, CA: Wadsworth.

Daniels, L. K. (2002). "It's just as easy to fall in love with a rich man . . .": The relationship between perceived social pressure and human mate preferences. *Dissertation Abstracts International: Section B: The Sciences and Engineering, 64*(1-B), 584.

Darling, C. A., Davidson, J. K., & Cox, R. P. (1991). Female sexual response and the timing of partner orgasm. *Journal of Sex & Marital Therapy, 17*, 3–21.

Darwin, C. (1965). *The expression of emotions in man and animals*. Chicago, IL: University of Chicago Press. (Original work published 1872.)

D'Augelli, A., & D'Augelli, J. F. (1985). The enhancement of sexual skills and competence: Promoting lifelong sexual unfolding. In L. L'Abate & M. A. Milan (Eds.), *Handbook of social skills training and research* (pp. 170–191). New York: John Wiley.

Davey, A., Fincham, F. D., Beach, S. R. H., & Brody, G. H. (2001). Attributions in marriage: Examining the entailment model in dyadic context. *Journal of Family Psychology, 15*, 721–734.

Davies, S., Katz, J., & Jackson, J. L. (1999). Sexual desire discrepancies: Effects on sexual and relationship satisfaction in heterosexual dating couples. *Archives of Sexual Behavior, 28*, 553–567.

Davis, D., & Holtgraves, T. (1984). Perceptions of unresponsive others: Attributions, attraction, understandability, and memory of their utterances. *Journal of Experimental Social Psychology, 20*, 383–408.

Davis, D., & Perkowitz, W. T. (1979). Consequences of responsiveness in dyadic interaction: Effects of probability of response and proportion of content-related responses on interpersonal attraction. *Journal of Personality and Social Psychology, 37*, 534–550.

Davis, J. A., & Smith, T. (1991). *General social surveys, 1972–1991*. Storrs, CT: University of Connecticut, Roper Center for Public Opinion Research.

Davis, K. E., Ace, A., & Andra, M. (2000). Stalking perpetrators and psychological maltreatment of partners: Anger-jealousy, attachment insecurity, need for control, and break-up context. *Violence and Victims, 15*, 407–425.

Davis, K. E., Coker, A. L., & Sanderson, M. (2002). Physical and mental health effects of being stalked for men and women. *Violence and Victims, 17*, 429–443.

Davis, K. E., & Latty-Mann, H. (1987). Love styles and relationship quality: A contribution to validation. *Journal of Social and Personal Relationships, 4*, 409–428.

Davis, M. (1973). *Intimate relations*. New York: Free Press.

Davis, S. N., Greenstein, T. N., & Gerteisen Marks, J. P. (2007). Effects of union type on division of household labor: Do cohabiting men really perform more housework? *Journal of Family Issues, 28*, 1246–1272.

De Becker, G. (1998). *The gift of fear: Survival signals that protect us from violence*. New York: Dell.

DeCasper, A. J., Lecanuet, J-P., Busnel, M-C., & Granier-Deferre, C. (1994). Fetal reactions to recurrent maternal speech. *Infant Behavior & Development, 17*, 159–164.

Deenen, A. A., Gijs, L., & van Naerssen, A. X. (1994). Intimacy and sexuality in gay male couples. *Archives of Sexual Behavior, 23*, 421–431.

Dekel, R., Enoch, G., & Solomon, Z. (2008). The contribution of captivity and post-traumatic stress disorder to marital adjustment of Israeli couples. *Journal of Social and Personal Relationships, 25*, 497–510.

De La Ronde, C., & Swann, W. B. Jr. (1998). Partner verification: Restoring shattered images of our intimates. *Journal of Personality and Social Psychology, 75*, 374–382.

DeMaris, A. (2007). The role of relationship inequity in marital disruption. *Journal of Social and Personal Relationships, 24*, 177–195.

Demo, D. H., & Supple, A. J. (2003). Divorce: Effects on children. In J. J. Ponzetti Jr. (Ed.), *International encyclopedia of marriage and family* (2nd ed., Vol. 1, pp. 475–480). New York: Macmillan Reference USA.

Dennerstein, L., Koochaki, P., Barton, I., & Graziottin, A. (2006). Hypoactive sexual desire disorder in menopausal women: A survey of Western European women. *Journal of Sexual Medicine, 3*, 212–222.

D'Entremont, B., & Muir, D. (1999). Infant responses to adult happy and sad vocal and facial expressions during face-to-face interactions. *Infant Behavior & Development, 22*, 527–539.

DePaulo, B. M., & Morris, W. L. (2006). The unrecognized stereotyping and discrimination against singles. *Current Directions in Psychological Science, 15*, 251–254.

Derlega, V. J., Winstead, B. A., & Greene, K. (2008). Self-disclosure and starting a close relationship. In S. Sprecher, A. Wenzel, & J. Harvey (Eds.), *Handbook of relationship initiation* (pp. 153–174). New York: Psychology Press.

Derrick, J. L., Gabriel, S., & Tippin, B. (2008). Parasocial relationships and self-discrepancies: Faux relationships have benefits for low self-esteem individuals. *Personal Relationships, 15*, 261–280.

DeSteno, D., Bartlett, M. Y., Braverman, J., & Salovey, P. (2002). Sex differences in jealousy: Evolutionary mechanism or artifact of measurement? *Journal of Personality and Social Psychology, 83*, 1103–1116.

DeSteno, D. A., & Salovey, P. (1996). Evolutionary origins of sex differences in jealousy? Questioning the "fitness" of the model. *Psychological Science, 7*, 367–372.

Dewberry, C., Ing, M., James, S., Nixon, M., & Richardson, S. (1990). Anxiety and unrealistic optimism. *The Journal of Social Psychology, 130*, 151–156.

DeYoung, R., & Buzzi, B. (2003). Ultimate coping strategies: The differences among parents of murdered or abducted, long-term missing children. *Omega: Journal of Death and Dying, 47*, 343–360.

Diener, E., & Oishi, S. (2005). The nonobvious social psychology of happiness. *Psychological Inquiry, 16*, 162–167.

Dimidjian, S., Martell, C. R., & Christensen, A. (2008). Integrative behavioral couple therapy. In A. S. Gurman (Ed.), *Clinical handbook of couple therapy* (4th ed., pp. 73–106). New York: Guilford Press.

Dindia, K. (2000). Relational maintenance. In C. Hendrick & S. S. Hendrick (Eds.), *Close relationships: A sourcebook* (pp. 287–299). Thousand Oaks, CA: Sage Publications.

Dion, K. K., Berscheid, E., & Walster, E. (1972). What is beautiful is good. *Journal of Personality and Social Psychology, 24*, 285–290.

Dion, K. L., & Dion, K. K. (1993). Gender and ethnocultural comparisons in styles of love. *Psychology of Women Quarterly, 17*, 463–473.

Dobash, R. E., & Dobash, R. P. (1979). *Violence against wives: A case against patriarchy*. New York: Free Press.

Doka, K. J. (1989). *Disenfranchised grief: Recognizing hidden sorrow*. Lexington, MA: Lexington Books.

Doka, K. J. (2008). Disenfranchised grief in historical and cultural perspective. In M. S. Stroebe, R. O. Hansson, H. Schut, W. Stroebe, & E. Van den Blink (Eds.), *Handbook of bereavement research and practice: Advances in theory and intervention* (pp. 223–240). Washington, DC: American Psychological Association.

Donn, J. E., & Sherman, R. C. (2002). Attitudes and practices regarding the formation of romantic relationships on the Internet. *CyberPsychology & Behavior, 5*, 107–123.

Donnellan, M. B., Assad, K. K., Robins, R. W., & Conger, R. D. (2007). Do negative interactions mediate the effects of Negative Emotionality, Communal Positive Emotionality, and Constraint on relationship satisfaction? *Journal of Social and Personal Relationships, 24*, 557–573.

Donnellan, M. B., Conger, R. D., & Bryant, C. M. (2004). The Big Five and enduring marriages. *Journal of Research in Personality, 38*, 481–504.

Donnellan, M. B., Larsen-Rife, D., & Conger, R. D. (2005). Personality, family history, and competence in early adult romantic relationships. *Journal of Personality and Social Psychology, 88*, 562–576.

Donnelly, D. A. (1993). Sexually inactive marriages. *Journal of Sex Research, 30*, 171–179.

Donovan, W., Taylor, N., & Leavitt, L. (2007). Maternal self-efficacy, knowledge of infant development, sensory sensitivity, and maternal response during interaction. *Developmental Psychology, 43*, 865–876.

Donovan, W. L., Leavitt, L. A., & Walsh, R. O. (2000). Maternal illusory control predicts socialization strategies and toddler compliance. *Developmental Psychology, 36*, 402–411.

Doss, B. D., Simpson, L. E., & Christensen, A. (2004). Why do couples seek therapy? *Professional Psychology: Research and Practice, 35*, 608–614.

Dostal, C., & Langhinrichsen-Rohling, J. (1997). Relationship-specific cognitions and family-of-origin divorce and abuse. *Journal of Divorce & Remarriage, 27*, 101–120.

Downey, G., Bonica, C., & Rincon, C. (1999). Rejection sensitivity and adolescent romantic relationships. In W. Furman, B. B. Brown, & C. Feiring (Eds.), *The development of romantic relationships in adolescence* (pp. 148–174). New York: Cambridge University Press.

Downey, G., Feldman, S., & Ayduk, O. (2000). Rejection sensitivity and male violence in romantic relationships. *Personal Relationships, 7*, 45–61.

Downey, G., & Feldman, S. I. (1996). Implications of rejection sensitivity for intimate relationships. *Journal of Personality and Social Psychology, 70*, 1327–1343.

Downey, G., Freitas, A. L., Michaelis, B., & Khouri, H. (1998). The self-fulfilling prophecy in close relationships: Rejection sensitivity and rejection by romantic partners. *Journal of Personality and Social Psychology, 75*, 545–560.

Dressing, H., Kuehner, C., & Gass, P. (2005). Lifetime prevalence and impact of stalking in a European population: Epidemiological data from a middle-sized German city. *British Journal of Psychiatry, 187*, 168–172.

Drigotas, S. M., Rusbult, C. E., & Verette, J. (1999). Level of commitment, mutuality of commitment, and couple well-being. *Personal Relationships, 6*, 389–409.

Driver, J. L., & Gottman, J. M. (2004). Daily marital interactions and positive affect during marital conflict among newlywed couples. *Family Process, 43*, 301–314.

Duck, S. (1982). A topography of relationship disengagement and dissolution. In S. Duck (Ed.), *Personal relationships, Vol. 4: Dissolving personal relationships* (pp. 1–30). London: Academic Press.

Duck, S., & Miell, D. (1986). Charting the development of personal relationships. In R. Gilmour & S. Duck (Eds.), *The emerging field of personal relationships* (pp. 133–143). Hillsdale, NJ: Lawrence Erlbaum Associates Inc.

Dunkel-Schetter, C. (1984). Social support and cancer: Findings based on patient interviews and their implications. *Journal of Social Issues, 40*, 77–98.

Dunkel-Schetter, C., & Brooks, K. P. (2009). Social support, nature of. In H. T. Reis & S. K. Sprecher (Eds.), *Encyclopedia of human relationships* (Vol. 3, pp. 1565–1570). Thousand Oaks, CA: Sage Publications.

Dunkel-Schetter, C., & Skokan, L. A. (1990). Determinants of social support provision in personal relationships. *Journal of Social and Personal Relationships, 7*, 437–450.

Dunn, J. L. (1999). What love has to do with it: The cultural construction of emotion and sorority women's responses to forcible interaction. *Social Problems, 46*, 440–459.

Dunn, R. L., & Schwebel, A. I. (1995). Meta-analytic review of marital therapy outcome research. *Journal of Family Psychology, 9*, 58–68.

Dutton, D. G. (1985). An ecologically nested theory of male violence toward intimates. *International Journal of Women's Studies, 8*, 404–413.

Dutton, D. G. (2007). Female intimate partner violence and developmental trajectories of abusive females. *International Journal of Men's Health, 6*, 54–70.

Dutton, L. B., & Winstead, B. A. (2006). Predicting unwanted pursuit: Attachment, relationship satisfaction, relationship alternatives, and break-up distress. *Journal of Social and Personal Relationships, 23*, 565–586.

Dworkin, S. L., & O'Sullivan, L. (2005). Actual versus desired initiation patterns among a sample of college men: Tapping disjunctures within traditional male sexual scripts. *The Journal of Sex Research, 42*, 150–158.

Dykstra, P. A. (2009). Kin relationships. In H. T. Reis & S. K. Sprecher (Eds.), *Encyclopedia of human relationships* (Vol. 2, pp. 951–954). Thousand Oaks, CA: Sage Publications.

Eagly, A. H. (1987). *Sex differences in social behavior: A social-role interpretation.* Hillsdale, NJ: Lawrence Erlbaum Associates Inc.

Eagly, A. H., Ashmore, R. D., Makhijani, M. G., & Longo, L. C. (1991). What is beautiful is good, but . . .: A meta-analytic review of research on the physical attractiveness stereotype. *Psychological Bulletin, 110*, 109–128.

Ebbesen, E. B., Kjos, G. L., & Konecni, V. J. (1976). Spatial ecology: Its effects on the choice of friends and enemies. *Journal of Experimental Social Psychology, 12*, 505–518.

Eckerman, C. O., & Rheingold, H. L. (1974). Infants' exploratory responses to toys and people. *Developmental Psychology, 10*, 255–259.

Edelstein, R. S., & Shaver, P. R. (2004). Avoidant attachment: Exploration of an oxymoron. In D. J. Mashek & A. Aron (Eds.), *Handbook of closeness and intimacy* (pp. 397–412). Mahwah, NJ: Lawrence Erlbaum Associates Inc.

Egland, K. L., Spitzberg, B. H., & Zormeier, M. (1996). Flirtation and conversational competence in cross-sex platonic and romantic relationships. *Communication Reports, 9*, 105–117.

Eibl-Eibesfeldt, I. (1975). *Ethology: The biology of behavior* (2nd ed.). New York: Holt, Rinehart, & Winston.

Eibl-Eibesfeldt, I. (1989). *Human ethology*. New York: Aldine de Gruyter.

Eidelson, R. J., & Epstein, N. (1982). Cognition and relationship maladjustment: Development of a measure of dysfunctional relationship beliefs. *Journal of Consulting and Clinical Psychology, 50*, 715–720.

Einarsen, S., & Hoel, H. (2001, May). *The Negative Acts Questionnaire: Development, validation and revision of a measure of bullying at work.* Paper presented at the 10th European Congress on Work and Organisational Psychology, Prague, Czech Republic.

Einarsen, S., Hoel, H., Zapf, D., & Cooper, C. L. (2003). The concept of bullying at work. In S. Einarsen, H. Hoel, D. Zapf, & C. L. Cooper, C. L. (Eds.), *Bullying and emotional abuse in the workplace: International perspectives in research and practice* (pp. 3–30). London & New York: Taylor & Francis.

Einarsen, S. & Raknes, B. (1997). Harassment in the workplace and the victimization of men. *Violence and Victims, 12*, 247–263.

Eisenberg, N., Murphy, B. C., & Shepard, S. (1997). The development of empathic accuracy. In W. J. Ickes (Ed.), *Empathic accuracy* (pp. 73–116). New York: Guilford Press.

Eisenman, R., & Dantzker, M. L. (2006). Gender and ethnic differences in sexual attitudes at a Hispanic-serving university. *The Journal of General Psychology, 133*, 153–162.

Ekman, P. (1993). Facial expression and emotion. *American Psychologist, 48*, 376–379.

Ekman, P. (1997). Expression or communication about emotion. In N. L. Segal, G. E. Weisfeld, & C. Cronin (Eds.), *Uniting psychology and biology: Integrative perspectives on human development* (pp. 315–338). Washington, DC: American Psychological Association.

Eldridge, K. A., & Christensen, A. (2002). Demand–withdraw communication during couple conflict: A review and analysis. In P. Noller & J. A. Feeney (Eds.), *Understanding marriage: Developments in the study of couple interaction* (pp. 289–322). New York: Cambridge University Press.

Eldridge, K. A., Sevier, M., Jones, J., Atkins, D. C., & Christensen, A. (2007). Demand–withdraw communication in severely distressed, moderately distressed, and nondistressed couples: Rigidity and polarity during relationship and personal problem discussions. *Journal of Family Psychology, 21*, 218–226.

Ellis, A. (1954). *The American sexual tragedy*. New York: Twayne.

Ellis, D., & Stuckless, N. (1996). *Mediating and negotiating marital conflicts*. Thousand Oaks, CA: Sage Publications.

Ellis, H. (1901–1928). *Studies in the psychology of sex* (Vols. 1–7). Philadelphia, PA: F. A. Davis. (Original work published 1897–1928.)

Ellis, H. (1963). *Psychology of sex*. New York: The New American Library of World Literature, Inc. (Original work published 1933.)

Ellsworth, C. P., Muir, D. W., & Hains, S. M. J. (1993). Social competence and person–object differentiation: An analysis of the still-face effect. *Developmental Psychology, 29*, 63–73.

Emerson, R. M., Ferris, K. O., & Gardner, C. B. (1998). On being stalked. *Social Problems, 45*, 289–314.

Emmelkamp, P. M., Krol, B., Sanderman, R., & Rüphan, M. (1987). The assessment of relationship beliefs in a marital context. *Personality and Individual Differences, 8*, 775–780.

Engedal, K. (1996). Mortality in the elderly—a 3-year follow-up of an elderly community sample. *International Journal of Geriatric Psychiatry, 11*, 467–471.

Epstein, N., & Eidelson, R. J. (1981). Unrealistic beliefs of clinical couples: Their relationship to expectations, goals, and satisfaction. *American Journal of Family Therapy, 9*, 13–22.

Erber, R., & Fiske, S. T. (1984). Outcome dependency and attention to inconsistent information. *Journal of Personality and Social Psychology, 47*, 709–726.

Etcheverry, P. E., Le, B., & Charania, M. R. (2008). Perceived versus reported social referent approval and romantic relationship commitment and persistence. *Personal Relationships, 15*, 281–295.

Eysenck, H. J. (1980). Personality, marital satisfaction, and divorce. *Psychological Reports, 47*, 1235–1238.

Farah, M. J. (2000). *The cognitive neuroscience of vision.* Malden, MA: Blackwell

Farah, M. J., Rabinowitz, C., Quinn, G. E., & Liu, G. T. (2000). Early commitment of neural substrates for face recognition. *Cognitive Neuropsychology, 17*, 117–123.

Farnsworth, J., Lund, D. A., & Pett, M. A. (1989). Management and outcomes of loss in later life: A comparison of bereavement and divorce. In D. A. Lund (Ed.), *Older bereaved spouses* (pp. 155–166). Washington, DC: Hemisphere.

Farrer, J., Tsuchiya, H., & Bagrowicz, B. (2008). Emotional expression in *tsukiau* dating relationships in Japan. *Journal of Social and Personal Relationships, 25*, 169–188.

Farroni, T., Johnson, M. H., & Csibra, G. (2004). Mechanisms of eye gaze perception during infancy. *Journal of Cognitive Neuroscience, 16*, 1320–1326.

Faulkner, R. A., Davey, M., & Davey, A. (2005). Gender-related predictors of change in marital satisfaction and marital conflict. *The American Journal of Family Therapy, 33*, 61–83.

Feeney, B. C., & Collins, N. L. (2003). Attachment: Couple relationships. In J. J. Ponzetti Jr. (Ed.), *International encyclopedia of marriage and family* (2nd ed., Vol. 1, pp. 96–103). New York: Macmillan Reference USA.

Feeney, J., Peterson, C., & Noller, P. (1994). Equity and marital satisfaction over the family life cycle. *Personal Relationships, 1*, 83–99.

Feeney, J. A. (2004). Hurt feelings in couple relationships: Towards integrative models of the negative effects of hurtful events. *Journal of Social and Personal Relationships, 21*, 487–508.

Feeney, J. A. (2005). Hurt feelings in couple relationships: Exploring the role of attachment and personal injury. *Personal Relationships, 12*, 253–271.

Feeney, J. A., & Hill, A. (2006). Victim-perpetrator differences in reports of hurtful events. *Journal of Social and Personal Relationships, 23*, 587–608.

Feeney, J. A., Noller, P., & Roberts, N. (2000). Attachment and close relationships. In C. Hendrick & S. S. Hendrick (Eds.), *Close relationships: A sourcebook* (pp. 185–201). Thousand Oaks, CA: Sage Publications.

Fehr, B. (1988). Prototype analysis of the concepts of love and commitment. *Journal of Personality and Social Psychology, 55*, 557–579.

Fehr, B. (1994). Prototype-based assessment of layperson's views of love. *Personal Relationships, 1*, 309–331.

Fehr, B. (1996). *Friendship processes.* Thousand Oaks, CA: Sage Publications.

Fehr, B. (2000). The life cycle of friendship. In C. Hendrick & S. S. Hendrick, *Close relationships: A sourcebook* (pp. 70–82). Thousand Oaks, CA: Sage Publications.

Fehr, B. (2004). Intimacy expectations in same-sex friendships: A prototype interaction-pattern model. *Journal of Personality and Social Psychology, 86*, 265–284.

Fehr, B. (2006). A prototype approach to studying love. In R. J. Sternberg & K. Weis (Eds.), *The new psychology of love* (pp. 225–246). New Haven, CT: Yale University Press.

Fehr, B. (2008). Friendship formation. In S. Sprecher, A. Wenzel, & J. Harvey (Eds.), *Handbook of relationship initiation* (pp. 29–54). New York: Psychology Press.

Fehr, B., & Russell, J. A. (1991). The concept of love viewed from a prototype perspective. *Journal of Personality and Social Psychology, 60*, 425–438.

Felmlee, D. H. (1995). Fatal attractions: Affection and disaffection in intimate relationships. *Journal of Social and Personal Relationships, 12*, 295–311.

Felmlee, D. H. (1998). Fatal attraction. In B. H. Spitzberg & W. R. Cupach (Eds.), *The dark side of close relationships* (pp. 3–31). Mahwah, NJ: Lawrence Erlbaum Associates Inc.

Felmlee, D. H. (2001a). From appealing to appalling: Disenchantment with a romantic partner. *Sociological Perspectives, 44*, 263–280.

Felmlee, D. H. (2001b). No couple is an island: A social network perspective on dyadic stability. *Social Forces, 79*, 1259–1287.

Feltey, K. M., Ainslie, J. J., & Geib, A. (1991). Sexual coercion attitudes among high school students: The influence of gender and rape education. *Youth & Society, 23*, 229–250.

Fincham, F. D., & Bradbury, T. N. (1992). Assessing attributions in marriage: The Relationship Attribution Measure. *Journal of Personality and Social Psychology, 3*, 457–468.

Fincham, F. D., Harold, G. T., & Gano-Phillips, S. (2000). The longitudinal association between attributions and marital satisfaction: Direction of effects and role of efficacy expectations. *Journal of Family Psychology, 14*, 267–285.

Fincham, F. D., Paleari, F. G., & Regalia, C. (2002). Forgiveness in marriage: The role of relationship quality, attributions, and empathy. *Personal Relationships, 9*, 27–37.

Finkelhor, D., & Dziuba-Leatherman, J. (1994). Victimization of children. *American Psychologist, 49*, 173–183.

Finkelhor, D., & Yllö, K. (1985). *License to rape: Sexual abuse of wives.* New York: Holt, Rinehart & Winston.

Fischer, K. W., Shaver, P. R., & Carnochan, P. (1990). How emotions develop and how they organise development. *Cognition and Emotion, 4*, 81–127.

Fisher, H. (2000). Lust, attraction, attachment: Biology and evolution of three primary emotion systems for mating, reproduction, and parenting. *Journal of Sex Education and Therapy, 25*, 96–104.

Fisher, H. (2006). The drive to love: The neural mechanism for mate selection. In R. J. Sternberg & K. Weis (Eds.), *The new psychology of love* (pp. 87–115). New Haven, CT: Yale University Press.

Fisher, H. E. (1989). Evolution of human serial pairbonding. *American Journal of Physical Anthropology, 78*, 331–354.

Fisher, H. E. (1992). *Anatomy of love: A natural history of mating, marriage, and why we stray.* New York: Fawcett Columbine.

Fisher, H. E. (1998). Lust, attraction, and attachment in mammalian reproduction. *Human Nature, 9*, 23–52.

Fisher, T. D., & McNulty, J. K. (2008). Neuroticism and marital satisfaction: The mediating role played by the sexual relationship. *Journal of Family Psychology, 22*, 112–122.

Fitness, J., & Strongman, K. (1991). Affect in close relationships. In G. J. O. Fletcher & F. D. Fincham (Eds.), *Cognition in close relationships* (pp. 175–202). Hillsdale, NJ: Lawrence Erlbaum Associates Inc.

Fletcher, G. J. O., & Fincham, F. D. (1991). Attribution processes in close relationships. In G. J. O. Fletcher & F. D. Fincham (Eds.), *Cognition in close relationships* (pp. 7–35). Hillsdale, NJ: Lawrence Erlbaum Associates Inc.

Fletcher, G. J. O., & Thomas, G. (1996). Close relationship lay theories: Their structure and function. In G. J. O. Fletcher & J. Fitness (Eds.), *Knowledge structures in close relationships: A social psychological approach* (pp. 3–24). Mahwah, NJ: Lawrence Erlbaum Associates Inc.

Flight attendant angered by Condit's definition of a "relationship." (2001, August 28). *Good Morning America: Ann Marie Smith interview transcript*. Retrieved April 11, 2009 from http://a.abcnews.com/GMA/story?id=126735&page=3

Forgas, J. P., Levinger, G., & Moylan, S. J. (1994). Feeling good and feeling close: Affective influences on the perception of intimate relationships. *Personal Relationships, 1*, 165–184.

Fowers, B. J., Lyons, E., Montel, K. H., & Shaked, N. (2001). Positive illusions about marriage among married and single individuals. *Journal of Family Psychology, 15*, 95–109.

Frayser, S. G. (1989). Sexual and reproductive relationships: Cross-cultural evidence and biosocial implications. *Medical Anthropology, 11*, 385–407.

Frazier, P., Arikian, N., Benson, S., Losoff, A., & Maurer, S. (1996). Desire for marriage and life satisfaction among unmarried heterosexual adults. *Journal of Social and Personal Relationships, 13*, 225–239.

Freud, S. (1963). "Civilized" sexual morality and modern nervousness. In P. Rieff (Ed.), *Sexuality and the psychology of love* (pp. 20–40). New York: Collier Books. (Original work published 1908.)

Freud, S. (1963). The most prevalent form of degradation in erotic life. In P. Rieff (Ed.), *Sexuality and the psychology of love* (pp. 58–70). New York: Collier Books. (Original work published 1912.)

Fricker, J., & Moore, S. (2002). Relationship satisfaction: The role of love styles and attachment styles. *Current Research in Social Psychology, 7*, 182–204.

Frieze, I. H. (1983). Investigating the causes and consequences of marital rape. *Signs, 8*, 532–553.

Frieze, I. H., & Browne, A. (1989). Violence in marriage. In L. Ohlin & M. Tonry (Eds.), *Family violence* (Vol. 11, pp. 163–218). Chicago, IL: The University of Chicago Press.

Frieze, I. H., & McHugh, M. C. (1992). Power and influence strategies in violent and nonviolent marriages. *Psychology of Women Quarterly, 16*, 449–465.

Frisén, A., Jonsson, A., & Persson, C. (2007). Adolescents' perception of bullying: Who is the victim? Who is the bully? What can be done to stop bullying? *Adolescence, 42*, 749–761.

Fromm, E. (1956). *The art of loving*. New York: Harper & Row.

Frye, N. E. (2006). Relationship problems and physical aggression: The moderating role of temporal comparison. *Personal Relationships, 13*, 303–315.

Furnham, A., Tan, T., & McManus, C. (1997). Waist-to-hip ratio and preferences for body shape: A replication and extension. *Personality and Individual Differences, 22*, 539–549.

Gagnon, J. H., & Simon, W. (1973). *Sexual conduct: The social sources of human sexuality*. Chicago: Aldine.

García, E. L., Banegas, J. R., Pérez-Regadera, A. G., Cabrera, R. H., & Rodríguez-Artalejo, F. (2005). Social network and health-related quality of life in older adults: A population-based study in Spain. *Quality of Life Research: An International Journal of Quality of Life Aspects of Treatment, Care & Rehabilitation, 14*, 511–520.

Garcia-Moreno, C., Jansen, H. A. F. M., Ellsberg, M., Heise, L., & Watts, C. H. (2006). Prevalence of intimate partner violence: Findings from the WHO multi-country study on women's health and domestic violence. *The Lancet, 368*, 1260–1269.

Gaunt, R. (2006). Couple similarity and marital satisfaction: Are similar spouses happier? *Journal of Personality, 74*, 1401–1420.

Gay y Blasco, P. (1997). A "different" body? Desire and virginity among Gitanos. *Journal of the Royal Anthropological Institute, 3*, 517–535.

Gelles, R. J., & Harrop, J. W. (1989). Violence, battering, and psychological distress among women. *Journal of Interpersonal Violence, 4*, 400–420.

Ghimire, D. J., Axinn, W. G., Yabiku, S. T., & Thornton, A. (2006). Social change, premarital nonfamily experience, and spouse choice in an arranged marriage society. *American Journal of Sociology, 111*, 1181–1218.

Gidycz, C. A., Warkentin, J. B., & Orchowski, L. M. (2007). Predictors of verbal, physical, and sexual violence: A prospective analysis of college men. *Psychology of Men & Masculinity, 8*, 79–94.

Gilbert, L. (1993). *Two careers/one family*. Newbury Park, CA: Sage Publications.

Gilford, R. (1984). Contrasts in marital satisfaction throughout old age: An exchange theory analysis. *Journal of Gerontology, 39*, 325–333.

Gilford, R., & Bengtson, V. (1979). Measuring marital satisfaction in three generations: Positive and negative dimensions. *Journal of Marriage & the Family, 41*, 387–398.

Givens, D. B. (1978). The nonverbal basis of attraction: Flirtation, courtship, and seduction. *Psychiatry, 41*, 346–359.

Glass, S. P., & Wright, T. L. (1977). The relationship of extramarital sex, length of marriage, and sex differences on marital satisfaction and romanticism: Athanasiou's data reanalyzed. *Journal of Marriage & the Family, 39*, 691–703.

Gleason, M. E. J., Iida, M., Shrout, P. E., & Bolger, N. (2008). Receiving support as a mixed blessing: Evidence for dual effects of support on psychological outcomes. *Journal of Personality and Social Psychology, 94*, 824–838.

Glenn, N. D., & Weaver, C. N. (1978). A multivariate, multisurvey study of marital happiness. *Journal of Marriage & the Family, 40*, 269–282.

Glenn, N. D., & Weaver, C. N. (1979). Attitudes toward premarital, extramarital, and homosexual relations in the U.S. in the 1970s. *Journal of Sex Research, 15*, 108–119.

Goldberg, A. E. (2008). Universal Grammar? Or prerequisites for natural language? *Behavioral and Brain Sciences, 31*, 522–523.

Goldberg, A. E., & Perry-Jenkins, M. (2007). The division of labor and perceptions of parental roles: Lesbian couples across the transition to parenthood. *Journal of Social and Personal Relationships, 24*, 297–318.

Goldfarb, W. (1947). Variations in adolescent adjustment of institutionally reared children. *American Journal of Orthopsychiatry, 17*, 449–457.

Golding, J. M. (1999). Intimate partner violence as a risk factor for mental disorders: A meta-analysis. *Journal of Family Violence, 14*, 99–132.

Gonzalez, R., & Griffin, D. (1997). On the statistics of interdependence: Treating dyadic data with respect. In S. Duck (Ed.), *Handbook of personal relationships: Theory, research and interventions* (2nd ed., pp. 271–302). Chichester, UK: Wiley.

Goodfriend, W., & Agnew, C. R. (2008). Sunken costs and desired plans: Examining different types of investments in close relationships. *Personality and Social Psychology Bulletin, 34*, 1639–1652.

Goodwin, R. (1999). *Personal relationships across cultures*. London: Routledge.

Goodwin, R., Christakopoulou, S., & Panagiotidou, V. (2006). Britain. In G. James, J. W. Berry, F. J. R. van de Vijver, Ç. Kagitçibasi, & Y. H. Poortinga (Eds.), *Families across cultures: A 30-nation psychological study* (pp. 267–274). New York: Cambridge University Press.

Goodwin, R., & Gaines, S. O. Jr. (2004). Relationship beliefs and relationship quality across cultures: Country as a moderator of dysfunctional beliefs and relationship quality in three former Communist societies. *Personal Relationships, 11*, 267–279.

Goodwin, R., & Tang, D. (1991). Preferences for friends and close relationship partners: A cross-cultural comparison. *Journal of Social Psychology, 131*, 579–581.

Gorchoff, S. M., John, O. P., & Helson, R. (2008). Contextualizing change in marital satisfaction during middle age: An 18-year longitudinal study. *Psychological Science, 19*, 1194–1200.

Gordon, C. L., & Baucom, D. H. (2009). Examining the individual within marriage: Personal strengths and relationship satisfaction. *Personal Relationships, 16*, 421–435.

Goren, C. C., Sarty, M., & Wu, P. Y. K. (1975). Visual following and pattern discrimination of face-like stimuli by newborn infants. *Pediatrics, 56*, 544–549.

Gottman, J. M. (1993). The roles of conflict engagement, escalation, and avoidance in marital interaction: A longitudinal view of five types of couples. *Journal of Consulting and Clinical Psychology, 61*, 6–15.

Gottman, J. M. (1994a). *What predicts divorce? The relationship between marital processes and marital outcomes.* Hillsdale, NJ: Lawrence Erlbaum Associates Inc.

Gottman, J. M. (1994b). *Why marriages succeed or fail . . . and how you can make yours last.* New York: Simon & Schuster.

Gottman, J. M. (1998). Psychology and the study of marital processes. *Annual Review of Psychology, 49*, 169–197.

Gottman, J. M. (1999). *The marriage clinic: A scientifically based marital therapy.* New York: W. W. Norton.

Gottman, J. M., & Driver, J. L. (2005). Dysfunctional marital conflict and everyday marital interaction. *Journal of Divorce & Remarriage, 43*, 63–77.

Gottman, J. M., & Krokoff, L. J. (1989). Marital interaction and satisfaction: A longitudinal view. *Journal of Consulting and Clinical Psychology, 57*, 47–52.

Gottman, J. M., & Levenson, R. W. (1988). The social psychophysiology of marriage. In P. Noller & M. A. Fitzpatrick (Eds.), *Perspectives on marital interaction* (pp. 182–200). Philadelphia: Multilingual Matters.

Gottman, J. M., & Levenson, R. W. (1992). Marital processes predictive of later dissolution: Behavior, physiology, and health. *Journal of Personality and Social Psychology, 63*, 221–233.

Grad, H. (2006). Spain. In G. James, J. W. Berry, F. J. R. van de Vijver, Ç. Kagitçibasi, & Y. H. Poortinga (Eds.), *Families across cultures: A 30-nation psychological study* (pp. 458–466). New York: Cambridge University Press.

Graham, J. M., & Conoley, C. W. (2006). The role of marital attributions in the relationship between life stressors and marital quality. *Personal Relationships, 13*, 231–241.

Graham-Kevan, N., & Archer, J. (2003). Intimate terrorism and common couple violence: A test of Johnson's predictions in four British samples. *Journal of Interpersonal Violence, 18*, 1247–1270.

Grammer, K., & Thornhill, R. (1994). Human (*homo sapiens*) facial attractiveness and sexual selection: The role of symmetry and averageness. *Journal of Comparative Psychology, 108*, 233–42.

Gravetter, F. J., & Wallnau, L. B. (2007). *Statistics for the behavioral sciences* (7th ed.). Florence, KY: Cengage/Wadsworth.

Green, L., Fein, D., Modahl, C., Feinstein, C., Waterhouse, L., & Morris, M. (2001). Oxytocin and autistic disorder: Alterations in peptide forms. *Biological Psychiatry, 50*, 609–613.

Green, S. K., & Sandos, P. (1983). Perceptions of male and female initiators of relationships. *Sex Roles, 9*, 849–852.

Greenberg, L. S., & Johnson, S. M. (1988). *Emotionally focused therapy for couples.* New York: Guilford Press.

Greenblat, C. S. (1983). The salience of sexuality in the early years of marriage. *Journal of Marriage and the Family, 45*, 289–299.

Greenwald, A. G. (1980). The totalitarian ego: Fabrication and revision of personal history. *American Psychologist, 35*, 603–618.

Griffin, D., & Gonzalez, R. (1995). Correlational analysis of dyad-level data in the exchangeable case. *Psychological Bulletin, 118*, 430–439.

Gros-Louis, J., West, M. J., Goldstein, M. H., & King, A. P. (2006). Mothers provide differential feedback to infants' prelinguistic sounds. *International Journal of Behavioral Development, 30*, 509–516.

Grossmann, T., Johnson, M. H., Farroni, T., & Csibra, G. (2007). Social perception in the infant brain: Gamma oscillatory activity in response to eye gaze. *Social Cognitive and Affective Neuroscience, 2*, 284–291.

Grote, N. K., & Clark, M. S. (2001). Perceiving unfairness in the family: Cause or consequence of marital distress? *Journal of Personality and Social Psychology, 80*, 281–293.

Groth, A. N. (1979). Patterns of rape. In A. N. Groth (Ed.), *Men who rape: The psychology of the offender* (pp. 174–180). New York: Plenum Press.

Guay, S., Boisvert, J-M., & Freeston, M. H. (2003). Validity of three measures of communication for predicting relationship adjustment and stability among a sample of young couples. *Psychological Assessment, 15*, 392–398.

Guerrero, L. K., Trost, M. R., & Yoshimura, S. M. (2005). Romantic jealousy: Emotions and communicative responses. *Personal Relationships, 12*, 233–252.

Gunaid, A. A., Hummad, N. A., & Tamim, K. A. (2004). Consanguineous marriage in the capital city Sana'a, Yemen. *Journal of Biosocial Science, 36*, 111–121.

Gurung, R. A. R., Sarason, B. R., & Sarason, I. G. (1997). Personal characteristics, relationship quality, and social support perceptions and behavior in young adult romantic relationships. *Personal Relationships, 4*, 319–339.

Haas, S. M., & Stafford, L. (1998). An initial examination of maintenance behaviors in gay and lesbian relationships. *Journal of Social and Personal Relationships, 15*, 846–855.

Haavio-Mannila, E., & Kontula, O. (2003). Single and double standards in Finland, Estonia, and St. Petersburg. *The Journal of Sex Research, 40*, 36–49.

Haden, S. C., & Hojjat, M. (2006). Aggressive responses to betrayal: Type of relationship, victim's sex, and nature of aggression. *Journal of Social and Personal Relationships, 23*, 101–116.

Haferkamp, C. J. (1994). Dysfunctional beliefs, self-monitoring, and marital conflict. *Current Psychology, 13*, 248–262.

Hahlweg, K., & Markman, H. J. (1988). Effectiveness of behavioral marital therapy: Empirical status of behavioral techniques in preventing and alleviating marital distress. *Journal of Consulting and Clinical Psychology, 56*, 440–447.

Hains, S. M. J., & Muir, D. W. (1996). Infant sensitivity to adult eye direction. *Child Development, 67*, 1940–1951.

Halford, W. K. (2001). *Brief therapy for couples: Helping partners help themselves.* New York: Guilford Press.

Halford, W. K., Keefer, E., & Osgarby, S. M. (2002). "How has the week been for you two?" Relationship satisfaction and hindsight memory biases in couples' reports of relationship events. *Cognitive Therapy and Research, 26*, 759–773.

Hall, J. H., & Andrzejewski, S. A. (2009). Interpersonal sensitivity. In H. T. Reis & S. K. Sprecher (Eds.), *Encyclopedia of human relationships* (Vol. 2, pp. 902–905). Thousand Oaks, CA: Sage Publications.

Hall, J. H., & Fincham, F. D. (2006). Relationship dissolution following infidelity. In M. A. Fine & J. H. Harvey (Eds.), *Handbook of divorce and dissolution* (pp. 153–168). Mahwah, NJ: Lawrence Erlbaum Associates Inc.

Hall, J. H., & Fincham, F. D. (2009). Psychological distress: Precursor or consequence of dating infidelity? *Personality and Social Psychology Bulletin, 35*, 143–159.

Hall, S. (2004, May 26). Halle Berry's stalker scare. *E! Online.* Retrieved April 11, 2009 from www.eonline.com/uberblog/b47532_halle_berrys_stalker_scare.html

Hällström, T., & Samuelsson, S. (1990). Changes in women's sexual desire in middle life: The longitudinal study of women in Gothenburg. *Archives of Sexual Behavior, 19*, 259–268.

Hamon, R. R., & Ingoldsby, B. B. (Eds.). (2003). *Mate selection across cultures.* Thousand Oaks, CA: Sage Publications.

Haning, R. V., O'Keefe, S. L., Randall, E. J., Kommor, M. J., Baker, E., & Wilson, R. (2007). Intimacy, orgasm likelihood, and conflict predict sexual satisfaction in heterosexual male and female respondents. *Journal of Sex & Marital Therapy, 33*, 93–113.

Harlow, H. F. (1958). The nature of love. *The American Psychologist, 13*, 673–685.

Harlow, H. F. (1959). Love in infant monkeys. *Scientific American, 200*, 68–74.

Harper, M. S., Dickson, J. W., & Welsh, D. P. (2006). Self-silencing and rejection sensitivity in adolescent romantic relationships. *Journal of Youth and Adolescence, 35*, 459–467.

Harris, C. R. (2002). Sexual and romantic jealousy in heterosexual and homosexual adults. *Psychological Science, 13*, 7–12.

Harris, C. R. (2003). A review of sex differences in sexual jealousy, including self-report data, psychophysiological responses, interpersonal violence, and morbid jealousy. *Personality and Social Psychology Review, 7*, 102–128.

Harris, C. R. (2009). Jealousy. In H. T. Reis & S. K. Sprecher (Eds.), *Encyclopedia of human relationships* (Vol. 2, pp. 937–941). Thousand Oaks, CA: Sage Publications.

Harris, C. R., & Christenfeld, N. (1996). Gender, jealousy, and reason. *Psychological Science, 7*, 364–366.

Harvey, J. H., & Fine, M. A. (2006). Social construction of accounts in the process of relationship termination. In M. A. Fine & J. H. Harvey (Eds.), *Handbook of divorce and dissolution* (pp. 189–199). Mahwah, NJ: Lawrence Erlbaum Associates Inc.

Harvey, J. H., Weber, A. L., Galvin, K. S., Huszti, H. C., & Garnick, N. N. (1986). Attribution in the termination of close relationships: A special focus on the account. In R. Gilmour & S. Duck (Eds.), *Theoretical frameworks for personal relationships* (pp. 109–132). Hillsdale, NJ: Lawrence Erlbaum Associates Inc.

Hassebrauck, M., & Fehr, B. (2002). Dimensions of relationship quality. *Personal Relationships, 9*, 253–270.

Hatch, L. R., & Bulcroft, K. (2004). Does long-term marriage bring less frequent disagreements? Five explanatory frameworks. *Journal of Family Issues, 25*, 465–495.

Hatfield, E. (1988). Passionate and companionate love. In R. J. Sternberg & M. L. Barnes (Eds.), *The psychology of love* (pp. 191–217). New Haven, CT: Yale University Press.

Hatfield, E. (2006, spring). Proxmire's golden fleece award. *Relationship Research News (Newsletter of the International Association for Relationship Research), 4*, 5–9.

Hatfield, E., Greenberger, D., Traupmann, J., & Lambert, P. (1982). Equity and sexual satisfaction in recently married couples. *Journal of Sex Research, 17*, 18–32.

Hatfield, E., & Rapson, R. L. (1993). *Love, sex, and intimacy: Their psychology, biology, and history.* New York: HarperCollins.

Hatfield, E., & Rapson, R. L. (1996). *Love and sex: Cross-cultural perspectives.* Needham Heights, MA: Allyn & Bacon.

Hatfield, E., & Sprecher, S. (1986a). Measuring passionate love in intimate relationships. *Journal of Adolescence, 9*, 383–410.

Hatfield, E., & Sprecher, S. (1986b). *Mirror, mirror: The importance of looks in everyday life.* Albany, NY: State University of New York Press.

Hatfield, E., Traupmann, J., & Sprecher, S. (1984). Older women's perceptions of their intimate relationships. *Journal of Social and Clinical Psychology, 2*, 108–124.

Hatfield, E., Utne, M. K., & Traupmann, J. (1979). Equity theory and intimate relationships. In R. L. Burgess & T. L. Huston (Eds.), *Social exchange in developing relationships* (pp. 99–133). New York: Academic Press.

Hatton, H., Donnellan, M. B., Maysn, K., Feldman, B. J., Larsen-Rife, D., & Conger, R. D. (2008). Family and individual difference predictors of trait aspects of negative interpersonal behaviors during emerging adulthood. *Journal of Family Psychology, 22*, 448–455.

Haugaard, J. J., & Seri, L. G. (2003). Stalking and other forms of intrusive contact after the dissolution of adolescent dating or romantic relationships. *Violence and Victims, 18*, 279–297.

Hawker, D. S. J., & Boulton, M. J. (2000). Twenty years' research on peer victimization and psychosocial maladjustment: A meta-analytic review of cross-sectional studies. *Journal of Child Psychology and Psychiatry, 41*, 441–455.

Hawkley, L. C., & Cacioppo, J. T. (2007). Aging and loneliness: Downhill quickly? *Current Directions in Psychological Science, 16*, 187–191.

Hawkley, L. C., & Cacioppo, J. T. (2009). Loneliness. In H. T. Reis & S. K. Sprecher (Eds.), *Encyclopedia of human relationships* (Vol. 2, pp. 985–990). Thousand Oaks, CA: Sage Publications.

Hayden, A., Bhatt, R. S., Reed, A., Corbly, C. R., & Joseph, J. E. (2007). The development of expert face processing: Are infants sensitive to normal differences in second-order relational information? *Journal of Experimental Child Psychology, 97*, 85–98.

Hays, R. B. (1988). Friendship. In S. Duck (Ed.), *Handbook of personal relationships: Theory, research, and interventions* (pp. 391–408). Chichester, UK: Wiley.

Haythornthwaite, C., Wellman, B., & Garton, L. (1998). Work and community via computer-mediated communication. In J. Gackenbach (Ed.), *Psychology and the Internet: Intrapersonal, interpersonal, and transpersonal implications* (pp. 29–42). San Diego, CA: Academic Press.

Hazan, C., & Shaver, P. (1987). Romantic love conceptualized as an attachment process. *Journal of Personality and Social Psychology, 52*, 510–524.

Heatherington, L., Tolejko, N., McDonald, M., & Funk, J. (2007). Now why'd he do that? The nature and correlates of mothers' attributions about negative teen behavior. *Journal of Family Psychology, 21*, 315–319.

Heavey, C. L., Christensen, A., & Malamuth, N. M. (1995). The longitudinal impact of demand and withdrawal during marital conflict. *Journal of Consulting and Clinical Psychology, 63*, 797–801.

Heavey, C. L., Layne, C., & Christensen, A. (1993). Gender and conflict structure in marital interaction: A replication and extension. *Journal of Consulting and Clinical Psychology, 61*, 16–27.

Henderson-King, D. H., & Veroff, J. (1994). Sexual satisfaction and marital well-being in the first years of marriage. *Journal of Social and Personal Relationships, 11*, 509–534.

Hendrick, C., & Hendrick, S. S. (1986). A theory and method of love. *Journal of Personality and Social Psychology, 50*, 392–402.

Hendrick, C., & Hendrick, S. S. (1988). Lovers wear rose colored glasses. *Journal of Social and Personal Relationships, 5*, 161–183.

Hendrick, C., & Hendrick, S. S. (1989). Research on love: Does it measure up? *Journal of Personality and Social Psychology, 56*, 784–794.

Hendrick, C., & Hendrick, S. S. (1990). A relationship-specific version of the Love Attitudes Scale. *Journal of Social Behavior and Personality, 5*, 239–254.

Hendrick, C., & Hendrick, S. S. (2006). Styles of romantic love. In R. J. Sternberg & K. Weis (Eds.), *The new psychology of love* (pp. 149–170). New Haven, CT: Yale University Press.

Hendrick, C., Hendrick, S. S., & Dicke, A. (1998). The Love Attitudes Scale: Short form. *Journal of Social and Personal Relationships, 15*, 147–159.

Hendrick, C., Hendrick, S. S., Foote, F. H., & Slapion-Foote, M. J. (1984). Do men and women love differently? *Journal of Social and Personal Relationships, 1*, 177–195.

Hendrick, C., Hendrick, S. S., & Reich, D. A. (2006). The brief sexual attitudes scale. *The Journal of Sex Research, 43*, 76-86.

Hendrick, S. S. (1988). A generic measure of relationship satisfaction. *Journal of Marriage and the Family, 50*, 93–98.

Hendrick, S. S., & Hendrick, C. (1987). Love and sex attitudes and religious beliefs. *Journal of Social and Clinical Psychology, 5*, 391–398.

Hendrick, S. S., & Hendrick, C. (1992). *Liking, loving, and relating* (2nd ed.). Pacific Grove, CA: Brooks/Cole.

Hendrick, S. S., & Hendrick, C. (1995). Gender differences and similarities in sex and love. *Personal Relationships, 2*, 55–65.

Hendrick, S. S., & Hendrick, C. (2000). Romantic love. In C. Hendrick & S. S. Hendrick (Eds.), *Close relationships: A sourcebook* (pp. 203–215). Thousand Oaks, CA: Sage Publications.

Hendrick, S. S., & Hendrick, C. (2002). Linking romantic love with sex: Development of the Perceptions of Love and Sex Scale. *Journal of Social and Personal Relationships, 19*, 361–378.

Hendrick, S. S., Hendrick, C., & Adler, N. L. (1988). Romantic relationships: Love, satisfaction, and staying together. *Journal of Personality and Social Psychology, 54*, 980–988.

Henley, K., & Pasley, K. (2003). Divorce: Effects on couples. In J. J. Ponzetti Jr. (Ed.), *International encyclopedia of marriage and family* (2nd ed., Vol. 1, pp. 480–486). New York: Macmillan Reference USA.

Henning, K., Renauer, B., & Holdford, R. (2006). Victim or offender? Heterogeneity among women arrested for intimate partner violence. *Journal of Family Violence, 21*, 351–368.

Henry, N. J. M., Berg, C. A., Smith, T. W., & Florsheim, P. (2007). Positive and negative characteristics of marital interaction and their association with marital satisfaction in middle-aged and older couples. *Psychology and Aging, 22*, 428–441.

Henss, R. (1995). Waist-to-hip ratio and attractiveness: Replication and extension. *Personality and Individual Differences, 19*, 479–488.

Herlitz, C., & Ramstedt, K. (2005). Assessment of sexual behavior, sexual attitudes, and sexual risk in Sweden (1989–2003). *Archives of Sexual Behavior, 34*, 219–229.

Herold, E. S., Mantle, D., & Zemitis, O. (1979). A study of sexual offenses against females. *Adolescence, 14*, 65–72.

Hess, J. A. (2002). Distance regulation in personal relationships: The development of a conceptual model and tests of representational validity. *Journal of Social and Personal Relationships, 19*, 663–683.

Hess, J. A., Fannin, A. D., & Pollom, L. H. (2007). Creating closeness: Discerning and measuring strategies for fostering closer relationships. *Personal Relationships, 14*, 25–44.

Hill, C. A., Blakemore, J. E. O., & Drumm, P. (1997). Mutual and unrequited love in adolescence and young adulthood. *Personal Relationships, 4*, 15–23.

Hill, C. T., Rubin, Z., & Peplau, L. A. (1976). Breakups before marriage: The end of 103 affairs. *Journal of Social Issues, 32*, 147–168.

Hill, R. (1945). Campus values in mate-selection. *Journal of Home Economics, 37*, 554–558.

Hiller, J. (2004). Speculations on the links between feelings, emotions and sexual behaviour: Are vasopressin and oxytocin involved? *Sexual and Relationship Therapy, 19*, 393–412.

Hinde, R. A. (1979). *Towards understanding relationships*. London: Academic Press.

Hinde, R. A. (1997). *Relationships: A dialectical perspective*. Hove, UK: Psychology Press.

Hines, D. A., Brown, J., & Dunning, E. (2007). Characteristics of callers to the Domestic Abuse Hotline for Men. *Journal of Family Violence, 22*, 63–72.

Hines, D. A., & Malley-Morrison, K. (2005). *Family violence in the United States: Defining, understanding, and combating abuse*. Thousand Oaks, CA: Sage Publications.

Hirschberger, G., Srivastava, S., Marsh, P., Pape Cowan, C., & Cowan, P. A. (2009). Attachment, marital satisfaction, and divorce during the first fifteen years of parenthood. *Personal Relationships, 16*, 401–420.

Hoel, H., Faragher, B., & Cooper, C. L. (2004). Bullying is detrimental to health, but all bullying behaviours are not necessarily equally damaging. *British Journal of Guidance & Counselling, 32*, 367–387.

Hogben, M., & Byrne, D. (1998). Using social learning theory to explain individual differences in human sexuality. *Journal of Sex Research, 35*, 58–71.

Holland, A. S., & Roisman, G. I. (2008). Big Five personality traits and relationship quality: Self-reported, observational, and physiological evidence. *Journal of Social and Personal Relationships, 25*, 811–829.

Holmes, J. G. (2000). Social relationships: The nature and function of relational schemas. *European Journal of Social Psychology, 30*, 447–495.

Homans, G. (1961). *Social behavior: Its elementary forms.* New York: Harcourt, Brace & World.

Homans, G. C. (1979). Foreword. In R. L. Burgess & T. L. Huston (Eds.), *Social exchange in developing relationships* (pp. xv–xxii). New York: Academic Press.

Hortaçsu, N. (2007). Family- versus couple-initiated marriages in Turkey: Similarities and differences over the family life cycle. *Asian Journal of Social Psychology, 2007*, 103–116.

Hortaçsu, N., Baştuğ, S. S., & Muhammetberdiev, O. (2001). Change and stability with respect to attitudes and practices related to marriage in Ashkabat, Baku, and Ankara: Three Turkic cultures. *International Journal of Psychology, 36*, 108–120.

House, J. S., Landis, K. R., & Umberson, D. (1988). Social relationships and health. *Science, 241*, 540–545.

Hoyt, L. L., & Hudson, J. W. (1981). Personal characteristics important in mate preference among college students. *Social Behavior and Personality, 9*, 93–96.

Hudson, J. W., & Henze, L. F. (1969). Campus values in mate selection: A replication. *Journal of Marriage & the Family, 31*, 772–775.

Huebner, A. J., Mancini, J. A., Wilcox, R. M., Grass, S. R., & Grass, G. A. (2007). Parental deployment and youth in military families: Exploring uncertainty and ambiguous loss. *Family Relations, 56*, 112–122.

Hughes, D. K., & Surra, C. A. (2000). The reported influence of research participation on premarital relationships. *Journal of Marriage & the Family, 62*, 822–832.

Hunt, M. (1974). *Sexual behavior in the 1970s.* Chicago: Playboy Press.

Huston, T. L. (1973). Ambiguity of acceptance, social desirability, and dating choice. *Journal of Experimental Social Psychology, 9*, 32–42.

Huston, T. L. (2009). What's love got to do with it? Why some marriages succeed and others fail. *Personal Relationships, 16*, 301–327.

Huston, T. L., Caughlin, J. P., Houts, R. M., Smith, S. E., & George, L. J. (2001). The connubial crucible: Newlywed years as predictors of marital delight, distress, and divorce. *Journal of Personality and Social Psychology, 80*, 237–252.

Huston, T. L., & Levinger, G. (1978). Interpersonal attraction and relationships. *Annual Review of Psychology, 29*, 115–156.

Huston, T. L., McHale, S. M., & Crouter, A. (1986). When the honeymoon's over: Changes in the marriage relationship over the first year. In R. Gilmour & S. Duck (Eds.), *Theoretical frameworks for personal relationships* (pp. 109–132). Hillsdale, NJ: Lawrence Erlbaum Associates Inc.

Hynie, M., Lalonde, R. N., & Lee, N. (2006). Parent–child value transmission among Chinese immigrants to North America: The case of traditional mate preferences. *Cultural Diversity and Ethnic Minority Psychology, 12*, 230–244.

Ickes, W. (Ed.). (1997). *Empathic accuracy.* New York: Guilford Press.

Ickes, W. (2003). *Everyday mind reading: Understanding what other people think and feel.* Amherst, NY: Prometheus Books.

Ihinger-Tallman, M., & Henderson, D. A. (2003). Marriage ceremonies. In J. J. Ponzetti Jr. (Ed.), *International encyclopedia of marriage and family* (2nd ed., Vol. 3, pp. 1091–1094). New York: Macmillan Reference USA.

Iida, M., Seidman, G., Shrout, P. E., Fujita, K., & Bolger, N. (2008). Modeling support provision in intimate relationships. *Journal of Personality and Social Psychology, 94*, 460–478.

Immerman, R. S., & Mackey, W. C. (1997). An additional facet of the incest taboo: A protection of the mating-strategy template. *Journal of Genetic Psychology, 158*, 151–164.

Ingoldsby, B., Schvaneveldt, P., & Uribe, C. (2003). Perceptions of acceptable mate attributes in Ecuador. *Journal of Comparative Family Studies, 34*, 171–185.

Insel, T. R. (1997). A neurobiological basis of social attachment. *American Journal of Psychiatry, 154*, 726–735.

Insel, T. R. (2000). Toward a neurobiology of attachment. *Review of General Psychology, 4*, 176–185.

Isikoff, M., & Thomas, E. (2001, September 3). From bad to worse. *Newsweek*, pp. 20–23.

Jack, D. C. (1991). *Silencing the self: Women and depression.* Cambridge, MA: Harvard University Press.

Jacobson, N. S., & Christensen, A. (1996). *Integrative couple therapy: Promoting acceptance and change.* New York: W. W. Norton & Co.

Jacobson, N. S., Christensen, A., Prince, S. E., Cordova, J., & Eldridge, K. (2000). Integrative behavioral couple therapy: An acceptance-based, promising new treatment for couple discord. *Journal of Consulting and Clinical Psychology, 68*, 351–355.

James, W. (1950). *The principles of psychology* (Vol. 1). New York: Dover. (Original work published 1890.)

James, W. H. (1981). The honeymoon effect on marital coitus. *Journal of Sex Research, 17*, 114–123.

Jamieson, L., Anderson, M., McCrone, D., Bechhofer, F., Stewart, R., & Li, Y. (2002). Cohabitation and commitment: Partnership plans of young men and women. *Sociological Review, 50*, 356–377.

Jankowiak, W. (Ed.). (1995). *Romantic passion: A universal experience?* New York: Columbia University Press.

Jankowiak, W., & Hardgrave, M. D. (2007). Individual and societal response to sexual betrayal: A view from around the world. *Electronic Journal of Human Sexuality, 10*, 1–7.

Jankowiak, W. R., & Fischer, E. F. (1992). A cross-cultural perspective on romantic love. *Ethnology, 31*, 149–155.

Jason, L. A., Reichler, A., Easton, J., Neal, A., & Wilson, M. (1984). Female harassment after ending a relationship: A preliminary study. *Journal of Family and Economic Issues, 6*, 259–269.

Jensen-Campbell, L. A., Adams, R., Perry, D. G., Workman, K. A., Furdella, J. Q., & Egan, S. K. (2002). Agreeableness, extraversion, and peer relations in early adolescence: Winning friends and deflecting aggression. *Journal of Research in Personality, 36*, 224–251.

Jockin, V., McGue, M., & Lykken, D. T. (1996). Personality and divorce: A genetic analysis. *Journal of Personality and Social Psychology, 71*, 288–299.

Johnson, A. J., Wittenberg, E., Villagran, M. M., Mazur, M., & Villagran, P. (2003). Relational progression as a dialectic: Examining turning points in communication among friends. *Communication Monographs, 70*, 230–249.

Johnson, H. D. (2004). Gender, grade and relationship differences in emotional closeness within adolescent friendships. *Adolescence, 39*, 243–255.

Johnson, M. D., & Bradbury, T. N. (1999). Marital satisfaction and topographical assessment of marital interaction: A longitudinal analysis of newlywed couples. *Personal Relationships, 6*, 19–40.

Johnson, M. H. (2001). Infants' initial "knowledge" of the world: A cognitive neuroscience perspective. In F. Lacerdo, C. von Hofsten, & M. Heimann (Eds.), *Emerging cognitive abilities in early infancy* (pp. 53–72). Mahwah, NJ: Lawrence Erlbaum Associates Inc.

Johnson, M. H., Dziurawiec, S., Ellis, H., & Morton, J. (1991). Newborns' preferential tracking of face-like stimuli and its subsequent decline. *Cognition, 40*, 1–19.

Johnson, M. P. (1999, November). *Two types of violence against women in the American family: Identifying patriarchal terrorism and common couple violence.* Paper presented at the annual meeting of the National Council on Family Relations, Irvine, CA.

Johnson, M. P. (2006). Conflict and control: Gender symmetry and asymmetry in domestic violence. *Violence Against Women, 12*, 1003–1018.

Johnson, M. P. (2008). *A typology of domestic violence: Intimate terrorism, violent resistance, and situational couple violence.* Boston, MA: Northeastern University Press.

Johnson, M. P., & Leone, J. M. (2005). The differential effects of intimate terrorism and situational couple violence: Findings from the National Violence Against Women survey. *Journal of Family Issues, 26*, 322–349.

Johnson, S. M. (2004). *The practice of emotionally focused couple therapy: Creating connection* (2nd ed.). New York: Brunner-Routledge.

Johnson, S. M. (2008). Emotionally focused couple therapy. In A. S. Gurman (Ed.), *Clinical handbook of couple therapy* (4th ed., pp. 107–137). New York: Guilford Press.

Johnson, S. M. (2009). Emotionally focused couple therapy. In H. T. Reis & S. K. Sprecher (Eds.), *Encyclopedia of human relationships* (Vol. 1, pp. 497–500). Thousand Oaks, CA: Sage Publications.

Johnson, S. M., & Greenberg, L. S. (1995). The emotionally focused approach to problems in adult attachment. In N. S. Jacobson & A. S. Gurman (Eds.), *Clinical handbook of couple therapy* (pp. 121–141). New York: Guilford Press.

Jones, D., & Hill, K. (1993). Criteria of facial attractiveness in five populations. *Human Nature, 4*, 271–296.

Jones, S. S., & Raag, T. (1989). Smile production in older infants: The importance of a social recipient for the facial signal. *Child Development, 60*, 811–818.

Jusczyk, P. W. (1985). The high-amplitude sucking technique as a methodological tool in speech perception research. In G. Gottlieb & N. A. Krasnegor (Eds.), *Measurement of audition and vision in the first year of postnatal life: A methodological overview* (pp. 195–222). Westport, CT: Ablex Publishing.

Kalmijn, M. (1997). A sociological analysis of marriage ceremonies between 1946 and 1994. *Mens en Maatschappij, 72*, 96–114.

Kamo, Y. (1993). Determinants of marital satisfaction: A comparison of the United States and Japan. *Journal of Social and Personal Relationships, 10*, 551–568.

Kane, H. S., Jaremka, L. M., Guichard, A. C., Ford, M. B., Collins, N. L., & Feeney, B. C. (2007). Feeling supported and feeling satisfied: How one partner's attachment style predicts the other partner's relationship experiences. *Journal of Social and Personal Relationships, 24*, 535–555.

Kanin, E. J. (1967). An examination of sexual aggression as a response to sexual frustration. *Journal of Marriage and the Family, 29*, 428–433.

Kanin, E. J. (1984). Date rape: Unofficial criminals and victims. *Victimology: An International Journal, 9*, 95–108.

Kanin, E. J. (1985). Date rapists: Differential sexual socialization and relative deprivation. *Archives of Sexual Behavior, 14*, 219–231.

Kaplan, H. S. (1979). *Disorders of sexual desire and other new concepts and techniques in sex therapy.* New York: Simon & Schuster.

Kaplan, H. S. (1996). Erotic obsession: Relationship to hypoactive sexual desire disorder and paraphilia. *American Journal of Psychiatry, 153*, 30–41.

Karney, B. R., & Bradbury, T. N. (1997). Neuroticism, marital interaction, and the trajectory of marital satisfaction. *Journal of Personality and Social Psychology, 72*, 1075–1092.

Karney, B. R., & Bradbury, T. N. (2000). Attributions in marriage: State or trait? A growth curve analysis. *Journal of Personality and Social Psychology, 78*, 295–309.

Karney, B. R., Bradbury, T. N., & Johnson, M. D. (1999). Deconstructing stability: The distinction between the course of a close relationship and its endpoint. In J. M. Adams & W. H. Jones (Eds.), *Handbook of interpersonal commitment and relationship stability* (pp. 481–499). New York: Kluwer Academic/Plenum.

Karney, B. R., & Coombs, R. H. (2000). Memory bias in long-term close relationships: Consistency or improvement? *Personality and Social Psychology Bulletin, 26*, 959–970.

Kashy, D. A., & Kenny, D. A. (2000). The analysis of data from dyads and groups. In H. T. Reis & C. M. Judd (Eds.), *Handbook of research methods in social psychology* (pp. 451–477). New York: Cambridge University Press.

Kauth, M. R. (2006). Sexual orientation and identity. In R. D. McAnulty & M. M. Burnette (Eds.), *Sex and sexuality. Vol. 1. Sexuality today: Trends and controversies* (pp. 153–184). Westport, CT: Praeger.

Kawabata, Y., & Crick, N. R. (2008). The role of cross-racial/ethnic friendships in social adjustment. *Developmental Psychology, 44*, 1177–1183.

Kayser, K. (1993). *When love dies: The process of marital disaffection.* New York: Guilford Press.

Kayser, K. (1996). The Marital Disaffection Scale: An inventory for assessing emotional estrangement in marriage. *The American Journal of Family Therapy, 24*, 83–88.

Kayser, K., & Rao, S. S. (2006). Process of disaffection in relationship breakdown. In M. A. Fine & J. H. Harvey (Eds.), *Handbook of divorce and dissolution* (pp. 201–221). Mahwah, NJ: Lawrence Erlbaum Associates Inc.

Kellas, J. K., & Manusov, V. (2003). What's in a story? The relationship between narrative completeness and adjustment to relationship dissolution. *Journal of Social and Personal Relationships, 20*, 285–307.

Kelley, H. H., Berscheid, E., Christensen, A., Harvey, J. H., Huston, T. L., Levinger, G., McClintock, E., Peplau, L. A., & Peterson, D. R. (Eds.). (1983). *Close relationships.* New York: W. H. Freeman & Company.

Kelley, H. H., Berscheid, E., Christensen, A., Harvey, J. H., Huston, T. L., Levinger, G., McClintock, E., Peplau, L. A., & Peterson, D. R. (2002). Analyzing close relationships. In H. H. Kelley, E. Berscheid, A. Christensen, J. H. Harvey, T. L. Huston, G. Levinger, E. McClintock, L. A. Peplau, & D. R. Peterson (Eds.), *Close relationships* (pp. 20–67). Clinton Corners, NY: Percheron Press. (Original work published 1983.)

Kelly, D. J., Quinn, P. C., Slater, A. M., Lee, K., Ge, L., & Pascalis, O. (2007). The other-race effect develops during infancy. *Psychological Science, 18*, 1084–1089.

Kelly, E. L., & Conley, J. J. (1987). Personality and compatibility: A prospective analysis of marital stability and marital satisfaction. *Journal of Personality and Social Psychology, 52*, 27–40.

Kelly, J. B., & Johnson, M. P. (2008). Differentiation among types of intimate partner violence: Research update and implications for interventions. *Family Court Review, 46*, 476–499.

Kenny, D. A. (1990). Design issues in dyadic research. In C. Hendrick & M. S. Clark (Eds.), *Review of personality and social psychology: Research methods in personality and social psychology* (Vol. 11, pp. 164–184). Newbury Park, CA: Sage Publications.

Kenny, D. A., & Judd, C. M. (1986). Consequences of violating the independence assumption in analysis of variance. *Psychological Bulletin, 99*, 422–431.

Kenny, D. A., Kashy, D. A., & Bolger, N. (1998). Data analysis in social psychology. In D. T. Gilbert, S. T. Fiske, & G. Lindzey (Eds.), *The handbook of social psychology* (4th ed., Vol. 1, pp. 233–265). Boston: McGraw-Hill.

Kenny, D. A., Kashy, D. A., & Cook, W. L. (2006). *Dyadic data analysis.* New York: The Guilford Press.

Kephart, W. M. (1967). Some correlates of romantic love. *Journal of Marriage & the Family, 29*, 470–474.

Kerckhoff, A. C. (1974). The social context of interpersonal attraction. In T. L. Huston (Ed.), *Foundations of interpersonal attraction* (pp. 61–76). New York: Academic Press.

Kerckhoff, A. C., & Davis, K. E. (1962). Value consensus and need complementarity in mate selection. *American Sociological Review, 27*, 295–303.

Kersten, K. K. (1990). The process of marital disaffection: Interventions at various stages. *Family Relations, 39*, 257–265.

Khallad, Y. (2005). Mate selection in Jordan: Effects of sex, socio-economic status, and culture. *Journal of Social and Personal Relationships, 22*, 155–168.

Kidd, T., & Sheffield, D. (2005). Attachment style and symptom reporting: Examining the mediating effects of anger and social support. *British Journal of Health Psychology, 10*, 531–541.

Kiecolt-Glaser, J. K., Bane, C., Glaser, R., & Malarkey, W. B. (2003). Love, marriage, and divorce: Newly-weds' stress hormones foreshadow relationship changes. *Journal of Consulting and Clinical Psychology, 71*, 176–188.

Kiernan, K. (2004). Cohabitation and divorce across nations and generations. In P. L. Chase-Lansdale, K. Kiernan, & R. J. Friedman (Eds.), *Human development across lives and generations: The potential for change* (pp. 139–170). New York: Cambridge University Press.

Kiesler, S., Siegel, J., & McGuire, T. W. (1984). Social psychological aspects of computer-mediated communication. *American Psychologist, 39*, 1123–1134.

Kim, B. S., Atkinson, D. R., & Yang, P. H. (1999). The Asian Values Scale: Development, factor analysis, validation and reliability. *Journal of Counseling Psychology, 46*, 342–352.

Kim, T. I., Shin, Y. H., & White-Traut, R. C. (2003). Multisensory intervention improves physical growth and illness rates in Korean orphaned newborn infants. *Research in Nursing & Health, 26*, 424–433.

King, C. E., & Christensen, A. (1983). The Relationship Events Scale: A Guttman scaling of progress in courtship. *Journal of Marriage & the Family, 45*, 671–678.

Kinsey, A. C., Pomeroy, W. B., & Martin, C. E. (1948). *Sexual behavior in the human male*. Philadelphia: W. B. Saunders.

Kinsey, A. C., Pomeroy, W. B., Martin, C. E., & Gebhard, P. H. (1953). *Sexual behavior in the human female*. Philadelphia, PA: W. B. Saunders Company.

Kir, T., Gulec, M., Bakir, B., Hosgonul, E., & Tumerdem, N. (2005). The frequency and effecting factors of consanguineous marriage in a group of soldiers in Ankara. *Journal of Biosocial Science, 37*, 519–523.

Kisilevsky, B. S., Hains, S. M. J., Lee, K., Muir, D. W., Xu, F., Fu, G., Zhao, Z. Y., & Yang, R. L. (1998). The still-face effect in Chinese and Canadian 3- to 6-month-old infants. *Developmental Psychology, 34*, 629–639.

Kisler, T. S., & Christopher, F. S. (2008). Sexual exchanges and relationship satisfaction: Testing the role of sexual satisfaction as a mediator and gender as a moderator. *Journal of Social and Personal Relationships, 25*, 587–602.

Kleiboer, A. M., Kuijer, R. G., Hox, J. J., Schreurs, K. M. G., & Bensing, J. M. (2006). Receiving and providing support in couples dealing with multiple sclerosis: A diary study using an equity perspective. *Personal Relationships, 13*, 485–501.

Kline, G. H., Stanley, S. M., Markman, H. J., Olmos-Gallo, P. A., St. Peters, M., Whitton, S. W., & Prado, L. M. (2004). Timing is everything: Pre-engagement cohabitation and increased risk for poor marital outcomes. *Journal of Family Psychology, 18*, 311–318.

Kline Rhoades, G., Stanley, S. M., & Markman, H. J. (2006). Pre-engagement cohabitation and gender asymmetry in marital commitment. *Journal of Family Psychology, 20*, 553–560.

Knee, C. R. (1998). Implicit theories of relationships: Assessment and prediction of romantic relationship initiation, coping, and longevity. *Journal of Personality and Social Psychology, 74*, 360–370.

Knee, C. R., Patrick, H., & Lonsbary, C. (2003). Implicit theories of relationships: Orientations toward evaluation and cultivation. *Personality and Social Psychology Review, 7*, 41–55.

Knox, D., Schacht, C., & Zusman, M. E. (1999). Love relationships among college students. *College Student Journal, 33*, 149–151.

Knox, D., Vail-Smith, K., & Zusman, M. (2008). "Men are dogs": Is the stereotype justified? Data on the cheating college male. *College Student Journal, 42*, 1015–1022.

Kobiella, A., Grossmann, T., Reid, V. M., & Striano, T. (2008). The discrimination of angry and fearful facial expressions in 7-month-old infants: An event-related potential study. *Cognition and Emotion, 22*, 134–146.

Kochanska, G., Forman, D. R., & Coy, K. C. (1999). Implications of the mother–child relationship in infancy for socialization in the second year of life. *Infant Behavior & Development, 22*, 249–265.

Koenig, B. L., Kirkpatrick, L. A., & Ketelaar, T. (2007). Misperception of sexual and romantic interests in opposite-sex friendships: Four hypotheses. *Personal Relationships, 14*, 411–429.

Koss, M. P., Gidycz, C. A., & Wisniewski, N. (1987). The scope of rape: Incidence and prevalence of sexual aggression and victimization in a national sample of higher education students. *Journal of Consulting and Clinical Psychology, 55*, 162–170.

Kotsoni, E., de Haan, M., & Johnson, M. H. (2001). Categorical perception of facial expressions by 7-month-old infants. *Perception, 30*, 1115–1125.

Kowalski, R. M. (1992). Nonverbal behaviors and perceptions of sexual intentions: Effects of sexual connotativeness, verbal response, and rape outcome. *Basic and Applied Social Psychology, 13*, 427–445.

Kowalski, R. M. (1993). Inferring sexual interest from behavioral cues: Effects of gender and sexually relevant attitudes. *Sex Roles, 29*, 13–36.

Krafft-Ebing, R. von (1945). *Psychopathia sexualis* (12th ed.). New York: Pioneer Publications. (Original work published 1886.)

Krantz, D. S., & McCeney, M. K. (2002). Effects of psychological and social factors on organic disease: A critical assessment of research on coronary heart disease. *Annual Review of Psychology, 53*, 341–369.

Kujala, A., Huotilainen, M., Hotakainen, M., Lennes, M., Parkkonen, L., Fellman, V., & Näätänen, R. (2004). Speech-sound discrimination in neonates as measured with MEG. *Neuroreport: For Rapid Communication of Neuroscience Research, 15*, 2089–2092.

Kumagai, F. (1995). Families in Japan: Beliefs and realities. *Journal of Comparative Family Studies, 26*, 135–163.

Kunkel, A. W., & Burleson, B. R. (1999). Assessing explanations for sex differences in emotional support: A test of the different cultures and skill specialization accounts. *Human Communication Research, 25*, 307–340.

Kurdek, L. A. (1991). Sexuality in homosexual and heterosexual couples. In K. McKinney & S. Sprecher (Eds.), *Sexuality in close relationships* (pp. 177–191). Hillsdale, NJ: Lawrence Erlbaum Associates Inc.

Kurdek, L. A. (1993). Predicting marital dissolution: A 5-year prospective longitudinal study of newlywed couples. *Journal of Personality and Social Psychology, 64*, 221–242.

Kurdek, L. A. (1994). Areas of conflict for gay, lesbian, and heterosexual couples: What couples argue about influences relationship satisfaction. *Journal of Marriage and the Family, 56*, 923–934.

Kurdek, L. A. (1998). Developmental changes in marital satisfaction: A 13-year prospective longitudinal study of newlywed couples. In T. N. Bradbury (Ed.), *The developmental course of marital dysfunction* (pp. 180–204). New York: Cambridge University Press.

Kurdek, L. A. (1999). The nature and predictors of the trajectory of change in marital quality for husbands and wives over the first 10 years of marriage. *Developmental Psychology, 35*, 1283–1296.

Kurdek, L. A. (2000). Attractions and constraints as determinants of relationship commitment: Longitudinal evidence from gay, lesbian, and heterosexual couples. *Personal Relationships, 7*, 245–262.

Kurdek, L. A. (2002). Predicting the timing of separation and marital satisfaction: An eight-year prospective longitudinal study. *Journal of Marriage and Family, 64*, 163–179.

Kurdek, L. A. (2003). Methodological issues in growth-curve analyses with married couples. *Personal Relationships, 10*, 235–266.

Kurdek, L. A. (2004). Are gay and lesbian cohabiting couples *really* different from heterosexual married couples? *Journal of Marriage and Family, 66*, 880–900.

Kurdek, L. A. (2005a). Gender and marital satisfaction early in marriage: A growth curve approach. *Journal of Marriage and Family, 67*, 68–84.

Kurdek, L. A. (2005b). What do we know about gay and lesbian couples? *Current Directions in Psychological Science, 14*, 251–254.

Kurdek, L. A. (2006a). Differences between partners from heterosexual, gay, and lesbian cohabiting couples. *Journal of Marriage and Family, 68*, 509–528.

Kurdek, L. A. (2006b). The nature and correlates of deterrents to leaving a relationship. *Personal Relationships, 13*, 521–535.

Kurdek, L. A. (2008). A general model of relationship commitment: Evidence from same-sex partners. *Personal Relationships, 15*, 391–405.

Kurup, R. K., & Kurup, P. A. (2003). Hypothalamic digoxin, hemispheric dominance, and neurobiology of love and affection. *International Journal of Neuroscience, 113*, 721–729.

Kushner, H. I., & Sterk, C. E. (2005). The limits of social capital: Durkheim, suicide, and social cohesion. *American Journal of Public Health, 95*, 1139–1143.

Lacey, R. S., Reifman, A., Scott, J. P., Harris, S. M., & Fitzpatrick, J. (2004). Sexual-moral attitudes, love styles, and mate selection. *The Journal of Sex Research, 41*, 121–128.

Lamm, H., & Wiesmann, U. (1997). Subjective attributes of attraction: How people characterize their liking, their love, and their being in love. *Personal Relationships, 4*, 271–284.

Laner, M. R., & Ventrone, N. A. (2000). Dating scripts revisited. *Journal of Family Issues, 21*, 488–500.

Langer, E. J. (1975). The illusion of control. *Journal of Personality and Social Psychology, 32*, 311–328.

Langlois, J. H., Kalakanis, L., Rubenstein, A. J., Larson, A., Hallam, M., & Smoot, M. (2000). Maxims or myths of beauty? A meta-analytic and theoretical review. *Psychological Bulletin, 126*, 390–423.

Langlois, J. H., & Roggman, L. A. (1990). Attractive faces are only average. *Psychological Science, 1*, 115–121.

Lannutti, P. J. (2005). For better or worse: Exploring the meanings of same-sex marriage within the lesbian, gay, bisexual and transgendered community. *Journal of Social and Personal Relationships, 22*, 5–18.

Laurenceau, J-P., Barrett, L. F., & Rovine, M. J. (2005). The interpersonal process model of intimacy in marriage: A daily-diary and multilevel modeling approach. *Journal of Family Psychology, 19*, 314–323.

Laursen, B. (1993). The perceived impact of conflict on adolescent relationships. *Merrill-Palmer Quarterly, 39*, 535–550.

Laursen, B., Coy, K. C., & Collins, W. A. (1998). Reconsidering changes in parent–child conflict across adolescence: A meta-analysis. *Child Development, 69*, 817–832.

LaVeist, T. A., Sellers, R. M., Brown, K. A. E., & Nickerson, K. (1997). Extreme social isolation, use of community-based senior support services, and mortality among African American elderly women. *American Journal of Community Psychology, 25*, 721–732.

Lawrance, K., & Byers, E. S. (1995). Sexual satisfaction in long-term heterosexual relationships: The interpersonal exchange model of sexual satisfaction. *Personal Relationships, 2*, 267–285.

Lawrence, E., & Bradbury, T. N. (2007). Trajectories of change in physical aggression and marital satisfaction. *Journal of Family Psychology, 21*, 236–247.

Lawrence, E., Bunde, M., Barry, R. A., Brock, R. L., Sullivan, K. T., Pasch, L. A., White, G. A., Dowd, C. E., & Adams, E. E. (2008). Partner support and marital satisfaction: Support amount, adequacy, provision, and solicitation. *Personal Relationships, 15*, 445–463.

Lawrence, E., Pederson, A., Bunde, M., Barry, R. A., Brock, R. L., Fazio, E., Mulryan, L., Hunt, S., Madsen, L., & Dzankovic, S. (2008). Objective ratings of relationship skills across multiple domains as predictors of marital satisfaction trajectories. *Journal of Social and Personal Relationships, 25*, 445–466.

Lawrence, E., Rothman, A. D., Cobb, R. J., Rothman, M. T., & Bradbury, T. N. (2008). Marital satisfaction across the transition to parenthood. *Journal of Family Psychology, 22*, 41–50.

Lawson, H. M., & Leck, K. (2006). Dynamics of internet dating. *Social Science Computer Review, 24*, 189–208.

Lay, C., Fairlie, P., Jackson, S., Ricci, T., Eisenberg, J., Sato, T., Teeäär, A., & Melamud, A. (1998). Domain-specific allocentrism–idiocentrism. *Journal of Cross-Cultural Psychology, 29*, 434–460.

Le, B., & Agnew, C. R. (2003). Commitment and its theorized determinants: A meta-analysis of the Investment Model. *Personal Relationships, 10*, 37–57.

Le, T. N. (2005). Narcissism and immature love as mediators of vertical individualism and ludic love style. *Journal of Social and Personal Relationships, 22*, 543–560.

Le Bourdais, C., & Lapierre-Adamcyk, E. (2004). Changes in conjugal life in Canada: Is cohabitation progressively replacing marriage? *Journal of Marriage and Family, 66*, 929–942.

Le Gall, A., Mullet, E., & Shafighi, S. R. (2002). Age, religious beliefs, and sexual attitudes. *The Journal of Sex Research, 39*, 207–216.

Leary, M. R. (2001). Toward a conceptualization of interpersonal rejection. In M. R. Leary (Ed.), *Interpersonal rejection* (pp. 3–20). New York: Oxford University Press.

Leary, M. R., & Cox, C. B. (2008). Belongingness motivation: A mainspring of social action. In J. Y. Shah & W. L. Gardner (Eds.), *Handbook of motivation science* (pp. 27–40). New York: Guilford Press.

Leckman, J. F., & Herman, A. E. (2002). Maternal behavior and developmental psychopathology. *Biological Psychiatry, 51*, 27–43.

Leckman, J. F., Hrdy, S. B., Keverne, E. B., & Carter, C. S. (2006). A biobehavioral model of attachment and bonding. In R. J. Sternberg & K. Weis (Eds.), *The new psychology of love* (pp. 116–145). New Haven, CT: Yale University Press.

Lee, J. A. (1973). *Colours of love: An exploration of the ways of loving.* Toronto: New Press.

Lee, J. A. (1977). A typology of styles of loving. *Personality and Social Psychology Bulletin, 3*, 173–182.

Lee, J. A. (1988). Love-styles. In R. J. Sternberg & M. L. Barnes (Eds.), *The psychology of love* (pp. 38–67). New Haven, CT: Yale University Press.

Lee, J. W., & Guerrero, L. K. (2001). Types of touch in cross-sex relationships between coworkers: Perceptions of relational and emotional messages, inappropriateness, and sexual harassment. *Journal of Applied Communication Research, 29*, 197–220.

Lee, R. E., & Whiting, J. B. (2007). Foster children's expressions of ambiguous loss. *The American Journal of Family Therapy, 35*, 417–428.

Lee, Y-S., & Waite, L. J. (2005). Husbands' and wives' time spent on housework: A comparison of measures. *Journal of Marriage and Family, 67*, 328–336.

Lehman, D. R., Ellard, J. H., & Wortman, C. B. (1986). Social support for the bereaved: Recipients' and providers' perspectives on what is helpful. *Journal of Consulting and Clinical Psychology, 54*, 438–446.

Leitz-Spitz, M. A. (2003). Stalking: Terrorism at our doors—how social workers can help victims fight back. *Social Work, 48*, 504–512.

Lemay, E. P. Jr., & Clark, M. S. (2008). How the head liberates the heart: Projection of communal responsiveness guides relationship promotion. *Journal of Personality and Social Psychology, 94*, 647–671.

Lemay, E. P. Jr., Clark, M. S., & Feeney, B. C. (2007). Projection of responsiveness to needs and the construction of satisfying communal relationships. *Journal of Personality and Social Psychology, 92*, 834–853.

Lennon, M. C., & Rosenfield, S. (1994). Relative fairness and the division of housework: The importance of options. *American Journal of Sociology, 100*, 5013–5031.

Lento, J. (2006). Relational and physical victimization by peers and romantic partners in college students. *Journal of Social and Personal Relationships, 23*, 331–348.

Lester, D. (1996). Trends in divorce and marriage around the world. *Journal of Divorce and Remarriage, 25*, 169–171.

Lester, D., Haig, C., & Monello, R. (1989). Spouses' personality and marital satisfaction. *Personality and Individual Differences, 10*, 253–254.

Lever, J. (1994, August 23). The 1994 *Advocate* survey of sexuality and relationships: The men. *The Advocate: The National Gay & Lesbian Newsmagazine*, pp. 17–24.

Lever, J. (1995, August 22). The 1995 *Advocate* survey of sexuality and relationships: The women. *The Advocate: The National Gay & Lesbian Newsmagazine*, pp. 22–30.

Levin, K., & Haines, S. (2007). Opportunities for the development of communicative competence for children in an orphanage in South Africa. *Child Care in Practice, 13*, 221–236.

Levine, D. (2000). Virtual attraction: What rocks your boat. *CyberPsychology & Behavior, 3*, 565–573.

Levine, R., Sato, S., Hashimoto, T., & Verma, J. (1995). Love and marriage in eleven cultures. *Journal of Cross-Cultural Psychology, 26*, 554–571.

Levinger, G. (1965). Marital cohesiveness and dissolution: An integrative view. *Journal of Marriage and the Family, 27*, 19–28.

Levinger, G. (1976). A social psychological perspective on marital dissolution. *Journal of Social Issues, 32*, 21–47.

Levinger, G. (1983). Development and change. In H. H. Kelley, E. Berscheid, A. Christensen, J. H. Harvey, T. L. Huston, G. Levinger, E. McClintock, L. A. Peplau, & D. R. Peterson (Eds.), *Close relationships* (pp. 315–359). New York: Freeman.

Levinger, G., Senn, D. J., & Jorgensen, B. W. (1970). Progress toward permanence in courtship: A test of the Kerckhoff-Davis hypothesis. *Sociometry, 33*, 427–443.

Levinger, G., & Snoek, J. D. (1972). *Attraction in relationship: A new look at interpersonal attraction.* Morristown, NJ: General Learning Press.

Levy, D. M. (1937). Primary affect hunger. *American Journal of Psychiatry, 94*, 643–652.

Lewis, C. S. (1988). *The four loves.* New York: Harcourt Brace. (Original work published 1960.)

Lewis, R. A. (1972). A developmental framework for the analysis of premarital dyadic formation. *Family Process, 11*, 17–48.

Lewis, R. A. (1973). A longitudinal test of a developmental framework for premarital dyadic formation. *Journal of Marriage & the Family, 35*, 113–125.

Leymann, H. (1990). Mobbing and psychological terror at workplaces. *Violence and Victims, 5*, 119–126.

Leymann, H., & Gustafsson, A. (1996). Mobbing at work and the development of post-traumatic stress disorders. *European Journal of Work and Organizational Psychology, 5*, 251–275.

Lieberman, D., & Hatfield, E. (2006). Passionate love: Cross-cultural and evolutionary perspectives. In R. J. Sternberg & K. Weis (Eds.), *The new psychology of love* (pp. 274–297). New Haven, CT: Yale University Press.

Lin, L. W., & Huddleston-Casas, C. A. (2005). Agape love in couple relationships. *Marriage and Family Review, 37*, 29–48.

Lindahl, K., Clements, M., & Markman, H. (1998). The development of marriage: A 9-year perspective. In T. N. Bradbury (Ed.), *The developmental course of marital dysfunction* (pp. 205–236). Cambridge, UK: Cambridge University Press.

Lindsey, E. W., Colwell, M. J., Frabutt, J. M., & MacKinnon-Lewis, C. (2006). Family conflict in divorced and non-divorced families: Potential consequences for boys' friendship status and friendship quality. *Journal of Social and Personal Relationships, 23*, 45–63.

Litzinger, S., & Gordon, K. C. (2005). Exploring relationships among communication, sexual satisfaction, and marital satisfaction. *Journal of Sex & Marital Therapy, 31*, 409–424.

Liu, L-J., & Guo, Q. (2007). Loneliness and health-related quality of life for the empty nest elderly in the rural areas of a mountainous county in China. *Quality of Life Research: An International Journal of Quality of Life Aspects of Treatment, Care & Rehabilitation, 16*, 1275–1280.

Ljungberg, T., Horowitz, L., Jansson, L., Westlund, K., & Clarke, C. (2005). Communicative factors, conflict progression, and use of reconciliatory strategies in pre-school boys—a series of random events or a sequential process? *Aggressive Behavior, 31*, 303–323.

Locke, H. J., & Wallace, K. M. (1959). Short marital-adjustment and prediction tests: Their reliability and validity. *Marriage and Family Living, 21*, 251–255.

Logan, T. K., Leukefeld, C., & Walker, B. (2000). Stalking as a variant of intimate violence: Implications from a young adult sample. *Violence & Victims, 15*, 91–111.

Loh, C., Orchowski, L. M., Gidycz, C. A., & Elizaga, R. A. (2007). Socialization and sexual aggression in college men: The role of observational influence in detecting risk cues. *Psychology of Men & Masculinity, 8*, 129–144.

Lorenz, K. (1952). *King Solomon's ring: New light on animal ways* (M. K. Wilson, Trans.). London: Methuen.

Loucks, E. B., Berkman, L. F., Gruenewald, T. L., & Seeman, T. E. (2005). Social integration is associated with fibrinogen concentration in elderly men. *Psychosomatic Medicine, 67*, 353–358.

Loucks, E. B., Sullivan, L. M., D'Agostino, R. B. Sr., Larson, M. G., Berkman, L. F., & Benjamin, E. J. (2006). Social networks and inflammatory markers in the Framingham Heart Study. *Journal of Biosocial Science, 38*, 835–842.

Love: The chemical reaction. (2006, February). *National Geographic Magazine.*

Lu, L. (2006). Postnatal adjustment of Chinese parents: A two-wave panel study in Taiwan. *International Journal of Psychology, 41*, 371–384.

Luepnitz, D. A. (1988). *The family interpreted.* New York: Basic Books.

Luo, S., & Klohnen, E. C. (2005). Assortative mating and marital quality in newlyweds: A couple-centered approach. *Journal of Personality and Social Psychology, 88*, 304–326.

Lutgen-Sandvik, P., Tracy, S. J., & Alberts, J. K. (2007). Burned by bullying in the American workplace: Prevalence, perception, degree and impact. *Journal of Management Studies, 44*, 837–862.

Maccoby, E. E. (1990). Gender and relationships: A developmental account. *American Psychologist, 45*, 513–520.

MacGeorge, E. L., Graves, A. R., Feng, B., Gillihan, S. J., & Burleson, B. R. (2004). The myth of gender cultures: Similarities outweigh differences in men's and women's provision of and responses to supportive communication. *Sex Roles, 50*, 143–175.

MacLean, K. (2003). The impact of institutionalization on child development. *Development and Psychopathology, 15*, 853–884.

MacNeil, S., & Byers, E. S. (2005). Dyadic assessment of sexual self-disclosure and sexual satisfaction in heterosexual dating couples. *Journal of Social and Personal Relationships, 22*, 169–181.

Madden, M., & Lenhart, A. (2006, March 5). *Online dating* (Report for the Pew Internet & American Life Project). Retrieved August 6, 2008, from http://www.pewinternet.org/pdfs/PIP_Online_Dating.pdf

Maisel, N. C., Gable, S. L., & Strachman, A. (2008). Responsive behaviors in good times and in bad. *Personal Relationships, 15*, 317–338.

Major, B. (1993). Gender, entitlement, and the distribution of family labor. *Journal of Social Issues, 49*, 141–159.

Mantovani, F. (2001). Networked seduction: A test-bed for the study of strategic communication on the Internet. *CyberPsychology & Behavior, 4*, 147–154.

Manusov, V. (1990). An application of attribution principles to nonverbal behavior in romantic dyads. *Communication Monographs, 57*, 104–118.

Marazziti, D., Akiskal, H. S., Rossi, A., & Cassano, G. B. (1999). Alteration of the platelet serotonin transporter in romantic love. *Psychological Medicine, 239*, 741–745.

Marcus, G. F., & Rabagliati, H. (2009). Language acquisition, domain specificity, and descent with modification. In J. Colombo, P. McCardle, & L. Freund (Eds.), *Infant pathways to language: Methods, models, and research disorders* (pp. 267–285). New York: Psychology Press.

Markey, P. M., & Markey, C. N. (2007). Romantic ideals, romantic obtainment, and relationship experiences: The complementarity of interpersonal traits among romantic partners. *Journal of Social and Personal Relationships, 24*, 517–533.

Markides, K. S., Roberts-Jolly, J., Ray, L. A., Hoppe, S. K., & Rudkin, L. (1999). Changes in marital satisfaction in three generations of Mexican Americans. *Research on Aging, 21*, 36–45.

Marquart, B. S., Nannini, D. K., Edwards, R. W., Stanley, L. R., & Wayman, J. C. (2007). Prevalence of dating violence and victimization: Regional and gender differences. *Adolescence, 42*, 645–657.

Marshall, A. D., & Holtzworth-Munroe, A. (2002). Varying forms of husband sexual aggression: Predictors and subgroup differences. *Journal of Family Psychology, 16*, 286–296.

Martin, E., & Gamella, J. F. (2005). Marriage practices and ethnic differentiation: The case of Spanish Gypsies. *The History of the Family, 10*, 45–63.

Martin, K. M., & Huebner, S. (2007). Peer victimization and prosocial experiences and emotional well-being of middle school students. *Psychology in the Schools, 44*, 199–208.

Martin, P. D., Specter, G., Martin, D., & Martin, M. (2003). Expressed attitudes of adolescents toward marriage and family life. *Adolescence, 38*, 359–367.

Martin, P. V., & Hummer, R. A. (1989). Fraternities and rape on campus. *Gender & Society, 3*, 457–473.

Maurer, D., & Salapatek, P. (1976). Developmental changes in the scanning of faces by young infants. *Child Development, 47*, 523–527.

Maurice, W. L. (2007). Sexual desire disorders in men. In S. R. Leiblum (Ed.), *Principles and practice of sex therapy* (4th ed., pp. 181–211). New York: Guilford Press.

McCabe, M. P., & Collins, J. K. (1984). Measurement of depth of desired and experienced sexual involvement at different stages of dating. *Journal of Sex Research, 20*, 377–390.

McCarthy, B. W., Ginsberg, R. L., & Fucito, L. M. (2006). Resilient sexual desire in heterosexual couples. *The Family Journal, 14*, 59–64.

McCormick, N. B. (1979). Come-ons and put-offs: Unmarried students' strategies for having and avoiding sexual intercourse. *Psychology of Women Quarterly, 4*, 194–211.

McCormick, N. B., & Jones, A. J. (1989). Gender differences in nonverbal flirtation. *Journal of Sex Education and Therapy, 15*, 271–282.

McGinnis, R. (1958). Campus values in mate selection: A repeat study. *Social Forces, 36*, 368–373.

McGonagle, K. A., Kessler, R. C., & Schilling, E. A. (1992). The frequency and determinants of marital disagreements in a community sample. *Journal of Social and Personal Relationships, 9*, 507–524.

McKenna, K. A. (2008). MySpace or your place: Relationship initiation and development in the wired and wireless world. In S. Sprecher, A. Wenzel, & J. Harvey (Eds.), *Handbook of relationship initiation* (pp. 235–247). New York: Psychology Press.

McNamara, J. R., & Grossman, K. (1991). Initiation of dates and anxiety among college men and women. *Psychological Reports, 69*, 252–254.

McNulty, J. K., & Fisher, T. D. (2008). Gender differences in response to sexual expectancies and changes in sexual frequency: A short-term longitudinal study of sexual satisfaction in newly married couples. *Archives of Sexual Behavior, 37*, 229–240.

McNulty, J. K., & Hellmuth, J. C. (2008). Emotion regulation and intimate partner violence in newlyweds. *Journal of Family Psychology, 22*, 794–797.

Medora, N. P. (2003). Mate selection in contemporary India: Love marriages versus arranged marriages. In R. R. Hamon & B. B. Ingoldsby (Eds.), *Mate selection across cultures* (pp. 209–230). Thousand Oaks, CA: Sage Publications.

Medora, N. P., Larson, J. H., Hortaçsu, N., & Dave, P. (2002). Perceived attitudes toward romanticism: A cross-cultural study of American, Asian-Indian, and Turkish young adults. *Journal of Comparative Family Studies, 33*, 155–178.

Meeks, B. S., Hendrick, S. S., & Hendrick, C. (1998). Communication, love and relationship satisfaction. *Journal of Social and Personal Relationships, 15*, 755–773.

Meloy, J. R. (1989). Unrequited love and the wish to kill: Diagnosis and treatment of borderline erotomania. *Bulletin of the Menninger Clinic, 53*, 477–492.

Meloy, J. R. (2007). Stalking: The state of the science. *Criminal Behaviour and Mental Health, 17*, 1–7.

Melson, G. F. (2001). *Why the wild things are: Animals in the lives of children*. Cambridge, MA: Harvard University Press.

Merrell, K. W., Gueldner, B. A., Ross, S. W., & Isava, D. M. (2008). How effective are school bullying intervention programs? A meta-analysis of intervention research. *School Psychology Quarterly, 23*, 26–42.

Metts, S. (1994). Relational transgressions. In W. R. Cupach & B. H. Spitzberg (Eds.), *The dark side of interpersonal communication* (pp. 217–240). Hillsdale, NJ: Lawrence Erlbaum Associates Inc.

Metts, S. (2003). Sexual communication: Couple relationships. In J. J. Ponzetti Jr. (Ed.), *International encyclopedia of marriage and family* (2nd ed., Vol. 3, pp. 1437–1443). New York: Macmillan Reference USA.

Metts, S. (2004). First sexual involvement in romantic relationships: An empirical investigation of communicative framing, romantic beliefs, and attachment orientation in the passion turning point. In J. Harvey, A. Wenzel, & S. Sprecher (Eds.), *The handbook of sexuality in close relationships* (pp. 135–158). Mahwah, NJ: Lawrence Erlbaum Associates Inc.

Metts, S., Sprecher, S., & Regan, P. C. (1998). Communication and sexual desire. In P. A. Andersen & L. K. Guerrero (Eds.), *Handbook of communication and emotion: Research, theory, applications, and contexts* (pp. 353–377). Orlando, FL: Academic Press.

Meyers, S., & Berscheid, E. (1996). The language of love: The difference a preposition makes. *Personality and Social Psychology Bulletin, 23*, 347–362.

Meyers, S. A., & Landsberger, S. A. (2002). Direct and indirect pathways between adult attachment style and marital satisfaction. *Personal Relationships, 9*, 159–172.

Mezulis, A. H., Abramson, L. Y., Hyde, J. S., & Hankin, B. L. (2004). Is there a universal positivity bias in attributions? A meta-analytic review of individual, developmental, and cultural differences in the self-serving attributional bias. *Psychological Bulletin, 130*, 711–747.

Michael, R. T., Gagnon, J. H., Laumann, E. O., & Kolata, G. (1994). *Sex in America: A definitive survey*. Boston: Little, Brown.

Michalski, J. H. (2005). Explaining intimate partner violence: The sociological limitations of victimization studies. *Sociological Forum, 20*, 613–640.

Mikkelsen, E. G., & Einarsen, S. (2002). Basic assumptions and symptoms of post-traumatic stress among victims of bullying at work. *European Journal of Work and Organizational Psychology, 11*, 87–111.

Mikulincer, M., & Shaver, P. R. (2009). An attachment and behavioral systems perspective on social support. *Journal of Social and Personal Relationships, 26*, 7–19.

Milardo, R. M. (1988). Families and social networks: An overview of theory and methodology. In R. M. Milardo (Ed.), *Families and social networks* (pp. 13–47). Newbury Park, CA: Sage Publications.

Milardo, R. M., & Helms-Erikson, H. (2000). Network overlap and third-party influence in close relationships. In C. Hendrick & S. S. Hendrick (Eds.), *Close relationships: A sourcebook* (pp. 33–46). Thousand Oaks, CA: Sage Publications.

Milkie, M. A., Bianchi, S. M., Mattingly, M. J., & Robinson, J. P. (2002). Gendered division of childrearing: Ideals, realities, and the relationship to parental well-being. *Sex Roles, 47*, 21–38.

Millings, A., & Walsh, J. (2009). A dyadic exploration of attachment and caregiving in long-term couples. *Personal Relationships, 16*, 437–453.

Mintz, E. E. (1980). Obsession with the rejecting beloved. *Psychoanalytic Review, 67*, 479–492.

Mischel, W. (1966). A social-learning view of sex differences in behavior. In E. E. Maccoby (Ed.), *The development of sex differences* (pp. 513–581). Stanford, CA: Stanford University Press.

Monden, C. (2007). Partners in health? Exploring resemblance in health between partners in married and cohabiting couples. *Sociology of Health & Illness, 29*, 391–411.

Mondloch, C. J., Lewis, T. L., Budreau, D. R., Maurer, D., Dannemiller, J. L., Stephens, B. R., & Kleiner-Gathercoal, K. A. (1999). Face perception during early infancy. *Psychological Science, 10*, 419–422.

Mongeau, P. A., Jacobsen, J., & Donnerstein, C. (2007). Defining dates and first date goals: Generalizing from undergraduates to single adults. *Communication Research, 34*, 526–547.

Mongeau, P. A., & Johnson, K. L. (1995). Predicting cross-sex first-date sexual expectations and involvement: Contextual and individual difference factors. *Personal Relationships, 2*, 301–312.

Mongeau, P. A., Morr Serewicz, M. C., & Therrien, L. F. (2004). Goals for cross-sex first dates: Identification, measurement, and the influence of contextual factors. *Communication Monographs, 71*, 121–147.

Monson, C. M., & Langhinrichsen-Rohling, J. (1998). Sexual and nonsexual marital aggression: Legal considerations, epidemiology, and an integrated typology of perpetrators. *Aggression and Violent Behavior, 3*, 369–389.

Montague, D. P. F., & Walker-Andrews, A. S. (2001). Peekaboo: A new look at infants' perception of emotion expressions. *Developmental Psychology, 37*, 826–838.

Montoya, R. M., Horton, R. S., & Kirchner, J. (2008). Is actual similarity necessary for attraction? A meta-analysis of actual and perceived similarity. *Journal of Social and Personal Relationships, 25*, 889–922.

Moore, M. M. (1985). Nonverbal courtship patterns in women: Context and consequences. *Ethology and Sociobiology, 6*, 237–247.

Moore, M. M. (1995). Courtship signaling and adolescents: "Girls just wanna have fun"? *The Journal of Sex Research, 32*, 319–328.

Moreland, R. L., & Beach, S. R. (1992). Exposure effects in the classroom: The development of affinity among students. *Journal of Experimental Social Psychology, 28*, 255–276.

Morrow, G. D., Clark, E. M., & Brock, K. F. (1995). Individual and partner love styles: Implications for the quality of romantic involvements. *Journal of Social and Personal Relationships, 12*, 363–387.

Morry, M. M. (2005). Allocentrism and friendship satisfaction: The mediating roles of disclosure and closeness. *Canadian Journal of Behavioural Science, 37*, 211–222.

Morse, B. J. (1995). Beyond the Conflict Tactics Scale: Assessing gender differences in partner violence. *Violence and Victims, 10*, 251–272.

Morton, J., & Johnson, M. H. (1991). CONSPEC and CONLERN: A two-process theory of infant face recognition. *Psychological Review, 98*, 164–181.

Mosher, D. L., & Anderson, R. D. (1986). Macho personality, sexual aggression, and reactions to guided imagery of realistic rape. *Journal of Research in Personality, 18*, 150–163.

Mosher, D. L., & Sirkin, M. (1984). Measuring a macho personality constellation. *Journal of Research in Personality, 18*, 150–163.

Muehlenhard, C. L., Goggins, M. F., Jones, J. M., & Satterfield, A. T. (1991). Sexual violence and coercion in close relationships. In K. McKinney & S. Sprecher (Eds.), *Sexuality in close relationships* (pp. 155–175). Hillsdale, NJ: Lawrence Erlbaum Associates Inc.

Muehlenhard, C. L., & Miller, E. N. (1988). Traditional and nontraditional men's responses to women's dating initiation. *Behavior Modification, 12*, 385–403.

Mullen, P. E., & Pathé, M. (1994). Stalking and the pathologies of love. *Australian and New Zealand Journal of Psychiatry, 28*, 469–477.

Munro, B., & Munro, G. (2003). Family, definition of. In J. J. Ponzetti Jr. (Ed.), *International encyclopedia of marriage and family* (2nd ed., Vol. 2, pp. 549–555). New York: Macmillan Reference USA.

Murdock, G. P. (1949). *Social structure.* New York: Macmillan.

Murdock, G. P. (1967). Ethnographic atlas: A summary. *Ethnology, 6*, 109–236.

Murnen, S. K., & Byrne, D. (1991). Hyperfemininity: Measurement and initial validation of the construct. *The Journal of Sex Research, 28*, 479–489.

Murray, C. I. (2003). Grief, loss, and bereavement. In J. J. Ponzetti Jr. (Ed.), *International encyclopedia of marriage and family* (2nd ed., Vol. 2, pp. 782–788). New York: Macmillan Reference USA.

Murray, S. L. (1999). The quest for conviction: Motivated cognition in romantic relationships. *Psychological Inquiry, 10*, 23–34.

Murray, S. L., & Holmes, J. G. (1999). The (mental) ties that bind: Cognitive structures that predict relationship resilience. *Journal of Personality and Social Psychology, 77*, 1228–1244.

Murray, S. L., Holmes, J. G., & Griffin, D. W. (1996a). The benefits of positive illusions: Idealization and the construction of satisfaction in close relationships. *Journal of Personality and Social Psychology, 70*, 79–98.

Murray, S. L., Holmes, J. G., & Griffin, D. W. (1996b). The self-fulfilling nature of positive illusions in romantic relationships: Love is not blind, but prescient. *Journal of Personality and Social Psychology, 71*, 1155–1180.

Murray, S. L., Holmes, J. G., & Griffin, D. W. (2003). Reflections on the self-fulfilling effects of positive illusions. *Psychological Inquiry, 14*, 289–295.

Murstein, B. I. (1970). Stimulus-value-role: A theory of marital choice. *Journal of Marriage & the Family, 32*, 465–481.

Murstein, B. I. (1976). *Who will marry whom? Theories and research in marital choice.* New York: Springer.

Murstein, B. I. (1980). Mate selection in the 1970s. *Journal of Marriage & the Family, 42*, 777–792.

Murstein, B. I. (1987). A clarification and extension of the SVR theory of dyadic pairing. *Journal of Marriage & the Family, 49*, 929–947.

Murstein, B. I. (1988). A taxonomy of love. In R. J. Sternberg & M. L. Barnes (Eds.), *The psychology of love* (pp. 13–37). New Haven, CT: Yale University Press.

Mwaba, K., & Naidoo, P. (2005). Sexual practices, attitudes toward premarital sex and condom use among a sample of South African university students. *Social Behavior and Personality, 33*, 651–656.

Nahemow, L., & Lawton, M. P. (1975). Similarity and propinquity in friendship formation. *Journal of Personality and Social Psychology, 32*, 205–213.

Namie, G. (2007). *Workplace Bullying Institute & Zogby International: U.S. workplace bullying survey, September 2007* [online]. Retrieved from http://bullyinginstitute.org/zogby2007/WBIsurvey2007.pdf

National Domestic Violence Hotline. (2008). *What is domestic violence?* [online]. Retrieved from http://www.ndvh.org/get-educated/what-is-domestic-violence

Neary, A., & Joseph, S. (1994). Peer victimization and its relationship to self-concept and depression among schoolgirls. *Personality and Individual Differences, 16*, 183–186.

Neff, L. A., & Karney, B. R. (2002). Judgments of a relationship partner: Specific accuracy but global enhancement. *Journal of Personality, 70*, 1079–1112.

Neff, L. A., & Karney, B. R. (2005). Gender differences in social support: A question of skill or responsiveness? *Journal of Personality and Social Psychology, 88*, 79–90.

Nemechek, S., & Olson, K. R. (1996). Personality and marital adjustment. *Psychological Reports, 78*, 26.

Neto, F., & Pinto, M. d. C. (2003). The role of loneliness, gender and love status in adolescents' love styles. *International Journal of Adolescence and Youth, 11*, 181–191.

Newcomb, T. M. (1961). *The acquaintance process*. New York: Holt, Rinehart, & Winston.

Neyer, F. J., & Asendorpf, J. B. (2001). Personality-relationship transaction in young adulthood. *Journal of Personality and Social Psychology, 81*, 1190–1204.

Neyer, F. J., & Voigt, D. (2004). Personality and social network effects on romantic relationships: A dyadic approach. *European Journal of Personality, 18*, 279–299.

Nishina, A., Juvonen, J., & Witkow, M. R. (2005). Sticks and stones may break my bones, but names will make me feel sick: The psychosocial, somatic, and scholastic consequences of peer harassment. *Journal of Clinical Child and Adolescent Psychology, 34*, 37–48.

Noller, P., Feeney, J. A., Bonnell, D., & Callan, V. J. (1994). A longitudinal study of conflict in early marriage. *Journal of Social and Personal Relationships, 11*, 233–252.

Nørretranders, T. (1998). *The user illusion* (J. Sydenham, Trans.). New York: Viking.

Norton, R. (1983). Measuring marital quality: A critical look at the dependent variable. *Journal of Marriage & the Family, 45*, 141–151.

Notelaers, G., Einarsen, S., De Witte, H., & Vermunt, J. K. (2006). Measuring exposure to bullying at work: The validity and advantages of the latent class cluster approach. *Work & Stress, 20*, 289–302.

Nylund, K., Bellmore, A., Nishina, A., & Graham, S. (2007). Subtypes, severity, and structural stability of peer victimization: What does latent class analysis say? *Child Development, 78*, 1706–1722.

O'Brien, M. (2007). Ambiguous loss in families of children with autism spectrum disorders. *Family Relations, 56*, 135–146.

Odimegwu, C. O. (2005). Sexual behavior of Nigerian university students. *Journal of Child and Adolescent Mental Health, 17*, 35–38.

O'Leary, K. D., & Williams, M. C. (2006). Agreement about acts of violence in marriage. *Journal of Family Psychology, 20*, 656–662.

Oliver, M. B., & Hyde, J. S. (1993). Gender differences in sexuality: A meta-analysis. *Psychological Bulletin, 114*, 29–51.

Olson, D. H. (1990). Marriage in perspective. In F. D. Fincham & T. N. Bradbury (Eds.), *The psychology of marriage: Basic issues and applications* (pp. 402–419). New York: Guilford Press.

Olweus, D. (1993). *Bullying at school: What we know and what we can do.* Cambridge, MA: Blackwell.

Olweus, D. (1995). Bullying or peer abuse at school: Facts and intervention. *Current Directions in Psychological Science, 4*, 196–200.

Orbuch, T. L., & Harvey, J. H. (1991). Methodological and conceptual issues in the study of sexuality in close relationships. In K. McKinney & S. Sprecher (Eds.), *Sexuality in close relationships* (pp. 9–24). Hillsdale, NJ: Lawrence Erlbaum Associates Inc.

Ortiz-Torres, B., Williams, S. P., & Ehrhardt, A. A. (2003). Urban women's gender scripts: Implications for HIV prevention. *Culture, Health & Sexuality, 5*, 1–17.

Orvis, B. R., Kelley, H. H., & Butler, D. (1976). Attributional conflict in young couples. In J. H. Harvey, W. J. Ickes, & R. F. Kidd (Eds.), *New directions in attribution research* (Vol. 1, pp. 353–386). Hillsdale, NJ: Lawrence Erlbaum Associates Inc.

Ostrov, J. M., & Crick, N. R. (2007). Forms and functions of aggression during early childhood: A short-term longitudinal study. *School Psychology Review, 36*, 22–43.

O'Sullivan, L. F. (1995). Less is more: The effects of sexual experience on judgments of men's and women's personality characteristics and relationship desirability. *Sex Roles, 33*, 159–181.

O'Sullivan, L. F., & Gaines, M. E. (1998). Decision-making in college students' heterosexual dating relationships: Ambivalence about engaging in sexual activity. *Journal of Social and Personal Relationships, 15*, 347–363.

Oswald, D. L., & Clark, E. M. (2006). How do friendship maintenance behaviors and problem-solving styles function at the individual and dyadic levels? *Personal Relationships, 13*, 333–348.

Oswald, D. L., Clark, E. M., & Kelly, C. M. (2004). Friendship maintenance: An analysis of individual and dyad behaviors. *Journal of Social and Clinical Psychology, 23*, 413–441.

Overall, N. C., & Sibley, C. G. (2009). When rejection sensitivity matters: Regulating dependence within daily interactions with family and friends. *Personality and Social Psychology Bulletin, 35*(8), 1057–1070.

Paavola, L., Kunnari, S., & Moilanen, I. (2005). Maternal responsiveness and infant intentional communication: Implications for the early communicative and linguistic development. *Child: Care, Health & Development, 31*, 727–735.

Pagelow, M. D. (1981). *Woman-battering: Victims and their experiences.* Beverly Hills, CA: Sage Publications.

Painter, K., & Farrington, D. P. (1998). Marital violence in Great Britain and its relationship to marital and non-marital rape. *International Review of Victimology, 5*, 257–276.

Palmer, D. C. (2000). Chomsky's nativism: A critical review. *Analysis of Verbal Behavior, 17*, 39–50.

Pam, A., Plutchik, R., & Conte, H. R. (1975). Love: A psychometric approach. *Psychological Reports, 37*, 83–88.

Paris, B. L., & Luckey, E. B. (1966). A longitudinal study in marital satisfaction. *Sociology & Social Research, 50*, 212–222.

Parish, W. L., Luo, Y., Laumann, E. O., Kew, M., & Yu, Z. (2007). Unwanted sexual activity among married women in urban China. *The Journal of Sex Research, 44*, 158–171.

Parks, M. R. (2007). *Personal relationships and personal networks.* Mahwah, NJ: Lawrence Erlbaum Associates Inc.

Parks, M. R., & Eggert, L. L. (1991). The role of social context in the dynamics of personal relationships. In W. H. Jones & D. Perlman (Eds.), *Advances in personal relationships: A research annual* (Vol. 2, pp. 1–34). Oxford, UK: Jessica Kingsley Publishers.

Parks, M. R., & Floyd, K. (1996). Making friends in cyberspace. *Journal of Communication, 46*, 80–97.

Parks, M. R., & Roberts, L. D. (1998). Making MOOsic: The development of personal relationships on line and a comparison to their off-line counterparts. *Journal of Social and Personal Relationships, 15*, 517–537.

Pasch, L. A., Bradbury, T. N., & Davila, J. (1997). Gender, negative affectivity, and observed social support behavior in marital interaction. *Personal Relationships, 4*, 361–378.

Pathé, M. (2002). *Surviving stalking.* Cambridge, UK: Cambridge University Press.

Pellegrini, A. D. (2002). Bullying, victimization, and sexual harassment during the transition to middle school. *Educational Psychologist, 37*, 151–163.

Pellegrini, A. D., & Long, J. D. (2002). A longitudinal study of bullying, dominance, and victimization during the transition from primary school through secondary school. *British Journal of Developmental Psychology, 20*, 259–280.

Pence, E., & Paymar, M. (1993). *Education groups for men who batter: The Duluth model.* New York: Springer Publishing Company.

Peplau, L. A. (1983). *Roles and gender.* In H. H. Kelley, E. Berscheid, A. Christensen, J. H. Harvey, T. L. Huston, G. Levinger, E. McClintock, L. A. Peplau, & D. R. Peterson (Eds.), *Close relationships* (pp. 220–264). New York: Freeman.

Peplau, L. A., Cochran, S. D., & Mays, V. M. (1997). A national survey of the intimate relationships of African American lesbians and gay men: A look at commitment, satisfaction, sexual behavior, and HIV disease. In B. Greene (Ed.), *Ethnic and cultural diversity among lesbians and gay men* (pp. 11–38). Thousand Oaks, CA: Sage Publications.

Peplau, L. A., Cochran, S., Rook, K., & Padesky, C. (1978). Loving women: Attachment and autonomy in lesbian relationships. *Journal of Social Issues, 34,* 7–27.

Peplau, L. A., Fingerhut, A., & Beals, K. P. (2004). Sexuality in the relationships of lesbians and gay men. In J. H. Harvey, A. Wenzel, & S. Sprecher (Eds.), *The handbook of sexuality in close relationships* (pp. 349–369). Mahwah, NJ: Lawrence Erlbaum Associates Inc.

Peplau, L. A., & Perlman, D. (Eds.). (1982). *Loneliness: A sourcebook of current theory, research, and therapy.* New York: Wiley.

Peplau, L. A., Rubin, Z., & Hill, C. T. (1977). Sexual intimacy in dating relationships. *Journal of Social Issues, 33,* 86–109.

Peplau, L. A., Russell, D., & Heim, M. (1979). The experience of loneliness. In I. H. Frieze, D. Bar-Tal, & J. S. Carroll (Eds.), *New approaches to social problems: Applications of attribution theory.* San Francisco: Jossey-Bass.

Peplau, L. A., & Spalding, L. (2000). The close relationships of lesbians, gay men, and bisexuals. In C. Hendrick & S. S. Hendrick (Eds.), *Close relationships: A sourcebook* (pp. 111–123). Thousand Oaks, CA: Sage Publications.

Perlman, D., & Oskamp, S. (1971). The effects of picture content and exposure frequency on evaluations of Negroes and Whites. *Journal of Experimental Social Psychology, 7,* 503–514.

Perlman, S. D., & Abramson, P. R. (1982). Sexual satisfaction among married and cohabiting individuals. *Journal of Consulting and Clinical Psychology, 50,* 458–460.

Perper, T., & Weis, D. L. (1987). Proceptive and rejective strategies of U.S. and Canadian college women. *Journal of Sex Research, 23,* 455–480.

Perren, S., von Wyl, A., Bürgin, D., Simoni, H., & von Klitzing, K. (2005). Intergenerational transmission of marital quality across the transition to parenthood. *Family Process, 44,* 441–459.

Perry, B. D. (2002). Childhood experience and the expression of genetic potential: What childhood neglect tells us about nature and nurture. *Brain & Mind, 3,* 79–100.

Peterson, D. R. (2002). Conflict. In H. H. Kelley, E. Berscheid, A. Christensen, J. H. Harvey, T. L. Huston, G. Levinger, E. McClintock, L. A. Peplau, & D. R. Peterson (Eds.), *Close relationships* (pp. 360–396). Clinton Corners, NY: Percheron Press. (Original work published 1983.)

Peterson, Z. D., & Muehlenhard, C. L. (2003). Rape. In J. J. Ponzetti Jr. (Ed.), *International encyclopedia of marriage and family* (2nd ed., Vol. 3, pp. 1293–1297). New York: Macmillan Reference USA.

Pierce, G. R., Sarason, I. G., & Sarason, B. R. (1991). General and relationship-based perceptions of social support: Are two constructs better than one? *Journal of Personality and Social Psychology, 61,* 1028–1039.

Pietropinto, A. (1986). Inhibited sexual desire. *Medical Aspects of Human Sexuality, 20,* 46–49.

Pimlott-Kubiak, S., & Cortina, L. M. (2003). Gender, victimization, and outcomes: Reconceptualizing risk. *Journal of Consulting and Clinical Psychology, 71,* 528–539.

Pinker, S. (1994). *The language instinct: How the mind creates language.* New York: William Morrow & Company.

Pinker, S. (1997). *How the mind works.* New York: W. W. Norton & Co.

Pinker, S., & Jackendoff, R. (2005). The faculty of language: What's special about it? *Cognition, 95,* 201–236.

Pinney, E. M., Gerrard, M., & Denney, N. W. (1987). The Pinney Sexual Satisfaction Inventory. *Journal of Sex Research, 23,* 233–251.

Prager, K. J. (2000). Intimacy in personal relationships. In C. Hendrick & S. S. Hendrick (Eds.), *Close relationships: A sourcebook* (pp. 228–242). Thousand Oaks, CA: Sage Publications.

Prager, K. J., & Buhrmester, D. (1998). Intimacy and need fulfillment in couple relationships. *Journal of Social and Personal Relationships, 15,* 435–469.

Prager, K. J., & Roberts, L. J. (2004). Deep intimate connection: Self and intimacy in couple relationships. In D. J. Mashek & A. Aron (Eds.), *Handbook of closeness and intimacy* (pp. 43–60). Mahwah, NJ: Lawrence Erlbaum Associates Inc.

Press, J. E., & Townsley, E. (1998). Wives' and husbands' housework reporting: Gender, class, and social desirability. *Gender & Society, 12*, 188–218.

Previti, D., & Amato, P. R. (2004). Is infidelity a cause or a consequence of poor marital quality? *Journal of Social and Personal Relationships, 21*, 217–230.

Proite, R., Dannells, M., & Benton, S. L. (1993). Gender, sex-role stereotypes, and the attribution of responsibility for date and acquaintance rape. *Journal of College Student Development, 34*, 411–417.

Proxmire, W. (1975, May). Romantic love studied. *Newsletter.* Retrieved July 14, 2008 from http://bulk.resource.org/courts.gov/c/F2/579/579.F2d.1027.77-1755.77-1677.html

Pryor, J. B., & Merluzzi, T. V. (1985). The role of expertise in processing social interaction scripts. *Journal of Experimental Social Psychology, 21*, 362–379.

Purdie, V., & Downey, G. (2000). Rejection sensitivity and adolescent girls' vulnerability to relationship-centered difficulties. *Child Maltreatment, 5*, 338–349.

Quinn, P. C., & Slater, A. (2003). Face perception at birth and beyond. In O. Pascalis & A. Slater (Eds.), *The development of face processing in infancy and early childhood: Current perspectives* (pp. 3–11). Hauppauge, NY: Nova Science Publishers.

Quinn, P. C., Yahr, J., Kuhn, A., Slater, A. M., & Pascalis, O. (2002). Representation of the gender of human faces by infants: A preference for female. *Perception, 31*, 1109–1121.

Rack, J. J., Burleson, B. R., Bodie, G. D., Holmstrom, A. J., & Servaty-Seib, H. (2008). Bereaved adults' evaluations of grief management messages: Effects of message person centeredness, recipient individual differences, and contextual factors. *Death Studies, 32*, 399–427.

Ramsey-Rennels, J. L., & Langlois, J. H. (2006). Infants' differential processing of male and female faces. *Current Directions in Psychological Science, 15*, 59–62.

Rao, K. V., & DeMaris, A. (1995). Coital frequency among married and cohabiting couples in the United States. *Journal of Biosocial Science, 27*, 135–150.

Raudenbush, S. W., Brennan, R. T., & Barnett, R. C. (1995). A multivariate hierarchical model for studying psychological change within married couples. *Journal of Family Psychology, 9*, 161–174.

Rayner, C., & Hoel, H. (1997). A summary review of literature relating to workplace bullying. *Journal of Community & Applied Social Psychology, 7*, 181–191.

Raz, A. E., & Atar, M. (2005). Perceptions of cousin marriage among young Bedouin adults in Israel. *Marriage & Family Review, 37*, 27–46.

Regan, P. C. (1998a). Of lust and love: Beliefs about the role of sexual desire in romantic relationships. *Personal Relationships, 5*, 139–157.

Regan, P. (1998b). Romantic love and sexual desire. In V. C. de Munck (Ed.), *Romantic love and sexual behavior: Perspectives from the social sciences* (pp. 91–112). Westport, CT: Praeger.

Regan, P. C. (1998c). What if you can't get what you want? Willingness to compromise ideal mate selection standards as a function of sex, mate value, and relationship context. *Personality and Social Psychology Bulletin, 24*, 1288–1297.

Regan, P. C. (2000). The role of sexual desire and sexual activity in dating relationships. *Social Behavior and Personality, 28*, 51–60.

Regan, P. (2008). *The mating game: A primer on love, sex, and marriage* (2nd ed.). Thousand Oaks, CA: Sage Publications.

Regan, P. C., & Berscheid, E. (1995). Gender differences in beliefs about the causes of male and female sexual desire. *Personal Relationships, 2*, 345–358.

Regan, P. C., & Berscheid, E. (1997). Gender differences in characteristics desired in a potential sexual and marriage partner. *Journal of Psychology and Human Sexuality, 9*, 25–37.

Regan, P. C., & Berscheid, E. (1999). *Lust: What we know about human sexual desire.* Thousand Oaks, CA: Sage Publications.

Regan, P. C., Durvasula, R., Howell, L., Ureño, O., & Rea, M. (2004). Gender, ethnicity, and the developmental timing of first sexual and romantic experiences. *Social Behavior and Personality, 32*, 667–676.

Regan, P. C., Kocan, E. R., & Whitlock, T. (1998). Ain't love grand! A prototype analysis of romantic love. *Journal of Social and Personal Relationships, 15*, 411–420.

Regan, P. C., Levin, L., Sprecher, S., Christopher, F. S., & Cate, R. (2000). Partner preferences: What characteristics do men and women desire in their short-term sexual and long-term romantic partners? *Journal of Psychology & Human Sexuality, 12*, 1–21.

Regan, P. C., Shen, W., De La Peña, E., & Gosset, E. (2007). "Fireworks exploded in my mouth": Affective reactions before, during, and after the very first kiss. *International Journal of Sexual Health, 19*, 1–16.

Regan, P. C., Snyder, M., & Kassin, S. M. (1995). Unrealistic optimism: Self-enhancement or person positivity? *Personality and Social Psychology Bulletin, 21*, 1073–1082.

Rehman, U. S., & Holtzworth-Munroe, A. (2006). A cross-cultural analysis of the demand–withdraw marital interaction: Observing couples from a developing country. *Journal of Consulting and Clinical Psychology, 74*, 755–766.

Reik, T. (1944). *A psychologist looks at love.* New York: Farrar & Rinehart.

Reik, T. (1945). *Psychology of sex relations.* New York: Grove Press.

Reinhardt, J. P., Boerner, K., & Horowitz, A. (2006). Good to have but not to use: Differential impact of perceived and received support on well-being. *Journal of Social and Personal Relationships, 23*, 117–129.

Reis, H. T. (1994). Domains of experience: Investigating relationship processes from three perspectives. In R. Erber & R. Gilmour (Eds.), *Theoretical frameworks for personal relationships* (pp. 87–110). Hillsdale, NJ: Lawrence Erlbaum Associates Inc.

Reis, H. T., Clark, M. S., & Holmes, J. G. (2004). Perceived partner responsiveness as an organizing construct in the study of intimacy and closeness. In D. J. Mashek & A. Aron (Eds.), *Handbook of closeness and intimacy* (pp. 201–225). Mahwah, NJ: Lawrence Erlbaum Associates Inc.

Reis, H. T., Collins, W. A., & Berscheid, E. (2000). The relationship context of human behavior and development. *Psychological Bulletin, 126*, 844–872.

Reis, H. T., & Gable, S. L. (2000). Event-sampling and other methods for studying daily experience. In H. T. Reis & C. Judd (Eds.), *Handbook of research methods in social and personality psychology* (pp. 190–222). Cambridge, UK: Cambridge University Press.

Reis, H. T., & Patrick, B. C. (1996). Attachment and intimacy: Component processes. In E. T. Higgins & A. Kruglanski (Eds.), *Social psychology: Handbook of basic principles* (pp. 523–563). New York: Guilford Press.

Reis, H. T., & Shaver, P. (1988). Intimacy as an interpersonal process. In S. Duck (Ed.), *Handbook of personal relationships: Theory, research, and interventions* (pp. 367–389). Chichester, UK: Wiley.

Reis, H. T., & Wheeler, L. (1991). Studying social interaction with the Rochester Interaction Record. In M. P. Zanna (Ed.), *Advances in experimental social psychology* (Vol. 24, pp. 269–318). San Diego, CA: Academic Press.

Reiss, I. L. (1960). Toward a sociology of the heterosexual love relationship. *Marriage and Family Living, 22*, 139–145.

Reiss, I. L. (1964). The scaling of premarital sexual permissiveness. *Journal of Marriage and the Family, 26*, 188–198.

Reiss, I. L. (1967). *The social context of premarital sexual permissiveness.* New York: Holt, Rinehart & Winston.

Reiss, I. L. (1980). *Family systems in America* (3rd ed.). New York: Holt, Rinehart & Winston.

Reiss, I. L. (1981). Some observations on ideology and sexuality in America. *Journal of Marriage & the Family, 43*, 271–283.

Reiss, I. L. (1986). *Journey into sexuality: An exploratory voyage.* Englewood Cliffs, NJ: Prentice Hall.

Renninger, L. A., Wade, T. J., & Grammer, K. (2004). Getting that female glance: Patterns and consequences of male nonverbal behavior in courtship contexts. *Evolution and Human Behavior, 25*, 416–431.

Repetti, R. L., Taylor, S. E., & Seeman, T. E. (2002). Risky families: Family social environments and the mental and physical health of offspring. *Psychological Bulletin, 128*, 330–366.

Richter, L. (2004). *The importance of caregiver–child interactions for the survival and healthy development of young children: A review.* Department of Child and Adolescent Health and Development, World Health Organization [online]. Retrieved from http://www.hsrc.ac.za/Document-1656.phtml

Ridge, R. D., & Berscheid, E. (1989, May). *On loving and being in love: A necessary distinction.* Paper presented at the meeting of the Midwestern Psychological Association, Chicago, IL.

Rini, C., Dunkel-Schetter, C., Hobel, C. J., Glynn, L. M., & Sandman, C. A. (2006). Effective social support: Antecedents and consequences of partner support during pregnancy. *Personal Relationships, 13*, 207–229.

Risley-Curtiss, C., Holley, L. C., & Wolf, S. (2006). The animal–human bond and ethnic diversity. *Social Work, 51*, 257–268.

Roche, J. P., & Ramsbey, T. W. (1993). Premarital sexuality: A five-year follow-up study of attitudes and behavior by dating stage. *Adolescence, 28*, 67–80.

Rodrigues, A. E., Hall, J. H., & Fincham, F. D. (2006). What predicts divorce and relationship dissolution? In M. A. Fine & J. H. Harvey (Eds.), *Handbook of divorce and dissolution* (pp. 85–112). Mahwah, NJ: Lawrence Erlbaum Associates Inc.

Rollie, S. S., & Duck, S. (2006). Divorce and dissolution of romantic relationships: Stage models and their limitations. In M. A. Fine & J. H. Harvey (Eds.), *Handbook of divorce and dissolution* (pp. 223–240). Mahwah, NJ: Lawrence Erlbaum Associates Inc.

Rollins, B. C., & Feldman, H. (1970). Marital satisfaction over the life cycle. *Journal of Marriage & the Family, 32*, 20–28.

Rosch, E. (1975). Cognitive representations of semantic categories. *Journal of Experimental Psychology, 104*, 192–233.

Rosch, E. (1978). Principles of categorization. In E. Rosch & B. B. Lloyd (Eds.), *Cognition and categorization* (pp. 27–48). Hillsdale, NJ: Lawrence Erlbaum Associates Inc.

Rosch, E. H. (1973). On the internal structure of perceptual and semantic categories. In T. E. Moore (Ed.), *Cognitive development and the acquisition of language* (pp. 111–144). New York: Academic Press.

Roscoe, B., Strouse, J. S., & Goodwin, M. P. (1994). Sexual harassment: Early adolescent self-reports of experiences and acceptance. *Adolescence, 29*, 515–523.

Rose, S. M. (1984). How friendships end: Patterns among young adults. *Journal of Social and Personal Relationships, 1*, 267–277.

Rosenblatt, P. C. (1983). *Bitter, bitter tears: Nineteenth-century diarists and twentieth century grief theories.* Minneapolis: University of Minnesota Press.

Rosenfeld, L. B., & Bowen, G. L. (1991). Marital disclosure and marital satisfaction: Direct-effect versus interaction-effect models. *Western Journal of Speech Communication, 55*, 69–84.

Ross, C. E., Mirowsky, J., & Goldsteen, K. (1990). The impact of the family on health: The decade in review. *Journal of Marriage & the Family, 52*, 1059–1078.

Ross, M., & Sicoly, F. (1979). Egocentric biases in availability and attribution. *Journal of Personality and Social Psychology, 37*, 322–336.

Rotenberg, K. J., & Korol, S. (1995). The role of loneliness and gender in individuals' love styles. *Journal of Social Behavior and Personality, 10,* 537–546.

Rubenstein, C. M., & Shaver, P. (1982). The experience of loneliness. In L. A. Peplau & D. Perlman (Eds.), *Loneliness: A sourcebook of current theory, research, and therapy* (pp. 206–223). New York: Wiley.

Rubin, L. (1976). *Worlds of pain: Life in the working class family.* New York: Basic Books.

Rubin, Z. (1970). Measurement of romantic love. *Journal of Personality and Social Psychology, 16,* 265–273.

Rubin, Z., Hill, C. T., Peplau, L. A., & Dunkel-Schetter, C. (1980). Self-disclosure in dating couples: Sex roles and the ethic of openness. *Journal of Marriage and the Family, 42,* 305–317.

Rubin, Z., & Mitchell, C. (1976). Couples research as couples counseling: Some unintended effects of studying close relationships. *American Psychologist, 31,* 17–25.

Rusbult, C. E. (1983). A longitudinal test of the investment model: The development (and deterioration) of satisfaction and commitment in heterosexual involvements. *Journal of Personality and Social Psychology, 45,* 101–117.

Rusbult, C. E. (1987). Responses to dissatisfaction in close relationships: The exit-voice-loyalty-neglect model. In D. Perlman & S. Duck (Eds.), *Intimate relationships: Development, dynamics, and deterioration* (pp. 209–237). Newbury Park, CA: Sage Publications.

Rusbult, C. E., Bissonnette, V. L., Arriaga, X. B., & Cox, C. L. (1998). Accommodation processes during the early years of marriage. In T. N. Bradbury (Ed.), *The developmental course of marital dysfunction* (pp. 74–113). Cambridge, UK: Cambridge University Press.

Rusbult, C. E., & Buunk, B. P. (1993). Commitment processes in close relationships: An interdependence analysis. *Journal of Social and Personal Relationships, 10,* 175–204.

Rusbult, C. E., Johnson, D. J., & Morrow, G. D. (1986a). Determinants and consequences of exit, voice, loyalty, and neglect: Responses to dissatisfaction in adult romantic involvements. *Human Relations, 39,* 45–63.

Rusbult, C. E., Johnson, D. J., & Morrow, G. D. (1986b). Predicting satisfaction and commitment in adult romantic involvements: An assessment of the generalizability of the investment model. *Social Psychology Quarterly, 49,* 81–89.

Rusbult, C. E., Martz, J. M., & Agnew, C. R. (1998). The Investment Model Scale: Measuring commitment level, satisfaction level, quality of alternatives, and investment size. *Personal Relationships, 5,* 357–391.

Rusbult, C. E., Verette, J., Whitney, G. A., Slovik, L. F., & Lipkus, I. (1991). Accommodation processes in close relationships: Theory and preliminary empirical evidence. *Journal of Personality and Social Psychology, 60,* 53–78.

Rusbult, C. E., Yovetich, N. A., & Verette, J. (1996). An interdependence analysis of accommodation processes. In G. J. O. Fletcher & J. Fitness (Eds.), *Knowledge structures in close relationships: A social psychological approach* (pp. 63–90). Mahwah, NJ: Lawrence Erlbaum Associates Inc.

Rusbult, C. E., Zembrodt, I. M., & Gunn, L. K. (1982). Exit, voice, loyalty, and neglect: Responses to dissatisfaction in romantic involvements. *Journal of Personality and Social Psychology, 43,* 1230–1242.

Russell, D., Peplau, L. A., & Cutrona, C. E. (1980). The revised UCLA Loneliness Scale: Concurrent and discriminant validity evidence. *Journal of Personality and Social Psychology, 39,* 472–480.

Rutledge, T., Linke, S. E., Olson, M. B., Francis, J., Johnson, B. D., Bittner, V., York, K., McClure, C., Kelsey, S. F., Reis, S. E., Cornell, C. E., Vaccarino, V., Sheps, D. S., Shaw, L. J., Krantz, D. S., Parashar, S., & Merz, C. N. B. (2008). Social networks and incident stroke among women with suspected myocardial ischemia. *Psychosomatic Medicine, 70,* 282–287.

Ryan, B., & DeMarco, J. R. G. (2003). Sexual orientation. In J. J. Ponzetti Jr. (Ed.), *International encyclopedia of marriage and family* (2nd ed., Vol. 3, pp. 1491–1499). New York: Macmillan Reference USA.

Sabini, J., & Green, M. C. (2004). Emotional responses to sexual and emotional infidelity: Constants and differences across genders, samples, and methods. *Personality and Social Psychology Bulletin, 30,* 1375–1388.

Sáez Sanz, P. (1984). Trayetoria de la satisfacción matrimonial a lo largo del ciclo vital. [Patterns of marital satisfaction over the life cycle.] *Revista de Psicología General y Aplicada, 39*, 983–995.

Sagrestano, L. M., Christensen, A., & Heavey, C. L. (1998). Social influence techniques during marital conflict. *Personal Relationships, 5*, 75–89.

Salin, D. (2001). Prevalence and forms of bullying among business professionals: A comparison of two different strategies for measuring bullying. *European Journal of Work and Organizational Psychology, 10*, 425–441.

Salin, D. (2003). Ways of explaining workplace bullying: A review of enabling, motivating and precipitating structures and processes in the work environment. *Human Relations, 56*, 1213–1232.

Samson, J. M., Levy, J. J., Dupras, A., & Tessier, D. (1991). Coitus frequency among married or cohabiting heterosexual adults: A survey in French-Canada. *Australian Journal of Marriage & Family, 12*, 103–109.

Sanders, M. R., Nicholson, J. M., & Floyd, F. J. (1997). Couples' relationships and children. In W. K. Halford & H. J. Markman (Eds.), *Clinical handbook of marriage and couples interventions* (pp. 225–253). Chichester, UK: Wiley.

Sanderson, C. A., Keiter, E. J., Miles, M. G., & Yopyk, D. J. A. (2007). The association between intimacy goals and plans for initiating dating relationships. *Personal Relationships, 14*, 225–243.

Sanford, K. (2006). Communication during marital conflict: When couples alter their appraisal, they change their behavior. *Journal of Family Psychology, 20*, 256–265.

Sangrigoli, S., & de Schonen, S. (2004). Recognition of own-race and other-race faces by three-month-old infants. *Journal of Child Psychology and Psychiatry, 45*, 1219–1227.

Sarason, B. R., Sarason, I. G., & Gurung, R. A. R. (2001). Close personal relationships and health outcomes: A key to the role of social support. In B. R. Sarason & S. Duck (Eds.), *Personal relationships: Implications for clinical and community psychology* (pp. 15–42). New York: Wiley.

Sarason, I. G., Sarason, B. R., & Pierce, G. R. (1994). Social support: Global and relationship-based levels of analysis. *Journal of Social and Personal Relationships, 11*, 295–312.

Scanzoni, J., Polonko, K., Teachman, J., & Thompson, L. (1989). *The sexual bond: Rethinking families and close relationships.* Newbury Park, CA: Sage Publications.

Schrodt, P., & Afifi, T. D. (2007). Communication processes that predict young adults' feelings of being caught and their associations with mental health and family satisfaction. *Communication Monographs, 74*, 200–228.

Schumm, W. R., Paff-Bergen, L. A., Hatch, R. C., Obiorah, F. C., Copeland, J. M., Meens, L. D., & Bugaighia, M. A. (1986). Concurrent and discriminant validity of the Kansas Marital Satisfaction Scale. *Journal of Marriage & the Family, 48*, 381–387.

Schvaneveldt, P. L., Kerpelman, J. L., & Schvaneveldt, J. D. (2005). Generational and cultural changes in family life in the United Arab Emirates: A comparison of mothers and daughters. *Journal of Comparative Family Studies, 36*, 77–91.

Schwartz, P. (1994). *Peer marriage: How love between equals really works.* New York: Free Press.

Schwartz, P., & Rutter, V. (1998). *The gender of sexuality.* Thousand Oaks, CA: Pine Forge.

Sedikides, C., Oliver, M. B., & Campbell, W. K. (1994). Perceived benefits and costs of romantic relationships for women and men: Implications for exchange theory. *Personal Relationships, 1*, 5–21.

Seeman, T. E. (2000). Health promoting effects of friends and family on health outcomes in older adults. *American Journal of Health Promotion, 14*, 362–370.

Segal, M. W. (1974). Alphabet and attraction: An unobtrusive measure of the effect of propinquity in a field setting. *Journal of Personality and Social Psychology, 30*, 654–657.

Serrano, J. M., Iglesias, J., & Loeches, A. (1995). Infants' responses to adult static facial expressions. *Infant Behavior & Development, 18*, 477–482.

Shadish, W. R., & Baldwin, S. A. (2005). Effects of behavioral marital therapy: A meta-analysis of randomized controlled trials. *Journal of Consulting and Clinical Psychology, 73*, 6–14.

Shanahan, L., McHale, S. M., Osgood, D. W., & Crouter, A. C. (2007). Conflict frequency with mothers and fathers from middle childhood to late adolescence: Within- and between-families comparisons. *Developmental Psychology, 43*, 539–550.

Shaver, P., Schwartz, J., Kirson, D., & O'Connor, C. (1987). Emotion knowledge: Further exploration of a prototype approach. *Journal of Personality and Social Psychology, 52*, 1061–1086.

Sheridan, L., Gillett, R., & Davies, G. (2002). Perceptions and prevalence of stalking in a male sample. *Psychology, Crime & Law, 8*, 289–310.

Sheridan, L., Gillett, R., Davies, G. M., Blaauw, E., & Patel, D. (2003). "There's no smoke without fire": Are male ex-partners perceived as more "entitled" to stalk than acquaintances or stranger stalkers? *British Journal of Psychology, 94*, 87–98.

Sherwin, R., & Corbett, S. (1985). Campus sexual norms and dating relationships: A trend analysis. *Journal of Sex Research, 21*, 258–274.

Shrout, P. E., Herman, C. M., & Bolger, N. (2006). The costs and benefits of practical and emotional support on adjustment: A daily diary study of couples experiencing acute stress. *Personal Relationships, 13*, 115–134.

Shulman, S., & Laursen, B. (2002). Adolescent perceptions of conflict in interdependent and disengaged friendships. *Journal of Research on Adolescence, 12*, 353–372.

Shye, D., Mullooly, J. P., Freeborn, D. K., & Pope, C. R. (1995). Gender differences in the relationship between social network support and mortality: A longitudinal study of an elderly cohort. *Social Science and Medicine, 41*, 915–947.

Sias, P. M., & Cahill, D. J. (1998). From coworkers to friends: The development of peer friendships in the workplace. *Western Journal of Communication, 62*, 273–299.

Siegert, J. R., & Stamp, G. H. (1994). "Our first big fight" as a milestone in the development of close relationships. *Communication Monographs, 61*, 345–360.

Sillars, A., Roberts, L. J., Leonard, K. E., & Dun, T. (2000). Cognition during marital conflict: The relationship of thought and talk. *Journal of Social and Personal Relationships, 17*, 479–502.

Simion, F., Valenza, E., & Umiltà, C. (1998). Mechanisms underlying face preference at birth. In F. Simion & G. Butterworth (Eds.), *The development of sensory, motor, and cognitive capacities in early infancy: From perception to cognition* (pp. 87–101). Hove, UK: Psychology Press.

Simon, W., & Gagnon, J. H. (1986). Sexual scripts: Permanence and change. *Archives of Sexual Behavior, 15*, 97–120.

Simpson, J. A., Campbell, B., & Berscheid, E. (1986). The association between romantic love and marriage: Kephart (1967) twice revisited. *Personality and Social Psychology Bulletin, 12*, 363–372.

Simpson, J. A., Rholes, W. S., & Nelligan, J. S. (1992). Support-seeking and support-giving within couple members in an anxiety-provoking situation: The role of attachment styles. *Journal of Personality and Social Psychology, 62*, 434–446.

Simpson, J. A., Winterheld, H. A., Rholes, W. S., & Oriña, M. M. (2007). Working models of attachment and reactions to different forms of caregiving from romantic partners. *Journal of Personality and Social Psychology, 93*, 466–477.

Simpson, L. E., Gattis, K. A., & Christensen, A. (2003). Therapy: Couple relationships. In J. J. Ponzetti Jr. (Ed.), *International encyclopedia of marriage and family* (2nd ed., Vol. 4, pp. 1626–1634). New York: Macmillan Reference USA.

Sinclair, H. C., & Frieze, I. H. (2002). Initial courtship behavior and stalking: How should we draw the line? In K. E. Davis, I. H. Frieze, & R. D. Maiuro (Eds.), *Stalking: Perspectives on victims and perpetrators* (pp. 186–211). New York: Springer Publishing Co.

Sinclair, H. C., & Frieze, I. H. (2005). When courtship persistence becomes intrusive pursuit: Comparing rejecter and pursuer perspectives of unrequited attraction. *Sex Roles, 52*, 839–852.

Singh, D. (1993). Adaptive significance of female physical attractiveness: Role of waist-to-hip ratio. *Journal of Personality and Social Psychology, 65*, 293–307.

Singh, D. (1994). Body fat distribution and perception of desirable female body shape by young Black men and women. *International Journal of Eating Disorders, 16*, 289–294.

Singh, D. (1995). Female judgment of male attractiveness and desirability for relationships: Role of waist-to-hip ratio and financial status. *Journal of Personality and Social Psychology, 69*, 1089–1101.

Singh, D., & Luis, S. (1995). Ethnic and gender consensus for the effect of waist-to-hip ratio on judgment of women's attractiveness. *Human Nature, 6*, 51–65.

Small, M. F. (1992). The evolution of female sexuality and mate selection in humans. *Human Nature, 3*, 133–156.

Smart, C. (2007). Same sex couples and marriage: Negotiating relational landscapes with families and friends. *Sociological Review, 55*, 671–686.

Smeaton, G., Byrne, D., & Murnen, S. K. (1989). The repulsion hypothesis revisited: Similarity irrelevance or dissimilarity bias? *Journal of Personality and Social Psychology, 56*, 54–59.

Smetana, J., & Gaines, C. (1999). Adolescent–parent conflict in middle-class African American families. *Child Development, 70*, 1447–1463.

Smith, J. D., Schneider, B. H., Smith, P. K., & Ananiadou, K. (2004). The effectiveness of whole-school anti-bullying programs: A synthesis of research evaluation. *School Psychology Review, 33*, 547–560.

Smith, T. W. (2006). Sexual behavior in the United States. In R. D. McAnulty & M. M. Burnette (Eds.), *Sex and sexuality. Vol. 1. Sexuality today: Trends and controversies* (pp. 103–132). Westport, CT: Praeger.

Smock, P. J., & Gupta, S. (2002). Cohabitation in contemporary North America. In A. Booth & A. C. Crouter (Eds.), *Just living together: Implications of cohabitation on families, children, and social policy* (pp. 53–84). Mahwah, NJ: Lawrence Erlbaum Associates Inc.

Soken, N. H., & Pick, A. D. (1999). Infants' perception of dynamic affective expressions: Do infants distinguish specific expressions? *Child Development, 70*, 1275–1282.

Solberg, M. E., & Olweus, D. (2003). Prevalence estimation of school bullying with the Olweus Bully/Victim Questionnaire. *Aggressive Behavior, 29*, 239–268.

Solomon, S. E., Rothblum, E. D., & Balsam, K. F. (2004). Pioneers in partnership: Lesbian and gay male couples in civil unions compared with those not in civil unions and married heterosexual couples. *Journal of Family Psychology, 18*, 275–286.

Solomon, S. E., Rothblum, E. D., & Balsam, K. F. (2005). Money, housework, sex, and conflict: Same-sex couples in civil unions, those not in civil unions, and heterosexual married siblings. *Sex Roles, 52*, 561–575.

Spanier, G. B. (1976). Measuring dyadic adjustment: New scales for assessing the quality of marriage and similar dyads. *Journal of Marriage & the Family, 38*, 15–28.

Spanier, G. B., & Margolies, R. L. (1983). Marital separation and extramarital sexual behavior. *Journal of Sex Research, 19*, 23–48.

Spitz, R. A. (1946). Hospitalism: A follow-up report on investigation described in Volume I, 1945. *The Psychoanalytic Study of the Child, 2*, 113–117.

Spitz, R. A. (1949). The role of ecological factors in emotional development in infancy. *Child Development, 20*, 145–156.

Spitzberg, B. H., & Cupach, W. R. (1996, July). *Obsessive relational intrusion: Victimization and coping.* Paper presented at the meeting of the International Society for the Study of Personal Relationships, Banff, Alberta.

Spitzberg, B. H., & Cupach, W. R. (Eds.). (1998). *The dark side of close relationships*. Mahwah, NJ: Lawrence Erlbaum Associates Inc.

Spitzberg, B. H., & Cupach, W. R. (2001). Paradoxes of pursuit: Toward a relational model of stalking-related phenomena. In J. A. Davis (Ed.), *Stalking crimes and victim protection: Prevention, intervention, and threat assessment* (pp. 97–136). Boca Raton, FL: CRC Press.

Spitzberg, B. H., & Cupach, W. R. (2002). The inappropriateness of relational intrusion. In R. Goodwin & D. Cramer (Eds.), *Inappropriate relationships: The unconventional, the disapproved, and the forbidden* (pp. 191–219). Mahwah, NJ: Lawrence Erlbaum Associates Inc.

Spitzberg, B. H., & Cupach, W. R. (2003). What mad pursuit? Obsessive relational intrusion and stalking related phenomena. *Aggression and Violent Behavior, 8*, 345–375.

Spitzberg, B. H., & Cupach, W. R. (2007). The state of the art of stalking: Taking stock of an emerging literature. *Aggression and Violent Behavior, 12*, 64–86.

Spreadbury, C. L. (1982). First date. *Journal of Early Adolescence, 2*, 83–89.

Sprecher, S. (1989). Importance to males and females of physical attractiveness, earning potential, and expressiveness in initial attraction. *Sex Roles, 21*, 591–607.

Sprecher, S. (1992). How men and women expect to feel and behave in response to inequity in close relationships. *Social Psychology Quarterly, 55*, 57–69.

Sprecher, S. (1998). Social exchange theories and sexuality. *Journal of Sex Research, 35*, 32–43.

Sprecher, S. (1999). "I love you more today than yesterday": Romantic partners' perceptions of changes in love and related affect over time. *Journal of Personality and Social Psychology, 76*, 46–53.

Sprecher, S. (2002). Sexual satisfaction in premarital relationships: Associations with satisfaction, love, commitment, and stability. *The Journal of Sex Research, 39*, 190–196.

Sprecher, S., Aron, A., Hatfield, E., Cortese, A., Potapova, E., & Levitskaya, A. (1994). Love: American style, Russian style, and Japanese style. *Personal Relationships, 1*, 349–369.

Sprecher, S., & Cate, R. M. (2004). Sexual satisfaction and sexual expression as predictors of relationship satisfaction and stability. In J. H. Harvey, A. Wenzel, & S. Sprecher (Eds.), *The handbook of sexuality in close relationships* (pp. 235–256). Mahwah, NJ: Lawrence Erlbaum Associates Inc.

Sprecher, S., & Chandak, R. (1992). Attitudes about arranged marriages and dating among men and women from India. *Free Inquiry in Creative Sociology, 20*, 59–69.

Sprecher, S., Christopher, F. S., & Cate, R. (2006). Sexuality in close relationships. In A. Vangelisti & D. Perlman (Eds.), *The Cambridge handbook on personal relationships* (pp. 463–482). New York: Cambridge University Press.

Sprecher, S., Felmlee, D., Orbuch, T. L., & Willetts, M. C. (2001). Social networks and change in personal relationships. In A. L. Vangelisti, H. T. Reis, & M. A. Fitzpatrick (Eds.), *Stability and change in relationships: Advances in personal relationships* (pp. 257–284). New York: Cambridge University Press.

Sprecher, S., Felmlee, D., Schmeeckle, M., & Shu, X. (2006). No breakup occurs on an island: Social networks and relationship dissolution. In M. A. Fine & J. H. Harvey (Eds.), *Handbook of divorce and dissolution* (pp. 457–478). Mahwah, NJ: Lawrence Erlbaum Associates Inc.

Sprecher, S., & Hatfield, E. (1995). Premarital sexual standards among U.S. college students: Comparison with Russian and Japanese students. *Archives of Sexual Behavior, 25*, 261–288.

Sprecher, S., & Hendrick, S. S. (2004). Self-disclosure in intimate relationships: Associations with individual and relationship characteristics over time. *Journal of Social and Clinical Psychology, 23*, 857–877.

Sprecher, S., & McKinney, K. (1993). *Sexuality*. Newbury Park, CA: Sage Publications.

Sprecher, S., McKinney, K., Walsh, R., & Anderson, C. (1988). A revision of the Reiss premarital sexual permissiveness scale. *Journal of Marriage & the Family, 50*, 821–828.

Sprecher, S., & Metts, S. (1989). Development of the "Romantic Beliefs Scale" and examination of the effects of gender and gender-role orientation. *Journal of Social and Personal Relationships, 6*, 387–411.

Sprecher, S., & Metts, S. (1999). Romantic beliefs: Their influence on relationships and patterns of change over time. *Journal of Social and Personal Relationships, 16*, 834–851.

Sprecher, S., Metts, S., Burleson, B., Hatfield, E., & Thompson, A. (1995). Domains of expressive interaction in intimate relationships: Associations with satisfaction and commitment. *Family Relations: Journal of Applied Family & Child Studies, 44*, 203–210.

Sprecher, S., & Regan, P. C. (1998). Passionate and companionate love in courting and young married couples. *Sociological Inquiry, 68*, 163–185.

Sprecher, S., & Regan, P. C. (2000). Sexuality in a relational context. In C. Hendrick & S. S. Hendrick (Eds.), *Close relationships: A sourcebook* (pp. 217–227). Thousand Oaks, CA: Sage Publications.

Sprecher, S., & Regan, P. C. (2002). Liking some things (in some people) more than others: Partner preferences in romantic relationships and friendships. *Journal of Social and Personal Relationships, 19*, 463–481.

Sprecher, S., Regan, P. C., & McKinney, K. (1998). Beliefs about the outcomes of extramarital sexual relationships as a function of the gender of the "cheating spouse." *Sex Roles, 38*, 301–311.

Sprecher, S., Regan, P. C., McKinney, K., Maxwell, K., & Wazienski, R. (1997). Preferred level of sexual experience in a date or mate: The merger of two methodologies. *Journal of Sex Research, 34*, 327–337.

Sprecher, S., Schmeeckle, M., & Felmlee, D. (2006). The principle of least interest: Inequality in emotional investment in romantic relationships. *Journal of Family Issues, 27*, 1255–1280.

Sprecher, S., & Schwartz, P. (1994). Equity and balance in the exchange of contributions in close relationships. In M. J. Lerner & G. Mikula (Eds.), *Entitlement and the affectional bond: Justice in close relationships* (pp. 11–42). New York: Plenum.

Sprecher, S., Schwartz, P., Harvey, J., & Hatfield, E. (2008). The BusinessofLove.com: Relationship initiation at Internet matchmaking services. In S. Sprecher, A. Wenzel, & J. Harvey (Eds.), *Handbook of relationship initiation* (pp. 249–265). New York: Psychology Press.

Sprecher, S., & Toro-Morn, M. (2002). A study of men and women from different sides of earth to determine if men are from Mars and women are from Venus in their beliefs about love and romantic relationships. *Sex Roles, 46*, 131–147.

Sroufe, L. A. (2005). Attachment and development: A prospective, longitudinal study from birth to adulthood. *Attachment & Human Development, 7*, 349–367.

Sroufe, L. A., & Fleeson, J. (1988). The coherence of family relationships. In R. A. Hinde & J. Stevenson (Eds.), *Relationships within families: Mutual influences* (pp. 27–47). Oxford, UK: Oxford University Press.

Stafford, L., Kline, S. L., & Rankin, C. T. (2004). Married individuals, cohabiters, and cohabiters who marry: A longitudinal study of relational and individual well-being. *Journal of Social and Personal Relationships, 21*, 231–248.

Sternberg, R. J. (1986). A triangular theory of love. *Psychological Review, 93*, 119–135.

Sternberg, R. J. (1988). Triangulating love. In R. J. Sternberg & M. L. Barnes (Eds.), *The psychology of love* (pp. 119–138). New Haven, CT: Yale University Press.

Sternberg, R. J. (1997). Construct validation of a triangular love scale. *European Journal of Social Psychology, 27*, 313–335.

Sternberg, R. J. (1998). *Cupid's arrow: The course of love through time*. Cambridge, UK: Cambridge University Press.

Sternberg, R. J. (2006). A duplex theory of love. In R. J. Sternberg & K. Weis (Eds.), *The new psychology of love* (pp. 184–199). New Haven, CT: Yale University Press.

Sternberg, R. J., & Barnes, M. L. (Eds.). (1988). *The psychology of love*. New Haven, CT: Yale University Press.

Sternberg, R. J., & Weis, K. (Eds.). (2006). *The new psychology of love*. New Haven, CT: Yale University Press.

Storch, E. A., & Esposito, L. E. (2003). Peer victimization and posttraumatic stress among children. *Child Study Journal, 33*, 91–98.

Straus, M. A. (2004). Prevalence of violence against dating partners by male and female university students worldwide. *Violence Against Women, 10*, 790–811.

Straus, M. A., Hamby, S. L., Boney-McCoy, S., & Sugarman, D. B. (1996). The revised Conflict Tactics Scales (STS2): Development and preliminary psychometric data. *Journal of Family Issues, 17*, 283–316.

Straus, M. A., & Ramirez, I. L. (2007). Gender symmetry in prevalence, severity, and chronicity of physical aggression against dating partners by university students in Mexico and USA. *Aggressive Behavior, 33*, 281–290.

Striano, T., Kopp, F., Grossmann, T., & Reid, V. M. (2006). Eye contact influences neural processing of emotional expressions in 4-month-old infants. *Social Cognitive and Affective Neuroscience, 1*, 87–94.

Stroebe, M. S., & Stroebe, W. (1987). *Bereavement and health: The psychological and physical consequences of partner loss*. London: Cambridge University Press.

Stuart, F. M., Hammond, D. C., & Pett, M. A. (1987). Inhibited sexual desire in women. *Archives of Sexual Behavior, 16*, 91–106.

Stuart, G. L., Moore, T. M., Gordon, K. C., Hellmuth, J. C., Ramsey, S. E., & Kahler, C. W. (2006). Reasons for intimate partner perpetration among arrested women. *Violence Against Women, 12*, 609–621.

Sueyoshi, S., & Ohtsuka, R. (2003). Effects of polygyny and consanguinity on high fertility in the rural Arab population in South Jordan. *Journal of Biosocial Science, 35*, 513–526.

Sullivan, B. F., & Schwebel, A. I. (1995). Relationship beliefs and expectations of satisfaction in marital relationships: Implications for family practitioners. *The Family Journal, 3*, 298–305.

Sunnafrank, M., & Ramirez, A. (2004). At first sight: Persistent relational effects of get-acquainted conversations. *Journal of Social and Personal Relationships, 21*, 361–379.

Surra, C. A. (1985). Courtship types: Variations in interdependence between partners and social networks. *Journal of Personality and Social Psychology, 49*, 357–375.

Surra, C. A., Curran, M. A., & Williams, K. (2009). Effects of participation in a longitudinal study of dating. *Personal Relationships, 16*, 1–21.

Suter, E. A., Bergen, K. M., Daas, K. L., & Durham, W. T. (2006). Lesbian couples' management of public-private dialectical contradictions. *Journal of Social and Personal Relationships, 23*, 349–365.

Swain, I. U., Zelazo, P. R., & Clifton, R. K. (1993). Newborn infants' memory for speech sounds retained over 24 hours. *Developmental Psychology, 29*, 312–323.

Swann, W. B. Jr., De La Ronde, C., & Hixon, J. G. (1994). Authenticity and positivity strivings in marriage and courtship. *Journal of Personality and Social Psychology, 66*, 857–869.

Swann, W. B. Jr., Hixon, J. G., & De La Ronde, C. (1992). Embracing the bitter "truth": Negative self-concepts and marital commitment. *Psychological Science, 3*, 118–121.

Sweeting, H., Young, R., West, P., & Der, G. (2006). Peer victimization and depression in early-mid adolescence: A longitudinal study. *British Journal of Educational Psychology, 76*, 577–594.

Swensen, C. H. (1961). Love: A self-report analysis with college students. *Journal of Individual Psychology, 17*, 167–171.

Swensen, C. H., & Gilner, F. (1963). Factor analysis of self-report statements of love relationships. *Journal of Individual Psychology, 19*, 186–188.

Symons, D. (1992). On the use and misuse of Darwinism in the study of human behavior. In J. H. Barrow, L. Cosmides, & J. Tooby (Eds.), *The adapted mind: Evolutionary psychology and the generation of culture* (pp. 137–159). Oxford, UK: Oxford University Press.

Tamis-LeMonda, C. S., Bornstein, M. H., & Baumwell, L. (2001). Maternal responsiveness and children's achievement of language milestones. *Child Development, 72*, 748–767.

Tamis-LeMonda, C. S., Bornstein, M. H., Baumwell, L., & Damast, A. M. (1996). Responsive parenting in the second year: Specific influences on children's language and play. *Early Development & Parenting, 5*, 173–183.

Tannen, D. (1990). *You just don't understand: Women and men in conversation.* New York: William Morrow.

Tashiro, T., & Frazier, P. (2003). "I'll never be in a relationship like that again": Personal growth following romantic relationship breakups. *Personal Relationships, 10*, 113–128.

Tashiro, T., & Frazier, P. (2007). The causal effects of emotion on couples' cognition and behavior. *Journal of Counseling Psychology, 54*, 409–422.

Tashiro, T., Frazier, P., & Berman, M. (2006). Stress-related growth following divorce and relationship dissolution. In M. A. Fine & J. H. Harvey (Eds.), *Handbook of divorce and dissolution* (pp. 361–384). Mahwah, NJ: Lawrence Erlbaum Associates Inc.

Taylor, S. Jr. (1982, July 9). Hinckley hails "historical" shooting to win love. *The New York Times.* Retrieved July 3, 2008 from http://query.nytimes.com

Taylor, S. E., & Brown, J. D. (1988). Illusion and well-being: A social psychological perspective on mental health. *Psychological Bulletin, 103*, 193–210.

Taylor, S. E., & Brown, J. D. (1994). Positive illusions and well-being revisited: Separating fact from fiction. *Psychological Bulletin, 116*, 21–27.

Teachman, J., Tedrow, L., & Hall, M. (2006). The demographic future of divorce and dissolution. In M. A. Fine & J. H. Harvey (Eds.), *Handbook of divorce and dissolution* (pp. 59–82). Mahwah, NJ: Lawrence Erlbaum Associates Inc.

Tellegen, A. (1985). Structures of mood and personality and their relevance to assessing anxiety, with an emphasis on self-report. In A. H. Tuma & J. D. Maser (Eds.), *Anxiety and the anxiety disorders* (pp. 681–706). Hillsdale, NJ: Lawrence Erlbaum Associates Inc.

Tennov, D. (1979). *Love and limerence.* New York: Stein & Day.

Tennov, D. (1998). Love madness. In V. C. de Munck (Ed.), *Romantic love and sexual behavior: Perspectives from the social sciences* (pp. 77–88). Westport, CT: Praeger.

Thibaut, J. W., & Kelley, H. H. (1959). *The social psychology of groups.* New York: John Wiley.

Thomas, L. A., De Bellis, M. D., Graham, R., & LaBar, K. S. (2007). Development of emotional facial recognition in late childhood and adolescence. *Developmental Science, 10*, 547–558.

Thompson, A. P. (1984). Emotional and sexual components of extramarital relations. *Journal of Marriage and the Family, 46*, 35–42.

Thompson, L. A., Madrid, V., Westbrook, S., & Johnston, V. (2001). Infants attend to second-order relational properties of faces. *Psychonomic Bulletin & Review, 8*, 769–777.

Thompson, S. C. (1999). Illusions of control: How we overestimate our personal influence. *Current Directions in Psychological Science, 8*, 187–190.

Thompson, S. C., & Kelley, H. H. (1981). Judgments of responsibility for activities in close relationships. *Journal of Personality and Social Psychology, 41*, 469–477.

Tjaden, P., & Thoennes, N. (2000). Prevalence and consequences of male-to-female and female-to-male intimate partner violence as measured by the National Violence Against Women Survey. *Violence Against Women, 6*, 142–161.

Tolhuizen, J. H. (1989). Communication strategies for intensifying dating relationships: Identification, use, and structure. *Journal of Social and Personal Relationships, 6*, 413–434.

Tooby, J., & Cosmides, L. (1992). The psychological foundations of culture. In J. H. Barrow, L. Cosmides, & J. Tooby (Eds.), *The adapted mind: Evolutionary psychology and the generation of culture* (pp. 19–136). Oxford, UK: Oxford University Press.

Toro-Morn, M., & Sprecher, S. (2003). A cross-cultural comparison of mate preferences among university students: The United States vs. The People's Republic of China (PRC). *Journal of Comparative Family Studies, 34*, 151–170.

Toyama, M. (2002). Positive illusions in close relationships among college students. *The Japanese Journal of Social Psychology, 18*, 51–60.

Tracy, J. K., & Junginger, J. (2007). Correlates of lesbian sexual functioning. *Journal of Women's Health, 16*, 499–509.

Treas, J. (2003). Infidelity. In J. J. Ponzetti Jr. (Ed.), *International encyclopedia of marriage and family* (2nd ed., Vol. 2, pp. 895–901). New York: Macmillan Reference USA.

Tronick, E. Z. (1989). Emotions and emotional communication in infants. *American Psychologist, 44*, 112–126.

Troy, M., & Sroufe, L. A. (1987). Victimization among preschoolers: Role of attachment relationship history. *Journal of the American Academy of Child and Adolescent Psychiatry, 26*, 166–172.

Trudel, G. (1991). Review of psychological factors in low sexual desire. *Sexual and Marital Therapy, 6*, 261–272.

True love. (2006, March). *National Geographic Magazine* (Letters, p. 1).

Tucker, J. S., Kressin, N. R., Spiro, A. III, & Ruscio, J. (1998). Intrapersonal characteristics and the timing of divorce: A prospective investigation. *Journal of Social and Personal Relationships, 15*, 210–225.

Turmanis, S. A., & Brown, R. I. (2006). The Stalking and Harassment Behaviour Scale: Measuring the incidence, nature, and severity of stalking and relational harassment and their psychological effects. *Psychology and Psychotherapy: Theory, Research and Practice, 79*, 183–198.

Turner, R. H. (1970). *Family interaction.* New York: John Wiley.

Twenge, J. M., Campbell, W. K., & Foster, C. A. (2003). Parenthood and marital satisfaction: A meta-analytic review. *Journal of Marriage and Family, 65*, 574–583.

Tyson, S. Y., Herting, J. R., & Randell, B. P. (2007). Beyond violence: Threat reappraisal in women recently separated from intimate-partner violent relationships. *Journal of Social and Personal Relationships, 24*, 693–706.

Uchino, B. N., Cacioppo, J. T., & Kiecolt-Glaser, J. K. (1996). The relationship between social support and physiological processes: A review with emphasis on underlying mechanisms and implications for health. *Psychological Bulletin, 119*, 488–531.

Uebelacker, L. A., Courtnage, E. S., & Whisman, M. A. (2003). Correlates of depression and marital satisfaction: Perceptions of marital communication style. *Journal of Social and Personal Relationships, 20*, 757–769.

Ullery, E. K., Millner, V. S., & Willingham, H. A. (2002). The emergent care and treatment of women with hypoactive sexual desire disorder. *The Family Journal: Counseling and Therapy for Couples and Families, 10*, 346–350.

Umberson, D., Williams, K., Powers, D. A., Chen, M. D., & Campbell, A. M. (2005). As good as it gets? A life course perspective on marital quality. *Social Forces, 84*, 487–505.

Umiltà, C., Simion, F., & Valenza, E. (1996). Newborn's preference for faces. *European Psychologist, 1*, 200–205.

U.S. Census Bureau. (1998). *Marital status and living arrangements: March 1998* (Current Population Reports, Series P20-514). Washington, DC: Government Printing Office.

U.S. Census Bureau. (2005a). *2005 American Community Survey. Table GCT1204. Median age at first marriage for men: 2005* [online]. Retrieved from http://factfinder.census.gov

U.S. Census Bureau. (2005b). *2005 American Community Survey. Table GCT1205. Median age at first marriage for women: 2005* [online]. Retrieved from http://factfinder.census.gov

U.S. Census Bureau. (2005c). *2005 American Community Survey. Table S1101. Households and families* [online]. Retrieved from http://factfinder.census.gov

U.S. Census Bureau. (2007a). Table 1: Marital history by sex for selected birth cohorts, 1935–39 to 1980–1984: 2004. *The 2008 statistical abstract: The national data book* [online]. Retrieved from http://www.census.gov/population/socdemo/marital-hist/2004/Table1.2004.xls

U.S. Census Bureau. (2007b). Table 3: Marital history for people 15 years and over, by age and sex: 2004. *The 2008 statistical abstract: The national data book* [online]. Retrieved from http://www.census.gov/population/socdemo/marital-hist/2004/Table3.2004.xls

U.S. Census Bureau. (2007c). Table 56: Marital status of the population by sex and age: 2006. *The 2008 statistical abstract: The national data book* [online]. Retrieved from http://www.census.gov/compendia/statab/tables/08s0056.pdf

U.S. Census Bureau. (2007d). Table 121: Marriages and divorces—number and rate by state: 1990 to 2005. *The 2008 statistical abstract: The national data book* [online]. Retrieved from http://www.census.gov/compendia/statab/tables/08s0121.pdf

U.S. Census Bureau. (2007e). Table 1312: Marriage and divorce rates, by country: 1980 to 2003. *Statistical abstract of the United States: 2007* [online]. Retrieved from http://www.census.gov/compendia/statab/tables/07s1312.xls

U.S. Department of Health and Human Services. (2004). *Guidelines for the conduct of research involving human subjects at the National Institutes of Health* [online]. Retrieved from http://ohsr.od.nih.gov/guidelines/GrayBooklet82404.pdf

U.S. Department of Justice. (2008a). *Domestic violence awareness handbook* [online]. Retrieved from http://www.da.usda.gov/shmd/aware.htm

U.S. Department of Justice. (2008b). Table 34: Family violence, 2006: Percent distribution of victimizations, by type of crime and relationship to offender. *Criminal victimization in the United States, 2006. Statistical tables. National Crime Victimization Survey, August 2008* [online]. Retrieved from http://jp.usdoj.gov/bjs/pub/pdf/cvus0602.pdf

Vaillant, C. O., & Vaillant, G. E. (1993). Is the U-curve of marital satisfaction an illusion? A 40-year study of marriage. *Journal of Marriage & the Family, 55*, 230–239.

van den Berghe, P. L. (1979). *Human family systems: An evolutionary view.* New York: Elsevier.

van IJzendoorn, M. H., & Sagi, A. (1999). Cross-cultural patterns of attachment: Universal and contextual dimensions. In J. Cassidy & P. R. Shaver (Eds.), *Handbook of attachment: Theory, research, and clinical applications* (pp. 713–734). New York: Guilford Press.

Van Lange, P. A. M., & Rusbult, C. E. (1995). My relationship is better than—and not as bad as—yours is: The perception of superiority in close relationships. *Personality and Social Psychology Bulletin, 21*, 32–44.

van Leeuwen, M., van den Berg, S. M., & Boomsma, D. I. (2008). A twin-family study of general IQ. *Learning and Individual Differences, 18*, 76–88.

van Ooijen, B., Bertoncini, J., Sansavini, A., & Mehler, J. (1997). Do weak syllables count for newborns? *Journal of the Acoustical Society of America, 102*, 3735–3741.

Vangelisti, A. L. (2001). Making sense of hurtful interactions in close relationships. In V. Manusov & J. H. Harvey (Eds.), *Attribution, communication behavior, and close relationships* (pp. 38–58). New York: Cambridge University Press.

Vangelisti, A. L. (2006). Hurtful interactions and the dissolution of intimacy. In M. A. Fine & J. H. Harvey (Eds.), *Handbook of divorce and dissolution* (pp. 133–152). Mahwah, NJ: Lawrence Erlbaum Associates Inc.

Vangelisti, A. L. (2009). Challenges in conceptualizing social support. *Journal of Social and Personal Relationships, 26,* 39–51.

Vanzetti, N. A., Notarius, C. I., & NeeSmith, D. (1992). Specific and generalized expectancies in marital interaction. *Journal of Family Psychology, 6,* 171–183.

Vartia, M. (2001). Consequences of workplace bullying with respect to the well-being of its targets and the observers of bullying. *Scandinavian Journal of Work Environment and Health, 27,* 63–69.

Vaughn, D. (1986). *Uncoupling: Turning points in intimate relationships.* New York: Vintage Books.

Vernberg, E. M., Beery, S. H., Ewell, K. K., & Abwender, D. A. (1993). Parents' use of friendship facilitation strategies and the formation of friendships in early adolescence: A prospective study. *Journal of Family Psychology, 7,* 356–369.

Veroff, J., Douvan, E., & Kulka, R. A. (1981). *The inner American: A self-portrait from 1957 to 1976.* New York: Basic Books.

Vinokur, A. D., Price, R. H., & Caplan, R. D. (1996). Hard times and hurtful partners: How financial strain affects depression and relationship satisfaction of unemployed persons and their spouses. *Journal of Personality and Social Psychology, 71,* 166–179.

Vogel, D. L., & Karney, B. R. (2002). Demands and withdrawals in newlyweds: Elaborating on the social structure hypothesis. *Journal of Social and Personal Relationships, 19,* 685–701.

Vorauer, J. D., Cameron, J. J., Holmes, J. G., & Pearce, D. G. (2003). Invisible overtures: Fears of rejection and the signal amplification bias. *Journal of Personality and Social Psychology, 84,* 793–812.

Vorauer, J. D., & Ratner, R. K. (1996). Who's going to make the first move? Pluralistic ignorance as an impediment to relationship formation. *Journal of Social and Personal Relationships, 13,* 483–506.

Vouloumanos, A., & Werker, J. F. (2007). Listening to language at birth: Evidence for a bias for speech in neonates. *Developmental Science, 10,* 159–171.

Wahab, A., & Ahmad, M. (2005). Consanguineous marriages in the Sikh community of Swat, NWFP, Pakistan. *Journal of Social Sciences, 10,* 153–157.

Wahab, A., Ahmad, M., & Shah, S. A. (2006). Migration as a determinant of marriage pattern: Preliminary report on consanguinity among Afghans. *Journal of Biosocial Science, 38,* 315–325.

Walker, A. S. (1982). Intermodal perception of expressive behaviors by human infants. *Journal of Experimental Child Psychology, 33,* 514–535.

Wallace, H., & Silverman, J. (1996). Stalking and posttraumatic stress syndrome. *Police Journal, 69,* 203–206.

Walster, E., Aronson, V., Abrahams, D., & Rottmann, L. (1966). Importance of physical attractiveness in dating behavior. *Journal of Personality and Social Psychology, 4,* 508–516.

Walster [Hatfield], E., & Berscheid, E. (1971). Adrenaline makes the heart grow fonder. *Psychology Today, 5,* 47–62.

Walster, E., Walster, G. W., & Berscheid, E. (1978). *Equity: Theory and research.* Boston: Allyn & Bacon.

Ward, C. C., & Tracey, T. J. G. (2004). Relation of shyness with aspects of online relationship involvement. *Journal of Social and Personal Relationships, 21,* 611–623.

Watson, D. (2002). Positive affectivity: The disposition to experience pleasurable emotional states. In C. R. Snyder & S. J. Lopez (Eds.), *Handbook of positive psychology* (pp. 106–119). New York: Oxford University Press.

Watson, D., & Clark, L. A. (1984). Negative affectivity: The disposition to experience aversive emotional states. *Psychological Bulletin, 96,* 465–490.

Weaver, S. E., & Ganong, L. H. (2004). The factor structure of the Romantic Beliefs Scale for African Americans and European Americans. *Journal of Social and Personal Relationships, 21*, 171–185.

Weber, A. L. (1998). Losing, leaving, and letting go: Coping with nonmarital breakups. In B. H. Spitzberg & W. R. Cupach (Eds.), *The dark side of close relationships* (pp. 267–306). Mahwah, NJ: Lawrence Erlbaum Associates Inc.

Wegner, H. Jr. (2005). Disconfirming communication and self-verification in marriage: Associations among the demand/withdraw interaction pattern, feeling understood, and marital satisfaction. *Journal of Social and Personal Relationships, 22*, 19–31.

Weinberg, M. K., & Tronick, E. Z. (1996). Infant affective reactions to the resumption of maternal interaction after the still-face. *Child Development, 67*, 905–914.

Weinfield, N. S., Sroufe, L. A., Egeland, B., & Carlson, E. A. (1999). The nature of individual differences in infant-caregiver attachment. In J. Cassidy & P. R. Shaver (Eds.), *Handbook of attachment: Theory, research, and clinical applications* (pp. 68–88). New York: Guilford Press.

Weinstein, N. D. (1980). Unrealistic optimism about future life events. *Journal of Personality and Social Psychology, 39*, 806–820.

Weinstein, N. D. (1982). Unrealistic optimism about susceptibility to health problems. *Journal of Behavioral Medicine, 5*, 441–460.

Weinstein, N. D. (1983). Reducing unrealistic optimism about illness susceptibility. *Health Psychology, 2*, 11–20.

Weinstein, N. D. (1984). Why it won't happen to me: Perceptions of risk factors and susceptibility. *Health Psychology, 3*, 431–457.

Weiss, R. L. (1980). Strategic behavioral marital therapy: Toward a model for assessment and intervention. In J. P. Vincent (Ed.), *Advances in family intervention, assessment, and intervention* (Vol. 1, pp. 229–271). Greenwich, CT: JAI Press.

Weiss, R. L., & Margolin, G. (1977). Assessment of marital conflict and accord. In A. R. Ciminero, K. S. Calhoun, & H. E. Adams (Eds.), *Handbook for behavioral assessment* (pp. 555–602). New York: Wiley.

Weiss, R. L., & Summers, K. J. (1983). Marital Interaction Coding System-III. In E. E. Filsinger (Ed.), *Marriage and family assessment: A sourcebook for family therapy* (pp. 85–115). Beverly Hills, CA: Sage Publications.

Weiss, R. S. (Ed.). (1973). *Loneliness: The experience of emotional and social isolation.* Cambridge, MA: MIT Press.

Wells, B. E., & Twenge, J. M. (2005). Changes in young people's sexual behavior and attitudes, 1943–1999: A cross-temporal meta-analysis. *Review of General Psychology, 9*, 249–261.

Wenger, A., & Fowers, B. J. (2008). Positive illusions in parenting: Every child is above average. *Journal of Applied Social Psychology, 38*, 611–634.

Whitaker, D. J., Haileyesus, T., Swahn, M., & Saltzman, L. S. (2007). Differences in frequency of violence and reported injury between relationships with reciprocal and nonreciprocal intimate partner violence. *American Journal of Public Health, 97*, 941–947.

White, G. L., & Mullen, P. E. (1989). *Jealousy: Theory, research, and clinical strategies.* New York: Guilford Press.

Whitty, M. T. (2004). Cyber-flirting: An examination of men's and women's flirting behaviour both offline and on the Internet. *Behaviour Change, 21*, 115–126.

Whitty, M. T., & Carr, A. N. (2003). Cyberspace as potential space: Considering the web as a playground to cyber-flirt. *Human Relations, 56*, 869–891.

Whitty, M. T., & Carr, A. N. (2006). *Cyberspace romance: The psychology of online relationships.* New York: Palgrave Macmillan.

Widmer, E. D. (2006). Who are my family members? Bridging and binding social capital in family configurations. *Journal of Social and Personal Relationships, 23*, 979–998.

Widmer, E. D., Treas, J., & Newcomb, R. (1998). Attitudes toward nonmarital sex in 24 countries. *The Journal of Sex Research, 35*, 349–358.

Wiederman, M. (2006). Sex research. In R. D. McAnulty & M. M. Burnette (Eds.), *Sex and sexuality. Vol. 1. Sexuality today: Trends and controversies* (pp. 1–15). Westport, CT: Praeger.

Wiederman, M. W. (1997). Extramarital sex: Prevalence and correlates in a national survey. *The Journal of Sex Research, 34*, 167–174.

Wiederman, M. W. (2004). Methodological issues in studying sexuality in close relationships. In J. Harvey, A. Wenzel, & S. Sprecher (Eds.), *The handbook of sexuality in close relationships* (pp. 31–56). Mahwah, NJ: Lawrence Erlbaum Associates Inc.

Wiederman, M. W., & Allgeier, E. R. (1996). Expectations and attributions regarding extramarital sex among young married individuals. *Journal of Psychology and Human Sexuality, 8*, 21–35.

Wiederman, M. W., & Kendall, E. (1999). Evolution, sex, and jealousy: Investigation with a sample from Sweden. *Evolution and Human Behavior, 20*, 121–128.

Wile, D. B. (1993). *After the fight: A night in the life of a couple.* New York: Guilford Press.

Wilkie, J. R., Ferree, M. M., & Ratcliff, K. S. (1998). Gender and fairness: Marital satisfaction in two-earner couples. *Journal of Marriage & the Family, 60*, 577–594.

Willetts, M. C., Sprecher, S., & Beck, F. D. (2004). Overview of sexual practices and attitudes within relational contexts. In J. H. Harvey, A. Wenzel, & S. Sprecher (Eds.), *The handbook of sexuality in close relationships* (pp. 57–85). Mahwah, NJ: Lawrence Erlbaum Associates Inc.

Williams, L., & Philipguest, M. (2005). Attitudes toward marriage among the urban middle-class in Vietnam, Thailand, and the Philippines. *Journal of Comparative Family Studies, 36*, 163–186.

Williams, S. L., & Frieze, I. H. (2005). Courtship behaviors, relationship violence, and breakup persistence in college men and women. *Psychology of Women Quarterly, 29*, 248–257.

Wilson, C. C., & Turner, D. C. (Eds.). (1998). *Companion animals in human health.* Thousand Oaks, CA: Sage Publications.

Wilson, T. D. (1994). The proper protocol: Validity and completeness of verbal reports. *Psychological Science, 5*, 249–252.

Wood, J. T. (2000). Gender and personal relationships. In C. Hendrick & S. S. Hendrick (Eds.), *Close relationships: A sourcebook* (pp. 300–313). Thousand Oaks, CA: Sage Publications.

Wood, J. T. (2007). *Gendered lives: Communication, gender, and culture* (7th ed.). Belmont, CA: Wadsworth Thomson Learning.

Wood, J. T. (2009). Communication, gender differences in. In H. T. Reis & S. K. Sprecher (Eds.), *Encyclopedia of human relationships* (Vol. 1, pp. 252–256). Thousand Oaks, CA: Sage Publications.

Wortman, C. B., & Dunkel-Schetter, C. (1979). Interpersonal relationships and cancer: A theoretical analysis. *Journal of Social Issues, 35*, 120–155.

Wortman, C. B., & Dunkel-Schetter, C. (1987). Conceptual and methodological issues in the study of social support. In A. Baum & J. Singer (Eds.), *Handbook of psychology and health. Volume 5. Stress* (pp. 63–108). Hillsdale, NJ: Lawrence Erlbaum Associates Inc.

Wright, P. H. (2003). Friendship. In J. J. Ponzetti Jr. (Ed.), *International encyclopedia of marriage and family* (2nd ed., Vol. 2, pp. 702–710). New York: Macmillan Reference USA.

Wu, Z., & Schimmele, C. M. (2003). Cohabitation. In J. J. Ponzetti Jr. (Ed.), *International encyclopedia of marriage and family* (2nd ed., Vol. 1, pp. 315–323). New York: Macmillan Reference USA.

Xu, X., & Whyte, M. K. (1990). Love matches and arranged marriages: A Chinese replication. *Journal of Marriage & the Family, 52*, 709–722.

Yan, Y. K. (2006). Sexual responses and behaviors of university students in Hong Kong. *International Journal of Adolescence and Youth, 13*, 43–54.

Yarab, P. E., Allgeier, E. R., & Sensibaugh, C. C. (1999). Looking deeper: Extradyadic behaviors, jealousy, and perceived unfaithfulness in hypothetical dating relationships. *Personal Relationships, 6*, 305–316.

Yeh, H-C., Lorenz, F. O., Wickrama, K. A. S., Conger, R. D., & Elder, G. H. Jr. (2006). Relationships among sexual satisfaction, marital quality, and marital instability at midlife. *Journal of Family Psychology, 20*, 339–343.

Young, M., Denny, G., Luquis, R., & Young, T. (1998). Correlates of sexual satisfaction in marriage. *Canadian Journal of Human Sexuality, 7*, 115–127.

Young-Browne, G., Rosenfeld, H. M., & Horowitz, F. D. (1977). Infant discrimination of facial expressions. *Child Development, 48*, 555–562.

Zaidi, A. U., & Shuraydi, M. (2002). Perceptions of arranged marriages by young Pakistani Muslim women living in a Western society. *Journal of Comparative Family Studies, 33*, 494–514.

Zajonc, R. B. (1968). Attitudinal effects of mere exposure. *Journal of Personality and Social Psychology, 9*, 1–27.

Zajonc, R. B. (2001). Mere exposure: A gateway to the subliminal. *Current Directions in Psychological Science, 10*, 224–228.

Zellman, G. L., & Goodchilds, J. D. (1983). Becoming sexual in adolescence. In E. A. Allgeier & N. B. McCormick (Eds.), *Changing boundaries: Gender roles and sexual behavior* (pp. 49–63). Palo Alto, CA: Mayfield.

Zuckerman, C. B., & Rock, I. (1957). A re-appraisal of the roles of past experience and innate organizing processes in visual perception. *Psychological Bulletin, 54*, 269–296.

Author index

351

Subject index

feature of passionate love, 183–184, 187
natural language concept, 181–182
reciprocity of negative, 276–277
relation to concept of love, 180–182
response to relationship dissolution, 268–270
role in relationship dissolution, 261–262
Emotional distress:
account making and relief from, 268
inequity, 99–100
infidelity, 224
relational transgressions, 213
relationship dissolution, 268, 269–270
sexual disinterest, 217
sexual jealousy, 225
unrequited love, 216–217
Emotional infidelity. *See* Infidelity
Emotional intensity:
relation to erotic love style, 176
relation to passionate love, 183–186, 187
Emotional intimacy:
bids for, 281
relation to companionate love, 191
See also Intimacy; Self-disclosure
Emotional isolation. *See* Loneliness
Emotional stability, evolved preferences for, 66. *See also* Negative affectivity
Emotional support, 56, 155
lack of, association with sexual disinterest, 218
Emotionally focused couple therapy, 285
Empathic accuracy, 48–50. *See also* Interpersonal sensitivity; Responsiveness
Empty love, 174–175
Engagement, as justification for sexual intercourse, 197, 204
Environment of evolutionary adaptedness, 65
Environmental factors:
definition of, 18
role in affiliation, 70–73
role in bullying, 243
role in conflict, 252
role in demand–withdraw, 279–280
role in infidelity, 223
role in interpersonal attraction, 65–67
role in marital satisfaction, 124–127
role in physical aggression, 236
role in relational stalking, 220
role in relationship development, 100–105
role in relationship dissolution, 262–263
role in sexual aggression, 239
role in social support, 159
types of, 17, 18

Equity:
definition of, 97–98
relationship quality, 97–98, 99–100
social support, 158
types of, 98
See also Social exchange theories
Eros:
Agape and, 177
cultural differences and, 177
intense emotion, 176
love style, 176
Mania and, 177
measurement of, 178
passionate love, 185
predictor of relationship satisfaction, 177
sexuality, 172
Erotic love. *See* Eros; Passionate love
Ethical procedures, 36–37
Ethnic differences. *See* Cultural differences
Ethnographic Atlas, 111
Event-contingent sampling, 33
Evolutionary principles:
attachment, 44–47
human nature, 42–52
interpersonal attraction, 65–66
language development, 51
mate selection, 114
selective attention, 62
sexual jealousy, 225–226
Exogamy, 112
Experiment, 29–30
Experimental control, 31
External validity, 26–27, 34
Extramarital sex. *See* Infidelity
Extrarelational sex. *See* Infidelity
Extraversion. *See* Positive affectivity
Eye contact:
as flirting behavior, 78–79
infant sensitivity to, 49
Eyebrow flash, as flirting behavior, 78–79

F

Face perceptual system, 47–48
Familiarity:
adaptive significance of, 67
role in interpersonal attraction, 67–68
role in love, 171
Family interaction lab, 258
Family relationships:
characteristics of, 10

CPSIA information can be obtained
at www.ICGtesting.com
Printed in the USA
BVHW01s1816280818
525846BV00011B/145/P